■ THE STUDY OF PHILOSOPHY

■ THE STUDY

ROWMAN & LITTLEFIELD PUBLISHERS, INC.

OF PHILOSOPHY

S. Morris Engel and Angelika Soldan

with Kevin Durand

Lanham • Boulder • New York • Toronto • Plymouth, UK

ROWMAN & LITTLEFIELD PUBLISHERS, INC.

Published in the United States of America
by Rowman & Littlefield Publishers, Inc.
A wholly owned subsidiary of The Rowman & Littlefield Publishing Group, Inc.
4501 Forbes Boulevard, Suite 200, Lanham, Maryland 20706
www.rowmanlittlefield.com

Estover Road
Plymouth PL6 7PY
United Kingdom

British Library Cataloguing in Publication Information Available

Library of Congress Cataloging-in-Publication Data:

Engel, S. Morris, 1931-
  The study of philosophy : an introduction / S. Morris Engel, Angelika Soldan, with the assistance of Kevin Durand. — 6th ed.
     p. cm.
  Includes bibliographical references and index.
  ISBN-13: 978-0-7425-4892-3 (pbk. : alk. paper)
  ISBN-10: 0-7425-4892-9 (pbk. : alk. paper)
     1. Philosophy—Introductions. I. Soldan, Angelika, 1953- II. Durand, Kevin K. J. III. Title.
BD21.E6 2008
100—dc22   2007020681

Printed in the United States of America

⊗™ The paper used in this publication meets the minimum requirements of American National Standard for Information Sciences—Permanence of Paper for Printed Library Materials, ANSI/NISO Z39.48-1992.

■ PART III PHILOSOPHY'S MAIN QUESTIONS

■ PART IV CONTEMPORARY DIRECTIONS

We do not go into this merely to be titillated by nice arguments or caught up in playing intellectual games. We are trying to find those things that will enhance our understanding of life, and even ennoble our minds and make our hearts better. It is really not too much to think that philosophy has this power.

—RICHARD TAYLOR

A TEACHER OF THE INTRODUCTORY COURSE in philosophy knows two things about his or her students: Most of them will come to the course with eagerness and anticipation, assuming that philosophy deals with the big questions of existence. But many of them will avoid any second course on the subject. They have left their philosophy course feeling deeply disappointed, even dismayed. Philosophy for them seems to lack a center—to be merely a hodgepodge of issues and questions, many seemingly pointless.

Because I believe that the students' expectations are valid, I have sought to provide a text that will neither disappoint nor dismay newcomers, without either oversimplifying philosophy or talking down to them. To achieve this it has seemed to me that the best way is simply to tell the story of philosophy.

This book thus begins with a discussion of the nature and scope of philosophy. Philosophy, this first chapter explains, is a critical examination of our basic values and beliefs. It is an attempt to discover what life is best worth living and what ideals are most worth pursuing. Philosophy, it goes on to point out, attempts to answer the following fundamental questions: What sort of world is it that we inhabit? Is it a world that is basically friendly or unfriendly to us? And what sorts of beings are we who inhabit this world, and what should our purpose be? How do we know about our world and ourselves? And how much faith can we place in this kind of knowledge? These questions are taken up in philosophy's three main areas: metaphysics, ethics, and epistemology.

But how did the attempt, using reason alone (logic) to gain an understanding of ourselves and the world we live in—the theme of this text and what lies at the heart of philosophy—all begin? And where? Who were the first philosophers, and what were some of their first questions? This is the subject of the second chapter. It tells the story of how the first philosophers, without any instruments to aid them or a scientific tradition to go by, came to ask the most fundamental question that can be asked about the universe: What is the nature of the stuff that it is made of? The chapter explores their struggle with this question, their defiance of tradition, the difficulties that confronted them, their sometimes bold and brilliant resolutions of these difficulties, and the answer they arrived at—one that, in its essentials, is still accepted by science today.

But is reason's purpose only to discover the secrets of nature? Isn't humankind itself a secret? And reason, too, whose possession distinguishes humans from all other beings in the world—what is it for? The person who turned philosophy's attention to these questions—and who earned the title of "father of philosophy" as a result—was Socrates, one of the most remarkable men who ever lived. Chapter 3 gives an account of his life, the times he lived in, his method of philosophizing, and the nature of his teaching. It also introduces us to one of the greatest philosophers of all time, Plato, whose dialogues about Socrates are among the most profound and eloquent literature ever written.

But if philosophy is an attempt to gain an understanding of the world we live in (metaphysics), of ourselves (ethics), and of the relations between the two (epistemology), using reason alone (logic), what precisely, indeed *is* reason? When can we know we have done it correctly and when not? What are its basic concepts and principles? These important questions are taken up in part II of the text, concerned with the science or discipline of logic, one first founded by Plato's pupil, Aristotle.

Having achieved an understanding of what philosophy is, where and how it began, who it was that gave it direction, and what its main method is, we next turn to the study of the first of its main questions: What sort of world is it that we find ourselves in? Is its existence simply a freak accident, or is there perhaps a deeper meaning in its existence? What are the signs of such meaning, and what are their implications? Chapter 6, on metaphysics, explores these ever-old and ever-new questions of philosophy. They involve questions about cosmology, about life after death, and finally, about God. The chapter explores what has been said and what can reasonably said about these matters.

Because the question of what can reasonably be believed is the key to philosophy's approach, in chapter 7 we turn again to an examination of the nature of reason. Is its role larger, perhaps, than we have suspected? One even more fundamental than as a guide to conduct, determining the very shape of that conduct, concerned with the very meaning of what it is to be a human being, existing in a universe, bound by time and space? These are the matters epistemology investigates.

They are among the most difficult in all philosophy and have absorbed and dominated philosophy for the past 300 years. Chapter 7 gives a detailed account of philosophy's struggles with these questions.

With this broad overview now in our possession, we turn in chapter 8, on ethics, to consider the question of the meaning and purpose of life. Here we explore the various answers that both ancient and modern philosophers have given to this question. It contrasts Aristotle's answer (that its purpose is happiness) with Kant's (worthiness) and Mill's (the happiness of all), and all three with some contemporary views (that it has no purpose). This last, as we will find, is not a totally satisfying answer. The questions regarding what we should do and what we should make of ourselves cannot be disposed of so easily. They continue to intrigue and challenge us.

Indeed, these concerns continue to reappear in our last chapter, chapter 9, which carries our account of the story of philosophy to its conclusion by describing in detail two major philosophical tendencies in our own century: analytic philosophy and existentialism. The former characterizes English philosophy, the latter the philosophy of the European continent. The chapter traces the origins of these movements and explores their similarities and divergences concerning the neverending exploration of what it is to be a human being.

Presented in this fashion, philosophy should neither disappoint nor dismay but elevate and inspire. Let me close this brief overview of the book with a short article written by Professor Samuel Gorovitz (from *Teaching Philosophy*, vol. 1, no. 3, 1976, p. 234; used by permission), with which I often begin my course: Undergraduate students are commonly uninformed or misinformed about the nature of philosophy to a greater extent than with any other academic subject. Unlike most disciplines studied in a university, philosophy is usually unknown to the entering college student. Although high school students are intellectually capable of studying philosophy, the curriculum seldom provides them with the opportunity to do so. Furthermore, the impressions that students pick up about philosophy are apt to be distorted: philosophy is sometimes confused with religion, with psychology, with studies of mystical experience, and so on.

Yet philosophy is one of the most important subjects a student can take. Students who—because the uses of philosophy have never been brought to their attention—leave college without taking a course in philosophy have been deprived of a valuable part of their intellectual heritage. Among the uses of philosophy are these:

- Philosophy develops your ability to reason clearly, to distinguish between good and bad arguments, to navigate through a complicated maze of issues, and to use intelligence and logic in situations all too often ruled by emotion and ignorance.
- Philosophy will help you grapple intelligently with such basic and yet elusive questions as What are rights? . . . What are our obligations to society? . . . How can we be sure of our beliefs? . . . What is the good life? . . . and so on.
- Philosophy will expand your horizons by enabling you to see beyond things as they presently appear and develop a controlled but imaginative awareness of how things might be. This will in turn enrich your understanding of how things are.
- Philosophy will make available to you a valuable portion of the world's greatest ideas, by introducing to you the philosophical thought of ancient and modern philosophers, and by making you aware of how our whole world is influenced by these ideas.

Apart from the extent to which philosophy enriches our lives, it is important, at a time when students are increasingly restless and uncertain about the world, themselves, and their relations to society, that they have access to the one kind of study that has a systematic concern with questions of just this sort.

My debts in writing the various editions of this text are both many and varied. I wish to acknowledge with thanks and fondness the inspiring teachers it was my good fortune to have both as an undergraduate and graduate student: K. W. Maurer and W. M. Sibley at the University of Manitoba, and Fulton H. Anderson, Emil Fackenheim, and David Savan at the University of Toronto. If I have succeeded in writing simply and not without feeling, shunning undue complexity and remoteness, I owe the art to them.

Important also have been the various distinguished teachers and scholars it has been my good fortune to meet during the course of my teaching career, among them Lionel Ruby, Paul Weiss, and Abraham Kaplan. They, too, in a very real sense, have been my "teachers," and much of what I have tried to achieve here has been deeply influenced by their teaching, writing, and example. Nor can I neglect here the great debt I owe to the impact of other philosophers whose writings have contributed to my own orientation and view of philosophy, its setting and teaching—among them John Wisdom, Walter Kaufmann, James K. Feibleman, and Richard Taylor.

Finally, may I say how fortunate I am that I have had again the help of Jackie Estrada, the editor of the earlier editions, to assist me with this new edition of the text. I feel very lucky indeed. May I also express my gratitude to Steven Barta, publisher of Collegiate Press, for his continued support and affection for this text.

S. Morris Engel

THOSE WHO USED PREVIOUS EDITIONS will note that for this edition, several new readings have been added to meet the requests from both teachers and students for original works of specific philosophers, such as Aristotle, Hume, and Rawls. Moreover, the chapters on ethics, metaphysics, epistemology, and contemporary philosophy have been greatly revised, and ethics has been moved to fall before the metaphysics and epistemology chapters. Now two chapters, 7 and 8, are devoted to metaphysical questions. Chapter 7 focuses on explanations of the nature of God and why there is evil in the world as well as what kinds of proofs for the existence of God have been given by medieval and modern thinkers, whereas chapter 8 elaborates on how free we are in our actions.

Part IV of the book has been expanded by adding a new chapter on fairness and feminism and splitting the former chapter 10 into two parts with the new chapter 10 dealing primarily with the analytic tradition and the new chapter 11 mainly with the continental tradition. Thereby, similarities and differences between the two traditions in contemporary philosophizing should become even more visible. Chapters 10 and 11 describe in detail two major contemporary philosophical tendencies: analytic and continental European philosophies and their quest for meaning and truth. Chapter 12 continues the discussion of human existence by contemplating what equality and recognition of the full humanity of all people mean: Isn't justice also a question of fairness, and would that not entail just and fair treatment of "the other half" of humanity, women? Do we need a fundamental shift in our notions of family, sex, gender, and justice? In the chapter, female philosophers, such as Wollstonecraft, Jaggar, and Moller Okin, are given the opportunity to voice their answers to these questions.

A full range of exercises for students are also included in this edition. Answer keys for the exercises are available for download at http://www.rowmanlittlefield.com/RL /books/Green/. All instructors are invited to e-mail textbooks@rowman.com to receive access to this password-protected site.

The presented changes could not have been made without Kevin Durand. Thanks to his ability to explain complex issues in a well-understandable way, this edition will be even more fun to study.

Many thanks to Ruth Gilbert and Ross Miller of Rowman & Littlefield for their assistance with this edition.

Angelika Soldan
The University of Texas at Brownsville
and Texas Southmost College
April 2007

PHILOSOPHY AND ITS BEGINNINGS

CHAPTER ONE

■ The Nature and Scope of Philosophy

FINDING HIMSELF ONE DAY at the Olympic games and looking about him, Pythagoras, an ancient Greek thinker, observed that three classes of people were present. First, a great mass of people had come to trade and barter. Lovers of gain, he called them. Then there were the people who had come to participate in the games in the hope of winning fame and fortune for both themselves and their cities. Pythagoras called them the lovers of honor. Finally, there were those who had come simply to watch. Pythagoras called them the lovers of the spectacle.

It then occurred to Pythagoras, the story goes, that one can find these same three classes of people everywhere. There are, first, the vast majority of people, whose main object is to try to gain as many material goods as possible. He did not think there was anything necessarily wrong with that. These are the lovers of gain. A second group, smaller than the first, contains those whose main goal is to achieve fame by distinguishing themselves in some pursuit. They are the lovers of honor. Finally, there is a third group, smaller even than the second group, who do not care that much for wealth or fame but whose main hope is to gain an understanding of this spectacle called life. Pythagoras thought a good name for these lovers of the spectacle was philosophers—a term meaning "lovers of wisdom." Including himself in this group, he went on to remark that it would not be appropriate to call them wise, for only God is wise, but some people may call themselves lovers of wisdom. And thus the word **philosophy** was coined.

> The philosophy of one century is the common sense of the next.
>
> **—Found in a fortune cookie**

Although few since Pythagoras's time have denied that philosophy is indeed somehow connected with the love of and search for wisdom, philosophers have not found it easy to say what this thing called "wisdom" is. Wisdom is not something that is achieved by discovering some new fact. In this respect philosophy is very unlike science. The failure to solve a scientific problem lies, in the great majority of cases, in our inability to get at some missing piece of information. But this is not the reason that some of our philosophical problems have continued to elude us. It is not for the lack of some fact, in other words, that a philosophic problem has escaped solution. The "facts" necessary to solve many of the most fundamental of philosophical problems, many philosophers would say, have been with us for a very long time, yet their solution continues to defy our best efforts. Discovering some further "fact" would not help at all. In many cases the trouble is that we already have too many facts.

It is like working at a massive jigsaw puzzle: Our inability to put the puzzle together does not lie in the fact that certain pieces are missing, it lies in the fact that we have before us, say, a thousand little pieces of various sizes and shapes and we do not know how they fit together. Adding another piece to the thousand would obviously be of no help at all. On the other hand, what would help would be a way to see how the pieces fit together, to see the thing whole.

As the British philosopher John Wisdom once put it, philosophy is not "knowledge of new fact" but "new knowledge of fact"—it is a deeper, more profound understanding of the facts we already have.

> Life can only be understood backwards; but it must be lived forwards.
>
> —Søren Kierkegaard

How do we go about getting at the true meaning of facts, at this deeper understanding of them? We do it by trying to see things not in isolation and separate but as they are connected and related in a whole of which they are merely parts. Seeing things whole in this way is to see them in proper perspective—and this is what wisdom is, both in philosophy and in life. That is why wisdom comes—if it does—only late in life, after much reflection and experience. For to see the true place and role of a thing—its true dimensions—requires that it be viewed from a distance and from different perspectives. And that takes time and maturity.

HOW PHILOSOPHY AND SCIENCE DIFFER

Ancient philosophical concerns laid the foundation for modern scientific inquiry, although the political implications for seeking answers to questions about the natural order of things without appeal to the gods could be quite dire. Socrates, for example, rightly felt that the prejudice against him because he was perceived to be a natural philosopher would be one of the things that would doom him to conviction for impiety. A natural philosopher was one who sought natural explanations for natural events. Thus, a natural philosopher would conduct multiple observations and extrapolate from those observations that lightning was a natural phenomenon with explainable origins that need not include the invocation of lightning-bolt-wielding Zeus. Such conclusions would increasingly erode the purview of the gods, slowly stealing from them one power after another. Such audacity was often seen as a form of impiety.

From such beginnings grew the work of Aristotle whose systematic treatment of natural phenomena from flora and fauna to constitutions and languages is the ancestor of the empirical sciences. His categorization of natural objects (e.g., trees, birds, humans, rocks, and so on) bequeathed to the biological sciences the divisions of genus and species and the many subdivisions within those. His systematization of **logic** into syllogistic forms is invaluable to mathematics to this day. The Aristotelian categories of literary analysis are still among the fundamental forms of grammar, literary criticism, and dramatic review. And his treatment of such questions as constitutional development and political interaction are not merely historical anachronisms but rather are seen as the quite perceptive and seminal work that must be taken into account even in the most current debates concerning political theory and practice.

Following Aristotle, the discipline of philosophy slowly fragmented into many pieces that had been constitutive of philosophical inquiry. Thus, the physical sciences, the social sciences, and the political sciences all have their birth in the unified approach of philosophical inquiry. For this reason, philosophy is often seen as that discipline that is deeply interested in the interconnectedness of the several realms of scientific inquiry. Or, perhaps more clearly, philosophers try to "see things whole."

> Some people see the way things are and ask: why? I dream of the way they might be and ask: why not?
>
> —Robert F. Kennedy

How do philosophers go about "seeing things whole"? They do so by enquiring not into the how or what of things but into their why. Let us, for example, take the question "Why is there evil in the world?" and note first how a scientist would answer it, then how a philosopher would do so.

A geologist who tried to answer this question strictly as a geologist might say to us, "Well, as far as natural evil is concerned, that is easy enough to say, for the earth has a certain mantle around it and there are various breaks in it. People—knowingly or unknowingly—build cities over or near these breaks or 'faults,' and when the breaks widen, buildings collapse, kill their occupants, and bring death, misery, and suffering."

Such an answer, assuming it was seriously proposed, would scarcely satisfy us because we know well enough how evil comes about. In asking the question, we were not asking for the causes of evil; we were asking the more general and basic question of why evil should exist at all.

It is in this respect that philosophy differs significantly from science. Philosophy tries to see things whole by asking questions that are more general—in the sense that their answers have far-reaching consequences for our understanding of ourselves and our world—than those asked by science. To consider another brief example, a scientist might be interested in the cause of a certain phenomenon (let us call it X). He or she may spend a lifetime pursuing this problem and, if fortunate, may discover the cause, in the process making an important contribution to our knowledge and, more than likely, to our welfare. While the philosopher would be interested in the discovery, he or she would ask a different set of questions. Those questions that concern the philosopher are the implications of the discovery to the larger picture of an understanding of the world, the nature of causation itself, and perhaps whether all things have causes.

Philosophy tries to see things whole, not only by asking questions that are more general and fundamental than those asked by science but also by asking questions that are concerned not so much with facts as with how different bodies of fact are re-

> The study of man is philosophy, and so is the study of time. But the study of man in America is sociology or anthropology, and the study of the seventeenth century is history.
>
> —Henry W. Johnstone Jr.

lated. Not only does the nature of the pieces of the puzzle pose a problem, but how they fit together does as well. The philosopher will thus wonder, for example, if we indeed accept science's basic assumption that cause and effect govern all of nature, including human nature, by what right, then, can we justify holding people legally and morally responsible for what they do?

Like the problem of evil, this is a long-standing question in philosophy, one still largely unresolved. Because it exemplifies the structural type of question (in contrast with the strictly factual type) so typical of many of philosophy's questions, let us spend a few more moments on it.

If it is the case that everything that happens in nature (and we are a part of that nature) is governed by the law of cause and effect, then it would seem that just as the stone one might throw into the air cannot help hitting the window that it shatters (as a result of the force used in sending it on its way) and finally falling to the ground (as the result of the force of gravity), so similarly one could argue that, given a certain background and nature, so and so could similarly not help shattering that window in the jeweler's store and helping himself to that enticing ring or watch. Were our knowledge of human psychology as secure as our knowledge of physics, we could easily have predicted the action in question—with the result that instead of the man who helps himself to the trinkets in question being brought to trial and no doubt eventually jailed, the real culprit and the one who deserves to be punished is not the window breaker but the jeweler, for placing such enticing trinkets in the window and tempting people who are constitutionally incapable of resisting the temptation.

But philosophy's questions are nonfactual in a further way as well. Take, for example, the question "When does life begin?" which is central in the discussion of the issue of abortion. Although this looks like an ordinary empirical or scientific question, subject to "expert" opinion, it is not really such a question at all. If it were simply such an empirical question, it would have a simple answer: that, biologically, life may be said to begin when an egg is fertilized by a sperm. But this is a different type of question, a philosophical question as we might say, one whose answer or solution depends on one's definition or "understanding" of "life," hence its difficulty.

And such a question is difficult to resolve because unlike ordinary, empirical questions, which are answered either directly by observation or indirectly by experimentation, this type of question involves the weighing of values and rights rather than facts. Facts, of course, are important to such questions as well, but facts alone cannot resolve or settle them. For example, we will be in no better position in, say, 100 years from now than we are today in solving the vexing question "Should there be censorship in a free society?" And the reason again is that this is not simply an empirical, or factual, question; what is involved here are matters of rights and values. And these are things that are tremendously difficult to resolve. Where they are concerned, it is all too easy to go overboard, to adopt extremist views, to make someone value the sole one—in short, to give in to fanaticism, as we may label it. For, indeed, a fanatic is a person for whom one particular value ("life" or "free speech") is so precious, so all-important, that other values cease to exist. The philosophic approach is to resist such fanaticism with all one's heart, to try rather to see things in proper perspective and balance.

> If the only tool you have is a hammer, you tend to treat everything as if it were a nail.
>
> **—Abraham Maslow**

Our ordinary understanding of what philosophy is captures this sense of philosophy very accurately. When, for example, we say of someone that "He took his defeat philosophically," what we mean is that he was a person who faced the vicissitudes of life serenely, that he did not allow himself to be destroyed by reversals of fortune, did not give in to defeat—did not allow that one incident (or that one value) to overshadow all the others (the whole of his life).

HOW PHILOSOPHY AND RELIGION DIFFER

Having seen how science and philosophy differ in their approaches, let us see how philosophy and religion approach things differently by returning to the problem of evil. No one has expressed the problem more succinctly than the ancient philosopher Epicurus, who put it in the form of the following dilemma: Is God willing to prevent evil but not able to do so? In that case He cannot be omnipotent. But is it perhaps the case that He is able but not willing to do so? In that case He is not a benevolent but a malevolent God. But if He is both willing and able to prevent evil, whence then comes evil?

Although this is an especially severe problem for believers who want to and do believe in a merciful and benevolent God but cannot shut their eyes to all the evil He apparently allows to exist in the world He created, one does not have to subscribe to any particular religion to find this problem of interest.

Certainly, prior to the Middle Ages, philosophy and religion were often conjoined, religion seen as perhaps a subset of philosophical inquiry or, after the ascendancy of the Church, the two seen as so closely intertwined that they could not easily be separated. For thinkers like St. Augustine, the concepts and worldview inherited from Plato and the neo-Platonists like Plotinus provided him the framework to systematize Church doctrine concerning the nature of God, humanity, sin, and grace and also to address the problem of evil in a careful and reasoned way.

During the latter part of the medieval period, fissures began to appear in the treatment of philosophy and religion. St. Thomas Aquinas reimagined the relationship between philosophical inquiry and religious questioning. For St. Thomas, religion had to do with the revelation of God and the careful study of that self-revelation. On his view, God reveals Himself directly and through sacred texts and through the mediation of the Church. Thus, religion is conceived as a top-down field where God's self-revelation to humanity is the focus. Philosophy, on the other hand, begins for St. Thomas with observation of natural phenomena. From the observation of particular objects, one could reasonably extrapolate upward to knowledge of God and of truth. Thus, philosophy and religion are related but substantially different fields. The former reasons from the created order upward toward God, while the latter reasons about God's self-revelation downward toward humanity. This distinction between the two fields is a wedge that ultimately separates the two rather completely, philosophers and theologians having little enough dialogue in the modern conversation.

Where Are We in the Universe?
We inhabit "a minor planet orbiting a very average star in the outer suburbs of a fairly typical spiral galaxy."

—Stephen Hawking, inaugural lecture: "Is the End in Sight for Theoretical Physics?"

Additionally, we are living in a period of intense fascination with the possibility of the existence of extraterrestrial life, a period in which we also have the means to extend our search deep into the outer reaches of space. Considering the staggering vastness of the universe, with the likelihood of planets like ours existing in the millions, the possibility of life existing elsewhere in the universe is very high. As rocket expert Wernher von Braun remarked, "Our sun is one of 100 billion stars in our galaxy. Our galaxy is one of billions of galaxies populating the universe. It would be the height of presumption to think that we are the only living things in that enormous immensity!"

Not only is the probability of such life very high, the likelihood of some of that life being of a type superior—perhaps much superior—to ours is also very high. This being so, we can sympathize strongly with the Jet Propulsion Laboratory scientist who on a clear evening some time ago, after scanning the sky, threw his hands up in despair and exclaimed, "Where is everybody?"

Where indeed is everybody? Some have, of course, thought that with the seemingly increasing UFO sightings and other such inexplicable phenomena, we have been and are increasingly watched and visited. Somewhat more skeptical people have answered this question in ways that do not compliment us very much. On our walks through the woods, they have said, we may have encountered some little colony of bugs or vermin—say, a colony apparently in the throes of some insurmountable difficulty (a boulder that has fallen in their path and crushed some of their members) or some other such disaster—one that we could so easily have resolved for them by expending some little energy on our part, becoming saviors in their eyes for doing so—yet, far from doing that, what we have in fact done is trample them to death.

The suggestion is that there is indeed intelligent life elsewhere in the universe, be-ings much, much superior to anything known to us. But because we are so far down the scale of evolution compared to them, they do not bother with us and simply pass us by—if not, in fact, in their contempt for us, visiting us with the evil we all know so well. And perhaps this is what Shakespeare had in mind when he had Gloucester say in *King Lear*, "As flies to wanton boys, are we to th' Gods; / They kill us for their sport."

One need not be a devout, religious person to wonder about the existence of higher beings, perhaps even the existence of some one supreme Being. And once having enter-tained the possibility of the existence of such beings or Being, the old philosophical question of the existence of evil begins to acquire new force.

But when dealing with such a question, one may well come to feel that not only is science not capable of throwing any light on it, but neither is philosophy, and perhaps only religion can help us here. "A little philosophy," Bacon once said, "makes a man an atheist; a great deal turns him to religion." Maybe in the case of a problem such as this, seeing how little illumination philosophy offers, we are indeed driven back to religion for the answers we seek and the consolation we need so badly. And if religion does man-age to provide answers that are satisfying, let us not look down our noses at it simply because, living in an age of science, we shall not attach much importance to the offer-ings of religion.

Still, the problem of evil captivates the mind. Why do bad things happen to good peo-ple? Popular treatments of the question as well as philosophical and religious/theological answers are regularly put forward from many varied quarters. Of all the answers proposed by religion to the question of evil, the most forceful is still the one first enunciated in the

According to Plato, man's life is a perpetual search for something he has not got, though without it he can never be at peace with himself. This something is "the good for man," "that which would make any man's life happy," if only he had the fruition of it. . . . Hence the need of "philosophy" for the direction of life; the whole object of philosophy is to lead us into a sure and abiding knowledge of good and evil, and so to make our judgment and the conduct which ensues from it, sound, and to restore the soul to health and unity with itself.

—**A. E. Taylor, *Platonism and Its Influence***

Book of Job. Job, having lost all his possessions, his friends, and his wife and children and now afflicted with a painful and odious disease, has removed himself from the city. Sitting on a refuse heap outside the city walls, he raises an accusing finger at God, demanding to know why this misery and agony has been visited on him. In reply to this demand, God appears to Job and in turn demands of him, "Where were you when I made all this?"—pointing to the stars, the earth, the heavens—the implication being that if He could do all that, then surely He could easily have prevented what has happened to Job, and if He did not, there was good reason. Although this does not make Job's suffering any more intelligible to him, it does make it more acceptable. And we can, of course, see why. If God appeared to any one of us (assuming we could be sure it was God) and gave us, as He did Job, His personal assurance that everything would be all right, our doubts, too, would be laid to rest and our faith restored.

And this is religion's greatest and perhaps only real answer to this problem of evil in a world presumably created and sustained by a good God. It comes up again in the New Testament. Jesus says to his disciples, trying to comfort them in their sorrow and doubts, that a sparrow could not fall to the ground without the good Father knowing about it. And when they ask him how they can be sure this is so, he gives them his personal assurance that "if it were not so, I would tell you."

To accept such an answer, to believe it and trust in it, requires, of course, enormous faith. Very few of us have that much faith or are capable of it. No doubt

> ### "Ah! Sweet Mystery of Life"
> Ah! sweet mystery of life, at last I've found
>   thee.
> Ah, I know at last the secret of it all.
> All the longing, seeking, striving, waiting,
>   yearning—
> The idle hopes, the joy and burning tears
>   that fall
> For 'tis love and love alone, the world is
>   seeking;
> And 'tis love, and love alone that can repay!
> 'tis the answer, 'tis the end and all of living—
> For it is love alone that rules for evermore!
> **—Victor Herbert, *Naughty Marietta* (1910)**

most of us are like the man who fell over the edge of a cliff but was able to catch hold of a tree. He hollered, "Hey, can somebody up there help me?" A deep voice answered, "This is God. I want you to follow My instructions. First, let go of the tree." At this the poor fellow's fear only increased, and he yelled back, "Is there anybody else up there?" That is not faith, certainly not the type religion says is necessary for understanding.

From what has been said, I think we can see that philosophy differs from religion in that it bases its belief on sound reasoning and evidence and not, like religion, on appeal to tradition and sacred authority. Philosophy, unlike religion, wants to find out "what it's all about," using reason alone. We can therefore define **philosophy** as an attempt, using reason alone, to gain an understanding of ourselves and of the world we live in. It is a search for what is the best kind of life to lead and what ideals are best worth pursuing.

PHILOSOPHY'S THREE MAIN AREAS

We have seen that philosophy differs from science in asking questions that are more general than those asked by science, and its answers differ from those given by religion in that they depend only on reason. But what sort of general questions does philosophy ask? As we will see in what follows, philosophy asks questions about ourselves and the nature of humanity, about the nature of the world we inhabit, and about the relations between the two, particularly related to how we have knowledge of ourselves or the world.

> There is nothing; and even if there were, we couldn't know it; and if we knew it, we couldn't communicate it!
>
> —Gorgias, Greek philosopher, fourth century B.C.

Questions about ourselves and the nature of humanity give rise to an area or discipline within philosophy called **ethics**. Here it asks such questions as What are we like? How should we order our lives? What goals should we seek? What should count with us most? What does it mean to live a good life?

Philosophy's questions about the world we live in give rise to an area within philosophy called **metaphysics**. Here philosophy asks such questions as What is the world like? Is the universe rational, purposive, evolving to some goal friendly to us and our needs? Or is it a nonrational, goalless thing—dead matter conforming to immutable law?

These two questions and studies entail two others to which they are intimately connected, namely, How do we know all this? How much faith can we place in this knowledge? These questions open the door to the branch of philosophical inquiry concerned with theories of knowledge, or **epistemology**. Central to questions of knowledge is the question of the nature of truth, or **logic**.

These three areas, although representing the core of philosophy and what is intrinsic to it, do not exhaust the traditional interests of philosophy. For philosophers have traditionally been interested not only in investigating the foundations of their own specific concerns but in exploring the foundations of the concerns of other thinkers as well—artists, scientists, historians, and so on. What is it that these people do, philosophers have asked, and what is its meaning? What are the methods, arguments, reasons, and presuppositions that lie at the foundations of their work, and how sound are they?

> The purpose of philosophy: To enhance our understanding of life, ennoble our minds, and to make our hearts better.
>
> —Richard Taylor, American scholar and philosopher

It is this further reach of philosophy that makes the subject appear so complicated and, sometimes, even amorphous. Although complicated, it is not amorphous. Everywhere, philosophy's concern is the same: to get at the deeper meaning of things. And so Pythagoras was, perhaps, right: philosophers are lovers of the spectacle—not there to profit from it, to participate in it, or even to enjoy it but only to understand it.

Lord Balfour, British prime minister at the turn of the twentieth century and noted author, in a moment of deep pessimism observed the following:

> The energies of our system will decay, the glory of the sun will be dimmed, and the earth, tideless and inert, will no longer tolerate the race which has for a moment disturbed its solitude. Man will go down into the pit, and all his thoughts will perish. The uneasy consciousness which in this obscure corner has for a brief space broken the contented silence of the universe, will be at rest. Matter will know itself no longer. "Imperishable monuments" and "immortal deeds," death itself, and love stronger than death, will be as if they had not been. Nor will anything that is, be better or worse for all that the labor, genius, devotion, and suffering of man have striven through countless ages to effect. (*The Foundations of Belief*)

It is this mood, captured so beautifully in Lord Balfour's remark, that leads some thinkers to take up science, others to turn to religion, and some few to pursue philosophy.

SUMMARY

1. *Philosophy* means "love of wisdom." The word was coined by Pythagoras.

2. Wisdom is a matter not of knowledge but of understanding and insight. It is achieved by inquiring into the why of things rather than into their how or what.

3. Such inquiries lead philosophy to ask questions that are more basic and fundamental than those asked by science: not "What is the cause of X?" but "Is it the case that everything has a cause?"

4. Unlike religion, philosophy wants to understand why things are the way they are and not simply to accept on faith that they must be so.

5. Philosophy may in part be defined as an attempt, by way of reason alone, to gain an understanding of our nature and the nature of the world we live in. To be a philosopher, therefore, is to be interested in the following three questions, which give rise to philosophy's three main areas:

- What sort of world is it that we inhabit? (metaphysics)
- What sort of beings are we? (ethics)
- How do we know all this? (epistemology)

KEY TERMS

epistemology	metaphysics
ethics	philosophy
logic	

REVIEW QUESTIONS

1. What is the origin of the term *philosophy*?
2. How does philosophical inquiry differ from scientific inquiry?
3. How are religion and philosophy different?
4. What are the three main branches of philosophy? What are some of the questions each branch tries to answer?

PHILOSOPHY BEGAN HERE, in the coastal city of Miletus, southeast of the Greek island of Samos, on the mainland of what is now Turkey. In the sixth century B.C., Miletus was a wealthy, prosperous Greek city, founded some 200 years earlier by the Athenians. What strikes one about this and the many other famous centers of ancient Greek civilization is the way it was surrounded by water. Everywhere there was water, and water was everywhere.

The center of the world for the Greeks was not a mass of land but a body of water—the Aegean Sea. On one side of this sea lay their European towns and cities; on the other side, their Asian settlements. In the middle, in the blue sea, were to be found the many islands with their now famous names: Melos, Delos, Rhodes, Samos, Chios, Lesbos.

If the waters separated these ancient Greeks within this great sea, the mountain ridges, which carved the landscape into tiny, island-like plains, did the same for their inland centers. The paradox of diversity and unity, of isolation and community, that came to characterize these ancient Greeks was to no small degree a result of this curious geography.

Although the country was rugged and isolated, its climate was mild and hospitable, allowing its inhabitants to spend much of the year outdoors and in each other's company. In addition, the towns and cities on the coastal plains, although separated from each other, lay at the crossroads of the world, with Asia to the east, Europe to the west, and the lands of the ancient civilizations of the Near East to the south. The rational and skeptical spirit that came to characterize them was nourished by this exposure to these diverse cultures.

At first, life could not have been easy for the average person. The basic occupation was farming, and both the land and the primitive methods used to cultivate it produced small if any surpluses. Most people lived a short, dismal existence, the usual life span for men being 35. Because of the risks and frequency of childbearing, women's life expectancy was even shorter, and that of infants was shorter still.

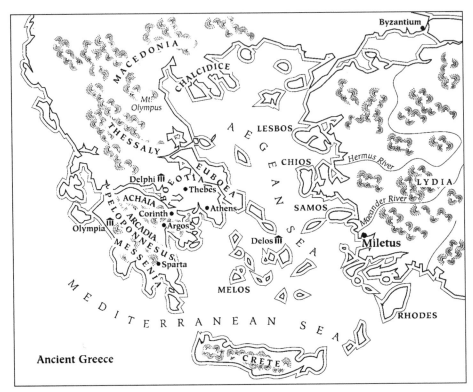

Map of Greece

This harsh, bitter, and uncertain life came to be reflected in their religion, a religion dominated by gods whose decrees were as arbitrary and uncertain as the lives they were thought to control; gods whose bitter conflicts with each other could not have been a source of comfort for those who worshipped them.

But with the development of industry and commerce, the situation of the people improved greatly. By exporting such natural resources as marble, copper, iron, lead, and silver (and later such manufactured items as pottery, statuary, and textile goods), they were able to import what their own land could not produce in adequate quantities. This commerce gave rise to an expanding population and for some a more prosperous existence. Prosperity gave birth to leisure, leisure to curiosity, and curiosity to science and philosophy.

The curiosity that gave rise to science and philosophy was, however, of a distinct sort, for other peoples at different times and periods had also achieved the leisure to pursue science and philosophy and yet had not done so. The rise of science and philosophy occurred only once and only here among these ancient Greeks. Why?

Aristotle, much closer to the event than we, although already some 300 years removed from it, tells us in a famous passage that it was the Greeks' "wonder" about their world and themselves that gave birth to science and philosophy.

Aristotle speaks of wonder, and later historians have tended to agree that that was certainly part of the answer, although not the whole of it. There were, they say, two contributions of these ancient Greeks, in addition to their curiosity, that were involved in the rise of philosophy and science. First, the Greeks asked new questions: they were curious about new sorts of things. In the older civilizations the questions were of a religious kind, concerned mainly with life in the hereafter. This world and this life interested them much less. What they principally wanted to know was what the life hereafter was like and what they could do so that their journey to that other world might be a successful one. The ancient Greeks, on the other hand, perhaps because of their own generally humbler station in life, were interested in investigating this world and this life, not the other world and the other life. In a very real sense we might say that they were the first to discover this world.

In addition to this new interest in the things of this world, the ancient Greeks pursued them in a new way. They were the first people to see the importance not only of collecting facts and knowledge but also of "systematizing" this knowledge. Take, for example, the science of geometry. Long before the Greeks, the ancient Egyptians knew many of the most important facts about geometry. The construction of their pyramids and temples would have been impossible without these rules. But in the hands of the ancient Egyptians, these facts remained merely scattered "observations" or "theorems." The Greeks were the first people to hit on the idea of trying to "prove" these theorems, of trying to find some basic and simple axioms from which they could be deduced. The concept of proof, of achieving a system, of bringing separate theorems into a single framework, was what distinguished their approach to these matters from that of their forerunners. As Herodotus, the first Greek historian, put it in a striking and revealing passage, the Greeks began to study these matters "for the sake of inquiry alone."

But pursuing these questions in a new way did not mean that these early Greek thinkers were able to start afresh, with a completely clean slate. Although in the main abandoning **supernaturalism** for **naturalism** and trying to explain events as the result not of the whim of the gods but of the working of law, these ancient Greeks inherited several assumptions or "myths" from the past that continued to have an impact on their thinking. This is not surprising, for no one, no matter how hard the effort, can be completely free of all past beliefs; some will always remain that will appear indubitable, and that was the case with these first scientists and philosophers.

Four basic assumptions restricted the thinking of the early Greeks. They believed first that the world was initially in a state of chaos but then that some god (or gods) brought order out of the chaos by fashioning the earth, the sun, the stars, and so forth. Second, they believed that the natural world, now so secured, was just, fair, and equitable and would continue to be so as long as each god (which was given a different portion of the universe to rule over) refrained from upsetting the balance by overstepping the boundary of some other god's territory. Third, they believed that strife and tension were present along with order. However, this tension and conflict (as between such opposing forces as Night and Day, Winter and Summer, Love and Hatred) never went too far, with one force permanently rising triumphant over the other. Were that to happen, the balance would be upset and chaos would again set in. They were certain, however, that that would never happen again. They believed, finally, that the world, so fashioned and so sustained, was composed of four different kinds of stuff (or elements, as they were later called): earth, air, fire, and water.

Before going on to consider the boundaries to thought that these myths posed to the first philosophers—known as the **pre-Socratics** because they came before the great philosopher Socrates—we should take note of a much more subtle boundary, one that was no less pervasive and similarly difficult to overcome. This was the linguistic boundary.

It has become commonly accepted in our day that language and its limits vastly affect thought and its possibilities. Consider the language introduced by the rulers in Orwell's novel *1984*. This language was designed to keep people thinking in patterns preferred by the rulers. Although the Greek language was constructed for no such purpose, it had an amazingly similar effect. At the beginning of the pre-Socratic era, Greece was still largely an oral culture. This meant that information was not written and read but spoken and heard. A book can be placed on a shelf and retrieved later, but without the written word, memory must play a singularly important role. To facilitate better memorization, Greek works in this period were composed almost exclusively in poetry, not prose, embodying rhythm and rhyme. The syntax also took on an interesting character: the basic units of the Greek language became not single words but groups of recurring words. Last, much of the vocabulary that is both necessary for serious philosophical consideration and helpful in spurring such discussion was lacking. Thus, we must credit these early philosophers with fighting not only restrictive cultural frameworks but also restrictive linguistic frameworks.

THE PROBLEM OF BEING

Miletus was home to the first thinkers to be considered philosophers: Thales, Anaximander, and Anaximenes.

Thales

The person credited with being the first philosopher and scientist was a man named Thales (pronounced "Thay-leez"), who, as historians like to put it, "flourished" in Miletus

---

When they reproached Thales because of his poverty, as though philosophy were no use, it is said that, having observed through his study of the heavenly bodies that there would be a large olive crop, he raised a little capital while it was still winter, and paid deposits on all the olive presses in Miletus and Chios, hiring them cheaply because no one bid against him. When the appropriate time came there was a sudden rush of requests for the presses; he then hired them out on his own terms and so made a large profit, thus demonstrating that it is easy for philosophers to be rich, if they wish, but that it is not in this that they are interested.

—**Aristotle, *Politics***

around 585 B.C. This is not the year of his birth but rather the year in which he predicted an eclipse of the sun would take place; according to our modern calculations, he was apparently off by only some minutes. Although this was a remarkable feat, Thales is remembered not so much for it as for the question he was the first to raise and the answer he proposed to it.

If we look around us, what strikes us, as indeed it must have struck Thales, is the enormous profusion and variety of things. Surely, Thales wondered, this infinite variety all around us must be different forms of the same basic and fundamental stuff. And if so, what, he asked, is the nature of that fundamental stuff out of which all of this variety arose? Having come to pose that question and having looked around him once more, the answer he offered seemed almost inevitable: it all arose, he said, from water.

Thales (640?–546 BCE)

Why water? We do not know for certain why he chose it as the prime element, but it is not difficult to imagine what may have played a role in his choice. It was, first, one of the elements singled out by tradition; second, there was a lot of it around; third, it was present in all living things and was essential to life; fourth, and probably most important, it was capable of taking on the other three forms identified in the traditional fourfold classification. Water freezes and so becomes a solid ("earth"), it evaporates into a mist and becomes "air," and it is used by the sun (which is a "fire") as a kind of fuel (when the sun "draws water to itself" or "burns off the mist"). Water was therefore a substance capable of becoming any one of the four fundamental elements out of which tradition said the world was composed.

Although still obviously much influenced by tradition, in choosing a physical element as his principle of explanation, Thales was no longer bound by that tradition but was, on the contrary, already in the process of establishing a complete new tradition, one that was to profoundly affect Western civilization from that time on. Nor, it may be interesting to observe, does he seem to have been far from wrong in choosing water as the fundamental element underlying all things. If our present understanding of the universe is correct, about 90 percent of the observable universe is hydrogen, with the remaining 10 percent consisting of helium, oxygen, nitrogen, and so on. A good part of the universe is indeed, therefore, "water" (hydrogen and oxygen).

> A witty and attractive Thracian servant-girl is said to have mocked Thales for falling into a well while he was observing the stars and gazing upwards, declaring that he was eager to know the things in the sky but that what was behind him and just by his feet escaped his notice.
>
> —Plato, *Theaetetus*

19

Lest we grant Thales more credit than he may deserve, let us remember that although he seems to have discarded mythological explanations, he did not yet succeed in entirely abandoning the language of mythology. In a fragment that has survived, he is quoted as having taught that "all things are full of the gods."

Anaximander

Thales was raising for the first time a question concerning, as it is generally referred to, the problem of Being. The second great early thinker to direct himself to this problem was a pupil of Thales by the name of Anaximander.

Anaximander (610–546 B.C.) seems to have been much bolder in his speculations than Thales. In considering what that fundamental stuff out of which everything arose might have been, he decided it could not have been any one of the four named by tradition. For had one of these four been elevated above the others, this would have involved, he reasoned, a kind of unfairness to the other three, with disastrous results. The basic element must have been, therefore, something more primitive than these four.

All this seems to be suggested in the sentence, the only one which has been preserved, from the prose treatise (the first to be written in European literature) that Anaximander wrote. Things return, that sentence runs, to their origins, "as is ordained, for they give satisfaction and reparation to one another for their injustice according to the ordering of time . . ."

> At first we worship God in things; later we worship things in God.
>
> —St. Thomas of Aquinas

The dominance of one thing over another, Anaximander seems to be saying here, is a kind of cosmic injustice for which a penalty (death) is exacted, the penalty being assessed by Time.

Such dark phrases as "ordained," "reparation," and "ordering" make us wish more of his writings had survived. But they did not.

If Anaximander seems still overly influenced by the ancient myths (in this case the idea of justice in Nature), such belief led him to a much more promising notion of the nature of that basic stuff than the one propounded by Thales.

Reasoning that whatever has definite qualities must in time lose them (die), and since the fundamental stuff from which everything else arose must be eternal and indestructible, it must have lacked all definite qualities. He came, therefore, to call that basic element "the *apeiron*," meaning a kind of neutral, indeterminate stuff, boundless in amount.

Initially (and what he says here is reminiscent of the idea of chaos in the old myths) there was, he speculated, nothing but this boundless, indeterminate matter. But as a result of a certain kind of shaking process, perhaps like that of a gigantic sieve (for it was not shaking because some god or gods were shaking it), the four elements separated off. The first to do so was the solid element, the earth, which fell to the center; second was water, which covered the earth; then followed air, which formed a sphere around the water; and finally appeared a sphere of fire.

Although nothing much remains of these speculations, the essential thing is that they are of the same kind as modern science and appeal to the same sorts of explanatory principles. They represent a kind of scientific or naturalistic account, in contrast to the mythopoetic or supernaturalistic, characteristic of previous stages of thought.

In another sphere Anaximander hit on the very modern idea of the evolution of man and animals from lower forms of life, using a concept of natural selection to explain the extinction of some species and the survival of others. He suggested that life began in the warm, moist slime at the edge of the sea—which is still a good guess—and that the first forms of life were marine creatures. He accordingly enjoined his students not to eat fish. Then, Anaximander speculated, some of these early forms of marine creatures began to live on land and gradually developed organs to enable them to survive outside water. Thus, land animals arose, and finally, the last to develop were humans. Anaximander further noted that during the course of evolution, very strange types of animals must have emerged, but some were fitted to cope with their environment and survived; other forms were not able to do so and thus died out.

> Whether our brethren of the deep cherish equally delicate sentiments towards us is not recorded.
>
> **—Bertrand Russell**

Another distinction Anaximander enjoys is that of having been the first, as far as we know, to draw a map of the known world.

Anaximenes

The last member of this so-called **Milesian school**, a generation younger than Anaximander and possibly his pupil, was Anaximenes (585–524 B.C.). In his search for the fundamental stuff, Anaximenes reverted back to the four elements and chose air—a choice motivated, it seems, by his desire to strike a balance between the views of his two predecessors and preserve what was best in each. First, air, although like water present and indispensable to all life, has the advantage that it does not have as specific and defined a nature as water and is therefore more capable of transforming itself into the great variety of objects around us. And, second, air is a more likely source of this variety than Anaximander's *apeiron* (the Boundless), for the Boundless seems too empty and vacuous a stuff to be capable of giving rise to such variety and profusion. Air, having none of the heaviness or solidity of water and being as infinite, as all-pervading, and as supple as the Boundless, must have been, Anaximenes concluded, the source of it all.

His efforts to explain how air could become any one of the other three elements led Anaximenes to hit on the notion of condensation and rarefaction, a notion that will become essential in later speculations. He argued that when particles of air get tightly packed together, the result is a fluid, and when they become still more tightly packed, the result is a solid. On the other hand, when the particles become rarefied and separated, the solid turns to a fluid, the fluid to a mist, and the mist (or air) to fire.

> No man knows or ever will know the truth about the gods and about everything I speak of: for even if one chanced to say the complete truth, yet oneself knows it not; but seeming is wrought over all things.
>
> Not from the beginning have the gods revealed all things to mortals, but by long seeking men find what is better.
>
> —Anaximenes

Seeing, apparently, that the thinner or rarer air is, the hotter it becomes, and that the thicker it is, the colder it becomes, Anaximenes conducted the first recorded experiment. Blow on your hand hard through compressed lips, he said, and you'll find the "thick" air feels cold. Now open your mouth wide and blow gently; the "thin" air is warm.

Although Anaximenes' physical explanation of the process whereby one fundamental substance gets transformed into another is superior to the moral explanation entailed in Anaximander's theory (the giving of satisfaction for some injustice), like Anaximander and Thales before him, his overall view was still not entirely free of **anthropomorphism**—the assignment of human characteristics to nonhuman beings. Air, he thought, was the more fundamental element because "just as our soul, being air, holds us together, so do breath and air encompass the whole world," which is its soul.

With Anaximenes, the Milesian school came to an end. Its speculations, which mark the beginning of science and with it the beginning of Western culture, were conducted in the shadows of the rise in the east of the great Persian Empire. Founded by Cyrus the Great in 550 B.C. with his conquest of the Near East, it spread to Lydia, ruled by its famous king Croesus, and then to the Greek cities on the east coast of the Aegean Sea. When, in 499 B.C., these Greek city-states revolted, the Persians put down the revolt and as a further warning and punishment destroyed its greatest city, Miletus.

> The major advances of civilization are processes that all but wreck the societies in which they occur.
>
> —Alfred North Whitehead

Although the Persians subsequently succeeded in extending their rule into Europe along the north coast of the Aegean as far as Macedonia, their attempts to extend it farther into Old Greece resulted in the great Athenian victories at Marathon (490 B.C.) and Salamis (480 B.C.), victories that marked the beginning of the Golden Age of Greece.

THE PROBLEM OF BECOMING

The first question raised by these early thinkers soon gave rise to a second, for the first question asked essentially, "What is it that is constantly changing or becoming?" and it was soon realized that change or becoming was itself a puzzling thing.

There is indeed something very curious about the idea of change. When something changes, it ceases to be what it was and becomes something else. But if this is so, what becomes of that original thing? Has it vanished from existence? And if it has, what sort of reality or being could it have had, seeing how it could lose it so completely and swiftly? Surely not real Being.

Furthermore, if we are to grant that things change, as our senses tell us is obviously the case, then we must assume there is something permanent continuing throughout the process, for otherwise we would not have change but first one thing then something else—something totally different from it. But to assume that there is something permanent in change is to embrace a contradiction, for the permanent, by definition, is that which does not change.

Parmenides

Such thoughts about being and change led one famous ancient philosopher and his followers to the very odd position of maintaining that change is really an impossibility. This philosopher was Parmenides, who was born in 515 B.C. in Elea, a city founded by Ionian refugees in southern Italy.

Parmenides had to agree, of course, that things do seem to change, but he held that logic could show that in reality they did not. And Parmenides' logic was simple and seemingly irrefutable. He started by laying down the following very simple and sound principle: what is, is (Being is); and what is not, is not (Non-Being—nothing—is not). Now consider, he reasoned, the possibilities:

(a) Being changing into Being.
(b) Non-Being changing into Non-Being.
(c) Being changing into Non-Being.
(d) Non-Being changing into Being.

Only one way remains; that it is. To this way there are very many signposts: that being has no coming-into-being and no destruction, for it is whole of limb, without motion, and without end. And it never was, nor will be, because it is now, a whole all together, one, continuous; for what creation of it will you look? How, whence sprung? Nor shall I allow you to speak or think of it as springing from not-being; for it is neither expressible nor thinkable that what-is-not is. Also, what necessity impelled it, if it did spring from nothing, to be produced later or earlier? Thus it must be absolutely, or not at all. Nor will the force of credibility ever admit that anything should come into being, beside being itself, out of not-being. So far as that is concerned, justice has never released (being) from its fetters and set it free either to come into being or to perish, but holds it fast. The decision on these matters depends on the following: it is, or it is not. It is therefore decided, as is inevitable: ignore the one way as unthinkable and inexpressible (for it is no true way) and take the other as the way of being and reality. How could being perish? How could it come into being? If it came into being, it is not; and so too if it is about-to-be at some future time. Thus coming-into-being is quenched, and destruction also into the unseen.

—**Parmenides**

Now, case (a) cannot occur, for this is not change at all. If we have the very same thing at the beginning and end, we do not have change. Case (b) cannot occur for the same reason. Also, this statement is unintelligible; the idea of Non-Being, or nothing, is impossible. How about case (c)? This, too, is impossible, for here we would have to suppose something is capable of being nothing, of disappearing into nothingness. How is *that* possible? And, finally, case (d) is equally impossible, for here we would have to suppose that what is *not* becomes what is, that *something* comes into being from *nothing*!

Parmenides, therefore, came to the conclusion that although our senses tell us that things change, our reason shows that this is impossible. His logic led Parmenides to the view that ultimate reality was an unchanging, unitary Being. Nothing determinate, of course, could be said of Being, which he spoke of simply as *It*.

Zeno

Parmenides' argument probably would not have convinced many people had it not been strongly reinforced by one of his followers, an exceptionally ingenious person named Zeno the Eleatic (ca. 490 B.C.). Zeno developed several famous paradoxes, designed to support the contention that change or motion is impossible: Achilles and the tortoise, the racetrack, and the flying arrow. All have to do with motion in space, with change of position.

Before we look at **Zeno's paradoxes**, let us note that a paradox is a very different sort of thing from a problem. A problem is solved; a paradox is resolved or even dissolved. It is not something real and genuine but rather something that arises from a confusion, when strands of thought become intertwined and entangled. That is not to say that all paradoxes are easy to disentangle.

Perhaps the most famous paradox comes from St. Paul. Writing to Titus (about A.D. 64), who had been left on the island of Crete to spread the gospel, Paul said, "Be careful of the Cretans. They are liars—a Cretan himself said so." (The Cretan he was referring to was a man named Epimenides; see Titus 1:12–13.) Now the trouble here is that if the Cretan was lying (in saying that "all Cretans are liars"), then he might have been telling the truth; and if he was telling the truth (that all Cretans are liars), then he was lying! So if he was lying, he was telling the truth, and if he was telling the truth, he was lying!

Graffito: What kind of nut writes on toilet walls?

A **paradox**, then, is a type of statement that tends to impugn its own correctness. How it does so, however, is not always easy to say. Let us take, first, Zeno's paradox of Achilles and the tortoise. Since Achilles is the fastest being in the world and the tortoise the slowest, let us give the latter a head start of 100 yards before we have them run the race. And now off they go! By the time Achilles reaches the 100-yard point, the tortoise will have gone, say, 10 yards; by the time Achilles reaches this point, the tortoise will have gone, say, another 1 yard; by the time Achilles gets to this point, the tortoise will have gone

Aristotle's criticism: Zeno's argument involves a confusion of infinite length with infinite divisibility of length. The argument attempts to prove that the space that Achilles must cover before overtaking the tortoise is an infinite magnitude; it does not prove this but rather that the space in question is divisible ad infinitum. Hence, the argument commits the fallacy of irrelevant thesis (see chapter 4).

---

another 1/10 of a yard. Since we are not going to run out of numbers, it is hard to see how Achilles can catch up to the tortoise—let alone overtake him. (As a wag once put it, when last seen, the tortoise was .000000005 of an inch ahead, and Achilles' tongue was hanging out half a yard.) Of course, mathematically, we can determine exactly when the two will meet, but once we begin to think about it along the lines Zeno suggested, we seem to run into difficulties.

Now let's take Zeno's racetrack paradox: Before I cover the full distance of a race, I must first cover the 1/2 distance; before I cover the 1/2, I must cover the 1/4; before the 1/4 the 1/8; before the 1/8 the 1/16; before the 1/16 the 1/32; then the 1/64, the 1/128, and so on. Since I'll never run out of numbers, I'm obviously never going to get to the end!

Or consider, finally, the flying arrow: at any given moment (aside from the fact that before it can cover the full distance, it must cover the 1/2, the 1/4, and so on) it must occupy a space equal to itself and

Joe: You know, there is no such thing as truth.

Sue: Is that the truth?

Joe: What I mean is, there are no such things as facts.

Sue: Is that a fact?

Joe: What I am trying to say is that there is no right or wrong!

Sue: Well, you're either right or wrong about that!

Joe: Listen, what I mean is that there are no *absolutes!*

Sue: Are you absolutely sure?

is therefore at rest or motionless. But if at every instant of its flight it is motionless, how can it move at all? Of course, the answer is that Parmenides was right—it doesn't!

These paradoxes have had a very long history: in fact, they are still being discussed by philosophers and mathematicians. The surprising fact is that although everyone seems to agree there is a fallacy somewhere, no two thinkers agree on just what it is.

Heraclitus

About the same time as Parmenides, there lived another famous thinker named Heraclitus (540–480 B.C.), who took a diametrically opposite view from that of Parmenides. So impressed was Heraclitus by the universality of change that he compared reality to a river. You cannot step into the same river twice, he asserted—to which one of his disciples soon added that you cannot even step into it once (for both you and the river are constantly changing). Defying logic, Heraclitus therefore went on to assert that "there is nothing permanent except change."

Concerning the nature of the underlying substance that is constantly in flux, Heraclitus thought it was fire. In doing so, Heraclitus was approaching more closely to our modern understanding of these matters than his predecessors. Of this view, the physicist Werner Heisenberg has written that

> modern physics is in some way extremely near to the doctrines of Heraclitus. If we replace the word "fire" by the word "energy" we can almost repeat his statements word for word from our modern point of view. Energy is in fact that substance from which all elementary particles, all atoms and therefore all things are made, and energy is that which moves. Energy is a substance, since its total amount does not change, and the elementary particles can actually be made from this substance as is seen from many experiments on the creation of elementary particles. Energy can be changed into motion, into heat, into light and into tension. Energy may be called the fundamental cause for all change in the world. (*Physics and Philosophy*)

Heraclitus's view that nothing is constant and unchanging is more in agreement with our sense experience than Parmenides', for our senses tell us that things do change. Yet from the point of view of reason, his idea is not satisfactory, for unless, as we clearly see with our minds, there is something permanent and unchanging, we cannot speak of change at all. We may not be able to step into the river twice (or once), but if there were no banks, there would be no river to begin with.

Change obviously involves permanence, and the difficulty is to see how they are related. Parmenides retained the permanent and this forced him to rule out change; Heraclitus attempted to get along without the idea of the permanent, but this seemed to fail, too.

In addition to being a brilliant thinker, Heraclitus was also a brilliant stylist and aphorist, many of whose sayings have survived. Among the briefer and more memorable ones are the following:

"A man's character is his destiny."
"Every beast is driven to the pasture with a blow."
"The way up and the way down is one and the same."

Sayings of Heraclitus

Fire lives the death of earth, and air the death of fire; water lives the death of air, earth that of water.

Immortals are mortal, mortals immortal, living each other's death, dying each other's life.

This cosmos, none of gods or men made, but it always was and is and shall be: an everlasting fire, kindling in measures and going out in measures.

The lord whose oracle is in Delphi neither speaks out nor conceals, but gives a sign.

After death things await men which they do not expect or imagine.

It is no doubt that remarks like the last led antiquity to refer to him as "The Dark." In view of the nature of the substance he had picked as underlying reality, the nickname strikes one as ironic.

THE THEORY OF ATOMISM: A SYNTHESIS

During the next 50 years, attempts were made to deduce change without resorting to the paradoxically extreme positions of either Heraclitus or Parmenides. The eventual outcome was an extremely ingenious answer, which, as far as the physical world is concerned, is still in its essentials accepted by science today.

This is the theory of **atomism**, propounded by Leucippus (490–430 B.C.) in a work titled *The Great World System* and improved and developed by Democritus (460– 370 B.C.) in a work titled *The Small World System*. This theory proved to be an excellent solution to both problems, Being and Becoming.

Leucippus began by criticizing Parmenides' conception of space. For Parmenides the notion of space presented a problem because he rejected the existence of Not-Being. Not-Being, he said, cannot be; it cannot even be thought of, for to think of Not-Being is to think of nothing (and to think of nothing is not to think). But space, being a part of the total It, could not be nothing; therefore, with no void between things, motion, as movement in empty space (and with it change or becoming), must be impossible. And if it appears to take place, this must be an illusion.

But Leucippus, admitting that in a sense the void or space is "what is not," a kind of nothing, nevertheless decided to go ahead and defy the logic of Parmenides and claim that in this case, "What is not, is." If we could think of space as a kind of receptacle, full in some parts and empty in others, Parmenides' difficulties about change and motion would not arise, he thought.

Leucippus's first assumption was therefore that space is real. His second assumption was that within this space, which he saw as extending infinitely, there moved originally an infinite number of tiny particles, which he called atoms—meaning "uncuttables."

How did he come to this notion? Matter, he reasoned, was obviously divisible into parts and those parts into lesser and lesser parts. Such division, however, must lead eventually to particles so tiny that, because they would be absolutely solid and have no space within them, they would resist further division. These would be the uncuttables,

---

Take our own bodies. I believe they are composed of myriads and myriads of infinitesimally small individuals, each in itself a unit of life, and that these units work in squads—or swarms, as I prefer to call them—and that these infinitesimally small units live forever. When we "die" these swarms of units, like a swarm of bees, so to speak, betake themselves elsewhere, and go on functioning in some other form or environment.

—Thomas Edison, modern-day "atomist"

As [the atoms] move, they collide and become entangled in such a way as to cling in close contact to one another, but not so as to form one substance of them in reality of any kind whatever; for it is very simple-minded to suppose that two or more could ever become one. The reason he gives for atoms staying together for a while is the intertwining and mutual hold of the primary bodies; for some of them are angular, some hooked, some concave, some convex, and indeed with countless other differences; so he thinks they cling to each other and stay together until such time as some stronger necessity comes from the surrounding and shakes and scatters them apart.

—**Aristotle on Democritus**

or atoms. Leucippus thought that there must be an infinite number of these particles, moving randomly about in infinite space.

These atoms were not thought of by Leucippus and Democritus as being regular in shape, like the tiny billiard balls envisioned by modern science. On the contrary, they thought of them as having irregular surfaces and some as being endowed with little hooks. Originally these tiny atoms flew in random directions through empty space, motion being natural to them. How often two such little particles would collide, only to bounce off and continue on their separate paths, no one, of course, could say. Sooner or later, however, two such atoms were bound to get entangled. Now hooked together, they would soon be joined by another tiny atom, with others then quickly following. As a large mass thus formed, a vortex was created that swept more and more matter into its orbit. And out of these larger masses there eventually arose a universe of stars, sun, moon, and planets.

In this view, then, every tangible and visible body that we find is simply an agglomeration, or collection, of atoms, all things of whatever kind being ultimately made of the same particles. But if so, why do things appear different? They appear different, the atomists explained—invoking here Anaximenes' theory of condensation and rarefaction—because of the different ways in which these particles or atoms are joined together. If they are loosely joined, we have a liquid; if tightly joined, we have a solid; and so on. Differences are also due, they explained, to the different patterns (or "atomic structure" as we would now put it) of the same particles.

Without a scientific tradition to draw on and no scientific instruments to aid them, armed with only their senses and reason, these first atomists not only solved the first two major problems bequeathed to them by their predecessors but did so in a way that is still astonishing.

Atomism was an ingenious answer to the first problem concerning Being, and it was an extremely satisfying solution to the problem of Becoming or change. Parmenides, it showed, was right in maintaining that what is real does not change, for atoms are indeed real and do not change; and Heraclitus was right in insisting on the existence of change, for change, too, is real, but it occurs only to complex bodies. Each, the theory

At the beginning of the century it was shown that matter was not continuous but was made up of atoms. Shortly thereafter it was discovered that these supposedly indivisible atoms were made up of electrons revolving about a nucleus. The nucleus in turn was found to be composed of so-called elementary particles, protons and neutrons. The latest episode in this story is that we have found that the proton and the neutron are made up of quarks.

—**Stephen Hawking, "Is the End in Sight for Theoretical Physics?"**

indicated, had been correct in what he asserted but wrong in what he denied—with both saying more than they knew.

Democritus, who expanded and developed the atomic theory first propounded by Leucippus, went on to make explicit the theory's mechanistic-materialist implications for religious orthodoxy, especially the fears, superstitions, and terrors such orthodoxy tended to generate. Fears and superstitions, he announced, need no longer plague us; all phenomena are easily explainable as being the product of the generation and dissolution of atoms. There is no place remaining in such a world for demonic forces and powers and the tortures and torments of hell.

Democritus (c. 460–c. 370 BCE)

An interesting story about Democritus illustrates very clearly what was characteristic of his approach. Considerable interest had been aroused by the strange death of a prominent man. While the man was strolling along the beach, an eagle dropped a turtle on his head and killed him. It was recalled that an oracle had once predicted that the man would die by a "bolt from Zeus," and although this was thought to mean that he would die by lightning, it was nevertheless felt that the prediction had been fulfilled since the eagle was a bird sacred to Zeus. But this explanation did not satisfy Democritus, who went out to the beach to observe the eagles. He noticed that they would swoop down and seize a turtle with their talons and then fly up with it and drop it on a rock in order to crack the shell to get at the meat. When Democritus recalled that the deceased had been bald, the solution immediately unfolded itself to him. There was obviously no need to appeal to the designs of unseen beings in order to solve the mystery; ordinary natural principles sufficed.

Democritus concluded that worlds come into being through the coming together of large collections of atoms isolated in a large patch of void. There are probably, therefore,

> Democritus holds the same view as Leucippus about the elements, full and void . . . he spoke as if the things that are were in constant motion in the void; and there are innumerable worlds which differ in size. In some worlds there is no sun and moon, in others they are larger than in our world, and in others more numerous. The intervals between the worlds are unequal; in some parts there are more worlds, in others fewer; some are increasing, some at their height, some decreasing; in some parts they are arising, in other failing. They are destroyed by colliding with each other. There are some worlds without any living creatures, plants, or moisture.
>
> —Hyppolytus

an infinite number of worlds such as ours, worlds in the process either of formation or of dissolution through the generation or destruction of their mass. And the same is the case with us, who are collections of smaller numbers of atoms.

This dimension of Democritus's atomic theory was later to be used by another ancient Greek, Epicurus of Samos (342–270 B.C.), as the basis of his famous moral philosophy; later still, it inspired the Roman poet and author Lucretius (94–55 B.C.) to write his *De Rerum Natura*—a long poem devoted to explaining "the nature of things" in terms of atomic and Epicurean science and ethics.

The achievements of these first philosophers and scientists must be measured not by the empirical validity of their specific findings (remarkable as these sometimes were) but rather by their choice of methods and assumptions. They tried to answer questions about nature without resorting to divine revelation by speculating in a rational way about the natural world and its possible origins. They replaced the older concept of a world governed by gods with the concept of nature as obedient to law, one intelligible to reason and amenable to its methods of investigation. That they achieved all this without the aid of scientific instruments and in the face of an opposing tradition is all the more remarkable.

But they were remarkable men living in a remarkable period of history. The sixth century B.C., when all this began, was a century unlike any other either before or after it. The last prophecies of Jeremiah (ca. 645–580 B.C.) date from this period; it also marked the rise of the Buddha in India (563–483 B.C.), of Confucius in China (551–479 B.C.), and of Zarathustra or Zoroaster (627–551 B.C.) in Persia, the founder and prophet of a religion that had an enormous impact on both Judaism and Christianity.

> I heard the voice of the Lord saying, whom shall I send, and who will go for us? Then said I, Here am I; send me.
>
> —Isaiah 6:8

It would be the fate of these two great traditions, the religious and scientific, with their separate rallying calls of faith and reason, to run headlong into each other in subsequent centuries as each grew in strength and followers.

SUMMARY

1. Philosophy and science arose in the sixth century B.C. in the ancient Greek city of Miletus in Asia Minor.

2. It was the wonder and curiosity of the Greeks about this world rather than concern about the next that led to the rise of philosophy and science. Discovering the world for the first time not only led these first thinkers to raise new questions about it but also led them to pursue these new questions in a new way. They sought natural rather than supernatural knowledge about the world, and their goal was the achievement of a system of unified knowledge rather than a collection of facts.

3. The first philosophers and scientists did not succeed in seeing the world entirely anew. There were a number of beliefs (concerning the genesis, government, and composition of the world) that they inherited from the past that continued to influence their thinking on the new questions they raised.

4. The first philosopher and scientist was Thales, who flourished around 585 B.C. The first question raised by Thales and his successors concerned the nature of "Being." The great variety and profusion of things surrounding us must all have arisen, Thales and his successors speculated, from some one fundamental substance. Picking one of the four elements mentioned by tradition, Thales said that it must all have come from water. Anaximander, believing that it would have been unjust (and a threat to the harmony of the cosmos) for one of the elements to be elevated above the others, speculated that it could not have been any one of the four but something more primitive and prior to them. He identified it as apeiron, or the Boundless—some neutral, indeterminate, and infinite stuff. Anaximenes, the last member of this school, trying to preserve and synthesize what seemed best in the thought of his two predecessors, suggested that the fundamental stuff was air—a substance not quite so definite as water and not so indefinite and empty as Anaximander's Boundless. The other three elements, he further suggested, arose from it by way of the principle of condensation and rarefaction.

5. Thinkers soon realized that the first question raised and discussed—What is the nature of that stuff which seems constantly to be changing or becoming something else?—entailed another, even more fundamental question: What is change itself?

6. The first to address the question of change was Parmenides, who argued that change or becoming, if we use reason as our guide and are not deceived by what our senses tell us, must be an illusion. Since space, logically, is nothing, and since nothing is not, it does not exist. If there is no space, there cannot be motion in which it can take place, and without motion there cannot be change. Furthermore, since for many things to exist there must be space between them and since there is no space, all there can be is just one thing. Parmenides called that unitary, unchanging being the It.

7. Parmenides' subtle and abstract arguments were strongly reinforced by one of his followers, Zeno the Eleatic, in the form of certain paradoxes that continue to baffle thinkers to this day.

8. Heraclitus, a thinker living at about the same time as Parmenides, adopted a diametrically opposite view. Far from change being unreal, it is the most real thing there is. "Everything flows—nothing abides," he said. Concerning the nature of that which is in constant flux, he said it was fire.

9. The effort on the part of subsequent thinkers to preserve what was correct in each extreme finally resulted in the theory of atomism, a theory that proved to be an ingenious solution not only to the problem of Becoming but also to the problem of Being. The atomists suggested that the basic stuff out of which everything arises is atoms—tiny, indestructible particles, infinite in number. Bodies, large and small, are collections of atoms and arise and disappear as a result of the generation or dissolution of atoms. Parmenides was correct in maintaining that the real is unchanging, for the real consists of atoms, and they do not change; and Heraclitus was correct in insisting on change, for change, too, is real but happens only to complexes of atoms. And the Milesians were correct in seeking a unitary source of Being. Atoms are that source.

10. Although it is remarkable that thinkers living in the fifth century B.C. should succeed in arriving at a physical theory that in its essentials is still accepted by science today, what is even more noteworthy about both them and their predecessors was the new spirit that guided their investigations. In them, for the first time, supernaturalism gave way to naturalism, making possible the birth of science and philosophy.

KEY TERMS

anthropomorphism	paradox
atomism	pre-Socratics
Milesian school	supernaturalism
naturalism	Zeno's paradoxes

REVIEW QUESTIONS

1. Where did philosophy begin? Who is considered to be the "first" philosopher?

2. What were the four basic assumptions that restricted early Greek thought?

3. What was "the apeiron," and who posited it?

4. Who were the members of the Milesian school, and what did each consider to be the fundamental "stuff"?

5. Name the three early Greek philosophers who addressed the problem of change and becoming. What approach did each of them take?

6. Briefly summarize the three paradoxes of Zeno discussed in the text.

7. How does a paradox differ from a problem?

8. What is the theory of atomism? Which early Greek thinkers are most closely connected with this theory?

■ Reading

"Ionian Science before Socrates"

F. M. CORNFORD

Excerpted F. M. Cornford, *Before and After Socrates* (Cambridge: Cambridge University Press, 1950), pp. 1–28. Reprinted with the permission of Cambridge University Press.

Socrates, in his youth, had been eager to learn how philosophers had accounted for the origin of the world and of living creatures. He soon gave up this science of Nature, because he could not be satisfied with the sort of explanations or reasons offered. Some, for instance, had found the origin of life in a process of fermentation set up by the action of heat and cold. Socrates felt that such explanations left him none the wiser, and he concluded that he had no natural talent for inquiries of this sort.

We can infer from the sequel why he was dissatisfied. In this earlier science a physical event was supposed to be "explained" when it was (so to say) taken to pieces and described in terms of other physical events preceding or composing it. Such an explanation offers a more detailed picture of *how* the event came about; it does not, Socrates thought, tell us *why* it came about. The kind of reason Socrates wanted was the reason why.

Socrates then heard someone reading aloud a book by Anaxagoras, the philosophic friend of Pericles, which said that the world had been ordered by an Intelligence. This raised his hopes to a high pitch. An Intelligence ordering all things will surely, he thought, dispose them "for the best." He expected to find that Anaxagoras would explain the world order as a work of design, not a result of blind mechanical necessity. The reason of that order would then be found, not in some previous state of things from which it had emerged, but in some end or purpose that it could be shown to serve. Reasons of that sort seemed to Socrates intelligible and satisfying. . . . On reading Anaxagoras, however, Socrates found that the action of this Intelligence was limited to starting motion in space; and for the rest Anaxagoras fell back on mechanical causes of the usual type. In this system the world, after all, was not designed for any good purpose. Socrates himself could not do what Anaxagoras had left undone. He gave up all hope of an intelligible system of Nature, and turned away from the study of external things.

Accordingly, we find the Socrates depicted by Plato and Xenophon conversing, not about Nature, but about human life in society, the meaning of right and wrong, the ends for which we ought to live. . . .

The life of Socrates found its appropriate motto in the Delphic inscription, "Know thyself." Why was it that, just at that time and place, man discovered in himself a problem of more pressing importance than the understanding of external Nature? We might have expected that philosophy should begin at home, with the understanding that man's own soul and the meaning of his own life are more to him than the natural history of lifeless things. Why did man study Nature first, and forget the need to know himself till Socrates proclaimed that need as his chief concern? To find an answer to that question, we must now consider the early Ionian science of Nature, its character, and how it arose.

This science is called "Ionian" because it was begun by Thales and his successors at Miletus, one of the Ionian colonies on the coast of Asia Minor. Thales lived at the beginning of the sixth century. The development of Ionian science culminated two centuries later in the Atomism of Democritus, a contemporary of Socrates and Plato.

All the histories of Greek philosophy, from Aristotle's time to this day, begin with Thales of Miletus. It is generally agreed that with him something new, that we call Western science, appeared in the world—science as commonly defined: the pursuit of knowledge for its own sake, not for any practical use it can be made to serve. Thales, traveling in the East, found that the Egyptians possessed some rough rules of land measurement. Every year the inundation of the Nile obliterated the landmarks, and the peasants' fields had to be marked out afresh. The Egyptians had a method of calculating rectangular areas, and so solved their practical problem. The inquisitive Greek was not interested in marking out fields. He saw that the method could be detached from that particular purpose and generalized into a method of calculating areas of any shape. So the rules of land measurement were converted into the science of geometry. The problem—something to be done—gave place to the theorem—something to be contemplated. Reason found a fresh delight in knowing that the angles at the base of an isosceles triangle are always equal, and why they must be equal. The land surveyor still makes use of this truth in constructing maps; the philosopher is content to enjoy it because it is true.

In the same way the Greeks turned the art of astrology into the science of astronomy. For many centuries the Babylonian priests had recorded the movements of the planets, in order to predict human events, which the stars were believed to govern. The Greeks borrowed the results of observation, and Thales predicted an eclipse which occurred in Asia Minor in 585 B.C. But they ignored the whole fabric of astrological superstition which had hitherto provided the practical motive for observing the heavens. There is hardly a trace of astrology in Greek thought before the fusion of East and West following the conquests of Alexander.

The rise of science, then, meant that the intelligence became disinterested and now felt free to voyage on seas of thought strange to minds bent on immediate problems of action. Reason sought and found truth that was universal, but might, or might not, be useful for the exigencies of life. Looking back across some 2500 years, we see the cosmogonies of the Milesian School as the dawn or infancy of science. Here the histories of philosophy start, after a few remarks on the earlier age of mythology and superstition. But, for our purpose of appreciating the Socratic revolution of thought, it will be useful to look at this starting point of philosophy from the other side—the farther side. If we could survey the whole development of mankind, these last twenty-five centuries of science from Thales to our own day would appear in a very different proportion and perspective. We should then see philosophy as the latest of man's great achievements. Pre-

Socratic speculation would no longer strike us as rudimentary and infantile, but as the crowning epoch in a development covering many more ages than history can record.

I have spoken of this epoch as the discovery of Nature—a phrase which calls for explanation. I mean the discovery that the whole of the surrounding world of which our senses give us any knowledge is natural, not partly natural and partly supernatural. Science begins when it is understood that the universe is a natural whole, with unchanging ways of its own—ways that may be ascertainable by human reason, but are beyond the control of human action. To reach that point of view was a great achievement. If we would measure its magnitude, we must take a backward glance at certain features of the pre scientific age. These are (1) the detachment of the self from the external object—the discovery of the object; (2) the preoccupation of intelligence with the practical needs of action in dealing with the object; (3) the belief in unseen, supernatural powers, behind or within the object to be dealt with.

(1) With regard to the first point—the detachment of the self from the object—if it is true that the individual still recapitulates in miniature the history of the race, we are here concerned with something that goes very far back in human development. It is only in the first weeks of life that the human baby is a solipsist, taking for granted that his environment is a part of himself. This infantile philosophy is soon disturbed by doubt. Something goes wrong: the food supply fails to appear in immediate response to hunger. The infant cries out in anger and distress. He has to exert himself to make the environment behave as he wants. The solipsistic dream is soon shattered. In a month or so, he will be aware that there are other things, outside himself, to be cajoled or circumvented. The baby (as nurses say) "begins to take notice," or (as Virgil says) to "recognize his mother with a smile." The rift has begun to open between the self and the external world.

This nascent belief in the independent existence of external objects is the foundation of the philosophy of common sense, forced on the infant by the breakdown of his naive solipsism. In the development of the race, the discovery that there are things outside the self must, as I said, lie very far back. But it is one thing to make this discovery, and quite another to reach the idea that these external objects have a nature of their own, foreign to man's nature, and having neither sympathy nor hostility towards his passions and desires. A very long time must elapse before the line between the self and the object will be drawn where science draws it, and the object will be completely detached.

(2) The reason is that the intelligence remains, for all this long period, immersed in the interests of action, and has no leisure for disinterested speculation. That is the second feature of the pre-scientific age. In man, as in the higher animals, the primary use of intelligence was to devise means to compassing practical ends that cannot be immediately achieved. If you offer a banana to an ape, the ape will take it and begin to eat; there is no call for reflection. But if you hang the banana out of reach, action is held up. Intelligence must be summoned to the aid of thwarted desire. There is a pause before action can be resumed. When we have observed the action that follows we fill in that pause with a rudimentary train of reasoning. We imagine that the ape has reflected: "How can I get that

banana? Here are some boxes. If I pile them up and climb on them, I shall be able to reach it." What really happened in the ape's mind we cannot know. But we do know that man has used intelligence to overcome unusual obstacles to action, and, by the invention of tools and implements of all sorts, has extended his natural powers by natural means, and is still extending them. Thus intelligence at all times serves the purposes of action; and we conjecture that at first it served those purposes exclusively.

The limitation of the intelligence to things that merit attention because they can be turned to some practical purpose is still characteristic of savages. Dr. Malinowsky[1] writes about the Melanesian:

> The outer world interests him in so far as it yields things useful. Utility here of course must be understood in its broadest sense, including not only what man can consume as food, use for shelter and implement, but all that stimulates his activities in play, ritual, war, or artistic production.

All such significant things stand out for the savage as isolated, detached units against an undifferentiated background. When moving with savages through any natural milieu—sailing on the sea, walking on a beach or through the jungle, or glancing across the starlit sky—I was often impressed by their tendency to isolate the few objects important to them, and to treat the rest as mere background. In a forest a plant or tree would strike me, but on inquiry I would be informed—"Oh, that is just 'bush.'" An insect or bird which plays no part in the tradition or the larder would be dismissed *"Mauna wala"*—"*merely* a flying animal." But if, on the contrary, the object happened to be useful in one way or another, it would be named; detailed reference to its uses and properties would be given, and the thing thus would be distinctly individualized. . . . Everywhere there is the tendency to isolate that which stands in some connection, traditional, ritual, useful to man, and to bundle all the rest into one indiscriminate heap.

(3) At first, then, the scope of thought was bounded by the imperious needs of action. External things were selected for notice in proportion as they entered into human activities. They were not interesting for what they are in themselves, but as things we can do something with, or that can act upon us. Let us now consider them in this second capacity, as agents.

To go back to our ape, pausing in his thwarted desire to seize the banana. In the interval of suspended action, we may imagine him feeling that things are opposing his desire with some contrary will of their own—an experience familiar enough in his dealings with his brother apes. There are resistances to be overcome—powers to be circumvented by his own power. And when he perceives that the boxes will help him to gain his end, he will feel that the world is not all against him: there are also things with benevolent intentions that sympathize with and forward his wishes. These helpful or harmful intentions, these unseen forces that further or thwart action, are fragmentary elements of personality. They are the raw material from which man, when he began to reflect, constructed the supernatural world. In Roman religion we find countless *numina*—powers whose whole content is expressed in abstract nouns, *nomina:* Janus is not a fully personal god presiding over doorways, but simply the spirit of "doorness," conceived as a power present in all doors, that can help or harm one who passes through them. From such elementary *numina* there is a scale ranging through spirits of various kinds up to the completely anthropomorphic god, like the gods of Homer.

These fragmentary elements of personality at first simply reside in things. In a sense, they are projected from man's self into the object; but we must not think of them as the creations of any conscious theory. In a census return, primitive man would not have entered his religion as "Animist," or even as "Pre-animist." The assumption that helpful or harmful things have the will to help or harm is made as unreflectingly as by the child who kicks a door that has pinched his finger, or by the man who curses his golf club for slicing a stroke. If such a man were logical, he would pray to his golf clubs before beginning a match; or he would murmur some spell to charm them into hitting straight. For these projected elements of personality are the proper objects of magical art. They are "supernatural" in that their behavior is not regular and calculable; you cannot be sure which way they will act, as you can be sure that if you touch flame you will be burnt. Magic includes a whole collection of practices designed to bring these supernatural forces under some measure of control. And if they are to be controlled, the more we can know of their nature and habits the better. Mythology supplies this need by fabricating a history of the supernatural, with the effect of fixing the unseen powers in more definite shape and endowing them with more concrete substance. They become detached from the things in which at first they resided, and are filled out into complete persons. So magic and mythology occupy the immense outer region of the unknown, encompassing the small field of matter-of-fact ordinary knowledge. The supernatural lies everywhere within or beyond the natural; and the knowledge of the supernatural which man believes himself to possess, not being drawn from ordinary direct experience, seems to be knowledge of a different and higher order. It is a revelation, accessible only to the inspired or (as the Greeks said) "divine" man—the magician and the priest, the poet and the seer.

Now the birth of science in Greece is marked by the tacit denial of this distinction between two orders of knowledge, experience and revelation, and between the two corresponding orders of existence, the natural and the supernatural. The Ionian cosmogonists assume (without even feeling the need to make the assertion) that the whole universe is natural, and potentially within the reach of knowledge as ordinary and rational as our knowledge that fire burns and water drowns. That is what I meant by the discovery of Nature. The conception of Nature is extended to incorporate what had been the domain of the supernatural. The supernatural, as fashioned by mythology, simply disappears; all that really exists is natural.

Enough, perhaps, has been said to justify the statement that the discovery of Nature was one of the greatest achievements of the human mind. Like all other great achievements, it was the work of a very few individuals with exceptional gifts. Why were these individuals Ionian Greeks of the sixth century?

The Ionian cities in Asia Minor were then at the height of Western civilization. There were men in them who had outgrown the magical practices that were never to die out among the peasantry. They had also outgrown the Olympian religion of Homer. Thanks to the poets, the anthropomorphic tendency of myth had over-reached itself. The Greek imagination was, perhaps, unique in visual clarity, far surpassing the Roman in this respect. The supernatural powers had taken human shapes so concrete and well defined that a Greek could recognize any god by sight. When the tall and bearded Barnabas and the restless eloquent Paul came to Lystra, the inhabitants at once identified them as Zeus and Hermes. It was inevitable that, when the gods had become completely human persons, some skeptical mind should refuse to believe that a thunderstorm in Asia Minor was really due to the anger of a deity seated on the summit of Olympus. In the sixth century Xenophanes attacked anthropomorphic polytheism with devastating finality:

> If horses or oxen had hands and could draw or make statues, horses would represent the forms of the gods like horses, oxen like oxen.

Henceforth natural science annexed to its province all that went on "aloft" in the sky or "under the earth." Thunder and lightning, Anaximander said, were caused by the blast of the wind. Shut up in a thick cloud, the wind bursts forth, and then the tearing of the cloud makes the noise, and the rift gives the appearance of a flash in contrast with the blackness of the cloud. This is a typically scientific "explanation." There is no longer a supernatural background, peopled with fragmentary or complete personalities accessible to prayer and sacrifice or amenable to magical compulsion. Intelligence is cut off from action. Thought is left confronting Nature, an impersonal world of things, indifferent to man's desires and existing in and for themselves. The detachment of self from the object is now complete.

To the few advanced intellects who had reached this point of view, it probably seemed that they had disposed of mythology, once for all, as simply false. It is important to bear in mind that they did not carry with them the rest of the Greek world. For a thousand years the smoke of sacrifice was still to rise from the altars of Zeus. Minds not less acute and possibly more profound felt that myth was not a baseless figment of superstition, but was like the Muses of Hesiod, who knew not only how to speak falsehood in the guise of truth, but also, when they would, how to utter the truth itself. The Aphrodite and Artemis of the *Hippolytus* and the Dionysus of the *Bacchae* were to Euripides something more than either projections of human psychology or fictitious personifications of natural forces. So myth was destined to survive the contempt of Ionian rationalism and to await reinterpretation.

But at the moment we are now considering science seems to have swept mythology away. The systems of the sixth century are cast in the form of cosmogony. Two principal questions are answered. First, how did the world we see come to be arranged as it is: at the center, the earth with the great masses of water in the hollow seas; round it the airy region of mist and cloud and rain; and beyond that the heavenly fires? Secondly, how did life arise within this order? The answer is a history of the birth of a world order out of an initial state of things (a "beginning," *arché*).

Take for illustration the most complete and daring of these cosmogonies, the system of Thales's successor, Anaximander, which set the pattern for the Ionian tradition. At first there was an unbounded and unordered mass of indiscriminate stuff, containing the antagonistic powers of heat and cold. This mass had the living property of eternal motion. At some point a nucleus, pregnant with these warring powers, took shape—a rationalized equivalent of the world-egg of mythical cosmogony. Perhaps because the hostility of the hot and the cold drove them apart, the nucleus was differentiated. The cold became a watery mass of earth enveloped in cloud; the hot, a sphere of flame enwrapping the whole, like bark round a tree. Then the sphere of flame burst, and was torn off to form rings of fire enclosed and hidden in dark mist. Sun, moon, and stars, the points of light we see in the sky, are spouts of fire issuing from holes in these opaque rings, as the air issues from the nozzle of a bellows. The earth was then dried by the heat of the heavenly fires, and the seas shrank into their hollow beds. At last, life arose in the warm slime. The first animals were like sea urchins enclosed in prickly shells. From these sea creatures, land animals, including man, were evolved.

The significance of this cosmogony lies not so much in what it contains as in what it leaves out. Cosmogony has been detached from theogony. There is not a word about the gods or any supernatural agency. This new form of thought brings into the field of everyday experience what had previously lain outside that field. We may see the difference by contrasting this history of the world with the old poetical theogony of Hesiod. As Hesiod looked back in time from his own age and the life he knew and dealt with every day, past the earlier ages—the Heroic Age, the Silver Age—to the dominion of Cronos and the elder gods, and beyond that to the birth of the gods themselves from the mysterious marriage of Heaven and Earth, it must have seemed that the world became less and less like the common world of familiar experience. The events—the marriage and birth of the gods, the war of the Olympians and the Titans, the legend of Prometheus—were not events of the same order as what happened in Boeotia in Hesiod's time. We may get the same impression by thinking of the Book of Genesis—all the events from creation down to the call of Abraham. As we follow the story we gradually emerge into the world we know, and the superhuman figures dwindle down to human proportions. That is how the past had looked to everyone before the rise of Ionian science. It was an extraordinary feat of rational thinking, to dissipate this haze of myth from the origins of the world and of life. Anaximander's system pushes back to the very beginning the operation of ordinary forces such as we see at work in Nature every day. The formation of the world becomes a natural, not a supernatural, event.

Such were the Ionian cosmogonies of the sixth century: they told how an ordered world was evolved out of an undifferentiated initial state of things. In the fifth century, science takes a somewhat different line, which it has followed ever since. Retaining the form of cosmogony, it becomes more particularly an inquiry into the ultimate constitution of material substance—the uniform and permanent "nature of things." Let us consider, in conclusion, the outcome of this inquiry—the Atomism of Democritus.

Atomism is a theory of the nature of tangible bodily substance. The notion of substance is taken from common sense. The belief in substantial things outside ourselves goes back to the original detachment of self from the object. A substance is something that exists independently of my seeing or touching it—something that endures, as the same thing, whether I am there to see it or not. The problem for science is: What is this substance that endures when it has ceased to yield us sensations? I have under my eyes what I call a sheet of paper. What I actually see is a white area with black marks. When I touch it, I feel the resistance of a smooth surface, and I can trace with my finger its rectangular shape. These sensations are my only assurance that something is there, outside me. If I turn my eyes in another direction, the whiteness and the black marks disappear. I have only the tactile sensations of the resistance of the smooth rectangular surface. If I lift my finger, these sensations also disappear. Yet I am absolutely certain that something is still there—a substance which does not depend upon my having sensations derived from it. Which of these properties—white and black, resistance, smoothness, shape—really belong independently to the thing outside me, and continue to exist when I am not looking and touching?

The Atomists held that the tactile properties are the real ones; the visual properties are not substantial or objective. They are not there when I am not looking. In a dark room the sheet of paper would lose its color; I should see nothing. But I should still feel the shape and resistance of the surface. If I could not detect those properties, I should feel nothing and be sure the thing was not there. If I did detect them, I should be certain that, when I turned on the light, the visual properties would spring into existence again.

By this train of thought common sense can be led towards the fundamental doctrines of Atomism. The atoms of Democritus are hard bodies, too small to be seen, and deprived of all properties except shape and resistance—the tangible properties necessary and sufficient to convince us that something real is there. A larger body is not destroyed when it is broken up into atoms. All the pieces are still there, and they can be reassembled. Also they can move in space without suffering any change of quality. Atomism held that the real—the enduring and unchanging core of substance—is nothing but atoms, moving in empty space. Not only are these atoms real, but they are the whole of reality.

I do not mean to suggest that the Atomism of Democritus was actually reached by the train of thought I have outlined. In historical fact, it arose as a mathematical theory that matter consists of discrete units. But the result is the same. The atoms of Democritus are tiny bodies, into which larger bodies can be cut up, but which cannot themselves be cut into smaller pieces. They are absolutely solid, compact, impenetrable.

Where scientific Atomism went beyond common sense was in its demand that the atoms of body shall be absolutely indestructible and unchanging. This was a requirement of the reason. Common sense, untutored by science, would suppose that bodies can be, and constantly are being, destroyed. A thing will remain the same thing for a time, though some of its properties change; but then it may simply cease to exist and something else will come into being. But ancient science, holding to the principle that nothing can come out of nothing, demanded some permanent and indestructible "being" behind the screen of shifting appearances. This postulate met the same rational need that has prompted the assertion by modern science of the principle of conservation in various forms: the law of inertia, the conservation of mass, the conservation of energy. It has been observed that all these propositions were at first announced either without proof of any sort or as the result of a priori demonstration, although later they have often been regarded as purely empirical laws.[2] The something—whatever it may be—of which modern science has required the conservation corresponds to the permanent "being" or "nature of things" required by the ancients. For the Atomists it was impenetrable particles of material substance.

Ancient science, having deduced the indestructible atom, thought it had arrived at the real nature of things. The variable qualities which things seem to have, but atoms have not—colors, tastes, and so forth—were disposed of as mere sensations which fall inside our organs of perception. They are not "substantial," for they depend on us for their existence. Atoms alone are real, with the void in which they move and strike one another.

The essential feature of this Atomism is that it is a materialist doctrine. By that I do not mean merely that it is an account of the nature of material substance or body. It is materialist in the sense that it declares that material substance, tangible body, is not only real but the whole of reality. Everything that exists or happens is to be explained in terms of these bodily factors. The world is resolved into an invisible game of billiards. The table is empty space. The balls are atoms; they collide and pass on their motion from one to another. That is all: nothing else is real. There are no players in this game. If three balls happen to make a cannon, that is a mere stroke of luck—necessary, not designed. The game consists entirely of flukes; and there is no controlling intelligence behind.

Considered as a theory of the nature of material substance, Atomism was a brilliant hypothesis. Revived by modern science, it has led to the most important discoveries in chemistry and physics. But, as I have said, ancient Atomism went farther than this. It claimed to be an account of the whole of reality—not a mere scientific hypothesis, but a complete philosophy. As such, it should include an account of the spiritual aspect of the world, as well as of the material. But when we consider the system from that standpoint, we find that anything we can recognize as spiritual has simply disappeared. When the Atomist is asked for an account of the soul, he replies that the soul (like everything else) consists of atoms. These soul-atoms are of the same impenetrable substance as all others; only they are spherical in shape, and so can move very easily and slip in between the angular and less mobile atoms of the body. Sensation is due to atoms from outside knocking up against the soul-atoms. The variety of qualities we perceive corresponds to the variety of atomic shapes. As late as 1675, a French chemist, whose treatise remained classical for half a century, wrote:

> The hidden nature of a thing cannot be better explained than by attributing to its parts shapes corresponding to all the effects it produces. No one will deny that the acidity of a liquid consists in pointed particles. All experience confirms this. You have only to taste it to feel a pricking of the tongue like that caused by some material cut into very fine points.[3]

That statement might have been written by Lucretius, and (so far as it goes) it is a reasonable explanation of the mechanical cause of a certain sensation. But if I turn from the mechanical cause to the sensation itself, and then to the soul which has the sensation, and also has feelings, thoughts, and desires, I am not so easily convinced that the soul itself consists of round atoms, and that nothing really happens except collisions. It is much harder to believe that a process of thought or an emotion of anger is either totally unreal or else actually consists of a number of solid particles banging together. If man had begun by studying himself, rather than external Nature, he would never have reached so fantastic a conclusion.

Perhaps what I said earlier about the peculiar visual clarity of Greek mythology, may explain how science came at last to ignore or deny the spiritual, as distinct from the material. If the world has a spiritual aspect, man can only give an account of it in terms of his own spirit or mind. At first he projected elements of his own personality into external things. Then the Greek imagination developed these elements into the complete human personalities of anthropomorphic gods. Sooner or later the Greek intelligence was bound to discover that such gods do not exist. Thus mythology overreached itself and discredited the very existence of a spiritual world. Science drew the conclusion, not that the spiritual world had been misconceived, but that there was no such thing: nothing was real except tangible body composed of atoms. The result was a doctrine that philosophers call materialism, and religious people call atheism.

The Socratic philosophy is a reaction against this materialistic drift of physical science. In order to rediscover the spiritual world, philosophy had to give up, for the moment, the search after material substance in external Nature, and turn its eyes inwards to the nature of the human soul. This was the revolution accomplished by Socrates, with his Delphic injunction "Know thyself."

NOTES

1. C. K. Ogden and I. A. Richards, *The Meaning of Meaning* (1930), Supplement 1, p. 331.

2. Cf. E. Meyerson, De l'explication dans les sciences (Paris, 1921), II, 327; Paul Tannery, Pour l'histoire de la science hellne (Paris, 1887), p. 264.

3. Lémery, Cours de Chymie, quoted by E. Meyerson, De l'explication dans les sciences (Paris, 1921), I, 285.

■ **Questions for Discussion**

1. Compare the break made by the pre-Socratics, beginning with Thales of Miletus, from previous thought to the break made by Socrates from the thinkers that preceded him. How are they similar? How do they differ?

2. Do you think one or the other had greater consequences or significance?

Socrates: "And so I go about the world . . ."

THE MAN WHO IS the subject of this chapter wrote not a single book, left not a scrap of written information for posterity, and is known only at secondhand through the writings of his contemporaries. Yet he was one of the most remarkable people who ever lived and was part of an age and culture whose profound and overwhelming effect on the Western world helped determine the form our civilization has taken. His name was Socrates.

In an absorbing series titled "The Miracle of Greece" that appeared in *Life* magazine, this age and this people were described in its opening lines:

It was sudden. It was miraculous. Nobody knows why it happened. But on a small rock-bound Mediterranean peninsula 2,500 years ago a handful of people called Greeks roused the human race to a new ambition and sense of purpose and launched it into history. (January 4, 1963, p. 28)

That the modern world still feels the impact of that awakening is in great part due to Socrates, who set Western thought on its course and gave it the tone and character it still bears.

The *Life* article went on to say that on the surface these ancient Greeks seem unlikely candidates for this momentous mission:

They were always fighting among themselves. They were garrulous and monstrously egocentric. They were often treacherous. They were so eager that they had to mount the slogan "Nothing to Excess" in big letters at Delphi to remind them to be less excessive. But they did have one idea, so novel and profound that a whole new age dawned in its light. It was simply that man's nature, even in its mortality, is the glory of creation, and that man

45

has a noble purpose: to live at the highest possible pitch of human perfection—physically, morally and intellectually. (p. 29)

To Socrates, who understood that idea probably better than anyone else and who may even be credited with being the first to articulate it, it consisted in the belief that humans possess a **psyche**, a soul, the part of them that is most truly the self. This was in fact his single greatest discovery—perhaps the single greatest discovery in the whole of philosophy—and one that more than anything else accounts for the obsessive urgency, gradually assuming the force of a compulsion with which he went about trying to reveal it to others.

Socrates was not, of course, the first to speak of the soul. Among the pre-Socratics, both Democritus and Heraclitus had in fact a good deal to say about it. Democritus, for example, maintained that the soul was composed of "finer" atoms, and Heraclitus believed that the most reasonable soul was the dry one, the one closest to that ultimate stuff, fire. Heraclitus added, as evidence, that imbibing liquor moistens the soul, with obvious results. Socrates' conception, however, went beyond these materialistic metaphors to what was genuinely important—the *excellence* of the soul and how to attain it. It is this attempt to discover what is truly unique about human beings and how we can preserve it that led F. M. Cornford to say that whereas "pre-Socratic philosophy begins with the discovery of Nature, Socratic philosophy begins with the discovery of man's soul" (see the reading in chapter 2) and A. E. Taylor to remark that "it was Socrates who, as far as can be seen, created the conception of the *soul*" (*Socrates*, Oxford University Press, 1933).

It was this new conception of the soul and the use he made of it that in the end cost Socrates his life. Why should people take the life of such a man?

As we will see, it was in part because of the increasing hostility engendered by the kind of activity he engaged in and partly because of the tragic social and political events of the final 30 years or so of the fifth century B.C., events ending in the defeat of Athens by Sparta and in the death of this great civilization.

Before turning to consider the ideas of Socrates, it will be useful to look for a few moments at a group of other thinkers—called **Sophists**—circulating in Athens at this time and with whom, unfortunately, Socrates tended to be confused.

THE SOPHISTS

It is ironic and sad that Socrates, who believed that the human soul was the only thing worth caring about, should be confused in the public mind with a group of people whose main concern was not the salvation of man's soul but the secret of worldly success.

Who were these Sophists? They were itinerant teachers who began to gravitate to Athens around the fifth century B.C. The Greek term that referred to them, reflecting the respect in which they were initially held, meant "expert" or "wise one." They did not, however, succeed in retaining this good name for very long. Becoming masters of the arts of political success, they offered to teach these skills to anyone able to afford their fees. Athens was now a democracy, and such skills were important tools for anyone wishing to succeed in life. Understandably, the demand for their services increased, and the Sophists grew wealthy from the large fees they received. The poor, who could not afford to pay their high fees but who needed these skills as much as anyone, if not more, came to despise them.

Although confining themselves at first to teaching only practical subjects, the Sophists began to explore and raise questions about matters of much wider implication and concern, regarding the state and its justification, traditional religion, and orthodox morality. As they became more and more radical, their attacks on the established system of political, social, and religious life became more and more severe. Might it not be the case, they began to ask their listeners, that our notions of

> How can man be the measure of all things when he is not the measure of himself?
> **Richard Taylor, American philosopher**

law, conduct, and religion are merely a matter of custom and convention? If so, by what right can we say one way is better than another? And if we have indeed merely agreed to adopt certain ways of conducting and governing ourselves, what stops us, should we be so inclined, from abandoning these ways or overthrowing them?

The result of the extreme subjectivism adopted by the Sophists is perhaps best epitomized in the famous line of Protagoras that "Man is the measure of all things."

From teaching how to win, by fair means or foul, the Sophists proceeded to enquire whether there was such a thing as fair or foul, right or wrong, to begin with and then finally to wonder whether perhaps winning is all. The public, scandalized by the expression of such views and questions, came to regard them with increasing suspicion and alarm.

Opposed to these Sophists, although no less critical than they, stood Socrates, who showered both them and the state with abuse for neglecting what he believed should be their chief and proper concern: knowledge of oneself and of the right way to live. For he believed there was a right way and that it was not all simply relative. Yet he was also certain it had not yet been found, at least in Athens.

SOCRATES THE MAN

The details of Socrates' life are unremarkable. He came from a middle-class Athenian family. His father was a bricklayer and his mother a midwife. Socrates himself seems to have been trained in his father's craft. Physically, he was by all accounts rather odd looking: short, ugly, pop-eyed, potbellied, pug-nosed, walking with a shambling gait. But he was also obviously a man of considerable bravery and vigor, well known for his courageous behavior in battle. Intellectually, needless to say, he was brilliant.

Socrates (470?–399 BCE)

But he does not seem to have worked very hard, if at all, at his trade, nor does he seem to have spent much time with his family, preferring to spend it in following his profession of philosophy, which took the form of questioning people concerning their beliefs and way of life.

Most of the accounts that have come down to us depict Socrates as engaged in this sort of investigation of his fellow Athenians. He believed they were occupied with all sorts of trivial pursuits and were neglecting the one thing that was really important, which for him was the pursuit of virtue and knowledge. He thought it was not possible to acquire virtue, to act rightly, without knowledge. This was why clear thinking about right conduct and the need to achieve exact definitions were of such importance to him. This was a necessary first step.

To this, however, he added a view that looks paradoxical to us: that if one does have this kind of knowledge, one cannot fail to *be* good and act as a good person should, regardless of the circumstances in which one may find oneself or the stresses one may be subjected to. Such, he believed and taught, was the power of knowledge—and deep within his fellows' hearts, he insisted, they knew he was right.

In maintaining all this, Socrates was really addressing two very different but related questions. The first concerned the role that learning performs in making a person good. Most of us would probably agree that learning does indeed play such a role. We believe, for instance, in trying to incorporate a "moral education" in our children's upbringing. Further, we tend to value a literary work more if it incorporates a moral tale. Also, we seem to believe that by example of those around us, we can assimilate some good traits. So, for most of us, the answer to the question cast at this level would be that learning is a necessary condition for becoming good. This would amount to the rather moderate claim that in order to become a person of good character, we must at some time have learned about what kinds of acts are right and what makes them right.

Socrates was, however, also making the much more ambitious claim that learning about such things was not only a necessary but also a sufficient condition for becoming a good person. This amounts to saying that should we come to such knowledge of good and bad, right and wrong, we could not help becoming a virtuous person. It also means that the morally undeveloped, and indeed the vicious, necessarily lack such knowledge and are as they are because they lack it. This position would seem to be very difficult to defend against empirical evidence. We hear of people daily committing vicious and barbarous acts and admitting that they knew they were wrong. We do not think, typically, of the murderer or rapist as one who is unfortunately short of knowledge of right or wrong but rather as a person who perpetrates the crime knowing full well that his or her deed is heinous.

However that may be, Socrates believed he still lacked this knowledge that would make him truly good and was hoping to find it with the help of others who might be, as he would add—perhaps ironically—"more gifted than himself."

Obviously, Socrates could not have run into very many, if indeed any, who were more gifted than he was, and very few no doubt could have been expected to respond kindly to this appeal to their better selves, if indeed they were not angered by it. So there were reasons enough for his own growing personal unpopularity with many of his fellow citizens.

Thus, it could not have been entirely unexpected either of him or of them that when he was brought to trial for heresy and for "corrupting the minds of the young," he took the opportunity to dwell again on their failures and past mistakes and to explain to them the real source of their animosity toward him. This stemmed, he told them, from his "philosopher's mission of searching into myself and other people," from his having been a gadfly to the state, urging its citizens to self-improvement, and from his search for wisdom, having exposed their ignorance. His true enemies were not his present prosecutors but all those who opposed the life of reason and virtue and who shrank before his conviction that "the unexamined life is not worth living."

To understand why Socrates was brought to trial and eventually executed for his teachings, it is necessary to understand the social and political events of the last 30 or so years of this fifth century B.C.

LIFE IN ATHENS AND CONQUEST BY SPARTA

Athens reached her peak development under the great democratic statesman Pericles (495–429 B.C.). She was a great naval and military power, had built an empire and possessed great wealth, and had advanced to a democratic form of government. It was the most brilliant society ancient times produced.

If you will think of a small city of about 130,000 inhabitants producing in a short span of time buildings unsurpassed in beauty to this day, two of the greatest historians of all time, some of the greatest dramatists the world has ever known, to say nothing of achievements in philosophy, sculpture, and music, you will have some idea of the splendor of the age. Pericles himself was not unaware of the greatness of the period over which he presided. "Future ages," he said, "will wonder at us, for our adventurous spirit has taken us to every sea and country, and everywhere we have left behind us everlasting monuments" (Thucydides, *The Peloponnesian War*, Book II).

But this high point of Athenian development was no sooner reached than its decline began. As is so often the case, the cause was war: here it was the Peloponnesian War (431–404 B.C.). Socrates was 38 when this long, exhausting war began, and it ended in the defeat of Athens by Sparta and her allies.

Located about 150 miles by land from Athens, Sparta occupied the southeast part of the Peloponnesus. The Spartans conquered the country at the time of the Dorian invasion and reduced the population to the condition of serfs. The serfs, called helots, were forced to work the land for their new masters. The helots bitterly resented their condition and, when they could, rebelled. The Spartans had a body of secret police to deal with this danger. In addition, once a year they would declare war on the helots so that their young men could legally kill any helot who seemed insubordinate.

Freed from labor, which they regarded as degrading, the Spartans devoted themselves, from birth, to becoming invincible warriors. Sickly children would be killed by exposure, and only those judged vigorous were allowed to live. Those so selected were then, to the age of 20, trained in one big school. The object of the training was to make them hardy, indifferent to pain, and submissive to authority.

At 20, actual military service began. Although marriage was permitted to anyone over 20, all men (including those who were married) had to live in the "men's house" until the age of 30. Homosexuality was encouraged in the belief that fighting next to one's lover would make one braver and more heroic. It was also the theory of the state that no Spartan should be poor or rich. No one was therefore allowed to own gold or silver, and money was made of iron. Spartan simplicity became proverbial.

Women were also treated differently in Sparta than they were anywhere else in Greece. Not secluded as elsewhere, they were given the same training as the boys, with the same design in mind—to turn them into wholly devoted citizens of the state. They were not allowed to show grief if their newborn child was condemned to death or if their son was killed in battle. If childless, they were trained to raise no objection if the state ordered them to see whether another man might be more successful than their husband in begetting children for the state. Children, once begotten, reared, trained, and sent off to battle, would be told by their mothers to come back *with* their shields or on them.

It was these people, who neither tried to make nor made any contribution to civilization but sacrificed everything to success in war, who finally, in 404 B.C., managed to defeat Athens. Driving out its whole population—men, women, and children—the Spartans forced the Athenians to submit to the final humiliation of tearing down the wall surrounding the city. That marked the end of that great Greek civilization.

But that empire and greatness, as glorious and inspiring as it might appear to us, had been achieved at a very high price. Greece's Golden Age began with the victories over Persian invaders at Marathon (490 B.C.) and Salamis (480 B.C.). After the Persians had been repulsed, the Greeks, under the leadership of Athens, formed a league whose aim was to protect the Aegean from further Persian attacks. In time, however, the Athenians, by threat and deception, converted this voluntary league into an empire, an empire that exacted with growing ruthlessness huge sums of money from its subject states, money that it used to increase its military might, beautify the city, and finance the expensive projects on the Acropolis. The statue of Athena in the Parthenon alone cost the equivalent of $10 million. All this occurred while some 20,000 slaves, many of them

Greeks, were worked to death in Athens and its silver mines, and many thousands of other Greeks led a dismal existence.

There was, then, much to criticize. Democracy with its glorious achievements was financed by imperialism abroad and exploitation at home, an imperialism and exploitation growing more oppressive and ruthless with each year. Dreams of world conquest and the good life corrupted the Athenians, proving that the democracy they had achieved—for the elite—was only skin deep after all. On the stage, their dramatists portrayed and taught how a surfeit of goods leads to pride, rashness, and ruin, and their audiences proved them right.

But however comforting it might be to believe that the Athenians knew the truth, recognized that they did not deserve to keep what they had so ignobly obtained, and desired Socrates' life because of the guilt he aroused in their hearts, it is probable that this is not the way the ordinary citizen of Athens and those in authority saw it. They undoubtedly regarded those who, like the Sophists, asked too many questions or those who, like Socrates, raised doubts about worldly gain, as subversives, busy undermining the loyalties of those, and especially the youth, on whom the city's continued happiness depended.

And so in 399 B.C., after the Thirty Tyrants (who had been installed to rule Athens by the Spartans) had been overthrown and the democrats returned to power, Socrates was indicted on the charge of "corrupting the minds of the young and introducing strange gods."

Although the charges strike us as ridiculous, they would not necessarily have appeared so to his fellow citizens: after all, Socrates did profess to be guided by a "voice," and there had been in the recent past the cases of Alcibiades, the gifted, charismatic leader of Athens, who had turned traitor in the course of the war, and Critias, the cruelest of the Thirty Tyrants, both of whom had attended on Socrates when they were young.

The "voice" in question here is one from which Socrates, we will see later, claimed to receive direction. He understood it to be of divine origin and as such always unquestionably correct. "I am subject," he said of it at his trial, "to a divine or supernatural experience, which Meletus [one of his accusers] saw fit to travesty in his indictment."

Socrates was obviously not unaware of the suspicion in which he was held, but at his trial he seemed less interested in defusing the suspicions than in using the occasion to once again explain to his fellow citizens what their mission in life should be.

Was he unaware of the more serious factors in the case against him and their dangerous potentials? No. Did he care? No. Did he seek martyrdom? Possibly.

SOCRATES' CHRONICLERS

The person who immortalized Socrates was his young pupil Plato. Born in 427 B.C.—in the early years of the Peloponnesian War—Plato was a young man when Athens was finally defeated by Sparta and may even have fought in the war.

Plato belonged to one of the best families in Athens, a family both wealthy and politically influential. On his mother's side he could claim descent from Solon, the great Athenian statesman and reformer; on his father's side he could claim descent from the last kings of Athens.

The normal career for Plato would have been in politics. But as we have seen, the political life of Athens had degenerated greatly in the last 30 years of the century. The Peloponnesian War had exhausted the city's resources, and Plato, after fulfilling his military service, steered clear of politics. He decided instead to develop a sound political philosophy. This remained a leading interest with him all his life; it is in the forefront of his speculations. He began by writing dialogues to commemorate the memory of his teacher and mentor, Socrates, in whose company (he was 28 when Socrates was executed) he had spent over 10 years.

> Plato has cast a spell on many generations, the sense of a quest on the verge of fulfillment, of wonderful things glimpsed, but never clearly seen, so that keeping company with him seems to carry a promise.
>
> —F. J. E. Woodbridge,
> *The Son of Apollo* (1929)

Plato's lifelong passion, acquiring the thrust it did as a result of the unjust and tragic death suffered by his beloved teacher, was to arrive at a conception of a state in which such an injustice could not be perpetrated. Justice, or the just state, is thus the subject of many of his works, including the greatest and best known of these, the *Republic*. It is in this work that he arrived at the solution that the just state will be achieved only when either philosophers become kings or kings become philosophers.

It is interesting that Plato's conception of justice, which leads to this conclusion, is reminiscent of one of the mythopoetic beliefs we explored in the previous chapter in connection with the thought of the first Greek thinkers. **Justice** is a kind of disposition existing in each member of the **just society** (rulers, soldiers, workers) to mind his or her own proper business and not meddle in the affairs of the others—affairs in which, by their nature, they lack competence. Put in contemporary terminology, it is to resist the Peter Principle—that is, to resist the temptation to rise to your level of incompetence. If your nature has provided you with the abilities to be a first-rate shoemaker, you and others should resist the temptation to accept the reward of promotion to a higher office for which you may lack any competence (e.g., the management of the entire shoe factory or president of the union). In Plato's view, a just society is a society where everything has its proper place and everyone does what is proper for him (what his nature or talents prepared him best for).

Plato had an opportunity to put his theories into practice. About 11 years after Socrates' death, Plato was invited by the tyrant of Syracuse, Dionysius I, to visit his court. Plato disliked the dissolute life there, and Dionysius did not care much for Plato, either. The result of the unfortunate encounter ended, if we can trust tradition, in Plato being sold into slavery. Friends, however, managed to ransom him. On his return to

Athens, they refused his offer to repay the money used in gaining his freedom, so Plato used his money to found the Academy. This school, of which he remained the leader until his death in 347 B.C., was in effect the first university in the Western world. He gathered around him a group of scholars and pupils. The scholars organized research projects and quite soon made brilliant contributions in such fields as mathematics and astronomy. The Academy continued for over 900 years before it was finally closed by the Roman emperor Justinian in A.D. 529—a record for unbroken existence never exceeded by any other university.

PLATON. PHILOSOPHE GREC.
Chap. 29.

Plato (427?-347 BCE)

Plato was the first philosopher whose literary output is largely (but not wholly) preserved. Most of his writings are in the form of **dialogues**, initiated as a means of paying tribute to Socrates. Socrates is the main speaker in all but a few, and he is represented as being present in all save one. Scholars have generally divided Plato's work into three periods.

The *early*, or *Socratic*, *period* includes a dozen or so dialogues, of which the *Euthyphro* and the *Apology* are good examples. These dialogues analyze the chief virtues and are characterized generally by Socratic irony, although the real answers to the questions raised are indicated rather clearly.

The *middle period* consists of somewhat longer works, and it is here that Plato reaches the height of his dramatic power. The *Republic*, to which we have already referred, and the *Phaedo*, which we will be looking at later, are good examples of the works of this period.

Finally, there are the works of the *late period*. These are drier in style and more technical. Plato was getting into questions here that Socrates probably did not discuss. The *Theaetetus* (a long dialogue about knowledge in which Plato attempted to demolish the view, ascribed to Protagoras, that knowledge is based on sense perception and is relative to the individual perceiver) and the *Timaeus* (a similarly long work dealing with cosmology) are typical of this period. Finally there is the *Laws*, Plato's last work, which is also concerned with the problem of constructing an ideal state. The deeply conservative view that Plato took in this longest of all his works has been a source of great puzzlement to its readers, leading some to regard him as one of the major Western proponents of totalitarianism.

Although Plato was obviously the deepest and most profound student of Socrates to write about him, he was not the only one. We have, in fact, two further main sources of information regarding Socrates: Aristophanes and Xenophon.

Of the three, Aristophanes was the only one to have written about Socrates while he was still alive. The other two wrote about Socrates only after his death: Plato soon after

Gorgias's Advice to Socrates

Here, then, you have the truth of the matter. You will become convinced of it if you only let philosophy alone and pass on to more important considerations. Of course, Socrates, philosophy does have a certain charm if one engages with it in one's youth and in moderation; but if one dallies overlong, it's the ruin of a fellow. If a man, however well endowed, goes on philosophizing throughout his life, he will never come to taste the experiences which a man must have if he's going to be a gentleman and have the world look up to him. You know perfectly well that philosophers know nothing about state laws and regulations. They are equally ignorant of the conversational standards that we have to adopt in dealing with our fellow men at home and abroad. Why, they are inexperienced even in human pleasures and desires! In a word, they are totally innocent of all human character. So, when they come to take part in either a private or a public affair, they make themselves ridiculous—just as ridiculous, I dare say, as men of affairs may be when they get involved in your quibbles, your "debates."

But the best course, no doubt, is to be a participant in both. It's an excellent thing to grasp as much philosophy as one needs for an education, and it's no disgrace to play the philosopher while you're young; but if one grows up and becomes a man and still continues in the subject, why, the whole thing becomes ridiculous, Socrates. My own feeling toward its practitioners is very much the same as the way I feel toward men who lisp and prattle like a child. When I see a child, who ought to be talking that way, lisping and prattling, I'm pleased, it strikes me as a pleasant sign of good breeding and suitable to the child's age; and when I hear a little lad speaking distinctly, it seems to me disagreeable and offends my ears as a mark of servile origin. So, too, when I hear a grown man prattling and lisping, it seems ridiculous and unmanly; one would like to strike him hard! And this is exactly the feeling I have about students of philosophy. When I perceive philosophical activity in a young lad, I am pleased; it suits him, I think, and shows that he has good breeding. A boy who doesn't play with philosophy I regard as illiberal, a chap who will never raise himself to any fine or noble action. Whereas when I see an older man still at his philosophy and showing no sign of giving it up, that one seems to me, Socrates, to be asking for some hard knocks! For, as I said just now, such a man, even if he's well endowed by nature, must necessarily become unmanly by avoiding the center of the city and the assemblies where, as the Poet says, "men win distinction." Such a fellow must spend the rest of his life skulking in corners, whispering with two or three little lads, never pronouncing any large, liberal, or meaningful utterance.

—**Plato, *Gorgias***

and Xenophon some 15 years later. Scholars do not generally attach too much significance to Aristophanes' picture of Socrates as contained in his comic drama *The Clouds*, for it was intended as a farce and Socrates was caricatured neither as a moral reformer nor as a political subversive but a kind of crack-brained scientist, running a shabby establishment called a Thinkery. The play was first performed in 426 B.C., about 25 years before Socrates' trial, when Socrates was 46 and the playwright 23. On the other hand, some 25,000 spectators viewed it when it was first performed, and although it failed to win a prize (coming in third), it is difficult to say what role this depiction of Socrates as a type of Sophist may have played in some people's minds—even at that much later date of 399 B.C. Plato himself hinted at some such connection.

Nor do scholars generally attach a great deal of significance to the much more voluminous body of writings devoted to Socrates by Xenophon, concerning whose intellectual abilities they appear to have many reservations. The 10,000 Greeks who had been in service to the Persians and then found themselves stranded in enemy territory apparently had a higher opinion of Xenophon, choosing him as one of the generals to lead them back to their homeland— a feat of some magnitude that he successfully accomplished and later wrote about in a work called the *Anabasis*. Although Xenophon is undoubtedly not a Plato, his writings about Socrates have a strong ring of truth about them.

> (In some scholars' opinion, the passage is autobiographical, Plato debating with himself—or perhaps with his family—whether to continue with philosophy or give it up.)
>
> The safest general characterization of the European philosophical tradition is that it consists in a series of footnotes to Plato.
>
> **—Alfred North Whitehead**

THE DIALOGUES: SOCRATES' TRIAL AND DEATH

We will follow tradition here and complete our account of the life and thought of Socrates by basing it on Plato's portrait of him as contained in the *Euthyphro*, the *Apology*, the *Crito*, and the *Phaedo*, all of which form a single story and were written to perpetuate and vindicate Socrates' memory.

Although the *Euthyphro* precedes the *Apology* and the *Crito* in the drama unfolded in these dialogues, it is generally regarded as having been written after them. The *Apology* is not really written in dialogue form: it is the speech (or series of speeches) delivered by Socrates at his trial. There can be little doubt that it is in substance a faithful record of what was said, for the dialogue was written soon after the event and was meant to be read to and by groups of people (some of whom had been present at the trial), and Plato would therefore not have tried to misrepresent facts that were familiar to large numbers of the Athenian people.

The same may be said of the *Crito*, which depicts Socrates in prison, although the conversations it contains may well be a dramatic summary of arguments with several friends on different occasions. The object of the dialogue is to explain and justify Socrates' attitude toward escape for the benefit of those friends who felt that he was sacrificing himself too easily. It also has the aim of displaying Socrates' loyal obedience to constitutional authority. The guilt for his condemnation was attached not to the state or its laws but to those enemies of the state who had perverted justice. The *Euthyphro* is the prologue of this drama. It shows us Socrates awaiting his trial and informs us of the charges preferred against him. The story of Euthyphro prosecuting his father for manslaughter is probably fictional. The dialogue illustrates Socrates' methods and suggests some ground for his unpopularity. Finally, the *Phaedo*, whose theme is the immortality of the soul (not an inappropriate theme for the occasion), carries the story to its conclusion by narrating, through the mouth of an eyewitness, Phaedo of Elis, the events and discussions of the last day in Socrates' life and the manner of his death.

Let us turn now to the first of these four dialogues.

Euthyphro

Outside the courtyard where he is shortly to stand his trial, Socrates meets Euthyphro, a seer and religious expert who says that he is going to charge his own father with manslaughter. Socrates is startled and inquires how Euthyphro can be sure that such conduct is consistent with his religious duty. There seems to be here an extreme clash of pieties; a kind of absurdity in itself. The result is a discussion of the true nature of piety or holiness.

Euthyphro is obviously sympathetic to Socrates. But he is also, obviously, just the kind of person to whom Socrates likes to apply his curative treatment, for Euthyphro claims to be an expert and feels supremely confident in his ability. Socrates is going to clear the young man's mind of some of these false assumptions and thus enable it to receive real knowledge. Poor Euthyphro is now his victim. The dialogue is only some 20 pages long.

Euthyphro is surprised to find Socrates before the religious courthouse and asks him why he is there and not, as is usual with him, at the Lyceum—the recreation grounds. "I don't suppose," he says, "that you have actually got a case before this court as I have." This gives both of them a chance to bring before us the two themes or lines of the dialogue: Euthyphro's prosecution of his father and the coming trial of Socrates. Socrates replies to Euthyphro's question:

> SOCRATES: No Euthyphro; the official name for it is not a private case but a public action.
> EUTHYPHRO: Really? I suppose that someone has brought an action against you; I won't insult you by suggesting that you have done it to somebody else.

(The translation here is from Hugh Tredennick, *Plato: The Last Days of Socrates* [Harmondsworth: Penguin, 1954]. Reproduced by permission.)

As you see, the dialogue is packed with irony. Euthyphro won't think so badly of Socrates as to suppose that he would initiate such a thing himself, yet he himself is now on his way to do just that—and to his own father!

Socrates tells Euthyphro that Meletus has brought charges against him and that these charges are rather serious. When Euthyphro complains that no one takes his predictions seriously—in fact, that they laugh at him even though his predictions generally come true—Socrates replies that he should consider himself lucky. For if ridicule were all that his prosecutors intended for him and planned no other harm, he wouldn't mind at all. In fact, it "wouldn't be at all unpleasant," he says, "to spend our time in the law-court joking and laughing. But if they are going to be serious, then there's no knowing how the case will turn out—except for you prophets."

The last remark is, of course, a dig at Euthyphro (who as a seer should know the future), but Euthyphro is undaunted and replies, "I dare say that it will come to nothing, Socrates, and you will conduct your case satisfactorily, as I expect to conduct mine." This last remark is a reminder to Socrates that Euthyphro wants to talk about himself. Socrates gets the message and enquires about the case. The next few interchanges are quite amusing as Euthyphro hesitates to reveal to Socrates what his lawsuit is about and against whom:

> SOCRATES: Oh, yes, Euthyphro, what is this lawsuit of yours? Are you defending yourself or prosecuting?
> EUTHYPHRO: Prosecuting.
> SOCRATES: Whom?
> EUTHYPHRO: Someone by prosecuting whom I am increasing my reputation for craziness.
> SOCRATES: Why, is he such a nimble opponent? [Notice the double play on the word "nimble."]
> EUTHYPHRO: Not at all nimble; actually he's quite an old gentleman.
> SOCRATES: Who is this person?
> EUTHYPHRO: My father.

(All matter in square brackets appearing from now on in the selections quoted is editorial comment and not part of the text.)

> SOCRATES: My good man! Your own father?
> EUTHYPHRO: Yes, indeed.
> SOCRATES: What is the charge? What is the trial for?
> EUTHYPHRO: Manslaughter, Socrates.
> SOCRATES: Good heavens!

When Socrates gets over the shock, he says to Euthyphro, with his tongue in his cheek, "Of course, most people have no idea, Euthyphro, what the rights of such a case are. I imagine that it isn't everyone that may take such a course, but only one who is far advanced in wisdom." To this Euthyphro replies: "Far indeed, Socrates." (A far-out fellow!)

Well, what happened? Euthyphro tells his story:

We were farming in Naxos and the deceased was working for us there. Well, he got drunk, lost his temper with one of our servants, and knifed him. So my father bound him hand and foot and threw him into a ditch; and then sent a man over here to ask the proper authority what has to be done. In the meantime he not only troubled himself very little about the prisoner but neglected him altogether, considering that he was a murderer, and it would not matter if he died. And that was just what happened; what with starvation and exposure and confinement, he died before the messenger came back from consulting the expert. That is why both my father and my other relatives are angry with me; because on the murderer's account I am prosecuting my father for manslaughter, whereas in the first place (as they maintain) he did not kill the man, and in the second, even supposing that he did kill him, since the dead man was a murderer, one ought not to concern one's self in defense of such a person, because it is an act of impiety for a son to prosecute his father for manslaughter. They have a poor comprehension, Socrates, of how the divine law stands with regard to piety and impiety.

But this leads Socrates to ask Euthyphro, "But tell me, Euthyphro, do you really believe that you understand the ruling of the divine law, and what makes actions pious and impious, so accurately that in the circumstances that you describe you have no misgivings; aren't you afraid that in taking your father into court you may turn out to be committing an act of impiety yourself?"

When Euthyphro assures Socrates that he indeed knows what piety and impiety are, Socrates remarks that in that case it might be a good idea for him to become Euthyphro's student, and before Meletus has a chance to bring charges against him, he will tell him that he has now become a student of Euthyphro; and if Meletus still thinks that he is guilty, then instead of bringing charges against him for corrupting the young, he had better bring charges against Euthyphro for corrupting the elderly! Although this would probably be enough to discomfort anyone, it does not disturb Euthyphro. He seems ready to take on anyone.

Socrates is ready to be instructed and asks Euthyphro to tell him what he was just insisting piety was. Euthyphro's first definition of piety is that it is "prosecuting a wrongdoer, whether the offender happens to be your father or anybody else." (In other words, it is what he is now in fact doing.) And Euthyphro supports his case by reminding Socrates that that is what the children of the gods do. And it is therefore absurd, as he adds with overweening vanity (to say nothing of impiety), to criticize him for doing the same. In taking Euthyphro to task, his family contradict themselves "by laying down one rule for the gods and another for me."

What Euthyphro has in mind here are such tales of the gods as that of Uranus (Heaven), who imprisoned his children, the Titans, deep in the body of his consort Gaia (Earth). She encouraged them to assert themselves, and Cronos, the youngest but most formidable of the Titans, attacked Uranus and castrated him. To avoid such a fate for himself, Cronos swallowed his own children as they were born. But his wife Rhea smuggled the infant Zeus away to Crete and put his baby clothes on a stone, which Cronos swallowed. The clothes acted as an emetic and made him vomit up the other children. Zeus later led a revolt against Cronos and put him in chains. These are some of the doings of the gods Euthyphro is referring to here.

Socrates is, of course, not very happy with this definition of piety offered by Euthyphro. In fact, as he points out to him, it is not so much a definition of piety as an example of it. Surely, Socrates tells him, there are other things that are pious in addition to bringing a wrongdoer to trial, and what is it that is common to all of them? To this new demand, Euthyphro offers this new definition: "Piety is what the gods love." To this Socrates replies that it is an excellent answer. Whether it is true is something they will have to see.

Socrates now goes on to cross-examine Euthyphro. Haven't we said a few moments ago, he asks him, that the gods are divided and disagree with one another and feel enmity toward one another? The question is, What sort of disagreement are the gods involved in?

There can be two sorts of disagreements: we can disagree about such things as the length or weight or number of things, in which case (these being matters of fact) we can settle our disputes by measuring, or weighing, or counting. This sort of disagreement wouldn't make us hostile and angry with one another. But since the gods apparently do disagree with one another, it must be about something else—about such things as right and wrong, good and bad. Disagreement over these sorts of things does make us hostile and angry. Well, seeing that the gods are hostile to one another, they must be in disagreement over what is right and wrong, and if they disagree over this, what sort of authority are they on these matters? We cannot appeal to them. For if you ask Uranus, he might say, "Yes, it is right," but if you ask Cronos, he might say "No, it is wrong!"

For a moment, Euthyphro feels beaten and does not know what to reply. He hesitates and then gets a brilliant idea. He says, "I imagine, Socrates, that none of the gods disagree with one another on this point, at any rate: that whoever kills without justification should be brought to justice"—in short, that the guilty should be punished.

At first this might look like a very good reply, for surely the gods indeed could not be in disagreement on this point. But if we look at this answer carefully, we will see that it really says nothing. And that, indeed, is what Socrates points out to Euthyphro. Of course, he says to him, the gods are not in disagreement over that! No one would dispute that the guilty should be punished. But what is in dispute on such occasions is whether the person is indeed guilty. Can Euthyphro prove that all the gods regard what his father has done as being wrong and reprehensible? In short, in saying that the guilty should be punished, Euthyphro had simply begged the question of his father's guilt.

"Come," says Socrates, "try to give me some definite proof that in these circumstances and beyond all doubt, all the gods regard this action as right; and if you prove it to my satisfaction, I shall never stop singing the praises of your wisdom."

But Socrates does not want to push this point too far. On the contrary, he realizes that even if it could be proven that all the gods find what Euthyphro is doing wrong or right, the question of what piety or impiety is would still be left unanswered. Euthyphro's proof would only supply information about some particular action but would reveal nothing, in general, about the meaning of these terms—unless, of course, one could generalize and say that "piety is what *all* the gods love." And so Socrates is willing to concede the point and willing to assume, for the sake of the argument, that all the gods regard this sort of homicide as wrong and detest it. Is Euthyphro willing to use this as his model for piety? In short, what this will mean is that whenever we find that all the gods love or approve of a certain thing, it is a sign that the thing or action in question is good or right, and when they are all agreed that it is wrong, this will be proof of its wrongness. (Of course, when the gods are in disagreement, then we will simply be in the dark about the things or actions in question.) Euthyphro agrees to adopt this as his position. This is what he had in mind all along, he says.

Very well, then, replies Socrates. Let us see now what this means, what the implications are of this. And so he asks Euthyphro, "Is what is pious [and here follows the most difficult part of the dialogue] loved by the gods because it is pious, or is it pious because it is loved by them?"

This question is one that occupied philosophers and religious thinkers a great deal during the Middle Ages. It then took the form, Is something good because God wills it, or does God will it because it is good?

At first sight this may seem to be an unimportant and quibbling question. One who does not take such matters very seriously may be tempted to say, "If God's will and the good coincide, what does it matter?" To this the believer may retort, "A great deal!" for one's answer really affects and reflects how we conceive of God. If our answer is that they are indeed the same, then we commit ourselves to the belief in the absolute omnipotence of God. Not only can this God create and order a world, but those acts that are right and wrong are so because he makes them that way. Indeed, such a believer might criticize someone maintaining the opposite by saying that such a view imposes a standard on God, one that is prior to and above Him and that governs His will. There is, however, something to be said for this line of thought. For instance, we do seem to have faith in a certain order to those acts we deem right and wrong. Saving an innocent life is typically right, whereas willfully killing an innocent is typically wrong. Yet if God willed just the opposite, would it then be so? Many, of course, would say, "No, it would not." But how would they justify this?

And there is, of course, the further difficulty of finding out what exactly God wills. There are many conflicting claims here and no very obvious way of mediating between them. Thus, we can see that much rides on the answer the believer may give to such a question.

The reply Euthyphro gives to the question is that "the gods love the pious thing because it is pious; it is not pious merely because they love it." Hearing this, Socrates is somewhat taken aback and says, "But if it is something else and not their *loving it* which makes it pious, then what is that something else about piety that makes the gods love it so?

What then, indeed, is piety? Aren't we back where we began—now saying again that piety is what the gods love?" (And we are still in the dark, as before, as to *why* they love it.)

Becoming understandably demoralized at this turn in the argument, Euthyphro says to Socrates, "But, Socrates, I don't know how to convey to you what I have in mind. Whatever we put forward somehow keeps on shifting its position and refuses to stay where we laid it down."

Socrates tries to come to his rescue again, but the solution continues to elude them. The dialogue finally ends with the following exchange between Socrates and Euthyphro:

> SOCRATES: We shall then have to start our inquiry about piety all over again from the beginning; because I shall never give up of my own accord until I have learnt the answer. Only don't refuse to take me seriously, but do your best to give me your closest attention, and tell me the truth, because you know it if any man does. If you didn't know all about piety and impiety you would never have attempted to prosecute your aged father for manslaughter; you would have been too much afraid of the gods, and too much ashamed of what men might think, to run such a risk, in case you should be wrong in doing so. As it is, I am sure that you think you know [note the qualifications] all about what is pious and what is not. So tell me your opinion, my most worthy Euthyphro, and don't conceal it. [Socrates pretends Euthyphro knows the answer but just won't tell it!]
> EUTHYPHRO: Another time, Socrates; at the moment I have an urgent engagement somewhere, and it's time for me to be off. [The universal excuse!]
> SOCRATES: What a way to treat me, my friend! Fancy you going off like this and dashing me from my great hope! I thought that if I learnt from you about piety and impiety I should both escape from Meletus' indictment (by demonstrating to him that I had now become instructed by Euthyphro in religion, and no longer in my ignorance expressed independent and unorthodox views) and also live better for the rest of my life.

And this is the way this dialogue ends. It shows how people's actions, which often have serious and even tragic consequences, are all too often based on ignorance. Here is Euthyphro about to prosecute his own father for impiety, and when asked what impiety is, he very soon becomes confused and must admit his ignorance. And similarly with Socrates: he is about to be prosecuted on the same charge by people who are probably as confused and ignorant as Euthyphro regarding this matter. But in Socrates' case, of course, it will lead to his condemnation and execution.

Apology

Let us now turn to the *Apology*. The title comes from the Greek word *apologia*, which was the technical term for a defendant's speech. What the dialogue contains is not an apology in our sense of the word. It is Socrates' defense of himself.

There are two persons in this dialogue: Socrates and Meletus. The charges against Socrates, however, were formally brought by three Athenians: Meletus, Anytus, and Lycon. The charges against Socrates were that he was, first, guilty of heresy or impiety and, second, guilty of corrupting the minds of the young by his teaching. These were standing charges, not invented for just this occasion.

The procedure in court was for the litigants to state their own cases. The prosecution spoke first and the defendant replied. The jury (consisting of 501 representative citizens) would then give its verdict by a majority vote. If the plaintiff received less than one-fifth of the total number, he was fined. If the verdict was guilty and, as in the present case, there was no penalty fixed by law, the plaintiff proposed one, the defendant proposed another, and the jury voted between them.

The *Apology* consists of three separate speeches: Socrates' defense, his counterproposal for the penalty, and a final address to the court (the complete text is presented at the end of this chapter).

We do not have the prosecutor's speech, but Socrates' sarcastic and ironic opening remarks tell us a good deal about its tone. The dialogue begins with these words of Socrates:

> I do not know what effect my accusers have had upon you, gentlemen, but for my own part I was almost carried away by them; their arguments were so convincing. On the other hand, scarcely a word of what they said was true. I was especially astonished at one of their many misrepresentations: I mean when they told you that you must be careful not to let me deceive you—the implication being that I am a skillful speaker. I thought that it was peculiarly brazen of them to tell you this without a blush, since they must know that they will soon be effectively confuted, when it becomes obvious that I have not the slightest skill as a speaker—unless, of course, by a skillful speaker they mean one who speaks the truth. If that is what they mean, I would agree that I am an orator, though not after their pattern.

Socrates now goes on to deal with his earliest accusers, those not present in court but who have been spreading false rumors about him for many years. This is his big task—to rid his listeners of these ancient prejudices and charges against him, prejudices and charges that are customarily made against all philosophers. He pretends to read out the affidavit his ancient critics would have drawn up had they brought him to trial: "Socrates is guilty of criminal meddling in that he inquires into things below the earth and in the sky, and teaches people to disbelieve in the gods." The accusation is, in other words, that Socrates is a student of natural philosophy or science and as such must be an atheist. To this he replies,

> I mean no disrespect for such knowledge, if anyone really is versed in it—I do not want any more lawsuits brought against me by Meletus—but the fact is, gentlemen, that I

take no interest in it. What is more, I call upon the greater part of you as witnesses to my statement, and I appeal to all of you who have ever listened to me talking (and there are a great many to whom this applies) to clear your neighbors' minds on this point. Tell one another whether anyone of you has ever heard me discuss such questions briefly or at length; and then you will realize that the other popular reports about me are equally unreliable. The fact is that there is nothing in any of these charges. But here perhaps one of you might interrupt me and say, "But what is it that you *do*, Socrates? How is it that you have been misrepresented like this? Surely all this talk and gossip about you would never have arisen if you had confined yourself to ordinary activities, but only if your behavior was abnormal. Tell us the explanation, if you do not want us to invent it for ourselves." This seems to be a reasonable request, and I will try to explain to you what it is that has given me this false notoriety; so please give me your attention. Perhaps some of you will think that I am not being serious; but I assure you that I am going to tell you the whole truth.

At this point he tells them of his friend's visit to the oracle at Delphi. Here follows a rather long section, but it is one of the most eloquent in all of Western literature and deserves to be quoted in full:

When I heard about the oracle's answer, I said to myself, "What does the god mean? Why does he not use plain language? I am only too conscious that I have no claim to wisdom, great or small; so what can he mean by asserting that I am the wisest man in the world? He cannot be telling a lie; that would not be right for him."

After puzzling about it for some time, I set myself at last with considerable reluctance to check the truth of it in the following way. I went to interview a man with a high reputation for wisdom, because I felt that here if anywhere I should succeed in disproving the oracle and pointing out to my divine authority: "You said that I was the wisest of men, but here is a man who is wiser than I am."

Well, I gave a thorough examination to this person—one of our politicians—and in conversation with him I formed the impression that although in many people's opinions, and especially in his own, he appeared to be wise, in fact he was not. Then when I began to try to show him that he only thought he was wise and was not really so, my efforts were resented both by him and by many of the other people present. However, I reflected as I walked away: "Well, I am certainly wiser than this man. It is only too likely that neither of us has any knowledge to boast of; but he thinks that he knows something which he does not know, whereas I am quite conscious of my ignorance. At any rate it seems that I am wiser than he is to this small extent, that I do not think that I know what I do not know."

After this I went on to interview a man with an even greater reputation for wisdom, and I formed the same impression again; and here too I incurred the resentment of the man himself and a number of others.

From that time on I interviewed one person after another. I realized with distress and alarm that I was making myself unpopular, but I felt compelled to put my religious duty first. Since I was trying to find out the meaning of the oracle, I was bound to interview everyone who had a reputation for knowledge. And by Dog, gentlemen! (For I must be frank with you) my honest impression was this: it seemed to me, as I pursued my investigation at the god's command, that the people with the greatest reputations were almost entirely deficient, while others who were supposed to be their inferiors were much better qualified in practical intelligence.

I want you to think of my adventures as a sort of pilgrimage undertaken to establish the truth of the oracle once and for all. After I had finished with the politicians I turned to the poets, dramatic, lyric, and all the rest, in the belief that here I should expose myself as a comparative ignoramus. I used to pick up what I thought were some of their most perfect works and question them closely about the meaning of what they had written, in the hope of incidentally enlarging my own knowledge. Well, gentlemen, I hesitate to tell you the truth, but it must be told. It is hardly an exaggeration to say that any of the bystanders could have explained those poems better than their actual authors. So I soon made up my mind about the poets too: I decided that it was not wisdom that enables them to write their poetry, but a kind of instinct or inspiration, such as you find in seers and prophets who deliver their sublime messages without knowing in the least what they mean. It seemed clear to me that the poets were in much the same case; and I also observed that the very fact that they were poets made them think that they had a perfect understanding of all other subjects, of which they were totally ignorant. So I left that line of inquiry too with the same sense of advantage that I had felt in the case of the politicians.

Last of all I turned to the skilled craftsmen. I knew quite well that I had practically no technical qualifications myself, and I was sure that I should find them full of impressive knowledge. In this I was not disappointed; they understood things which I did not, and to that extent they were wiser than I was.

But, gentlemen, these professional experts seemed to share the same failing which I had noticed in the poets; I mean that on the strength of their technical proficiency they claimed a perfect understanding of every other subject, however important; and I felt that this error more than outweighed their positive wisdom. So I made myself spokesman for the oracle, and asked myself whether I would rather be as I was—neither wise with their wisdom nor stupid with their stupidity—or possess both qualities as they did. I replied through myself to the oracle that it was best for me to be as I was.

The effect of these investigations of mine, gentlemen, has been to arouse against me a great deal of hostility, and hostility of a particularly bitter and persistent kind, which has resulted in various malicious suggestions, including the description of me as a professor of wisdom. This is due to the fact that whenever I succeed in disproving another person's claim to wisdom in a given subject, the bystanders assume that I know everything about that subject myself. But the truth of the matter, gentlemen, is pretty certainly this: that real wisdom is the property of God, and this oracle is his way of telling us that human wisdom has little or no value. It seems to me that he is not referring literally to Socrates, but has merely taken my name as an example, as if he would say to us "The wisest of you men is he who has realized, like Socrates, that in respect of wisdom he is really worthless."

And so I go about the world, obedient to the god, and search and make enquiry into the wisdom of anyone, whether citizen or stranger, who appears to be wise; and if he is not wise, then in vindication of the oracle I show him that he is not wise.

With these remarks, Socrates ends his defense against the charges brought by the first class of his accusers and turns to his present prosecutors—in particular to Meletus ("high-principled and patriotic as he claims to be"). He questions Meletus on the new charges and in a short time shows him to be as confused about these questions as Euthyphro was—if not, indeed, more so. So he leaves off questioning him. Knowing, however, there are still many questions troubling the jury, he turns and addresses himself directly to them:

But perhaps someone will say, "Do you feel no compunction, Socrates, at having followed a line of action which puts you in danger of the death penalty?" I might fairly reply to him, "You are mistaken, my friend, if you think that a man who is worth anything ought to spend his time weighing up the prospects of life and death. He has only one thing to consider in performing any action; that is, whether he is acting rightly or wrongly, like a good man or a bad one. The truth of the matter is this, gentlemen. Where a man has once taken up his stand, either because it seems best to him or in obedience to his orders, there I believe he is bound to remain and face the danger, taking no account of death or anything else before dishonor."

This being so, Socrates, who has faced death in battle, will not make any concessions in order to save his own life, for he does not know whether death is a good or an evil. Then he goes on to raise, on their behalf, another question:

Suppose you said to me, "Socrates, on this occasion we shall disregard Anytus and acquit you, but only on one condition, that you give up spending your time on this quest and stop philosophizing. If we catch you going on in the same way, you shall be put to death." Well, supposing, as I said, that you should offer to acquit me on these terms, I should reply, "Gentlemen, I am your very grateful and devoted servant, but I owe a greater obedience to God than to you; and so long as I draw breath and have my faculties, I shall never stop practicing philosophy and exhorting you and elucidating the truth for everyone that I meet. I shall go on saying, in my usual way, 'My very good friend, you are an Athenian and belong to a city which is the greatest and most famous in the world for its wisdom and strength. Are you not ashamed that you give your attention to acquiring as much money as possible, and similarly with reputation and honor, and give no attention or thought to truth and understanding and the perfection of your soul?' . . . It is my belief that no greater good has ever befallen you in this city than my service to my God; for I spend all my time going about trying to persuade you, young and old, to make your first and chief concern not for your bodies nor for your possessions, but for the highest welfare of your souls, proclaiming as I go 'Wealth does not bring goodness, but goodness brings wealth and every other blessing, both to the individual and to the State.' Now if I corrupt the young by this message, the message would seem to be harmful; but if anyone says that my message is different from this, he is talking nonsense." And so, Gentlemen, I would say: "You can please yourselves whether you listen to Anytus or not, and whether you acquit me or not; you know that I am not going to alter my conduct, not even if I have to die a hundred deaths."

He throws out a challenge to them. If he has indeed corrupted anyone, then surely they will rise and say so. A good many of his listeners are here in court. And if they won't speak up, perhaps their brothers, uncles, or kinsmen will do so. These are the people Meletus should have produced as his witnesses. "If he forgot to do so then," Socrates says with sarcasm, "let him do it now." He will not appeal to the pity of his judges or make a scene in court such as he has often witnessed. The judge should not be influenced by his feelings but convinced by his reason.

A vote is taken and the verdict is "guilty": 281 against Socrates, 220 for. Since there is no penalty fixed by law, each side has the option of proposing one. The prosecution proposes the death penalty. Socrates argues that since he has really been a benefactor of the state, the only just penalty would be to pension him off, like the Olympic heroes, in one of the fancy "hotels" of Athens, for he has done more for the people than the heroes have, and besides he needs the money more than they do. His friends—Plato among them—become alarmed and urge him to propose a fine, which he does—first a ridiculously low one (arguing that he cannot afford more) and then, at the urging of Plato and others who will guarantee it, a larger one.

A vote is taken, and Socrates is condemned to death, this time by an even larger majority: 301 against, 200 for him.

The dialogue ends with a short closing address by Socrates in which he prophecies that they will be accused of killing a wise man. And why could they not wait a few more years? He is an old man and certainly has not much longer to live. They are about to kill him because he has been their accuser, but other accusers will rise up and denounce them even more vehemently. He believes that what is happening to him will be good because that inner voice, which always restrains him when he is about to do something that he should not, gives no sign of opposition. Death, he finally argues, is either good or is nothing; it is either a profound sleep or a prelude to another life. If the latter, then how wonderful it would be to rejoin and converse with Homer and Hesiod, to see the heroes of Troy, and to continue the search after knowledge in another world. He adds that nothing can harm a good man either in life or in death, and his fortunes are not a matter of indifference to the gods.

He has, finally, only one wish to make: "Do to my sons as I have done to you."

In Xenophon's *Symposium*, Socrates declared that women are inferior to men only in physical strength and in the training given to them in Athens. "Therefore," he continued, "let any man teach his wife whatever he desires." "How is it then, Socrates," a fellow guest asked, "that you haven't trained Xanthippe? I think she is the hardest to get along with of all women who have ever lived—or ever will." Socrates smiled. "Very early in my life," he replied, "I determined to get along with everybody. I noticed that all who became fine horsemen chose the most spirited horses. So I chose Xanthippe."

Crito

In Athens, sentence of execution was normally carried out at once. But the day before Socrates' trial was also the first day of the annual mission to Delos (Apollo's birthplace). This was a state holiday, during which no executions were permitted in commemoration of the legendary deliverance of the city from the Minotaur by Theseus, Prince of Athens.

Because of bad weather, the mission to Delos in 399 B.C. took so long that Socrates remained in prison for a month. (This delay in the execution, some scholars have argued, must have been foreseen, with the hope, they have suggested, that Socrates would use the occasion to escape.)

In the *Crito* the ship returning from Delos has now been sighted and is about to reach Athens. Crito, who has not been able to sleep, has been watching for the ship's return and has now come to tell Socrates the bad news. It is ironic that while Crito is wakeful and in distress, he finds Socrates soundly and peacefully asleep.

Crito is a wealthy Athenian. He is an old man and Socrates' oldest and closest friend. He has come now to beseech Socrates to let his friends save him. They are ready with money, and a refuge can easily be found. There is plenty of money to buy off the guards, and Crito knows men who will take Socrates out of the country where friends will take good care of him. He mustn't worry about the risks involved. They are willing and ready to take them. They are prepared to risk a large fine, loss of property, or other punishment. Socrates must come and do so quickly, for time is running out.

By submitting to the sentence imposed by the Athenian court, Crito tells Socrates, he is playing into the hands of his enemies, deserting his children, and allowing the world to believe his friends are deficient in courage. "Look here, Socrates," Crito tells him, "it is still not too late to take my advice and escape."

Your death means a double calamity for me. I shall not only lose a friend whom I can never possibly replace, but besides a great many people who don't know you and me very well will be sure to think that I let you down, because I could have saved you if I had been willing to spend the money; and what could be more contemptible than to get a name for thinking more of money than of your friends? Most people will never believe that it was you who refused to leave this place although we tried our hardest to persuade you.

67

To this Socrates replies, "My dear Crito, I appreciate your warm feelings very much—that is, assuming that they have some justification. Very well, then, we must consider whether we ought to follow your advice or not."

With characteristic irony, Socrates adds that since Crito is in no danger of death, he will be more likely to be impartial and objective in such a discussion than he himself!

Crito has argued that Socrates should consider the *consequences* of his staying, but what Socrates wants to consider are only the *principles* on which he has always acted—whatever the consequences. These two positions have acquired separate names in philosophy: the former is called **teleological**, the latter **deontological**. If you are a teleologist, you evaluate the rightness or wrongness of proposed actions by the kind of results you think will issue from them. If the results are good, the proposed action, in your view, is good. On the other hand, if you are a deontologist, you tend to evaluate the rightness or wrongness of proposed actions in accordance with whether they conform to certain principles you feel bound to obey or follow regardless of their consequences.

Thus, to Crito's remark "See now, Socrates, how sad and discreditable are the consequences, both to us and to you," of your staying, Socrates replies, "The principles which I have hitherto honored and revered I still honor, and unless we can at once find other and better principles, I am certain not to agree with you."

> Shall we be acting rightly in paying money and showing gratitude to these people who are going to rescue me, and in escaping or arranging the escape ourselves; or shall we really be acting wrongly in doing all this? If it becomes clear that such conduct is wrong, I cannot help thinking that the question whether we are sure to die, or to suffer any other ill effect for that matter, if we stand our ground and take no action, ought not to weigh with us at all in comparison with the risk of doing what is wrong.

We have no right, he goes on to say, to return evil for evil—"whatever the provocation." For it is "never right to do a wrong or return a wrong or defend one's self against injury by retaliation." "I know," he adds, "that there are and always will be few people who think like this; and consequently between those who do think so and those who do not there can be no agreement on principles; they must always feel contempt when they observe one another's decisions."

For him to try to escape now would be to reverse the whole conduct of his past life, to say nothing of making a hypocrisy of his statement at the trial that he would prefer death to exile. For although he has been a critic of the state, he recognizes the authority of law as well as of his own conscience. The trial may have been unjust and the charges false, but the sentence was pronounced by the law of Athens, and it is therefore his duty to submit.

Going on to reinforce his point, Socrates explains to Crito that in wrongly convicting him of an offense he had not committed, the culprit was not the law but those who abused it. If Socrates were now to take Crito's advice and flee, however, *he* would be the culprit—not only by violating the law but also by weakening its very fabric and authority.

"Compared with your mother and father and all the rest of your ancestors, your country," Plato has Socrates exclaim, "is something far more precious, more venerable, more sacred, and held in greater honor both among gods and among all reasonable men."

This remark (as well as a few others that Plato reports Socrates as expressing) has occasioned much discussion. In fact, it embodies one side of a debate that has been carried on in political philosophy for centuries. Among those holding the view expressed here perhaps the greatest and best known was a German philosopher of the nineteenth century, Hegel. Proponents of this view tend to revere the state as something holy and magnificent, regarding it as a creation separate from and higher than any individuals that compose it. As such, it is much more worthy than the persons who make it up, whose good must always be subordinate and rightly sacrificed when required for the good of the state. Nazi Germany was able to exploit this idea to the extreme, with well-known devastating results for all concerned.

The other side of the debate has been represented by those who have taken what we might call an institutionalist approach—a much less romantic and heroic view, one typified by historical and contemporary libertarian movements. According to this view, the state is nothing more than a human institution. It is an instrument designed to do the necessary jobs of offering services to a populace and protecting its citizens from each other. Indeed, this approach maintains that it might be better if there were no need for this instrument at all. But, as there is a need, we must do our best to see to it that it does not get out of hand. Under this view the state is obviously no entity at all and serves merely to enhance the liberty and protect the rights of individuals. To revere it, then, even in the form of superpatriotism, is not only dangerous but a form of madness—dangerous, perhaps, because irrational.

Socrates' further argument here, however, is that if he did not like the law of Athens, he was free to go to another city or state. By staying, as the laws themselves seem to be saying to him now, he has entered into a kind of pact with them that he is not at liberty to break at his pleasure. If he does, he will only harm his friends and disgrace himself. He must think of justice first and of life and children afterward—so that when he enters the next world he may have all this to plead in his defense before the authorities there.

"That, my dear Crito," Socrates tells his friend, "I do assure you, is what I seem to hear them saying. And the sound of their arguments rings so loudly in my head that I cannot hear the other side. However, if you think you will do any good by it, say what you like."

"Socrates," Crito replies, "I have nothing to say." "Then, Crito, let us follow this course, since God points out the way."

And so with sadness and resignation, Crito gives in.

Phaedo

The last hours of Socrates' life are described in Plato's dialogue the *Phaedo*. Unlike the *Crito*, the *Phaedo* is very long and very difficult. It has two themes: the death of Socrates and the immortality of the soul. These two themes are tied together, for it is Socrates' firm belief in the latter that enables him to meet his death so courageously and hopefully.

The scene is Socrates' prison room on the day set by the Athenian court for his death. His friends have come to take their leave of him. He uses the occasion to talk to them about the nature of the soul. Toward the evening, the jailor brings in the fatal cup of hemlock.

All this is told by an eyewitness, Phaedo of Elis, to a group of fellow philosophers, only one of whom is named and speaks. Plato, we are told, was not present at the execution; he is at home ill (an illness brought on, no doubt, by the event about to happen to his teacher and master).

The friends gathered around Socrates in these last few hours of his life express surprise that he remains as calm and reasonable as ever in the face of approaching death, but he argues that the philosopher has nothing to fear: philosophy, which is always trying to release the soul from the limitations of the body, is, in effect, the study of death.

What Socrates means by this seemingly paradoxical definition of philosophy is that it is only at death, when the soul is freed from the body, that it is at long last able to see things as they really are. For so long as our soul is embedded in the body, it must view reality only through the distortions of our bodily organs. At death, however, the soul is finally released from its prison, the human body, and at long last is able to see things as they are in themselves.

The arguments in support of immortality that Socrates proposes and discusses in this dialogue are very difficult. Involved in one of the main arguments is the idea, a popular one of Plato's, that "our birth is but a sleep and a forgetting," that to learn is in part to remember knowledge that must have been gained in another life. Another argument involves the idea that the soul is immortal because it can perceive and have a share in Truth, Beauty, and Goodness, which are immortal and eternal. Man can know God, the Eternal, because he has something in him that is Godlike.

At death, Socrates goes on to argue, the soul retires into another world. In the beautiful Myth of the Earthly Paradise and the Myth of the Destination of Souls, he makes some attempts to describe the other world. The description, he ends by saying, provides ground enough "for leaving nothing undone to attain during life some measure of goodness and wisdom; for the prize is glorious and the hope great."

It is typical of Plato and his works that where he reaches a certain point in his thought at which he can only guess and speculate, where he is no longer certain of himself, he chooses to present his account in the form of a story or a myth. It is as if he were saying that what you are about to hear is only a story; here is where philosophy ends and fiction begins. But, of course, it is not mere fiction for him. It is certainly a product of his imagination, but there may be, for all we know, much truth in the account.

These myths from the *Phaedo* should be read together with the account of similar matters given in Plato's *Republic*—especially the Myth of Er toward the end of the work. Er, having died before his time was really up and having already seen part of what lies ahead on this journey, was sent back to tell his fellows what awaits them. After telling his tale, Plato adds these concluding words:

And so Glaucon, the tale was saved from perishing; and if we will listen, it may save us, and all will be well when we cross the River of Lethe. Also we shall not defile our souls; but, if you will believe with me that the soul is immortal and able to endure all good and ill, we shall keep always to the upward way and in all things pursue justice with the help of wisdom. Then we shall be at peace with heaven and with ourselves, both during our sojourn here and when, like victors in the Games collecting gifts from their friends, we receive the prize of justice; and so, not here only, but in the journey of a thousand years of which I have told you, we shall fare well.

"Of course," Socrates says here in the *Phaedo*, "no reasonable man ought to insist that the facts are exactly as I have described them."

But that either this or something very like it is a true account of our souls and their future habitations—since we have clear evidence that the soul is immortal—this, I think, is both a reasonable contention and a belief worth risking; for the risk is a noble one. We

Socrates (c. 450–c. 380 BCE)

should use such accounts to inspire ourselves with confidence; and that is why I have already drawn out my tale so long.

The last few pages of the *Phaedo*, describing Socrates' death, are among the most moving in Western literature; they are written with a plainness and simplicity that is always the mark of great writing. There is, however, a certain allusion made toward the end of the passages about to be quoted that needs explaining to a contemporary reader. To Crito's question whether he has any last requests to make, Socrates replies that he is to make sure to offer a sacrifice of a cock to Asclepius. Asclepius was the God of Healing. People who had been through a serious illness would offer a sacrifice to him in gratefulness. And so what this means is that now that he, Socrates, is about to enter a greater life *The Death* (death releasing him from the "fitful fever" of this one), he wants to thank the God of Healing by offering a sacrifice. It is Socrates' final irony: he has been accused of impiety; he is about to die because of it. Yet his last deed is one of deep piety. Now, the conclusion:

> When he had finished speaking, Crito said, "Very well, Socrates. But have you no directions for the others or myself about your children or anything else? What can we do to please you best?"
>
> "Nothing new, Crito," said Socrates, "just what I am always telling you. Look after yourselves and follow the line of life as I have laid it down now and in the past."
>
> "We shall try our best to do as you say," said Crito. "But how shall we bury you?"
>
> "Any way you like," replied Socrates, "that is, if you can catch me and I don't slip through your fingers." He laughed gently as he spoke, and turning to us went on: "I can't persuade Crito that I am this Socrates here who is talking to you now and marshalling all the arguments; he thinks that I am the one whom he will see presently lying dead; and he asks how he is to bury me! As for my long and elaborate explanation that I shall depart to a state of heavenly happiness, this attempt to console both you and myself seems to be wasted on him. You must assure him that when I am dead I shall not stay, but depart and be gone. That will help Crito to bear it more easily, and keep him from being distressed on my account when he sees my body being burned or buried, as if something dreadful were happening to me; or from saying at the funeral that it is Socrates whom he is laying out or carrying to the grave or burying. No, you must keep up your spirits and say that it is only my body that you are burying; and you can bury it as you please, in whatever way you think is most proper."
>
> With these words he got up and went into another room to bathe; and Crito went after him, but told us to wait. So we waited, discussing and reviewing what had been said, or else dwelling upon the greatness of the calamity which had befallen us; for we felt just as though we were losing a father and should be orphans for the rest of our lives. Meanwhile when Socrates had taken his bath, his children were brought to see him—he had two little sons and one big boy—and the women of his household—you know—arrived. He talked

to them in Crito's presence and gave them directions about carrying out his wishes; then he told the women and children to go away, and came back himself to join us.

It was now nearly sunset, because he had spent a long time inside. He came and sat down, fresh from the bath; and he had only been talking for a few minutes when the prison officer came in, and walked up to him. "Socrates," he said, "at any rate I shall not have to find fault with you, as I do with others, for getting angry with me and cursing when I tell them to drink the poison—carrying out Government orders. I have come to know during this time that you are the noblest and the gentlest and the bravest of all the men that have ever come here, and now especially I am sure that you are not angry with me, but with them; because you know who are responsible. So now—you know what I have come to say; try to bear what must be as easily as you can." As he spoke he burst into tears, and turning around, went away.

Socrates looked up at him and said: "We will do as you say." Then addressing us he went on "What a charming person! All the time I have been here he has visited me, and sometimes had discussions with me, and shown me the greatest kindness, and how generous of him now to shed tears for me at parting! But come, Crito, let us do as he says. Someone had better bring in the poison if it is ready prepared; if not, tell the man to prepare it."

"But surely, Socrates," said Crito, "the sun is still upon the mountains; it has not gone down yet. Besides, I know that in other cases people have dinner and enjoy their wine and sometimes the company of those whom they love, long after they receive the warning; and only drink the poison quite late at night. No need to hurry; there is still plenty of time."

"It is natural that these people whom you speak of should act in that way, Crito," said Socrates, "because they think that they gain by it. And it is also natural that I should not; because I believe that I should gain nothing by drinking the poison a little later—I should only make myself ridiculous in my own eyes if I clung to life and hugged it when it has no more to offer. Come, do as I say and don't make difficulties."

At this Crito made a sign to his servant, who was standing near. The servant went out and after spending a considerable time returned with the man who was to administer the poison; he was carrying it ready prepared in a cup. When Socrates saw him he said "Well, my good fellow, you understand these things, what ought I to do?"

"Just drink it," he said, "and then walk about until you feel a weight in your legs, and then lie down. Then it will act of its own accord."

As he spoke he handed the cup to Socrates, who received it quite cheerfully, without a tremor, without any change of color or expression, and said, looking up under his brows with his usual steady gaze, "What do you say about pouring a libation from this drink? Is it permitted, or not?"

"We only prepare what we regard as the normal dose, Socrates," he replied.

"I see," said Socrates. "But I suppose I am allowed, or rather bound, to pray the gods that my removal from this world to the other may be prosperous. This is my prayer, then;

and I hope that it may be granted." With these words, quite calmly and with no sign of distaste, he drained the cup in one breath.

Up till this time most of us had been fairly successful in keeping back our tears; but when we saw that he was drinking, that he had actually drunk it, we could do so no longer; in spite of myself the tears came pouring out, so that I covered my face and wept brokenheartedly—not for him, but for my own calamity in losing such a friend. Crito had given up even before me, and had gone out when he could not restrain his tears. But Apollodorus, who had never stopped crying even before, now broke out into such a storm of passionate weeping that he made everyone in the room break down, except Socrates himself, who said:

"Really, my friends, what a way to behave! Why, that was my main reason for sending away the women, to prevent this sort of disturbance; because I am told that one should make one's end in a tranquil frame of mind. Calm yourselves and try to be brave."

This made us feel ashamed, and we controlled our tears. Socrates walked about, and presently, saying that his legs were heavy, lay down on his back—that was what the man recommended. The man kept his hand upon Socrates, and after a little while examined his feet and legs; then pinched his foot hard and asked if he felt it. Socrates said no. Then he did the same to his legs; and moving gradually upwards in this way let us see that he was getting cold and numb. Presently he felt him again and said that when it reached the heart, Socrates would be gone.

The coldness was spreading about as far as his waist when Socrates uncovered his face—for he had covered it up—and said (they were his last words):

"Crito, we ought to offer a cock to Asclepius. See to it, and don't forget."

"No, it shall be done," said Crito. "Are you sure there is nothing else?"

Socrates made no reply to this question, but after a little while he stirred; and when the man uncovered him, his eyes were fixed. When Crito saw this, he closed the mouth and eyes.

Such was the end of our comrade, who was, we may fairly say, of all those whom we knew in our time, the bravest and also the wisest and most upright man.

It would not be until some 400 years later that humanity would be left with another equally deeply moving account of a martyrdom, one strangely similar to it in so many ways.

SUMMARY

1. Socrates differed from previous Greek philosophers in being concerned not with the external world but with the inner world of man and his nature.

2. Believing that the most precious thing about man is his *psyche*, or soul, Socrates went about Athens trying to persuade others of its care and value. It was unworthy of them, he insisted, to devote themselves to pursuing wealth and glory and to neglect what really mattered most.

3. The public confused Socrates with other kinds of critics, itinerant teachers circulating at Athens at this time called Sophists. Although at first highly respected, these "experts" or "wise men" gradually lost their good name as a result of their increasingly severe attacks on the established system of law, ethics, and religion.

4. Hostility toward Socrates was aggravated as the result of the disastrous social and political events surrounding the Peloponnesian War and its aftermath. Eventually, he was arrested and brought to trial for impiety and corruption of youth. Although Socrates might have gotten off with a fine or by apologizing, he used the opportunity of his trial to speak instead about his "philosopher's mission to search into myself and others."

5. The person who immortalized the name of Socrates was his young pupil Plato, all of whose works were written in the form of dialogues and featured Socrates (with whom he had been associated for over ten years) as the main speaker. Of these, four dialogues—the *Euthyphro*, the *Apology*, the *Crito*, and the *Phaedo*—form a unit and are devoted to describing Socrates' thought, trial, and death.

6. After some good-natured banter, Socrates' discussion with Euthyphro turns to the question of the nature of piety. To Euthyphro's first definition—that piety is "prosecuting a wrongdoer"—Socrates remarks that although this may be an example of piety, it is not a definition of it. Euthyphro's second definition of piety—that it is "what is pleasing to the gods"—also proves unsatisfactory because, as Socrates reminds him, the same things please some gods and displease others. To Euthyphro's rejoinder here that the gods surely do not disagree with each other on the point that the guilty should be punished, Socrates replies that of course no one would dispute that. But what is disputed at such occasions is whether the person in question is guilty. But, as Socrates himself recognizes, even if Euthyphro could prove that all the gods agree that what his father did was wrong and that what he, Euthyphro, is doing is right or pious, this still would not tell us what piety in general is—unless we could generalize here and say that "piety is what all the gods love." Euthyphro accepts this as his new definition. The question that now emerges, however, is this: "Is what is pious loved by the gods *because it is pious*, or is it pious *because it is loved by them*?" When Euthyphro replies that the gods love a thing because it is pious (and not the other way around), Socrates replies in surprise, "If that is so, then what is it about such things which make the gods love them? Aren't we back at the beginning, wondering what is piety and saying, as you did then, that it is what is pleasing to the gods!" Despite Socrates' plea that he try again, Euthyphro declines, saying he has an urgent engagement and must be off. The dialogue shows us how people's actions are often based on ignorance, and these actions can have serious, even tragic, consequences.

7. Socrates begins his defense against the charges of "corrupting the minds of the young and not worshipping the gods the state worships" by saying that he wants to deal first with his earliest accusers, those not in court now but who nevertheless have been spreading false rumors about him for many years. These rumors accuse him of

speculating about the earth and the stars in the tradition of his predecessors and assert that he is, like them, no doubt, an atheist. Socrates argues that these accusations are simply false, that he has never had any interest in these matters. But if he has not been spending his time doing that, what is it that he does? In answer to this question, he relates the story of his friend's visit to the oracle; the oracle's pronouncement that Socrates is the wisest man in the world, what he did to determine the meaning of the pronouncement, and how this aroused hostility against him. These investigations, he tells them, led to the discovery that the oracle was indeed right: he is the wisest of them all, for unlike everyone else, he knows that he knows nothing, whereas they are equally ignorant but do not know it. Sensing that the jury might think he has failed to recognize the seriousness of his position, he assures them he is fully aware of the implications of the charges. It is simply that having faced death before he is not afraid to die now, nor is he about to give up the one thing that is more precious to him than life itself: the pursuit of wisdom. If he has corrupted anyone as a result of this pursuit, let that person (or his kin) rise and say so. The jury votes and finds him guilty. Condemned to die, his last request is that they "do to my sons as I have done to you."

8. Socrates is now in prison awaiting execution. Crito, a wealthy Athenian and Socrates' oldest friend, has come to plead that he escape. Socrates, while appreciating Crito's warm feelings, wants to consider the matter only on its merits. Crito urges Socrates to consider all the bad consequences that would result from his staying, but Socrates wants to consider only what his duty is, regardless of the consequences. The question we should always ask, he tells Crito, is whether we are acting rightly or wrongly, risking doing something wrong or not, not forgetting that it is never right to do a wrong or to return evil for evil. He is not, of course, guilty, but nevertheless when a person is legally but wrongly convicted of an offense he has not committed, the wrong is inflicted not by the law but by those who have misused the law. The prison breaker, however, in doing what he does, challenges the whole fabric of law. Besides, if he did not like living in Athens, he was free to go; by staying, he had entered into a pact that he is not now at liberty to break at his pleasure. When Crito is at a loss to reply, Socrates says to him, "Then, Crito, let us follow this course, since God points the way."

9. The *Phaedo*'s two main themes are the death of Socrates and the question of the immortality of the soul. The scene is Socrates' cell on the day set by the Athenian court for his death. The friends who have come to bid farewell to Socrates are surprised to find him calm and cheerful at this hour. In reply Socrates explains why the philosopher does not fear death (living, as he does, constantly with it). Several arguments for the soul's immortality are examined, and through the medium of myth an attempt is made to explore the nature of the soul's destination. The dialogue ends with a detailed and moving account of Socrates' last moments and death.

KEY TERMS

deontological   psyche
dialogues   Sophists
just society   teleological
justice

REVIEW QUESTIONS

1. Who were the Sophists, and what was their main concern?
2. What were Socrates' two main concerns?
3. What was the Academy, and who founded it?
4. What was Plato's lifelong passion?
5. What was the main form that Plato's writings took?
6. Name the four dialogues that are devoted to the life and teachings of Socrates. What is the theme of each of these dialogues?
7. What is the moral of the *Euthyphro*? What lesson does it try to teach?
8. How does Socrates defend himself against the charges he is being tried for?

■ Reading
Apology
Plato

From *The Dialogues of Plato*, translated by Benjamin Jowett.

How you, O Athenians, have been affected by my accusers, I cannot tell; but I know that they almost made me forget who I was—so persuasively did they speak; and yet they have hardly uttered a word of truth. But of the many falsehoods told by them, there was one which quite amazed me; I mean when they said that you should be upon your guard and not allow yourselves to be deceived by the force of my eloquence. To say this, when they were certain to be detected as soon as I opened my lips and proved myself to be anything but a great speaker, did indeed appear to me most shameless—unless by the force of eloquence they mean the force of truth; for if such is their meaning, I admit that I am eloquent. But in how different a way from theirs! Well, as I was saying, they have scarcely spoken the truth at all; but from me you shall hear the whole truth.

First, I have to reply to the older charges and to my first accusers, and then I will go on to the later ones. For of old I have had many accusers, who have accused me falsely to you during many years; and I am more afraid of them than of Anytus and his associates, who are dangerous, too, in their own way. But far more dangerous are the others, who began when you were children, and took possession of your minds with their falsehoods, telling of one Socrates, a wise man, who speculated about the heaven above, and searched into the earth beneath, and made the worse appear the better cause. The disseminators of this tale are the accusers whom I dread; for their hearers are apt to fancy that such enquirers do not believe in the existence of the gods. And they are many, and their charges against me are of ancient date, and they were made by them in the days when you were more impressible than you are now—in childhood, or it may have been in youth—and the cause when heard went by default, for there was none to answer. And hardest of all, I do not know and cannot tell the names of my accusers; unless in the chance case of a comic poet.

Well, then, I must make my defense, and endeavor to clear away in a short time, a slander which has lasted a long time. May I succeed, if to succeed be for my good and yours, or likely to avail me in my cause! The task is not an easy one; I quite understand the nature of it. And so leaving the event with God, in obedience to the law I will now make my defense.

I will begin at the beginning, and ask what is the accusation which has given rise to the slander of me, and in fact has encouraged Meletus to prefer this charge against me. Well, what do the slanderers say? They shall be my prosecutors, and I will sum up their words in an affidavit: "Socrates is an evildoer, and a curious person, who searches into things under the earth and in heaven, and he makes the worse appear the better cause; and he teaches the aforesaid doctrines to others." Such is the nature of the accusation: it is just what you have yourselves seen in the comedy of Aristophanes,[1] who has introduced a man whom he calls Socrates, going about and saying that he walks in air, and talking a deal of nonsense concerning matters of which I do not pretend to know either much or little—not that I mean to speak disparagingly of anyone who is a student of natural philosophy. I should be very sorry if Meletus could bring so grave a charge against me. But the simple truth is, O Athenians, that I have nothing to do with physical speculations.

Very many of those here present are witnesses to the truth of this, and to them I appeal. Speak then, you who have heard me, and tell your neighbors whether any of you have ever known me hold forth in few words or in many upon such matters. . . . You hear their answer. And from what they say of this part of the charge you will be able to judge of the truth of the rest.

As little foundation is there for the report that I am a teacher, and take money; this accusation has no more truth in it than the other. Although, if a man were really able to instruct mankind, to receive money for giving instruction would, in my opinion, be an honor to him. Had I the same, I should have been very proud and conceited; but the truth is that I have no knowledge of the kind.

I dare say, Athenians, that someone among you will reply, "Yes, Socrates, but what is the origin of these accusations which are brought against you; there must have been something strange which you have been doing? All these rumors and this talk about you would never have arisen if you had been like other men: tell us, then, what is the cause of them, for we should be sorry to judge hastily of you." Now, I regard this as a fair challenge, and I will endeavor to explain to you the reason why I am called wise and have such an evil fame. Please to attend then. And although some of you may think that I am joking, I declare that I will tell you the entire truth. Men of Athens, this reputation of mine has come of a certain sort of wisdom which I possess. If you ask me what kind of wisdom, I reply, wisdom such as may perhaps be attained by man, for to that extent I am inclined to believe that I am wise; whereas the persons of whom I was speaking have a superhuman wisdom, which I may fail to describe, because I have it not myself; and he who says that I have, speaks falsely, and is taking away my character. And here, O men of Athens, I must beg you not to interrupt me, even if I seem to say something extravagant. For the word which I will speak is not mine. I will refer you to a witness who is worthy of credit; that witness shall be the god of Delphi—he will tell you about my wisdom, if I have any, and of what sort it is. You must have known Chaerephon; he was early a friend of mine, and also a friend of yours, for he shared in the recent exile of the people, and returned with you. Well, Chaerephon, as you know, was very impetuous in all his doings, and he went to Delphi and boldly asked the oracle to tell him whether— as I was saying, I must beg you not to interrupt—he asked the oracle to tell him whether anyone was wiser than I was, and the Pythian prophetess answered that there was no man wiser. Chaerephon is dead himself; but his brother, who is in court, will confirm the truth of what I am saying.

Why do I mention this? Because I am going to explain to you why I have such an evil name. When I heard the answer, I said to myself, What can the god mean? and what is the interpretation of his riddle? for I know that I have no wisdom, small or great. What then can he mean when he says that I am the wisest of men? And yet he is a god, and cannot lie; that would be against his nature. After long consideration, I thought of a method of trying the question. I reflected that if I could only find a man wiser than myself, then I might go to the god with a refutation in my hand. I should say to him, "Here is a man who is wiser than I am; but you said that I was the wisest." Accordingly I went to one who had the reputation of wisdom, and observed him—his name I need not mention; he was a politician whom I selected for examination—and the result was as follows: When I began to talk with him, I could not help thinking that he was not really wise, although he was thought wise by many, and still wiser by himself; and thereupon I tried to explain to him that he thought himself wise, but was not really wise; and the consequence was that he hated me, and his enmity was shared by several who were present and heard me. So I left him, saying to myself, as I went away: Well, although I do not suppose that either of us knows anything really beautiful and good, I am better off than he is—for he knows nothing, and thinks that he knows; I neither know nor think that I know. In this latter particular, then, I seem to have slightly the advantage of him. Then I went to another who had still higher pretensions to wisdom, and my conclusion was exactly the same. Whereupon I made another enemy of him, and of many others besides him.

Then I went to one man after another, being not unconscious of the enmity which I provoked, and I lamented and feared this: but necessity was laid upon me—the word of God, I thought, ought to be considered first. And I said to myself, Go I must to all who appear to know, and find out the meaning of the oracle. And I swear to you, Athenians, by the dog I swear!—for I must tell you the truth—the result of my mission was just this: I found that the men most in repute were all but the most foolish; and that others less esteemed were really wiser and better. I will tell you the tale of my wanderings and of the "Herculean" labors, as I may call them, which I endured only to find at last the oracle irrefutable. After the politicians, I went to the poets; tragic, dithyrambic, and all sorts. And there, I said to myself, you will be instantly detected; now you will find out that you are more ignorant than they are. Accordingly I took them some of the most elaborate passages in their own writings, and asked what was the meaning of them—thinking that they would teach me something. Will you believe me? I am almost ashamed to confess the truth, but I must say that there is hardly a person present who would not have talked better about their poetry than they did themselves. Then I knew that not by wisdom do poets write poetry, but by a sort of genius and inspiration; they are like diviners or soothsayers who also say many fine things, but do not understand the meaning of them. The poets appeared to me to be much in the same case; and I further observed that upon the strength of their poetry they believed themselves to be the wisest of men in other things in which they were not wise.

So I departed, conceiving myself to be superior to them for the same reason that I was superior to the politicians.

At last I went to the artisans. I was conscious that I knew nothing at all, as I may say, and I was sure that they knew many fine things; and here I was not mistaken, for they did know many things of which I was ignorant, and in this they certainly were wiser than I was. But I observed that even the good artisans fell into the same error as the poets; because they were good workmen they thought that they also knew all sorts of high matters, and this defect in them overshadowed their wisdom; and therefore I asked myself on behalf of the oracle, whether I would like to be as I was, neither having their knowledge nor their ignorance, or like them in both; and I made answer to myself and to the oracle that I was better off as I was.

This inquisition has led to my having many enemies of the worst and most dangerous kind, and has given occasion also to many calumnies. And I am called wise, for my hearers always imagine that I myself possess the wisdom which I find wanting in others: but the truth is, O men of Athens, that God only is wise; and by his answer he intends to show that the wisdom of men is worth little or nothing; he is not speaking of Socrates, he is only using my name by way of illustration, as if he said, He, O men, is the wisest, who, like Socrates, knows that his wisdom is in truth worth nothing. And so I go about the world obedient to the god, and search and make enquiry into the wisdom of anyone, whether citizen or stranger, who appears to be wise; and if he is not wise, then in vindication of the oracle I show him that he is not wise; and my occupation quite absorbs me, and I have no time to give either to any public matter of interest or to any concern of my own, but I am in utter poverty by reason of my devotion to the god.

Someone will say: And are you not ashamed, Socrates, of a course of life which is likely to bring you to an untimely end? To him I may fairly answer: There you are mistaken: a man who is good for anything ought not to calculate the chance of living or dying; he ought only to consider whether in doing anything he is doing right or wrong—acting the part of a good man or of a bad. Whereas, upon your view, the heroes who fell at Troy were not good for much, and the son of Thetis above all, who altogether despised danger in comparison with disgrace; and when he was so eager to slay Hector, his goddess mother said to him, that if he avenged his companion Patroclus, and slew Hector, he would die himself—"Fate," she said, in these or the like words, "waits for you next after Hector"; he, receiving this warning, utterly despised danger and death, and instead of fearing them, feared rather to live in dishonor, and not to avenge his friend. "Let me die forthwith," he replies, "and be avenged of my enemy, rather than abide here by the beaked ships, a laughing stock and a burden of the earth." Had Achilles any thought of death and danger? For wherever a man's place is, whether the place which he has chosen or that in which he has been placed by a commander, there he ought to remain in the hour of danger; he should not think of death or of anything but of disgrace. And this, O men of Athens, is a true saying.

Strange, indeed, would be my conduct, O men of Athens, if I, who, when I was ordered by the generals whom you chose to command me at Potidaea and Amphipolis and Delium, remained where they placed me, like any other man, facing death—if now, when, as I conceive and imagine, God orders me to fulfill the philosopher's mission of searching into myself and other men, I were to desert my post through fear of death, or any other fear; that would indeed be strange, and I might justly be arraigned in court for denying the existence of the gods, if I disobeyed the oracle because I was afraid of death, fancying that I was wise when I was not wise. For the fear of death is indeed the pretense of wisdom, and not real wisdom, being a pretense of knowing the unknown; and no one knows whether death, which men in their fear apprehend to be the greatest evil, may not be the greatest good. Is not this ignorance of a disgraceful sort, the ignorance which is the conceit that a man knows what he does not know? And in this respect only I believe myself to differ from men in general, and may perhaps claim to be wiser than they are: that whereas I know but little of the world below, I do not suppose that I know: but I do know that injustice and disobedience to a better, whether God or man, is evil and dishonorable, and I will never fear or avoid a possible good rather than a certain evil. And therefore if you let me go now, and are not convinced by Anytus, who said that since I had been prosecuted I must be put to death (or if not that I ought never to have been prosecuted at all); and that if I escape now, your sons will all be utterly ruined by listening to my words—if you say to me, Socrates, this time we will not mind Anytus, and you shall be let off, but upon one condition, that you are not to enquire and speculate in this way anymore, and that if you are caught doing so again you shall die; if this was the condition on which you let me go, I should reply: Men of Athens, I honor and love you; but I shall obey God rather than you, and while I have life and strength I shall never cease from the practice and teaching of philosophy, exhorting anyone whom I meet and saying to him after my manner: You, my friend, a citizen of the great and mighty and wise city of Athens, are you not ashamed of heaping up the greatest amount of money and honor and reputation, and caring so little about wisdom and truth and the greatest improvement of the soul, which you never regard or heed at all? And if the person with whom I am arguing, says: Yes, but I do care; then I do not leave him or let him go at once; but I proceed to interrogate and examine and cross examine him, and if I think that he has no virtue in him, but only says that he has, I reproach him with undervaluing the greater, and overvaluing the less. And I shall repeat the same words to everyone whom I meet, young and old, citizen and alien, but especially to the citizens, inasmuch as they are my brethren. For know that this is the command of God; and I believe that no greater good has ever happened in the State than my service to the God. For I do nothing but go about persuading you all, old and young alike, not to take thought for your persons or your properties, but first and chiefly to care about the greatest improvement of the soul. I tell you that virtue is not given by money, but that from virtue comes money and every other good of man, public as well as private. This is my teaching, and if this is the doctrine which corrupts the youth, I am a mischievous person. But if anyone says that this is not my teaching, he is speaking an untruth. Wherefore, O men of Athens, I say to you, do as Anytus bids or not as Anytus bids, and either acquit me or not; but whichever you do, understand that I shall never alter my ways, not even if I have to die many times.

And now, Athenians, I am not going to argue for my own sake, as you may think, but for yours, that you may not sin against the God by condemning me, who am his gift to you. For if you kill me you will not easily find a successor to me, who, if I may use such a ludicrous figure of speech, am a sort of gadfly, given to the State by God; and the State is a great and noble steed who is tardy in his motions owing to his very size, and requires to be stirred into life. I am that gadfly which God has attached to the State, and all day long and in all places am always fastening upon you, arousing and persuading and reproaching you. You will not easily find another like me, and therefore I would advise you to spare me. I dare say that you may feel out of temper (like a person who is suddenly awakened from sleep), and you think that you might easily strike me dead as Anytus advises, and then you would sleep on for the remainder of your lives, unless God in his care of you sent you another gadfly. When I say that I am given to you by God, the proof of my mission is this: if I had been like other men, I should not have neglected all my own concerns or patiently seen the neglect of them during all these years, and have been doing yours, coming to you individually like a father or elder brother, exhorting you to regard virtue; such conduct, I say, would be unlike human nature. If I had gained anything, or if my exhortations had been paid, there would have been some sense in my doing so; but now, as you will perceive, not even the impudence of my accusers dares to say that I have ever exacted or sought pay of anyone; of that they have no witness. And I have a sufficient witness to the truth of what I say—my poverty.

Someone may wonder why I go about in private giving advice and busying myself with the concerns of others, but do not venture to come forward in public and advise the State. I will tell you why. You have heard me speak at sundry times and in divers places of an oracle or sign which comes to me, and is the divinity which Meletus ridicules in the indictment. This sign, which is a kind of voice, first began to come to me when I was a child; it always forbids but never commands me to do anything which I am going to do. This is what deters me from being a politician. And rightly, as I think. For I am certain, O men of Athens, that if I had engaged in politics, I should have perished long ago, and done no good either to you or to myself. And do not be offended at my telling you the truth: for the truth is, that no man who goes to war with you or any other multitude, honestly striving against the many lawless and unrighteous deeds which are done in a State, will save his life; he who will fight for the right, if he would live even for a brief space, must have a private station and not a public one.

I can give you convincing evidence of what I say, not words only, but what you value far more—actions. Let me relate to you a passage of my own life which will prove to you that I should never have yielded to injustice from any fear of death and that "as I should have refused to yield" I must have died at once. I will tell you a tale of the courts, not very interesting perhaps, but nevertheless true. The only office of State which I ever held, O men of Athens, was that of senator: the tribe Antiochis, which is my tribe, had the presidency at the trial of the generals who had not taken up the bodies of the slain after the battle of Arginusae; and you proposed to try them in a body, contrary to law, as you all thought afterwards; but at the time I was the only one of the Prytanes who was opposed to the illegality, and I gave my vote against you; and when the orators threatened to impeach and arrest me, and you called and shouted, I made up my mind that I would run the risk, having law and justice with me, rather than take part in your injustice because I feared imprisonment and death. This happened in the days of the democracy. But when the oligarchy of the Thirty was in power, they sent for me and four others into the rotunda, and bade us bring Leon the Salaminian from Salamis, as they wanted to put him to death. This was a specimen of the sort of commands which they were always giving with the view of implicating as many as possible in their crimes; and then I showed, not in word only but in deed, that, if I may be allowed to use such an expression, I cared not a straw for death, and that my great and only care was lest I should do an unrighteous or unholy thing. For the strong arm of that oppressive power did not frighten me into doing wrong; and when we came out of the rotunda the other four went to Salamis and fetched Leon, but I went quietly home. For which I might have lost my life, had not the power of the Thirty shortly afterwards come to an end. And many will witness to my words.

Now, do you really imagine that I could have survived all these years, if I had led a public life, supposing that like a good man I had always maintained the right and had made justice, as I ought, the first thing? No, indeed, men of Athens, neither I nor any other man. But I have been always the same in all my actions, public as well as private, and never have I yielded any base compliance to those who are slanderously termed my disciples, or to any other. Not that I have any regular disciples. But if anyone likes to come and hear me while I am pursuing my mission, whether he be young or old, he is not excluded. Nor do I converse only with those who pay; but anyone, whether he be rich or poor, may ask and answer me and listen to my words; and whether he turns out to be a bad man or a good one, neither result can be justly imputed to me; for I never taught or professed to teach him anything. And if anyone says that he has ever learned or heard anything from me in private which all the world has not heard, let me tell you that he is lying.

Well, Athenians, this and the like of this is all the defense which I have to offer. . . .

[Socrates is convicted.]

There are many reasons why I am not grieved, O men of Athens, at the vote of condemnation. I expected it, and am only surprised that the votes are so nearly equal; for I had thought that the majority against me would have been far larger; but now, had thirty votes gone over to the other side, I should have been acquitted. And I may say, I think, that I have escaped Meletus. I may say more; for without the assistance of Anytus and Lycon, anyone may see that he would not have had a fifth part of the votes, as the law requires, in which case he would have incurred a fine of a thousand drachmae.

And so he proposes death as the penalty. And what shall I propose on my part, O men of Athens? Clearly that which is my due. And what is my due? What returns shall be made to the man who has never had the wit to be idle during his whole life; but has been careless of what the many care for—wealth, and family interests, and military offices, and speaking in the assembly, and magistracies, and plots, and parties. Reflecting that I was really too honest a man to be a politician and live, I did not go where I could do no good to you or to myself; but where I could do the greatest good privately to every one of you, thither I went, and sought to persuade every man among you that he must look to himself, and seek virtue and wisdom before he looks to his private interests, and look to the State before he looks to the interests of the State; and that this should be the order which he observes in all his actions. What shall be done to such a one? Doubtless some good thing, O men of Athens, if he has his reward; and the good should be of a kind suitable to him. What would be a reward suitable to a poor man who is your benefactor, and who desires leisure that he may instruct you? There can be no reward so fitting as maintenance in the Prytaneum, O men of Athens, a reward which he deserves far more than the citizen who has won the prize at Olympia in the horse or chariot race, whether the chariots were drawn by two horses or by many. For I am in want, and he has enough; and he only gives you the appearance of happiness, and I give you the reality. And if I am to estimate the penalty fairly, I should say that maintenance in the Prytaneum is the just return.

Perhaps you think that I am braving you in what I am saying now, as in what I said before about the tears and prayers. But this is not so. I speak rather because I am convinced that I never intentionally wronged anyone, although I cannot convince you—the time has been too short; if there were a law at Athens, as there is in other cities, that a capital cause should not be decided in one day, then I believe that I should have convinced you. But I cannot in a moment refute great slanders; and, as I am convinced that I never wronged another, I will assuredly not wrong myself. I will not say of myself that I deserve any evil, or propose any penalty. Why should I? Because I am afraid of the penalty of death which Meletus proposes? When I do not know whether death is a good or an evil, why should I propose a penalty which would certainly be an evil? Shall I say imprisonment? And why should I live in prison, and be the slave of the magistrate of the year—of the Eleven? Or shall the penalty be a fine, and imprisonment until the fine is paid? There is the same objection. I should have to lie in prison, for money I have none, and cannot pay. And if I say exile (and this may possibly be the penalty which you will affix), I must indeed be blinded by the love of life, if I am so irrational as to expect that when you, who are my own citizens, cannot endure my discourses and words, and have found them so grievous and odious that you will have no more of them, others are likely to endure me. No, indeed, men of Athens, that is not very likely. And what a life should I lead, at my age, wandering from city to city, ever changing my place of exile, and always being driven out! For I am quite sure that wherever I go, there, as here, the young men will flock to me; and if I drive them away, their elders will drive me out at their request; and if I let them come, their fathers and friends will drive me out for their sakes.

[A vote is taken, and Socrates is condemned to death. Socrates makes a closing address to those assembled.]

Not much time will be gained, O Athenians, in return for the evil name which you will get from the detractors of the city, who will say that you killed Socrates, a wise man; for they will call me wise, even although I am not wise, when they want to reproach you. If you had waited a little while, your desire would have been fulfilled in the course of nature. For I am far advanced in years, as you may perceive, and not far from death. I am speaking now not to all of you, but only to those who have condemned me to death. And I have another thing to say to them: You think that I was convicted because I had no words of the sort which would have procured my acquittal—I mean, if I had thought fit to leave nothing undone or unsaid. Not so; the deficiency which led to my conviction was not of words—certainly not. But I had not the boldness or impudence or inclination to address you as you would have liked me to do, weeping and wailing and lamenting, and saying and doing many things which you have been accustomed to hear from others, and which, as I maintain, are unworthy of me. I thought at the time that I ought not to do anything common or mean when in danger: nor do I now repent of the style of my defense; I would rather die having spoken after my manner, than speak in your manner and live. For neither in war nor yet at law ought I or any man to use every way of escaping death. Often in battle there can be no doubt that if a man will throw away his arms, and fall on his knees before his pursuers, he may escape death; and in other dangers there are other ways of escaping death, if a man is willing to say and do anything. The difficulty, my friends, is not to avoid death, but to avoid unrighteousness; for that runs faster than death. I am old and move slowly, and the slower runner has overtaken me, and my accusers are keen and quick, and the faster runner, who is unrighteousness, has overtaken them. And now I depart hence condemned by you to suffer the penalty of death; they too go their ways condemned by the truth to suffer the penalty of villainy and wrong; and I must abide by my award—let them abide by theirs. I suppose that these things may be regarded as fated—and I think that they are well.

Wherefore, O judges, be of good cheer about death, and know of a certainty, that no evil can happen to a good man, either in life or after death. He and his are not neglected by the gods; nor has my own approaching end happened by mere chance. But I see clearly that the time had arrived when it was better for me to die and be released from trouble; wherefore the oracle gave no sign. For which reason, also, I am not angry with my condemners, or with my accusers; they have done me no harm, although they did not mean to do me any good; and for this I may gently blame them.

Still, I have a favor to ask of them. When my sons are grown up, I would ask you, O my friends, to punish them; and I would have you trouble them, as I have troubled you, if they seem to care about riches, or anything, more than about virtue; or if they pretend to be something when they are really nothing—then reprove them, as I have reproved you, for not caring about that for which they ought to care, and thinking that they are something when they are really nothing. And if you do this, both I and my sons will have received justice at your hands.

The hour of departure has arrived, and we go our ways—I to die, and you to live. Which is better God only knows.

NOTE

1. Aristophanes, Clouds, 225 ff.

■ Questions for Discussion

1. Do you think Socrates was correct in accepting his sentence? Could you have done the same?

2. What did Socrates mean when he called himself a gadfly?

3. How would Socrates be regarded by society today? How would you regard such a person? Can you think of any modern individuals who are similar to Socrates?

PART II

PHILOSOPHY'S METHOD

CHAPTER FOUR

■ Aristotle and the Science of Logic

One can acquire no greater skill in life than the ability to think. Contrary to what many believe, this is not a skill that comes naturally to us, nor is it one we exercise a great deal. As George Bernard Shaw once remarked, few people think more than two or three times a year. He had managed to achieve an international reputation by thinking as often as once a week.

Although thinking is not a natural skill, it is one, as we have had occasion to see, that has been integral to the activity of philosophy from its very beginning—so much so, in fact, that to philosophize and to think have come to be regarded as almost synonymous.

Although this is so, thinking did not assume the importance that it came to possess and its study did not achieve the rank of a separate and distinct discipline until the arrival of Aristotle, whose investigations transformed it into the important discipline it has become.

Who was Aristotle and how did this happen?

ARISTOTLE

Aristotle (384–322 B.C.) was born at Stagira, a Macedonian city some 200 miles to the north of Athens. When he was born, Plato was 43, and Socrates had been dead 15 years.

Aristotle's father was court physician to the King of Macedonia. However, his parents died while he was still young, and he was given a home and an education by a friend of the family.

At the age of 18, he was sent to Plato's Academy in Athens, where he remained for the next 20 years, first as a pupil and then as a colleague of Plato's. When Plato died in 327 B.C. and the leadership of the Academy passed to Plato's nephew, Aristotle left. He

Aristotle (384–322 BCE)

went to Assos, a town on the coast of Asia Minor opposite the island of Lesbos, to teach at a school established by its philosophically sympathetic ruler, Hermias. Aristotle taught there for the next three years. He married Hermias's daughter and they had two children, a son, Nicomachus, and a daughter, Pythias, named after her mother.

After spending another two years on the neighboring island of Lesbos, Aristotle was invited by Philip of Macedonia to superintend the education of his son Alexander, a boy of 13.

Aristotle spent seven years as tutor to the young prince. His assignment came to an end with the death of Philip in 336 B.C. Alexander ascended to the throne of Macedonia, which by then dominated all Greece, and began his spectacular career as the conquerer of Persia, earning his name of Alexander the Great.

Aristotle returned to Athens and founded his own school. It was called the Lyceum, and his system of philosophy came to be known as the peripatetic philosophy—apparently from his habit of teaching while walking up and down its covered walk. Aristotle spent the next 12 years at the Lyceum, where he started a library (the first in history), made vast collections of scientific data (much of the material coming to him from Alexander's expeditions), and built residential halls to accommodate the growing number of students. The Lyceum quickly outstripped the Academy in fame. The two schools were very different in their orientation, each tending to reflect the temperament of its founder: the Academy was devoted to the study of the rational sciences—mathematics and astronomy—while the Lyceum focused on the study of the empirical sciences, especially biology.

Aristotle's work at the Lyceum came to an end in 323 B.C. with Alexander's sudden death. In a wave of anti-Macedonian feeling, he was marked down as an associate of Alexander by the rebellious Athenians, and they drew up a charge against him—one similar to the accusation that had been brought against Socrates in 399 B.C. Not wanting, as he said, "to give the Athenians a second chance of sinning against philosophy," he returned to his country estate, where he died a few months later at the age of 63.

Aristotle's ability was recognized by Plato, who called him the *nous* (the "brain" or "mind") of the school. And Aristotle always spoke highly of Plato. He said of him that he was a man "whom bad men have not even the right to praise and who showed in his life and teachings how to be happy and good at the same time."

Aristotle is known variously as "The Stagirite," after his birthplace; "The Peripatetic," from his habit of teaching; and "The Philosopher," the name given to him by St. Thomas Aquinas to indicate that there was no other.

The Sophists Again

The study of **logic**, or thinking—which, as we have said, has come to be considered so integral a part of philosophy—can be said to have begun some 2,000 years ago when Aristotle, while a student at Plato's Academy and following Plato around as the latter engaged in discussion with the still ubiquitous Sophists, found himself baffled and challenged by their ability to outwit and outsmart all comers. He decided to examine what it was that enabled these "experts," as they were called, to accomplish their feats.

The result was a work on logic (one of six he was to devote to the study of thinking) titled *Of Sophistical Refutations*. The title hints at its contents, for what we have here is a manual in which Aristotle sets out to expose the strategy and tactics the Sophists often resorted to in order to gain their verbal victories.

To call someone a sophist today is not, of course, to pay them a compliment. As the dictionary tells us, a sophist is someone who is clever and tricky, who engages in fallacious reasoning, and who tries to outmaneuver and take advantage of an opponent in every possible way. But, as we saw in chapter 3, the meaning was not always so.

Aristotle's teacher Plato has left us some graphic descriptions of these "experts" in action. Probably the most memorable of these, although it is the least subtle of them and hardly does them justice, is in the dialogue titled the *Euthydemus*. Since it contains the kinds of logical points in argumentation that formed part of the basis for Aristotle's work in logic—work that will occupy us for most of this chapter—let us spend some moments with it.

The dialogue opens with Socrates relating his encounter with two recent arrivals in Athens, the Sophists Euthydemus and Dionysodorous. They have encountered a young boy, Cleinias, and are busy questioning him. Socrates is there, and so is Cleinias's close friend, a youth called Ctessippus, who will later get clobbered when he tries to come to his friend's rescue. The Sophists always attracted a large crowd, and there is one here, too.

The questioning begins with Euthydemus asking Cleinias who learns things best—the wise or the unwise? The boy, understanding the word "wise" to mean "intelligent," naturally replies that it is the wise who learn best and not the unwise. By playing fast and loose with the meaning of the word, quickly shifting from one meaning to another, the Sophists soon get Cleinias to deny what he has just affirmed, subsequently to affirm it once again, then to deny it, until he is naturally completely befuddled—to the great amusement of the crowd that has gathered to watch the spectacle. Having finished off Cleinias, they turn next to Socrates:

DIONYSODOROUS: Reflect, Socrates: you may have to deny your words.
SOCRATES: I have reflected, and I shall never deny my words.
DIONYSODOROUS: Well, and so you say that you wish Cleinias to become wise?
SOCRATES: Undoubtedly.
DIONYSODOROUS: And he is not wise as yet?

SOCRATES: At least his modesty will not allow him to say that he is.

DIONYSODOROUS: You wish him to become wise and not to be ignorant? You wish him to be what he is not, and no longer to be what he is? . . . You wish him no longer to be what he is? Which can only mean that you wish him to perish! Pretty lovers and friends they must be who want their favorite not to be, that is, to perish!

[Socrates is thrown into consternation at this and quite baffled. While in this state, a friend of Cleinias's, Ctessippus, intervenes, and the Sophists turn to him.]

DIONYSODOROUS: If you will answer my questions, I will soon extract the same admissions from you, Ctessippus. You say you have a dog.

CTESSIPPUS: Yes, a villain of a one.

DIONYSODOROUS: And he has puppies?

CTESSIPPUS: Yes, and they are very like himself.

DIONYSODOROUS: And the dog is the father of them?

CTESSIPPUS: Yes, I certainly saw him and the mother of the puppies come together.

DIONYSODOROUS: And he is not yours?

CTESSIPPUS: To be sure he is.

DIONYSODOROUS: Then he is a father, and he is yours; ergo, he is your father, and the puppies are your brothers.

EUTHYDEMUS: Ctessippus, let me ask you one little question: you beat this dog?

CTESSIPPUS: (Laughing) Indeed I do; and I only wish I could beat you instead of him.

EUTHYDEMUS: Then you beat your father!

Plato is in a Neil Simon mood here, engaging in broad comedy. In the course of the dialogue, he has the Sophists prove, among other things, that it is impossible to tell a lie since a lie is "that which is not" and thus can have no existence, that good men speak evil since they would not be good if they did not speak evil of evil things, and that everything visible "has the quality of vision" and hence can see. Not all Sophists were as easy to ridicule, nor were the fallacies committed by them always as easy to track down as those represented here. Nevertheless, this was the task that Plato's able student Aristotle set himself.

Aristotle's *Of Sophistical Refutations* led to a whole new type of investigation, one that continued to be pursued by other philosophers after him. They recognized, like him, that errors in logic, although often amusing, nevertheless can cause serious problems—for individuals, for groups, and for nations.

> Tweedledum: I know what you're thinking about; but it isn't so, nohow.
>
> Tweedledee: Contrariwise. If it was so, it might be; and if it were so, it would be; but as it isn't, it ain't. That's logic.
>
> —Lewis Carroll, *Through the Looking Glass*

The Science of Logic

In his other logical works, Aristotle discovered something else about language and thinking that was to prove of enormous importance. Certainly we can be led astray easily by people like the Sophists or by their modern-day counterparts, and a study of their tactics is absolutely essential. But we must also learn to develop a healthy respect for the structures built into our language and even the content packed into our words and idioms. Rules govern the use of language, rules that are binding on all of us and determine what we may or may not say. We violate these rules only at our peril.

Aristotle went on to show how very limited and bound in fact we are by the way we talk. He demonstrated this limitation by examining the main units of language with which we do most of our thinking—the categorical proposition and the arguments, called syllogisms, that employ those propositions.

By **categorical proposition**, Aristotle meant simply the declarative sentence, the common sentence we all speak: "The table is brown," or "The sky is clear." A **syllogism** is an argument composed of such sentences. Like Molière's gentleman who didn't realize he had been speaking prose all his life, few of us are aware that most of the reasoning we engage in is syllogistic.

This fact easily escapes us because our reasoning is often highly abbreviated and its formal structure is not always clear to us. Even an epithet like "Liar!" hurled at someone is in essence an argument—and a formally valid one at that. For, unpacked, what it contains is the following reasoning:

All people who try to deceive others by uttering what they know to be false are liars.
You are such a person.
Therefore, you are a liar.

Although the categorical proposition is only one way in which we can organize our thought, it is nevertheless the main one, accounting for perhaps as much as 90 percent of our reasoning. Aristotle discovered a surprising thing about it: although we might believe that the vast number of words in our language would allow us to compose an unlimited number of different propositions and arguments, the fact is that the number of different *types* of propositions we can construct is severely limited, and their combinations in possible argument forms can be determined exactly.

> Thinking consists of journeys through the mazes of our linguistic forms, and logic is the study of the relations that obtain in and among these forms.
>
> —**Source unknown**

Aristotle went on to determine just how many argument forms the various combinations of categorical propositions make possible. He found the number to be exactly 256. So much for freedom of thought. More depressing still was the further discovery that of these 256 argument forms, only some 15 are valid!

Long before Aristotle arrived on the scene, people had engaged in and reflected on reasoning, but he is considered the founder of logic, and we can see why. He was the first to make a science of it.

LOGIC AS THE STUDY OF ARGUMENT

Logic is the study of **argument**. As used in this sense, the word means not a quarrel (as when we "get into an argument") but a piece of reasoning in which one or more statements are offered as support for some other statement. The statement being supported is the **conclusion** of the argument. The reasons given in support of the conclusion are called **premises**. We may say, "This is so (conclusion) because that is so (premise)." Or, "This is so and this is so (premises), therefore that is so (conclusion)." Premises are generally preceded by such words as *because, for, since,* or *on the ground that.* Conclusions, on the other hand, are generally preceded by such words as *therefore, hence, consequently,* and *it follows that.*

The first step toward understanding arguments, therefore, is learning to identify premises and conclusions. To do so, look for the indicator words, as they are called, just listed. In arguments where such indicator words are absent, try to find the conclusion by determining the main thrust of the argument: the point the argument is trying to establish. That will be its conclusion; the rest will be supporting grounds or premises.

Distinguishing the conclusion from the premise or premises in the following two arguments is easy, for in the first case one of the statements is preceded by the word *for* (which tells us that what follows is a premise and what remains must be its conclusion), while in the second, one of the statements is preceded by the word *hence* (which tells us that what follows is a conclusion and what remains must be its premise):

> Jones will not do well in this course, for he is having a hard time concentrating on course work this semester and has hardly attended any classes.
>
> She has antagonized nearly everyone on the committee; hence it is unlikely that she will be granted the promotion.

In the following two examples, however, no such helpful indicator words are present:

> There are no foxes in this area. We haven't seen one all day.
> All communists favor public housing. Senator Smith favors it; he must be a communist.

To distinguish the premise from the conclusion in cases of this sort, ask yourself such questions as, What is being *argued for*? and What is the person trying to *persuade us of*? In the first example what is being argued for is not that "we haven't seen a fox all day"—for the other person obviously already knows this and is simply being reminded of it—but rather that, in light of this known fact, there *must* be no foxes in this area.

That is the conclusion of the argument. Similarly, with the second example what is being argued for is not that "all communists favor public housing," nor that "Senator Smith favors it"—for in this argument these are assumed to be shared statements of fact and stated as such—but rather that, in the light of these facts, Smith must be a communist.

The following is a somewhat more difficult example:

It is an incontestable fact that our country is the ultimate, priceless goal of international communism. The leaders of international communism have vowed to achieve world domination. This cannot be until the Red Flag is flown over the United States. (J. Edgar Hoover on communism)

To distinguish the premises from the conclusion in this argument, ask yourself what the main thrust of this argument is. Is it to persuade us of the fact that "the leaders of international communism have vowed to achieve world domination"? This hardly seems so, being offered, as it is, as a simple statement of fact. Is it that such world domination cannot be achieved "until the Red Flag is flown over the United States"? Again, hardly so since this, too, is offered as a presumed fact, one entailed by the statement that immediately precedes it. We come, then, to the remaining statement, the one with which the argument opens: that it is "an incontestable fact that our country is the ultimate, priceless goal of international communism." Despite the use of the rhetorical phrase *incontestable fact*, what we have here is not a statement of fact but a conclusion gathered from the facts offered. From both its tone and its content, this is what the argument aims to establish and convince us of.

Finding the conclusion when it has no obvious indications will not always be easy or certain. Our best aid will be attending carefully to the content and tone of the argument and to the direction of its reasoning.

■ EXERCISES*

Distinguish between the conclusion and the premises in the following arguments.

1. Since all rational beings are responsible for their actions and since all human beings are rational, it follows that all human beings are responsible for their actions.

2. Mario does not attend church, for he is an atheist, and atheists do not attend church.

3. If people are successful, then they are keenly interested in their work and not easily distracted from it. We may therefore conclude that no one who is successful is easily distracted when working.

---

*Answers appear at the end of the chapter.

4. The city should reimburse him for his hospital expenses for the simple reason that the accident took place while he was engaged on city business.

5. Because only those who can quote large chunks of that material can pass a test on it, it is useless for me to try, for I know hardly any of it by heart.

6. Today I will be master of my emotions. The tides advance; the tides recede. Winter goes and summer comes. Summer wanes and the cold increases. The sun rises; the sun sets. The moon is full; the moon is black. The birds arrive; the birds depart. Flowers bloom; flowers fade. Seeds are sown; harvests are reaped. All nature is a circle of moods and I am a part of nature and so, like the tides, my moods will rise; my moods will fall. Today I will be master of my emotions. (Og Mandino, *The Greatest Salesman in the World*)

7. Steve ought to exercise more. It would be good for his condition.

8. Sheila must have left already. She doesn't answer her phone.

9. I no longer believe those who say that a poor politician could be a good president, "if he could only be appointed to the job." Without the qualities required of a successful candidate—without the ability to rally support, to understand the public, to express its aspirations—without the organizational talent, the personal charm, and the physical stamina required to survive the primaries, the convention, and the election—no man would make a great president, however wise in other ways he might be. (Theodore G. Sorensen, *Decision-Making in the White House*)

10. The day *may* come when the rest of the animal creation may acquire those rights which never could have been withholden from them by the hand of tyranny. The French have already discovered that the blackness of the skin is no reason why a human being should be abandoned without redress to the caprice of a tormentor. It may one day come to be recognized that the number of the legs, the villosity of the skin, or the termination of the *os sacrum*, are reasons equally insufficient for abandoning a sensitive being to the same fate. What else is it that should trace the insuperable line? Is it the faculty of reason, or perhaps the faculty of discourse? But a full-grown horse or dog is beyond comparison a more rational, as well as a more conversable animal, than an infant of a day, or a week, or even a month, old. But suppose they were otherwise, what would it avail? The question is not, Can they *reason*? nor Can they *talk*? but, Can they *suffer*? (Jeremy Bentham, *The Principles of Morals and Legislation*, 1789)

DISTINGUISHING ARGUMENTS FROM NONARGUMENTS

As we have seen, an argument is a piece of reasoning in which one or more statements are offered as support for some other statement. If a piece of writing makes no claim supported by such reasons, it is not an argument. Thus questions are not arguments, nor are announcements, complaints, compliments, or apologies.

Such writings are not arguments because, again, they make no effort to persuade by offering reasons in support of their claims. For example, to write and ask whether actor

Hugh Grant is any relation to Cary Grant is merely to pose a question, not an argument. It requests information, not assent to some claim.

The same is true of the following representative types of communication we all engage in from time to time:

(a) Every scene of *Mistral's Daughter*, the CBS miniseries, was filled with excitement and expectancy for me. Those paintings were marvelous for me as I do portraits in oil. I just must know who did this artwork.

(b) I spent $125 to attend a reincarnation seminar and the leader appeared in a racing jacket, jeans, and a T-shirt advertising a California guitar shop. I consider that bad taste in Philadelphia. He is certainly the best regressionist I've seen in my 60 years, but you can have his kung-fu approach to spirituality.

(c) The sincerest satisfaction in life is doing and not in dodging duty; in meeting and solving problems, in facing facts, in being a dependable person.

Example (a) is an expression of support and enthusiasm, (b) is a complaint, and (c) is merely a statement of a point of view without any attempt either to argue or persuade us of it.

None of these, then, is an argument. That does not mean such passages are bad arguments; it simply means that they are not arguments at all. They fulfill other legitimate—and often necessary—functions.

More difficult are those cases in which reasons are indeed offered but more in way of clarification rather than justification. Although appearing like arguments, such passages are often no more than a collection of statements, one expanding on the other. Consider, for example, the following remark by nationally syndicated televangelist James Robinson:

> Women have great strengths, but they are strengths to help the man. A woman's primary purpose in life and marriage is to help her husband succeed, to help him be all God wants him to be.

Robinson's main point is that women's role in life is to help the man, a point he then simply reaffirms and expands on in the rest of his comment. What we have here then is, essentially, merely a slightly elaborated but unsupported statement of an opinion—not an argument.

The same is true of the following oft-quoted aphorism of Francis Bacon:

> He that hath wife and children hath given hostages to fortune; for they are impediments to great enterprise, either of virtue or mischief.

Rather than offering reasons why, in his view, women and children stand in a man's way (are "hostages to fortune"), Bacon simply explains himself by expanding and repeating the point. So this, too, is not an argument.

But cases will not always be so clear-cut, and often enough, one will encounter examples where explanation and justification simply blend into each other:

> We are sorry but we tried and tried but we find that the stains on this garment cannot be removed without possible injury to the color or fabric. This has been called to your attention so that you will know it has not been overlooked.

This passage can be said both to explain that the stains have not been removed as well as to offer a reason why they have not. Although the former is probably its main object, the explanation is of such a nature that it can function as a reason—that is, constitute an argument—as well (and would, no doubt, be invoked as such were the need to arise).

It would seem best to evaluate examples like these in light of their primary intention. If, as in the case above, the intention is to explain rather than justify, then, strictly speaking, the passage is not an argument.

■ EXERCISES

Which of the following are arguments, and which are nonarguments? If they are not arguments, explain what they are; if they are arguments, say why.

11. Back in the mid-1950s there was an actor named John Bromfield. I believe he was married to actress Corinne Calvet. I can't think of any movies that he was in, but he seemed quite popular for a year or so in TV. What happened to him?

12. We must stop the homosexuals dead in their tracks—before they get one step further toward warping the minds of our youth. The time for us to attack is now! The enemy is in our camp! (Jerry Falwell, founder of the Moral Majority)

13. The main issue in life is not the victory but the fight. The essential thing is not to have won but to have fought well. (Baron Pierre de Coubertin, founder of the modern Olympic Games)

14. Sex deepens love and love deepens sex, so physical intimacy transforms everything and playing with it is playing with fire. Men try to ignore the fact that making love creates bonds, creating dependencies where there were none before, and women who try to ignore it with them deny their basic needs. (Merle Shain, *Some Men Are More Perfect Than Others*)

15. I must study politics and war, that my sons may have liberty to study mathematics and science. My sons ought to study mathematics and science, geography, natural history and engineering, commerce, and agriculture, in order to give their children a right to study painting, poetry, music, architecture, literature, and philosophy.

16.   Oh, come with old Khayyam, and leave the Wise
      To talk; one thing is certain, that life flies;
      One thing is certain, and the Rest is Lies;

The Flower that once has blown for ever dies.
Ah, make the most of what we yet may spend,
Before we too into the Dust descend;
Dust into Dust, and under Dust, to lie,
Sans Wine, sans Song, sans Singer—and sans End!
(Edward Fitzgerald)

17. You shouldn't have legislation against a thing that the majority of the population does. And today the majority smokes marijuana. So marijuana should be legalized.

18. It is important that you study this book thoroughly and with diligence. The state insurance departments which administer insurance examinations take seriously their responsibility to protect the public from unqualified persons. For that reason, life insurance examinations cannot be considered easy to pass. Prospective agents who take their task of studying lightly have been surprised to learn that they have failed examinations. Fortunately, those prospective agents who were qualified undertook study with more earnestness and passed examinations on subsequent occasions. While examinations cannot be considered easy, neither should they be considered unreasonably difficult. The purpose of the examination is to test your knowledge of the type of information contained in this book. If you study thoroughly, you have a good chance of passing. (Gary H. Snouffer, *Lit Insurance Agent*)

19. The only creatures on earth that have bigger—and maybe better—brains than humans are the Cetacea, the whales and dolphins. Perhaps they could one day tell us something important, but it is unlikely that we will hear it. Because we are coldly, efficiently and economically killing them off. (Jacques Cousteau)

20. What happens to cigarette smoke in the air? The logical and obvious thing: cigarette smoke is immediately diluted by surrounding air. And measurements of cigarette smoke in the air, taken under realistic conditions, show again and again that there is minimal tobacco smoke in the air we breathe. In fact, based on one study, which measured nicotine in the air, it has been said that a nonsmoker would have to spend 100 straight hours in a smoke-filled room to consume the equivalent of a single filter-tipped cigarette. That's what we mean by minimal. So, does cigarette smoke endanger nonsmokers? In his most recent report, the Surgeon General, no fan of smoking, said that the available evidence is not sufficient to conclude that other people's smoke causes disease in nonsmokers. In our view, smoking is an adult custom and the decision to smoke should be based on mature and informed individual freedom of choice.

21. Although we do not know if other influenza vaccines can cause Guillain-Barre syndrome (GBS), this risk may be present for all of them. Little is known about the exact causes of GBS, but clearly the great majority of the several thousand GBS cases that occur each year in the United States are not due to influenza vaccine. The risk of GBS from the vaccine is very small. This risk should be balanced against the risk of influenza and its complications. The risk of death from influenza during a typical epidemic is more than 400 times the risk of dying from any possible complications of influenza vaccine injections.

ELIMINATING VERBIAGE

Arguments as ordinarily expressed are encumbered with a great deal of repetition, verbosity, and irrelevance. To see more clearly what such arguments are about it is necessary to scrape away a good deal of this deadwood from them. Sometimes this may simply involve ignoring a rather long, drawn-out introduction, as in the following example from Og Mandino's classic salesmen's manual *The Greatest Salesman in the World* (you'll recognize this as exercise 6):

> Today I will be master of my emotions. The tides advance; the tides recede. Winter goes and summer comes. Summer wanes and the cold increases. The sun rises; the sun sets. The moon is full; the moon is black. The birds arrive; the birds depart. Flowers bloom; flowers fade. Seeds are sown; harvests are reaped. All nature is a circle of moods and I am a part of nature and so, like the tides, my moods will rise; my moods will fall. Today I will be master of my emotions.

What this argument basically asserts is contained in its second-to-last sentence: "All nature is a circle of moods and I am part of nature and so, like the tides, my moods will rise; my moods will fall." For purposes of logical evaluation, all the preceding material is irrelevant, however poetic and moving it may be.

What applies to introductions applies similarly to conclusions that may needlessly repeat what has already been adequately stated. The insurance example in exercise 18 is characteristic of such unnecessary repetition:

> It is important that you study this book thoroughly and with diligence. The state insurance departments which administer insurance examinations take seriously their responsibility to protect the public from unqualified persons. For that reason, life insurance examinations cannot be considered easy to pass. Prospective agents who take their task of studying lightly have been surprised to learn that they have failed examinations. Fortunately, those prospective agents who were qualified undertook study with more earnestness and passed examinations on subsequent occasions. While examinations cannot be considered easy, neither should they be considered unreasonably difficult. The purpose of the examination is to test your knowledge of the type of information contained in this book. If you study thoroughly, you have a good chance of passing.

Do the last three sentences of the passage say anything that has not been said previously?

Often, however, an example is simply verbose throughout and needs to be abbreviated drastically before its structure can be observed clearly, as in the cigarette smoke example in exercise 20. Before such arguments can be properly evaluated, they need to be rewritten as concisely as possible and their premises and conclusion arranged in their logical order.

Revising the three arguments in exercises 6, 18, and 20 along such lines, we find that they essentially state the following:

6. All nature is a circle of moods: I am part of nature; therefore, I, too, must accept the fact that I will be subject to such swings of mood.

18. Insurance examinations are not easy to pass without proper preparation. Therefore, prepare yourself for them—by buying and carefully reading this book—if you desire to pass them.

20. According to a recent study, cigarette smoke is immediately diluted by surrounding air; this is also affirmed by the Surgeon General; therefore, cigarette smoke in the air does not represent a serious danger to nonsmokers.

In eliminating verbiage from arguments, you will at times be forced to discard some of the "poetry" or literary elegance of the original. This is a sacrifice, however, you will need to make for the sake of logical clarity.

■ **EXERCISES**

Rewrite the following arguments as concisely as possible, clarifying their meaning and arranging the premises and conclusion in their logical order. (You will recognize some of these passages from earlier exercises.)

22. I no longer believe those who say that a poor politician could be a good president, "if he could only be appointed to the job." Without the qualities required of a successful candidate—without the ability to rally support, to understand the public, to express its aspirations—without the organizational talent, the personal charm, and the physical stamina required to survive the primaries, the convention, and the election—no man would make a great president, however wise in other ways he might be. (Theodore G. Sorensen, *Decision-Making in the White House*)

23. The day *may* come when the rest of the animal creation may acquire those rights which never could have been withholden from them by the hand of tyranny. The French have already discovered that the blackness of the skin is no reason why a human being should be abandoned without redress to the caprice of a tormentor. It may one day come to be recognized that the number of the legs, the villosity of the skin, or the termination of the *os sacrum*, are reasons equally insufficient for abandoning a sensitive being to the same fate. What else is it that should trace the insuperable line? Is it the faculty of reason, or perhaps the faculty of discourse? But a full-grown horse or dog is beyond comparison a more rational, as well as a more conversable animal, than an infant of a day, or a week, or even a month, old. But suppose they were otherwise, what would it avail? The question is not, Can they *reason*? nor Can they *talk*? but, Can they *suffer*? (Jeremy Bentham, *The Principles of Morals and Legislation*, 1789)

24. Although we do not know if other influenza vaccines can cause Guillain-Barre syndrome (GBS), this risk may be present for all of them. Little is known about the ex-

act causes of GBS, but clearly the great majority of the several thousand GBS cases that occur each year in the United States are not due to influenza vaccine. The risk of GBS from the vaccine is very small. This risk should be balanced against the risk of influenza and its complications. The risk of death from influenza during a typical epidemic is more than 400 times the risk of dying from any possible complications of influenza vaccine injections.

25.   Oh, come with old Khayyam, and leave the Wise
       To talk; one thing is certain, that life flies;
       One thing is certain, and the Rest is Lies;
       The Flower that once has blown for ever dies.
       Ah, make the most of what we yet may spend,
       Before we too into the Dust descend;
       Dust into Dust, and under Dust, to lie,
       Sans Wine, sans Song, sans Singer—and sans End!
       (Edward Fitzgerald)

26. Because the father of poetry was right in denominating poetry an imitative art, these metaphysical poets will, without great wrong, lose their right to the name of poets, for they copied neither nature nor life. (Samuel Johnson, *Life of Cowley*)

27. The Abbé, talking among friends had just said, "Do you know, ladies, my first penitent was a murderer," when a nobleman of the neighborhood entered the room and exclaimed, "You there, Abbé? Why, ladies, I was the Abbé's first penitent, and I promise you my confession astonished him." (story by Thackeray)

28. Surely also there is something strange in representing the man of perfect blessedness as a solitary or a recluse. Nobody would deliberately choose to have all the good things in the world, if there was a condition that he was to have them all by himself. Man is a social animal, and the need for company is in his blood. Therefore the happy man must have company, for he has everything that is naturally good, and it will not be denied that it is better to associate with friends than with strangers, with men of virtue than with the ordinary run of persons. We conclude then that the happy man needs friends. (Aristotle, *Ethics*)

29. Forty years ago, it took farmers three to four months and five pounds of natural feed to produce one pound of chicken meat. Today, it takes nine weeks and two and a half pounds of "doctored feed" to achieve the same results. The breeders are experimenting with techniques to do it with two pounds of feed. Today, 90 percent of all chickens eat arsanilic acid, an arsenic substance that is mixed into the feed as a growth stimulant. This substance is toxic to humans but apparently not to the chickens. To help chickens resist disease before they make it to the supermarket, they are automatically given antibiotics. The Food and Drug Administration also permits breeders to dip the slaughtered hens into an antibiotic solution designed to increase the shelf life of the chicken. Many other drugs and additives are often added to poultry feed, among them tranquilizers, aspirin, and hormones. How many of these chemicals come to affect us no one really knows.

30. *Nothing* in the world—indeed nothing even beyond the world—can possibly be conceived which could be called good without qualification except a *good will*. Intelligence, wit, judgment, and the other talents of the mind, however they may be named, or courage, resoluteness, and perseverance as qualities of temperament, are doubtless in many respects good and desirable. But they can become extremely bad and harmful if the will, which is to make use of these gifts of nature and which in its special constitution is called character, is not good. It is the same with the gifts of fortune. Power, riches, honor, even health, general well-being, and the contentment with one's condition which is called happiness, make for pride and even arrogance if there is not a good will to correct their influence on the mind and on its principles of action so as to make it universally conformable to its end. It need hardly be mentioned that the sight of a being adorned with no feature of a pure and good will, yet enjoying uninterrupted prosperity, can never give pleasure to a rational impartial observer. Thus the good will seems to constitute the indispensable condition even of worthiness to be happy. (Immanuel Kant, *Foundations of the Metaphysics of Morals*)

SUPPLYING MISSING COMPONENTS

An argument's basic structure, as we have seen, may be obscured by verbiage, an excess that needs to be cut so that premises and conclusion stand out clearly. But an argument's structure may also be obscured (and as a result may possibly be misleading and deceptive) because it has missing components. Such arguments may appear sounder than they are because we are unaware of important assumptions on which they rest. Such assumptions need to be dug out, if hidden, or made explicit, if unexpressed. Once made explicit, it will be easier to determine the role these missing components play in the argument and to what degree the argument depends on them.

It will be easier to find such missing components of an argument if we keep in mind that many arguments consist of a statement of a general principle, the citing of a case of it, and a conclusion inferring that what is true of the general principle is true of the case in question. The following is a classic example:

> All men are mortal. (the general principle)
> Socrates is a man. (the case)
> Socrates is mortal. (the conclusion)

In the previous exercises, the examples from Samuel Johnson (exercise 26) and Aristotle (exercise 28) conform very much to this pattern. In abbreviating and putting them into proper logical form, what you probably got was the following:

> Poetry is an imitative art.
> Metaphysical poetry is not imitative.
> Metaphysical poetry, therefore, is not poetry.

To be happy is to have the things you need.
One of the things you need is friends.
To be happy, therefore, you need friends.

Arguments of this type may lack the statement of the general principle (called in logic the *major premise*), explicit reference to the case in question (the *minor premise*), or the inference (the *conclusion*). Here are some typical examples:

1. These are natural foods and therefore good for you.
   Omitted here is the major premise: All natural foods are good for you.
   > All natural foods are good for you.
   > These foods are natural foods.
   > Therefore these foods are good for you

2. You'll make an excellent kindergarten teacher. People who are fond of children always do, you know.
   Omitted here is the minor premise: You are fond of children.
   > All who are fond of children make excellent teachers.
   > You are fond of children.
   > You'll make an excellent kindergarten teacher.

3. Yon Cassius has a lean and hungry look; such men are dangerous.
   Omitted here is the conclusion: Cassius is dangerous.
   > All who have lean and hungry looks are dangerous.
   > Cassius has such a look.
   > Cassius is dangerous.

   Not all such omissions are innocent or done for the sake of literary elegance or brevity. Often what is omitted is highly questionable and omitted for that very reason:

4. This must be a good book; it was chosen by the Book-of-the-Month Club.
   What has been left unstated here is the major premise: All books chosen by the Book-of-the-Month Club are good. It has been implied for understandable reasons, for to state it explicitly is to call attention to it and risk having it questioned. The same is true of the following two examples:

5. All alcoholics are short lived; therefore Jim won't live long.

6. Cowardice is always contemptible, and this was clearly a case of cowardice.

Although the missing components easily spring to mind in these brief examples, it is still an advantage not to state them explicitly, for to do so is, again, to call attention to them and risk a challenge.

More difficult to unravel—and far more frequent—are the longer and more verbose examples. Often, benefits hang in the balance—the opportunity for gain, influence, deception—and hence a greater effort is made to hide the assumptions on which the argument rests. Because such arguments are more complicated, it is easy to lose track of the missing components. The following is an advertisement for a tape dealing with loneliness:

> Almost everyone feels lonely at times, and for many it is a constant companion. From the little child who feels he has no friends to the elderly who feel resigned to a cold empty feeling. Teenagers often feel they are nobody and young adults feel friendless. This remarkable tape is not only comforting news but also contains an innovative approach to resolving this emptiness.

Restating this argument, we find that it asserts the following:

Everyone suffers from loneliness.
This tape is a cure for loneliness.
This tape will relieve your loneliness.

It is the conclusion that we now see has been omitted—and for good reason. To state it explicitly possibly raises a question in the reader's mind as to whether indeed this tape—although it supposedly has helped others—will help us.

Not all omissions of this sort are, of course, questionable. Usually a person will omit a component because it is simply too obvious to state explicitly. Sometimes it may be done for dramatic reasons, and occasionally it occurs because the person wishes to be somewhat guarded and cautious. Two of the examples in the exercises were of this last sort: the Guillain-Barre syndrome (GBS) example (exercise 24) and the poultry example (exercise 29). Both writers seem hesitant to state their conclusions. In the GBS announcement we are told that the risk of death from influenza during a typical epidemic is far greater than the risk of dying from the complications of influenza vaccine injection, and it is left to us to infer that, this being so, vaccination is the wiser choice. In the poultry example, we are informed that to stimulate growth and increase shelf life, poultry are now fed and treated with large doses of a variety of potentially dangerous chemicals; the conclusion that, this being so, it would be wiser to investigate the risks of these new breeding and marketing methods is, again, merely implied and not explicitly stated.

Such hesitancy, if that is all it is, may be defensible from the point of view of scientific reserve or legal caution; in logic, however, one must always make it a point to know clearly what is being asserted and what one is being asked to assent to.

■ EXERCISES

Supply the missing components in the following arguments. If these components, required by the argument, throw the argument into suspicion, explain how and why.

31. The speaker criticizes free enterprise; he must be a communist.

32. She is a Phi Beta Kappa, so she must have been a bookworm.

33. The energy crisis, being human made, can be human solved.

34. Our ideas reach no farther than our experience; we have no experience of divine attributes and operations; I need not conclude my syllogism; you can draw the inference yourself. (David Hume)

35. We do not want a democracy in this land, because if we have a democracy a majority rules. (televangelist Charles Staney)

36. Death cannot be an evil, being universal. (Goethe)

37. No man is free, for every man is a slave either to money or to fortune.

38. Nothing intelligible puzzles me, but logic puzzles me.

39. He cannot possibly have a telephone since he's not listed in the directory.

40. He would not take the crown; therefore 'tis certain he was not ambitious. (Shakespeare, *Julius Caesar*)

41. Blessed are the meek, for they shall inherit the earth.

DISTINGUISHING DEDUCTIVE AND INDUCTIVE ARGUMENTS

Having separated premises from conclusions, distinguished between arguments and nonarguments, eliminated excess verbiage, and supplied missing components, it now remains for us to ask two important and crucial questions of an argument: are the premises true, and does the conclusion really follow from them?

Regarding the first question, we want to know whether the facts stated by the argument are really so or whether the statements perhaps misrepresent or falsify the facts, prejudge them, or are misleading. Premises, after all, are the foundation of an argument; if they are unreliable or shaky, the argument built on them will be no better.

There is, however, another way an argument can go wrong, and that is when the relationship between the premises and conclusion is such that the premises fail to support the conclusion in question. A premise can support a conclusion fully:

All men are mortal.
Socrates is a man.
Socrates is mortal.

Partially:

Most Scandinavians are blond.
My cousin Christine is Scandinavian.
She must be blond.

Or not at all:

> "Be sure to use American Express.
> Jerry Seinfeld wouldn't think of using any other card."

We will consider arguments of the third type—*seductive* arguments, let us call them—in great detail in the next chapter. Here let us consider the first two: the first is called deductive, the second inductive. **Deductive arguments** are arguments in which the conclusion is presented as following from the premises with *necessity*. **Inductive arguments**, on the other hand, are arguments in which the conclusion is presented as following from the premises with a *high degree of probability*.

Two examples will help illustrate this distinction between necessary and probable inference:

> All the beans in this bag are black.
> All these beans are from this bag.
> All these beans must be black.

> All these beans are from this bag.
> All these beans are black.
> All the beans in the bag must be black.

Of these two arguments, only the first (a deductive argument) has a conclusion that follows with certainty from its premises; the conclusion of the second argument (an inductive argument) follows only with some degree of probability from its premises.

One difference between deductive and inductive arguments is that the premises in a deductive argument contain all the information needed to reach a conclusion that follows with necessity. Nothing in the conclusion refers outside the premises. In the conclusion of an inductive argument, on the other hand, we must venture beyond information contained in the premises. Thus, our conclusion can never be certain, although it can have a high probability of being true.

A classic example of inductive argument highlights this issue of certainty:

> The sun has risen every morning since time immemorial.
> Therefore the sun will rise tomorrow morning.

We feel sure that the sun will rise tomorrow, yet logically speaking the relation of this conclusion to its premises is one of probability, not necessity. (As the renowned logician Bertrand Russell once put it, in *The Problems of Philosophy*, "The man who has fed the chicken every day throughout its life at last wrings its neck instead.") In inductive arguments, we assert in the conclusion a fact not itself contained in the premises. In the argument about the sun rising, for example, the premises make assertions only about the past; they assert nothing about what will happen in the future. Therefore, the premises do not rule out the possibility of the conclusion being false since they yield a conclusion whose truth is only *probable* with respect to these premises, not necessary. It is in the nature of inductive arguments to carry us beyond what is asserted in the premises so that we may see what implications those premises have for other events.

Deductive reasoning is precisely the reverse. With it, the premises contain all the information that we seek to draw out or unfold. We attempt not to go beyond the premises but to understand more specifically what they contain. In the following example, everything contained in the conclusion is contained, either explicitly or implicitly, in the premises:

> If there are 50,001 people in a town,
> And if no person can have more than 50,000 hairs on his or her head,
> And if no one is completely bald,
> Then at least two people in the town have the same number of hairs on their heads.

This example illustrates the precision of which deduction is capable. Whereas inductive arguments expand the content of their premises at the sacrifice of necessity, deductive arguments achieve necessity by sacrificing expansion of content. Most of the arguments one encounters in daily affairs are of the inductive type. Both types of arguments, however, are alike in having premises and a conclusion, and hence both must be evaluated in light of our two basic questions: (1) are the premises true, and (2) does the conclusion follow from them?

■ EXERCISES

Determine whether each of the following arguments is deductive or inductive. Give your reasons for your answer in each case.

42. There are no foxes in this area. We haven't seen one all day.

43. Tom must have left already. He doesn't answer his phone.

44. Because the father of poetry was right in denominating poetry an imitative art, these metaphysical poets will, without great wrong, lose their right to the name of poets, for they copied neither nature nor life. (Samuel Johnson, *Life of Cowley*)

45. Everyone in the chemistry class needed to have had one year of high school chemistry as a prerequisite. Since John is a member of that class, he must have had one year of high school chemistry.

46. The house across the street has shown no signs of life for several days. Some rain-soaked newspapers lie on the front steps. The grass badly needs cutting. The people across the street therefore must be away on a trip.

47. All life requires water. There is no water on the planet Venus. Therefore, there is no life on that planet.

48. Tom will be ineligible to vote in this state, for he is 19 years old and only persons over the age of 21 are eligible to vote here.

49. "How, in the name of good fortune, did you know all that, Mr. Holmes?" he asked. "How did you know, for example, that I did manual labor? It's true as gospel, for I began as a ship's carpenter."

"Your hands, my dear sir. Your right hand is quite a size larger than your left. You have worked with it and the muscles are more developed." (Arthur Conan Doyle, "The Red-Headed League")

50. Our ideas reach no farther than our experience; we have no experience of divine attributes and operations; I need not conclude my syllogism; you can draw the inference yourself. (David Hume)

51. Since many drug addicts who came through the courts admit that they started on pot, pot likely causes hard-core drug addiction.

52.   . . . You are wise;
      Or else you love not, for to be wise and love
      Exceed man's might; that dwells with gods above.
      (Shakespeare, *Troilus and Cressida*)

EVALUATING ARGUMENTS: TRUTH, VALIDITY, AND SOUNDNESS

People are sometimes heard to say, "That may be logical, but it's not true" or "What's logical isn't always right." Both of these views are correct, yet they do not mean that logic is unconcerned with truth or is somehow opposed to it. Indeed, logic defines truth rigorously and separates it from two other concepts—validity and soundness—with which it is sometimes confused in ordinary speech. Together, these three concepts provide a basis for evaluating any argument.

Validity refers to the correctness with which a conclusion has been inferred from its premises, with whether the conclusion *follows* from its premises. **Truth**, on the other hand, refers to whether those premises and conclusion accord *with the facts*. It is thus possible in logic to start with true premises but reach a false conclusion (because we reason badly with those premises) or to reason correctly or validly without reaching a true conclusion (because our premises are false). **Soundness** results when the premises of an argument are true and its conclusion validly derives from them. Otherwise, the argument is *unsound*.

To accept the conclusion of an argument as sound, therefore, we must be sure of two things. First, we need to know that the premises are true, not false. Premises, after all, are the foundation of an argument; if they are unreliable or shaky, the argument built on them will be no better. Second, we need to know that the inference from the premises is valid—that is, that the conclusion *follows* from them.

The important point to grasp here, then, is that a conclusion may be valid though false ("That may be logical, all right, but it's not true"). Some people imagine that correct reasoning can never result in false conclusions. However, the fact that something follows from something else doesn't necessarily mean it is true; it may be false if the statement from which it follows is itself false and thus infects it with its own falsity.

An inference, then, can be valid whether the premises are true or false. And the same is the case when an inference is invalid; it is invalid regardless of whether the premises are true or false. It should be borne in mind, therefore, that a conclusion validly inferred is not necessarily on that account true (since the premise might have been false), and a conclusion invalidly inferred is not on that account false (since it might happen to be true for other reasons).

Knowing that something can follow from something else even though what it follows from is false can be enormously useful. For this means that if you are uncomfortable with a conclusion seemingly validly derived from a premise, it is possible you are not in full agreement with the premise from which it is, apparently, correctly deduced. The trouble may therefore lie in the premise.

Consider, for example, the following argument:

> Abortion is the destruction of a human fetus, and the destruction of a human fetus is the taking of a human life. If, therefore, the taking of a human life is murder, then so is abortion.

What are the premises of this argument? What is the conclusion? Does the conclusion follow validly from the premises? If so, how might you still challenge this argument? (Hint: Do you agree that destroying a fetus is the same as destroying a human life?)

We have seen how a conclusion may follow from given premises fully, partially, or not at all. In those cases where the conclusion does not follow at all from its premises, what we are confronted with is neither a deductive nor an inductive argument but a seductive one—an argument where the problem lies not in the conclusion (and whether or to what degree it follows from its premises) but in the premises themselves. The study of such arguments is what we will turn to in chapter 5.

■ EXERCISES

Do the conclusions in the following arguments follow validly from their premises? If so, how might you still challenge their soundness?

53. Every event in the world is caused by other events. Human actions and decisions are events in the world. Therefore, every human action and decision is caused by other events.

54. Thinking is a function of man's immortal soul. God has given an immortal soul to every man and woman, but not to any other animal or to machines. Hence no animal or machine can think. (A. M. Turing)

55. Our ideas reach no farther than our experience; we have no experience of divine attributes and operations; I need not conclude my syllogism; you can draw the inference yourself. (David Hume)

56. . . . You are wise;
Or else you love not, for to be wise and love
Exceed man's might; that dwells with gods above.
(Shakespeare, *Troilus and Cressida*)

SUMMARY

1. Aristotle founded the science of logic. Among Aristotle's works on logic was *Of Sophistical Refutations*, which dealt with arguments that appear sound but that for one reason or another are not.

2. Logic is the study of argument. Every argument consists of two basic elements: premises and a conclusion. This is what distinguishes arguments from nonarguments.

3. Not all arguments display their structure simply. As ordinarily expressed, arguments are encumbered with excessive verbiage and irrelevance and often rest on hidden or unexpressed assumptions. In order to judge the soundness of arguments, one must learn how to recognize and eliminate verbiage and how to identify hidden and unstated assumptions.

4. In deductive arguments, the premises contain all the information necessary for the conclusion; in inductive arguments the conclusion goes beyond the data contained in the premises. Thus, even in the best inductive arguments, the conclusion is only probable, whereas the conclusion in a deductively valid argument follows with necessity.

5. An argument has three characteristics on which it may be evaluated. The first is the truth or falsity of the premises. The second is the validity or invalidity of the reasoning from the premises. The third is the argument's soundness (which exists whenever the premises are true and the reasoning valid) or unsoundness (which exists if truth and/or validity is lacking).

6. Something may indeed follow from something else without it necessarily being true. Whether or not a conclusion is true will depend on whether the premises it follows from are true. In short, a conclusion may be valid (i.e., may follow from a premise) but be false.

KEY TERMS

argument	premises
categorical proposition	soundness
conclusion	syllogism
deductive argument	truth
inductive argument	validity
logic	

REVIEW QUESTIONS

1. Whose system of philosophy was known as "the peripatetic philosophy"?
2. What was the Lyceum?
3. The study of the strategies and tactics of what school led Aristotle to develop the science of logic?
4. What did Aristotle mean by "categorical proposition"?
5. What are the two basic elements of an argument?
6. What is the difference between a deductive argument and an inductive argument?
7. What are the three concepts used in evaluating arguments?

ANSWERS TO EXERCISES

1. Premise 1: All rational beings are responsible for their actions.
   Premise 2: All human beings are rational.
   Conclusion: All human beings are responsible for their actions.
2. Premise 1: Atheists do not attend church.
   Premise 2: Mario is an atheist.
   Conclusion: Mario does not attend church.
3. Premise: If people are successful, then they are keenly interested in their work and not easily distracted from it.
   Conclusion: No one who is successful is easily distracted when working.
4. Premise 1: The city should reimburse for hospital expenses anyone injured in an accident that takes place while he or she is engaged on city business.
   Premise 2: He was injured in an accident that took place while he was engaged on city business.
   Conclusion: The city should reimburse him for his hospital expenses.
5. Premise 1: Only those who can quote large chunks of that material can pass a test on it.
   Premise 2: I know hardly any of it by heart.
   Conclusion: It is useless for me to try to pass a test on it.
6. Premise 1: All nature is a cycle of moods.
   Premise 2: I am part of nature.
   Conclusion: I, too, am subject to such swings of mood.
7. Premise 1: Exercise is good for people with that condition (assumed).
   Premise 2: Steve has that condition.
   Conclusion: Steve ought to exercise more.
8. Premise: Sheila doesn't answer her phone.
   Conclusion: She must have left already.
9. Premise 1: To be a great president requires organizational talent, personal charm, physical stamina, and so on.

Premise 2: Only good politicians have all these qualities.

Conclusion: Only a good politician can make a good president.

10. Premise 1: Animals are similar to humans in being sensitive creatures, susceptible to suffering.

Premise 2: This is a crucial similarity.

Conclusion: Basic rights enjoyed by humans should not be withheld from animals.

11. An inquiry, not an argument.

12. A diatribe, not an argument; at most, an announcement of intentions.

13. Not an argument. The passage consists of two statements, the second elaborating on the first.

14. An argument attempting to persuade us that "physical intimacy transforms everything and playing with it is playing with fire."

15. Appears to be more of an explanation than an argument, more interested in expressing a certain point of view rather than persuading us of a particular conclusion.

16. An argument: Life passes one by very quickly into an endless death; therefore, make the most of what remains.

17. This is an argument, consisting of a conclusion (that marijuana should be legalized) and two premises (the rest).

18. An argument: Insurance examinations are not easy to pass without proper preparation. Therefore, prepare yourself for them—by carefully studying this book—if you desire to pass them.

19. More of an explanation than an argument, lamenting a certain state of affairs.

20. An argument attempting to persuade us that secondary cigarette smoke is not harmful to nonsmokers.

21. An argument attempting to convince us that the benefits of taking the vaccine far outweigh its risks.

22. To be a great president requires organizational talent, personal charm, physical stamina, and so on.

Good politicians have these qualities.

Good politicians can make a good president.

23. Animals are similar to humans in being sensitive creatures, susceptible to suffering.

This is a crucial similarity.

The basic rights enjoyed by humans should, therefore, not be denied to animals.

24. Vaccines protect against influenza with minimal side effects.

The risk of death from influenza is great without vaccine.

People should be vaccinated against influenza.

25. Life passes one by very quickly into an endless death.

Make the most, therefore, of what is yet left.

26. Poetry has been denominated an imitative art.

    Metaphysical poets imitate neither life nor nature.

    Metaphysical poets have no right to be called poets.

27. The Abbé's first penitent was a murderer.

    The nobleman was the Abbé's first penitent.

    The nobleman was a murderer.

28. Man is a social animal and needs the company of other men to be happy.

    The company of friends is better than that of strangers.

    To be happy man needs friends.

29. Today chickens are fed chemical additives that are toxic to humans.

    Slaughtered hens are also dipped in antibiotic solutions that may also be toxic to humans.

    Eating commercially bred chickens may be hazardous to one's health.

30. Intelligence, wit, judgment, courage, and so on are good but not without qualification.

    They can become bad if combined with a bad will. This leaves only a good will itself as the only good thing without qualification in the world.

31. Major premise: All who criticize free enterprise are communists. (An obviously questionable premise, not allowing for the possibility of loyal opposition.)

32. Major premise: All Phi Beta Kappans as bookworms. (We cannot assume that all PBKs are bookworms.)

33. Major premise: All human-made crises can be human solved. (Some human-made crises—such as a nuclear holocaust—may result in the extinction of all life on earth.)

34. Conclusion: We can have no ideas of divine attributes and operations.

35. Minor premise: We don't want the majority to rule. (Reverend Staney may not want this but the rest of us may feel differently about it.)

36. Major premise: Nothing that is universal is evil. (A very large assumption.)

37. Major premise: To be a slave to either money or fortune is not to be free. (The truth of this premise will depend on how we understand the words *slave, fortune,* and *free.*)

38. Conclusion: Logic is not intelligible. (This does follow from the premises. Our recourse, then, as we will learn subsequently, is to question the truth of the premise or premises.)

39. Major premise: All who have telephones are listed in the directory. (If stated thus, the argument is not sound, for he may have a telephone despite not being listed.)

40. Major premise: All who are ambitious are people who would take the crown. (The assumption seems reasonable.)

41. Major premise: All who inherit the earth are blessed. (Again, the assumption seems reasonable.)

42. Inductive. The fact that they haven't seen any foxes all day makes it only probable, not certain, that there aren't any in the area. (They may not be very observant, or the foxes may be avoiding them.)

43. Inductive. The fact that he doesn't answer his phone doesn't necessarily mean he has left already. He may be in the shower or can't get to it for some other reason.

44. Deductive. The conclusion is asserted to follow necessarily from the premises. (And, indeed, if all poetry is imitative and their poetry is not imitative, then it is not poetry. But is it the case that all poetry is imitative?)

45. Deductive. Given that the premises are true, the conclusion follows from them with certainty: if everyone in that class absolutely had to have had one year of high school chemistry in order to get into the class, and he is a member of it, then he must have had one year of high school chemistry.

46. Inductive. The people may be at home but too ill to take care of these things at the moment.

47. Deductive. If it is the case that all life—meaning all organic life—requires water and there is no water on Venus, then it follows necessarily that there is no life on that planet.

48. Deductive. If only people over 21 can vote and Tom is only 19, then it follows necessarily that he cannot vote in that state.

49. Inductive. He may have been born with one hand larger than the other.

50. Deductive. The conclusion is asserted to follow necessarily from the premises.

51. Inductive. That conclusion does not necessarily follow from those premises.

52. Deductive. The premise states that it is not possible to be wise and to love at the same time; the conclusion merely restates this (and hence does not go beyond what is asserted in the premise).

53. The conclusion does follow with certainty from the premises in this argument. But is it the case that human actions and decisions are just like other (physical) events? The law of causality may apply to physical but not to mental events.

54. If thinking is a function of man's immortal soul, and if God has given an immortal soul only to human beings, then it follows that only human beings can think. But perhaps God has also given this capacity—in varying degrees—to other creatures as well.

55. If all our ideas come from experience and if we have no experience of God, then it follows that we can have no idea of God. But is it the case that absolutely all our ideas come from (or originate only from) experience?

56. If it is indeed impossible to be both wise and to love (at the same time), then it follows that if I love, I am not wise, and if I am wise, I do not love. But is it truly impossible to do both or have both?

■ Reading

Prior Analytics

ARISTOTLE

Excerpted from Aristotle, *Prior Analytics*, Book 1, Chapters 1–4, translated by A. J. Jenkinson, http://classics.mit.edu//Aristotle/prior.html

BOOK 1

Chapter 1

We must first state the subject of our inquiry and the faculty to which it belongs: its subject is demonstration and the faculty that carries it out demonstrative science. We must next define a premiss, a term, and a syllogism, and the nature of a perfect and of an imperfect syllogism; and after that, the inclusion or noninclusion of one term in another as in a whole, and what we mean by predicating one term of all, or none, of another.

A premiss then is a sentence affirming or denying one thing of another. This is either universal or particular or indefinite. By universal I mean the statement that something belongs to all or none of something else; by particular that it belongs to some or not to some or not to all; by indefinite that it does or does not belong, without any mark to show whether it is universal or particular, e.g. 'contraries are subjects of the same science', or 'pleasure is not good'. The demonstrative premiss differs from the dialectical, because the demonstrative premiss is the assertion of one of two contradictory statements (the demonstrator does not ask for his premiss, but lays it down), whereas the dialectical premiss depends on the adversary's choice between two contradictories. But this will make no difference to the production of a syllogism in either case; for both the demonstrator and the dialectician argue syllogistically after stating that something does or does not belong to something else. Therefore a syllogistic premiss without qualification will be an affirmation or denial of something concerning something else in the way we have described; it will be demonstrative, if it is true and obtained through the first principles of its science; while a dialectical premiss is the giving of a choice between two contradictories, when a man is proceeding by question, but when he is syllogizing it is the assertion of that which is apparent and generally admitted, as has been said in the *Topics*. The nature then of a premiss and the difference between syllogistic, demonstrative, and dialectical premisses, may be taken as sufficiently defined by us in relation to our present need, but will be stated accurately in the sequel.

I call that a term into which the premiss is resolved, i.e. both the predicate and that of which it is predicated, 'being' being added and 'not being' removed, or vice versa.

A syllogism is discourse in which, certain things being stated, something other than what is stated follows of necessity from their being so. I mean by the last phrase that they produce the consequence, and by this, that no further term is required from without in order to make the consequence necessary.

I call that a perfect syllogism which needs nothing other than what has been stated to make plain what necessarily follows; a syllogism is imperfect, if it needs either one or more propositions, which are indeed the necessary consequences of the terms set down, but have not been expressly stated as premises.

That one term should be included in another as in a whole is the same as for the other to be predicated of all of the first. And we say that one term is predicated of all of another, whenever no instance of the subject can be found of which the other term cannot be asserted: 'to be predicated of none' must be understood in the same way.

Chapter 2

Every premiss states that something either is or must be or may be the attribute of something else; of premisses of these three kinds some are affirmative, others negative, in respect of each of the three modes of attribution; again some affirmative and negative premises are universal, others particular, others indefinite. It is necessary then that in universal attribution the terms of the negative premiss should be convertible, e.g. if no pleasure is good, then no good will be pleasure; the terms of the affirmative must be convertible, not however, universally, but in part, e.g. if every pleasure is good, some good must be pleasure; the particular affirmative must convert in part (for if some pleasure is good, then some good will be pleasure); but the particular negative need not convert, for if some animal is not man, it does not follow that some man is not animal.

First then take a universal negative with the terms A and B. If no B is A, neither can any A be B. For if some A (say C) were B, it would not be true that no B is A; for C is a B. But if every B is A then some A is B. For if no A were B, then no B could be A. But we assumed that every B is A. Similarly too, if the premiss is particular. For if some B is A, then some of the As must be B. For if none were, then no B would be A. But if some B is not A, there is no necessity that some of the As should not be B; e.g. let B stand for animal and A for man. Not every animal is a man; but every man is an animal.

Chapter 3

The same manner of conversion will hold good also in respect of necessary premisses. The universal negative converts universally; each of the affirmatives converts into a particular. If it is necessary that no B is A, it is necessary also that no A is B. For if it is possible that some A is B, it would be possible also that some B is A. If all or some B is A of necessity, it is necessary also that some A is B: for if there were no necessity, neither would some of the Bs be A necessarily. But the particular negative does not convert, for the same reason which we have already stated.

In respect of possible premisses, since possibility is used in several senses (for we say that what is necessary and what is not necessary and what is potential is possible), affirmative statements will all convert in a manner similar to those described. For if it is possible that all or some B is A, it will be possible that some A is B. For if that were not possible, then no B could possibly be A. This has been already proved. But in negative statements the case is different. Whatever is said to be possible, either because B necessarily is A, or because B is not necessarily A, admits of conversion like other negative statements, e.g. if one should say, it is possible that man is not horse, or that no garment is white. For in the former case the one term necessarily does not belong to the other; in the latter there is no necessity that it should: and the premiss converts like other negative statements. For if it is possible for no man to be a horse, it is also admissible for no horse to be a man; and if it is admissible for no garment to be white, it is also admissible for nothing white to be a garment. For if any white thing must be a garment, then some garment will necessarily be white. This has been already proved. The particular negative also must be treated like those dealt with above. But if anything is said to be possible because it is the general rule and natural (and it is in this way we define the possible), the negative premises can no longer be converted like the simple negatives; the universal negative premiss does not convert, and the particular does. This will be plain when we speak about the possible. At present we may take this much as clear in addition to what has been said: the statement that it is possible that no B is A or some B is not A is affirmative in form: for the expression 'is possible' ranks along with 'is', and 'is' makes an affirmation always and in every case, whatever the terms to which it is added, in predication, e.g. 'it is not-good' or 'it is not-white' or in a word 'it is not-this'. But this also will be proved in the sequel. In conversion these premisses will behave like the other affirmative propositions.

Chapter 4

After these distinctions we now state by what means, when, and how every syllogism is produced; subsequently we must speak of demonstration. Syllogism should be discussed before demonstration because syllogism is the general: the demonstration is a sort of syllogism, but not every syllogism is a demonstration.

Whenever three terms are so related to one another that the last is contained in the middle as in a whole, and the middle is either contained in, or excluded from, the first as in or from a whole, the extremes must be related by a perfect syllogism. I call that term middle which is itself contained in another and contains another in itself: in position also this comes in the middle. By extremes I mean both that term which is itself contained in another and that in which another is contained. If A is predicated of all B, and B of all C, A must be predicated of all C: we have already explained what we mean by 'predicated of all'. Similarly also, if A is predicated of no B, and B of all C, it is necessary that no C will be A.

But if the first term belongs to all the middle, but the middle to none of the last term, there will be no syllogism in respect of the extremes; for nothing necessary follows from the terms being so related; for it is possible that the first should belong either to all or to none of the last, so that neither a particular nor a universal conclusion is necessary. But if there is no necessary consequence, there cannot be a syllogism by means of these premisses. As an example of a universal affirmative relation between the extremes we may take the terms animal, man, horse; of a universal negative relation, the terms animal, man, stone. Nor again can syllogism be formed when neither the first term belongs to any of the middle, nor the middle to any of the last. As an example of a positive relation between the extremes take the terms science, line, medicine: of a negative relation science, line, unit.

If then the terms are universally related, it is clear in this figure when a syllogism will be possible and when not, and that if a syllogism is possible the terms must be related as described, and if they are so related there will be a syllogism.

But if one term is related universally, the other in part only, to its subject, there must be a perfect syllogism whenever universality is posited with reference to the major term either affirmatively or negatively, and particularity with reference to the minor term affirmatively: but whenever the universality is posited in relation to the minor term, or the terms are related in any other way, a syllogism is impossible. I call that term the major in which the middle is contained and that term the minor which comes under the middle. Let all B be A and some C be B. Then if 'predicated of all' means what was said above, it is necessary that some C is A. And if no B is A but some C is B, it is necessary that some C is not A. The meaning of 'predicated of none' has also been defined. So there will be a perfect syllogism. This holds good also if the premiss BC should be indefinite, provided that it is affirmative: for we shall have the same syllogism whether the premiss is indefinite or particular.

But if the universality is posited with respect to the minor term either affirmatively or negatively, a syllogism will not be possible, whether the major premiss is positive or negative, indefinite or particular: e.g. if some B is or is not A, and all C is B. As an example of a positive relation between the extremes take the terms good, state, wisdom: of a negative relation, good, state, ignorance. Again if no C is B, but some B is or is not A or not every B is A, there cannot be a syllogism. Take the terms white, horse, swan: white, horse, raven. The same terms may be taken also if the premiss BA is indefinite.

Nor when the major premiss is universal, whether affirmative or negative, and the minor premiss is negative and particular, can there be a syllogism, whether the minor premiss be indefinite or particular: e.g. if all B is A and some C is not B, or if not all C is B. For the major term may be predicable both of all and of none of the minor, to some of which the middle term cannot be attributed. Suppose the terms are animal, man, white: next take some of the white things of which man is not predicated-swan and snow: animal is predicated of all of the one, but of none of the other. Consequently there cannot be a syllogism. Again let no B be A, but let some C not be B. Take the terms inanimate, man, white: then take some white things of which man is not predicated-swan and snow: the term inanimate is predicated of all of the one, of none of the other.

Further since it is indefinite to say some C is not B, and it is true that some C is not B, whether no C is B, or not all C is B, and since if terms are assumed such that no C is B, no syllogism follows (this has already been stated) it is clear that this arrangement of terms will not afford a syllogism: otherwise one would have been possible with a universal negative minor premiss. A similar proof may also be given if the universal premiss is negative.

Nor can there in any way be a syllogism if both the relations of subject and predicate are particular, either positively or negatively, or the one negative and the other affirmative, or one indefinite and the other definite, or both indefinite. Terms common to all the above are animal, white, horse: animal, white, stone.

It is clear then from what has been said that if there is a syllogism in this figure with a particular conclusion, the terms must be related as we have stated: if they are related otherwise, no syllogism is possible anyhow. It is evident also that all the syllogisms in this figure are perfect (for they are all completed by means of the premisses originally taken) and that all conclusions are proved by this figure, viz. universal and particular, affirmative and negative.

■ Questions for Discussion

1. What is a premise? What sorts of premises are there?

2. What is the relationship between universals and particulars (see especially chapter 3)?

3. Why is it that every demonstration is a syllogism, but every syllogism is not a demonstration?

■ Common Fallacies

FALLACIES ARE ARGUMENTS that appear to be sound but that for various reasons are not. Aristotle, who was the first to explore these common errors of reasoning, divided them into two groups: those that have their source in language (*in dictione*) and those whose source lies outside language (*extra dictionem*). Although many writers have tended to follow Aristotle's classification, neither the list of fallacies he compiled nor their treatment has remained fixed.

In departing from Aristotle's twofold classification here, I have attempted to stress the fact that all the fallacies have their source in some dimension of language. What distinguishes them cannot therefore be the fact that some have their source *in dictione* while others have their source *extra dictionem*. Although all have their source in language, the fallacies differ in that different aspects of language are responsible for the three large groups we will be distinguishing.

In one group of **fallacies**—we will call them **fallacies of ambiguity**—it is the ambiguity of the words used that proves deceiving. In another group—**fallacies of presumption**—what deceives is their similarity to the valid argument forms. Finally, in still another group—**fallacies of relevance**—it is the emotional appeal of the language that deceives.

Often the very thing responsible for the fallacy is what makes the argument appealing to us. That is why we are so often deceived by fallacies. In other words, although they are unsound, fallacies are psychologically persuasive. And this is so not only because they evoke such attitudes as pity, fear, reverence, disapproval, and enthusiasm (which tends to blind us to the purely logical merits of the case being argued) but also because they are often extremely subtle and complex.

To learn how to deal more easily with these more complex and subtle cases, it will sometimes be helpful to use somewhat absurd examples. Using such examples should not be misunderstood as meaning that the reader or anyone else is ever likely to commit the fallacies in these extreme and absurd guises. These examples serve rather the same purpose in logic as the telescope and microscope serve in their respective fields: they magnify the structure and nature of the difficulty under examination so that we may see it more clearly.

Let us consider, for example, the following absurd argument: "Everything that runs has feet; the river runs; therefore, the river has feet." This argument may appear sound because we do say such things as "the river *runs*." Of course, when we do so, we do not mean that it has feet on which it runs. We mean that it *flows*. Although this is an absurd and obvious example, the persuasiveness of many subtle arguments depends on this same device: a key term switched in meaning at a critical point in an argument.

Consider the case of the fellow with a Bible tract under his arm who comes knocking at your door and says, "If you believe in the miracles of science, how come you don't believe in the miracles of the Bible? As a student of science and logic, you ought to be consistent." If he truly believes in this argument, he has come to do so by failing to see that the word *miracle* used in the context of science is quite different from its biblical meaning. Used in the biblical and literal sense, a miracle is any occurrence that goes against, or interrupts, the laws of nature. But as used metaphorically in the context of "miracles of science," the term means "great discovery" or "outstanding achievement." This being so, as you might therefore reply, you are not being inconsistent in believing in the so-called miracles of science and not in the miracles of the Bible.

Unlike the example of the river running, this one is more subtle and more difficult. The absurd example, however, will be found useful in learning how to deal with the more difficult arguments you will ordinarily encounter.

We can use the same devices responsible for these logical traps for the expression of our sense of humor. "Good steaks are rare these days, so don't order yours well done"; "Diamonds are seldom found in this country, so be careful not to mislay your engagement ring"; "Your argument is sound, nothing but sound." In these cases we are not deceiving with the words *rare*, *found*, and *sound*; we are punning with them. Sometimes the pun can be very pointed, as in Benjamin Franklin's famous quip: "We must all hang together, or assuredly we shall all hang separately."

THE FALLACIES OF AMBIGUITY

The fallacies generally discussed under the category of ambiguity include amphiboly, accent, and equivocation. What tends to deceive us in these fallacies is the confusing nature of the language in which the argument is expressed. Each type of confusion arises from an important aspect of the nature of sentences: *amphiboly* explores the consequences of not taking sufficient care with the way we structure our statements, *accent* explores what can go wrong when we mistake the context of a sentence or statement and as a result fail to understand it in the way it was intended to be understood, and *equivocation* explores the errors we are prone to commit when we fail to recognize that many of our words have multiple meanings.

One of the benefits of studying these three fallacies is that it helps people develop their ability to express themselves with greater clarity and precision. In dealing with these fallacies, your goal, therefore, should not simply be to identify the fallacy in question (tag it with some appropriate label) but rather to develop the skill of explaining with clarity and precision why this or that particular argument is less than sound.

Amphiboly

Language admits of different sorts of ambiguity and each major kind has come to receive its own name. **Amphiboly** is the term attached to fallacies or deceptions that result from faulty or careless sentence structure. The carelessness may be intentional, as in the case of the title of the record album *Best of the Beatles*, which misled many people into buying it, thinking they were getting a record featuring the best songs of the Beatles. In fact, what they had purchased was a record featuring Pete Best, who had been a member of the Beatles early in their career.

Shakespeare loved to exploit this particular ambiguity of language—in his case not, of course, for gain but simply for dramatic effect. In *Henry VI* (part II, scene iv) a witch prophesies that "The Duke yet lives that Henry shall depose," which leaves it unclear whether the Duke will depose Henry or Henry will depose the Duke. To make it clear which is which, the word *that* would have to be replaced with either *who* or *whom*.

A more striking use of this kind of ambiguity by Shakespeare occurs in the play *Macbeth*. The witches tell Macbeth,

> Be bloody, bold, and resolute; laugh to scorn
> The power of man, for none of woman born
> Shall harm Macbeth.

The phrase "none of woman born" turns out to be a ghastly deception when Macbeth discovers, all too late, that his murderer, Macduff, had been "untimely ripped from his mother's womb" and thus torn of woman and not literally born of her.

It is because of the inherent ambiguity in our language that when we are asked to swear an oath, we promise not only to tell the truth (for we might then only tell part of it) and not only to tell the whole truth (for we might then throw in a few lies as well) but "to tell the truth, the whole truth, and nothing but the truth," which takes care of all contingencies.

■ EXERCISES

Explain in two or three sentences how the following examples illustrate amphiboly.

1. It would be a great help toward keeping the churchyard in good order if others would follow the examples of those who clip the grass on their own graves.

2. Mrs. Manning's are the finest pork and beans you ever ate. So when you order pork and beans, be sure Mrs. Manning is on the can.

3. *Sign on window:* Wanted Smart Young Man for Butcher. Able to Cut, Skewer, and Serve a Customer.

4. *Headline:* Nude Patrol OK'd for Muir Beach

5. *Report of Social Worker:* Woman still owes $45 for a funeral she had recently.

6. Dr. William Smith read an interesting paper on "Idiots from Birth." There were over 200 present.

Accent

Accent is the name logicians have come to attach to those fallacies or deceptions that arise from ambiguity or confusion in emphasis. The fallacy can take three forms: (1) It can result from confusion concerning the *tone of voice* a certain statement was meant to be spoken in. (2) It can result from confusion concerning where the *stress* was meant to be placed in a remark. (3) It can arise when a passage is taken out of context and thus given an emphasis it was not meant to have.

In one of the transcripts of the Watergate tapes, John Dean warns Richard Nixon against getting involved in a cover-up, and Nixon replies, "No—it is wrong, that's for sure." But what inflection was in Nixon's voice when he made this remark? Was it said in a serious and straightforward tone of voice, or was it said ironically? If it was uttered ironically, this remark would represent additional evidence of his involvement in the cover-up.

It is because tone of voice adds a further dimension to language that clerks of court usually read testimony in a deliberate monotone, trying in this way to keep out any inadvertent indications of their own feelings about the matter read.

The following are somewhat more mundane examples of the fallacy in this first form. "I cannot praise this book too highly" (meaning what? that it is impossible to praise it at all or enough?); "You never looked better" (meaning what? that you always look that way—namely, bad; or that you were never more beautiful?); "I wish you all the good fortune you deserve" (meaning what?).

Ambiguities with tone of voice apply to stress as well. Thus, to consider a somewhat artificial example, if we were to emphasize the word *friends* in the statement "We should not speak ill of our friends," we might succeed in conveying the thought that it is all right to speak ill of our enemies; if we emphasize the word *speak*, we might convey the idea that is all right to *think* ill of them; and so on. The same applies to such a statement as "men were created equal." If we stressed *men*, we might thereby imply that *women* were not created equal, and if we stressed *were created*, we might suggest that although that is the way they started out, they are no longer so.

As these examples indicate, the fallacy of accent arises either when a wrong or unintended stress is placed on some word or phrase in a statement or when a statement is read in a tone of voice different from the one that was intended for it. As such, the fallacy is unlike amphiboly, whose ambiguity is due not to misplaced emphasis or intonation but to misplaced words or faulty sentence structure.

How can we avoid this fallacy? Sometimes it will simply be unavoidable. We cannot foretell how our words will be used or abused or understood or misunderstood on some future occasion. We can, however, take some precautions. We can provide a background or context that will be difficult to distort. It need not be anything very elaborate. The addition of another emphatic word will sometimes do it.

Sometimes to avoid misunderstanding we must avoid using terms that tend to call too much of the wrong sort of attention to themselves, as in the following example involving the word *hope:* "They will be married Sunday. Then they will spend a few weeks in a cottage by the sea, and by the time the honeymoon is over, the groom hopes to be in the army." (The word *expects* would be much more advisable here.)

As with the fallacy of amphiboly, the fallacy of accent can also be exploited for humorous purposes. A notable example is the poor worker in Charlie Chaplin's film *The Great Dictator* who growled, "This is a *fine* country to live in" and was promptly arrested by the dictator's police. He managed to get himself off, however, by pleading that all he said was "This is a fine country to live in"—meaning that it was a lovely, wonderful place.

Accent is obviously more a reader's than a writer's fallacy. The authors of a particular remark or statement presumably know what emphasis they wish to give to it or how they want it to be understood, and were they present to translate it into spoken words, they would be able to make that meaning clear to readers.

The fallacy of accent can be found in one further form. This occurs whenever the meaning of a statement or the content of a book, a speech, or a review is distorted by removing or quoting not merely a word or a phrase but sentences or portions of sentences out of context. This is a favorite device not only of propagandists but also of blurb writers and newspaper reporters. Since very few people ever bother or have the time to read everything in their newspapers or other reports, the damage and misinformation conveyed by dishonest captions, misleading headlines, and misquotations is probably enormous. The same applies to advertisements. How many of us have not at one time or another been misled into buying a certain book or seeing a certain movie as a result of misleading blurbs and quotations?

A drama critic might write that he "liked all of the play except the lines, the acting, and the scenery," only to find himself quoted the next morning that he "liked all of the play . . ." Or, to take a sadder example, a schoolteacher might tell her civics class that "Communism is the best type of government if you care nothing for your liberty or your material welfare," only to discover that Johnny has quoted her at home as saying that "Communism is the best type of government."

There is probably no way to be sure what Johnny will take back from school with him, but responsible writers who make a direct quotation should always indicate any omission of words or phrases by the use of ellipsis points. Not to do so is to tell only half the story and with it only half the truth. In addition, they should make a sincere effort to capture both the tone and flavor of the original in their paraphrase, providing as well the proper context of the remark in question.

■ **EXERCISES**

Explain in two or three sentences how the following sentences illustrate the fallacy of accent.

7. Only Hollywood could produce a film like this.

8. Member of audience after sitting through a five-hour performance of Wagner's opera *Parsifal:* "I can't believe I heard the whole thing!"

9. What are you doing this weekend? The usual?

10. Thou shalt not bear false witness against thy neighbor.

11. Be courteous to strangers.

12. *Federal regulation:* Warning: Under Title 18 U.S. Code: It Is a Federal Offense to Assault a Postal Employee While on Duty.

13. *School sign:* Slow Children Crossing.

14. *Speaker:* Lincoln could not have been such a fine man, for didn't he say that "You can fool some of the people all of the time"?

Equivocation

We have seen how ambiguity of sentence structure gives rise to the fallacy of amphiboly and how ambiguity concerning emphasis gives rise to the fallacy of accent. Now we want to note how confusion arises from the ambiguity of the words and phrases themselves.

The fallacy of **equivocation** consists in using a word with two or more meanings during the course of an argument while acting as if the meaning of the word is being held constant. If the change in meaning is subtle, the conclusion of such an argument will seem to follow from the premises, and the argument will appear a good deal more convincing than it deserves to be.

A rather obvious and absurd example uses the term *man* equivocally to construct a seemingly sound argument: "Only man is rational; no woman is a man; therefore, no woman is rational." This argument would be valid if the term *man* had the same meaning each time it occurred. However, for the first premise to be true, *man* must mean "human being," whereas for the second premise to be true, *man* must mean "male." Thus, if the premises are to have any plausibility, the term *man* must shift its meaning.

A good test to apply to arguments we suspect turn on the fallacy of equivocation is to make them stick to the original meanings of their terms and see whether by so doing the arguments still make sense. An argument that turns on equivocation will not. If we make the term *man* mean "male" throughout the example argument, it will then read, "Only males are rational . . ." We need not go further because we immediately reject this premise as either false or a matter of assuming the very point to be proven. On the other hand, if we make the term *man* mean "human being" throughout the argument, we get the following result: "Only human beings are rational; no woman is a human being . . ." Here again, we need go no further, for we have already committed an absurdity.

The fallacy of equivocation is especially easy to commit when the key term happens to be a figure of speech or a metaphor. By interpreting the metaphor literally, we can sometimes persuade ourselves that our argument is sounder than it really is. Consider the following example:

> It is the clear duty of the press to publish such news as it shall be in the public interest to have published. There can be no doubt about the public interest taken in the brutal murder of the Countess and concerning the details of her private life that led up to the murder. The press would have failed in their duty if they had refrained from publishing these matters.

The arguer here apparently does not seem to realize that what is "in the public interest" is not quite the same thing as what the public is interested in. The former is a metaphorical expression meaning "what is for the public good," while the latter simply means what the public is curious about.

The warning against being misled by figures of speech should not be mistaken to imply a warning against their use. Language is shot through with figures of speech, and it is not possible to avoid them entirely. Nor should we try to. Our speech and writing would be much poorer without them. Not only do they make for pungent expression, economy, and tact, but very often a figure of speech is the only way yet devised of saying precisely what we wish to say.

Equivocation, however, is not confined to figurative expressions. On the contrary, since the vast majority of our words have more than one meaning, any one of them (and not merely those that are figures of speech) can occasion the fallacy. An absurd example would be the following: "Some birds are domesticated; my parrot is domesticated; my parrot, therefore, is some bird!" As this example shows, even such a common and simple word as *some* can lend itself to equivocation. Here *some* is used first in a quantitative sense, meaning "a number of," and in the conclusion in a qualitative sense, meaning "a magnificent bird." Although probably no one would ever become confused over such a word as *some*, the example brings out the important point that almost any word in our language can either be exploited for its ambiguity or be itself ambiguous, so that it occasions mistakes in thinking.

Ironically, this inherent ambiguity of language is not really a defect we should wish to remedy. It is one of the major vehicles for the expression of our wit and would be sorely missed were it possible to eliminate it from language.

■ EXERCISES

Explain how the following arguments illustrate the fallacy of equivocation.

15. There are laws of nature. Law implies a lawgiver. Therefore, there must be a cosmic lawgiver.

16. I have the right to publish my opinions concerning the present administration. What is right for me to do I ought to do. Hence I ought to publish them.

17. *Jane:* That old copper kettle isn't worth anything. You can't even boil water in it.
Mary: It is worth something. It's an antique.

18. Birth control is race suicide, for when no children are born, as happens when you practice birth control, the human race must die out.

19. Anyone who is considered old enough to go into the army and fight for his country is a mature person, and anyone old enough to vote is a mature person, too. Hence, anyone old enough to fight is old enough to vote.

20. I do not believe in the possibility of eliminating the desire to fight from humankind because an organism without fight is dead or moribund. Life consists of tensions. There must be a balance of opposite polarities to make a personality, a nation, a world, or a cosmic system.

21. In our democracy all men are equal. The Declaration of Independence states this clearly and unequivocally. But we tend to forget this great truth. Our society accepts the principle of competition. And competition implies that some men are better than others. But this implication is false. The private is just as good as the general; the file clerk is just as good as the corporation executive; the scholar is no better than the dunce; the philosopher is no better than the fool. We are all born equal.

THE FALLACIES OF PRESUMPTION

Whereas confusing language is what deceives in the case of the fallacies of ambiguity, it is the misleading resemblance to valid argument forms (achieving this deception by misrepresenting the facts disclosed in the argument) that deceives in the case of the fallacies under the category of *presumption*. For example, the argument "Exercise is good; Jones therefore should do more of it, for it will be good for him" looks deceptively like the classic argument "All men are mortal; Socrates is a man; therefore, Socrates is mortal." However, the statement "Exercise is good" is an unqualified generalization that may not apply to Jones, who may suffer from a heart condition and has been told specifically by his doctor not to exercise.

What is most characteristic of the fallacies of presumption is that facts relevant to the argument have not been represented correctly in the premises. This inappropriate treatment of the facts may take the form of overlooking, evading, or distorting them. Overlooking the facts gives rise to the fallacies of sweeping generalization, hasty generalization, and bifurcation. Evading the facts takes the form of begging the question. Distorting the facts occurs with the fallacies of false analogy and false cause.

Overlooking the Facts

In the fallacy of **sweeping generalization**, the error lies in assuming that what is true under certain conditions must be true under all conditions. Consider this example:

> Everyone has a right to his or her own property. Therefore, even though Smith has been declared insane, you had no right to take away his weapon.

The first premise in this argument is a general principle that is widely accepted. It does not apply, however, in the specific case in which a person has lost his reason—especially when the piece of property is a weapon.

The source of this fallacy's persuasive power is that it resembles valid arguments in which individual cases do fall under a general rule. The point to remember is that a generalization is designed to apply only to individual cases that properly fall under it. It is not designed to apply to all individual cases.

To argue, therefore, that "since horseback riding and mountain climbing are healthful exercises, Harry Jones ought to do more of it because it will be good for his heart trouble" would be to commit this fallacy, for what is good for a person's health normally is not good where special conditions prevail. And the same is true of the following argument: "It is my duty to do unto others as I would have them do unto me. If I were puzzled by a question in an examination, I would like my neighbor to help me out. So it is my duty to help this person beside me who is stuck." Here our reply should be that to try to do one's duty in such circumstances would not be to help the person. This is an examination, and the point of it is to find out what each one knows by himself or herself.

Arguments of the kind we are examining here have two parts to them: a rule and a case. If the argument in question is invalid, it is because the case to which the rule is being applied is exceptional and therefore does not fall under the given rule. To expose them, therefore, all one needs to do is to isolate the rule and show that, understood properly, it cannot be applied to the case in question.

■ EXERCISES

Explain how each of the following arguments demonstrates the fallacy of sweeping generalization.

22. I don't care if he did weigh three times as much as you. A good scout always tries to help. You should have jumped in and tried to save him.

23. Narcotics are habit forming. Therefore, if you allow your physician to ease your pain with an opiate you will become a hopeless drug addict.

24. No man who lives on terms of intimate friendship and confidence with another is justified in killing him. Brutus, therefore, did wrong in assassinating Caesar.

25. The president should get rid of his advisers and run the government by himself. After all, too many cooks spoil the broth.

26. American secretary of state, refusing to grant asylum to Jewish refugees on the ship the *St. Louis*, whose forced return to Germany meant certain death: "I took an oath to protect the flag and obey the laws of my country and you are asking me to break those laws."

The fallacy of **hasty generalization** is the reverse of the fallacy we have just examined. This fallacy is committed whenever some isolated or exceptional case or event is used as the basis for a general conclusion.

Let us look at some examples. A woman argues, "I had a bad time with my ex-husband. From that experience I learned that men were no good." And someone else complains, "I've only known one union representative, and he was a louse. I wouldn't trust any of them." The arguments in both cases are invalid because they assume that what is true under certain conditions is true under all conditions. At most, the evidence (if one may call it that) warrants only a specific, not a general, conclusion. And this is typical of the fallacy: unlike sweeping generalization, which results when a rule or a generalization is misapplied, the fallacy of hasty generalization results when a particular case is misused.

Of course, in generalizing we should remember that it is not possible (or necessary) to consider all the cases involved. Nevertheless, unless a sufficiently large number of cases are examined, the conclusion cannot be relied upon. A small sample may not be at all representative. On the contrary, it may be quite exceptional. The following would be an absurd example: "They just don't care about traffic law enforcement in this town, for they let ambulances go at any speed they like and let them run red lights, too." This is absurd, of course, because there are good reasons for permitting these vehicles to do these things. No such conclusion can therefore be built on the basis of such unrepresentative examples of supposed law violation.

The fallacy of hasty generalization is also committed when we select and consider only the evidence that favors our position and ignore all the evidence that would tend to throw doubt on it. The following would be a typical example: "State owned industries encourage featherbedding and absenteeism. All state-owned industries should therefore be abolished." Even if it were true that state-owned industries encourage featherbedding and absenteeism, this is hardly a sufficient basis for the kind of drastic action recommended. To try to get rid of these abuses by abolishing the industries in which they tend to flourish would be like throwing out the baby with the bathwater.

■ **EXERCISES**

Explain how each of the following arguments demonstrates the fallacy of hasty generalization.

27. The clerks in Mason's Department Store are incompetent. They got two of my orders mixed up during the last Christmas rush season.

28. Doctors are all alike. They really don't know any more than you or I do. This is the third case of faulty diagnosis I have heard of in the last month.

29. She is very fond of children and so will undoubtedly make a fine kindergarten teacher.

30. He speaks so beautifully that anyone can see he must have studied acting.

31. High tariffs enable our industries to grow strong; they ensure high wages to the workers, and they increase federal revenues. High tariffs, therefore, are a benefit to the nation.

The term **bifurcation** refers to a fallacy that presumes a certain distinction or classification is exhaustive and exclusive when other alternatives are possible. The fallacy is sometimes referred to as the "either/or fallacy" or the "black or white fallacy." All these names, as we will see, are appropriate.

In some cases of either/or, the situation is such that there is no middle course between the two extremes noted. The two poles of the proposition exhaust all the possibilities, and therefore if one of them is true, the other must be false and vice versa: "Either the man is dead or he is alive"; "Either it is your birthday today or it is not."

However, polar terms that go into the formation of many propositions or arguments do not exhaust all the possibilities and are therefore not logical contradictories (but rather contraries). The result is the fallacy of bifurcation. The debates in 1948 over the atomic bomb, in which the great British philosopher Bertrand Russell figured prominently, gave rise to many examples of the fallacy. In this debate Russell argued that either we must have war against Russia before she has the atom bomb or we will have to lie down and let Russia govern us. In other words, what he was saying was, as the position came to be tagged, "Better dead than Red." Others who disagreed with him retorted, "Better Red than dead"; both parties were overlooking, as still others added, "Better pink than extinct." That would be the middle course between the two extremes.

In the same vein we have all seen the bumper stickers that read "America: Love It or Leave It" and the reply "America: Change It or Lose It." Or perhaps even the sign near an Indian reservation "America: Love It or Give It Back."

Because our vocabulary is replete with polar terms, the tendency to bifurcate is all too common. We are thus prone to people the world with the *rich* and the *poor*, the *haves* and the *have-nots*, the *good* and the *bad*, the *normal* and the *abnormal*, the *heroes* and the *villains*, forgetting that between these extremes are to be found numerous gradations that lead from one to the other—any one of which could be further alternatives to the either/or proposed.

The rich/poor polarity leads to such statements as "Only the rich and the poor need be of any concern to the government: the rich because they will try to influence our legislatures through the power of their wealth; the poor because they must be cared for by the state." Of course, since most people are neither rich nor poor, their voice is as important, if not more so, than these two groups.

From a logical point of view, what is objectionable about such arguments is that there is no necessary connection between the two alternatives proposed in them. The fact that we do not want our soup cold does not mean, nor does it logically follow, that we want it hot; it is not necessarily the case that if something is not good it must be bad. It could be neither good nor bad but a bit of both.

It is, however, in the context of political debate that the fallacy is most often committed. It is typical in such debates for opponents to adopt extreme positions. Extreme positions, unfortunately, seem more attractive than the saner middle-of-the-road positions. But the middle of the road is not an exciting area, and one meets few fascinating creatures there in comparison with the gutter and the ditch. On the other hand, one can get along faster there and arrive at one's destination more quickly.

■ **EXERCISES**

Explain how the following arguments illustrate the fallacy of bifurcation.

32. There are only two kinds of people in the world: winners and losers.

33. Either he knew everything that was going on, in which case he's a liar, or, alternatively, he's a fool.

34. God doesn't tolerate fence-riders in the cosmic sense. You must be either committed to Christ or fall in with the Devil. There are only two places to spend eternity: Heaven and Hell. You can't be somewhere in between.

35. It seems to me that now more than ever before in our history, one is either for law enforcement or against it. He is either for mob rule or he is for the law. He either loves a cop or he hates him.

36. We can become independent of Arab oil only by ruining our environment.

Evading the Facts

In the second category of the fallacies of presumption, evading the facts, the error lies not in overlooking facts, as in the first category, but in seeming to deal with all relevant facts without actually doing so. Such arguments deceive by inviting us to assume that the facts are as they have been stated in the argument when they are quite otherwise.

In its rudimentary form, the fallacy of **begging the question** is committed when instead of providing proof for our assertion we simply repeat it. If the statement or argument is brief, not many will be taken in by it. Thus, if we should argue, "The belief in God is universal because everybody believes in God," it would be apparent to almost everyone that since *universal* means "everybody," all we have done is reaffirm that the belief in God is universal without having confirmed or proved it. The same would be true if we argued, "Honesty is praiseworthy because it deserves the approval of all." Again, since *praiseworthy* means "deserving of approval," we have merely repeated in our premise (which should contain our evidence) the very conclusion ("Honesty is praiseworthy") to be established. The argument, therefore, lacks evidence and is no real argument. The same would be true if, finally, we argued, "Miracles are impossible, for they cannot happen." Here, too, all we have done is reassert the very point we began with.

Of course, to assert, or even reassert, something is not in itself objectionable. What makes arguments of this sort objectionable is that they suggest they have done more than this; they imply that by reasserting the point they have somehow established or confirmed it. It is this that makes them fallacious.

As obvious as this error may seem, it is a surprisingly common one. Nor does it spare the mighty. It was one of President Calvin Coolidge's misfortunes to provide logicians with a rather classic example. He once remarked, "When large numbers of people are out of work, unemployment results." Perhaps we should not think too harshly of Coolidge for this absurdity; arguments of this sort are fallacious, we should remember, not because they argue a point invalidly but because they do not argue it at all.

Although this is essentially all one can and need say regarding the logic of such an argument as begging the question, this hardly exhausts the uses, both sound and unsound, to which this form is often put. Politics provides us with a rich source of further uses of the fallacy. Thus, in reply to a reporter's question as to why presidential candidate Hubert Humphrey lost Illinois in the 1968 elections, Mayor Richard Daley of Chicago replied, "He lost it because he didn't get enough votes." Although it may appear as if Mayor Daley was falling victim to the same fallacy as President Coolidge, he was rather cleverly using it as a humorous dodge in order to avoid an embarrassing question. Obviously, fallacy and wit have much in common. Mayor Daley's reply is amusing and meant to be so. That is why it is not a fallacy, for to feign an error is not to commit it.

Often quite flagrant examples of this fallacy will escape detection if the statements involved are somewhat drawn out. Our memories, not always very good, fail to make the repetition immediately apparent to us. Consider the following example:

> Free trade will be good for this country. The reason for this is patently clear. Is it not obvious that unrestricted commercial relations would bestow upon all sections of this community the advantages and benefits which result when there is an unimpeded flow of goods between nations?

Since "unrestricted commercial relations" is simply a more verbose way of saying "free trade," and "would bestow upon all sections of this community the advantages and benefits" is a more verbose way of saying "good for this country," the argument merely says, in effect, that "free trade will be good for this country, because free trade will be good for this country." Unfortunately, a good many of our arguments often consist of such restatements. Language hides this from us and makes it easy for us to forget that this is so because of the numerous synonyms it contains. Although the existence of English's large body of words makes it possible to make our speech seem less dull, it also makes it seem more cogent than it often really is.

To see even more clearly why these arguments are fallacious, we might note a further form in which they sometimes appear. A person will occasionally try to establish a particular proposition by subsuming it under a generalization. Should the generalization itself be questionable, then the argument is fallacious. Consider the following argument: "Communism is the best form of government because it alone takes care of the interests of the common people." Here the conclusion ("Communism is the best form of government") is made to rest upon a principle ("it alone takes care . . .") that is much wider and much more questionable than the conclusion itself. Obviously, if the conclusion needs proving, how much more so does the premise.

■ **EXERCISES**

Explain how each of the following illustrates the fallacy of begging the question.

37. School isn't worthwhile because book learning doesn't pay off.

38. Death for traitors is properly justified because it is right to put to death those who betray our country.

39. To allow every man an unbounded freedom of speech must always be, on the whole, advantageous to the state. You ask why? Well, it is highly conducive to the interest of the community that each individual should enjoy a liberty, perfectly unlimited, of expressing his sentiments.

40. He talks with angels.
   How do you know?
   He said he did.
   But suppose that he lied!
   O, perish the thought! How could any man lie who is capable of talking with angels?

41. Barry cannot have told you a lie when he said he was my cousin, for no cousin of mine would ever tell a lie.

42. Moral beliefs are unjustified because they are not verifiable in sense experience.

Distorting the Facts

The third type of fallacies of presumption includes those that, rather than overlooking or evading relevant facts, actually distort them. In the fallacy of *false analogy*, certain cases are made to appear more similar than they really are. The fallacy of *false cause* makes it appear that two events are causally connected in a way they are not.

Perhaps no other technique of reasoning has been more helpful or harmful than reasoning by analogy. **Analogy** is a method of reasoning in which facts that are obscure or difficult to understand are explained by comparing them to facts that are already known or better understood and to which they bear some likeness. In an argument, analogy suggests that because two things or situations are similar in certain respects, they must therefore be similar in other respects. Now, drawing attention to such similarities can be extremely useful, as long as we are careful that the two things being compared resemble each other in important respects and differ only in trifling ones. If, on the contrary, they resemble each other in unimportant ways and differ from each other in important ones, then there is no analogy between them. Merely to seize upon some slight similarity between two things and then to conclude on that basis that what is true of one is also true of the other leads to the fallacy of **false analogy**.

Consider the following extreme but not necessarily absurd example:

> It is praiseworthy to force people to accept the gospel for their own good, just as force must be used to prevent a delirious person from throwing himself over the edge of a steep cliff.

Actually this is not much of an argument—even for those for whom the existence of a heaven (as espoused in the gospel) is not a matter of doubt. In the one case it is a matter of saving a delirious person from doing away with himself, and in the other, the person involved presumably is not delirious. In other words, even if we were to grant that just as we are obligated to do all we can to save people for this life, so we are similarly obligated to do all we can to save them for the afterlife, it still would not follow that just as force is allowed in the case of the delirious person and where this life is concerned, so force should be permitted in the case of other people and the other life. In the one case we are dealing with a person who has lost his reason, and in the other we are dealing, presumably, with people who have not lost their reason and should be allowed, therefore, to make up their own minds about such things.

Incidentally, if someone should say in reply that surely anyone who did not believe in the gospel must be out of his or her mind (must be delirious), that would be a matter of committing the fallacy of begging the question. (The mere fact that one says so is no proof that it is so.)

As in all cases of imperfect or false analogy, the one we have just examined is faulty because the two things that are compared resemble each other only in trifling ways and differ in significant ones. To expose imperfect analogy, all one must do is simply point this out. In the case of some analogies this is not at all difficult. Consider the following example:

> Why should we sentimentalize over a few thousand people who were cheated or ruined when our great industrial enterprises, railroads, and pipelines were being built? It may be that they suffered an injustice, but, after all, you can't make an omelet without breaking a few eggs.

Here one might point out that even if it were true that it is just as impossible to build great industrial enterprises without causing pain and suffering as it is to make an omelet without breaking a few eggs, the two cases are not comparable, for to break eggs is not to cause them any pain, while to build great empires by destroying people's lives is.

Of course, not every analogy is an argument by analogy. Often analogies are constructed merely for illustrative purposes or to lend color to a position supported in other ways. Such analogies may still mislead, of course, but no more weight should be placed on them than their authors intended them to carry. The following passage from Karl Marx is a case in point:

> As the heavenly bodies, once thrown into a certain definite motion, always repeat this, so it is with social production as soon as it is once thrown into this movement of alternate expansion and contraction.

Unlike the examples we have been looking at thus far, the cyclic and periodic behavior of the heavenly bodies is used here merely as an illustration of economic cycles and not as the reason for their occurrence.

For the sake of completeness, we should add here that it is not really possible to argue by analogy at all. Two things may be similar in a half dozen different ways, and these similarities may make possible a number of interesting metaphors, but the similarities noted cannot form the basis for assuming that the two things will resemble each other in some further property. Analogy may help us see that it is likely that they will, but it cannot establish that they will.

It is the capacity of language to do double service that enables many arguments by analogy to appear more forceful than they really are. It was obviously a misleading analogy, due to the use of a misleading metaphor, that led King James I to argue,

> If you cut off the head of a body, the other organs cannot function, and the body dies. Similarly, if you cut off the head of the State, the State may flop around awhile, but it is due to perish in time or become easy prey to its neighbors.

King James apparently overlooked the fact that while a body certainly cannot grow a new head, a state easily can—by appointing another ruler.

■ **EXERCISES**

Explain how each of the following illustrates the fallacy of false analogy:

43. President Truman: "We should never have stopped it [atmospheric testing of nuclear weapons]. Where would we be today if Thomas Edison had been forced to stop his experiments with the electric bulb?"

44. Why should we criticize and punish human beings for their actions? Whatever they do is an expression of their nature, and they cannot help it. Are we angry with the stone for falling and the flame for rising?

45. Philosopher Sidney Hook: "A philosopher in his own life need be no more wise than a physician needs to be healthy."

46. Advertisement for skin lotion: "You've seen land crack and dry when it loses its essential moisture; the same thing can happen to your skin when it loses its moisture."

47. If we find it necessary to tip bellmen, maids, and other hotel employees, why should we not similarly reward the bus driver, the saleslady, or the doctor? Either they should be included or hotel tipping should be abolished.

Although the fallacy of **false cause** can assume a variety of different forms, all are essentially a matter of mistakenly believing that because something occurred just prior to something else, it was therefore its cause. Much more knowledge is required to be able to identify the cause than the mere fact that it occurred a second, or even a split second, before the given event. In short, sequence alone is no proof of consequence.

Although formerly the most widespread of fallacies, false cause has tended to slip in prominence because of the impact of education on the general public. This is not to say that we are no longer inclined to commit it. We are, but the tendency to do so does not reveal itself any longer in the crude forms in which it once did. We have no doubt become too sophisticated to argue, as the nineteenth-century English reformer did, that because every sober and industrious farmer owned at least one or two cows and those who had no cows were usually lazy and drunken, a cow should be given to any farmer who had none in order to make him sober and industrious.

Today we encounter more subtle versions of the fallacy, as in the following:

In 1995 the number of television programs depicting crimes of violence increased 12 percent as compared with the figures of 1994. Subsequently, the Department of Justice index of juvenile delinquency showed a corresponding increase. Hence, the evidence shows that a stricter control of television crime programs would result in a lowering of the juvenile crime rate.

What we might say in response to this argument is that the fact that a rise in the crime rate followed a rise in the number of crime programs is not sufficient to establish a causal connection. The rise in crime might have been due to any number of different factors, such as a rise in population or changes in economic conditions.

It is important to remember that two events may be causally related though neither is the cause of the other if both are effects of a third event. Consider the ibis. The ancient Egyptians worshipped this bird because at a certain time each year, shortly after ibises migrated to the banks of the Nile, the river would overflow its banks and irrigate the land. The birds were credited with magical powers, when in fact both their migration and the overflow of the river were effects of a common cause, the change in seasons.

Let us consider a more modern example. Twenty-five years after graduation, male alumni of Harvard have an average income five times that of men of the same age who have no college education. Conclusion: If a man wants to be wealthy, he should enroll at Harvard. Although going to a school such as Harvard no doubt contributes to the kind of income a person is likely to make, we must remember that since Harvard attracts or takes only the most outstanding students or students who already come from wealthy homes, they would probably earn a high income regardless of where they went to college or whether they went at all. Going to Harvard is no guarantee, therefore, that anyone will do as well. The causes at work here are again somewhat more complicated than is assumed by the author of this argument. Harvard is not the sole, simple, immediate, or direct cause of higher income.

If immediate temporal succession is an insufficient basis for establishing causal connection, it goes without saying, of course, that somewhat more remote temporal succession gives even less warrant of assuming this. Thus, the fact, to take some very broad examples, that humans follow the apes in the succession of primates is no proof that we are descended from apes; nor is the fact that because the Roman Empire declined and fell after the appearance of Christianity proof that Christianity was the cause of its decline and fall.

■ **EXERCISES**

Explain how each of the following illustrates the fallacy of false cause.

48. No sooner did the government start to fluoridate the water but my friends began dying of heart disease. It just doesn't pay to tamper with nature.

49. Your boss has a bigger vocabulary than you have. That's one good reason why he's your boss.

50. From early Greek physics: Night is the cause of the extinction of the sun, for as evening comes on, the shadows arise from the valleys and blot out the sunlight.

51. If strong law enforcement really prevented crime, then those areas where police patrols are most frequent would be the safest and the best protected. Actually, the very reverse is true, for in such areas even one's life is in danger, and crimes of all kinds are more common than in other areas where police patrols are infrequent.

52. The president of the Women's Christian Temperance Union said Sunday that people were turning to drink to escape the worries of the troubled national economy. "Liquor dealers admit that since the energy crisis began, the consumption of alcoholic beverages has greatly increased," said Mrs. Fred Tooze, head of the national antialcohol group. Mrs. Tooze said the need to conserve gasoline would cause people to stay home and drink more, creating broken homes and harming the mental capacity of the nation's workforce.

FALLACIES OF RELEVANCE

Fallacies of relevance are arguments in which the premises, despite appearances, do not bear upon the conclusions drawn in the arguments. These fallacies might well be called fallacies of *irrelevance*, for all of them introduce some piece of irrelevance that tends to confuse. What unites this last set of fallacies is that in all of them the irrelevance is an attempt to obscure the real issue by stirring up our emotions. Fallacies of relevance derive their persuasive power from the fact that, when feelings run high, almost anything will pass as an argument.

The five fallacies selected for examination here include the genetic fallacy, abusive ad hominem, circumstantial ad hominem, tu quoque, and poisoning the well. This list is far from exhaustive and probably represents only a small fraction of the types of irrelevance often appealed to. The Latin names that the fallacies carry go back some centuries and have become part of our language.

Genetic Fallacy

Genetic fallacy is a type of argument in which an attempt is made to prove a conclusion false by condemning its source, or genesis. Such arguments are fallacious because how an idea originated is irrelevant to its viability. Thus, it would be fallacious to argue that since chemical elements are involved in all life processes, life is therefore nothing more than a chemical process, or that since the early forms of religion were matters of magic, religion is nothing but magic. Genetic accounts of an issue may be true, and they may be illuminating as to why the issue has assumed its present form, but they are irrelevant to its merits. Here are some examples:

This scholarship aid proposal is calculated to exploit poor students, for it was written by a committee composed only of members of the faculty and administration. No scholarship students were on that committee.

We must take Schopenhauer's famous essay denouncing women with a grain of salt. Any psychiatrist would at once explain this essay by reference to the strained relationship between Schopenhauer and his mother.

The spread of psychoanalysis has tended to promote the appeal to underlying motivations that is found in this last argument. Through an unfavorable psychological account of how or why the advocate of a certain view came to hold it, one might claim to undermine any argument whatsoever. Although it may be true that a source's motives may weaken his or her credibility, motives are irrelevant to the credibility of an argument itself. Arguments are sound not because of who proposes them but by virtue of their internal merit. If the premises of an argument prove its conclusion, they do so no matter who happens to formulate the argument. If they do not, the greatest logician cannot make them sound.

Abusive ad Hominem

A variant of the genetic fallacy is the **abusive ad hominem** (argument against the man), which, in addition to drawing attention to the source of an idea, attacks the advocate of that idea with insult or abuse. For example:

> This theory about a new cure for cancer has been introduced by a woman known for her Marxist sympathies. I don't see why we should extend her the courtesy of our attention.

> Oglethorp is now saying that big corporations shouldn't pay more taxes. That's what you'd expect from a congressman who's lived in Washington for a couple of years and has forgotten all about the people back home.

> In reply to the gentleman's argument, I need only say that two years ago he vigorously defended the very measure he now opposes so adamantly.

Turning attention away from the facts in arguments to the people participating in them is characteristic not only of everyday discussions but of many of our political debates as well. Rather than discuss political issues soberly, rivals may find it easier to discuss personalities and engage in mudslinging. This tactic can be effective because a suspicion once raised is difficult to put to rest. It is not surprising, therefore, that abusive ad hominem is all too common in debates among people seeking office.

When feelings run high, such abusive tactics can persuade. Making an opponent appear suspicious, ridiculous, or inconsistent suggests that his or her argument must be unsound because he or she cannot be trusted.

Circumstantial ad Hominem

Occasionally, instead of engaging in direct abuse, an opponent will try to undercut a position by suggesting that the views being advanced merely serve the advocate's own interests. Logicians call this the **circumstantial ad hominem** argument.

Someone might point out, for example, that a manufacturer's argument in favor of tariff protection should be rejected on the ground that, as a manufacturer, the individual would naturally favor a protective tariff. Rather than offering reasons for the truth of the conclusion being asserted, such arguments offer only reasons for expecting one's opponent to view the conclusion as he or she does.

Although charging an opponent with having vested interests can be seen as a form of reproach, the nonabusive form of this fallacy differs from the abusive form in that abuse is only incidental, not central, to circumstantial ad hominem. Take this argument:

> It is true that several college professors have testified that these hallucinogenic drugs are harmless and nonaddictive, but these same professors have admitted to taking drugs themselves. We should certainly disregard their views.

Here again, an irrelevancy has been introduced in order to divert attention from the real issue.

Tu Quoque

We have now examined three ways to destroy a person's credibility: deflation (the genetic fallacy), straight-out insult (the abusive ad hominem), and insinuation (the circumstantial ad hominem). The remaining two types of fallacies of relevance are somewhat more complicated.

The first of these tactics goes by the quaint Latin name **tu quoque** (pronounced "tu kwokway"), meaning "you, also." In idiomatic English, it means "look who's talking." This is an argument in which the person advocating a position is charged with acting in a manner that contradicts the position taken. The thrust of the tu quoque fallacy is that an opponent's argument is worthless because the opponent has failed to follow his or her own advice: "Look who's telling me to stop smoking! You smoke more than I do." Although the fact that the suggestion comes from a fellow smoker tends to weaken its moral force, it does not undermine the argument. The contention that smoking is unhealthful may still be true whether or not the person saying so is a smoker.

We have a natural tendency to want others to practice what they preach. But practice is irrelevant to the merits of an argument. The following retort seems reasonable enough at first glance, but it has no place in logical discourse: "If you think communal living is such a great idea, why aren't you living in a commune?" Those who resort to this kind of attack often draw courage from another cliché: that people who live in glass houses shouldn't throw stones. There is no reason, however, why a stone thrown from a glass house cannot find its mark.

It is only a step from an argument charging, "You do it, too!" to one that charges, "You would do the same thing if you got a chance." Notice this shift between the next two arguments:

> Far too much fuss has been made over the CIA's espionage abroad. Other countries are just as deeply engaged in spying as we are.

143

It may be true that Kuwait hasn't yet carried out any espionage activities in the United States, but it would if it had the chance. Let's beat Kuwait to it, I say.

The fallacy is fundamentally the same in each case. Whether someone else is already acting in a manner counter to the conclusion at issue or whether someone else would act in such a manner if the opportunity arose has no bearing on whether the conclusion in question is right or wrong. As in all fallacies based on personal attack, any considerations of those who hold a position or who originated a position or who are opposed to a position must be viewed as irrelevant.

Poisoning the Well

The final fallacy of this sort is known as **poisoning the well**. The expression goes back to the Middle Ages, when waves of anti-Jewish prejudice and persecution were common. If a plague struck a community, the people blamed it on the Jews, whom they accused of "poisoning the wells." In the poisoning-the-well fallacy, an attempt is made to place the opponent in a position from which he or she is unable to reply. This form of the fallacy was identified by John Henry Cardinal Newman, a nineteenth-century British churchman, in one of his frequent controversies with the clergyman and novelist Charles Kingsley. During the course of their dispute, Kingsley suggested that Newman, as a Roman Catholic priest, did not place the highest value on truth. Newman protested that such an accusation made it impossible for him or for any other Catholic to state his case. For how could he prove to Kingsley that he had more regard for truth than for anything else if Kingsley presupposed that he did not? Kingsley had automatically ruled out anything that Newman might offer in defense. Kingsley, in other words, had poisoned the well of discourse, making it impossible for anyone to partake of it.

Consider how these accusations poison the well:

Don't listen to him; he's a scoundrel!

I beg of you, ladies and gentlemen, to remember when you hear members of the opposition that a person opposing this move does not have the welfare of our community at heart.

This man denies being a member of the opposition. But we know that members of the opposition have been brainwashed to deny under any circumstances that they belong to the opposition.

Those who disagree with me when I say that mankind is corrupt prove that they are already corrupted. (Friedrich Nietzsche)

Anyone attempting to rebut these arguments would be hard pressed to do so, for anything he or she said would only seem to strengthen the accusation against the person saying it. The very attempt to reply succeeds only in placing someone in an even more impossible position. It is as if, being accused of talking too much, one cannot argue against the accusation without condemning oneself; the more one talks, the more one helps establish the truth of the accusation. And that is perhaps what such unfair tactics are ultimately designed to do: by discrediting in advance the only source from which evidence either for or against a particular position can arise, they seek to avoid opposition by precluding discussion.

It should be pointed out in connection with the fallacies we have just considered that there *are* occasions on which it is appropriate to question a person's character. In a court of law, for example, it would not be irrelevant to point out that a witness is a convicted perjurer or a chronic liar. If the assertion is true, this information is relevant. Although this information would tend to reduce the credibility of the person's testimony, it would not in itself prove that testimony false. Even chronic liars have been known to tell the truth, and we would be guilty of a breach of logic were we to argue that what a person says is a lie because he or she has lied in the past.

■ **EXERCISES**

Identify which relevance fallacy each of the following illustrates and explain how it commits that fallacy.

53. Present economic policies are rapidly placing this country in a bad condition. This is mainly due to some of the ex–White House advisers connected with the former administration, plus some of the eggheads still in power. These people are evidently very egotistical and smug, entirely out of contact with the American people and Congress.

54. Humans are made of nothing but atoms, and since atoms have no free will, therefore, humans don't either.

55. *Smith:* Of course you would be in favor of reduced real estate taxes because you would benefit personally by such a reduction.

Jones: Of course you are against such a reduction because you own no real estate.

56. A top Chinese authority on U.S. affairs showed irritation at Americans over the humanitarian issue. "What moral right do they have to act as preachers of freedom and democracy, especially in the light of events that occurred in America itself?" asked Georgy Arbatov, listing Watergate and Wounded Knee.

57. *She:* I don't think I really matter to you.

He: Now why are you saying that? I'm doing the best I can.

She: Well, I just feel taken for granted.

He: I think you are insatiable. There is never enough.

She: See, this is proof of what I just said. I don't really matter to you. If I did you wouldn't talk this way to me.

SUMMARY

1. Traditionally, the common fallacies have been divided into three groups: fallacies of ambiguity, fallacies of presumption, and fallacies of relevance.

2. Fallacies of ambiguity are linguistic fallacies in that they stem from the use of language having more than one meaning. The best way to unravel such fallacies is to clarify the language in question. Among the fallacies of ambiguity are amphiboly, accent, and equivocation.

3. *Amphiboly* results from ambiguity in sentence structure, as when Macbeth draws the wrong conclusion from the witch's prophecy that "none of woman born / Shall harm Macbeth." *Accent* results from ambiguity of stress or tone. *Equivocation is* the name given to fallacies stemming from a shift in meaning of a key term during an argument.

4. Fallacies of presumption are arguments in which unfounded or unproven assumptions are smuggled in under the guise of valid argument forms. These fallacies are divided into three types: those in which the error lies in overlooking the facts, those in which the facts are evaded, and those in which they are distorted.

5. Fallacies that involve overlooking the facts include sweeping generalization, hasty generalization, and bifurcation. *Sweeping generalization* results when a generalization is applied to a special case that properly falls outside of it. *Hasty generalization* is the opposite of sweeping generalization. Here, an isolated or exceptional case is used erroneously to support a universal conclusion, as when a bad experience with a former husband is used to prove that all men are no good. *Bifurcation* overlooks a range of possibilities that lie between two polar alternatives, as in the assertion that something is either good or bad.

6. A type of fallacy that involves evading the facts is *begging the question*, which occurs when the premises of an argument assume the very conclusion that the argument is supposed to prove.

7. The third type of presumptive fallacy distorts the facts. *False analogy* distorts by making the facts under discussion appear more similar to another set of facts than they really are. An example is King James I's comparison of cutting off the head of a body with removing the head of a state. *False cause* distorts facts by assuming that two events are causally connected when in fact they may not be, as when the Egyptians worshipped the ibis because its appearance preceded the annual Nile flooding.

8. Fallacies of relevance are arguments in which the emotional appeal deceives us into believing that what is said is relevant to the conclusion being urged. Many of these fallacies involve personal attacks, including genetic fallacy, abusive ad hominem, circumstantial ad hominem, tu quoque, and poisoning the well. Rather than attacking the issue itself, the arguer attacks the person or persons associated with the issue.

KEY TERMS

abusive ad hominem
accent
amphiboly
analogy
begging the question
bifurcation
circumstantial ad hominem
equivocation
fallacies
fallacies of ambiguity

fallacies of presumption
fallacies of relevance
false analogy
false cause
genetic fallacy
hasty generalization
poisoning the well
sweeping generalization
tu quoque

REVIEW QUESTIONS

1. What are the three major categories of fallacies, and what distinguishes each of them?
2. Identify the three fallacies of ambiguity.
3. What fallacies are included under the category of presumption?
4. Which of the fallacies of presumption discussed in the text evade the facts? Which overlook the facts? Which distort the facts?
5. What is reasoning by analogy?
6. What are the five fallacies of relevance examined in the text?

ANSWERS TO EXERCISES

1. Whose example are we asked to follow here: the dead who clip the grass on "their" own graves, or those who keep the graves of "their" loved ones trimmed so neatly?

2. Failure to adjust our words to changing contexts is a frequent source of the fallacy. Sometimes this can be avoided by addition of another word, here by writing "be sure Mrs. Manning's *picture* is on the can."

3. By adding what word after *serve* might this butcher shop avoid losing all its customers?

4. Here it is unclear whether the word *nude* refers to the patrol or the beach.

5. If it is the woman's own funeral they really mean here, they are going to find it hard to collect.

6. Juxtaposing the two sentences as done here makes it appear that the 200 present were also the subject of the paper.

7. Said in a serious tone of voice, this remark means that only Hollywood could produce such a great film; said sarcastically, it means that only Hollywood could produce such a terrible film.

8. Said in an excited tone of voice, the remark is an expression of great satisfaction; said in a dreary tone of voice, it is an expression of disbelief and disgust.

9. Said in an expectant tone of voice, it means one thing; said in a tone of boredom it means quite another sort of thing.

10. If the stress is on *thou*, the implication is that although you may not bear false wit ness, someone else may; if the stress is on *thy neighbor*, the implication is that it may be all right to bear false witness against someone else's neighbor; if the stress is on *false witness*, then the intended meaning is conveyed—that you must not speak falsehoods against others, but you may always, of course, speak the truth.

11. Stress the word *strangers*, and it implies that one should be courteous only to strangers (but not to family or friends); unstressed, the intent expressed is that one should be courteous to everyone, including strangers.

12. Does this mean it is a federal offense to assault a postal employee only while he or she is on duty? That it is a federal offense only in the case of a postal employee?

13. If the word *slow* is stressed, the statement directs motorists to reduce their speed to prevent hitting youngsters crossing the street; if the word is left unstressed, the purpose is to inform motorists of the type of children in the area.

14. Lincoln is being quoted out of context. What he reputedly said was, "You can fool all the people some of the time, and some of the people all of the time, but you cannot fool all the people all of the time." In context, then, Lincoln's remark carries just the opposite implication here attributed to him.

15. Since by "laws of nature" we mean "sets of observations" and not commands, it does not follow that their existence implies a cosmic law giver.

16. *Right* can mean privilege as well as duty. Here in its first occurrence it is used in the former sense; in the second occurrence, it is used in the latter sense.

17. Jane and Mary are speaking at cross-purposes here: Mary is using the word *worth* in its monetary sense, Jane in its practical sense.

18. What does the author of this argument think birth control stands for? What was it meant to stand for?

19. The argument turns on the equivocal use of the word *mature*: just because a person may be physically mature to perform a certain task at a certain age does not mean that he or she is necessarily mentally mature at that age as well.

20. Since by the phrase "desire to fight" we mean violence, pugalism, and war and not merely drive or spirit ("without fight"), it may be possible to eliminate the one (violence) without necessarily doing away with the other—the will to live.

21. Since by the phrase "all men are equal" we mean all are equal before the law and not that all are born with the same abilities ("born equal"), we are not being inconsistent in believing in the one (that the law should treat everyone alike) and not in the other (that society should reward everyone the same).

22. Certainly we ought to try to come to one another's assistance, but in this particular case, unless the accused Boy Scout is a powerful swimmer, the attempt to save a

bigger boy might have resulted in tragedy for both. It would have been better for the scout to have tried to throw the drowning boy a rope or to have run for help.

23. Narcotics are habit forming, but the circumstances here are special: the drug will apparently be administered by one with the proper knowledge and under guarded conditions and for probably a limited period of time. It is therefore not likely to lead to the same results as self-administered doses.

24. Of course, normally a person who lives with another on terms of friendship should not wish to harm him. Here, however, the person involved was a threat to Rome and the lives of its citizens.

25. Running a government is not like making a broth. No one person can master all that is involved but must depend on the advice and skill of many different people. What applies to a broth hardly therefore applies to the duties and responsibilities of a president.

26. The Secretary of State's reasoning was specious, as he was undoubtedly aware, since the circumstances were special and mitigating. The *St. Louis's* sad mission ended in the ship's return to Europe and subsequently in the demise of most of its passengers in Auschwitz, Treblinka, and other death camps.

27. Two mixed-up orders are hardly sufficient to condemn every clerk in the store. An added factor was the time when this occurred—the Christmas rush season.

28. When one considers how many doctors there are and how many diagnoses are made in the course of a month, three such faulty diagnoses hardly justify the general conclusion that all doctors are alike or that they do not know any more than we do.

29. Although being fond of children is an important factor here, it alone could not guarantee the person would make a fine kindergarten teacher. Intelligence, dedication, patience, perseverance—these may be even more important qualities.

30. Many people make an effort to speak "beautifully"; doing so is not necessarily proof of having studied acting. More evidence would be needed to confirm that they did so.

31. What is stated is no doubt true, but it is only part of the story. What is neglected is some recognition of the need and value of international trade. Other nations are able to do some things better and more economically than the United States can, and it may make better sense to let them produce these things and sell them in the United States in exchange for things we have that they need or that we can produce more economically than they.

32. This is an especially destructive cliché. No one is always either a "winner" or a "loser." Sometimes we succeed, sometimes we do not. And on some occasions when we think we have won, we discover later that we really (or wish) we hadn't.

33. Another possibility overlooked here is that his lack of awareness of what was going on does not necessarily make him a fool, for the evidence may have been cleverly hidden from him or was simply not very easy to get at.

34. Since Christians represent a minority of the world's population, this argument condemns the rest to a life of torment in hell. One may not believe in Christ or even know of him and yet be a good person, deserving God's favor.

35. A typical example of oversimplification and of thinking in absolute terms. If one does not "love" a cop, does that mean one "hates" him or her? Most of us just expect our police officers to do what they are paid to do: serve their communities to the best of their abilities.

36. Are these indeed the only possibilities? What about solar energy? In addition, safeguards to protect our natural resources can be found, and we are not necessarily bound to deal only with Arab states. Furthermore, new reserves keep being discovered and the world supply appears to be greater than first believed.

37. Since "school" is essentially the same as "book learning" and "not worthwhile" the same as "does not pay off," the second part of the statement (the premise) simply repeats the first part (the conclusion), with the result being that nothing is confirmed.

38. Since "those who betray our country" is another way of saying "traitor" and "right" is the same as "properly justified," the premises of the "argument" simply repeat what has been asserted in the conclusion. This is therefore only an assertion and not an argument.

39. "Each individual should enjoy a liberty perfectly unlimited, of expressing his sentiments" is simply another way of expressing "every man" should be allowed "an unbounded freedom of speech," and the phrase "highly conducive to the interests of the community" is another way of saying "advantageous to the State"; thus, nothing new is presented in support of the original claim.

40. If we could be sure he indeed does talk with angels, then we could accept his word for it. But does he really talk with them? That question is begged. In other words, no one "capable of talking with angels" would lie; but first we need to find out whether he does talk with them.

41. How do we know that no cousin of his would lie? Or that that person, claiming to be his cousin, is his cousin? Both these questions are begged.

42. This statement assumes that only things verifiable in sense experience are justifiable. What evidence is there for this large assumption? Here it is only begged, not established.

43. It is absurd to compare these two vastly different cases. Experimenting with electric bulbs posed no great danger to anyone, whereas the testing of nuclear weapons threatens the lives of thousands, possibly of millions.

44. One cannot compare a human being to a stone or a fire. Stones and fires perform as they do as the result of the force of natural law on them. Human beings, having intelligence, have a measure of choice and therefore can be held at least partly responsible for their actions.

45. A doctor may not be entirely healthy, yet he may still be able to help his patients by imparting his knowledge to them; a philosopher who is totally lacking in wisdom may have little to impart to his students and be able to shed little light on anything.

46. The same thing cannot happen to skin that can happen to land. The body produces its own natural moisturizers and oils, while the land is dependent solely on external sources for such moisture. Our skin has internal sources that naturally prevent it from cracking and drying up completely, as opposed to what the advertisement would like us to believe.

47. Bellmen and hotel maids receive a lower wage because employers anticipate that their employees will be tipped in relation to how friendly or helpful they are. Clerks, doctors, or bus drivers receive a wage or payment for a specified job in which extending an extra friendly smile, say, or some other courtesy is not a necessary or relevant part of the work; tipping would therefore be inappropriate.

48. The simultaneous occurrence of fluoridation and heart disease does not mean that one is the cause of the other. His friends may have died from heart disease because they did not take proper care of themselves.

49. It takes more than just a large vocabulary to achieve success, although a large vocabulary certainly helps. His being your boss (or your continuing to be just an employee) cannot be attributed solely to the size of your respective vocabularies. Such work roles are more often than not attributable to such characteristics as experience, intelligence, initiative, perseverance, and so on.

50. Cause and effect are reversed here: the sun setting causes the shadows, which then seem to blot out the sunlight—and not the other way around (night with its shadows causing the setting of the sun).

51. Although it is true that in areas where police patrols are frequent, crimes are more common, it is not because law enforcement does not prevent crime. More likely, it is because a high-crime area is more frequently patrolled—otherwise the crime rate would be even higher. If the police stay long enough, the crime rate will go down.

52. As in exercise 48, a simultaneous increase in alcoholism along with the energy crisis does not mean a causal relationship exists between them.

53. Abusive ad hominem. Instead of examining the economic policies to find out why the country is in a "bad condition," the arguer attacks the "advisers" and "eggheads" who devised the policies.

54. Genetic fallacy. Because we are composed or made up of atoms (which lack free will), it does not follow that we are identical with atoms and their properties (i.e., that we lack free will).

55. Circumstantial ad hominem. In this interchange, each believes that the other will take a certain position on the tax issue because of his or her circumstances, when this may not be the case at all. Whose case is worthier can only be decided on its merits, not on the motives or merits of its proposers.

56. Tu quoque. It may be true that we in America may have violated various basic humanitarian rights, but this does not invalidate our belief or contention that such practices, wherever they may occur, are reprehensible.

57. Poisoning the well. Matters are arranged in such a way that anything the other person says is taken as proof of the original contention—here that he or she doesn't matter very much.

PART III

PHILOSOPHY'S MAIN QUESTIONS

Ethics: What Are We Like, and What Should We Do?

THE NEWSPAPER ARTICLE WAS TITLED "Doctor's Choice Causes Furor." Its subtitle let the reader know why: "Life or Death for Brain-Damaged Infant?" Although its author probably did not intend it, his account of the hospital incident touched on almost every major ethical question that all of us, at one time or another, in one context or another, have had to face.

The baby was born with serious birth defects and, after five agonizing days, the doctor decided the best thing to do was to let him die "mercifully."

Last Friday, after determining the infant was near death because of what appears to be a seriously defective brain, the doctor withdrew food from the baby.

Instead of following the standard practice of writing feeding orders the physician wrote nothing—in effect telling the staff the baby would be allowed to die.

The baby was not fed Saturday or Sunday but on Monday another physician in the hospital countermanded the orders and once more placed the infant on food.

Today the baby is still alive and apparently in no imminent danger of dying. He is taking some food by mouth but it is too early to tell whether he is growing. He has a good heart, lungs, and kidneys—the essentials of physical life.[1]

It is apparently not easy to determine how near to death anyone may be. On Friday one doctor thought the baby was at death's doorstep; by Monday the baby seemed to be doing quite well.

The case has become a cause celebre among the staff at the hospital, which is in Southern California. Some of the nursing staff believe the decision not to feed the baby was tantamount to euthanasia. Some call it murder. Others, perhaps the majority, are in total agreement with the initial decision.

A rabbi who has learned of the case from a distraught nurse is shocked that physicians take it upon themselves to make decisions that he believes to be moral, not medical.

"The medical profession cannot presume to make moral judgments with impunity," the rabbi says. "It may be that the decision not to feed the baby was morally correct, but I don't think any physician has the right to make such a decision exclusively."

Not an unimportant point. Whose decision should this be? All of us would probably agree that it should not be the doctor's exclusively. But should it be only the mother's? the church's? society's?

A cross-section of medical school pediatricians queried by the Times—at least those willing to comment on such a sensitive issue—said they would never under any circumstances fail to feed a baby.

This sounds as if they would never fail to do so in the case of an infant. Would they feel the same concern if the patient were a decrepit old man? Should such questions be decided on the basis of the pity that was aroused?

It is not rare for doctors in a large population area like Los Angeles to be confronted with a decision as the one this physician was forced to make. Not all of them—possibly not even the majority—would have made an identical decision. But this case and the decision reached could have occurred in many hospitals.

Usually such cases involve persons with terminal diseases or head injuries—whether the machines and drugs being used to keep them alive should be withdrawn, allowing the patient to die quietly.

Sometimes, as in this case, the patient is a baby born with severe impairments. Often nature takes care of things by allowing the infant to die, no matter what the doctors may try.

In other cases, the defects may be such that the child will live for years, but with physical and mental defects that place him at an enormous disadvantage.

What should the doctor—and the parents if they are around—do?

But to return to the baby:

The baby's doctor said Thursday that epileptic seizures which a week ago were occurring frequently have been controlled with drugs and that dosage is being diminished. He admits that he miscalculated in determining that death was imminent when he withdrew food and says he agrees that the baby should be fed.

The doctor now recognizes he had "miscalculated." I don't think we would want to stop feeding him because he had made a mistake, but such "mistakes" strengthen the case of those who argue that we have no right "to play God" and would be opposed to the action taken by this physician under any circumstances.

He said he cannot say with 100% certainty that the baby is mentally retarded, but tests indicate his brain is structurally abnormal. The baby is believed to be blind. He has a double cleft palate and lip and his arms are tiny stubs.

This is getting even worse: it cannot, apparently, even be determined that the baby is mentally retarded, nor even whether he is blind! Some facts are, of course, not very easy to establish. He is obviously, however, not very pretty—but that is scarcely a good reason not to feed him. Nor has fortune smiled on him in other respects:

The infant's mother is unwed. She did not share directly in the decision not to feed her baby. However, when the baby was admitted to the hospital, she told the doctor she wouldn't care if she did not see the baby again.

"Some doctors believe that a 100% effort must be made on all babies to sustain life. To me this is reasonable, but it's a copout. It doesn't take into consideration the circumstances that surround a baby's life," the doctor said in an interview.

"The mother has had a very tough time in life. She's unwed. She has three children at home. She said, 'How can I help this baby through a tough life with all these defects laid on him?'

"If she had showed some concern, some willingness to care for the baby, my decision would have been influenced."

The doctor's argument is stronger here and his action, perhaps, more understandable, but why would his decision have been merely "influenced" had the mother shown more concern? Why would it not have proven decisive in keeping the baby alive? Shouldn't the mother's rights in such a case be absolute? And if not, why not?

The physician said he does not think of his decision as being euthanasia, a practice against which his hospital has a strong policy.

"I had a picture of euthanasia as doing something to kill someone—an overt action. For example, giving an overdose of drugs to a terminal cancer patient who is in deep pain.

"In that case the doctor is doing an action. I was doing an inaction—I was refraining from writing feeding orders. I was saying I am not going to contribute to continuing this particular problem.

"On the other hand, suppose I had a baby who was not responding to treatment for hyaline membrane disease, a potentially lethal lung disorder, and who was having seizures and heart arrests. If someone told me to turn off the respirator, I would have a hard time doing that."

This shows us how easy it is to deceive even ourselves: to fail to see, in this case, that "doing an inaction" and "doing an action" are both species of action. Some might even feel that of the two, the former was more culpable; the writer of the article in fact discovered just such a person:

Of four pediatricians consulted by the Times, all indicated a strong aversion to withholding food from defective babies.

But one of them—a woman physician—who was the most adamant against that course of action said that she would have far less inhibition against pulling the plug on a respirator if she thought the case was hopeless—the exact opposite of the situation with the physician in this story.

On the other hand we should not make light of this active–passive distinction invoked by the physician in charge. Like the woman physician consulted by the Times, many have argued that in some cases active euthanasia is preferable to passive. Although, for example, it is often the practice in severe cases of Down syndrome to allow the patients to die by dehydration and unchecked infection, some have argued that a lethal injection would be far more humane.

But to return to the baby:

It is expected that the baby, whose care is being paid by the Medicaid program, soon will be moved from the hospital because he is not sick enough to stay and the cost—about $80 a day—is prohibitive.

He probably will be transferred to a nursing home. What happens then will involve other difficult medical and possibly moral decisions.

The basic moral decision is, of course, what is to be done? What should the doctor have done in this case?

If you had said, as is likely, that he should have done everything he could to keep the baby alive, for life is precious and must be preserved at all costs, it is also likely that he or someone else might have raised the question of whether this principle applies to all life (including, say, livestock) or only to human life; and if only to human life, does it apply, you might have been asked, to all human life, even the most vicious of criminals? And if you were now tempted to begin to draw lines between those who are worthy of life and those who are not, it is more than likely that someone else might have reminded you that this indeed was how it began in Nazi Germany, where they went from mental defectives to political enemies to, finally, whole races of people whom they judged as "material" unworthy of life.

On the other hand, it could be argued that, independent of the abuses people have made in judging life's quality, such issues as euthanasia, abortion, and capital punishment necessitate these judgments. One might add that in a society like our own, such judgments can be made rationally and held to firmly. To argue that to make any such judgments is to allow "the thin edge of the wedge" to enter is considered inapplicable by some people. This is still not to say that extreme caution is not to be taken in light of historical disasters.

Whatever direction such a discussion might take, it is obvious that this question of life would be central to it. And once it is raised, you would very quickly find yourself embroiled in such related questions as, "What sort of life?" "What should matter most in life?" "How should one best conduct it?" and so on. To become concerned with such questions is to become concerned with the philosophical study of ethics.

The study of ethics during the course of the centuries has tended to take three different directions. It has occupied itself with the practical problem of what is to be done (with what we might call morality proper), it has gone on to consider the possible theoretical reasons for various lines of conduct (ethics proper), and, last, it has become concerned with inquiry into the nature of those theories themselves (metaethics). Although all great philosophers who have written on ethics have been concerned with all three types of investigation, it is characteristic of today's writers to be concerned with the third (questions of meaning), of writers of recent centuries to be occupied with the second (with ethical theories), and of ancient writers with the first (with what we ought to do or what life is best to live).

One of the first philosophers to leave us a memorable account of the life he thought most worthy to live was Aristotle, whose name is already familiar to us. Let us begin by examining his classic work, the *Nicomachean Ethics*.

ARISTOTLE'S THEORY OF ETHICS

Aristotle believed that all living things—from trees and shrubs to humans—are endowed with certain capacities or potentialities and that their well-being lies in realizing these potentialities. The acorn has the potentiality of becoming an oak tree, and its well-being lies in attaining that final state, which it is drawn to achieve by its nature. What is true of the rest of nature is true of humans, who have the added capacity of being conscious of the goals they try to realize.

Ethics, which is the study of human conduct, must therefore begin with an investigation of the goals at which people aim. There is basically, however, only one goal people aim at: happiness. But since nobody can be happy without being good, the investigation of happiness must entail an investigation of goodness. The 10 books of the *Nicomachean Ethics* are therefore devoted to an exploration of these two major goals.

Goodness and Happiness

Aristotle begins by distinguishing between two types of ends: (1) those that are good in themselves and that are desired for themselves alone and (2) those that are good as means toward such ends. Some ends are, as we would now put it, "intrinsically good," while other ends are only "instrumentally good." Money, for example, is for most of us an example of an instrumental good, being desired not for itself but for the things it enables us to obtain; a miser, on the other hand, might turn it into an intrinsic good by desiring it for itself alone.

Yet even here we must be very clear, for the miser is typically someone who derives a great deal of pleasure from hoarding money. If he hoards the money in order to get this

Tell me, Socrates, what does he desire who loves good things? That he may have them, said I. And what will he have when he has the good things? This is easier to answer, said I; he will be happy. Yes, he said, it is through getting good things that the happy become happy. And now we have no need to go on and ask why man wishes to be happy, for we have come to the final point in our inquiry.

—Plato, *Symposium*

pleasure, the money is still only an instrumental good—good only in its capacity to get something else, pleasure. If, on the other hand, he wants the money independent of anything it might gain him—material goods, security, or pleasure—he is considering it an intrinsic good, something to be obtained purely for itself.

Not all goods, obviously, are desired only as means, for this would involve an infinite and meaningless progression—one thing desired only because of some other thing, desired only because of still some other thing, and so on. There must be some things that are desired for their own sake. And among these, there must be one that is valued more than the others.

There is, indeed, according to the common opinion of mankind, says Aristotle, such a final and supremely valued good. It is "happiness."

> Since there are evidently more ends than one, and of these we choose some (e.g. wealth or musical instruments or tools generally) as means to something else, it is clear that not all of them are final ends, whereas the supreme good is obviously something final. So if there is only one final end, this will be the good of which we are in search; and if there are more than one, it will be the most final of these. Now we call an object pursued for its own sake more final than one pursued because of something else, and one which is never choosable because of another more final than those which are choosable because of it as well as for their own sakes; and that which is always choosable for its own sake and never because of something else we call final without qualifications.
>
> Well, happiness more than anything else is thought to be just such an end, because we always choose it for itself, and never for any other reason. It is different with honor, pleasure, intelligence and good qualities generally. We do choose them partly for themselves (because we should choose each one of them irrespectively of any consequences); but we choose them also for the sake of our happiness, in the belief that they will be instrumental in promoting it. On the other hand nobody chooses happiness for their sake, or in general for any other reason. (Book I, vii)[2]

Although everyone, as Aristotle notes, seems to be in agreement about this, not everyone has quite the same conception of happiness, and so further analysis is necessary.

Before proceeding to this deeper analysis, Aristotle cautions the reader not to expect that the results of such an investigation will have the neatness and precision found in a science like mathematics. We should demand absolutely certain proofs from a mathematician. But in complex and difficult matters such as this, we cannot expect hard-and-fast rigorous statements. We must look for precision in a subject to the degree that the subject admits. It is the mark of an educated person to do this. Such precision is not possible in ethics or human affairs generally.

Now we may note as a beginning that happiness is not some momentary, fleeting feeling or sensation. It is something more substantial and lasting. When we remark of someone that he has had a happy life, what we mean is that he has had a full life, that he has lived well, that he has realized his aims and ambitions as a man—in short, that he has been, as we might say, a success. The question is, What is it to live well, to be a success?

Plato and Aristotle

To answer this question Aristotle returns to his basic premise about the nature of living things. A living thing, he says, lives well, has a fortunate life, if it has attained its nature, if it has realized its potentialities. Since the potentialities of different things are different (the potentiality of an acorn being different from the potentiality of a cow and that of a cow different from that of a human being), living well will be different for different things. In each case, however, the organism will "live well" only by attaining its highest potentialities, by attaining what is distinctive of it.

A human could not be said to live well if he or she only realized those capacities or potentialities shared with other living things; if, say, he or she lived a life of only eating and drinking. For a human to be happy the potentialities that are distinctive of a human being must be attained. In the case of humankind this is obviously **reason**—our ability to think and draw conclusions—which is a human's distinctive capacity. The truly good life for a human being must therefore in some way involve the exercise, development, and perfection of reason.

If one were in a particularly critical or unsympathetic mood, one might argue here against Aristotle, as others have in the past, that reason is not the only thing peculiar to humankind. What is peculiar to humans, in addition, is that they have a moral sense and a sense of anguish, and even that they are capable of laughter. Further, it seems more and more apparent that reason is not even itself peculiar to humankind but is shared by a number of "lower" primates. Yet even if reason is not peculiar to humans, it is peculiar in the degree to which it is present, and, further, although not the only distinguishing characteristic, it is nevertheless the chief one.

Aristotle stresses here that it is not enough to possess these higher potentialities or capacities, for happiness is not a state of being but a state of doing, of being involved, of achieving. The capacities we have must be exercised, not simply possessed, if we are to achieve happiness.

But although our happiness lies in the development, perfection, and exercise of these higher capacities, we must remember that our other needs must nevertheless also be satisfied. In fact, they have to be satisfied first. For even if we do not live to eat, we have to eat to live. Nor is it only a matter of merely eating; a truly happy life requires the sunshine of prosperity:

> Happiness needs the addition of external goods, for it is difficult if not impossible to do fine deeds without any resources. Many can only be done by the help of friends, or wealth, or political influence. There are also certain advantages, such as good ancestry or good children, or personal beauty, the lack of which mars our felicity; for a man is scarcely happy if he is very ugly to look at, or of low birth, or solitary and childless; and presumably even less so if he had good ones who are now dead. So, as we said, happiness seems to require this sort of prosperity too. (Book I, viii)

Aristotle ends this passage by reminding us not to make the mistake of equating happiness with the possession of such external goods. Although they are necessary conditions for attaining happiness, they are not sufficient ones. All of us know many who have had material goods in abundance and yet have missed happiness.

To summarize Aristotle's argument: The supreme aim of life is happiness, and in the case of humankind this means living a life that is distinctive and that can be lived only by humans. This cannot consist merely of a life of eating and drinking, for that can be done equally well by all other creatures. It means the development and perfection of reason.

The perfection of our reason, Aristotle goes on to explain, enables us to develop two main kinds of desirable qualities (or virtues, as he calls them), whose exercise brings us happiness. The first set, tied to our intelligence and called the **intellectual virtues** by Aristotle, includes our ability to discover and recognize the rules of life we ought to follow; the second set, tied to our character and called the **moral virtues**, deals with our ability to check our appetites and passions so that they will obey the rules recognized as good.

Moral Virtues

Aristotle first takes up the moral virtues, which deal with our feelings, emotions, and impulses, whose training makes possible the effective use of our intelligence. Unchecked, these emotions and passions may prevent us from recognizing the right thing to do, let alone from doing it.

Learning to check our emotions and passions, Aristotle says, is something we acquire slowly and gradually; it is not something we are born with. We are not, for example, born brave; we must learn to become so, and we learn by doing brave things. Furthermore, these passions of ours are in themselves neither good nor bad; they become so depending on the degree of their expression. Dampening our sense of fear to such a degree that we become rash and foolhardy is just as bad as allowing this fear to overwhelm us so that we become timid and cowardly. Both extremes are equally bad. The person of good character is one who has learned to act bravely not by despising fear but by controlling it.

This is the case with the other moral qualities. They are, in the main, means or points of balance between two extremes, each extreme being a vice either of excess or of defect. Modesty is thus the mean between pride (resulting from too much vanity) and humility (resulting from too little); ambition, between greed (the excess) and sloth (the defect); and so forth.

> It is in the nature of moral qualities that they are destroyed by deficiency and excess, just as we can see (since we have to use the evidence of visible facts to throw light on those that are invisible) in the case of bodily health and strength. For both excessive and insufficient exercise destroy one's strength, and both eating and drinking too much or too little destroy health, whereas the right quantity produces, increases and preserves it. So it is the same with temperance, courage and the other virtues. The man who shuns and fears everything and stands up to nothing becomes a coward; the man who is afraid of nothing at all, but marches up to every danger, becomes foolhardy. Similarly the man who indulges in every pleasure and refrains from none becomes licentious; but if a man behaves like a boor and turns his back on every pleasure, he is a case of insensibility. Thus temperance and courage are destroyed by excess and deficiency and preserved by the mean. (Book II, ii)
>
> . . .
>
> We have now said enough to show that moral virtue is a mean, and in what sense it is so: that it is a mean between two vices, one of excess and the other of deficiency, and that it is such because it aims at hitting the mean point in feelings and actions. For this reason it is a difficult business to be good; because in any given case it is difficult to find the midpoint—for instance, not everyone can find the center of a circle; only the man who knows how. So too it is easy to get angry—anyone can do that—or to give and spend money; but to feel or act towards the right person to the right extent at the right time for the right reason in the right way—that is not easy, and it is not everyone that can do it. Hence to do these things well is a rare, laudable and fine achievement. (Book II, ix)

Although much of the *Nicomachean Ethics* is devoted to the analysis of this doctrine of the **golden mean** (as it has come to be called), Aristotle's most memorable illustration of it is to be found not in the *Nicomachean Ethics* but in his *Rhetoric*, in the description of the three main stages of life as represented in the Youthful Man, the Elderly Man, and the Man in His Prime. In terms of the major virtues, the Youthful Man represents the excess, the Elderly Man the defect, and the Man in His Prime the mean.

> I will omit quoting here his sketch of the Youthful Man, since it contains the opposite of his description of the Elderly Man. Aristotle, however, finds the Youthful Man's innocence,

163

ignorance, and inexperience engaging. The Youthful Man, he says, is also passionate, brave, noble, and disinterested, but only because he does not yet know life as it is. And this is precisely what the elderly do know, and that knowledge has a desolating effect:

They have lived many years; they have often been taken in, and often made mistakes; and life on the whole is a bad business. The result is that they are sure about nothing and underdo everything. They "think" but they never "know"; and because of their hesitancy they always add a "possibly" or a "perhaps," putting everything this way and nothing positively.

They are cynical; that is, they tend to put the worst construction on everything. Further, their experience makes them distrustful and therefore suspicious of evil. Consequently they neither love warmly nor hate bitterly, but following the hint of Bias, they love as though they will some day hate and hate as though they will some day love.

They are small-minded, because they have been humbled by life: their desires are set upon nothing more exalted or unusual than what will help them to keep alive. They are not generous, because money is one of the things they must have, and at the same time their experience has taught them how hard it is to get and how easy to lose. They are cowardly, and are always anticipating danger; unlike that of the young, who are warm-blooded, their temperament is chilly; old age has paved the way for cowardice; fear is, in fact, a form of chill. . . .

They are too fond of themselves; this is one form that small-mindedness takes. Because of this, they guide their lives too much by consideration of what is useful and too little by what is noble—for the useful is what is good for oneself, and the noble what is good absolutely.

They are not shy, but shameless rather; caring less for what is noble than for what is useful, they feel contempt for what people may think of them. . . . Old men may feel pity, as well as young men, but not for the same reason. Young men feel it out of kindness, old men out of weakness, imagining that anything that befalls anyone else might easily happen to them, which is a thought that excites pity. . . .

Their fits of anger are sudden but feeble. Their sensual passions have altogether gone or have lost their vigor: consequently they do not feel their passions much, and their actions are inspired less by what they do feel than by the love of gain. Hence men at this time of life are often supposed to have a self-controlled character; the fact is that their passions have slackened and they are slaves to the love of gain. (*Rhetoric*, Book II, Chapter 13)[3]

Few current descriptions of the elderly are as impressive in their insights as this. He seems to know this life and to have observed it closely. His sketch of the Man in His Prime is briefer:

As for Men in their Prime, clearly we shall find that they have a character between that of the young and that of the old, free from the extremes of either. They have neither that excess of confidence which amounts to rashness, nor too much timidity, but the right amount of each. They neither trust everybody nor distrust everybody, but judge people correctly. Their lives will be guided not by the sole consideration either of what is noble or what is useful, but by both; neither by parsimony nor by prodigality, but by what is fit and proper. So, too, in regard to anger and desire; they will be brave as well as temperate, and temperate as well as brave; these virtues are divided between the young and the old; the young are brave but intemperate, the old temperate but cowardly. To put it generally, all the valuable qualities that youth and age divide between them are united in the prime of life, while all their excesses or defects are replaced by moderation and fitness. The body is in its prime from thirty to five-and-thirty; the mind about forty-nine. (*Rhetoric*, Book II, Chapter 14)

It is important to realize that the mean is not a rigid mathematical middle but a relative thing, differing for people of different temperaments and under different conditions. Finding one's mean, therefore, requires experience and maturity: after a certain amount of practice in, say, generosity or courage, one comes to find the mean in any given case almost instinctively. But it is not instinct, although with practice it can become habitual.

Aristotle is careful to point out that there are some moral virtues to which the doctrine of the mean does not apply, for their very nature already implies either their badness or goodness. Theft, envy, and spite would be typical examples. Here it is not a matter of too much or too little. They are simply bad. The same is true of such qualities as goodness and honesty.

There is one famous example in the Greek list of virtues that we would not regard as a virtue: it is what they called "high-mindedness" or "magnanimity." This is the quality of a person who, as Aristotle describes him, is superior in talents, who knows he is superior, and who takes good care to let you know it, too. He claims honor and public respect, but great honor will only mildly please him because he deserves this and a lot more. He is quite ready to confer benefits on other people but is too lofty to accept benefits from others. He keeps aloof from public matters, unless there is important business that demands his talents. He is not petty; he loves beautiful and useless possessions. "His step," Aristotle says, "is slow, his voice deep, and his speech sedate." Needless to say, this is hardly our notion of the ideal man, and we would tend to regard such a person as somewhat less than charming. One only hopes Aristotle is not describing himself in this sketch.

Intellectual Virtues

If the mean is a relative thing that differs for different people (and even for the same people in different situations), so that no precise rules can be laid down as to what it might be at any one time, how does one go about determining it? Aristotle replies that it requires knowledge and wisdom, and thus to attain happiness we need to attend not only to the moral virtues but also to the intellectual virtues (such as prudence, foresight, and wisdom).

However, what Aristotle now says about the attainment of these intellectual virtues is discouraging, for it soon becomes apparent that if he is right, only few of us can hope to achieve true happiness. For the perfection of the intellectual virtues, although indispensable in keeping the passions in check, is described as having a value and purpose all its own. The goodness of intellect that makes possible the goodness of character, which brings happiness, is itself, we are now told, intrinsically finer and higher than anything else available to us.

What follows is not an elaborate account of the use of intelligence in the formation of character but an eloquent defense and description of the contemplative life. Summarizing its values, Aristotle declares that this theoretic or contemplative life is superior to the merely practical life because "the intellect is the highest thing in us, and the objects that it apprehends are the highest things that can be known"; it is more lasting than other activities and purer and more pleasurable than them, and, as the highest human activity, it is most like that of the gods and tends to bring us closer to them:

> The man who exercises his intellect and cultivates it seems likely to be in the best state of mind and to be most loved by the gods. For if, as is generally supposed, the gods have some concern for human affairs, it would be reasonable to believe also that they take pleasure in that part of us which is best and most closely related to themselves (this being the intellect), and that they reward those who appreciate and honor it most highly; for they care for what is dear to them, and what they do is right and good. Now it is not hard to see that it is the wise man that possesses these qualities in the highest degree; therefore he is dearest to the gods. And it is natural that he should also be the happiest of men. So on this score too the wise man will be happy in the highest degree. (Book X, viii)

Aside from the irony that the highest activity a human is capable of and that is most characteristic turns out to be divine rather than human, this opinion must strike us as overly intellectual and elitist. Also, we have gotten very far away from that severely afflicted infant with whom we began this chapter, who will obviously never achieve the kind of happiness, let alone blessedness, here described. Does this mean its life is of no value, or will be of no value, to itself or others?

The position taken by Aristotle excludes not only that unfortunate infant but many others as well. For if Aristotle is correct, it means that the "good life" is possible only to a very few people, those who have the requisite degree of intellect as well as the combination of several other qualities—health, wealth, family, and so on. One is tempted to ask, Why should we believe that there is only one true road to happiness and that it is produced only by this single activity? Why should not a life devoted to service and good works, to the appreciation and production of beautiful things, lead to an equally happy and fulfilling life? Certainly most of us would be inclined to believe that composers, sculptors, painters, and so on, no less than scientists and philosophers, have it in their power to achieve the same heights of human perfection. And why draw the line at artists? The social activist, the reformer, the teacher, even the craftsperson—why should we think that true happiness (assuming their work is satisfying to them) is eternally closed to them?

It is difficult to resist the thought that Aristotle's selection of the intellectual life as the supremely happy one displays an element of egocentrism. This does not mean that the view must therefore be mistaken; although biased, it may nevertheless be true.

But what seems even more revealing is that we have in Aristotle's ethics an example of the characteristic relation between a philosopher's thought and the cultural setting in which it arises. For it is difficult not to see in Aristotle's elaborate analysis and definition of virtue as a mean between extremes an attempt to provide a philosophical justification of the moral convictions of his own age and culture, as conveyed, for example, in the famous Delphic exhortation "Nothing in excess."

Although living at a different time and place, we still find this rule commendable. But what a modern reader may find somewhat less commendable about Aristotle's ethical doctrine is not its cultural ethnocentrism but its egoism. Apparently, the happiness the virtuous man is to seek is not anyone else's but his own. I am obliged, says Aristotle, to look after only myself. Aristotle does indeed instruct us in such altruistic virtues as honesty, generosity, friendship, and so on, but their justification is not that they will increase the general happiness but that these things are desirable for the individual to have.

Yet on a more sympathetic note and in Aristotle's defense, we can see that if it is true that in order to obtain happiness one must cultivate and realize certain potentialities, then such happiness can be obtained only by attending to oneself. And if such happiness were realized, the society could not help but benefit.

However, we might nevertheless ask, What happens when one person's good and the good of others come into conflict? What ought one to do then? It is one of the major limitations of Aristotle's ethics that he hardly addressed this problem, much less giving an indication of the way he would have been inclined to answer it.

The attempt to deal with this very sort of problem—Whose good ought I choose in case of conflict?—is what distinguishes the ethics of the modern period from that of the ancient period.

KANT'S THEORY OF ETHICS

"Ethics," Kant says, putting himself in strict opposition to Aristotle's view, "is not the doctrine of how to make ourselves happy, but of how we are to be worthy of happiness." To make happiness, as Aristotle does, the supreme principle of morality is to miss what is central to it—the obligation we are all under to do what is right. For there is nothing morally admirable (or for that matter moral) about a person seeking his own happiness, but there is something worthy of admiration about a person who, in the face of overwhelming dangers, does his duty and does it for no other reason than that it is his duty. The difference between the moral and immoral person, furthermore, is not

Immanuel Kant (1724-1804)

that one is wise and the other foolish, that one knows what will lead to happiness and the other doesn't, but that one is good and the other is bad; one does what is right, whether it will bring him happiness or not, and the other is concerned only with his welfare.

A Good Will

But what makes a person good? Possession, Kant answers, of the only thing that is good without qualification, and this is a "good will." What this "good will" is and how we might come to recognize it is the task Kant sets himself to explain in his little book that bears the imposing title *Foundations of the Metaphysics of Morals*. It opens with these remarks:

Nothing can possibly be conceived in the world, or even out of it, which can be called good, without qualification, except a Good Will. Intelligence, wit, judgment, and the other talents of the mind, however they may be named, or courage, resolution, perseverance, as qualities of temperament, are undoubtedly good and desirable in many respects; but these gifts of nature may also become extremely bad and mischievous if the will which is to make use of them, and which, therefore, constitutes what is called character, is not good. It is the same with the gifts of fortune. Power, riches, honor, even health, and the general well-being and contentment with one's condition which is called happiness, inspire pride, and often presumption, if there is not a good will to correct the influence of these on the mind, and with this also to rectify the whole principle of acting, and adapt it to its end. The sight of a being who is not adorned with a single feature of a pure and good will, enjoying unbroken prosperity, can never give pleasure to an impartial rational spectator. Thus a good will appears to constitute the indispensable condition even of being worthy of happiness.

Kant does not deny, as we see from this opening statement, that there are many things in the world that may be regarded as good, and he lists a number of them for us, but he maintains that none of them is absolutely good. These things, he suggests, are morally good only if the will that directs them is good, and unless so directed they may in fact turn out to be bad (as in the case of great intelligence in a criminal).

A **good will**, then, does not derive its goodness, according to Kant, from being directed to the achievement of intelligence, courage, or wealth, for these things are good only when directed by a will that is already good. The goodness of the will is derived rather from the use of such faculties and gifts as intelligence, courage, and wealth in the service of duty.

What does this mean? A will to act from duty, Kant explains, follows the dictates not of desire or inclination but of pure reason. It is the will of one who does the right thing not because that is what he or she wants to do or because of the good consequences that will follow from it but because it is what pure reason demands of him or her. And only actions springing from such a motive are, according to Kant, deserving of moral praise and respect.

Let us consider some examples. Suppose you were accosted by a beggar and you gave him money, but only because you wished to be rid of him. Kant would say of such an action that, although not morally bad, it does not deserve moral praise. You may have acted, he would say, in accordance with duty (you did what was right) but not from a sense of duty (because it was right).

The following example will make the meaning of this distinction clearer. Suppose you are playing chess and a child walks up to the table and without knowing the game, its rules, or even taking time to consider his action moves your knight two squares up and one to the right (which is, as we know, the prescribed manner for the movement of a knight). Suppose further that the move is not only a permissible one but an excellent one as well. Now, we can say of the child that he has made a move, a good move, in accordance with the rules. However, to make a move from the rules (or duty) would require not only knowledge of the game, its permitted moves, and its goals but also the will to follow its strictures.

Let us return now to our beggar example. Suppose you were a completely warm-hearted person who delighted in spreading joy around you, and you gave this beggar money for no other reason than simply because you wanted to. Kant would say of this action that it was the gratification of some desire. Certainly what you did, he would say, was not bad, but it was not morally praiseworthy, either. You did it, he would say, merely for your own satisfaction. Such actions, he would add, may deserve encouragement but not moral esteem.

But now suppose that you gave this beggar money not because you wanted to get rid of him or because you felt kindly disposed toward him but rather because you felt duty bound to do so. Then and only then, says Kant, would your action have moral worth, for an action arising from that motive springs from a good will.

The Categorical Imperative

To make the meaning of such a will still clearer, Kant goes on to distinguish between two major types of imperatives, as he calls them, that may direct our will. The first of these are what we might call **technical imperatives** that command us to do certain things if we want to achieve certain ends. Thus, if it is our ambition to become a concert artist, such an imperative tells us that we must practice at least so many hours each day. However, we do not absolutely have to become concert artists, and should we decide not to, we are under no obligation to practice. Similarly, there are certain **prudential imperatives** that tell us, for example, that if we want to enjoy ourselves, we ought to go see the new play. But again, it is not absolutely necessary that we enjoy ourselves, and if we don't care to, we are under no obligation to do what we are inclined to.

These technical and prudential imperatives, Kant points out, are purely "hypothetical"; that is, they are conditional on certain wishes we may have, and should we cease to have the wishes, they cease to bind us. The "oughts" that figure in them are therefore not moral oughts: if we don't care to become concert artists or to be entertained, we are not doing anything wrong in not practicing or not going to the new play.

But when *ought* is used in a distinctly moral sense, the imperative is not hypothetical but categorical. For example, when we say to someone, "You ought to pay your debts," we mean that he ought to do so whether or not he wants to or whether or not he will gain something by doing it. Such a **categorical imperative** is unconditional and is not preceded or followed by an *if*. On the contrary, should we add an *if* to it (as in, "If you want people to trust you"), it immediately becomes a hypothetical, or conditional, imperative and ceases to be moral. People who pay their debts for that reason, Kant would say, are not acting from a pure motive and therefore are not acting morally. That is not to say, of course, that they are acting immorally. It is merely that an act motivated in this way is not worthy of moral esteem.

But why, one might ask, should we be moral, honest, pay our debts, and so forth? Why should we do what these categorical imperatives command?

It is interesting that Kant's answer is not unlike that given by Aristotle, although its elaboration is very different. It is that it would be unworthy of us as human beings to do otherwise. For to be human, as Kant explains, is to be rational, and to act as a human being, therefore, is to act rationally. It is, he explains, to possess a will that is motivated to act not by impulses or feeling but by reason. Since the essence of reason (unlike impulse and feeling) is consistency and the test of consistency is universal validity, an action in order to be rational must be motivated by a principle of conduct that is universally valid and binding. For just as it is characteristic of reason in the realm of science and mathematics to produce principles that are universally and necessarily true, so it must be characteristic of the principles issued by reason in the realm of human action and conduct to be universally valid and binding.

So to be rational in conduct, according to Kant, is to act on principles that can be willed to be universal; it is to act on principles that apply to every situation and to everyone equally. The person who is rational will not act on one principle in one situation and on another in a precisely similar situation, for that would be inconsistent and irrational. Nor would the rational person try to make an exception in his or her own case, for that, too, would be inconsistent and irrational. For the rational (and therefore moral) person will realize that whatever is morally right for him or her is right for all and that whatever is morally wrong for him or her is also morally wrong for all. That, for Kant, is the essence of what it is to be moral.

Kant's basic and fundamental principle of morality thus becomes a philosophical version of the golden rule: do unto others what you would have them do unto you. Or, as Kant expressed it, "Act on that maxim and that maxim only, which you can at the same time will to be a universal law."

This, finally, is Kant's supreme principle of morality, his principle of universality, as it has come to be called. It is also, as we can now see more clearly, what he means when he says that to have a good will is to act out of respect for law—not out of respect for some particular law but for law as such; respect for universality, which is the form of law; respect for a law that has no exceptions and is the same for all. Those who succeed in acting in this manner can be said to act from a sense of duty (they do what reason demands of them) and from a motive that is pure.

Kant offers the following example:

A man finds himself forced by need to borrow money. He well knows that he will not be able to repay it, but he also sees that nothing will be loaned him if he does not firmly promise to repay it at a certain time. He desires to make such a promise, but he has enough conscience to ask himself whether it is not improper and opposed to duty to relieve his distress in such a way. Now, assuming he does decide to do so, the maxim of his action would be as follows: When I believe myself to be in need of money, I will borrow money and promise to repay it, although I know I shall never do so. Now this principle of self-love or of his own benefit may very well be compatible with his whole future welfare, but the question is whether it is right. He changes the pretension of self-love into a universal law and then puts the question: How would it be if my maxim became a universal law? He immediately sees that it could never hold as a universal law of nature and be consistent with itself; rather it must necessarily contradict itself. For the universality of a law which says that anyone who believes himself to be in need could promise what he pleased with the intention of not fulfilling it would make the promise itself and the end to be accomplished by it impossible; no one would believe what was promised to him but would only laugh at any such assertion as vain pretense. (p. 40)

Just as Kant's principle of universality will be recognized as a philosophical version of the golden rule, so his question "How would it be if my maxim became a universal law?" will be recognized as our ordinary question "What if everybody behaved that way?"

Kant's formulation of this question, however, makes us see a good deal more clearly that what is wrong with everybody behaving that way is not that it would be unpleasant if they did or even that if it would be wrong for them it would be wrong for you but rather that it would make lying, breaking promises, and so on self-defeating and pointless. For if everybody lied, nobody would believe anybody, and lying promises would defeat themselves. That is why, as Kant insists, willing such a thing is a contradiction, for obviously if there is to be any point to lying, it must occur as the exception, not as the rule.

But this is precisely what the immoral person does, in fact, want. He wants to make an exception in his own favor in respect to a rule that others must observe if he is to

It is important to be clear about what Kant is saying here. He is not arguing against lying on the grounds that if I lie, others will soon lose confidence in me and eventually won't believe my promises. Nor is he arguing against lying on the grounds that my lie will contribute to a general practice of lying, which in turn will lead to a breakdown of trust and the destruction of the practice of promising. These considerations are basically utilitarian. Kant's point is more subtle. He is saying that there is something covertly self-contradictory about the state of affairs in which, as a law of nature, everyone makes a false promise when in need of a loan. Perhaps Kant's point is this: Such a state of affairs is self-contradictory because, on the one hand, in such a state of affairs everyone in need would borrow money on a false promise, and yet, on the other hand, in that state of affairs no one could borrow money on a false promise—for if promises were always violated, who would be silly enough to loan any money? . . . in that (allegedly impossible) state of affairs there would be promises, since those in need would make them, and there would also not be promises, since no one would believe that anyone was really committing himself to future payment by the use of the words "I promise." So, as Kant says, the generalized form of the maxim "annuls itself." It cannot be a law of nature.

—Fred Feldman, *Introductory Ethics* (1978)

succeed in gaining his ends. It is not that he doesn't know the principle behind his action or the nature of the principle it would contradict. He knows all this but wishes to be treated differently. On the other hand, the moral person does not try to make any exceptions for himself. He treats himself and others on the same basis. And for Kant that is ultimately the test of what is right and wrong, moral and immoral.

As inspiring and elevated an account of ethics as this may be, it is not without its difficulties. Let us consider here only those surrounding the ambiguity of the term *universal*. Suppose one were to agree to act on Kant's principle of universality. One agreed, that is to say, to do only those things that can be universalized and not do anything that cannot. But by taking specific circumstances into account, we could easily cheat: we could will that if anyone ever found himself in exactly the circumstances we now find ourselves in, we may lie. In such a case the principle would not appear to forbid lying, yet by extending to anyone in this kind of situation the same privilege, it would continue to be "universal."

It is apparent, however, from Kant's writings that his intention was to forbid such a thing as lying entirely. But that would be possible only if his principle were taken in its most general sense (do not lie now, unless you are willing that anyone should lie at any time in any situation). But taken in such an unqualified sense, the principle suffers from the opposite difficulty—it is now too rigorous for most people. For suppose telling a lie will save an innocent life? Most of us would probably justify such a lie.

For most people, Kant's principle seems either too restrictive or too permissive, and in cases of conflict between maxims (between telling the truth or saving an innocent life) it appears unhelpful. In the case of the severely afflicted baby in the hospital, all

Kant's Reply to This Kind of Criticism

The moral law must not indulge man and make allowances for his limited capacity, since it contains the standard of moral perfection, and the standard must be exact, invariable and absolute. A rule of ethics must, like a rule in mathematics, be defined with theoretical accuracy and irrespective of how far man can observe it. The center of a circle, or any mathematical point, is defined, but it cannot actually be made small enough to comply with the definition. So it is with the rules of ethics. These are measuring-rules of action and ought to set before us the standard of moral necessity. They ought not to be trimmed in consideration of man's capacity. Any system of ethics which accommodates itself to what man can do corrupts the moral perfection of humanity. The moral law must be pure.

—Kant, *Lectures on Ethics*, p. 74

parties could probably invoke Kant's principle in their support: the physician who stopped feeding orders and the mother of the baby could justify their decision by applying the principle narrowly; their critics could condemn their decision by applying Kant's principle with no exceptions.

The Role of Reason

But let us return to Kant's theory and note the way it deals with another type of objection. Suppose someone enquired of Kant's theory, "But why should we treat each other equally? Why indeed tell the truth, try to avoid the contradiction involved in making false promises, and so on?" To this sort of question Kant would answer that it is wrong to treat people otherwise because to do so would be to turn each other into things when we are not things but persons, possessing absolute intrinsic worth. I am not, Kant would say, merely a source of money for someone but a person, and being a person I am an end in myself, not a means or an instrument for someone else's end. When, however, we do such things as lie and cheat, we treat each other as things, and this is both demeaning and unworthy of us.

The principle of universality instructs us, therefore, in Kant's new formulation of this principle, "Act so that you treat humanity, whether in your own person or in that of another, always as an end and never as a means only." The principle doesn't say never treat anyone "as a means"; it says never treat anyone "as a means only." There are times when we serve each other's needs. This is unavoidable. But we can avoid treating each other as mere means.

We hear a great deal nowadays about the "human condition," but what seems to have interested Kant most was not so much the human condition as the condition under which we are human. For him that condition was our reason.

To make it even clearer how the possession of reason endows humans with absolute worth and places them in a unique position in the hierarchy of creation, Kant compares humans first with animals, then with God. Central to his view and description are, again, the claims made on us by the emotional and rational sides of our nature.

As we saw, a good will does not derive its goodness from being directed to the achievement of intelligence, courage, wealth, and so on; its goodness comes rather from the use of these faculties in the service of duty. Reason, however, as we well know, does not always and infallibly determine the direction of our will but does so only within limits. Not having full control over their will, humans come to experience the dictates of reason, Kant points out, as obligation—a feeling only they can experience, that comes to them in the form of a command or an imperative. Now when people follow the dictates of reason against the urges of desire and inclination and do what it demands, then their will can be said to be morally good.

Animals, not being subject to this conflict between duty and inclination, are incapable of that experience of obligation. An animal may indeed find itself torn between one want and another but never between want and duty. An animal, therefore, being wholly determined by its natural inclinations, can be said to be innocent and not, like humans, either morally good or evil.

God, being perfect, has a will that is perfectly rational. His will and His reason coincide, and there is never any tension between them. While an animal therefore is below the level of duty, God is above it. God, furthermore, may know the moral law, but He can have no desires that could possibly conflict with that law. God, that is, acts in conformity with the moral law, but He does so as a matter of course. God's will is therefore holy. Humans, on the other hand, who never perform their duty as a matter of course but are always subject to desire, may be morally good but never holy. People, therefore, unlike animals or God, are creatures who belong to two worlds at once—the world of sense and the world of reason—and unlike both are neither innocent nor holy but, depending on whether they do what reason commands, are either good or evil.

We are thus inevitably led to the question, the most fundamental of all, "Are people, however, free to do what reason demands?" Although Kant touches on this question here, he takes it up more fully in the *Critique of Practical Reason*, his second major work dealing with ethics. The conclusions he arrives at are as follows: (1) we must be free since the obligation to be moral (to do what reason demands) would make no sense were we not free to carry out such demands; (2) our souls must be immortal, for we are enjoined by reason to seek perfection, but this life alone is too brief to achieve it; hence, we must survive this life to continue our striving toward that goal; and (3) God must exist, for reason tells us that a good man ought to be happy. But goodness and happiness do not go together in this world; hence, there must be a Being who is all-knowing (and therefore can see through to our inner motives) and all-powerful (and therefore can reward us for them) and who, being also all-good, will apportion happiness to goodness.

Kant is careful to point out that these are only postulates; he has no proof of what they assert is so. But if we cannot know that they are true, he urges, we also cannot know that they are not; hence, belief in them is not irrational.

Whether true or not, however, these postulates are certainly not unfamiliar to us. They represent, obviously, some of the major tenets of Judeo-Christian teaching about our earthly duties and future rewards. Kant's ethics, no less than Aristotle's, are, therefore, in good part a reflection of his age and culture.

But a philosophy is not merely a summary and reflection of the thought and experience of a particular period and people. Often it is groundbreaking, anticipating developments yet to take place or whose full impact has yet to be felt, and this is certainly the case with Kant's philosophy. If it is not difficult, therefore, to recognize in his postulates and in his principle of universality the influence of his religious heritage, so similarly it is not difficult for us recognize in his further formulation of his fundamental principle (that we treat all men as ends and never merely as means) a philosophical expression of the equalitarian ideal represented by the two great social and political events of his age: the Industrial Revolution on the one hand and the American and French revolutions on the other.

THE UTILITARIAN THEORY

Although the full impact of the vast social and political changes of the late 1700s did not go unrecognized by Kant, their implications were not fully comprehended at Kant's writing. When their impact was fully realized in the next century, ethical theories arose that were better suited than Kant's to take account of the new phenomena created by these events. A society of plenty with a growing awareness of its rights had arisen, and utilitarianism became its philosophical voice.

Jeremy Bentham

Jeremy Bentham (1748–1832) was the founder of utilitarianism. The son of a well-to-do London lawyer, Bentham was sent to Oxford, destined for a legal career. But his temperament and his awareness of the plight of the working people of his time made him abandon the idea of a legal career. He decided instead to devote himself to the task of legal reform.

There was much to reform. The existing condition of England, soon to be so realistically described by Charles Dickens, with its workhouses, debtors' prisons, and slums, was shocking, and Bentham determined to correct them. He set about doing so not by taking to the streets but by working out a scientific system of law.

His father's generosity provided him with the financial independence to carry out the program he set himself. There now flowed from his pen a series of writings, the most famous of which was his *Principles of Morals and Legislation*, published in 1789. These works and the ideas they proclaimed gained him wide recognition, and there soon formed around him a group of like-minded intellectuals who, fired by his humanitarian ideals, pressed for social and political reforms.

Bentham died in 1832, aware that Parliament was about to pass its first reform bill—a landmark piece of legislation and a notable personal triumph for the man who, more than anyone else, had paved the way for its realization.

Bentham's main work, *Principles of Morals and Legislation*, opens with this statement: "Nature has placed mankind under the governance of two sovereign masters, pain and pleasure. It is for them alone to point out what we ought to do, as well as to determine what we shall do."

Bentham's brief opening statement asserts two separate doctrines. One is descriptive, claiming that the motive that governs our actions is desire for pleasure; the other is ethical or normative, stating what our standard for action ought to be. One is a statement concerning the way things are, the other is a proposal concerning the way they ought to be.

This would seem to be an inauspicious way to open a work on ethics, for if pain and pleasure determine our decisions, there would seem to be no point—the matter having already been decided—to go on to say what we ought to do. The advice would seem to be either unnecessary or futile.

But Bentham embraces these two standpoints purposely, their contradiction being for him only apparent. Nature has indeed arranged things so that we are guided by our desire for happiness, but unfortunately we are burdened with mistaken notions of what happiness is, and an investigation to see how it might best be secured is therefore neither unnecessary nor doomed to failure.

Jeremy Bentham (1748–1832)

The pleasure or happiness Bentham has in mind, as he very soon tells us, is not each person's own happiness or pleasure (as his predecessors, the ancient Greek hedonists, had maintained) but rather, in the words of his famous slogan, "the greatest happiness of the greatest number." In considering a course of action, what we have to be concerned with, he argues, is not merely our own pleasure but the amount of pleasure the action is likely to bring to all those whose interests are at stake.

This is Bentham's **principle of utility**. It maintains that there is only one way to determine whether something is right or wrong, good or bad, and this is by considering its usefulness or "utility" in bringing about pleasant results. An action is right if it brings about more happiness than any other possible action; it is wrong if some other possible action could have produced more happiness.

Since, according to Bentham, what is right, good, and best is that which produces the most happiness, and happiness is simply a condition in which pain is outweighed by pleasure, it is obviously important to try to arrive at as clear an understanding of the nature of pleasure as possible. And this is what Bentham now proceeds to do. He proposes a kind of "hedonistic calculus," as he calls it, that we might use in evaluating pleasures, based on the seven ways in which, according to him, pleasures vary.

Before a particular course of action is adopted, to conform to the new principle of utility he is recommending, we should evaluate the pleasurable results anticipated by asking ourselves such questions as the following:

(1) How intense are the pleasures?
(2) How long can we expect them to last?
(3) How certain are we they will occur?
(4) How immediate or remote are they?
(5) What is their chance of being followed by sensations of the same kind?
(6) What is their chance of being followed by sensations of the opposite kind?
(7) How many other people will share in them?

If after considering these seven different factors (the intensity of the pleasures, their duration, certainty, propinquity, fecundity, purity, and extent) it is discovered that the pleasures exceed the pains, then the action is right; if not, then it is wrong.

What strikes one most about Bentham's list is that an important ingredient of pleasure—namely, its quality—seems to be missing and that this omission must be an oversight. But this is not so. Desiring to keep his standard as simple and as practicable as possible and being by nature suspicious of undue complexity, Bentham purposely omits it from the calculus. The only thing that matters as far as pleasures and pains are concerned, he asserts, is their quantity, not their quality. Pushpin is as good as poetry, he was bold to remark, the quantity of pleasure being equal. This remark led his critics to call his new version of hedonism a "pig philosophy." But Bentham was undaunted: the source of pleasure, he felt, is irrelevant; what matters is the amount of it after any unpleasantness or pain has been subtracted.

Bentham proposes, therefore, that we begin to measure and calculate our pleasures and pains in the same way and in the same spirit scientists measure and calculate the motion of bodies in space. Anticipating the question of whether anyone ever has or would engage in this kind of calculation, Bentham replies,

> There are some who may look upon the nicety employed in the adjustment of such rules as so much labor lost: for gross ignorance, they will say, never troubles itself about laws, and passion does not calculate. But the evil of ignorance admits of cure: and when matters of such importance as pain and pleasure are at stake, and these in the highest degree, who is there that does not calculate? Men calculate, some with less exactness, indeed, and some with more: but all men calculate. (Introduction to *Principles of Morals and Legislation*, p. 4)

Although all men thus calculate, they do not unfortunately all do so in the right way, for they calculate their own pleasure or happiness, not, as they should, the greatest happiness of the greatest number. It would be a simple matter to get them to calculate properly, says Bentham, if they were not by nature egoistic and selfish, but they are and we cannot change them.

What, then, is to be done? How are we to reconcile this ideal of universalism or altruism with the reality of egoism?

Seeing this as the main problem not only of ethics but of government as well, Bentham makes a proposal designed as a corrective for both. It is true, he says, we must leave men the way they are, for we cannot change them. Nevertheless, we can get them to behave in a manner that will be for the good of all by making this course of action pay them personally. We can see to it, he says, that to deviate from the path of social good costs a man so much that he won't do so. By seeking his own good, such a person will then act in a way as to realize the maximum good for society.

Bentham did not need to look far to observe such a system of "sanctions," as he calls them, already at work. There were, first of all, the sanctions to be found in physical nature, operating to bring happiness to people who act in one way and pain (e.g., when they overeat) when they act in another; then there were the political and legal sanctions exacted by the law, the social sanctions of public opinion, and, finally, the sanctions of religion with its fear of divine punishment and promise of heavenly reward.

But the trouble is, Bentham argues, that in any existing society the sanctions applying to conduct are irrational. They have developed haphazardly and are now themselves the cause of much misery. They need to be made more reasonable by being brought into an orderly system on the basis of some first principle. Take, for example, he says, the penal laws. Describing the shocking conditions in the prisons, Bentham points out the unnecessary severity of the punishments. They inflict more pain than necessary in order to redirect conduct into socially desirable lines. Since pain is always evil, this is wrong. We need to inflict, he says, just that amount necessary to prevent a greater evil. To use more is unjustified and irrational.

The same is true, he urges, of the other areas of our life, arguing in the process, among other things, for a different sort of government (a democracy instead of a monarchy, for only where there is an identity between the rulers and the ruled will their interests be the same and the greatest happiness of the greatest number be assured) and less of it (since much that the government tries to control is really a matter of private morals and not its business at all).

Although we are here interested only in Bentham's moral theory, it becomes obvious when he comes to talk about problems of legislation, prison reform, theory of punishment, and so on that everything in his writings up to this point has been preparatory and that the whole purpose of the analysis of pleasure, the calculus, and the nature of human motivation has been to expose the abuses of his day and to bring about a more humane and just society.

This reformist tendency and dual interest was characteristic of all the utilitarians who gathered around Bentham. Feeling compassion for the misery of the poor laboring long hours in the rising network of workhouses and factories, angered by the complacency of many of the owners of these factories, and offended by the injustice of the prevailing system of distribution of profits, they set out to change the social, legal, and economic organization of society that gave rise to these conditions and that, despite the cruelties, people generally continued to tolerate.

Like Bentham, however, they were convinced that reform could be achieved only if based on sound principles concerning the nature of human motivation, law, society, and government. They therefore set about to study such disciplines as psychology, ethics, education, and politics, making profound contributions to each. In all these investigations, their basic principle was and remained the same: the principle of utility—only those actions, practices, and codes of law are worthy that promote the greatest happiness of the greatest number.

If that principle seems obvious to us now, it was far from appearing so to Bentham's contemporaries. To make it more acceptable, Bentham's followers went about the task of refining it. The most famous of these thinkers was John Stuart Mill.

John Stuart Mill

Bentham's most important immediate disciple was James Mill (1773–1836), the father of John Stuart Mill. In addition to writing the first comprehensive history of India, a work that brought him fame and fortune and eventually a high post in the East India Company, James Mill devoted his talents to studies in psychology and education, believing that education could change life and that the civil liberties and democratic ideals he shared with Bentham could be realized by properly conducted education.

The birth of his son in 1806 gave James Mill an opportunity to test his theories. He subjected the boy to a course of studies that still seems remarkable to us—and with remarkable results. Sending him neither to school nor university, James set his son to learn Greek at the age of three, arithmetic and English grammar soon afterward, and Latin not until the boy reached the ripe old age of four. By age six and a half, John had composed a work on the history of Rome, replete with footnotes. Some

John Stuart Mill (1806–1873)

years later, at the age of 12, John set to work on logic, economics, and philosophy. Much of this work young Mill had to do by himself, discussing what he had learned with his father during their walks. To master these subjects further, he was assigned the task of teaching them to his younger brothers and sisters. Nor, of course, was he spared the systematic study of utilitarian principles: at the age of 18 he landed in jail for handing out birth control pamphlets in a working-class slum. So intense was his personal tutoring that Mill was later to say that it put him a quarter of a century ahead of his contemporaries. It also, however, took its toll, for at the age of 20 he suffered a mental breakdown that he attributed to the overemphasis on analysis in his upbringing without a parallel development of the emotions. He tried to correct this imbalance by immersing himself in the writings of Coleridge, Carlyle, and Wordsworth—the English romantic poets and essayists.

Although he claimed this study helped him, what undoubtedly helped him even more to achieve the balance—which enabled him to go on to hold down a full-time position at the East India Company (rising eventually, like his father before him, to become its chief administrative officer), become the founder and editor of the important and influential *Westminster Review*, become a member of Parliament, and so on—was his long romance with Mrs. Harriet Taylor, which began when he was 25 and whom he married many years later when her husband died. Aside from Bentham, she was the most dominant influence in his life and, essentially, the coauthor of a number of his works.

Of Mill's works, apart from his groundbreaking and historically significant *System of Logic* (1843), his best known is the classic *On Liberty* (1859), whose elaborately reasoned and passionately asserted defense of the right of individuals to think and act for themselves has never been surpassed. The case for liberty, Mill argues here, is its utility—its power to create, maintain, and augment the greatest happiness of the greatest number. In striking and memorable words, he says of this work,

> The object of this Essay is to assert one very simple principle as entitled to govern absolutely the dealings of society with the individual in the way of compulsion and control, whether the means used be physical force in the form of legal penalties, or the moral coercion of public opinion. That principle is, that the sole end for which mankind are warranted, individually or collectively, in interfering with the liberty of action of any of their

---

Mill's Dedication of On Liberty

To the beloved and deplored memory of her who was the inspirer, and in part the author, of all that is best in my writings—the friend and wife whose exalted sense of truth and right was my strongest incitement, and whose approbation was my chief reward—I dedicate this volume. Like all that I have written for many years, it belongs as much to her as to me; but the work as it stands has had, in a very insufficient degree, the inestimable advantage of her revision; some of the most important portions having been reserved for a more careful reexamination, which they are now never destined to receive. Were I but capable of interpreting to the world one half the great thoughts and noble feelings which are buried in her grave, I should be the medium of a greater benefit to it, than is ever likely to arise from anything that I can write, unprompted and unassisted by her all but unrivaled wisdom.

---

number, is self-protection. That the only purpose for which power can be rightly exercised over any member of a civilized community, against his will, is to prevent harm to others. His own good, either physical or moral, is not a sufficient warrant. He cannot rightfully be compelled to do or forbear because it will be better for him to do so, because it will make him happier, because, in the opinions of others, to do so would be wise or even right. These are good reasons for remonstrating with him or reasoning with him, or persuading him, or entreating him, but not for compelling him, or visiting him with any evil in case he do otherwise. To justify that, the conduct from which it is desired to deter him must be calculated to produce evil to someone else. The only part of the conduct of anyone, for which he is amenable to society, is that which concerns others. In the part which merely concerns himself, his independence is, of right, absolute. Over himself, over his own body and mind, the individual is sovereign.

With this ideal of liberty still uppermost in his mind, Mill went on to defend it in a work written two years later, *Considerations on Representative Government* (1861). Those who are to live under laws, he argues here, should choose those who are to make and administer the laws, for only a government of such elected representatives can ensure the greatest happiness of the greatest number.

Finally, in another work, almost a century ahead of its time—*The Subjection of Women* (1869)—he went on to extend the argument of his treatise *On Liberty* to the position of women in the modern world. This work contains a protest against their political, economic, professional, and social subjection and an impassioned plea for their emancipation. In the long run and from an overall point of view, he argues here, women's subjection works against the greatest happiness of the greatest number, and their emancipation works for it.

Mill died in 1873 at the age of 67. A religious publication noted his death with these words: "His death is a loss to no one, for he was a crass infidel, however harmless he may have seemed, and a very dangerous person. The sooner those 'luminaries of thought' who hold the same views as his go where he is gone, the better it will be for the Church and the State."

Reading Bentham's works and assimilating the principle of utility made a profound impression on Mill. As he tells us in his *Autobiography*, which was published after his death,

This principle gave unity to my conceptions of things. I now had opinions, a creed, a doctrine, a philosophy, in one among the best senses of the word a religion; the inculcation and diffusion of which could be made the principal outward purpose of a life. And I had a grand conception laid before me of changes to be effected in the condition of mankind through that doctrine. The vista of improvement which Bentham opened was sufficiently large and brilliant to light up my life as well as to give a definite shape to my aspirations. (pp. 66–67)

But Bentham's version of the principle had stirred up many critics, and in his own work, *Utilitarianism* (1863), Mill set out to try to restate it in a way that would answer these critics and make it more convincing and appealing. Mill proceeded to introduce two major modifications in Bentham's theory, one concerning Bentham's psychological hedonism (his view of the way we are), the other concerning his ethical hedonism (what ought to count with us).

Concerning the first, Mill argued that we are not necessarily so made as to seek only our own happiness. Whereas Bentham tended to reduce our altruistic feelings, on those rare occasions when he even acknowledged their existence, to feelings of self-interest, Mill believed they were founded in a certain primitive, gregarious instinct characteristic of all of us. We are naturally, he says, altruistic and self-sacrificing and find our individual happiness by promoting the happiness of the group. Human beings, in short, according to Mill, are capable of impartial action.

Nevertheless it takes all kinds of people to make a world, and the more room the world has in it for the self-development and expression of different individual characters, the better chance everyone has to be happy. The greatest happiness of the greatest number can thus be attained only under conditions of the greatest possible individual freedom, hence Mill's advocacy, as we have seen, of the freedom of the individual, his defense of civil liberties, and his abhorrence of any form of regimentation and paternalism.

Second, Mill asserted that pleasures do differ in quality, and this difference affects their value. Instead of Bentham's quantitative hedonism, Mill thus posited a qualitative hedonism. Some pleasures are intrinsically superior to others.

Human beings have vast capacities for enjoying pleasures of many kinds. They have animal appetites, to be sure, but they also have higher faculties. And the pleasures derived from the exercise of these higher faculties are better than the purely sensuous pleasures. (This distinction was actually already present much earlier in philosophy. Epicurus, a Greek philosopher of the third and fourth centuries B.C., distinguished between the "higher pleasures," the rational and the aesthetic, and the "lower pleasures," eating, drinking, and generally sensual pleasures.) Persons who have experienced both of these kinds of pleasure know this to be so:

Few human creatures would consent to be changed into any of the lower animals, for a promise of the fullest allowance of a beast's pleasures; no intelligent human being would

It is quite compatible with the principle of utility to recognize the fact, that some kinds of pleasure are more desirable and more valuable than others. It would be absurd that while, in estimating all other things, quality is considered as well as quantity, the estimation of pleasures should be supposed to depend on quantity alone.

—John Stuart Mill, *Utilitarianism*

consent to be a fool, no instructed person would be an ignoramus, no person of feeling and conscience would be selfish and base, even though they should be persuaded that the fool, the dunce, or the rascal is better satisfied with his lot than they are with theirs.

And so Mill comes to the conclusion that he expressed in the following famous words:

> It is better to be a human being dissatisfied than a pig satisfied; better to be Socrates dissatisfied than a fool satisfied. And if the fool, or the pig, are of a different opinion, it is because they only know their own side of the question. The other party to the comparison knows both sides.

This issue is, of course, of tremendous practical consequence. In distributing tax money, for example, how we decide such questions will determine whether to subsidize opera houses and art galleries that cater to very refined tastes and that few people enjoy or use such monies to build sports arenas.

But aside from the obvious practical consequences entailed, the modification would seem to constitute an abandonment of pure hedonism, for if pleasures are now to be graded not for their quantity but for their quality, then pleasure is no longer the standard or criterion determining our choices. If pleasures, in other words, have to be judged in the light of some quality or qualities they have or have not, pleasure as such then ceases to be the standard of value, and this quality or these qualities become the new standard by which pleasure—and therefore human conduct—is to be judged.

It is strange that Mill does not appear to realize the difficulty he has placed himself in by introducing this modification, which in effect constitutes an abandonment of pleasure as the criterion of true happiness and therefore of human goodness.

This difficulty emerges again most clearly when Mill comes to deal with the question of what is the most "desirable" mode of conduct for human beings and argues that it is happiness, as utilitarianism teaches. But how can we prove that happiness is indeed the true and desirable end of human life and conduct? To this Mill replies (in what has become one of the most quoted passages in modern philosophical literature for the remarkable error it contains),

> The only proof capable of being given that an object is visible, is that people actually see it. The only proof that a sound is audible, is that people hear it: and so of the other sources of our experience. In like manner, I apprehend, the sole evidence it is possible to produce that anything is desirable, is that people do actually desire it.

Obviously, however, *desirable* and *visible* and *audible* do not run on all fours since *desirable* is not related to desired in the same way that visible is to seen. One involves a moral distinction that the other does not, for whereas *visible* means simply that something is *capable of being seen*, *desirable* implies that something is *worthy of being desired*, that it *ought* to be desired. This being so, it may be quite true that a thing's being seen proves that it is visible, but it does not follow that because a thing is desired it is for that reason desirable. Many people may desire heroin, but that does not prove that heroin is therefore *desirable*.

To establish that some pleasure is desirable (or more desirable than some other) involves therefore more than establishing the bare fact that many desire it, and if this is so, then pleasure as such ceases to be the standard of value, and something else takes its place. And this is the surprising consequence of Mill's modification of Bentham's version of hedonism.

Hedonism

Hedonism, the view that the end of human activity is or ought to be pleasure or happiness, is probably the most widespread ethical theory we have, and so it might perhaps be well to spend a little longer on it.

Concerning its ancient form—conveyed in the well-known saying "Eat, drink and be merry, lest tomorrow we die"—little need be said except perhaps that we may be around tomorrow to suffer the consequences, and so perhaps we had better eat, drink, and be merry in moderation.

Concerning the pursuit of pleasure, it has often been pointed out that "the best way to get pleasure is to forget pleasure," that pleasure or happiness is like a butterfly, which when pursued is always just beyond our grasp. But this objection is really somewhat beside the point, for the question is not how we can best get pleasure but rather whether pleasure is worth getting or pursuing.

Of course, in Bentham's view, as we have seen, we would seem to have no choice in this matter, for we are so endowed by nature that we cannot help but pursue pleasure. On the contrary, it is, in his view, the goal of all our striving.

In the view of many people, however, this would appear to be an astounding generalization to make about human motivation. As many critics have pointed out, it is one thing to say that a person gets pleasure from accomplishing the end of his action but quite another to say that the expectation of that pleasure is the reason for acting. For example, I frequently eat because I am hungry. I may get pleasure from the food, but that is not my reason for eating. Sometimes, however, I eat even though I am not hungry because I like the food that is offered and hope to get pleasure from eating it. But it is obviously wrong to confuse these two cases and claim that I always eat in order to get pleasure.

Similarly, I help my friend when he is ill and go to a lot of trouble to do so. When he finally gets well, I derive a great deal of pleasure. Now obviously my reason for helping him is to see that he gets well, not I. Were an egoist to suggest that I went to all this trouble only because of the pleasure I knew I would get from seeing my friend get well, we might reply that if I am the kind of person who gets pleasure from that sort of thing—from making other people happy—then that is what is meant by saying that some people are capable of impartial action or **altruism**.

To disprove psychological hedonism, all we need is to find one case of a true altruistic act. Are there such acts? We must first note that as psychological hedonism and altruism refer to motives, our finding of such an act and labeling it "altruistic" will be inferential. That is to say, we do not see, feel, smell, or touch motives; rather, we infer them from acts. Consider the case, for instance, of the happy, easygoing soldier who though in the prime of his life, financially well off, and with a generally bright future covers a hand grenade with his body to save his fellow soldiers. Such cases have happened more than once and are well recorded. The psychological hedonist cannot say that the soldier did it for any future pleasure, for not only will he not have any future pleasure, but he will not even have a future, and he was well aware of that. Nor can the psychological hedonist say that he did it to escape a bleak future or to end some great pain or sorrow since neither is true. It would thus seem we can find at least one class of acts that are both altruistic and clearly count against psychological hedonism. These acts could be roughly described as those done for another's good and to the exclusion of our own. If this is so, which seems obvious, then the psychological hedonist is refuted. On this issue of psychological hedonism, therefore, Mill rather than Bentham would seem to be closer to the truth.

Ethical hedonism, to turn to this doctrine, maintains two main theses: (1) that pleasure is always intrinsically good and (2) that it is the only thing that is intrinsically good. But if the first thesis is correct, what shall we say of the sadist who derives his pleasure from torturing others? We would normally regard such pleasure as bad, derived as it is from pain. So pleasure is not always good. And if the second thesis is correct, that pleasure is the only thing that is intrinsically good, what shall we say about such things as the development of our intellectual or artistic capacities? Are these not good in themselves? Many would claim that they indeed are. And of those ethical hedonists who, like Bentham, equate happiness with pleasure, might we not ask whether happiness does not ordinarily include more than just pleasure? And if it includes only pleasure, would we call a world in which we could produce it medically and did so, one in which happiness had finally been achieved?

Utilitarianism, to turn to it finally, instructs us that our goal is to seek the happiness of all. But, we might ask, first, does anyone know what happiness is? Doesn't the diversity of individual interests hint at the multiplicity of human goals? In addition, may not Bentham's critics have touched on an important point in suggesting that in trying to achieve the greatest happiness for the greatest number, we may succeed only in achieving the lowest denomination of happiness and ultimately a "pig philosophy"?

Second, we might note that in fulfilling what we feel to be our obligation, the general welfare is not always what is uppermost in our minds. At such times, what we are concerned about are such things as personal loyalty, the sanctity of promise keeping, and so forth—things that have little or nothing to do with promoting the general good.

Third, according to utilitarianism, we must take the total number of effects of our action into consideration before describing it as right. But the effects may be far reaching, and we may have to wait infinitely long before we can describe an act as right. The principle of utility, therefore, would seem to lose its utility, its practical value, in such circumstances.

Fourth, the theory would also seem to lead to various logical contradictions: an action X looks as if it will have the best consequences, so you do it; but tomorrow you discover its consequences are really very bad. Does this mean the act was right when you did it but wrong now?

Finally, can any teleological theory, such as utilitarianism—that is, any theory that evaluates the rightness and wrongness of an action by the consequences likely to result from it—be ultimately adequate? For suppose we could somehow succeed in making everyone happy except one innocent person, who would be tortured in hell. Would anyone be satisfied to say this is right? Presumably not.

GOODNESS AND HAPPINESS

We began our investigation of ethics by noting that one of its major concerns is to define the nature of the good life, the sort of life that is worth living. In each of the major treatments of this problem, we also noted that goodness (however differently each philosopher may have defined it) is regarded as somehow indispensable to the realization of such a life. But, curiously, we also noted that each philosopher seemed to have thought that happiness and goodness are somehow intimately connected, that it is not possible to achieve the one without the other. It is true, of course, that each major figure tended to define goodness differently: Aristotle defined it in the sense of becoming as knowledgeable and as wise as possible, Kant defined it in the sense of becoming worthy in God's eyes, and Bentham and Mill defined it in terms of utility for as many as possible. What was common to each, however, was the view that happiness somehow involves the notion of approval, of being able to think well of oneself—of being able to applaud oneself.

In stressing this aspect of happiness, these philosophers anticipated many of the discoveries and insights that have been achieved only in our own age and time. For practically all modern psychologists and psychotherapists have come to believe that a satisfying life is possible only in proportion to the esteem (to use a contemporary term) one feels for oneself. They regard this as a basic human need. Some call this sense of esteem for oneself self-love, others call it self-appreciation, and still others call it self-celebration. All, however, are agreed that without it, the prospect of one's personality suffering a breakdown (let alone failing to achieve happiness) is very great.

They have come to believe, further, that many, if not all, our psychological problems, from the slightest neuroses to the deepest psychoses, are symptomatic of the frustration of this fundamental human need for a sense of personal worth. The depth and duration of the symptomatic problems engendered (whether phobias, guilt complexes, or feelings of paranoia) are indicative of the depth and duration of the deprivation of this sense of self-esteem.

These psychologists and psychotherapists also seem to agree that the main and fundamental source of this self-appreciation is the love of others. But this love, so essential to our sense of well-being, they say, is not something that can be banked and drawn on when needed. To maintain a state of well-being and be happy, we need a steady flow of this reassurance and love from others. Without it we come to feel empty, bankrupt, and worthless.[4]

They have shown that those who fail to find this flow of love and approval from others lapse into one of several well-defined and increasingly better understood mental states. The most common is depression—a feeling of morbid dejection and sadness, ranging from mild discouragement to despair. Depression, they say, is the organism's defense against the pain of rejection; it is an idling of the human organism that prevents the violent pain from tearing it completely apart. It is a substitute form of suffering, more tolerable than the one it masks.

Another response to our sense of worthlessness is anger and violence. Feeling unsuccessful as persons, we vent our frustrations on others, making them pay for our sense of inadequacy and failure.

A third response, the most common of all, is physical illness. Here the psychological pain of failure is translated into physical symptoms that seem easier to bear. Many sicknesses formerly regarded as organic are really psychosomatic in origin, brought on by the severe judgments we pass on our secret selves.

Finally, a fourth common response to the failure to find love and a sense of worth in the public world is to escape to our own private world, a world of our own making, in which we no longer need to cope with our personal failure, having come to deny its very existence. This is a high price to pay for this liberation from failure, for unlike the retreat into fantasy by children when faced with disappointment, this escape is long lasting, painful, and often permanent. Yet in desperation, many choose it.

These alternatives to the admission of failure, although camouflaging and alleviating the original agony, do not do away with the pain we suffer. Still continuing to hurt, we try to kill the pain by resorting to such widely used but debilitating painkillers as food, alcohol, and drugs. All are desperate attempts to dull the pain of a seemingly worthless existence, and all are addictive and destructive.

The saddest aspect of this final attempt to solve our sense of failure as persons is that, if we succeed and remove the pain, we no longer feel the need to try to find our worth as persons, and we withdraw from life, preferring our addiction to everything and everyone else.

Well, what about the baby? Did the physician do right or wrong in stopping feeding orders? As we have seen, the answer one is likely to give to this question will depend on whether one takes a teleological or a deontological attitude toward ethical questions.

If you are a teleologist, for whom the results of an action determine its rightness, you would tend to side with the physician; if you are a deontologist, you would no doubt see the physician's action as wrong and condemn it.

Is there, then, no way in which these three different attitudes and solutions can be reconciled? Are there no further arguments to offer? There does not seem to be an easy or obvious way in which this can be done and no revolutionary arguments appear left to offer. Yet there is a consideration, already alluded to, that at least to this writer seems to offer hope of such a reconciliation.

Strangely enough, it consists in undertaking a form of argument made use of by Kant for which he has been criticized. Let us recall what Kant said in reply to the question, "Why ought I to be moral?" Rather than giving a typically deontological answer, Kant gives a teleological one. For example, he argues that it would be wrong to make a lying promise because if everyone made promises without intending to fulfill them, promises would not be believed and there would be no point in making them. (This argument was criticized by Bertrand Russell, who said that Kant argued that it was wrong to borrow money, for if we all did so, there would be no money left to borrow.) If, on the other hand, Kant goes on to argue, I find myself in prosperity, see all the wretchedness and poverty around me, but say, "What concern is it of mine?" it would be immoral to act on that thought or even harbor it, for some day I might find myself in distress and wish I had not been so rash. On the same grounds it would be wrong, Kant says, for a man out of laziness to fail to develop talents he possesses, for such talents "serve him, and have been given him, for all sorts of possible purposes."

It is obvious what seems to have gone wrong here and why a Kantian must be embarrassed by these examples. For Kant's theory demands, of course, a categorical reason as to why we should be moral, but the reasons given are hypothetical and prudential— reasons in keeping with a teleological position and not a deontological one.

But while to hold this position might seem logically embarrassing, nevertheless there is something very persuasive and convincing about it. Another example that comes to mind may make it clearer what this is. Several years ago, Dr. Robert R. Wilson, director of the large Fermi Accelerator Laboratory, was repeatedly pressed before a Senate hearing to come up with some national security application of the research being conducted there. To the dismay of the supporters of the laboratory, Wilson continued to insist that it had none. Finally, Wilson told the senators, "The Accelerator Laboratory only has to do with the respect with which we regard one another. It has nothing to do with defending our country except to help make it worth defending." Similarly, perhaps, here. Perhaps the decision should have been to keep the baby alive, regardless of cost or its own prospects, not so much for its sake as for our own.

SUMMARY

1. Ethics is the study of human conduct. It asks itself questions such as, What sort of life is most worth living? How should one best conduct it? What in it should matter most?

2. The investigation of these questions has tended to take three distinct directions: (1) it has occupied itself with the strictly practical problems of how the most worthwhile life can best be achieved (morality proper), (2) it has gone on to consider the possible theoretical reasons for choosing various lines of conduct (ethics proper), and (3) it has become occupied with an inquiry into the nature and meaning of those theories (*metaethics*).

3. Although in its typical form an ethical treatise consists of moralizing with the help of an ethical theory, defended on methodological or metaethical grounds, it is especially characteristic of ancient writers to be concerned with the question of what life is best to live (morality proper), of more recent writers to be concerned with the question how such choices can best be justified (ethics proper), and of today's writers to be occupied with the question of the meaning and validity of the judgments proposed (metaethics).

4. Aristotle believed that the best thing to strive for in life was happiness; but happiness, he believed, cannot be achieved without realizing our highest capacities and potentialities, and in the case of humans this is reason. The happy life, therefore, according to Aristotle, is one devoted to the exercise, development, and perfection of reason, one guided by its dictates.

5. Kant argued that the basic question of ethics is not how to achieve happiness but rather how we might become worthy of it. To become so worthy, he argued, the rule to follow is not the golden mean (practicing moderation in all things), as Aristotle had suggested, but rather the golden rule—doing unto others as we would have them do unto us. Kant therefore offered as his fundamental principle of morality the *categorical imperative* or the *principle of universality*: So act that the maxim of your action may be willed as a universal law. That alone is right which unconditionally permits everyone else to do it, one in which no exceptions are made for oneself. In another formulation, designed to bring out the notion that respect for each other as persons is central to ethical conduct, Kant stated his basic principle as follows: "Act so that you treat humanity, whether in your own person or in that of another, always as an end and never as a means only."

6. Utilitarianism, rejecting both personal happiness and the dictates of duty as the criterion of morality, argued that the only fit and proper standard is the principle of the greatest happiness of the greatest number, happiness being generally equated with pleasure. If an action, this principle of utility states, produces the greatest balance of pleasure (considered quantitatively by Bentham but qualitatively by Mill) over pain for the greatest number of people concerned, then it is right and ought to be done; otherwise, it is wrong and should be avoided.

7. Although utilitarians sought to arrive at a principle that would enable them to determine with scientific objectivity and accuracy whether an act is morally justifiable, the group of contemporary writers on ethics, known as logical positivists, by applying their principle of verification cast doubt on the validity and objective reality of the subject as a whole with its questionable notions of right and wrong, moral and immoral, and so forth. They concluded that these terms are cognitively meaningless and serve only to express our feelings and emotions or arouse similar feelings and emotions in others.

8. The problems remain and refuse to go away. And they remain because, of course, we remain, and the goals we set ourselves continue to elude us. We continue to believe with Aristotle that the goal is indeed happiness; we continue to believe both with him and many of the other great philosophers (as well as contemporary psychologists and psychotherapists) that it is somehow bound up with goodness. How and why are questions that still continue to intrigue and challenge us.

KEY TERMS

altruism	moral virtues
categorical imperative	principle of universality
deontological theory	principle of utility
ethical hedonism	prudential imperatives
ethics	reason
golden mean	skepticism
good will	technical imperatives
hedonism	teleological theory
intellectual virtues	verification principle
logical positivism	utilitarianism
metaethics	

REVIEW QUESTIONS

1. What are the three directions ethical investigation has taken in philosophy's history? What questions characterize each type of investigation? What historical period is associated with each type?

2. What distinction did Aristotle make between ends that are intrinsically good and ends that are instrumentally good?

3. What did Aristotle conclude is necessary for a human being to attain happiness?

4. What is the doctrine of the golden mean?

5. What is the difference between a hypothetical moral imperative and a categorical moral imperative?

6. Compare the place of reason in the ethical systems of Aristotle and Kant.

7. Describe Bentham's psychological hedonism and his ethical hedonism. How did Mill modify them?

8. What did Aristotle, Kant, and the utilitarians each see as the proper criterion of morality?

9. Distinguish between deontological and teleological approaches to ethics. Give examples of philosophers to exemplify each approach.

■ Reading

Nicomachean Ethics

ARISTOTLE

Excerpted from Aristotle, *Nicomachean Ethics*, translated by Terence Irwin (Indianapolis: Hackett Publishing Co., 1985).

1. The Highest Good: Happiness
    1.1 The Highest Good Is Supreme in the Hierarchy of Goods
    Goods correspond to ends

Every craft and every investigation, and likewise every action and decision, seems to aim at some good; hence the good has been well described as that at which everything aims.

However, there is an apparent difference among the ends aimed at. For the end is sometimes an activity, sometimes a product beyond the activity; and when there is an end beyond the action, the product is by nature better than the activity.

THE HIERARCHY OF GOOD CORRESPONDS TO THE HIERARCHY OF ENDS

Since there are many actions, crafts and sciences, the ends turn out to be many as well; for health is the end of medicine, a boat of boatbuilding, victory of generalship, and wealth of household management.

But whenever any of these sciences are subordinate to some one capacity—as e.g. bridlemaking and every other science producing equipment for horses are subordinate to horsemanship, while this and every action in warfare are in turn subordinate to generalship, and in the same way other sciences are subordinate to further ones—in each of these the end of the ruling science is more choiceworthy than all the ends subordinate to it, since it is the end for which those ends are also pursued. And here it does not matter whether the ends of the actions are the activities themselves, or some product beyond them, as in the sciences we have mentioned.

The highest good

Suppose, then, that (a) there is some end of the things we pursue in our actions which we wish for because of itself and because of which we wish for the other things; and (b) we do not choose everything because of something else, since (c) if we do, it will go on without limit, making desire empty and futile; then clearly (d) this end will be the good, i.e. the best good.

1.2 The Ruling Science Studying the Highest Good Is Political Science

The importance of finding the science of the highest good

Then surely knowledge of this good is also of great importance for the conduct of our lives, and if, like archers, we have a target to aim at, we are more likely to hit the right mark. If so, we should try to grasp, in outline at any rate, what the good is, and which science or capacity is concerned with it.

The relevant science is political science

It seems to concern the most controlling science, the one that, more than any other, is the ruling science. And political science apparently has this character.

(1) For it is the one that prescribes which of the sciences ought to be studied in cities, and which ones each class in the city should learn, and how far.

(2) Again, we see that even the most honored capacities, e.g. generalship, household management and rhetoric, are subordinate to it.

(3) Further, it uses the other sciences concerned with action, and moreover legislates what must be done and what avoided. Hence its end will include the ends of the other sciences, and so will be the human good.

[This is properly called political science;] for though admittedly the good is the same for a city as for an individual, still the good of the city is apparently a greater and more complete good to acquire and preserve. For while it is satisfactory to acquire and preserve the good even for an individual, it is finer and more divine to acquire and preserve it for a people and for cities. And so, since our investigation aims at these [goods, for an individual and for a city], it is a sort of political science.

1.3 The Method of Political Inquiry

The demand for exactness must be limited by the nature of ethics

Our discussion will be adequate if its degree of clarity fits the subject-matter; for we should not seek the same degree of exactness in all sorts of arguments alike, any more than in the products of different crafts.

Moreover, what is fine and what is just, the topics of inquiry in political science, differ and vary so much that they seem to rest on convention only, not on nature. Goods, however, also vary in the same sort of way, since they cause harm to many people; for it has happened that some people have been destroyed because of their wealth, others because of their bravery.

The proper aim of ethical theory

Since these, then, are the sorts of things we argue from and about, it will be satisfactory if we can indicate the truth roughly and in outline; since [that is to say] we argue from and about what holds good usually [but not universally], it will be satisfactory if we can draw conclusions of the same sort.

How to judge an ethical theory

Each of our claims, then, ought to be accepted in the same way [as claiming to hold good usually], since the educated person seeks exactness in each area to the extent that the nature of the subject allows; for apparently it is just as mistaken to demand demonstrations from a rhetorician as to accept [merely] persuasive arguments from a mathematician.

Further, each person judges well what he knows, and is a good judge about that; hence the good judge in a particular area is the person educated in that area, and the unconditionally good judge is the person educated in every area.

Qualifications of the student of ethics

This is why a youth is not a suitable student of political science; for he lacks experience of the actions in life which political science argues from and about.

Moreover, since he tends to be guided by his feelings, his study will be futile and useless; for its end is action, not knowledge. And here it does not matter whether he is young in years or immature in character, since the deficiency does not depend on age, but results from being guided in his life and in each of his pursuits by his feelings; for an immature person, like an incontinent person, gets no benefit from his knowledge.

If, however, we are guided by reason in forming our desires and in acting, then this knowledge will be of great benefit. These are the preliminary points about the student, about the way our claims are to be accepted, and about what we intend to do.

1.4 Common Beliefs About the Highest Good Are Inadequate

1.41 Most people identify the good with happiness, but disagree about the nature of happiness

Let us, then, begin again. Since every sort of knowledge and decision pursues some good, what is that good which we say is the aim of political science? What [in other words] is the highest of all the goods pursued in action?

As far as its name goes, most people virtually agree [about what the good is], since both the many and the cultivated call it happiness, and suppose that living well and doing well are the same as being happy. But they disagree about what happiness is, and the many do not give the same answer as the wise.

For the many think it is something obvious and evident, e.g. pleasure, wealth or honor, some thinking one thing, others another; and indeed the same person keeps changing his mind, since in sickness he thinks it is health, in poverty wealth. And when they are conscious of their own ignorance, they admire anyone who speaks of something grand and beyond them.

[Among the wise,] however, some used to think that besides these many goods there is some other good that is something in itself, and also causes all these goods to be goods.

1.51 Characteristics of the good

(1) The good is the end of action

But let us return once again to the good we are looking for, and consider just what it could be, since it is apparently one thing in one action or craft, and another thing in another; for it is one thing in medicine, another in generalship, and so on for the rest.

What, then, is the good in each of these cases? Surely it is that for the sake of which the other things are done; and in medicine this is health, in generalship victory, in housebuilding a house, in another case something else, but in every action and decision it is the end, since it is for the sake of the end that everyone does the other things.

And so, if there is some end of everything that is pursued in action, this will be the good pursued in action; and if there are more ends than one, these will be the goods pursued in action.

Our argument has progressed, then, to the same conclusion [as before, that the highest end is the good]; but we must try to clarify this still more.

(2) The good is complete

Though apparently there are many ends, we choose some of them, e.g. wealth, flutes and, in general, instruments, because of something else; hence it is clear that not all ends are complete. But the best good is apparently something complete. Hence, if only one end is complete, this will be what we are looking for; and if more than one are complete, the most complete of these will be what we are looking for.

CRITERIA FOR COMPLETENESS

An end pursued in itself, we say, is more complete than an end pursued because of something else; and an end that is never choiceworthy because of something else is more complete than ends that are choiceworthy both in themselves and because of this end; and hence an end that is always [choiceworthy, and also] choiceworthy in itself, never because of something else, is unconditionally complete.

(3) Happiness meets the criteria for completeness, but other goods do not

Now happiness more than anything else seems unconditionally complete, since we always [choose it, and also] choose it because of itself, never because of something else.

Honor, pleasure, understanding and every virtue we certainly choose because of themselves, since we would choose each of them even if it had no further result, but we also choose them for the sake of happiness, supposing that through them we shall be happy. Happiness, by contrast, no one ever chooses for their sake, or for the sake of anything else at all.

(4) The good is self-sufficient; so is happiness

The same conclusion [that happiness is complete] also appears to follow from self-sufficiency, since the complete good seems to be self-sufficient.

Now what we count as self-sufficient is not what suffices for a solitary person by himself, living an isolated life, but what suffices also for parents, children, wife and in general for friends and fellow-citizens, since a human being is a naturally political [animal]. Here, however, we must impose some limit; for if we extend the good to parents' parents and children's children and to friends of friends, we shall go on without limit; but we must examine this another time.

Anyhow, we regard something as self-sufficient when all by itself it makes a life choiceworthy and lacking nothing; and that is what we think happiness does.

(5) The good is most choiceworthy; so is happiness

Moreover, [the complete good is most choiceworthy, and] we think happiness is most choiceworthy of all goods, since it is not counted as one good among many. If it were counted as one among many, then, clearly, we think that the addition of the smallest of goods would make it more choiceworthy; for [the smallest good] that is added becomes an extra quantity of goods [so creating a good larger than the original good], and the larger of two goods is always more choiceworthy. [But we do not think any addition can make happiness more choiceworthy; hence it is most choiceworthy.]

Happiness, then, is apparently something complete and self-sufficient, since it is the end of the things pursued in action.

1.52 A clearer account of the good: the human soul's activity expressing virtue

But presumably the remark that the best good is happiness is apparently something [generally] agreed, and what we miss is a clearer statement of what the best good is.

(1) If something has a function, its good depends on its function

Well, perhaps we shall find the best good if we first find the function of a human being. For just as the good, i.e. [doing] well, for a flautist, a sculptor, and every craftsman, and, in general, for whatever has a function and [characteristic] action, seems to depend on its function, the same seems to be true for a human being, if a human being has some function.

(2) What sorts of things have functions?

Then do the carpenter and the leatherworker have their functions and actions, while a human being has none, and is by nature idle, without any function? Or, just as eye, hand, foot and, in general, every [bodily] part apparently has its functions, may we likewise ascribe to a human being some function besides all of theirs?

(3) The human function

What, then, could this be? For living is apparently shared with plants, but what we are looking for is the special function of a human being; hence we should set aside the life of nutrition and growth. The life next in order is some sort of life of sense-perception; but this too is apparently shared, with horse, ox and every animal. The remaining possibility, then, is some sort of life of action of the [part of the soul] that has reason.

Clarification of "has reason" and "life"

Now this [part has two parts, which have reason in different ways], one as obeying the reason [in the other part], the other as itself having reason and thinking. [We intend both.] Moreover, life is also spoken of in two ways [as capacity and as activity], and we must take [a human being's special function to be] life as activity, since this seems to be called life to a fuller extent.

(4) The human good is activity expressing virtue

(a) We have found, then, that the human function is the soul's activity that expresses reason [as itself having reason] or requires reason [as obeying reason]. (b) Now the function of F, e.g. of a harpist, is the same in kind, so we say, as the function of an excellent F, e.g. an excellent harpist. (c) The same is true unconditionally in every case, when we add to the function the superior achievement that expresses the virtue; for a harpist's function, e.g. is to play the harp, and a good harpist's is to do it well. (d) Now we take the human function to be a certain kind of life, and take this life to be the soul's activity and actions that express reason. (e) [Hence by (c) and (d)] the excellent man's function is to do this finely and well. (f) Each function is completed well when its completion expresses the proper virtue.

(g) Therefore [by (d), (e) and (f)] the human good turns out to be the soul's activity that expresses virtue.

(5) The good must also be complete

And if there are more virtues than one, the good will express the best and most complete virtue. Moreover, it will be in a complete life. For one swallow does not make a spring, nor does one day; nor, similarly, does one day or a short time make us blessed and happy.

1.91 An account of happiness requires an account of virtue

Since happiness is an activity of the soul expressing complete virtue, we must examine virtue; for that will perhaps also be a way to study happiness better.

Moreover, the true politician seems to have spent more effort on virtue than on anything else, since he wants to make the citizens good and law-abiding. We find an example of this in the Spartan and Cretan legislators and in any others with their concerns. Since, then, the examination of virtue is proper for political science, the inquiry clearly suits our original decision [to pursue political science].

1.92 A discussion of virtue requires a discussion of the soul

It is clear that the virtue we must examine is human virtue, since we are also seeking the human good and human happiness. And by human virtue we mean virtue of the soul, not of the body, since we also say that happiness is an activity of the soul. If this is so, then it is clear that the politician must acquire some knowledge about the soul, just as someone setting out to heal the eyes must acquire knowledge about the whole body as well. This is all the more true to the extent that political science is better and more honorable than medicine—and even among doctors the cultivated ones devote a lot of effort to acquiring knowledge about the body. Hence the politician as well [as the student of nature] must study the soul.

But he must study it for the purpose [of inquiring into virtue], as far as suffices for what he seeks; for a more exact treatment would presumably take more effort than his purpose requires. [We] have discussed the soul sufficiently [for our purposes] in [our] popular works as well [as our less popular], and we should use this discussion.

1.93 The rational and nonrational parts of the soul

We have said, e.g., that one [part] of the soul is nonrational, while one has reason. Are these distinguished as parts of a body as everything divisible into parts are? Or are they two only in account, and inseparable by nature, as the convex and the concave are in a surface? It does not matter for present purposes.

The nonrational part: (a) One part of it is unresponsive to reason

Consider the nonrational [part]. One [part] of it, i.e. the cause of nutrition and growth, is seemingly plantlike and shared [with other living things]: for we can ascribe this capacity of the soul to everything that is nourished, including embryos, and the same one to complete living things, since this is more reasonable than to ascribe another capacity to them.

Hence the virtue of this capacity is apparently shared, not [specifically] human. For this part and capacity more than others seem to be active in sleep, and here the good and the bad person are least distinct, which is why happy people are said to be no better off than miserable people for half their lives.

And this lack of distinction is not surprising, since sleep is inactivity of the soul in so far as it is called excellent or base, unless to some small extent some movements penetrate [to our awareness], and in this way the decent person comes to have better images [in dreams] than just any random person has. Enough about this, however, and let us leave aside the nutritive part, since by nature it has no share in human virtue.

(b) Another part is also nonrational

Another nature in the soul would also seem to be nonrational, though in a way it shares in reason.

[Clearly it is nonrational.] For in the continent and the incontinent person we praise their reason, i.e. the [part] of the soul that has reason, because it exhorts them correctly and towards what is best; but they evidently also have in them some other [part] that is by nature something besides reason, conflicting and struggling with reason.

For just as paralysed parts of a body, when we decide to move them to the right, do the contrary and move off to the left, the same is true of the soul; for incontinent people have impulses in contrary directions. In bodies, admittedly, we see the part go astray, whereas we do not see it in the soul; nonetheless, presumably, we should suppose that the soul also has a [part] besides reason, contrary to and countering reason. The [precise] way it is different does not matter.

But it is responsive to reason

However, this [part] as well [as the rational part] appears, as we said, to share in reason. At any rate, in the continent person it obeys reason; and in the temperate and the brave person it presumably listens still better to reason, since there it agrees with reason in everything.

Hence it differs both from the wholly unresponsive part . . .

The nonrational [part], then, as well [as the whole soul] apparently has two parts. For while the plant-like [part] shares in reason not at all, the [part] with appetites and in general desires shares in reason in a way, in so far as it both listens to reason and obeys it.

It listens in the way in which we are said to "listen to reason" from father or friends, not in the way in which we ["give the reason"] in mathematics.

The nonrational part also [obeys and] is persuaded in some way by reason, as is shown by chastening, and by every sort of reproof and exhortation.

And from the wholly rational part

If we ought to say, then, that this [part] also has reason, then the [part] that has reason, as well [as the nonrational part] will have two parts, one that has reason to the full extent by having it within itself, and another [that has it] by listening to reason as to a father.

1.94 The division of the virtues corresponds to the parts of the soul

The distinction between virtues also reflects this difference. For some virtues are called virtues of thought, others virtues of character; wisdom, comprehension and intelligence are called virtues of thought, generosity and temperance virtues of character.

For when we speak of someone's character we do not say that he is wise or has good comprehension, but that he is gentle or temperate. [Hence these are the virtues of character.] And yet, we also praise the wise person for his state, and the states that are praiseworthy are the ones we call virtues. [Hence wisdom is also a virtue.]

2. Virtues of Character in General

2.1 How a Virtue of Character Is Acquired

Virtue, then, is of two sorts, virtue of thought and virtue of character. Virtue of thought arises and grows mostly from teaching, and hence needs experience and time. Virtue of character [i.e. of ethos] results from habit [ethos]; hence its name "ethical," slightly varied from "ethos."

Virtue comes about, not by a process of nature, but by habituation

Hence it is also clear that none of the virtues of character arises in us naturally.

(1) What is natural cannot be changed by habituation

For if something is by nature [in one condition], habituation cannot bring it into another condition. A stone, e.g., by nature moves downwards, and habituation could not make it move upwards, not even if you threw it up ten thousand times to habituate it; nor could habituation make fire move downwards, or bring anything that is by nature in one condition into another condition.

Thus the virtues arise in us neither by nature nor against nature, but we are by nature able to acquire them, and reach our complete perfection through habit.

(2) Natural capacities are not acquired by habituation

Further, if something arises in us by nature, we first have the capacity for it, and later display the activity. This is clear in the case of the senses; for we did not acquire them by frequent seeing or hearing, but already had them when we exercised them, and did not get them by exercising them.

Virtues, by contrast, we acquire, just as we acquire crafts, by having previously activated them. For we learn a craft by producing the same product that we must produce when we have learned it, becoming builders, e.g., by building and harpists by playing the harp; so also, then, we become just by doing just actions, temperate by doing temperate actions, brave by doing brave actions.

(3) Legislators concentrate on habituation

What goes on in cities is evidence for this also. For the legislator makes the citizens good by habituating them, and this is the wish of every legislator; if he fails to do it well he misses his goal. [The right] habituation is what makes the difference between a good political system and a bad one.

(4) Virtue and vice are formed by good and bad actions

Further, just as in the case of a craft, the sources and means that develop each virtue also ruin it. For playing the harp makes both good and bad harpists, and it is analogous in the case of builders and all the rest; for building well makes good builders, building badly, bad ones. If it were not so, no teacher would be needed, but everyone would be born a good or a bad craftsman.

It is the same, then, with the virtues. For actions in dealing with [other] human beings make some people just, some unjust; actions in terrifying situations and the acquired habit of fear or confidence make some brave and others cowardly. The same is true of situations involving appetites and anger; for one or another sort of conduct in these situations makes some people temperate and gentle, others intemperate and irascible.

Conclusion: The importance of habituation

To sum up, then, in a single account: A state [of character] arises from [the repetition of] similar activities. Hence we must display the right activities, since differences in these imply corresponding differences in the states. It is not unimportant, then, to acquire one sort of habit or another, right from our youth; rather, it is very important, indeed all-important.

2.23 Definition of virtue

Virtue, then, is (a) a state that decides, (b) [consisting] in a mean, (c) the mean relative to us, (d) which is defined by reference to reason, (e) i.e., to the reason by reference to which the intelligent person would define it. It is a mean between two vices, one of excess and one of deficiency.

It is a mean for this reason also: Some vices miss what is right because they are deficient, others because they are excessive, in feelings or in actions, while virtue finds and chooses what is intermediate.

Hence, as far as its substance and the account stating its essence are concerned, virtue is a mean; but as far as the best [condition] and the good [result] are concerned, it is an extremity.

The definition must not be misapplied to cases in which there is no mean

But not every action or feeling admits of the mean. For the names of some automatically include baseness, e.g. spite, shamelessness, envy [among feelings], and adultery, theft, murder, among actions. All of these and similar things are called by these names because they themselves, not their excesses or deficiencies, are base.

Hence in doing these things we can never be correct, but must invariably be in error. We cannot do them well or not well—e.g. by committing adultery with the right woman at the right time in the right way; on the contrary, it is true unconditionally that to do any of them is to be in error.

[To think these admit of a mean], therefore, is like thinking that unjust or cowardly or intemperate action also admits of a mean, an excess and a deficiency. For then there would be a mean of excess, a mean of deficiency, an excess of excess and a deficiency of deficiency. Rather, just as there is no excess or deficiency of temperance or of bravery, since the intermediate is a sort of extreme [in achieving the good], so also there is no mean of these [vicious actions] either, but whatever way anyone does them, he is in error. For in general there is no mean of excess or of deficiency, and no excess or deficiency of a mean.

2.3 The Definition of Virtue as a Mean Applies to the Individual Virtues

However, we must not only state this general account but also apply it to the particular cases. For among accounts concerning actions, though the general ones are common to more cases, the specific ones are truer, since actions are about particular cases, and our account must accord with these.

2.31 Classification of virtues of character

Virtues concerned with feelings

(1) First, in feelings of fear and confidence the mean is bravery. The excessively fearless person is nameless (and in fact many cases are nameless), while the one who is excessively confident is rash; the one who is excessively afraid and deficient in confidence is cowardly.

(2) In pleasures and pains, though not in all types, and in pains less than in pleasures, the mean is temperance and the excess intemperance. People deficient in pleasure are not often found, which is why they also lack even a name; let us call them insensible.

Virtues concerned with external goods

(3) In giving and taking money the mean is generosity, the excess wastefulness and the deficiency ungenerosity. Here the vicious people have contrary excesses and defects; for the wasteful person spends to excess and is deficient in taking, whereas the ungenerous person takes to excess and is deficient in spending. At the moment we are speaking in outline and summary, and that suffices; later we shall define these things more exactly.

(4) In questions of money there are also other conditions. Another mean is magnificence; for the magnificent person differs from the generous by being concerned with large matters, while the generous person is concerned with small. The excess is ostentation and vulgarity, and the deficiency niggardliness, and these differ from the vices related to generosity in ways we shall describe later.

(5) In honor and dishonor the mean is magnanimity, the excess something called a sort of vanity, and the deficiency pusillanimity.

(6) And just as we said that generosity differs from magnificence in its concern with small matters, similarly there is a virtue concerned with small honors, differing in the same way from magnanimity, which is concerned with great honors. For honor can be desired either in the right way or more or less than is right. If someone desires it to excess, he is called an honor-lover, and if his desire is deficient he is called indifferent to honor, but if he is intermediate he has no name. The corresponding conditions have no name either, except the condition of the honor-lover, which is called honor-loving.

This is why people at the extremes claim the intermediate area. Indeed, we also sometimes call the intermediate person an honor-lover, and sometimes call him indifferent to honor; and sometimes we praise the honor-lover, sometimes the person indifferent to honor.

Virtues concerned with social life

(7) Anger also admits of an excess, deficiency and mean. These are all practically nameless; but since we call the intermediate person mild, let us call the mean mildness. Among the extreme people let the excessive person be irascible, and the vice be irascibility, and let the deficient person be a sort of inirascible person, and the deficiency be inirascibility.

6.13 The Virtuous Person Has Correct Decision and Therefore Must Have the Virtue of Practical Thought

. . . Now the origin of an action—the source of the movement, not the action's goal—is decision, and the origin of decision is desire together with reason that aims at some goal. Hence decision requires understanding and thought, and also a state of character, since doing well or badly in action requires both thought and character.

Thought by itself, however, moves nothing; what moves us is thought aiming at some goal and concerned with action. For this is the sort of thought that also originates productive thinking; for every producer in his production aims at some [further] goal, and the unconditional goal is not the product, which is only the [conditional] goal of some [production], and aims at some [further] goal. [An unconditional goal is] what we achieve in action, since doing well in action is the goal.

Now desire is for the goal. Hence decision is either understanding combined with desire or desire combined with thought; and what originates movement in this way is a human being.

13.3 Theoretical Study Is the Supreme Element of Happiness

If happiness, then, is activity expressing virtue, it is reasonable for it to express the supreme virtue, which will be the virtue of the best thing.

The best is understanding, or whatever else seems to be the natural ruler and leader, and to understand what is fine and divine, by being itself either divine or the most divine element in us.

Hence complete happiness will be its activity expressing its proper virtue; and we have said that this activity is the activity of study. This seems to agree with what has been said before, and also with the truth.

13.31 The activity of theoretical study is best

For this activity is supreme, since understanding is the supreme element in us, and the objects of understanding are the supreme objects of knowledge.

13.32 It is most continuous

Besides, it is the most continuous activity, since we are more capable of continuous study than of any continuous action.

13.33 It is pleasantest

We think pleasure must be mixed into happiness; and it is agreed that the activity expressing wisdom is the pleasantest of the activities expressing virtue. At any rate, philosophy seems to have remarkably pure and firm pleasures; and it is reasonable for those who have knowledge to spend their lives more pleasantly than those who seek it.

3.34 It is most self-sufficient

Moreover, the self-sufficiency we spoke of will be found in study above all. For admittedly the wise person, the just person and the other virtuous people all need the good things necessary for life. Still, when these are adequately supplied, the just person needs other people as partners and recipients of his just actions; and the same is true of the temperate person and the brave person and each of the others.

But the wise person is able, and more able the wiser he is, to study even by himself; and though he presumably does it better with colleagues, even so he is more self-sufficient than any other [virtuous person].

3.35 It aims at no end beyond itself

Besides, study seems to be liked because of itself alone, since it has no result beyond having studied. But from the virtues concerned with action we try to a greater or lesser extent to gain something beyond the action itself.

13.36 It involves leisure

Happiness seems to be found in leisure, since we accept trouble so that we can be at leisure, and fight wars so that we can be at peace. Now the virtues concerned with action have their activities in politics or war, and actions here seem to require trouble.

This seems completely true for actions in war, since no one chooses to fight a war, and no one continues it, for the sake of fighting a war; for someone would have to be a complete murderer if he made his friends his enemies so that there could be battles and killings.

But the actions of the politician require trouble also. Beyond political activities themselves these actions seek positions of power and honors; or at least they seek happiness for the politician himself and for his fellow-citizens, which is something different from political science itself, and clearly is sought on the assumption that it is different.

Hence among actions expressing the virtues those in politics and war are preeminently fine and great; but they require trouble, aim at some [further] end, and are choiceworthy for something other than themselves.

But the activity of understanding, it seems, is superior in excellence because it is the activity of study; aims at no end beyond itself; has its own proper pleasure, which increases the activity; and is self-sufficient, leisured and unwearied, as far [as these are possible] for a human being. And whatever else is ascribed to the blessedly happy person is evidently found in connection with this activity.

Hence a human being's complete happiness will be this activity, if it receives a complete span of life, since nothing incomplete is proper to happiness.

13.37 It is a god-like life

Such a life would be superior to the human level. For someone will live it not in so far as he is a human being, but in so far as he has some divine element in him. And the activity of this divine element is as much superior to the activity expressing the rest of virtue as this element is superior to the compound. Hence if understanding is something divine in comparison with a human being, so also will the life that expresses understanding be divine in comparison with human life.

We ought not to follow the proverb-writers, and "think human, since you are human," or "think mortal, since you are mortal." Rather, as far as we can, we ought to be pro-immortal, and go to all lengths to live a life that expresses our supreme element; for however much this element may lack in bulk, by much more it surpasses everything in power and value.

[A variant rendering of this passage:

We must not, as people advise, think humanly, being human, nor as mortals, being mortal, but as far as may be, we must put on the life of the Immortals and do all that we can to live according to what is best in us.]

13.38 It realizes the Supreme element in human nature

Moreover, each person seems to be his understanding, if he is his controlling and better element; it would be absurd, then, if he were to choose not his own life, but something else's. And what we have said previously will also apply now. For what is proper to each thing's nature is supremely best and pleasantest for it; and hence for a human being the life expressing understanding will be supremely best and pleasantest, if understanding above all is the human being. This life, then, will also be happiest.

[A variant rendering of this passage:

That which is proper to each thing is by nature best and most pleasant for each thing; for man, therefore, the life according to reason is best and pleasantest, since reason more than anything else is man. This life therefore is also the happiest.]

■ Questions for Discussion

1. Aristotle says that youths are not suitable students of the human good because they tend to be guided by their feelings and because they lack experience. Do you agree?

2. Are there benefits such a study might have in spite of these objections?

3. Do you think the young of Aristotle's era and culture differed significantly in these respects from American youth today?

NOTES

1. Copyright, 1972, *Los Angeles Times*. Reprinted by permission.

2. *The Ethics of Aristotle*, trans. J. A. K. Thomson (London: Allen and Unwin, 1953). Reproduced by permission.

3. Aristotle's *Rhetoric*, trans. W. Rhys Roberts, in Richard McKeon, ed., *The Basic Works of Aristotle* (New York: Random House, 1941). Reproduced by permission.

4. My account of these matters here follows that found in the very fine book by John Powell, *The Secret of Staying in Love* (Niles, Ill.: Angus Communications, 1974).

Religion: What Is the Nature of God?

I N AUGUST OF A.D. 410, the Visigoths under Alaric finally broke through the defenses of Rome and took the city. Historians mark this date, the fall of the Eternal City, as the beginning of the Middle Ages. Our history, of course, does not really fall into such neat divisions as those used by historians, but the periods themselves are real and distinct enough.

The Middle Ages differed from modern times economically, politically, and religiously. Economically, the Middle Ages were mainly agricultural, while the modern world is primarily commercial and industrial. Politically, medieval states were feudal, while most modern governments are bureaucratic—that is, run and controlled by a system of officials and bureaus. And religiously—which is most relevant for our story—the Christianity of the Middle Ages was united under the authority of the Catholic Church, while Christianity in modern times is divided among many denominations.

The fall of Rome was a great psychological shock, seeming to many people of the time to mark the end not only of civilization but also of the world itself. How could such a disaster have taken place, people wondered. Some traced the misfortune to the displeasure of the ancient deities who had stood guard over the city during its long history before being displaced by the Christian God. It had been scarcely a generation since Emperor Theodosius I had proscribed the ancient cults and declared Christianity to be the empire's official faith. The old gods, it was now said, were taking their revenge.

ST. AUGUSTINE AND ST. THOMAS

It fell to St. Augustine (354–430), Bishop of Hippo, one of the most penetrating thinkers of his age, to defend the rise of the Christian faith. The result was *The City of God*, which he began in 413 and took some 13 years to complete. It was the first important work of the Middle Ages, one largely responsible for shaping Christianity into the powerful force it became for the next thousand years.

St. Augustine's argument was that history was a drama involving God and humanity. God created the earth for people, but Adam sinned against God, and he and Eve were driven out of the paradise God had created for them. But God gave humanity a second chance after flooding the world to destroy everyone in it except Noah and his family and then a third chance by entering into a covenant with the Jews. But the Jews, St. Augustine argued, did not live up to the agreement they made with God, and so God allowed them to be captured by their enemies. God then sought to redeem not only the Jews but all humankind by sending the Messiah Jesus to die as an atonement for the sinfulness of humanity. Those who have accepted the sacrifice make up the new community, the Church. The Church (the City of God) and those who do not accept the sacrifice of Jesus (the City of Man) now exist side by side and will do so until the Day of Judgment, when God will destroy those who have not accepted Jesus as their savior and will create a new earth for those who have.

The church fathers were at first divided on the use of coercion. However, St. Augustine's view that the state, like a benevolent father, was required to encourage heretics to return to orthodoxy and thus save their souls in time became the dominant one. It was finally institutionalized in the Inquisition, with burning at the stake as its innovative method of execution.

If St. Augustine's writings mark the beginning of the Middle or Dark Ages, the work of another Church leader, St. Thomas Aquinas (1225–1274), universally regarded as the greatest intellectual figure of this thousand-year period, marks its height. St. Thomas took it upon himself to reconcile the truths of revelation with the truths of reason. The teachings of St. Augustine, which by this time had dominated Western thought for more than 800 years, had insisted that in the search for truth humans must depend on inner thought rather than on sensory experience. But the works of Aristotle, which were now becoming known once again, stressed the importance and value of experience and empirical knowledge in the search for truth. St. Thomas set about to synthesize and harmonize Aristotelian science with Christian revelation. The truths of faith and those of sense experience, he argued, are not only compatible but even complementary: some truths, such as the mystery of the Incarnation, can be known only through revelation, while others, such as knowledge of the composition of earthly things, can be known only through sense experience; still others—such as human awareness of God—require both revelation and sense experience for their perception.

St. Thomas's main work (famous for its five proofs for the existence of God) was his *Summa Theologica* (1265). Its synthesis of philosophy and theology became in time the accepted teachings of the Roman Catholic Church. He was canonized in 1328 and declared a doctor of the Church in 1567. Pope Leo XIII made his teaching, called **Thomism**, the basis of instruction in all Roman Catholic schools.

While the thought during the Middle Ages seems particularly tied to religious questions, to suppose that this is the sole focus would be misleading. Significant contributions to questions concerning freedom and **determinism**, logic, and the nature of the world (questions of **metaphysics**) also received considerable and thorough treatment. However, the questions of religion are not exclusively metaphysical ones. While St. Augustine and St. Thomas clearly demarcate the lines within which the questions concerning the *nature* of God and reality are contained, they also open the door for discussions of the nature of religious *knowledge* and *belief*. To struggle with the latter is to encounter David Hume and William James. To address the former questions—the existence, creativity, and goodness of God—is to wrestle with the work of St. Augustine and St. Thomas. In this wrestling, we also encounter the quite contemporary discussion of intelligent design and the ancient conflict between religion and natural philosophy made new.

Saint Thomas Aquinas (1225?–1274)

RELIGION: THE STUDY OF THE NATURE OF GOD AND BELIEF

It is not difficult to appreciate the development of the subject. The most fundamental questions we can ask—and we have a profound need to ask them—are the questions of our existence. What are we and why are we here? What should—and what can—we do? And why must we die? Why do bad things happen to good people? Why is there evil?

To reflect on our existence, on its approaching end, on the nature of the world in which it has been passed, and on whether one shall return to it or some other one is to reflect on metaphysics. The religions of the world have arisen in response to our need to answer these questions.

Philosophy's answers differ from those offered by religion in that philosophy's goal is not reassurance but understanding. But the questions are nevertheless the same, and over the centuries philosophers have devised special labels for each of the main questions that naturally arise in such discussions.

Thus, **cosmology** deals with the problem of what the universe as a whole is really like. "Why is there a universe?" it asks, "and where did it come from?" Rational psychology deals with the nature of the soul and asks such questions as "Why are we here, and what is to become of us?" And **rational theology**, finally, is concerned with the question of God's existence. The study of nature, the soul, and God have thus traditionally formed the three main subdivisions of metaphysics.

Although these three topics, which formed the main preoccupation of the thought of the Middle Ages, were replaced in modern times with our own obsession with questions of knowledge (e.g., how and whether we can know any such matters), these questions have by no means disappeared.

The Idea of God

Let us finally turn to the last of the three questions metaphysics traditionally poses to itself: the existence of God. Does such a divine Being exist, metaphysics asks? And how do we know that He does? Can we prove it? In entering this area of metaphysics, we are in reality entering the realm of theology. It may seem strange that as students of philosophy we should occupy ourselves with such essentially theological questions. Isn't philosophy (and science) opposed to religion and theology (which is its study), we may be tempted to ask? Although this may seem so, many teachers of philosophy have believed that there are few better ways of introducing students to philosophy than by way of an examination of such theological questions. In an older, classic student text on philosophy (*An Introduction to Modern Philosophy in Six Philosophical Problems*), first published by Macmillan in 1943, Alburey Castell explains why in the following words:

> The reason is that in most ages men have sought to answer philosophical questions in terms of theological beliefs. "What shall I believe?" has frequently been answered by "The word of God." "What shall I do?" has frequently been answered by "Obey the Will of God." "Where did the world come from?" has frequently been answered by "It was created by God." "What happens to me when I die?" has frequently been answered by "You return to God." In these and countless other ways, the notion of God has entered into the very texture of men's thinking; and wherever it has entered, it has always been to answer some ultimate and highly critical question. We can generalize all of this by saying that the idea of God has functioned as an ultimate principle of explanation and an ultimate principle of criticism. Now, inasmuch as philosophy (literally, "the love of wisdom") is the systematic inquiry into our ultimate principles of explanation and criticism, in every department of life and thought, there has always been a close connection between it and theology. If the answers to ultimate questions of explanation and evaluation are to be found in theology, it is a man's philosophical business to know this. If there is reasonable doubt about these matters, it is likewise a man's philosophical business to inform himself that such is the case. (pp. 11–12)

It is for this reason, Castell explains further, that theology provides a good beginning in philosophy. "The questions which define philosophy," he adds, "have frequently been answered by theology." In what follows, we will examine some of these answers and see to what degree they meet reason's demands.

The Problem of Evil

What of the existential problems of death? Of pain? Of evil? St. Augustine comes to these questions through reflecting on his own experiences, his own theological journey, and his philosophical commitments. In the *Confessions*, St. Augustine goes to considerable lengths to plumb the depths of his own motivations and to understand his desires and his will. Easily the most famous of his examples of his misspent youth is the story of the pear tree. He and some friends, all of them thugs, hooligans, hoodlums, and ruffians, raided a pear tree near the fields of St. Augustine's family. It was late at night, and they had been out looking for trouble to cause and doing so purely for the sake of causing trouble. They stripped the pear tree of its fruit, which St. Augustine points out was not at all good. It was ugly and did not taste good at all. They did not steal the pears because they needed pears—indeed, St. Augustine writes that he had an abundance of fruit, and so there was no need. They did not steal the pears out of spite for the farmer whose pears they were. They did not steal the pears for any other reason than the stealing. It would have been the same had the pears been plums or olives or apples. It was not the pears but the act of stealing itself that was the pleasurable experience. In fact, St. Augustine does not even seem to remember whether they ate any of the pears at that time, but he does remember taking them and throwing them at pigs, thus tormenting another creature with their ill-gotten gain. In this experience, St. Augustine realizes that it is the evil that is attractive, and he wonders from whence this evil comes given that God is in no way evil.

St. Augustine goes further in the *Confessions* in his description of God than the list of characteristics commonly associated with God by philosopher/theologians. The list—omnipotent, omnibenevolent, eternal, infinite, creator of all that exists—is a standard but fairly dry list. The portrait of the relationship with God that St. Augustine paints in the *Confessions* is a very different one. This is not to say that St. Augustine disagrees with any of these. However, the way St. Augustine describes God reveals a depth of feeling and connection that is not readily apparent in a simple listing of properties. For example, St. Augustine agrees that God is omnipresent, but he describes God as infusing all of creation with God's very presence. This is more than simply "being everywhere at once." Instead, God is thought to be completely and intimately related to all that exists. That presence is not simply in the midst of all that exists but also surrounding all existent things. This is more than simply bounding them on all sides, but St. Augustine conveys a sense of deep care, almost an embrace rather than a sterile fencing in. Thus, the God of St. Augustine's *Confessions* is a profoundly caring God, deeply concerned with all that God has created and called "good."

This deeper and more intimate portrait of God serves to exacerbate the Problem of Evil, however. If God is so deeply connected to God's creation, creating everything good from the fountain of God's own goodness, then how can evil come to be? Did it sneak in? Did it arise from the goodness of God's creation? Is evil some *thing*? Or is evil nothing?

St. Augustine's encounter with the pear tree is sufficient cause for him to think that there is something deeply and profoundly wrong. While the robbing of the pear tree may seem like a mischievous prank, St. Augustine sees it differently. He was taken not by the object but by the act of doing something wrong. Thus, whether it is stealing pears or some other wrongdoing, the very act of doing something wrong is the source of St. Augustine's youthful pleasure. He labels this *sin* and sin is wrong and evil. So, on the one hand, we have a good and powerful and caring God who creates all things good, and, on the other, we have clear and present evidence of evil. How can these two seemingly incommensurate hands be true?

In this question, St. Augustine frames the problem that has come to be known as the Problem of Evil. While the *Confessions* demonstrates the depth of the problem clearly and poignantly, the clearest Augustinian response to it is not in the *Confessions*. His clearest assessment of the Problem of Evil and his proposal for a solution to it is in his weighty tome *The City of God*. Before turning to the Augustinian solution, let us formulate the question as clearly as possible. The pernicious dilemma that is the Problem of Evil can be expressed as a series of propositions, all of which are supposed to be true but which, taken together, seem to be incommensurate. Generally speaking, the list of properties of God is taken as a single proposition, but we will separate them here to clearly illustrate the possible ways in which the problem can be attacked and which of those possibilities St. Augustine employs.

The Problem of Evil

1. God is good.
2. God is omniscient (all-knowing).
3. God is omnibenevolent (of infinitely good will).
4. God is omnipotent (all-powerful).
5. God is omnipresent (everywhere).
6. God is the infinite creator of all that exists.
7. Evil exists.

The problem should be quite straightforward. If God is omnipotent, then God has sufficient power to enact anything God wills to be the case. If God is omnibenevolent, then God always wills the good in any and all situations. If this is so, then when John sets out to murder Tom, John acts against God's will and against God's power. However, since God would not will that John kill Tom, indeed, would will that John not kill Tom, then if John kills Tom, this would suggest that God is not truly omnipotent. On the other hand, if we hold that God is indeed omnipotent, then if John kills Tom, this must either be in accord with the will of God or at least not opposed to it. Thus, God would not always will the good. The incommensurate nature of the propositions poses a quandary.

To address this quandary, St. Augustine offers a **theodicy**. The word *theodicy* comes from two Greek words—*theos* and *dike*—meaning "God" and "justice." Thus, a theodicy is a justification of the goodness of God given that there is evil in the world. The Augustinian theodicy has come to be known as a *Free Will Defense*. This means that, ultimately, St. Augustine sees the origin of evil within the human will, thus making human beings responsible for evil rather than God. However, before he can come to this conclusion, he must first do some heavy metaphysical lifting, particularly with respect to the understanding of the nature of God, the human nature, and the nature of evil.

To understand the nature of evil, it is first necessary that we consider the ontology of holes. This may seem an odd place to start; however, the importance of this digression will become clear. If we consider a hole and ask, "Does a hole exist?" it would certainly seem clear that it does. For example, Kenny could step in a hole and twist his ankle. If we asked Kenny if the hole exists, he might well think we had become addled to ask such a silly and obvious question. "Of course it exists," he might say, "after all, I just stepped in it, and I couldn't very well have stepped in something that doesn't exist!" However, if we consider the matter a bit further, an oddity within the reality of holes becomes apparent. A hole, it seems, exists differently from, say, a tree. The tree defines its own boundaries, it exists independently of other entities, and it has physical extension. A hole, on the other hand, does not exist independently. While we might say, "I stepped in a hole," it is clear that what is meant there is that "I stepped in a hole *in the ground*." A hole is always a hole *in something else*. Thus, it does not establish its own boundaries, it does not exist independently of the entity within which it is, and it does not have physical extension. A hole does not take up space; rather, it is an absence or a privation. Thus, a hole is not a *something*; it is a *nothing*.

With this understanding of the ontology of holes, we are ready for the first step of the Augustinian theodicy. The first thing to understand is the nature of evil. Evil is not a something; it is a nothingness. So, evil is a hole, not a physically existent thing. If we understand this, then the first premises of St. Augustine's *Free Will Defense Theodicy* will be as follows that evil is not a physical thing with some sort of positive existence (a *something*); rather, it is like a hole or an absence or a lack (a *nothing*).

From this, it follows that we can conceive evil separately from the good things that God has created. It is not in the power of God to create evil (as a physical object), but God could quite easily and perhaps justifiably create in such a way that there were interstices. That is, God could create something that was only as large as it is, not any larger. So one might imagine that God could create the human will as a sort of Swiss cheese. Every part of the will that has actual existence is good because God creates nothing that is not good. But God could well leave gaps and thus provide for the will to fill those in itself—either in ways that comport with the will of God or not. In this way, God does not abrogate God's own freedom but at the same time creates a space for the operation of the free human will to self-determine. This being the case, the rest of the *Free Will Defense Theodicy* proceeds apace.

If evil has this sort of negative existence that always consists in the malfunctioning of something that has positive existence and is itself good (e.g., a disease in an otherwise healthy body) and if freedom of will is bestowed upon human beings by God, then it follows that we can utilize that freedom in either good ways or destructive, evil ones. Since God acts creatively to provide for the human operation of the will, the operations of that will have consequences, the responsibility for which lie completely with the acting agent's will. Thus, we have the following two claims that depend for their justification on the nature of the human will and its activity. It should be noted that St. Augustine holds the view that the human will cannot act in any truly good ways apart from the grace of God. This is an implication of the Augustinian doctrine of Original Sin. Given that humanity is in a fallen state and thus wholly bound by the inherent failings of the fallen will, only God can overcome those failings to enable that will to will rightly. Thus, when St. Augustine holds the view that when an agent acts in good ways, he is acting under and because of the grace of God, he is merely extending his understanding of Original Sin to cover all actions that a free and willing agent might make. If the will directs in bad ways, then the responsibility lies completely with the agent. This is because the human will cannot help but act in bad ways because it is corrupt from the outset, an inheritance from the human condition. So the human will may act freely prior to the imposition of God's grace, but it will always choose to act in pursuit of evil pleasures rather than in accordance with the will of God. After the infusion of God's grace, the will can act in accord with the divine will. Thus, we have the next two claims in the Augustinian theodicy.

From the doctrine of Original Sin, if a person acts in good ways, then it is by the grace of God and reflects the health of the individual will. Similarly, if a person acts in bad ways, then the responsibility for those actions is solely with the person and is a reflection of the disease in the will of that person.

The upshot of this argument is that, ultimately, evil is not a physical thing and that, because it is a privation or a lack that exists within the human will, it is a nothingness that nevertheless corrupts that will. This corruption lies in the will acting on its own volition and apart from the direction of God. If this is so, then evil things that occur within the world are not the responsibility of God but rather are the fault of human beings, and we have that encapsulated in St. Augustine's conclusion: Evil is the fault of human beings and not of God.

Perhaps the most interesting thing about St. Augustine's theodicy is that it accepts all of the premises but in fact suggests that there is an equivocation between the proposition that "God is the infinite creator of all that exists" and that "Evil exists." In the first of these, the word *exists* does not mean the same thing it does in the second. In the former proposition, *exist* designates a physical existence, indeed, all of the things that have actual substantial existence, either physically or spiritually/mentally. In the latter, *exist* designates a dependent state of existence, a state that is dependent on the type of existence specified by the same word in the first. This equivocation, on one interpretation of St. Augustine, renders the Problem of Evil a pseudoproblem, which is to say, a problem that is not really a dilemma but merely a failure to be clear in one's terms. Clarity there will make the problem dissolve. This *free will theodicy* became the dominant approach to the Problem of Evil from the medieval Catholic Church through the contemporary Catholic and Protestant incarnations of the faith.

Despite its dominant position within the theological doctrines of the Church, Catholic and Protestant, the Augustinian theodicy has not been without its detractors. One of those was the German philosopher and theologian Friedrich Schleiermacher. On Schleiermacher's view, we must start with the understanding that God is omnipotent and omnibenevolent. These are two of the characteristics of God that Schleiermacher rightly takes as unassailable and nonnegotiable for St. Augustine. It seems, though, that the following proposition, "God would create flawlessly," follows directly from the omnipotence and omnibenevolence of God. Thus, God would not create entities that possess holes, which could cause all manner of grief later. If these are true, then there are only two options to explain the presence of evil. Either creation went wrong spontaneously, or the ultimate responsibility for evil belongs to God. In the former case, Schleiermacher wants to rule out the spontaneous devolution into evil because this would suggest that creation is somehow out of the control of God. This would deny the omnipotence of God, which St. Augustine cannot do and would not accept. In the latter case, responsibility for evil would lie with God because to omnisciently create with the great holes into which the human will can wander, causing all manner of mischief and grief, is to fail to will the good. Consider this example. If a parent knowingly places his child in a room where there is apple juice and radiator fluid and allows the child to pick whichever the child will freely pick, it seems rather clear that the parent bears responsibility if the child makes a tragic choice. We assume that the parent has the power to stop the child from picking the antifreeze (else the analogy would fail). Thus, if the parent possesses the power and does nothing, then we could reasonably conclude that the parent was not benevolent. Thus, if we deny that creation spontaneously went awry (and thus uphold the omnipotence of God), then, on Schleiermacher's view, we are left with denying the omnibenevolence of God. Thus, the presence of evil, physical or nonphysical, along with the assumption of the omnipotence and omnibenevolence of God form a trio of incommensurate propositions. If this is so, then, persuasive as it is, the Augustinian theodicy would ultimately fail as a justification of God.

Whether the Augustinian theodicy ultimately succeeds or fails, what is abundantly clear is that St. Augustine shifts the philosophical conversation and the emphasis within the branches of philosophy. The first question is no longer about the nature of humankind but rather about the nature of God and reality. From this metaphysical standpoint, St. Augustine radically reenvisions the big questions of philosophy and straightforwardly confronts some of the difficulties that arise (e.g., the Problem of Evil). The questions that follow, historically, in the process of human ideas concern whether God's existence can be demonstrated and what the nature of religious belief is like. In the proofs for the existence of God from the medieval era, we have the kernel of the contemporary philosophical, religious, and scientific question of intelligent design.

St. Augustine's *free will defense* is not the only theodicy offered by those confronted by the Problem of Evil. Indeed, St. Augustine's view is developed partly in response to an earlier theodicy. The third-century C.E. theologian Irenaeus (130–202) advanced a view commonly called a "soul-making" or "person-making" theodicy. This approach to the Problem of Evil is one that has received considerable attention in contemporary discussions of philosophy of religion.

A common and familiar saying often offered in the face of daunting obstacles goes something like this: "What doesn't kill us, makes us stronger." This is too colloquial to be a complete picture of the Irenaean theodicy, but it captures a central feature of it, namely, that God is constantly creating, working and reworking God's human beings, and refining the gold of the human soul in the heat of a refiner's fire. On this view, then, suffering and "evil" is not only a feature of the world with which to be dealt but also an essential feature of creation being used by God to perfect human souls.

In his theodicy, Irenaeus makes an intriguing theological distinction. For Irenaeus, God's work of creation is a work in progress. Initially, human beings are created "in the image of God." This *imago dei*, however, is not a final stage in human development. The human soul is still incomplete or unrefined. It must be cultivated and grow, eventually, until the person is not only created in the image of God but refined into the "likeness of God."

The strength of Irenaeus's view is that it gives an account for the tension experienced in life—a tension between a natural selfishness on the one hand and a call toward morality on the other. The latter has been understood in many ways, perhaps most commonly as a conscience, but that development from selfish actor to moral self is the centerpiece of the Irenaean theodicy.

In order to develop a moral character, Irenaeus recognizes that a person must be able to freely choose to develop, that is, to freely move toward God. If this is so, then God must have provided that freedom as a necessary feature of creation. A further feature in moral development is the existence of actual moral choices. Thus, in order to have the opportunity to behave morally, a person must have the opportunity to behave in the opposite fashion. Thus, not only is freedom a necessary feature of the world, but so too is what humans perceive as evil.

If this is so, then it would require a different view of the nature of creation itself. When God creates and calls that creation "good," Irenaeus thinks that God cannot possibly mean that it is good in the sense of absence of evil, suffering, and/or pain. Instead, it is created for a good *purpose*. That purpose, the creation of mature and moral souls, is such that it requires a diverse and potentially painful world. However, the purpose is good, and that good purpose puts into context any of the suffering necessary for the refining of the soul.

There are some rather powerful complaints lodged against soul-making theodicies, either Irenaean or more contemporary. These can generally be divided into three camps. The first of these notes that obstacles and hardships need not breed strength or moral goodness. This is a straightforward denial of the "whatever doesn't kill us makes us stronger" platitude. Instead, it recognizes that whatever doesn't kill us may well make us into a twisted, bitter, and immoral actor, bent on revenge and destruction. As a matter of empirical observation, it certainly seems that hardship is as likely to produce the opposite of moral strength as it is to produce strong and good character.

A second criticism of Irenaean soul-making theodicies is that it certainly seems an a priori claim that, even in the event of a good character produced by torment, the suffering and pain are worthwhile. Is a strong and moral character sufficient payoff for the cost of tremendous suffering? Further, is the system in which one does not have the choice whether to ask that question fair? As it happens, on Irenaeus's view, one has the choice of development of moral or immoral character, but one does not have the option of answering the "Is it worth all this?" question with a resounding "no."

Even if the answer is "Yes, it is worth the pain and suffering," an Irenaean theodicy requires the postulation of an afterlife. For example, should someone be subjected to intense and incredible suffering from the moment of birth until a death only hours after birth, an afterlife in which the payoff of continued soul making could continue is quite clearly required. Further, the claim of human freedom in making moral decisions is perhaps ultimately abrogated in that afterlife. Irenaeus was something of a universalist. That is, he was of the view that, ultimately, all souls created by God eventually are refined, purified, and purged of the dross and enter into a state of blessedness. Indeed, a sort of universalism is inherent in most forms of soul-making theodicies. However, if this is the case, then it would seem that human freedom, at least ultimately, is an illusion. The final destination, a morally developed soul, is never truly in play, and all of the choices in the interim are merely varied stations on the way. While this is, perhaps, a hopeful and positive vision that may overcome some of the earlier criticisms, it seems to place Irenaeus's views outside the heart of orthodoxy represented by philosopher/theologians like St. Augustine and St. Thomas.

PROOFS FOR THE EXISTENCE OF GOD

We will begin the examination of the proofs for the existence of God with St. Thomas and examine his five proofs for God's existence. We will then go on to look at the thought of that most enigmatic of thinkers, Blaise Pascal, who argued that far from human reason being capable of proving God's existence (as St. Thomas believed), the case is rather that our reason is totally inadequate to this task. And fortunately so, for it is this fact—our very helplessness without God—that is the surest proof of His existence! After examining this great seventeenth-century thinker's impassioned writing on this theme of our profound need for God, we will turn to the eighteenth century (the "century of reason") and to the Scottish philosopher David Hume, whose argument (one conveyed in no less eloquent terms) is that it is futile to try to prove God's existence, for human reason is simply incapable of doing so, all previous efforts showing this only too clearly. Leaving Hume, we will turn to the work of John Stuart Mill, a British thinker of the nineteenth century who tried to salvage something of Hume's devastating criticism by arguing not for an infinite, all-powerful, all-knowing God but for a finite and limited God governing our world with difficulty. In the process, we will reflect on the ways in which St. Thomas's Fifth Way, the Watchmaker Argument of Hume's contemporary William Paley, and the current conversation surrounding intelligent design are all inter-related. We will end our account, however, on a more positive note by examining the work of the great twentieth-century American psychologist and philosopher William James, whose arguments for God's existence will remind us once again of that remark-able French philosopher/mystic Blaise Pascal.

St. Thomas Aquinas

Certain features of the world we inhabit present a problem and challenge to us, St. Thomas noted. They seem mysterious and inexplicable and beg for explanation. For ex-ample, wherever we look in our world, we observe things in constant motion and change. Movement is everywhere. How did it come to be so? Of course, we can account for any particular movement by observing what adjacent object set it in motion. But how about *that* object—what set *it* in motion? On the other hand, there is no point in trying to locate what set it in motion, for this will only lead us to ask the same question again and again ad infinitum. What are we therefore to say about this? How are we to explain it? We may recall here that the same question confronted the first Western scientists—the atomists (see chapter 2). What made the tiny little particles of matter of which the uni-verse is composed fly about in empty space the way they do? Was someone moving them about, pushing them? No, the ancient atomists said, that was not the reason; the particles move about the way they do because motion is simply natural to them. But this is not the answer St. Thomas offers. The source of all this motion, he says, is God, the Unmoved Mover of all there is.

This is St. Thomas's first argument ("First Way") of the five that he offers for God's existence. The second argument, from Cause, is very similar: Everything that happens has a cause, and this cause in turn has a cause and so on. But either we go on in this way ad infinitum (which is unintelligible) or come to a First Cause, which, indeed, reason compels us to do.

These features of the world that we observe all around us (we have noted thus far only *motion* and *cause*, but St. Thomas goes on to note three others: *contingency*, *degrees of excellence*, and *harmony*) are fortunate for us. Without these signs, we would be com-pletely in the dark regarding God's existence. For God's existence is not something we can know of *directly*. We have no direct insight, or intuition, or vision of God. We can arrive at Him or infer His existence only from the peculiar features of the world He cre-ated and that point to Him. St. Thomas's account of these features of the world (these

"Effects" in the world that point to Him as their Cause) is contained in his major opus, a multivolume work titled *Summa Theologica*. These "proofs" ("the Five Ways") are among the most famous of that work:

The First Way:
The Argument from Change

The existence of God can be shown in five ways. The first and clearest is taken from the idea of motion. (1) Now it is certain, and our senses corroborate it, that some things in this world are in motion. (2) But everything which is in motion is moved by something else. (3) For nothing is in motion except in so far as it is in potentiality in relation to that towards which it is in motion. (4) Now a thing causes movement in so far as it is in actuality. For to cause movement is nothing else than to bring something from potentiality to actuality; but a thing cannot be brought from potential to actuality except by something which exists in actuality, as, for example, that which is hot in actuality, like fire, makes wood, which is only hot in potentiality to be hot in actuality, and thereby causes movement in it and alters it. (5) But it is not possible that the same thing should be at the same time in actuality and potentiality in relation to the same thing, but only in relation to different things; for what is hot in actuality cannot at the same time be hot in potentiality, though it is at the same time cold in potentiality. (6) It is impossible, therefore, that in relation to the same thing and in the same way anything should both cause movement and be caused, or that it should cause itself to move. (7) Everything therefore that is in motion must be moved by something else. If therefore the thing which causes it to move be in motion, this too must be moved by something else, and so on. (8) But we cannot proceed to infinity in this way, because in that cause there would be no first mover, and in consequence, neither would there be any other mover; for secondary movers do not cause movement except they be moved by a first mover, as, for example, a stick cannot cause movement unless it is moved by the hand. Therefore it is necessary to stop at some first mover which is moved by nothing else. And this is what we all understand God to be.

The Second Way:
The Argument from Causation

The Second Way is taken from the idea of the Efficient Cause. (1) For we find that there is among material things a regular order of efficient causes. (2) But we do not find, nor indeed is it possible, that anything is the efficient cause of itself, for in that case it would be prior to itself, which is impossible. (3) Now it is not possible to proceed to infinity in efficient causes. (4) For if we arrange in order all efficient causes, the first is the cause of the intermediate, and the intermediate the cause of the last, whether the intermediate be many or only one. (5) But if we remove a cause the effect is removed; therefore, if there is no first among efficient causes, neither will there be a last or an intermediate. (6) But if we proceed to infinity in efficient causes there will be no first efficient cause, and thus there will be no ultimate effect, nor any intermediate efficient causes, which is clearly false. Therefore it is necessary to suppose the existence of some first efficient cause, and this men call God.

The Third Way:
The Argument from Contingency

The Third Way rests on the idea of the "contingent" and the "necessary" and is as follows: (1) Now we find that there are certain things in the Universe which are capable of existing and of not existing, for we find that some things are brought into existence and then destroyed, and consequently are capable of being or not being. (2) But it is impossible for all things which exist to be of this kind, because anything which is capable of not existing, at some time or other does not exist. (3) If therefore all things are capable of not existing, there was a time when nothing existed in the Universe. (4) But if this is true there would also be nothing in existence now; because anything that does not exist cannot begin to exist except by the agency of something which has existence. If therefore there was once nothing which existed, it would have been impossible for anything to begin to exist, and so nothing would exist now. (5) This is clearly false. Therefore all things are not contingent, and there must be something which is necessary in the Universe. (6) But everything which is necessary either has or has not the cause of its necessity from an outside source. Now it is not possible to proceed to infinity in necessary things which have a cause of their necessity, as has been proved in the case of efficient causes. Therefore it is necessary to suppose the existence of something which is necessary in itself, not having the cause of its necessity from any outside source, but which is the cause of necessity in others. And this "something" we call God.

The Fourth Way:
The Argument from Degrees of Excellence

The Fourth Way is taken from the degrees which are found in things. (1) For among different things we find that one is more or less good or true or noble; and likewise in the case of other things of this kind. (2) But the words "more" or "less" are used of different things in proportion as they approximate in their different ways to something which has the particular quality in the highest degree—e.g., we call a thing hotter when it approximates more nearly to that which is hot in the highest degree. There is therefore something which is true in the highest degree, good in the highest degree and noble in the highest degree; (3) and consequently there must be also something which has being in the highest degree. For things which are true in the highest degree also have being in the highest degree (see Aristotle, Metaphysics, 2). (4) But anything which has a certain quality of any kind in the highest degree is also the cause of all the things of that kind, as, for example, fire which is hot in the highest degree is the cause of all hot things (as is said in the same book). (5) Therefore there exists something which is the cause of being, and goodness, and of every perfection in all existing things; and this we call God.

The Fifth Way:
The Argument from Harmony

The Fifth Way is taken from the way in which nature is governed. (1) For we observe that certain things which lack knowledge, such as natural bodies, work for an End. This is obvious, because they always, or at any rate very frequently, operate in the same way so as to attain the best possible result. (2) Hence it is clear that they do not arrive at their goal by chance, but by purpose. (3) But those things which have no knowledge do not move towards a goal unless they are guided by someone or something which does possess knowledge and intelligence—e.g., an arrow by an archer. Therefore, there does exist something which possesses intelligence by which all natural things are directed to their goal; and this we call God.

Although St. Thomas's language is elliptic, difficult, and elusive (some of his arguments were greatly elaborated on by others, as we will soon note), the basic idea conveyed is that there are signs all around us that unmistakably point to Him. That is in essence his basic observation and argument. A short passage from that same work summarizes this briefly and elegantly:

The existence of God is not self-evident to us. . . . Yet from every effect the existence of the cause can be clearly demonstrated, and so we can demonstrate the existence of God from His effects. Hence the existence of God, in so far as it is not self-evident to us, can be demonstrated from those of His effects which are known to us. (Second Article)

However, this passage also reveals what is most questionable and worrisome in St. Thomas's argument. Logicians would say that it is a classic example of the fallacy of begging the question. You will recall from our work on fallacies (chapter 5) that people beg a question when instead of proving a point at issue, they simply, in the course of their argument or presentation, assume it. For example, to argue that "God exists because the Bible says so" is to commit the fallacy, for the proof given ("the Bible says so") simply assumes the very thing that needs to be proven (namely, the existence of God who "wrote" it)—for if He did not exist, He did not write it. The proof that He exists therefore cannot be assumed but needs to be established. And precisely the same thing can be said of St. Thomas's argument: Certainly if God did indeed create the world, then what we see all around us are "His effects." But until we prove that He did so, we cannot appeal to these supposed "effects of His" to establish His existence—without, as we say, begging the question.

More simply still, as critics of St. Thomas have traditionally pointed out, his arguments are flawed because in each case he excludes the possibility of an infinite regress (either of motions or of causes) and so concludes that there must be a First Mover or a First Cause. But what good reason is there for excluding such a possibility? Because it makes the world seem unintelligible to us otherwise? But is God, with which it is replaced, any less unintelligible? Can we resist raising the child's notorious retort (to our reply that God made the world), Who made God? Why, indeed, not simply assume with the ancient atomists that the world simply is the way it is! In short, St. Thomas argues that either there exists a necessary being, God, who created the universe, or the universe is indeed ultimately unintelligible.

A more recent objection lodged against St. Thomas's view is that even if one takes the arguments to establish what they claim, there is nothing within them that compels the reader to suppose that each is a discussion of the same entity. That is, why must one suppose that the First Mover is also the First Cause or the Intelligent Designer of the Fifth Way? However, this objection is readily overcome by remembering the framework of the Five Ways. While it is true that St. Thomas does distinguish five arguments, it is not clear at all that these five arguments are five *distinct* arguments. Indeed, perhaps it is more in line with St. Thomas's intentions to read them as five aspects of a single argument. After all, the first and second proofs are exactly the same except that in the former the observed state of affairs is *motion*, while in the second it is some set of *effects*. One might wonder why St. Thomas would have two proofs, identical except for the object observed, in a set of five proofs that were all supposed to be distinct from one another. However, reading closely, one would notice that *motion* is but a *type* or a *kind* of *effect*. So, the first proof actually folds into the second like a nesting doll.

If the first proof folds into the second (as *motion* is a species of *effect*), we might suspect that the second would fold into the third and so on. Careful observation underscores this interpretation. If *motion* folds into *effect*, we might ask what sorts of causes there are to produce those effects. There can be but two kinds of causes—a necessary one or a contingent one. As the Third Way specifies the nature of the cause that must be the First Cause (which we discovered must exist in the Second Way) as necessary, we see that the second proof folds into the third. Similarly, the next proof deals not with the metaphysical character of the First Cause/First Mover but with the normative or moral nature of it, concluding that it is the standard by which all good things are called good; and more than the standard, it is the source of that goodness—or it *causes* it. The final question then becomes the basis for which those good things are caused. The cause of the universe is argued to be intelligent rather than random or brute. Thus, each of the proofs folds into the next, revealing for St. Thomas a deeper truth about the nature of the entity that is the First Mover, the First Cause, a Necessary Being, the source of all goodness, and the intelligent designer of the cosmos.

David Hume

Born in 1711 in Edinburgh, David Hume entered Edinburgh University at age 11, intending to pursue a career in law. But he abandoned all thoughts of a legal career when at the age of 18 he became convinced he had made a major philosophical discovery. He threw all his energies into its investigation, with the result that a year later he suffered a severe nervous breakdown.

Recovering, he went on to pursue his studies in philosophy and to incorporate his findings in a book, *A Treatise of Human Nature*, which finally appeared in 1739, when he was still only in his twenties. To his great disappointment, the book, as he put it, "fell deadborn from the press." He was more fortunate with his next, *Essays Moral and Political*, published in 1741–1742, which was an immediate success. This encouraged him to revise his *Treatise*, believing it was its style that originally held it back from achieving the success it deserved. Published under the new title *An Enquiry concerning Human Understanding* (1748), it drew more attention, although it again failed to become the popular success he had hoped it would be. What, however, finally did bring him the fame and popularity he craved were his political and historical writings, especially his immensely popular and widely acclaimed *History of England* (1754–1762), which went through many editions during his lifetime.

David Hume (1711–1776)

His writings having won for him a wide reputation, he was offered and served in a number of public offices: secretary to the British ambassador to France in 1763 and undersecretary of state from 1767 to 1769.

In 1769, Hume returned to Edinburgh, where his house became the meeting place and center for the most distinguished members of society. He died there in 1776, widely mourned.

In addition to his other works, Hume also wrote a book titled *Dialogues concerning Natural Religion*, which he resisted publishing during his lifetime, fearing it would prove too shocking to the public. Instead, he left instructions that it be published as soon as practicable after his death.

The excerpts from this work that are reprinted at the end of this chapter contain Hume's classic critique of the traditional arguments for God's existence—in particular the argument from design. The characters of the *Dialogues* are Cleanthes, who is a natural theologian; Demea, who is an orthodox believer; and Philo (who, in the main, represents Hume's own views, although the other two on occasion speak for him as well), a skeptic.

Hume's basic objections to the arguments offered by natural theology (such as those by St. Thomas) are that (1) they are questionable and that (2) even if they were not flawed, they are far from proving what they claim to prove. It is important to observe that Hume is not attempting to prove that God does not exist. His whole intention is much more modest: it is to show that the arguments that have been produced to prove His existence are far from compelling or convincing. What he is arguing for, in short, is skepticism, not atheism.

The traditional argument from design, Hume points out, is based on the principle of causal analogy—that is, that similar effects imply similar causes. "The curious adapting of means to ends, throughout all nature," Cleanthes declares, "resembles exactly, though it much exceeds, the productions of human contrivance—of human design, thought, wisdom, and intelligence. Since, therefore, the effects resemble each other, we are led to infer, by all the rules of analogy, that the causes also resemble, and that the Author of Nature is somewhat similar to the mind of man, though possessed of much larger faculties, proportioned to the grandeur of the work which he has executed." But an analogy is only as strong as the similarity between the two things being compared. But how similar, indeed, is the universe to a human-made product such as, say, a house? On the contrary "the dissimilitude is so striking that the utmost you can here pretend to is a guess, a conjecture, a presumption concerning a similar cause." What follows is therefore a detailed and searching analysis of the analogy. (For an account of the fallacy of false analogy, see chapter 5.)

Well, then, let us see how much trust we can place in this analogy between man's work and God's. Now, in the case of a house we know that in the majority of cases it is the product not of one builder but of many. Are we to say the same of the universe—that it required the effort of many Gods? Furthermore, the product of human hands is far from perfect, not surprisingly since the makers themselves are imperfect. Since the universe, too, is full of imperfections, are we to say, as the analogy would lead us to, that its Maker or Makers are similarly deficient? Or consider the case of the construction of a ship. Its success as a final product is the result of the contribution of carpenters, mechanics, and shipwrights over a long period of trial and error. Are we to say the same of the universe? Before arriving at this one, were many other universes bungled and botched before this one was finally arrived at? And again, in representing the Creator of the universe on the analogy of a house builder or shipwright, possessed of purpose and reason, we are modeling Him after ourselves. But how far are we to carry the comparison? Are we to say that, like us, the Supreme Being is possessed of such further human characteristics as hate, envy, enmity, scorn, and so on?

But perhaps we are mistaken about all this. Perhaps the universe is more comparable to an organism than to an artifact, that it more closely resembles a living organism like the human body than an artificial object like a house or ship. For, after all, do not Nature's cycles, its powers of regeneration and of self-repair together with its internal principles of change and motion, seem to suggest that its Maker is more aptly to be described as "the soul of the world" rather than as its architect? When Cleanthes is asked by Philo what he thinks of this new hypothesis, he rises to the occasion by suggesting that since the world has no sense organs, no nervous system, and such, it is perhaps more like a vegetable than an animal!

In the passages that follow the participants go on to have great fun with this new notion—milking it for all it is worth.

What, consequently, is the upshot of all this? Is the analogy totally without value? No, it is not entirely useless, nor is it too encouraging, either. All we can say with any confidence about it is that a person who follows it may perhaps allow himself "to assert, or conjecture, that the universe, sometime, arose from something like design." That is the utmost, unfortunately, we can say.

John Stuart Mill

In the next century, John Stuart Mill attempted to save natural theology from the skepticism to which it had been reduced by Hume by advancing the view that reason can with justice support the belief in a limited or finite Deity.

Mill can be considered the father of modern liberalism; his influence in this direction has been enormous. From his pen there flowed such works as *Principles of Political Economy, On Liberty, Utilitarianism, Considerations on Representative Government, The Subjection of Women*, and *Socialism*. In all these he attempted to persuade his fellow human beings to be kind, fair, and reasonable with one another. By doing so, he thought, they would surely come to realize that, for example, women have as much right to a life of their own and to have careers as men (as he argued eloquently in his book *The Subjection of Women*); that government by elected representative is preferable to any other form of government (his theme in his *Considerations on Representative Government*); that the greatest happiness of the greatest number should be our guiding principle in all our actions (as he argues in his essay *Utilitarianism*); that the motto "live and let live" is indeed still our best guide in our dealing with one another (in *On Liberty*); and so on.

Let us now see, then, what Mill says it is reasonable to believe regarding the existence of God. As Mill argues in the last of his *Three Essays on Religion* (1875), an essay titled "Theism," there are four central things in particular that reason leads us to believe: (1) that God is a Being of "great but limited power," (2) that He is a Being of "great and perhaps unlimited [but not infinite] knowledge and intelligence," (3) that benevolence but not justice is one of His attributes, and finally (4) that seeing God in this manner has several things to recommend it over the traditional view of Him.

In turning to Mill's essay "Theism," we find that he concentrates his attention entirely on the argument from design, preferring it to the others because it "is grounded wholly on our experience of the appearances of the universe," which we ourselves can observe all around us, whereas we have no experience whatever of such things as first causes and unmoved movers. The argument from design is therefore, he says, "a far more important argument for theism than any other."

Because it is, in his view, more important and more cogent than the others, he presents it in great and elaborate detail, as follows:

> The order of nature exhibits certain qualities that are found to be characteristic of such things as are made by an intelligent mind for a purpose. We are entitled from this great similarity in the effects to infer similarity in the cause, and to believe that things which it is beyond the power of man to make, but which resemble the works of man in all but power, must also have been made by intelligence armed with a power greater than human.

The argument from design is not drawn from mere resemblances in nature to the works of human intelligence, but from the special character of those resemblances. The circumstances in which it is alleged that the world resembles the works of man are not circumstances taken at random, but are particular instances of a circumstance which experience shows to have a real connection with an intelligent origin; the fact, namely, of conspiring to an end or purpose.

To show this, it will be convenient to handle, not the argument from design as a whole, but some one of the most impressive cases of it, such as the structure of the eye or the ear. It is maintained that the structure of the eye proves a designing mind. The argument may be analyzed as follows:

1. The parts of which the eye is composed, and the arrangement of these parts, resemble one another in this very remarkable respect, that they all conduce to enabling the animal to see. These parts and their arrangement being as they are, the animal sees. This is the only marked resemblance we can trace among the different parts of the eye; beyond the general likeness in composition which exists among all other parts of the animal.

2. Now, the combination of the parts of the eye had a beginning in time and must therefore have been brought together by a cause or causes. The number of instances (of such parts being brought together to enable organisms to see) is immensely greater than is required to exclude the possibility of a random or chance concurrence of independent causes. We are therefore warranted in concluding that what has brought all these parts together was some cause common to them all. And, since the parts agree in the single respect of combining to produce sight, there must be some connection between the cause which brought the parts together, and the fact of sight.

3. Now sight, being a fact which follows the putting together of the parts of the eye, can only be connected with the production of the eye as a final cause, not an efficient cause; since all efficient causes precede their effects. But a final cause is a purpose, and at once marks the origin of the eye as proceeding from an intelligent will.

Before proceeding to evaluate the argument as thus presented, Mill, assuming the role of the devil's advocate for a moment, offers what many would perhaps consider a cogent, alternative account of the phenomena supporting the notion of divine design. This alternative to "creative forethought" or "intelligent will" is the hypothesis of "natural selection" suggested by Mill's contemporary, Charles Darwin:

Of what value is this argument? Is intelligent will, or creative forethought, the only hypothesis that will account for the facts? I regret to say that it is not. Creative forethought is not the only link by which the origin of the mechanism of the eye may be connected with the fact of sight. There is another connecting link on which attention has been greatly fixed by recent speculation. This is the principle of natural selection, of "the survival of the fittest."

This principle of the survival of the fittest does not pretend to account for the origin of sensation, or of animal or vegetable life. It assumes the existence of some one or more very low forms of organic life, in which there are no complex adaptations. It next assumes, as experience warrants us in doing, that many small variations from those simple types would be thrown out, which would be transmissible by inheritance, some of which would be advantageous to the creature in its struggle for existence and others disadvantageous. The forms which are advantageous would always tend to survive; and those which are disadvantageous, to perish. Thus there would be a constant, though slow, general improvement of the type as it branched out into many different varieties, until it might attain to the most advanced examples which now exist.

It must be acknowledged that there is something very startling, and prima facie improbable in this hypothetical history of nature.

With reference to the eye, for example, it would require us to suppose that the primeval animal could not see, and had at most such slight preparation for seeing as might be constituted by some chemical action of light upon its cellular structure; that an accidental variation (mutation) would produce a variety that could see in some imperfect manner; that this peculiarity would be transmitted by inheritance while other variations continued to take place in other directions; that a number of races would thus be produced who, by the power of even imperfect sight, would have a great advantage over all other races which could not see and would in time extirpate them from all places except perhaps from a few very peculiar situations underground. Fresh variations would give rise to races with better and better seeing powers until we might at last reach as extraordinary a combination of structures and functions as are seen in the eye of man and of the more important animals.

Although Mill finds this new hypothesis intriguing and challenging, he regards it as less probable than the former, older theory:

> Of this theory, when pushed to this extreme point, all that can now be said is that it is not so absurd as it looks; and that the analogies which have been discovered in experience, favorable to its possibility, far exceed what anyone could have supposed beforehand. Whether it will ever be possible to say more than this is at present uncertain.
>
> Leaving this remarkable speculation to whatever fate the progress of discovery may have in store for it, I think it must be allowed that, in the present state of our knowledge, the adaptions in nature afford a large balance of probability in favor of creation by intelligence. It is equally certain that this is no more than a probability.

Assuming the theory of "creation by intelligence" is true, what can we say, further, about the nature of that intelligence responsible for the universe as we find it?

"What attributes," Mill asks, "are we warranted, by the evidence which nature accords of a creative mind, in assigning to that mind?" The first attribute we can assign to that Being, Mill goes on to argue, is great but *limited power*:

> Every indication of design in the cosmos is so much evidence against the omnipotence of the designer. For what is meant by *design*? Contrivance, the adaptation of means to end.

225

But the necessity for contrivance, the need of employing "means" to achieve an "end," is a consequence of the limitation of power.

Who would have recourse to means, to attain his end, if his mere wish or word was enough? The very idea of *means* implies that the means have an efficacy which the direct action of the being who employs them has not. Otherwise, they are not means but an encumbrance.

A man does not use machinery to move his arms; unless he is paralyzed, i.e., has not the power to do so directly by his volition.

But, if the use of contrivance is a sign of limited power, how much more so is the careful and skillful choice of contrivance? Could we speak of "wisdom in the selection of means," if he who selects them could, by his mere will, have achieved the same results without them, or by any other means? Wisdom and contrivance are shown in overcoming difficulties, and there is no room for difficulties, and so no room for wisdom or contrivance, in an omnipotent being.

Any evidences of design in nature, therefore, distinctly imply that the author of nature worked under limitations; that he was obliged to adapt himself to conditions independent of his will, and to attain his ends by such arrangements as those conditions admitted of.

On this hypothesis, the Deity had to work out His ends by combining materials of given nature and properties. This did require skill and contrivance; and the means by which it is effected are often such as justly excite our wonder and admiration. But, exactly because it requires wisdom, skill, contrivance, it implies limitation of power.

It may be said: An omnipotent Creator, though under no necessity of employing contrivances such as man must use, thought fit to do so in order to leave traces by which man might recognize his Creator's hand.

The answer is: This equally supposes a limit to the Deity's omnipotence, for it is a contrivance to achieve an end. Moreover, if it was His will that man should know that they and the world are His work, He, being omnipotent, had only to will that they should be aware of it.

From the question of God's power, Mill turns to the question of His knowledge and wisdom and argues that there are probably no grounds for ascribing infinite knowledge or intelligence to Deity:

Omnipotence, therefore, cannot be predicated of the Creator on the evidences of design in nature. But what of omniscience? If we suppose limitation of power, must we also suppose limitation of knowledge and wisdom?

To argue that Deity possesses only limited power does not preclude us from ascribing unlimited knowledge and wisdom to Him. But there is nothing to prove it. The knowledge and wisdom necessary to planning and arranging the cosmos are, no doubt, as much in excess of human knowledge as the power implied is in excess of human power. But nothing obliges us to suppose that either the knowledge or the skill is infinite.

We are not even obliged to suppose that the contrivances and arrangements were always the best possible. If we judge them as we judge the work of human artificers, we find abundant defects. The human body, for example, is one of the most striking instances of artful and ingenious contrivance which nature offers. But we may well ask whether so complicated a machine could not have been made to last longer, and not get out of order so easily and frequently.

We may ask why the human race should have been so constituted as to grovel in wretchedness and degradation for countless ages before a small portion of it was enabled to lift itself into the very imperfect state of intelligence, goodness, and happiness which we enjoy.

If, however, Deity, like human rule, had to adapt Himself to a set of conditions which He did not make, it is as unphilosophical, as presumptuous in us to call Him to account for any imperfections in His work; to complain that he left anything in it contrary to what (if indications of design prove anything) He must have intended.

So much for the attributes of omnipotence and omniscience. But what about the traditional moral attribute assigned to God? Is God, perhaps, similarly limited concerning His goodness? To settle this question—and Mill devotes a good deal of space to it—he suggests we try to discover the answer by again examining the evidence we find all around us and the purposes of the Creator that we may find revealed in that evidence. What Mill finds revealed is, as he puts it, "some benevolence but no justice."

Assuming then, that while we confine ourselves to the evidence of design in nature, there is no ground for ascribing infinite power, and probably no grounds for ascribing infinite knowledge or intelligence to Deity, the question arises as to the same evidence afforded with regard to His moral attributes. What indications does nature give of the purposes of its author?

This question bears a very different aspect to us from what it bears to those who are encumbered with the doctrine of the omnipotence of Deity. We do not have to attempt the impossible problem of reconciling infinite benevolence and justice with infinite power and knowledge in such a world as this. The attempt to do so involves a contradiction, and exhibits to excess the revolting spectacle of a jesuitical defense of enormities.

To what purpose, then, do the expedients and contrivances in the construction of animals and vegetables appear to tend? These are the "adaptations" which most excite our admiration. If they afford evidence of design, of purpose, in nature, we can best hope to be enlightened by examining such parts of nature.

There is no blinking the fact that these animal and vegetable adaptations tend principally to no more exalted object than to make the structure remain in life and in working order for a certain time: the individual for a few years, the species for a longer but still limited period.

The greater part of the design or adaptation in nature, however wonderful its mechanism, is, therefore, no evidence of any moral attributes in the author of nature; because the end to which it is directed is not a moral end: it is not the good of any creature but the qualified permanence, for a limited period of the work itself.

The only inference that can be drawn from most of nature, respecting the character of the author of nature, is that He does not wish His work to perish as soon as created. He wills them to have a certain duration.

In addition to the great number of adaptations which have no apparent object but to keep the organism going, there are a certain number of provisions for giving pleasure and a certain number for giving pain. These, perhaps, should be included among the contrivances for keeping the creature or its species in existence; for both the pleasures and the pains are generally so disposed as to attract to the things which maintain existence and deter from the things which would destroy it.

When these matters are considered, a vast deduction must be made from the facts usually cited as evidence of the benevolence of the Creator; so vast, indeed, that some may doubt whether any remains.

Yet, viewing the matter impartially, it does appear that there is a preponderance of evidence that the Creator desired the pleasure of His creatures. This is indicated by the fact, which cannot itself be denied, that pleasure of one description or another, is afforded by almost all of the powers, mental and physical, possessed by the creature.

The author of these pleasure-giving and pain-preventing adaptations is no doubt accountable for having made the creature susceptible of pain. But this may have been a necessary condition of its susceptibility to pleasure: a supposition which avails nothing on the theory of an omnipotent creator, but is extremely probable in the case of a limited creator.

There is, therefore, much evidence that the creature's pleasure is agreeable to the Creator; while there is very little if any evidence that its pain is so. There is, then, justification for inferring that benevolence is one of the attributes of the Creator.

But to jump from this to the inference that his sole or chief purposes are those of benevolence, and that the single end and aim of creation was the happiness of his creatures, is not only not justified by any evidence but is a conclusion in opposition to such evidence as we have.

If the motive of the Deity for creating sentient beings was the haziness of those beings, His purpose, in our corner of the universe at least, must be pronounced to have been thus far an ignominious failure. If God had no purpose but our happiness, and that of other living creatures, it is incredible that He would have called them into existence with the prospect of being so completely baffled.

If man had not the power, by the exercise of his own energies, to improve himself and his circumstances, to do for himself and other creatures vastly more than God had in the first instance done, then He [God] would deserve something very different from thanks at his [man's] hands.

Of course, it may be said that this very capacity of improving himself was given to man by God, and that the changes which man will be able ultimately to effect will be worth purchasing by the sufferings and wasted lives.

This may be so; but to suppose that God could not have procured these blessings for man at a less frightful cost is to make a very strange supposition concerning the Deity. It is to suppose that God could not, in the first instance, create anything better than a primitive savage, and was yet able to endow this primitive savage with power of raising himself into a Newton or a Fénelon. We do not know the nature of the barriers which limit the divine omnipotence; but it is a very odd notion of them that they enable the Deity to confer on a primitive savage the power of producing what God Himself had no other means of creating.

Such are the indications respecting the divine benevolence. If we look for any other moral attribute, for example, justice, we find a total blank. There is no evidence whatever in nature of divine justice, whatever standard of justice we may hold. There is no shadow of justice in the general arrangements of nature. Whatever justice exists in human society is the work of man himself, struggling upwards against immense natural difficulties into civilization, and making to himself a second, and far better and more unselfish nature than he was created with.

And, finally, Mill summarizes his findings in these words:

These, then, are the net results of natural theology on the question of the divine attributes. A Being of great but limited power, how or by what limited we cannot even conjecture; of great and perhaps unlimited intelligence; who desires, and pays some regard to the happiness of His creatures, but who scorns to have other motives of action which He cares more for, and who can hardly be supposed to have created the universe for that purpose alone.

Such is the Deity whom natural religion points to; and any idea of God more captivating than this comes only from human wishes, or from the teaching of either real or imaginary revelation.

But Mill does not end on this discouraging and despairing note. The idea of a finite God—so unlike the traditional view—is not, he says, without its compensating and edifying aspect.

This religious idea admits of one elevated feeling, which is not open to those who believe in the omnipotence of the good principle in the universe, the feeling of helping God—of requiting the good He has given by a voluntary cooperation which He, not being omnipotent, really needs, and by which a somewhat nearer approach may be made to the fulfillment of His purposes. This is the most invigorating thought which can inspire a human creature.

229

Intelligent Design

Although within the halls of academic philosophy, the arguments for the existence of God and the responses to them have gotten considerably less attention than, for example, questions of metaphysics, epistemology, and ethics over the past hundred years or so, the arguments are very much alive and well in the wranglings of popular philosophical discussion. From creationism (from the Scopes Trial to contemporary attempts to revise biology textbooks) to intelligent design, the arguments for the existence of God seem never very far from the public consciousness. Interestingly enough, most of the conversation of the early twenty-first century has centered around arguments for the existence of God that have their origin in the work of St. Thomas of Aquinas, particularly his Fifth Way.

The Proof from Harmony goes by many different names and has been incarnated in many different philosophical schemes since St. Thomas. Indeed, descendants of the proof continue to crop up within debates over the teaching of theories about the origins of human existence within various and sundry school districts even in the early parts of the twenty-first century. Few arguments have shown the subtlety and sophistication of St. Thomas's, however. Alternatively known as the Proof from Intelligent Design and the Teleological Proof, a version of the Fifth Way became part of the popular vernacular in the hands of eighteenth-century philosopher and theologian William Paley. Paley's Watchmaker Argument for the existence of God is essentially a pale and rather quick imitation of St. Thomas's. Paley's argument proceeds from an analogy. Given that a watch is a rather intricately ordered thing and that its order is imparted to it by the watchmaker, so too must the intricately ordered cosmos demonstrate, by inference, the delicate hand of the cosmic designer. Paley's Watchmaker Argument, though, suffers from a fatal and equally quick flaw. Recalling that for any analogy to hold, the related features of the argument must bear the same relationship to one another and that one cannot go beyond that relationship to introduce new items in one not found in the other, we can quickly discard Paley. As David Hume points out, the two relata that form the first half of the analogy—the watch and the watchmaker—are finite, and because, at the very least, our experience of the cosmos is similarly finite, it is impossible, then, to impute infinitude to the presumably analogous designer of that cosmos. In other words, while the designer of the universe could be conceived as tremendously large, it would be impossible to suppose that designer to be infinite, based on the analogy itself. Hence, the Watchmaker proof fails to demonstrate its conclusion.

The failure of Paley's Watchmaker Argument, however, points out a strength of St. Thomas's Fifth Way. The Watchmaker Argument fails because it appeals to an analogy that is ultimately unsupportable. St. Thomas's final proof does not appeal to an analogy, although the natural teleology of Paley's argument is clearly present in St. Thomas's. This final piece of the larger argument that is the Five Ways begins with the claim that inanimate things have ends. Here, we need to recall that St. Thomas follows an Aristotelian distinction that has fallen out of favor. By "inanimate" here, St. Thomas does not mean "without life." He simply means, as did Aristotle, that there are objects in the world that do not possess the ability to move themselves. So, plants, for example, are inanimate on this interpretation. Whatever the case, this is a semantic matter than can cause confusion but does not affect the argument itself.

Let us consider an acorn. An acorn has as its natural end the oak tree that it has the power to become. However, a necessary condition of possessing a natural end is the ability to tend toward that end or to form intentions the goal of which is that natural end. Thus, it would be necessary for the acorn to form the intention to become an oak tree. It is commonly granted that intelligence is a necessary condition of intention formation. If this is so, then it would seem to follow that inanimate things cannot possess natural ends because they do not possess intelligence. Thus, the acorn could not form intentions because it does not possess intelligence, and because it cannot form intentions, it must be without a natural end. However, this is counter to the observation with which this proof began, and therefore there must be some explanation for the possession of ends by inanimate entities. Suppose we assume, however, that inanimate things do not have ends, as would seem to follow from the requirement that intention formation requires an intelligence that acorns do not possess. As this would contradict the observable evidence, this assumption must be rejected. Thus, the only explanation for the end possessed by the acorn is that there must be some external entity who possesses both intelligence and the capacity to form intentions for acorns and to implant that intention into the acorn. By extension, since all natural objects have ends well before they are able to form intentions toward those ends, the relationship of this intelligent designer must be the same whether the object for whom the intentions is formed is an acorn or a human being. Thus, there must exist some intelligent designer who is the author of the natural ends of all things.

Most of the very contemporary discussions of intelligent design are more of the variety of William Paley's rather than St. Thomas's. While attention to the subtleties of the Proof from Harmony is beneficial for improving the conversation about the nature of God and intelligent design as a theological matter, a distinction that St. Thomas recognized cuts deeply into the desire to use intelligent design as an alternative to Darwinian evolutionary theory and its varied descendants. Indeed, prior to St. Thomas, the distinction between offering natural explanations for natural phenomena and offering supernatural explanations for the same natural phenomena was recognized by the ancient Greek philosophers. When Socrates argued that he was not a natural philosopher in the *Apology*, he was exploiting this distinction.

Simply put, at the end of the day, any argument that invokes God as an explanatory tool fails to adhere to the strict definition of science, or natural philosophy. The natural philosophers of the ancient period (e.g., Thales) understood that to use supernatural explanations for natural phenomena was to make a category mistake. That is, supernatural things and natural things are fundamentally different kinds of things. Science is properly concerned exclusively with natural things and natural explanations of them.

Thus, any theory that purports to be a competitor to evolutionary theory or theories of gravity, inertia, and motion must likewise remain firmly and exclusively within the realm of natural things and natural explanations. However subtle and theologically satisfying intelligent design arguments may be, they are ultimately outside the purview of science and thus not, strictly speaking, scientific theories.

CAN PROOFS FOR THE EXISTENCE OF GOD SUCCEED?

At this juncture, the question of the potential success of any argument for the existence of God comes into play more and more. Might it be the case that no proof for God's existence is possible? Immanuel Kant wades into this conversation, following Hume and St. Thomas and asking whether the proposition that "there exists a necessary being" can be demonstrated deductively. With regard to this particular proposition, Hume has already addressed it at some length in his *Dialogues concerning Natural Religion*, in which he showed that the common proofs offered to his day for God's existence each failed to demonstrate that existence. Hume's *Dialogues* had great influence on Kant, who wrote that Hume had awakened him from his dogmatic slumbers. Part of the genius of Kant's work is that he moves beyond Hume's own view to a stronger one. While Hume showed that all the proofs to his day had failed, Kant demonstrates not only that all proofs had failed but that they would always fail as well. In other words, that it is impossible to deductively demonstrate that God exists.

This is not a new idea. Boethius had held something similar, arguing that notions about God were the proper realm of faith and not of deductive argument. Indeed, Hume's own limited conclusion anticipates Kant's stronger one. Kant's argument is rather straightforward. Anything that might count as evidence for an inductive proof for the existence of God (e.g., a proof in the empirical vein of St. Thomas's) will never be able to point, conclusively, beyond the physical world of which it is a part. So, an appeal to the beauty or order of nature can point no further than the realm within which it is, namely, the physical world. Further, given that there are infinitely many possible explanations for the evidence, explanations that cannot be ruled out without question begging or circularity or dogmatic ad hominem, the deistic explanation is merely one possibility among several.

Any proof that approaches the proposition from the rationalistic side is likewise eliminated. At most, any rationalistic proof is completely dependent upon unargued axioms and postulates. While deductively certain, within the scope of those axioms, the axioms can simply be rejected, and no argument can establish them (else they are not axioms but theorems). Thus, there is no deductively certain foundation from which to argue for the proposition. Thus, since it is impossible to demonstrate inductively or deductively that "there exists a necessary being," we can conclude that the proposition is without proof.

It is important to note a logical consequence of any conclusion. If any proposition is demonstrated to be beyond proof, then its contradiction must likewise be beyond proof. If it were not, then a logician could simply assume the contradictory principle, demonstrate it to be either true or false, and in virtue of syllogistic inference demonstrate that the original proposition is either false or true. So, any proposition shown to be beyond deductive proof entails that its contradiction is also. Thus, since it is impossible to prove that "there exists a necessary being," it is also impossible to prove the contradiction, "there does not exist a necessary being."

RELIGIOUS BELIEF

If proof for God's existence is beyond the scope of deductive proof, the question becomes whether one ought to believe in God. Some who have pointed out that one proof for the existence of God or another does not succeed in proving what it claims have been labeled *infidel* or *atheist*. For example, when Hume's *Dialogues* was published, he was roundly called "The Great Infidel" by several members of the clergy of his home, Scotland. Yet careful reading of his *Dialogues* reveals that the furthest Hume goes is to argue that none of the arguments for the existence of God heretofore offered was successful; he does not argue that God does not exist, only that the proofs so far offered fail. More careful and fair-minded philosophical approaches turn to the question not of God's existence but of the nature of religious belief itself. Among these careful thinkers are early modern philosophers like Blaise Pascal and twentieth-century philosophers like William James.

Blaise Pascal

Blaise Pascal was born in Clermont, France, on June 19, 1623, to a devout, well-to-do Catholic family. Very early on—he was educated at home—he displayed a remarkable talent in physics and mathematics. By age 15, he had already begun to compose works on geometry and physics that were highly admired by the learned world of his age.

In 1650, when Pascal was 27, his father died and left him and his sister, Jacqueline, a large inheritance. Jacqueline entered a convent and he went off to Paris, where for the next several years he led a somewhat dissolute life. Then on November 23, 1654—at the age of 31—he had a mystical experience that transformed him completely. He began to lead now a life of austerity and self-denial, of almsgiving and prayer. He spent his days reflecting on the meaning of the Christian faith, on the purpose of life, and on our longing for God. He jotted down his thoughts in the form of short fragments or paragraphs that he hoped some day to publish in completed form. Death came (at age 39) before the project and book could be completed. What was left were hundreds of loosely grouped thoughts, aphorisms, and jottings on what it means to be a Christian, how to find God, and the secret of human happiness. These fragments were subsequently published under the French title *Pensées* (Thoughts).

Strictly speaking, Pascal's Wager is not strictly an argument for the *existence* of God. Rather, Pascal's argument has more to do with the belief that an individual ought to

Blaise Pascal (1623–1662)

adopt *about* the existence of God. That is, whether or not God exists, *should* one believe that God exists. The reason for this shift in focus is because Pascal is deeply ambiguous about what sorts of evidence might be marshaled to argue for the existence of God, an ambiguity that we find Kant later employing to great effect. In a sense, here, Pascal is reacting against the natural theology of St. Thomas to one degree or another. Natural theology, the kind of investigation that we find engaged in by St. Thomas, attempts to support religious beliefs with arguments and evidence. Pascal says, however, that such attempts are useless because the arguments and evidence cannot truly convince and are far from compelling. Such attempts are suspect because they rely on reason, which is not ultimate. A much more superior resource is faith, and our appeal should be directed to it. As he puts it, "Proofs only convince the mind"; they make "little impression" on the heart.

Such proofs may establish the existence of "a God considered as great, powerful, and eternal," but they cannot establish the existence of "the God of Abraham, the God of Isaac, the God of Jacob." This is not to say that God is not great, powerful, and eternal. He is. But he is also "a God of love and comfort . . . who fills the soul and heart of those whom He possesses," and our attention should be drawn to that.

Pascal doesn't deny that the world reveals some evidence of God's presence. The evidence, however, is ambiguous, as there are traces everywhere of design and order but also of disorder, evil, and chaos. Whether the one (the order) or the other (the chaos) impresses itself on us depends on prior faith on our part. In short, the evidence is real enough, but it is sufficient to convince only those who approach it with a deep need and longing for God. For God can be grasped only by the heart; He is not present to those who don't love Him.

On the night of November 23, Pascal was alone in his bedroom reading the seventeenth chapter of the Gospel of John, the high-priestly prayer of Jesus spoken before his final suffering and sacrifice. As Pascal read and reread these words he was caught up in an experience of burning, radiant ecstasy. The vacuum in his desperate life was suddenly and mysteriously filled. From that moment onward he knew in his heart of hearts what he had to do and to become. As the ecstasy began to fade he reached for the nearest piece of paper and began to write quickly, fervently:

The year of grace, 1654

Monday, 23rd November, feast of Saint Clement,

Pope and Martyr, and of others in the martyrology

Vigil of Saint Chrysogonus, Martyr, and others,

From about half past ten until about half past twelve

FIRE

God of Abraham, God of Isaac, God of Jacob,

not of the philosophers and *savants*

Certitude. Certitude. Feeling. Joy. Peace.

God of Jesus Christ.

My God and Thy God

"Thy God shall be my God"

Forgetfulness of the world, and of everything except God

He is to be found only in the ways taught in the Gospel

Grandeur of the human soul

Righteous Father, the world hath not known Thee,

but I have known Thee

Joy, joy, joy, tears of joy

I have fallen from Him

"They have forsaken me, the fountain of living water"

My God, wilt Thou forsake met?

May I not fall from Him for ever

This is eternal life, that they might know Thee, the only

true God, and Jesus Christ whom Thou hast sent

Jesus Christ

Jesus Christ

I have fallen away; I have fled from Him,

denied Him, crucified Him

May I not fall away from Him for ever

We hold Him only by the ways taught in the Gospel

Renunciation total and sweet

Total submission to Jesus Christ and to my director

Eternally in joy for a day's exercise on earth

I will not forget Thy word. Amen.

Shortly after Pascal's death eight years later, this paper and a parchment copy he had made were discovered sewn into the lining of his jacket. He had kept his Memorial of the experience close to him during all that time.

—**Roger Hazelton, *Blaise Pascal: The Genius of His Thought* (1974)**

If such arguments cannot prove God's existence what, we may ask, can? Our strongest proof for God's existence, Pascal replies, is the great need felt by the human soul for His sustaining presence. Without that presence, our life is meaningless—filled with boredom, anxiety, and wretchedness. It is God and God alone who can fill this emptiness. God made us so that we might enter into a relationship with Him and enjoy Him forever. Our wretchedness comes from having turned away from God and sought our satisfaction in other things. The result of this *rebellion* is the human misery we all experience. We must come to realize that only God can truly satisfy us.

Unfortunately, we are not helped much by the ambiguity of the physical evidence of God's existence. The evidence *is* ambiguous but for good reason: were it otherwise, the evidence of His reality would overwhelm us and *compel* us to acknowledge Him. He withholds such evidence, therefore, for He wants us to come to Him freely and willingly and on our own accord.

Seeing that the evidence for God's existence is ambiguous, what is such a person to do? To convince such people that they have nothing to lose by turning to God, Pascal proposes his famous wager. Man cannot know whether God does or does not exist, but he can take his stand and stake his life on God's side. This is not a rational solution but a mystical one, one dictated by our heart, which, we must remember "has its reasons, which reason does not know at all." Why not then bet that God indeed does exist, for what can one lose in so doing? Either God exists or He does not exist; if you bet that He exists and He in fact does exist, you gain all; if you lose the bet because He in fact does not exist, you lose nothing. In wagering on God's existence, your stake is zero; your reward, if God exists, is infinite. To follow only one's reason is to end in doubt and despair and to leave unsatisfied our deepest longings. On the other hand, in religious feeling we directly experience God and find peace.

> A disciple once approached his Hassidic master to complain about a companion who was passing himself off as a saint. The master replied: fear not, such a person has a severe punishment awaiting him—if he keeps it up long enough, he may become one!

But can a person take that first step—make himself or make herself believe in God? Pascal answers that it is possible: it may take time and effort, but it can be done. Start, he urges, by going to church, saying prayers, going to mass, giving alms, and so on—before long you'll find you've truly come to believe.

William James

William James was born in New York City in 1842 to a wealthy and highly cultured family. The family traveled a great deal, and William, his sister, and his three brothers were educated in various schools in Europe and America. Unlike his brother Henry (the famous novelist), who showed a definite inclination toward literature at an early age, William was slow to find his way. He tried painting, then studied chemistry and biology at Harvard. Still unable to reach a choice of a career, he went on a scientific expedition to Brazil with Louis Agassiz, the great naturalist. He returned to America and completed his work for his doctor's degree at Harvard.

During all this time, James suffered from poor health and deep depression—at times even considering suicide. This depression did not begin to lift until the age of 30, when he finally achieved his first permanent teaching post as instructor in physiology at Harvard, and did not leave entirely, apparently, until his marriage, six years later in 1878, to Alice Gibbens.

While James was teaching anatomy and physiology at Harvard, his interest began to turn to psychology and philosophy, which he felt was his true vocation. In 1880 he transferred to the philosophy department and began to compose his famous work *The Principles of Psychology*, on which he labored for over a decade. James had hoped to write an equally accomplished work in philosophy but he never came to complete such a systematic tome in that subject, writing instead (aside from his classic master work in religion, *Varieties of Religious Experience*) a series of essays on various topics in philosophy—essays that became famous in their own right. James died in his New Hampshire home in 1910. James's aim in his essay "The Will to Believe" (which he thought might better have been titled "The Right to Believe") is to point out that, under certain circumstances, where the evidence is insufficient to justify belief on strictly "rational" grounds, there may exist other grounds on which one may justifiably profess belief—in short, that ordinary evidence is not the only thing that gives one a "right to believe." What these other things may be and why he believes they are compelling is the subject of his essay.

James begins with a few remarks about **hypotheses**, explaining how some may be alive or dead. He then explains what he means by an **option**, which is a decision between two rival hypotheses. But options may be either *living* or *dead, forced* or *avoidable, momentous* or *trivial*. An option that is *living, forced,* and *momentous* he calls *genuine*. What James wants to say now is that when we are forced with a genuine option to choose between rival hypotheses (e.g., between believing in God or not believing in Him), neither of which is backed by sufficient evidence, we are justified in such circumstances to follow the dictates of our hearts or passional nature.

It may be true that God exists, or it may be false that He does. There is obviously no conclusive evidence here either way. But this is one of those hypotheses that is alive, and its options are both forced and momentous—so much so, in fact, that anyone who so desires has the right to stake his or her life on the belief that He does exist, for if He does exist, then this is the most important truth about reality there can be, a truth

William James (1842–1910)

tremendously vital to us, one we all feel deeply and passionately in need of. And that is justification enough.

Does this mean then that according to James anything that we wish or "will" deeply and are emotionally committed to we may justifiably believe exists and is true? If by "anything" we mean just anything at all, the answer, of course, is no. But if the "willing" and the yearning is something deeply and widely shared, then such passional feeling, integral to our nature, may indeed prove reliable. For not only our intellect but our heart, too, is an equally credible instrument. In addition, we must realize that "truths" are not only ascertained or discovered; they may be realized or achieved by people that value them, adopt them, and fulfill their lives by acting on them. As James himself declares in *The Varieties of Religious Experience*, "My first act of free will shall be to believe in free will." And similarly with faith in God.

But what sort of God does such faith and deliberate willing reveal? What sort of Being does our moral and passional nature with its needs, concerns, fears, and hopes seem to point to and require? What this temperament and nature of ours seems to reveal, says James, is a God who is part of our universe, a sympathetic and powerful helper, a great Companion and Friend. He is a conscious, personal, and moral Being of the same nature as ourselves—one with whom we can come into communion, as certain experiences, such as sudden conversions, show. He is a finite God to whom the evils in the world are as real as they are to us.

SUMMARY

1. The area of philosophy concerned with questions regarding the nature of God, and religious belief/knowledge is sometimes called "religion" and at others "philosophy of religion." Finally, it is concerned with whether the world is ruled by a supreme Being, a God, who guides it on its course and metes out rewards and punishments (rational theology).

2. The attempt to unravel the design of the universe has always been fraught with danger for philosophers. Tending to challenge established religion and deeply held convictions, their discoveries about the nature of the universe have dismayed their contemporaries and sometimes led to their deaths.

3. St. Augustine offers a very careful exposition of the Problem of Evil and offers a *Free Will* theodicy that seeks to provide a defense for the goodness, omnipotence, and omnibenevolence of God despite the existence of evil. The argument turns on an ontological distinction between different sorts of existence and a conception of the human will and human freedom.

4. According to St. Thomas, certain facts of nature are compelling evidence of God's existence. St. Thomas notes five such facts in particular, which, he believes, cry out for explanation, the only acceptable one being God. He argues, accordingly, that nothing can adequately account for the fact of motion or change—rejecting the idea that change

or motion is simply an ultimate, mysterious fact of nature neither requiring nor permitting any explanation—except God, its Unmoved Prime Mover. And similarly with such further, seemingly ultimate and mysterious facts of nature as Cause (that the series of causes in nature must have had their beginning in a First Cause, itself uncaused), Contingency (the fact that the things in nature all seem to be dependent on other things for their existence and thus imply the existence of a being not so dependent or contingent but "Necessary"), degrees of Excellence or Imperfection (which imply the existence of a being who is Perfect or Excellent in every way), and, finally, Harmony (the fact that things in nature are perfectly adapted for their particular function—the eyes for seeing, thick fur as protection against the cold, and so on, which imply the existence of a Being who has seen to this adaptation). These five facts of nature provide us thus with the following account or description of God's nature: He is unchanging; He is uncaused; He is necessary; He is perfect; and, finally, He is providential (He looks out for his creatures).

5. Hume admits that there is indeed "a curious adaptation of means to ends" throughout all nature, but is this resemblance between the things in nature and the things produced by human beings (such as machines) exact enough and strong enough to prove that the universe, too (like the things made by man), is the product of an intelligent Maker? In a detailed and close examination of the features of the universe that might support this conjecture, Hume concludes that the evidence for the existence of such a Grand Designer is far from certain. On the contrary, what the evidence tends to show is that if the universe was indeed made by some such deity, it must have been by a minor one, possessed of limited skill and intelligence who doubtless botched and bungled several previous attempts at world making (the products of which had consequently to be trashed) before finally producing our current highly imperfect one. Hume concludes, therefore, that the argument—that the universe, being like a human artifact, such as a watch or a house, therefore must have been created by a similarly intelligent Being—has implications that are far from encouraging. Indeed, judging by the world such a Deity has created, we can only conclude that He is neither all powerful, nor all wise, nor all good.

6. According to Mill, of all the arguments for God's existence, the one that has a measure of cogency is the argument from design. Unlike the other arguments, which appeal to such matters as first causes and first movers that we can know nothing about, its appeal is to things in our world that all of us know and can observe all around us. But, unfortunately, the argument, although superior to the Darwinian one, does not prove everything its supporters have claimed for it. Certainly it does not confirm the existence of an all-powerful, all-knowing, all-good God but seems to point to a somewhat more limited Being, finite both in power and in intelligence and possibly even in goodness—whose purpose does not seem to be the happiness of the creatures He created but some other mysterious goal to whose realization He is apparently more committed. If this is not an entirely comforting picture, let us remember that the evidence seems to indicate that God's work is still unfinished and that He both wants and needs

our help in bringing it to completion. And this cannot but be an elevating and invigorating thought.

7. There is a very important distinction that often confuses the distinction between religion and science. The first of these is that science deals in natural explanations for natural events and objects, while religion often makes use of supernatural explanations for the same or similar events and objects. As such, intelligent design arguments are not strictly competitors with purely scientific theories. Immanuel Kant (and Pascal) point out that the ambiguity of evidence that might be employed to argue for the existence of God ultimately thwarts both the arguments for God's existence and the arguments against God's existence.

8. Unlike St. Thomas, Pascal argues that it is impossible for man to demonstrate the existence of God and that philosophic proofs are of no real value. Reason may have its place in science, he says, but not in religion. Not being a sensible or an intellectual thing or being but a spirit, God can be reached only spiritually through our emotions and feelings. Indeed, the strongest proof for His existence is the great need felt by the human soul for Him. For without God, our lives are empty, wretched, and poor—an emptiness and wretchedness that only He can still. It is true that the evidence for His existence is ambiguous, but there are good reasons for this. Besides, with so much at stake here, why not open our hearts to Him and wager that He does indeed exist!

9. James argues that our rational intellects are incapable of deciding the question of the existence of God, either because there is no good evidence on either side of the question or because what evidence there is on one side is balanced out by equally good evidence on the other side. On the other hand, we find ourselves subject to a powerful desire to believe in God. This wish and desire, emanating from our passionate nature, is one that is both deeply and widely shared. Perhaps it is not, therefore, entirely subjective but is revelatory of something truly existent that is of vital importance to us. So vital, in fact, that belief in it is more than justified and entirely worth risking.

KEY TERMS

cosmology	option
determinism	rational theology
hypotheses	theodicy
metaphysics	Thomism

REVIEW QUESTIONS

1. What is the Problem of Evil, and how does St. Augustine's theodicy attempt to solve it?

2. Which of St. Thomas's five arguments do you find the clearest and most convincing? Why?

3. How is the intelligent design argument of the early twenty-first century similar to the Proof from Harmony?

4. Hume finds the argument from design almost totally wanting but not so Mill. Whom do you find more convincing here, Hume or Mill? Why?

5. Why, according to Pascal, should we believe in God?

6. Mill's and James's arguments for God's existence share much in common. In which respect or respects do they differ?

■ Reading

Dialogues Concerning Natural Religion

DAVID HUME

Excerpted from *The Philosophical Works of David Hume*, vol. 2 (Edinburgh: Adam Black and William Tait; Charles Tait, 1876).

Part II

Look round the world: contemplate the whole and every part of it: You will find it to be nothing but one great machine, subdivided into an infinite number of lesser machines, which again admit of subdivisions to a degree beyond what human senses and faculties can trace and explain. All these various machines, and even their most minute parts, are adjusted to each other with an accuracy which ravishes into admiration all men who have ever contemplated them. The curious adapting of means to ends, throughout all nature, resembles exactly, though it much exceeds, the productions of human contrivance; of human design, thought, wisdom, and intelligence. Since therefore the effects resemble each other, we are led to infer, by all the rules of analogs, that the causes also resemble; and that the Author of Nature is somewhat similar to the mind of man, though possessed of much larger faculties, proportioned to the grandeur of the work which he has executed. By this argument a posteriori, and by this argument alone, do we prove at once the existence of a Deity, and his similarity to human mind and intelligence.

I shall be so free, Cleanthes, said Demea, as to tell you, that from the beginning I could not approve of your conclusion concerning the similarity of the Deity to men; still less can I approve of the mediums by which you endeavour to establish it. What! No demonstration of the Being of God! No abstract arguments! No proofs a priori! Are these, which have hitherto been so much insisted on by philosophers, all fallacy, all sophism? Can we reach no farther in this subject than experience and probability? I will not say that this is betraying the cause of a Deity: But surely, by this affected candour, you give advantages to Atheists, which they never could obtain by the mere dint of argument and reasoning.

What I chiefly scruple in this subject, said Philo. is not so much that all religious arguments are by Cleanthes reduced to experience, as that they appear not to be even the most certain and irrefragable of that inferior kind. That a stone will fall, that fire will burn, that the earth has solidity we have observed a thousand and a thousand times; and when any new instance of this nature is presented, we draw without hesitation the accustomed inference. The exact similarity of the cases gives us a perfect assurance of a similar event; and a stronger evidence is never desired nor sought after. But wherever you depart, in the least, from the similarity of the cases, you diminish proportionably the evidence; and may at last bring it to a very weak analogy, which is confessedly liable to error and uncertainty. After having experienced the circulation of the blood in human creatures, we make no doubt that it takes place in Titius and Maevius: But from its circulation in frogs and fishes, it is only a presumption, though a strong one, from analogy, that it takes place in men and other animals. The analogical reasoning is much weaker, when we infer the circulation of the sap in vegetables from our experience that the blood circulates in animals; and those, who hastily followed that imperfect analogy, are found, by more accurate experiments, to have been mistaken.

If we see a house, Cleanthes, we conclude, with the greatest certainty, that it had an architect or builder; because this is precisely that species of effect which we have experienced to proceed from that species of cause. But surely you will not affirm, that the universe bears such a resemblance to a house, that we can with the same certainty infer a similar cause, or that the analogy is here entire and perfect. The dissimilitude is so striking, that the utmost you can here pretend to is a guess, a conjecture, a presumption concerning a similar cause; and how that pretension will be received in the world, I leave you to consider.

It would surely be very ill received, replied Cleanthes; and I should be deservedly blamed and detested, did I allow, that the proofs of a Deity amounted to no more than a guess or conjecture. But is the whole adjustment of means to ends in a house and in the universe so slight a resemblance? The economy of final causes? The order, proportion, and arrangement of every part? Steps of a stair are plainly contrived, that human legs may use them in mounting; and this inference is certain and infallible. Human legs are also contrived for walking and mounting; and this inference, I allow, is not altogether so certain, because of the dissimilarity which you remark; but does it, therefore, deserve the name only of presumption or conjecture?

Good God! cried Demea, interrupting him, where are we? Zealous defenders of religion allow, that the proofs of a Deity fall short of perfect evidence! And you, Philo, on whose assistance I depended in proving the adorable mysteriousness of the Divine Nature, do you assent to all these extravagant opinions of Cleanthes? For what other name can I give them? or, why spare my censure, when such principles are advanced, supported by such an authority, before so young a man as Pamphilus?

You seem not to apprehend, replied Philo, that I argue with Cleanthes in his own way; and, by showing him the dangerous consequences of his tenets, hope at last to reduce him to our opinion. But what sticks most with you, I observe, is the representation which Cleanthes has made of the argument a posteriori; and finding that that argument is likely to escape your hold and vanish into air, you think it so disguised, that you can scarcely believe it to be set in its true light. Now, however, much I may dissent, in other respects, from the dangerous principles of Cleanthes, I must allow that he has fairly represented that argument; and I shall endeavour so to state the matter to you, that you will entertain no farther scruples with regard to it.

Were a man to abstract from every thing which he knows or has seen, he would be altogether incapable, merely from his own ideas, to determine what kind of scene the universe must be, or to give the preference to one state or situation of things above another. For as nothing which he clearly conceives could be esteemed impossible or implying a contradiction, every chimera of his fancy should be upon an equal footing; nor could he assign any just reason why he adheres to one idea or system, and rejects the others which are equally possible.

Again; after he opens his eyes, and contemplates the world as it really is, it would be impossible for him at first to assign the cause of any one event, much less of the whole of things, or of the universe. He might set his fancy a rambling; and she might bring him in an infinite variety of reports and representations. These would all be possible; but being all equally possible, he would never of himself give a satisfactory account for his preferring one of them to the rest. Experience alone can point out to him the true cause of any phenomenon.

Now, according to this method of reasoning, Demea, it follows (and is, indeed, tacitly allowed by Cleanthes himself), that order, arrangement, or the adjustment of final causes, is not of itself any proof of design; but only so far as it has been experienced to proceed from that principle. For aught we can know a priori, matter may contain the source or spring of order originally within itself, as well as mind does; and there is no more difficulty in conceiving, that the several elements, from an internal unknown cause, may fall into the most exquisite arrangement, than to conceive that their ideas, in the great universal mind, from a like internal unknown cause, fall into that arrangement. The equal possibility of both these suppositions is allowed. But, by experience, we find, (according to Cleanthes), that there is a difference between them. Throw several pieces of steel together, without shape or form; they will never arrange themselves so as to compose a watch. Stone, and mortar, and flood, without an architect, never erect a house. But the ideas in a human mind, we see, by an unknown, inexplicable economy, arrange themselves so as to form the plan of a watch or house. Experience, therefore, proves, that there is an original principle of order in mind, not in matter. From similar effects we infer similar causes. The adjustment of means to ends is alike in the universe, as in a machine of human contrivance. The causes, therefore, must be resembling.

I was from the beginning scandalized, I must own, with this resemblance, which is asserted, between the Deity and human creatures; and must conceive it to imply such a degradation of the Supreme Being as no sound Theist could endure. With your assistance, therefore, Demea, I shall endeavour to defend what you justly call the adorable mysteriousness of the Divine Nature, and shall refute this reasoning of Cleanthes, provided he allows that I have made a fair representation of it.

When Cleanthes had assented, Philo, after a short pause, proceeded in the following manner.

That all inferences, Cleanthes, concerning fact, are founded on experience; and that all experimental reasonings are founded on the supposition that similar causes prove similar effects, and similar effects similar causes; I shall not at present much dispute with you. But observe, I entreat you, with what extreme caution all just reasoners proceed in the transferring of experiments to similar cases. Unless the cases be exactly similar, they repose no perfect confidence in applying their past observation to any particular phenomenon. Every alteration of circumstances occasions a doubt concerning the event; and it requires new experiments to prove certainly that the new circumstances are of no moment or importance. A change in bulk, situation, arrangement, age, disposition of the air, or surrounding bodies; any of these particulars may be attended with the most unexpected consequences: And unless the objects be quite familiar to us, it is the highest temerity to expect with assurance, after any of these changes, an event similar to that which before fell under our observation. The slow and deliberate steps of philosophers here, if any where, are distinguished from the precipitate march of the vulgar, who, hurried on by the smallest similitude, are incapable of all discernment or consideration.

But can you think, Cleanthes, that your usual phlegm and philosophy have been preserved in so wide a step as you have taken, when you compared to the universe houses, ships, furniture, machines, and, from their similarity in some circumstances, inferred a similarity in their causes? Thought, design, intelligence, such as we discover in men and other animals, is no more than one of the springs and principles of the universe, as well as heat or cold, attraction or repulsion, and a hundred others, which fall under daily observation. It is an active cause, by which some particular parts of nature, we find, produce alterations on other parts. But can a conclusion, with any propriety, be transferred from parts to the whole? Does not the great disproportion bar all comparison and inference? From observing the growth of a hair, can we learn any thing concerning the generation of a man? Would the manner of a leaf's blowing, even though perfectly known, afford us any instruction concerning the vegetation of a tree?

But, allowing that we were to take the operations of one part of nature upon another, for the foundation of our judgment concerning the origin of the whole (which never can be admitted), yet why select so minute, so weak, so bounded a principle, as the reason and design of animals is found to be upon this planet? What peculiar privilege has this little agitation of the brain which we call thought, that we must thus make it the model of the whole universe? Our partiality in our own favour does indeed present it on all occasions; but sound philosophy ought carefully to guard against so natural an illusion.

So far from admitting, continued Philo, that the operations of a part can afford us any just conclusion concerning the origin of the whole, I will not allow any one part to form a rule for another part, if the latter be very remote from the former. Is there any reasonable ground to conclude, that the inhabitants of other planets possess thought, intelligence, reason, or any thing similar to these faculties in men? When nature has so extremely diversified her manner of operation in this small globe, can we imagine that she incessantly copies herself throughout so immense a universe? And if thought, as we may well suppose, be confined merely to this narrow corner, and has even there so limited a sphere of action, with what propriety can we assign it for the original cause of all things? The narrow views of a peasant, who makes his domestic economy the rule for the government of kingdoms, is in comparison a pardonable sophism.

But were we ever so much assured, that a thought and reason. resembling the human, were to be found throughout the whole universe, and were its activity elsewhere vastly greater and more commanding than it appears in this globe; yet I cannot see, why the operations of a world constituted, arranged, adjusted, can with any propriety be extended to a world which is in its embryo-state, and is advancing towards that constitution and arrangement. By observation, we know somewhat of the economy, action, and nourishment of a finished animal; but we must transfer with great caution that observation to the growth of a foetus in the womb, and still more to the formation of an animalcule in the loins of its male parent. Nature we find, even from our limited experience, possesses an infinite number of springs and principles, which incessantly discover themselves on every change of her position and situation. And what new and unknown principles would actuate her in so new and unknown a situation as that of the formation of a universe, we cannot, without the utmost temerity, pretend to determine.

A very small part of this great system, during a very short time, is very imperfectly discovered to us; and do we thence pronounce decisively concerning the origin of the whole?

Admirable conclusion! Stone, wood, brick, iron, brass, have not, at this time, in this minute globe of earth, an order or arrangement without human art and contrivance; therefore the universe could not originally attain its order and arrangement, without something similar to human art: But is a part of nature a rule for another part very wide of the former? Is it a rule for the whole? Is a very small part a rule for the universe? Is nature in one situation, a certain rule for nature in another situation vastly different from the former?

And can you blame me, Cleanthes, if I here imitate the prudent reserve of Simonides, who, according to the noted story, being asked by Hiero, What God was? desired a day to think of it, and then two days more; and after that manner continually prolonged the term, without ever bringing in his definition or description?

Could you even blame me, if I had answered at first, that I did not know, and was sensible that this subject lay vastly beyond the reach of my faculties? You might cry out sceptic and rallier, as much as you pleased: but having found, in so many other subjects much more familiar, the imperfections and even contradiction of human reason, I never should expect any success from its feeble conjectures, in a subject so sublime, and so remote from the sphere of our observation. When two species of objects have always been observed to be conjoined together, I can infer, by custom, the existence of one wherever I see the existence of the other; and this I call an argument from experience. But how this argument can have place, where the objects, as in the present case, are single, individual, without parallel, or specific resemblance, may be difficult to explain. And will any man tell me with a serious countenance, that an orderly universe must arise from some thought and art like the human, because we have experience of it? To ascertain this reasoning, it were requisite that we had experience of the origin of worlds; and it is not sufficient, surely, that we have seen ships and cities arise from human art and contrivance.

Philo was proceeding in this vehement manner, somewhat between jest and earnest, as it appeared to me, when he observed some signs of impatience in Cleanthes, and then immediately stopped short. What I had to suggest, said Cleanthes, is only that you would not abuse terms, or make use of popular expressions to subvert philosophical reasonings. You know, that the vulgar often distinguish reason from experience, even where the question relates only to matter of fact and existence; though it is found, where that reason is properly analyzed, that it is nothing but a species of experience. To prove by experience the origin of the universe from mind, is not more contrary to common speech, than to prove the motion of the earth from the same principle. And a caviller might raise all the same objections to the Copernican system, which you have urged against my reasonings. Have you other earths, might he say, which you have seen to move? Have . . .

Yes! cried Philo, interrupting him, we have other earths. Is not the moon another earth, which we see to turn round its centre? Is not Venus another earth, where we observe the same phenomenon? Are not the revolutions of the sun also a confirmation, from analogy, of the same theory? All the planets, are they not earths, which revolve about the sun? Are not the satellites moons, which move round Jupiter and Saturn, and along with these primary planets round the sun? These analogies and resemblances, with others which I have not mentioned, are the sole proofs of the Copernican system; and to you it belongs to consider, whether you have any analogies of the same kind to support your theory.

In reality, Cleanthes, continued he, the modern system of astronomy is now so much received by all inquirers, and has become so essential a part even of our earliest education, that we are not commonly very scrupulous in examining the reasons upon which it is founded. It is now become a matter of mere curiosity to study the first writers on that subject, who had the full force of prejudice to encounter, and were obliged to turn their arguments on every side in order to render them popular and convincing. But if we peruse Galileo's famous Dialogues concerning the system of the world, we shall find, that that great genius, one of the sublimest that ever existed, first bent all his endeavours to prove, that there was no foundation for the distinction commonly made between elementary and celestial substances. The schools, proceeding from the illusions of sense, had carried this distinction very far; and had established the latter substances to be ingenerable, incorruptible, unalterable, impassible; and had assigned all the opposite qualities to the former. But Galileo, beginning with the moon, proved its similarity in every particular to the earth; its convex figure, its natural darkness when not illuminated, its density, its distinction into solid and liquid, the variations of its phases, the mutual illuminations of the earth and moon, their mutual eclipses, the inequalities of the lunar surface, etc. After many instances of this kind, with regard to all the planets, men plainly saw that these bodies became proper objects of experience; and that the similarity of their nature enabled us to extend the same arguments and phenomena from one to the other.

In this cautious proceeding of the astronomers, you may read your own condemnation, Cleanthes; or rather may see, that the subject in which you are engaged exceeds all human reason and inquiry. Can you pretend to show any such similarity between the fabric of a house. and the generation of a universe? Hare you ever seen nature in any such situation as resembles the first arrangement of the elements? Have worlds ever been formed under your eye; and have you had leisure to observe the whole progress of the phenomenon, from the first appearance of order to its final consummation? If you have, then cite your experience, and deliver your theory . . .

Part V

But to show you still more inconveniences, continued Philo, in your Anthropomorphism, please to take a new survey of your principles. Like effects prove like causes. This is the experimental argument; and this, you say too, is the sole theological argument. Now, it is certain, that the liker the effects are which are seen, and the liker the causes which are inferred, the stronger is the argument. Every departure on either side diminishes the probability, and renders the experiment less conclusive. You cannot doubt of the principle; neither ought you to reject its consequences.

All the new discoveries in astronomy, which prove the immense grandeur and magnificence of the works of Nature, are so many additional arguments for a Deity according to the true system of Theism; but, according to your hypothesis of experimental Theism, they become so many objections, by removing the effect still farther from all resemblance to the effects of human art and contrivance . . .

If this argument, I say, had any force in former ages, how much greater must it have at present, when the bounds of Nature are so infinitely enlarged, and such a magnificent scene is opened to us? It is still more unreasonable to form our idea of so unlimited a cause from our experience of the narrow productions of human design and invention.

The discoveries by microscopes, as they open a new universe in miniature, are still objections, according to you, arguments, according to me. The farther we push our researches of this kind, we are still led to infer the universal cause of all to be vastly different from mankind, or from any object of human experience and observation.

And what say you to the discoveries in anatomy, chemistry, botany? . . . These surely are no objections, replied Cleanthes; they only discover new instances of art and contrivance. It is still the image of mind reflected on us from innumerable objects. Add, a mind like the human, said Philo. I know of no other, replied Cleanthes. And the liker the better, insisted Philo. To be sure, said Cleanthes.

Now, Cleanthes, said Philo, with an air or alacrity and triumph, mark the consequences. First, By this method of reasoning, you renounce all claim to infinity in any of the attributes of the Deity. For, as the cause ought only to be proportioned to the effect, and the effect, so far as it falls under our cognizance, is not infinite; what pretensions have we, upon your suppositions, to ascribe that attribute to the Divine Being? You will still insist, that, by removing him so much from all similarity to human creatures, we give in to the most arbitrary hypothesis, and at the same time weaken all proofs of his existence.

Secondly, You have no reason, on your theory for ascribing perfection to the Deity, even in his finite capacity, or for supposing him free from every error, mistake, or incoherence, in his undertakings. There are many inexplicable difficulties in the works of Nature, which, if we allow a perfect author to be proved a priori, are easily solved, and become only seeming difficulties, from the narrow capacity of man, who cannot trace infinite relations. But according to your method of reasoning, these difficulties become all real; and perhaps will be insisted on, as new instances of likeness to human art and contrivance. At least, you must acknowledge, that it is impossible for us to tell, from our limited views, whether this system contains any great faults, or deserves any considerable praise, if compared to other possible, and even real systems. Could a peasant, if the Aeneid were read to him, pronounce that poem to be absolutely faultless, or even assign to it its proper rank among the productions of human wit, he, who had never seen any other production?

But were this world ever so perfect a production, it must still remain uncertain, whether all the excellences of the work can justly be ascribed to the workman. If we survey a ship, what an exalted idea must we form of the ingenuity of the carpenter who framed so complicated, useful, and beautiful a machine? And what surprise must we feel, when we find him a stupid mechanic, who imitated others, and copied an art, which, through a long succession of ages, after multiplied trials, mistakes, corrections, deliberations, and controversies, had been gradually improving? Many worlds might have been botched and bungled, throughout an eternity, ere this system was struck out; much labour lost, many fruitless trials made; and a slow, but continued improvement carried on during infinite ages in the art of world-making. In such subjects, who can determine, where the truth; nay, who can conjecture where the probability lies, amidst a great number of hypotheses which may be proposed, and a still greater which may be imagined?

And what shadows of an argument, continued Philo, can you produce, from your hypothesis, to prove the unity of the Deity? A great number of men join in building a house or ship, in rearing a city, in framing a commonwealth; why may not several deities combine in contriving and framing a world? This is only so much greater similarity to human affairs. By sharing the work among several, we may so much farther limit the attributes of each, and get rid of that extensive power and knowledge, which must be supposed in one deity and which, according to you, can only serve to weaken the proof of his existence. And if such foolish, such vicious creatures as man, can yet often unite in framing and executing one plan, how much more those deities or demons, whom we may suppose several degrees more perfect!

To multiply causes without necessity is indeed contrary to true philosophy: but this principle applies not to the present case. Were one deity antecedently proved by your theory, who were possessed of every attribute requisite to the production of the universe; it would be needless, I own (though not absurd), to suppose any other deity existent. But while it is still a question, Whether all these attributes are united in one subject, or dispersed among several independent beings, by what phenomena in nature can we pretend to decide the controversy? Where we see a body raised in a scale, we are sure that there is in the opposite scale, however concealed from sight, some counterposing weight equal to it; but it is still allowed to doubt, whether that weight be an aggregate of several distinct bodies, or one uniform united mass. And if the weight requisite very much exceeds any thing which we have ever seen conjoined in any single body, the former supposition becomes still more probable and natural. An intelligent being of such vast power and capacity as is necessary to produce the universe, or, to speak in the language of ancient philosophy so prodigious an animal exceeds all analogy, and even comprehension.

But farther, Cleanthes: Men are mortal, and renew their species by generation; and this is common to all living creatures. The two great sexes of male and female, says Milton, animate the world. Why must this circumstance, so universal. so essential, be excluded from those numerous and limited deities? Behold, then, the theogeny of ancient times brought back upon us.

And why not become a perfect Anthropomorphite? Why not assert the deity or deities to be corporeal, and to have eyes, a nose, mouth, ears, &c.? Epicurus maintained, that no man had ever seen reason but in a human figure; therefore the gods must have a human figure. And this argument, which is deservedly so much ridiculed by Cicero, becomes, according to you, solid and philosophical.

In a word, Cleanthes, a man who follows your hypothesis is able perhaps to assert, or conjecture, that the universe, sometime, arose from something like design: but beyond that position he cannot ascertain one single circumstance; and is left afterwards to fix every point of his theology by the utmost license of fancy and hypothesis. This world, for aught he knows, is very faulty and imperfect, compared to a superior standard; and was only the first rude essay of some infant deity, who afterwards abandoned it, ashamed of his lame performance: it is the work only of some dependent, inferior deity; and is the object of derision to his superiors: it is the production of old age and dotage in some superannuated deity; and ever since his death, has run on at adventures, from the first impulse and active force which it received from him. You justly give signs of horror, Demea, at these strange suppositions; but these, and a thousand more of the same kind, are Cleanthes's suppositions, not mine. From the moment the attributes of the Deity are supposed finite, all these have place. And I cannot, for my part, think that so wild and unsettled a system of theology is, in any respect, preferable to none at all.

These suppositions I absolutely disown, cried Cleanthes: they strike me, however, with no horror, especially when proposed in that rambling way in which they drop from you. On the contrary, they give me pleasure, when I see, that, by the utmost indulgence of your imagination, you never get rid of the hypothesis of design in the universe, but are obliged at every turn to have recourse to it. To this concession I adhere steadily; and this I regard as a sufficient foundation for religion.

Part VI

It must be a slight fabric, indeed, said Demea, which can be erected on so tottering a foundation. While we are uncertain whether there is one deity or many; whether the deity or deities, to whom we owe our existence, be perfect or imperfect, subordinate or supreme, dead or alive, what trust or confidence can we repose in them? What devotion or worship address to them? What veneration or obedience pay them? To all the purposes of life the theory of religion becomes altogether useless: and even with regard to speculative consequences, its uncertainty, according to you, must render it totally precarious and unsatisfactory.

To render it still more unsatisfactory, said Philo, there occurs to me another hypothesis, which must acquire an air of profitability from the method of reasoning so much insisted on by Cleanthes. That like effects arise from like causes: this principle he supposes the foundation of all religion. But there is another principle of the same kind, no less certain, and derived from the same source of experience; that where several known circumstances are observed to be similar, the unknown will also be found similar. Thus, if we see the limbs of a human body, we concluded that it is also attended with a human head, though hid from us. Thus, if we see, through a chink in a wall, a small part of the sum, we conclude, that, were the wall removed, we should see the whole body. In short, this method of reasoning is so obvious and familiar, that no scruple can ever be made with regard to its solidity.

Now, if we survey the universe, so far as it falls under our knowledge, it bears a great resemblance to an animal or organized body and seems actuated with a like principle of life and motion. A continual circulation of matter in it produces no disorder: a continual waste in every part is incessantly repaired: the closest sympathy is perceived throughout the entire system: and each part or member. in performing its proper offices, operates both to its own preservation and to that of the whole. The world, therefore, I infer, is an animal, and the Deity is the SOUL of the world, actuating it, and actuated by it.

You have too much learning, Cleanthes, to be at all surprised at this opinion, which, you know, was maintained by almost all the Theists of antiquity, and chiefly prevails in their discourses and reasonings. For though, sometimes, the ancient philosophers reason from final causes, as if they thought the world the workmanship of God; yet it appears rather their favourite notion to consider it as his body whose organization renders it subservient to him. And it must be confessed, that, as the universe resembles more a human body than it does the works of human art and contrivance, if our limited analogy could ever, with any propriety, be extended to the whole of nature, the inference seems juster in favour of the ancient than the modern theory.

There are many other advantages, too, in the former theory, which recommended it to the ancient theologians. Nothing [was] more repugnant to all their notions, because nothing [was] more repugnant to common experience, than mind without body; a mere spiritual substance, which fell not under their senses nor comprehension, and of which they had not observed one single instance throughout all nature. Mind and body they knew, because they felt both: an order, arrangement, organization, or internal machinery, in both, they likewise knew, after the same manner: and it could not but seem reasonable to transfer this experience to the universe; and to suppose the divine mind and body to be also coeval, and to have, both of them, order and arrangement naturally inherent in them, and inseparable from them.

Here, therefore, is a new species of Anthropomorphism, Cleanthes, on which you may deliberate; and a theory which seems not liable to any considerable difficulties. You are too much superior, surely, to systematical prejudices, to find any more difficulty in supposing an animal body to be originally, of itself, or from unknown causes, possessed of order and organization, than in supposing a similar order to belong to mind. But the vulgar prejudice, that body and mind ought always to accompany each other, ought not, one should think, to be entirely neglected; since it is founded on vulgar experience, the only guide which you profess to follow in all these theological inquiries. And if you assert, that our limited experience is an unequal standard, by which to judge of the unlimited extent of nature; you entirely abandon your own hypothesis, and must thenceforward adopt our Mysticism, as you call it, and admit of the absolute incomprehensibility of the Divine Nature.

This theory, I own, replied Cleanthes, has never before occurred to me, though a pretty natural one; and I cannot readily, upon so short an examination and reflection, deliver any opinion with regard to it. You are very scrupulous, indeed, said Philo: were I to examine any system of yours, I should not have acted with half that caution and reserve, in starting objections and difficulties to it. However, if any thing occur to you, you will oblige us by proposing it.

Why then, replied Cleanthes, it seems to me, that, though the world does, in many circumstances, resemble an animal body; yet is the analogy also defective in many circumstances the most material: no organs of sense; no seat of thought or reason; no one precise origin of motion and action. In short, it seems to bear a stronger resemblance to a vegetable than to an animal, and your inference would be so far inconclusive in favour of the soul of the world.

■ Questions for Discussion

1. Philo raises the argument from design. If you had been a member of this small group discussing this question, how would you have responded to Philo's criticisms?

2. Philo declares that by this argument we make ourselves the model. Why so? Why shouldn't we?

3. Trying to bring us down a notch or two, Philo declares (Part II), "What peculiar privilege has this little agitation of the brain which we call thought, that we must thus make it the model of the whole universe?" What does this mean? How might we reply to this criticism?

■ Reading

"The Will to Believe"

WILLIAM JAMES

Excerpted from William James, "The Will to Believe," an address to the Philosophical Clubs of Yale and Brown universities (first published in the New World, 1896).

Let us give the name of hypothesis to anything that may be proposed to our belief; and just as the electricians speak of live and dead wires, let us speak of any hypothesis as either live or dead. A live hypothesis is one which appeals as a real possibility to him to whom it is proposed. If I ask you to believe in the Mahdi, the notion makes no electric connection with your nature,—it refuses to scintillate with any credibility at all. As an hypothesis it is completely dead. To an Arab, however (even if he be not one of the Mahdi's followers), the hypothesis is among the mind's possibilities: it is alive. This shows that deadness and liveness in an hypothesis are not intrinsic properties, but relations to the individual thinker. They are measured by his willingness to act. The maximum of liveness in an hypothesis means willingness to act irrevocably. Practically, that means belief; but there is some believing tendency wherever there is willingness to act at all.

Next, let us call the decision between two hypotheses an option. Options may be of several kinds. They may be—1, living or dead; 2, forced or avoidable; 3, momentous or trivial; and for our purposes we may call an option a genuine option when it is of the forced, living, and momentous kind.

A living option is one in which both hypotheses are live ones. If I say to you: "Be a theosophist or be a Mohammedan," it is probably a dead option, because for you neither hypothesis is likely to be alive. But if I say, "Be an agnostic or be a Christian," it is otherwise: trained as you are, each hypothesis makes some appeal, however small, to your belief.

Next, if I say to you: "Choose between going out with your umbrella or without it," I do not offer you a genuine option, for it is not forced. You can easily avoid it by not going out at all. Similarly, if I say, "Either love me or hate me," "Either call my theory true or call it false," your option is avoidable. You may remain indifferent to me, neither loving nor hating, and you may decline to offer any judgment as to my theory. But if I say, "Either accept this truth or go without it," I put on you a forced option, for there is no standing place outside of the alternative. Every dilemma based on a complete logical disjunction, with no possibility of not choosing, is an option of this forced kind. . . .

The thesis I defend is, briefly stated, this: Our passional nature not only lawfully may, but must, decide an option between propositions, whenever it is a genuine option that cannot by its nature be decided on intellectual grounds; for to say, under such circumstances, "Do not decide, but leave the question open," is itself a passional decision,—just like deciding yes or no,—and is attended with the same risk of losing the truth. . . .

Wherever the option between losing truth and gaining it is not momentous, we can throw the chance of gaining truth away, and at any rate save ourselves from any chance of believing falsehood, by not making up our minds at all till objective evidence has come. In scientific questions, this is almost always the case; and even in human affairs in general, the need of acting is seldom so urgent that a false belief to act on is better than no belief at all. Law courts, indeed, have to decide on the best evidence attainable for the moment, because a judge's duty is to make law as well as to ascertain it, and (as a learned judge once said to me) few cases are worth spending much time over: the great thing is to have them decided on any acceptable principle, and got out of the way. But in our dealings with objective nature we obviously are recorders, not makers, of the truth; and decisions for the mere sake of deciding promptly and getting on to the next business would be wholly out of place. Throughout the breadth of physical nature facts are what they are quite independently of us, and seldom is there any such hurry about them that the risks of being duped by believing a premature theory need be faced. The questions here are always trivial options, the hypotheses are hardly living (at any rate not living for us spectators), the choice between believing truth or falsehood is seldom forced. The attitude of sceptical balance is therefore the absolutely wise one if we would escape mistakes. What difference, indeed, does it make to most of us whether we have or have not a theory of the Röntgen rays, whether we believe or not in mind-stuff, or have a conviction about the causality of conscious states? It makes no difference. Such options are not forced on us. On every account it is better not to make them, but still keep weighing reasons pro et contra with an indifferent hand. . . .

. . . Religions differ so much in their accidents that in discussing the religious question we must make it very generic and broad. What then do we now mean by the religious hypothesis? Science says things are; morality says some things are better than other things; and religion says essentially two things.

First, she says that the best things are the more eternal things, the overlapping things, the things in the universe that throw the last stone, so to speak, and say the final word. "Perfection is eternal,"—this phrase of Charles Secrétan seems a good way of putting this first affirmation of religion, an affirmation which obviously cannot yet be verified scientifically at all.

The second affirmation of religion is that we are better off even now if we believe her first affirmation to be true.

Now, let us consider what the logical elements of this situation are in case the religious hypothesis in both its branches be really true. (Of course, we must admit that possibility at the outset. If we are to discuss the question at all, it must involve a living option. If for any of you religion be a hypothesis that cannot, by any living possibility be true, then you need go no farther. I speak to the 'saving remnant' alone.) So proceeding, we see, first that religion offers itself as a momentous option. We are supposed to gain, even now, by our belief and to lose by our nonbelief, a certain vital good. Secondly, religion is forced option, so far as that good goes. We cannot escape the issue by remaining sceptical and waiting for more light, because, although we do avoid error in that way if religion be untrue, we lose the good, if it be true, just as certainly as if we positively chose to disbelieve. It is as if a man should hesitate indefinitely to ask a certain woman to marry him because he was not perfectly sure that she would prove an angel after he brought her home. Would he not cut himself off from that particular angel-possibility as decisively as if he went and married some one else? Scepticism, then, is not avoidance of option; it is option of a certain particular kind of risk. Better risk loss of truth than chance of error,—that is your faith-vetoer's exact position. He is actively playing his stake as much as the believer is; he is backing the field against the religious hypothesis, just as the believer is backing the religious hypothesis against the field. To preach scepticism to us as a duty until 'sufficient evidence' for religion be found, is tantamount therefore to telling us, when in presence of the religious hypothesis, that to yield to our fear of its being error is wiser and better than to yield to our hope that it may be true. It is not intellect against all passions, then; it is only intellect with one passion laying down its law. And by what, forsooth, is the supreme wisdom of this passion warranted? Dupery for dupery, what proof is there that dupery through hope is so much worse than dupery through fear? I, for one, can see no proof; and I simply refuse obedience to the scientist's command to imitate his kind of option, in a case where my own stake is important enough to give me the right to choose my own form of risk. If religion be true and the evidence for it be still insufficient, I do not wish, by putting our extinguisher upon my nature (which feels to me as if it had after all some business in this matter), to forfeit my sole chance in life of getting upon the winning side,—that chance depending, of course, on my willingness to run the risk of acting as if my passional need of taking the world religiously might be prophetic and right.

All this is on the supposition that it really may be prophetic and right, and that, even to us who are discussing the matter, religion is a live hypothesis which may be true. Now, to most of us religion comes in a still further way that makes a veto on our active faith even more illogical. The more perfect and more eternal aspect of the universe is represented in our religions as having personal form. The universe is no longer a mere It to us, but a Thou, if we are religious; and any relation that may be possible from person to person might be possible here. For instance, although in one sense we are passive portions of the universe, in another we show a curious autonomy, as if we were small active centres on our own account. We feel, too, as if the appeal of religion to us were made to our own active goodwill, as if evidence might be forever withheld from us unless we met the hypothesis halfway. To take a trivial illustration: just as a man who in a company of gentlemen made no advances, asked a warrant for every concession, and believed no one's word without proof, would cut himself off by such churlishness from all the social rewards that a more trusting spirit would earn,—so here, one who should shut himself up in snarling logicality and try to make the gods extort his recognition willy-nilly, or not get it at all, might cut himself off forever from his only opportunity of making the gods' acquaintance. This feeling, forced on us we know not whence, that by obstinately believing that there are gods (although not to do so would be so easy both for our logic and our life) we are doing the universe the deepest service we can, seems part of the living essence of the religious hypothesis. If the hypothesis were true in all its parts, including this one, then pure intellectualism, with its veto on our making willing advances, would be an absurdity; and some participation of our sympathetic nature would be logically required. I, therefore, for one, cannot see my way to accepting the agnostic rules for truthseeking, or wilfully agree to keep my willing nature out of the game. I cannot do so for this plain reason, that a rule of thinking which would absolutely prevent me from acknowledging certain kinds of truth if those kinds of truth were really there, would be an irrational rule.

That for me is the long and short of the formal logic of the situation, no matter what the kinds of truth might materially be.

I confess I do not see how this logic can be escaped. But sad experience makes me fear that some of you may still shrink from radically saying with me, in abstracto, that we have the right to believe at our own risk any hypothesis that is live enough to tempt our will. I suspect, however, that if this is so, it is because you have got away from the abstract logical point of view altogether, and are thinking (perhaps without realizing it) of some particular religious hypothesis which for you is dead. The freedom to 'believe what we will' you apply to the case of some patent superstition; and the faith you think of is the faith defined by the schoolboy when he said, "Faith is when you believe something that you know ain't true." I can only repeat that this is misapprehension. In concreto, the freedom to believe can only cover living options which the intellect of the individual cannot by itself resolve; and living options never seem absurdities to him who has them to consider. When I look at the religious question as it really puts itself to concrete men and when I think of all the possibilities which both practically and theoretically it involves, then this command that we shall put a stopper on our heart, instincts, and courage, and wait—acting of course meanwhile more or less as if religion were not true—till doomsday, or till such time as our intellect and senses working together may have raked in evidence enough,—this command, I say, seems to me the queerest idol ever manufactured in the philosophic cave. Were we scholastic absolutists, there might be more excuse. If we had an infallible intellect with its objective certitudes, we might feel ourselves disloyal to such a perfect organ of knowledge in not trusting to it exclusively, in not waiting for its releasing word. But if we are empiricists, if we believe that no bell in us tolls to let us know for certain when truth is in our grasp, then it seems a piece of idle fanasticality to preach so solemnly our duty of waiting for the bell. Indeed we may wait if we will.—I hope you do not think that I am denying that,—but if we do so, we do so at our peril as much as if we believed. In either case we act, taking our life in our hands. . . .

■ Questions for Discussion

1. What does James mean by a living option? A forced option? A momentous and genuine one?

2. Under what conditions, according to James, is it rationally permissible to believe on faith that God exists? What are James's reasons for thinking so?

3. It has been said of James's theory that it amounts to an encouragement to us all to believe, at our own risk, whatever we like and that this would validate any and every belief that anyone feels an inclination to hold as long as it is not capable of being proved or disproved. Do you think this is an accurate representation of his view?

METAPHYSICS: THE STUDY OF NATURE, THE SELF, AND REALITY

Of the three main branches of philosophy, metaphysics is often the most difficult to isolate from the others. As traditionally conceived, metaphysics concerns itself with the question of the nature of the universe, asking, What is there and what is it like? Is the world rational and purposive, evolving toward some goal that is friendly to us and to our needs? Or is it essentially arational, goalless, and alien—dead matter conforming to immutable laws? In short, what metaphysics asks is, How is it with the world? However, answers to such questions tend to have an inherently speculative quality and, as a result, to suffer from a skeptical challenge: How do we know any of this? That challenge, encapsulated in the skepticism of sixteenth-century philosopher like Michel Montaigne and his classical predecessor, Pyrrho, demonstrates how quickly answers to metaphysical questions turn into epistemological questions.

In addition to the close connection between epistemology and metaphysics, there is a similar connection between metaphysics and ethics. As we will see later in the chapter, metaphysical issues like causation, freedom, and determinism have significant ethical implications. If we make the claim that we *ought* to do some action or other, it seems to follow rather quickly that it is the case that we *can* do it. In other words, to make an ethical claim is to say something about the metaphysical structure of the universe. Beyond this, metaphysics has also been interested in inquiring into the sort of beings we are. What are we really like? it asks. Do we possess souls that survive the death of our bodies and wills that are free, or are we determined by the same forces that govern other bodies in

> Nothing is certain, concluded Pyrrho (360–270 b.c.); and when he died his students, though they loved him, did not mourn him, for they could not be sure that he was dead.
>
> **—Will Durant, *The Story of Philosophy***

the universe and like them are devoid of choice and freedom and perish in time? Reactions to these kinds of questions have been mixed, to say the least. Here are some representative opinions:

> Metaphysics is without a doubt the most difficult of all human studies; only no metaphysics has yet been written.
>
> —*Immanuel Kant*

> Metaphysics is the finding of bad reasons for what we believe on instinct—but the finding of these reasons is no less an instinct.
>
> —*F. H. Bradley*

> In Tibet the second official in the state is called the "metaphysician in chief." Elsewhere philosophy is no longer held in such high esteem.
>
> —*Bertrand Russell*

Metaphysics is a subject the knowledge of which, like that of a sunken reef, serves chiefly to enable us to keep clear of it.

—**C. S. Peirce**

The British philosopher J. E. McTaggart identified the nature of this discipline and the reason for its powerful hold on us in these words: "The utility of metaphysics," he said, coming closer to describing it than any of the other writers, "is to be found in the comfort it can give us . . . in the chance that it may answer this supreme question [whether good or evil predominates in the universe] in a cheerful manner, that it may provide some solution which shall be a consolation and an encouragement."

We can perhaps see from these quotations why this part of philosophy, so reminiscent of what has traditionally been the goal of religion, has come to be identified with medieval thought—that period of our history that more than any other was obsessed with religious speculation.

The subject, of course, has a longer history and is not confined merely to the question of salvation. The term itself was first used around 70 B.C. by one of the editors of

Metaphysics never lets you down. You can never come to the end of it. It is as various as the soul of man. It has greatness, for it deals with nothing less than the whole of knowledge. It treats of the universe, of God and immortality, of the properties of the human reason and the end and purpose of life, of the power and limitations of man, and if it cannot answer the questions that assail him on his journey through this dark and mysterious world it persuades him to support his ignorance with good humor.

—**W. Somerset Maugham, *The Summing Up***

Aristotle's manuscripts, Andronicus of Rhodes. Andronicus found a series of works among Aristotle's papers that followed his discussion of physics but bore no title. Not knowing what to call them, he simply gave them the label "metaphysics"—meaning works coming after physics. In time the word came to be used to describe any philosophical work treating the same material as Aristotle did in these writings—"What is being?" "How is it known?" and so on. Later the prefix *meta* was extended to cover not only discussions about the general nature of reality (what one would normally go on to consider after physics) but also discussions of matters lying beyond physics—the existence of God, freedom of the will, and causation.

Before examining and reflecting on these events, we ought perhaps to remind ourselves that although the questions posed by metaphysics seem esoteric and perhaps of interest only to occupants of ivory towers, this is not at all the case. Let us consider for a moment one of its main problems—What is the universe made of?—and see the profound effects on our lives of the way this question has been answered (and indeed the very asking of it).

As we saw at the very beginning of this journey into philosophy, What is the universe made of? was in fact the first question the earliest philosophers posed: Thales said it was water, Anaximenes that it was air, and Heraclitus that it was fire. Democritus and Leucippus finally resolved the problems raised by these conflicting answers by suggesting that the ultimate particles of reality were atoms. This metaphysical theory, first proposed by these ancient Greek philosophers, formed the foundation of scientific investigation into the ultimate building blocks of the universe well into the nineteenth and early twentieth centuries.

By the late nineteenth century, physicists no longer supposed that these tiny particles had hooks on them, of course, but they did assume that atoms were spherical, resembling tiny billiard balls or marbles. Later, in the twentieth century, a fundamental revision regarding the conception of the nature of these atoms took place, a change that resulted in a profound revolution in physics with vast implications for humanity as a whole. Then it was discovered that the atom is not the ultimate particle but is constructed of still smaller particles—electrons, which revolve around a nucleus much as the planets revolve about the sun. More recently still, it was discovered that the nucleus itself is composed of still tinier pieces of matter—neutrons and protons—and these of even smaller ones.

Of course, no physicist has ever claimed to have "seen" a neutron or a proton or any of the other particles. What scientists are able to observe is simply the behavior of these particles. This very fact itself has enormous implications, for it has led investigators to the notion of a nuclear force as responsible for the observed motion, which in turn has led to the conception of atoms as points or poles of energy and to the motivation to release the energy—with results all too familiar to us.

It was this transformation of the conception of the atom from a tiny marble (harbored by Democritus and his successors) to the idea of it as "congealed energy" (essentially a change in metaphysical theory) that led to the creation of the atomic and thermonu-clear bombs—those mighty symbols of modern humanity's supremacy over nature. None of this would have been possible in the old Democritean atomic theory; however, it would have been impossible without it, either, for the old provided impetus for the new, and both were and are metaphysical theories.

CAUSATION

Before a discussion of determinism and human freedom, it is good to first analyze what it is we mean by the notion of a *cause*. The simple and perhaps prephilosophical under-standing of a cause is some event or object that produces some subsequent event or ob-ject. However, simple though such a definition might be, isolating precisely what event or object is in fact the cause of some observed event is considerably more tricky. During the outbreak of an influenza epidemic, researchers struggle to differentiate between po-tential causes of the outbreak on the one hand and observations of phenomena that are merely correlations or coincidences on the other. Distinguishing between causes, corre-lations, and coincidences can be a matter of life and death. Thus, some analysis of what it is that makes a *cause* actually *causal* is required.

Aristotle

The first philosopher to systematically address the notion of **causation** was Aristo-tle, whom we have encountered many times previously in the course of this text. Aristo-tle's analysis of causation is rather foreign to modern ears. Generally, modern or con-temporary notions of causation are limited to a notion of cause and effect. That is, event A *causes* event B, or event B is the *effect* of event A. For example, we might well say something like, "The bowling ball caused the pins to fall down," or "The pins fell down because they were struck by the bowling ball." Aristotle addresses this conception of a cause; however, his theory of causation is considerably broader. On Aristotle's view, there are four things that can legitimately be called a cause. Indeed, his view is often simply called "The Four Cause Doctrine" because he isolates four distinct causes—the Formal, Efficient, Material, and Final causes.

Not only is it a bit odd that he treats *causation* more broadly than is harmonious to contemporary readers, but it also seems a bit strange to modern eyes that the treat-ment of this critical metaphysical topic is not exclusively, and perhaps not even con-clusively, treated in either the *Physics* or the *Metaphysics*. Indeed, some of Aristotle's most detailed discussion of the notion comes in the *Politics* and *Nicomachean Ethics*. In the *Politics*, Aristotle treats perhaps the oddest of the *causes* as his primary concern is the proper or natural end of human beings, or their **Final Cause**. In other words, what is it that human beings are *for*, what is the *purpose* of a human being. In the *Nico-machean Ethics*, he returns to this notion of a Final Cause or a function in order to ar-gue that the proper natural function of human beings is *reason* and that as a rational animal, the virtuous or excellent human being is one in which the human function is fulfilled excellently.

Another way of understanding the Final Cause is by way of example. Imagine an acorn. The proper natural end of an acorn is to become an oak tree. One might object that acorns also serve the purpose of being food for squirrels. To this objection, Aristotle would respond that a very important distinction has been overlooked. It is the distinction between an **essential property** and an **accidental property**. An essential property of some entity is something that the entity *itself* has the power to do. Thus, the acorn, under proper natural circumstances, will grow into an oak tree because of the power within it. Thus, an acorn's capacity to become an oak tree is *essential* to the acorn. Something that is done *to* the acorn is not an essential property of the acorn but rather an *accidental* property. The squirrel's eating of the acorn is a power not possessed by the acorn but an act done to it. Thus, it is not an essential property of the acorn. Anything that is not an essential property of a natural object, like acorns or humans, is something that is accidental to them. The Final Cause picks out an essential property of a natural object.

By first treating the strangest of the Aristotelian causes, we have shed some light on the others as well. Each of the causes isolates some essential property of the object being examined. In other words, Aristotle's concern in specifying the four causes of any natural object is to analyze the *essence* of the thing. The essence of something is that property of the thing without which it would not be what it is. A formal example may look like this. The essence of E is R. If something does not have the property R, then it is not an E. Or, perhaps another, less formal example will help.

By asking the **Formal Cause** of an object, Aristotle is specifying the organizing principle of that object. For example, the organizing principle of Philbert the dog is "dog." Notice that if by some means we could change the answer to that question and say, for example, that Philbert's Formal Cause was "fish," then something very important has happened to Philbert. He is no longer what he had previously been—he has been transmogrified from "dog" to "fish." Since he is no longer the same kind of thing he had been before, an *essential* property has been altered. If we merely changed his color, say, from brown to green, his *essential* nature would not have changed, although his coat's color did. Thus, like the Final Cause, the Formal Cause picks out an essential property. Similarly, if one were to ask for Philbert's **Material Cause**, that cause would be flesh. Again, if the stuff of his makeup (flesh) were changed, he would no longer be Philbert, the dog. The **Efficient Cause** of the dog is fairly straightforward, although Aristotle's understanding of reproduction is somewhat arcane. Philbert's Efficient Cause is his biological parents. And finally, to return again to the Final Cause, the Final Cause of Philbert has to do with the dog's telos, or natural end or purpose. If any of these causes is altered, then so too is the dog, and altered in such a way that he is no longer Philbert the dog but some other thing entirely. Thus, the Four Cause doctrine serves as a way of specifying essential properties of a particular object, and each cause, in turn, serves as an explanation for the essential property it specifies.

David Hume

The great empiricist philosopher David Hume provides us with perhaps the most comprehensive and careful analysis of causation. Indeed, Hume's analysis is generally regarded as the starting point for modern investigations of the nature of causation and what we can know about it. Hume's work also shows the close connection between what we can say about metaphysical notions and what can be known about them.

While Aristotle is rather confident that we can not only know and identify the effective cause of natural objects, Hume is considerably more agnostic with respect to the notion of "causation," or at least how we come to *know* of cause and effect. As Kenneth R. Merrill has written, "Hume correctly answers the question 'How can we have knowledge of cause . . . if our direct experience contains no evidence of causal connections?'" The answer is that there is no way. Yet for Hume, *cause* is of considerable importance. Hume maintains that knowledge of matters of fact depends largely upon *cause* and *effect*. Indeed, he writes in *An Enquiry concerning Human Understanding* that "all reasonings concerning matter of fact seem to be founded on the relation of *Cause and Effect*." Further, it is only this relation that allows individuals to "go beyond the evidence of our memory and senses." Or, as Hume writes in the *Treatise*, "we can never infer the existence of one object from another, unless they be connected together, either mediately or immediately. In order therefore to understand these reasonings, we must be perfectly acquainted with the idea of a cause."

Given that so much rests upon *cause* and *effect*, it behooves Hume to give some reckoning of how we come to know *cause* and *effect*. Obviously knowledge of *cause* and *effect* cannot arise from a priori reasonings on Hume's view. Neither can such knowledge arise from any abstract reasoning apart from experience itself. Instead, custom and habit form the foundation of knowledge of *cause* and *effect*. Hume conceives the cause-and-effect relation as one of three general principles by which ideas are associated. The others are *contiguity* and *resemblance*. These principles, while neither infallible nor sole causes of ideas and the unions of ideas, are nevertheless the three principles by which Hume understands the mind to conjoin distinct and separable ideas. Hume then endeavors to demonstrate how we may judge of causes and effects by setting out some general rules that are necessary conditions of the cause-and-effect relation. These briefly are (1) contiguity in space and time, (2) priority, (3) constant conjunction, and (4) necessary connection.

The imagination gives rise to an idea of cause and effect because we grow accustomed to seeing event B follow event A in time, we observe that event B never precedes event A, and we note that whenever A occurs, it is followed immediately by B. In another way, in our experience of events A and B, suppose we find them to be contiguous in space and time and constantly conjoined. Further, suppose we find that A always precedes B. From these empirically observable features, we become habituated to anticipating event B whenever we observe A, and thus we expect B to follow upon it. However, the rule of *necessary connection*, that is, that the same cause always produces the same effect, is *not* empirically observable. Ultimately, Hume thinks it impossible to prove these causal connections.

Hume thinks a great deal of the difficulty in demonstrating the existence of cause and effect lies in the fact that events A and B can be conceived of independently in the mind. This is not an idea novel to Hume; for example, Descartes argued for such an independent conceivability relative to minds and bodies in the *Meditations*. But Descartes does not apply this principle to cause and effect. Hume does.

On Hume's view, event A does not include any notion of a cause, either as cause of itself or as cause of another. If it did, then it would not be completely conceivable independent of the other. But perceptions are separable, distinct, and distinguishable. Hence, they are conceivable independent of one another. Thus, the notion of cause cannot be inherent in the event or object itself. So on Hume's view, one cannot get cause and effect from analysis of the events or objects themselves.

Ultimately, cause-and-effect reasoning rests upon experience. As a result, Hume seems to believe that eventually one comes to recognize that constant conjunction, however meager a notion of causation that may be, is all that there is. That is, there is no further explanation of cause and effect than constant conjunction. As he writes in the *Enquiry concerning Human Understanding*, "As to the causes of these general causes [e.g., elasticity, gravity, etc.] we should in vain attempt their discovery; nor shall we ever be able to satisfy ourselves, by any particular explication of them. The ultimate springs and principles are totally shut up from human curiousity and enquiry."

With this view of cause and effect, then, it is not difficult to see how the impossibility of proving that the future will resemble the past follows. For Hume, induction rests upon a supposition of the uniformity of nature. That supposition itself rests upon the custom and habit that, in our imagination, give rise to an idea of cause and effect. However, we have no immediate experience (and hence no simple impression) of the cause-and-effect relation. Thus, there is no ground upon which to build a proof that past causal connections, that is, connections that up until now have been only constant conjunctions, will hold in the future. It is not intuitively false to assume that these causal connections will hold, but neither can it be demonstrated that they must hold.

We return now specifically to the idea of *necessary connection*. Hume never denies that there is a real connection between cause and effect. However, he does deny that one is to find necessary connection in an instance of one billiard ball striking another and the second ball moving or in repeated instances of sufficiently similar sorts, for example. Given his understanding of causation as a general principle by which ideas are conjoined, albeit not infallibly nor necessarily, it is little wonder that Hume would not depend upon necessary connection for a doctrine of cause and effect. Instead, on his view, the mind is presented with distinct perceptions that in themselves possess no notion of cause. An idea of necessary connection must have at its base an impression. From an idea of necessary connection, if one were derivable from a particular impression, one would be able to tell with certainty which event would follow. In that sense, the second event would be dependent on and inseparable from the first. But each perception is separable, distinct, and distinguishable. Hence, there is no impression from which the idea of necessary connection could arise. In another way, it is true that we may discover that certain events are constantly conjoined in time and space. We may further discover that each time we encounter those events, the circumstances of our encounter sufficiently resemble past ones. However, it is not possible from this constant conjunction of events to suppose the arising of a new idea (e.g., necessary connection). Indeed, since such an idea was not present in any particular events or their conjunctions, no such idea would arise from a regular series of those conjunctions. The idea of cause and effect, however, arises from the experience, "which informs us, that such particular objects, in all past instances, have been constantly conjoin'd with each other." That is, we become accustomed to anticipating the second object whenever we encounter the first. This constant conjunction and our habituated anticipation of events called "effects" form the general principle of association of ideas known as *Cause* and *Effect*.

> We must believe in free will. We have no choice.
>
> —Isaac Bashevis Singer

FREEDOM AND NECESSITY

Determinism, Indeterminism, and Compatibilism

Free will is one of the most written about and explored problems in all of philosophy. The question is simply, Are we or are we not free to decide the course of our lives? Because this is one of the central questions in metaphysics, let us conclude our account of this part of philosophy by looking at it in some detail.

First, let us note the main terms generally used in the discussion of **freedom** versus determinism, or necessity.

Determinism is the view that the whole realm of nature, including humans, is governed by the law of cause and effect. Given the cause, the effect necessarily follows, and every event, the law asserts, has causes. These causes produce the event, form it, and determine it. This is a necessary assumption of science, whose whole object is to seek order or law in nature, "law" simply entailing the discovery of causes (which specify that whenever A happens, B must follow).

Indeterminism is a denial of determinism. It is the belief that some events do not have causes but spring into being by pure chance without any relation to anything preceding.

The problem is that we find ourselves trying to hold onto two positions about human nature that seem incompatible. On the one hand, we assume in science—and to a large extent in practice—that human nature is determined. We do so, for example, when we pick the people we want as our friends, the neighborhood to live in, the schools to attend, and so on, believing that human nature has a certain stability and that the people in question are people we will be able to count on, the neighborhood will have the characteristics expected, and the schools will live up to their reputations.

But the consequences of this assumption seem unfortunate, for if determinism is true, given the past, no one can help doing whatever they do, and the belief that they could have acted differently—the idea of freedom—must be a delusion. Those who hold that determinism and freedom are compatible are called *compatibilists*, while those who argue that the two are incompatible and that one or the other or both must be false are called *incompatibilists*. Incompatibilists come in two varieties— hard determinists and libertarians.

Nevertheless, in many of our practical and moral judgments, we do assume that a person could have acted differently. Thus, we say, "You ought not to have done that!" implying that someone could have acted otherwise. If we did not believe the person could have acted differently, we would not blame him or her for the action. Similarly, when we deliberate about a future course of action, we implicitly believe the future is not yet settled, that our present deliberation makes a difference. But if determinism were true, the future would have to be regarded as settled, for the future is determined by the present, the present is determined by the past, and everything is already settled and finished. But this idea seems difficult to accept.

> In the mind there is no absolute or free will; but the mind is determined to wish this or that by a cause, which also has been determined by a cause, and this last by another cause and so on to inanity.
>
> —Baruch Spinoza, *Ethics*

We find ourselves therefore in the dilemma of either accepting determinism and being unable to justify basic moral and practical judgments or rejecting determinism and being unable to justify some basic scientific principles. But we seem to be compelled to accept one or the other, with the result that we are unable to justify either some very basic moral and practical judgments or some basic scientific judgments.

This is not a comfortable dilemma. No one wants to take up an antiscientific standpoint, nor does anyone want to give up basic moral and practical judgments. We do not want to become strict determinists and say that becoming, say, an alcoholic is like catching tuberculosis. We do want to say that while catching tuberculosis does not depend on my choice and is unavoidable, becoming an alcoholic is avoidable and does depend on choice. And still we do want to be sufficiently scientific (and deterministic) and say that there are reasons that some people turn to drink.

Is there any way, then, out of this dilemma? There is no easy solution to this problem, and the two most obvious ones are each very clearly unsatisfactory. These are either to give up determinism or to give up freedom.

Suppose we tried the first "solution" and just denied that all events are caused by past events and assumed instead that some events have no causes, that they spring into existence without any cause at all—just out of the blue, as we say. Scientifically, there seems to be some justification for such a view, since at the microcosmic level events of an uncaused nature do seem to take place, the regularity normally observed being merely the result of averaging out billions of these random events.

Now even if these suppositions regarding random, uncaused events were true, they would be useless as a solution to the problem of freedom, for the problem arises because, from the moral point of view, we need to fix responsibility for certain actions on certain people. But if an event happens for which there is no cause, no one can be held responsible. One could simply claim that the event sprung into being from nowhere and that, being a freak occurrence, one should not be held responsible for it. Indeterminism therefore proves too much.

Nor could one act on such an assumption. All our predictions about the future are based on the assumption that the future will be like the past, that there are laws at work in nature, and that nature is orderly. But if an event could merely spring into being uncaused, one cannot be held responsible for it, having had no control over it. Such "free" actions, if granted, would bring chaos into nature and make it impossible to hold anyone responsible for anything. If responsibility cannot be saved by arguing that some events are uncaused, then this solution to the problem proves to be no solution at all.

But if we cannot solve the problem by denying determinism, let us see whether we can solve it by denying freedom.

When we deliberate about what we will do, we assume that the future is still open and not yet settled. If we believe things to be settled, we do not bother to deliberate; we merely wait for them to happen. But if determinism were true, the future really would be settled, and thinking would have to be regarded as merely useless. The future, we would have to say, is determined by the present, the present by the past, and the past by something that occurred at a point in time when, perhaps, one did not even exist. And how can one be held responsible for something that occurred before one was even born?

And we can apply the same thinking to "thinking" itself. Is that, we might ask, also determined? If it is, then in a sense the thought in question, having no other rationale, is false, and we need pay no attention to it. And if it is not determined, then there is at least one thing that is not determined, and the statement that thinking (meaning all thinking) is determined must be false. So in either case, determinism would be false.

Obviously, then, the dilemma cannot be resolved by either rejecting determinism or rejecting freedom. These "solutions" prove to be no solutions. Some people have thought that the solution to this problem lies in the fact that human beings possess the power of reason. Even on a practical level, they have pointed out, one can see this criterion at work. Thus, the law does not hold a person responsible for his actions until he is, as the saying goes, of the "age of reason." And if one becomes legally insane, if one "loses one's reason," one ceases to be held responsible for what one does.

Human freedom, they have said, is therefore somehow bound up with our possession of the ability to reason. We are not like animals or inanimate objects, who presumably behave as they do because of the force of instinct or the laws of nature. Our possession of reason and ability to deliberate give us a degree of power, of freedom, to select alternative courses of action. It is in this sense, therefore, that we can be said to have choice and be free.

Freedom, they have therefore said, can be made compatible with determinism. One's conduct is indeed determined, but it is determined by one's reason—that is, by oneself—and in this sense it can be said to be self-determined. Since each of us has reason, each of us is therefore free and can and should therefore be held responsible for what we do.

While, however, the possession of reason does obviously make a difference to our condition and distinguishes us from other beings and things in nature, it does not quite solve the problem. One could, for example, still ask, Why are some people rational and others not? Or, if that does not seem entirely accurate, we might put the question in this form: Why are some people more rational than others? Was this difference caused or not? If it was caused, then we are back to determinism, and if it was not caused, if it was due entirely to chance, then we are left in the equally unsatisfactory position of complete indeterminism, and this, as we saw, is no better than determinism. And so the problem remains.

The question of determinism/indeterminism perhaps becomes most pointed when we turn to questions of personal choices and praise and blame. To say that one actually has a *choice* is to say that freedom must exist. Further, suppose we want to blame John for acting badly toward Frida. To suppose that we are acting reasonably is to suppose that freedom exists, that is, that John had a choice in how he acted—he could have acted as he did, or he could have acted differently. Thus, it seems that freedom is necessary if we want to assign moral responsibility for acting to a person. For this reason, perhaps the application of questions of morality to questions of freedom and determinism is a fruitful place to continue our examination of various approaches to address the dilemma.

If we ask the question, Can we say that people are free even if the natural world (of which we are a part) is completely determined by natural forces and physical laws? and we respond with a "yes," we must focus our attention on the compatibilist/incompatibilist debate and, even further, on the compatibilist position to which our "yes" commits us.

It would seem quite odd to blame John (or, if he has done something good, to praise him) if he was completely constrained by circumstance and held in total thrall, without freedom. Indeed, Kant argues that without freedom, of some sort, one cannot even ascribe morality, much less responsibility for morality. This is not an uncommon position, as it is reflected in much contemporary thought, including that of P. F. Strawson and Harry Frankfurt, to name but a few. Further, this would be of significant interest only if the answer to the first question were "no" or at the very least "maybe not." As Strawson writes, one area in which both pessimists and optimists concerning freedom agree is that just punishment and moral condemnation imply moral guilt and guilt implies moral responsibility and moral responsibility implies freedom. If we accept this, then it is clear that if we say that freedom does not exist (the pessimists' position), then we must also reject praise and blame as meaningless. Or, in other words, without freedom, it is at least inappropriate to ascribe moral responsibility to agents.

Let us turn now to the more interesting question of whether freedom of action is compatible with being subject to causal explanations. It will be helpful to first examine the views of Kant, who quite nicely demonstrates the importance of the dialogue concerning freedom with respect to human agency, autonomy, and ethics.

Immanuel Kant—Freedom and Autonomy

Kant's notion of autonomy (or self-directed self-development) is absolutely critical in the development of his ethical theory. The opposite of autonomy is *heteronomy*. If we imagine that Dawn cannot choose to drive to work because a blizzard has buried her car, we can say that her actions have been heteronomously affected. That is, she has no choice but to stay home, and that lack of choice was imposed on her from outside of her will and outside of her control. So, in this case, her staying home from work was not a choice but rather an imposition.

Kant's conception of autonomy limits that which he can call the Good. Suppose, for a moment, that being happy or having fully developed talents is taken to be intrinsically good. In such a case, a right act would be defined as one that brings about such a happy state of affairs. Thus, right acts themselves have instrumental value as regards the Good (or, in other words, they help to bring about the Good). Kant rejects this view out of hand because of his understanding of autonomy. His rejection happens because if this were the case, goodness would occur independently of the will of any particular person. Thus, the moral person would be compelled to conform to the good dictated from outside of his will. As a result, such a person is not a self-directing agent because the standard of what is called Good is external to him. Such conformity is an example of heteronomy and **compulsion**. If one is compelled to act, then it is not completely appropriate to assign praise and blame to the person. Indeed, any such pursuit of a Good extrinsic to the will of the autonomous self devolves rapidly, on Kant's view, into heteronomy and compulsion. Since Kant views the heteronomous individual as that which stands in direct contrast to the truly moral and autonomous person, Kant must locate the Good in the moral and autonomous person, and one characteristic of that autonomy must be freedom, in some sense or other. And since any "good" extrinsic to the will would tend toward heteronomy, Kant must locate the Good in the will. Hence, his position that the only unconditionally good thing is the good will and moral responsibility is dependent upon autonomous freedom.

Without autonomy, a person cannot be said to be responsible for her actions, and as a result even the appearance of morality crumbles. This is not to say that autonomy is equal to or even equivalent with freedom. Kant clearly distinguishes between the freedom to do as one pleases and the freedom to determine what one is in oneself. The self-determining type of freedom is what Kant equates with autonomy. The autonomous person acts in accordance with the moral law—a moral law that arises from within the person's own will. In this way, autonomy is also distinct from heteronomy in that the universal moral law, while objective, is not outside the person, imposing itself upon the agent. Rather, an autonomous person constructs the moral law from within herself and freely chooses to impose it upon herself.

One question that arises from this account concerns the "from whence" of this autonomy. Since Kant accepts the causal principles of Newtonian science, autonomy cannot reside or arise from the physical world. On Kant's view, the concept of autonomy involves an Idea of Freedom under which the autonomous moral person acts. As it cannot be a part of the **phenomenal** world (or the world we experience through sense perception), it must arise from the **noumenal** self. This noumenal world (a world out of space, time, and the causation of the physical world) is the center of autonomy for Kant. The noumenal world is the world of the mind, and the world of the mind is not in the complete grip of physical causation. To surrender the noumenal realm is, for Kant, to eliminate the possibility of freedom. Such a move would eliminate the possibility for a rational moral theory, as praise and blame cease to be justifiable without autonomous freedom on which to hang responsibility for action.

Kant's account has some obvious difficulties from a determinist perspective (either incompatibilist or compatibilist). Quite simply, Kant must be able to account for the noumenal world. As he accepts a universal determinism within the phenomenal world, he must explain or justify holding a concept like the noumenon. Further, even if one has the kind of negative freedom available in the distinction between autonomy and heteronomy, Kant must show how the move is made from negative freedom, that is, freedom from *heteronomous* imposition of moral or causal laws, to an account of positive freedom, that is, the freedom to choose to act.

Kant overcomes the determinist claims, it seems, by supposing that it is the case that praise and blame are assessed and that agents are held responsible for their actions. Thus, society (specifically practical reason) shows that freedom is assumed. Since freedom can be neither proven nor disproven by pure reason, the assumptions and demonstrations of practical reason should suffice.

Having established Kant's very perceptive and thorough discussion of the problem, it will be helpful to examine, then, two contemporary philosophers and a third philosopher who was a contemporary of Kant.

P. F. Strawson

P. F. Strawson argues that even if the determinist is correct about the absence of human freedom, it is ultimately impossible for human beings to order their lives in such a way as to reflect that determinism. This impossibility can be observed by attention to what Strawson calls **reactive attitudes**. The reactive attitudes are those expressions within human life that involve participation with others in interpersonal human relations, such as resentment and gratitude. By contrast, the objective attitudes are those expressions that view others solely as objects. For Strawson, the reactive attitudes are linked directly to our conception of freedom because the very conception of freedom arises from the experience of the reactive attitudes and their complement in the set of all human attitudes, the objective attitudes.

For Strawson, these attitudes are at the heart of human interaction. Individuals and society can and do choose to regard certain individuals (e.g., small children, the mentally disabled, and criminals) from an objective perspective. That is to say that within society there are individuals who society, as a whole, and other individuals treat with a certain detachment and without (or with a minimal amount of) interpersonal involvement with the objectified individual. However, Strawson argues that it is not possible to begin, maintain, or cultivate such objective attitudes toward all other individuals within society and retain what are considered "normal" human relationships. Such basic interactions as friendship and intimacy require, according to Strawson, the reactive attitudes to flourish or to develop at all.

By using the interplay of the reactive and objective attitudes, Strawson recasts the question of freedom and determinism in terms of what he sees as intrinsic properties of human nature and relationships. In so doing, he argues that the illusion of rationality is removed from the moral pessimist's question, If determinism is true, what is it rational to do? He argues that no general thesis of determinism is "ever" relevant to the suspending of the reactive attitudes that occurs when one views another objectively. And similarly, it is not rational to assume that human life can be reduced to one of only objective attitudes upon the discovery that such a thesis were true. Indeed, even if human life could be so reduced, it would not remain human.

The links between the reactive attitudes and the concept of freedom are important because they assist in defining, for the moral optimist at least, those actions that are free actions whether or not some general thesis of determinism holds true. The moral optimist can now argue for more than a negative definition of freedom as regards human action. In other words, the moral optimist can argue that freedom is more than merely the absence of certain conditions that would make punishment appropriate. In addition, the moral optimist is not limited to advocating moral praise or censure based solely upon their perceived efficacy. Rather than the truth or falsity of determinism (and the attendant conversation about which determined actions count as free and thus for which moral responsibility can be assigned), concern centers about those choices, in terms of enrichment or impoverishment of human life, that it is rational to make.

These links are profoundly important, and Strawson would probably argue more important than "we often suppose." This is so because, as he argues, it is not possible to imagine a world in which the reactive attitudes were reduced only to objective ones. Strawson argues that what remained, should such a reduction be possible, would not be what is normally meant by "human life" because meaningful human interaction, reflected in the reactive attitudes, would not be possible. Further, it is not possible, or at least it is highly improbable, that a general thesis of determinism could, even if it received wide acceptance, so radically alter the basic interactions between people that these interpersonal interactions would disappear into the barren shallowness of solely objective attitudes. In Strawson's view, to suppose that some thesis of determinism could affect this alteration is simply not rational. Thus, these links enable discussion of what actions are morally permissible, praiseworthy, or blameworthy by dismissing the moral skeptic's "rational" appeal to some general thesis of determinism.

Henry Frankfurt

Another contemporary philosopher, Henry Frankfurt, has put forward a view of freedom that is developed in light of his conceptions of the will and the person. He argues for a conception of the will that allows the philosopher to differentiate the will from the immediate wants of the individual. To understand what Frankfurt is suggesting, it is probably helpful to think about a model that describes human actions. All humans have **desires**. Indeed, we all have desires that may be quite contrary to each other—the desire to go to the lake and the desire to study for an upcoming philosophy exam. All of these desires are the kind that we can call "first-order desires." From among all of our desires, one of them will become effective (i.e., we will act on that desire). The desire we act on we can call an **intention**. So an intention is a desire upon which we act.

For Frankfurt, the will is identical to some first-order desire. However, the will is not simply that first-order desire. The will is an effective desire, that is, a desire that moves the individual to act.

From this view, Frankfurt argues for a notion of what it means to be a person. Crucial to being a person are features of the will that are desires, but ones different from first-order desires; let us call them "second-order desires." A second-order desire is not a desire to go to the lake or a desire to study for an exam. A second-order desire has to do with the sorts of desires that involve what kind of person we want to be. Do we desire to be the sort of person who studies for our exams when we have them upcoming, or do we desire to be the sort of person who, when an exam looms on the horizon, abandons our desk for the lake?

It only makes sense, on Frankfurt's view, to use the phrase "freedom of the will" if we are dealing with a person and with a person's second-order desires. So freedom of the will is distinguished from freedom of action. Freedom of action is simply the ability to actualize a first-order desire. A person is free to act if the person can go to the lake or study for the exam. When a person exercises freedom of action, he acts on some first-order desire. However, because there is no second-order desire involved, necessarily, the individual cannot even be said to have a will and thus cannot be said to exercise free will. Freedom of the will corresponds with a person's ability to have the will that they want to have, that is, to be free to translate a second-order desire into a second-order volition. Or, in other words, freedom of the will has to do with the freedom to choose to be a particular sort of person.

Frankfurt recognizes that this construction is not yet completely clear. There are persons who have second-order volitions that are frustrated because of the strength of a countervening first-order desire. Imagine a person who is addicted to morphine and who became addicted following a horrible accident. In this imagined case, the person had no choice in the first application of the drug (because following his accident he was unconscious), and because the drug was introduced into his system, his body has become completely addicted. Thus, he is compelled by the desire for the drug (a first-order desire) and compelled to the point that it overwhelms his second-order desire to be the sort of person who is not addicted to drugs. Such an individual is a person who has a will, but the will is not free because the person acts by a will he wants to be without. Obviously, this person is not in the same boat as the person who ditches his study time for a trip to the lake. However, the unwilling addict has neither freedom of will nor freedom of action because he is moved to action by a will he wants to be without to act on first-order desires that are themselves unwanted. The free person, by contrast, is moved by the will he wants, which in turn leads to acting on first-order desires he wants to be effective.

This view of freedom makes it possible, whether determinism is true or not, to define those actions and those wills that count as free and to differentiate between the two. On that basis, responsibility, blame, praise, and the like can be assigned. Further, as relates to responsibility, it becomes possible to differentiate between being fully responsible and solely responsible.

David Hume

This brings us back to the eighteenth century and to a contemporary of Immanuel Kant's, David Hume. Given the earlier discussion of Hume's view of causation, it is appropriate to conclude the section on freedom by returning to his work. On Hume's view, the question of determinism versus freedom is quite simply the wrong question. Hume seems to be a rather thoroughgoing determinist. Although he does not argue for "every effect has a cause," he seems to believe such a principle. Thus, there is no event for which there is no cause. And, further, if there is no cause, then there is no event. Hence, events can be seen to have a cause of necessity. Indeed, for Hume, it is not only the case that every event has a cause but that the results of that cause could in no way be different from what they are.

Hume, however, has a significant place for freedom (**liberty**) within his system as well. Hume defends the idea that liberty and necessity are compatible on the basis that the two have nothing to do with one another. On Hume's view, it is given, for the most part, that causation is a fact of existence and further that things could in no way be different than they are. However, causation is not compulsion on Hume's view. And it is here that Hume's point is made. Freedom, on his view, is understood as freedom from constraint, compulsion, and/or coercion. In other words, should an individual choose to lift his arm, he could do so. In short, that there is a causal chain that precedes the lifting of the arm is a fact about the world. It is also irrelevant. So, on Hume's view, necessity obtains in the world, but it has nothing to do with coercion or compulsion and as such has nothing to do with freedom. At the same time, liberty is freedom from coercion and/or compulsion but has nothing to do with the law of universal causality. As such, it has nothing to do with necessity. So, on Hume's view of liberty and necessity, there is no conflict because the two do not involve one another.

This position, then, seems reflected in the positions of Strawson and Frankfurt in that both of the later philosophers seem to carve particular niches for the operation of freedom and the operation of causal explanation while arguing that a causal explanation for a series of events does not compromise the freedom that obtains in those events. At the very least, as Strawson seems to argue, even if causal explanations did compromise freedom, human beings could not ultimately conform life to such a reality.

SUMMARY

1. The distinction between causation, correlation, and coincidence is one of the more important distinctions when trying to understand the nature of the world, its patterns, and possibly its laws. Isolating a cause or the causes of any object is a tricky matter. Aristotle's view of causation is another way of isolating essential properties and accidental properties of any given event. Hume provides a framework for carefully and deliberately evaluating concurrent events that often are referred to colloquially as "cause" and "effect."

2. If we are part of a universe that is governed, as it appears, by immutable laws and if, furthermore, we are compelled to live lives that are shaped by factors beyond our knowledge and control, then the question arises, To what degree can we be said to be free? This is the ancient problem of freedom versus determinism, and on its resolution rests the question of whether we are ever justified in holding people accountable for their actions.

3. The attempt to solve the problem by either denying freedom or denying determinism proves to be no solution, for the former, although succeeding in reaffirming the principles of science, tends to undermine those of morality, and the latter, although at first seeming to reaffirm the principles of morality, in the end tends to undermine both them and those of science as well.

4. Contemporary treatments of the question of freedom and determinism generally approach the matter by analyzing the nature of freedom and our intuitional stance toward it. Frankfurt's careful analysis of the desires, volitions, and the human will builds on Kant's notions of the good and the good will. Strawson also echoes a Kantian strain as he argues that humans cannot help but live as if freedom is an actuality because it is impossible to live as if determinism is true. Hume's distinction between two sorts of freedom is also helpful in understanding how the word is often used to refer to several phenomena.

KEY TERMS

accidental property   freedom
causation   intention
compulsion   liberty
desires   Material Cause
Efficient Cause   noumenal
essential property   phenomenal
Final Cause   reactive attitudes
Formal Cause

REVIEW QUESTIONS

1. What are the three major topics within metaphysics?

2. What is determinism?

3. How has the fact that we possess the ability to reason been used by some in an attempt to reconcile freedom and determinism?

4. How do the reactive attitudes and the analysis of the will carve out a space for freedom?

5. What are Hume's two types of freedom, and which is compatible with the notion that determinism is true?

■ Reading

Physics

ARISTOTLE

Excerpted from Aristotle, *Physics*, Book 2, Chapter 2, translated by R. P. Hardie and R. K. Gaye, http://classics.mit.edu/Aristotle/physics.html.

Book II

Part 1

Of things that exist, some exist by nature, some from other causes.

'By nature' the animals and their parts exist, and the plants and the simple bodies (earth, fire, air, water)—for we say that these and the like exist 'by nature.'

All the things mentioned present a feature in which they differ from things which are not constituted by nature. Each of them has within itself a principle of motion and of stationariness (in respect of place, or of growth and decrease, or by way of alteration). On the other hand, a bed and a coat and anything else of that sort, qua receiving these designations i.e. in so far as they are products of art—have no innate impulse to change. But in so far as they happen to be composed of stone or of earth or of a mixture of the two, they do have such an impulse, and just to that extent which seems to indicate that nature is a source or cause of being moved and of being at rest in that to which it belongs primarily, in virtue of itself and not in virtue of a concomitant attribute.

I say 'not in virtue of a concomitant attribute,' because (for instance) a man who is a doctor might cure himself. Nevertheless it is not in so far as he is a patient that he possesses the art of medicine: it merely has happened that the same man is doctor and patient—and that is why these attributes are not always found together. So it is with all other artificial products. None of them has in itself the source of its own production. But while in some cases (for instance houses and the other products of manual labour) that principle is in something else external to the thing, in others those which may cause a change in themselves in virtue of a concomitant attribute—it lies in the things themselves (but not in virtue of what they are).

'Nature' then is what has been stated. Things 'have a nature' which have a principle of this kind. Each of them is a substance; for it is a subject, and nature always implies a subject in which it inheres.

The term 'according to nature' is applied to all these things and also to the attributes which belong to them in virtue of what they are, for instance the property of fire to be carried upwards—which is not a 'nature' nor 'has a nature' but is 'by nature' or 'according to nature.'

What nature is, then, and the meaning of the terms 'by nature' and 'according to nature,' has been stated. That nature exists, it would be absurd to try to prove; for it is obvious that there are many things of this kind, and to prove what is obvious by what is not is the mark of a man who is unable to distinguish what is self-evident from what is not. (This state of mind is clearly possible. A man blind from birth might reason about colours. Presumably therefore such persons must be talking about words without any thought to correspond.)

Some identify the nature or substance of a natural object with that immediate constituent of it which taken by itself is without arrangement, e.g. the wood is the 'nature' of the bed, and the bronze the 'nature' of the statue.

As an indication of this Antiphon points out that if you planted a bed and the rotting wood acquired the power of sending up a shoot, it would not be a bed that would come up, but wood—which shows that the arrangement in accordance with the rules of the art is merely an incidental attribute, whereas the real nature is the other, which, further, persists continuously through the process of making.

But if the material of each of these objects has itself the same relation to something else, say bronze (or gold) to water, bones (or wood) to earth and so on, that (they say) would be their nature and essence. Consequently some assert earth, others fire or air or water or some or all of these, to be the nature of the things that are. For whatever any one of them supposed to have this character—whether one thing or more than one thing—this or these he declared to be the whole of substance, all else being its affections, states, or dispositions.

Every such thing they held to be eternal (for it could not pass into anything else), but other things to come into being and cease to be times without number.

This then is one account of 'nature,' namely that it is the immediate material substratum of things which have in themselves a principle of motion or change.

Another account is that 'nature' is the shape or form which is specified in the definition of the thing.

For the word 'nature' is applied to what is according to nature and the natural in the same way as 'art' is applied to what is artistic or a work of art. We should not say in the latter case that there is anything artistic about a thing, if it is a bed only potentially, not yet having the form of a bed; nor should we call it a work of art. The same is true of natural compounds. What is potentially flesh or bone has not yet its own 'nature', and does not exist until it receives the form specified in the definition, which we name in defining what flesh or bone is. Thus in the second sense of 'nature' it would be the shape or form (not separable except in statement) of things which have in themselves a source of motion. (The combination of the two, e.g. man, is not 'nature' but 'by nature' or 'natural.')

The form indeed is 'nature' rather than the matter; for a thing is more properly said to be what it is when it has attained to fulfillment than when it exists potentially. Again man is born from man, but not bed from bed. That is why people say that the figure is not the nature of a bed, but the wood is—if the bed sprouted not a bed but wood would come up. But even if the figure is art, then on the same principle the shape of man is his nature. For man is born from man.

We also speak of a thing's nature as being exhibited in the process of growth by which its nature is attained. The 'nature' in this sense is not like 'doctoring,' which leads not to the art of doctoring but to health. Doctoring must start from the art, not lead to it. But it is not in this way that nature (in the one sense) is related to nature (in the other). What grows qua growing grows from something into something. Into what then does it grow? Not into that from which it arose but into that to which it tends. The shape then is nature.

'Shape' and 'nature,' it should be added, are in two senses. For the privation too is in a way form. But whether in unqualified coming to be there is privation, i.e. a contrary to what comes to be, we must consider later.

Part 2

We have distinguished, then, the different ways in which the term 'nature' is used.

The next point to consider is how the mathematician differs from the physicist. Obviously physical bodies contain surfaces and volumes, lines and points, and these are the subject-matter of mathematics.

Further, is astronomy different from physics or a department of it? It seems absurd that the physicist should be supposed to know the nature of sun or moon, but not to know any of their essential attributes, particularly as the writers on physics obviously do discuss their shape also and whether the earth and the world are spherical or not.

Now the mathematician, though he too treats of these things, nevertheless does not treat of them as the limits of a physical body; nor does he consider the attributes indicated as the attributes of such bodies. That is why he separates them; for in thought they are separable from motion, and it makes no difference, nor does any falsity result, if they are separated. The holders of the theory of Forms do the same, though they are not aware of it; for they separate the objects of physics, which are less separable than those of mathematics. This becomes plain if one tries to state in each of the two cases the definitions of the things and of their attributes. 'Odd' and 'even,' 'straight' and 'curved,' and likewise 'number,' 'line,' and 'figure,' do not involve motion; not so 'flesh' and 'bone' and 'man'—these are defined like 'snub nose,' not like 'curved.'

Similar evidence is supplied by the more physical of the branches of mathematics, such as optics, harmonics, and astronomy. These are in a way the converse of geometry. While geometry investigates physical lines but not qua physical, optics investigates mathematical lines, but qua physical, not qua mathematical.

Since 'nature' has two senses, the form and the matter, we must investigate its objects as we would the essence of snubness. That is, such things are neither independent of matter nor can be defined in terms of matter only. Here too indeed one might raise a difficulty. Since there are two natures, with which is the physicist concerned? Or should he investigate the combination of the two? But if the combination of the two, then also each severally. Does it belong then to the same or to different sciences to know each severally?

If we look at the ancients, physics would to be concerned with the matter. (It was only very slightly that Empedocles and Democritus touched on the forms and the essence.)

But if on the other hand art imitates nature, and it is the part of the same discipline to know the form and the matter up to a point (e.g. the doctor has a knowledge of health and also of bile and phlegm, in which health is realized, and the builder both of the form of the house and of the matter, namely that it is bricks and beams, and so forth): if this is so, it would be the part of physics also to know nature in both its senses.

Again, 'that for the sake of which,' or the end, belongs to the same department of knowledge as the means. But the nature is the end or 'that for the sake of which.' For if a thing undergoes a continuous change and there is a stage which is last, this stage is the end or 'that for the sake of which.' (That is why the poet was carried away into making an absurd statement when he said 'he has the end for the sake of which he was born.' For not every stage that is last claims to be an end, but only that which is best.)

For the arts make their material (some simply 'make' it, others make it serviceable), and we use everything as if it was there for our sake. (We also are in a sense an end. 'That for the sake of which' has two senses: the distinction is made in our work On Philosophy.)

The arts, therefore, which govern the matter and have knowledge are two, namely the art which uses the product and the art which directs the production of it. That is why the using art also is in a sense directive; but it differs in that it knows the form, whereas the art which is directive as being concerned with production knows the matter. For the helmsman knows and prescribes what sort of form a helm should have, the other from what wood it should be made and by means of what operations. In the products of art, however, we make the material with a view to the function, whereas in the products of nature the matter is there all along.

Again, matter is a relative term: to each form there corresponds a special matter. How far then must the physicist know the form or essence? Up to a point, perhaps, as the doctor must know sinew or the smith bronze (i.e. until he understands the purpose of each): and the physicist is concerned only with things whose forms are separable indeed, but do not exist apart from matter. Man is begotten by man and by the sun as well. The mode of existence and essence of the separable it is the business of the primary type of philosophy to define.

Part 3

Now that we have established these distinctions, we must proceed to consider causes, their character and number. Knowledge is the object of our inquiry, and men do not think they know a thing till they have grasped the 'why' of (which is to grasp its primary cause). So clearly we too must do this as regards both coming to be and passing away and every kind of physical change, in order that, knowing their principles, we may try to refer to these principles each of our problems.

In one sense, then, (1) that out of which a thing comes to be and which persists, is called 'cause,' e.g. the bronze of the statue, the silver of the bowl, and the genera of which the bronze and the silver are species.

In another sense (2) the form or the archetype, i.e. the statement of the essence, and its genera, are called 'causes' (e.g. of the octave the relation of 2:1, and generally number), and the parts in the definition.

Again (3) the primary source of the change or coming to rest; e.g. the man who gave advice is a cause, the father is cause of the child, and generally what makes of what is made and what causes change of what is changed.

Again (4) in the sense of end or 'that for the sake of which' a thing is done, e.g. health is the cause of walking about. ('Why is he walking about?' we say. 'To be healthy,' and, having said that, we think we have assigned the cause.) The same is true also of all the intermediate steps which are brought about through the action of something else as means towards the end, e.g. reduction of flesh, purging, drugs, or surgical instruments are means towards health. All these things are 'for the sake of' the end, though they differ from one another in that some are activities, others instruments.

This then perhaps exhausts the number of ways in which the term 'cause' is used.

As the word has several senses, it follows that there are several causes of the same thing not merely in virtue of a concomitant attribute (e.g., both the art of the sculptor and the bronze are causes of the statue). These are causes of the statue qua statue, not in virtue of anything else that it may be—only not in the same way, the one being the material cause, the other the cause whence the motion comes. Some things cause each other reciprocally, e.g. hard work causes fitness and vice versa, but again not in the same way, but the one as end, the other as the origin of change. Further the same thing is the cause of contrary results. For that which by its presence brings about one result is sometimes blamed for bringing about the contrary by its absence. Thus we ascribe the wreck of a ship to the absence of the pilot whose presence was the cause of its safety.

All the causes now mentioned fall into four familiar divisions. The letters are the causes of syllables, the material of artificial products, fire, &c., of bodies, the parts of the whole, and the premisses of the conclusion, in the sense of 'that from which.' Of these pairs the one set are causes in the sense of substratum, e.g. the parts, the other set in the sense of essence—the whole and the combination and the form. But the seed and the doctor and the adviser, and generally the maker, are all sources whence the change or stationariness originates, while the others are causes in the sense of the end or the good of the rest; for 'that for the sake of which' means what is best and the end of the things that lead up to it. (Whether we say the 'good' itself or the 'apparent good' makes no difference.)

Such then is the number and nature of the kinds of cause.

Now the modes of causation are many, though when brought under heads they too can be reduced in number. For 'cause' is used in many senses and even within the same kind one may be prior to another (e.g. the doctor and the expert are causes of health, the relation 2:1 and number of the octave), and always what is inclusive to what is particular.

Another mode of causation is the incidental and its genera, e.g. in one way 'Polyclitus,' in another 'sculptor' is the cause of a statue, because 'being Polyclitus' and 'sculptor' are incidentally conjoined. Also the classes in which the incidental attribute is included; thus 'a man' could be said to be the cause of a statue or, generally, 'a living creature.' An incidental attribute too may be more or less remote, e.g. suppose that 'a pale man' or 'a musical man' were said to be the cause of the statue.

All causes, both proper and incidental, may be spoken of either as potential or as actual; e.g. the cause of a house being built is either 'house-builder' or 'house-builder building.'

Similar distinctions can be made in the things of which the causes are causes, e.g. of 'this statue' or of 'statue' or of 'image' generally, of 'this bronze' or of 'bronze' or of 'material' generally. So too with the incidental attributes. Again we may use a complex expression for either and say, e.g. neither 'Polyclitus' nor 'sculptor' but 'Polyclitus, sculptor.'

All these various uses, however, come to six in number, under each of which again the usage is twofold. Cause means either what is particular or a genus, or an incidental attribute or a genus of that, and these either as a complex or each by itself; and all six either as actual or as potential. The difference is this much, that causes which are actually at work and particular exist and cease to exist simultaneously with their effect, e.g. this healing person with this being-healed person and that house-building man with that being-built house; but this is not always true of potential causes—the house and the housebuilder do not pass away simultaneously.

In investigating the cause of each thing it is always necessary to seek what is most precise (as also in other things): thus man builds because he is a builder, and a builder builds in virtue of his art of building. This last cause then is prior: and so generally.

Further, generic effects should be assigned to generic causes, particular effects to particular causes, e.g. statue to sculptor, this statue to this sculptor; and powers are relative to possible effects, actually operating causes to things which are actually being effected.

This must suffice for our account of the number of causes and the modes of causation.

■ Questions for Discussion

1. What does it mean to "have a nature" on Aristotle's view?

2. What sorts of causes are there? How do these specify essential properties of natural objects?

3. Why is it "always necessary to seek what is most precise" when investigating the cause of some object?

■ Reading

Treatise on Human Nature

DAVID HUME

Excerpted from David Hume, *Treatise on Human Nature*, Book 1, Section 4.

Sect. IV.
Of the Connection or Association of Ideas.

As all simple ideas may be separated by the imagination, and may be united again in what form it pleases, nothing wou'd be more unaccountable than the operations of that faculty, were it not guided by some universal principles, which render it, in some measure, uniform with itself in all times and places. Were ideas entirely loose and unconnected, chance alone wou'd join them; and 'tis impossible the same simple ideas should fall regularly into complex ones (as they commonly do) without some bond of union among them, some associating quality, by which one idea naturally introduces another. This uniting principle among ideas is not to be consider'd as an inseparable connection; for that has been already excluded from the imagination: Nor yet are we to conclude, that without it the mind cannot join two ideas; for nothing is more free than that faculty: but we are only to regard it as a gentle force, which commonly prevails, and is the cause why, among other things, languages so nearly correspond to each other; nature in a manner pointing out to every one those simple ideas, which are most proper to be united in a complex one. The qualities, from which this association arises, and by which the mind is after this manner convey'd from one idea to another, are three, viz. RESEMBLANCE., CONTIGUITY in time or place, and CAUSE and EFFECT.

I believe it will not be very necessary to prove, that these qualities produce an association among ideas, and upon the appearance of one idea naturally introduce another. 'Tis plain, that in the course of our thinking, and in the constant revolution of our ideas, our imagination runs easily from one idea to any other that resembles it, and that this quality alone is to the fancy a sufficient bond and association. 'Tis likewise evident that as the senses, in changing their objects, are necessitated to change them regularly, and take them as they lie *contiguous* to each other, the imagination must by long custom acquire the same method of thinking, and run along the parts of space and time in conceiving its objects. As to the connection, that is made by the relation of cause and effect, we shall have occasion afterwards to examine it to the bottom, and therefore shall not at present insist upon it. 'Tis sufficient to observe, that there is no relation, which produces a stronger connection in the fancy, and makes one idea more readily recall another, than the relation of cause and effect betwixt their objects.

That we may understand the full extent of these relations, we must consider, that two objects are connected together in the imagination, not only when the one is immediately resembling, contiguous to, or the cause of the other, but also when there is interposed betwixt them a third object, which bears to both of them any of these relations. This may be carried on to a great length; tho' at the same time we may observe, that each remove considerably weakens the relation. Cousins in the fourth degree are connected by causation, if I may be allowed to use that term; but not so closely as brothers, much less as child and parent. In general we may observe, that all the relations of blood depend upon cause and effect, and are esteemed near or remote, according to the number of connecting causes interpos'd betwixt the persons.

Of the three relations above-mention'd this of causation is the most extensive. Two objects may be considered as plac'd in this relation, as well when one is the cause of any of the actions or motions of the other, as when the former is the cause of the existence of the latter. For as that action or motion is nothing but the object itself, consider'd in a certain light, and as the object continues the same in all its different situations, 'tis easy to imagine how such an influence of objects upon one another may connect them in the imagination.

We may carry this farther, and remark, not only that two objects are connected by the relation of cause and effect, when the one produces a motion or any action in the other, but also when it has a power of producing it. And this we may observe to be the source of all the relation, of interest and duty, by which men influence each other in society, and are plac'd in the ties of government and subordination. A master is such-a-one as by his situation, arising either from force or agreement, has a power of directing in certain particulars the actions of another, whom we call servant. A judge is one, who in all disputed cases can fix by his opinion the possession or property of any thing betwixt any members of the society. When a person is possess'd of any power, there is no more required to convert it into action, but the exertion of the will; and that in every case is considered as possible, and in many as probable; especially in the case of authority, where the obedience of the subject is a pleasure and advantage to the superior.

These are therefore the principles of union or cohesion among our simple ideas, and in the imagination supply the place of that inseparable connection, by which they are united in our memory. Here is a kind of ATTRACTION, which in the mental world will be found to have as extraordinary effects as in the natural, and to shew itself in as many and as various forms. Its effects are every where conspicuous; but as to its causes, they are mostly unknown, and must be resolv'd into original qualities of human nature, which I pretend not to explain. Nothing is more requisite for a true philosopher, than to restrain the intemperate desire of searching into causes, and having established any doctrine upon a sufficient number of experiments, rest contented with that, when he sees a farther examination would lead him into obscure and uncertain speculations. In that case his enquiry wou'd be much better employ'd in examining the effects than the causes of his principle.

Amongst the effects of this union or association of ideas, there are none more remarkable, than those complex ideas, which are the common subjects of our thoughts and reasoning, and generally arise from some principle of union among our simple ideas.

■ Questions for Discussion

1. How are simple ideas associated in order to form more complex ones?
2. What is a cause? How is the notion of a "cause" constructed from simple ideas?

Epistemology: How Do We Know All This?

CHAPTER NINE

D r. Wayne Dyer, in his popular book *Your Erroneous Zones*, relates the following story:

A speaker stood before a group of alcoholics determined to demonstrate to them, once and for all, that alcohol was an evil beyond compare. On the platform he had what appeared to be two identical containers of clear fluid. He announced that one contained pure water and the other was filled with undiluted alcohol. He placed a small worm in the water container while everyone watched as it swam around and headed for the side of the glass, whereupon it simply crawled to the top of the glass. He then took the same worm and placed it in the container with alcohol. The worm disintegrated right before their eyes. "There," said the speaker. "What's the moral?" A voice from the rear of the room said quite clearly, "I see that if you drink alcohol, you'll never have worms." (p. 11)

The moral of Dyer's story is, of course, what all of us know so well: that we see what we want to see. But we do not always recognize how pervasive and far-reaching that simple truth is. Let us consider some further examples.

In 1955, social psychologist Solomon Asch performed an experiment with college students that is still regarded as a classic. Asch told the students that they were going to be subjects in an experiment on visual judgment. Each subject was then put in a room, along with seven or eight other "subjects" who were really the experimenter's collaborators. Pairs of cards were then passed around, and each "subject" (including, of course, the experimenter's planted subjects) was asked to pick out which of three lines on card B matched in length the single line of card A. The real subject was not aware, of course, that his fellow subjects were the experimenter's collaborators, and the idea was to see what influence, if any, group pressure would have on his judgment. The results were that the subjects—all of them intelligent, perceptive, alert students—almost uniformly went along with the group and picked out the wrong answer from card B even when the wrong line was so wrong that nobody, seemingly, could possibly choose incorrectly.

A similar experiment devised to study the influence of sex prejudice on our attitudes and judgments produced similar results. Students were handed a brief essay on some difficult economic problem and were asked to give their opinions of the clarity and persuasiveness of the argument. Half the students were given copies identifying the author as "John Miller," and the other half were given copies with the author as "Joan Miller." Even though the essays were identical, except for the name, the students with the John Miller version rated the essay higher than those with the Joan Miller version.

This latter experiment is perhaps more impressive than Asch's since it may be argued that the subjects in his experiment really did see that the lines were unequal but went along with the dominant opinion in order not to cause trouble; in the second experiment, no such overt pressure was exerted, and the subjects apparently actually believed they were judging the words fairly and objectively.

One last example: It might not perhaps seem too surprising that when teachers are told that their students are "late bloomers" and are expected to make dramatic gains in their work, that is indeed what happens. But it surely would be surprising if *rats*

Two centuries ago, a fictional young poet in Germany, torn by his hopeless passion for the "perfect" woman, drank a glass of wine, raised a pistol, and put a bullet through his head. It was a shot heard round the world. The lovelorn dropout who fired it was the hero of Goethe's novel *The Sorrows of Young Werther*, which contributed to the romantic movement that colors our expectations of love to this day. Goethe himself was a poet of 25 when he wrote the story. And like the fictional Werther, he suffered from an infatuation with a married woman, an unreachable woman, whose very mystery invited his fantasies of perfection. Goethe's hero struck such a chord in young people throughout Europe that a wave of suicides followed the book's publication.

Today, as then, it's enlightening to speculate on the degree to which a young man invents his romanticized version of the loved woman. She may be seen as the magical chameleon who will be a mother when he needs it and in the next instant the child requiring his protection, as well as the seductress who proves his potency, the soother of anxieties (who shall have none of her own), the guarantor of his immortality through the conversion of his seed. And to what degree does the young woman invent the man she marries? She often sees in him possibilities that no one else recognizes and pictures herself within his dream as the one person who truly understands. Such illusions are the stuff of which the twenties are made.

—Gail Sheehy, *Passages*

---

performed better when experimenters are falsely informed that the rats have been specially bred for intelligence. Yet this has proven to be the case.

The lesson these examples teach is obvious. There is no such thing as an "innocent eye." Our perception is selective, filtered, and screened. What we receive is usually what we expect or want, believe, or are used to. What comes to be "seen," in short, depends on experience, context, and interpretation; it is a joint product of the observer and the observed.

We have been considering so far the influence of psychological or cultural factors on our perceptions. In addition, biological factors limit us in striking and universal ways.

First of all, sensory awareness varies profoundly among species. Some species have senses we lack, such as sensitivity to radio waves or to magnetic fields. Certain fish, for example, sense their surroundings by the deformation of electric fields, and some birds do so by changes in the barometric pressure.

The kind of information available to each creature, furthermore, is determined not only by its senses but also by the range of sensitivity. Human beings can hear sounds ranging from about 16 to 20,000 cycles per second, but some moths can hear up to 200,000 cycles; human sensitivity to odors is minimal, but salmon can smell their way home through countless miles of trackless water; humans can see a spectrum of colors ranging from violet to red, but this relatively small range of visible light lies within a vast continuous range of similar electromagnetic waves visible to insects, for example, but not to us.

Not only are certain avenues of stimuli either completely closed or greatly limited for humans, but some are either highly ambiguous or downright deceptive. Grass is green, we say, but is it green on a cloudy day? Or under a microscope? Or to one who is color-blind? And what about dreams, illusions, and hallucinations—and phantom pain in amputated limbs? In these cases it is not a matter of something appearing other than it is (an oar appearing bent when submerged) but of having perceptions to which no physical objects correspond.

Our commonsense beliefs—that we perceive physical objects directly, that these objects exist independently of us, and that the character of these objects is as we perceive them to be—become highly suspect when these psychological, cultural, and biological phenomena are considered.

The truth seems to be that every organism lives in a world shaped for it by the nature of its sensory apparatus. **Epistemology**, or the study of the theory of knowledge, is that area of philosophy concerned with investigating the implications of this truth. It is the study of the ways in which the knower knows the known. The following are the main questions it has traditionally posed to itself:

What are the principal grounds of knowledge?
How certain can we properly be of what we think we know?
Are there limits beyond which we cannot reasonably hope to extend knowledge?

Actually, no problem is ever *understood* till we have foreseen how to solve it and pass beyond it.

—**Denis de Rougemont**,
Love in the Western World

Sense and reason have traditionally been regarded as our two main sources of knowledge, and in modern times, when philosophic interest in epistemology reached a peak, replacing the medieval absorption with metaphysics, two schools tended to form around this issue. One, called **rationalism**, emphasized the role of reason in knowledge; the other, called **empiricism**, emphasized the role of sense or experience.

THE RATIONALISTS

It is to the first of these two schools, beginning with Descartes, the father of modern philosophy and the champion of rationalism, that we now turn.

René Descartes

René Descartes was born in 1596 in La Haye, a small town in Touraine, France, now called La Haye-Descartes, or simply Descartes.

The seventeenth century in which Descartes lived was a period of great intellectual activity and achievement, and among his contemporaries were such giants of the world of the intellect as Shakespeare, who had just finished *The Merchant of Venice*, and Galileo, who had just conducted his famous experiments.

Descartes's family belonged to the lesser nobility, with a long tradition of government service, his father being a councillor of the Parliament of Brittany. Upon his father's death, Descartes inherited sufficient property to be financially independent for the rest of his life.

René Descartes (1596–1650)

From 1604 to 1612, Descartes attended the Jesuit college of La Flèche, where he studied ancient languages, philosophy, and mathematics. He found himself deeply drawn to mathematics, to which he was later to make notable contributions, and deeply dissatisfied with the other studies, which he determined to abandon and to seek only after such science "as he might discover in himself or in the great book of the world."

From La Flèche, Descartes proceeded to the University of Poitiers, where in 1616 he graduated in law. Weary of study, he went to live in Paris, where for a period he led a life of indulgence: traveling, gambling, and dueling. Tiring of this, too, he enlisted as a soldier in the armies fighting the Thirty Years' War, eventually serving on both sides, the Protestant and the Catholic.

Leaving the army in 1621, he devoted himself to further study and travel. Feeling finally the need of solitude, he decided to settle down in Holland, a center of culture and intellectual freedom. It was there that in the next 20 years (1629–1649) he wrote the works upon which his fame rests: *Discourse on Method* (1637), *Meditations on First Philosophy* (1641), *Principles of Philosophy* (1644), and *The Passions of the Soul* (1649).

By 1649, Descartes's fame was so great that Queen Christina of Sweden, just 22 years old, summoned him to teach her philosophy. He hesitated to go, but she was insistent and sent a ship to fetch him, and he came. The only time she could spare for instruction in philosophy was five o'clock in the morning. Descartes—who, because of frail health, had been in the habit of staying in bed until noon—found the new regimen a great ordeal. In addition, the lessons were conducted in a cold library. Descartes caught pneumonia and died. He was 54 years old.

He had been educated, Descartes tells us, at one of the most celebrated schools in Europe, yet in thinking back on his studies, he could not help but wonder about their value. The charming fables of ancient literature, although intellectually stimulating, were, after all, only fables that, portraying behavior of a superhuman kind, could obviously not be emulated by humans. Nor was poetry any more helpful: certainly poets had the ability to make the truth "shine forth more brightly" than the philosophers, but their works were the product of inspiration, not the result of the application of a special method that we could adopt to further our knowledge. Nor could one find such a method in theology, whose "revealed truths are quite above our intelligence." Finally, the philosophy taught him was not any more helpful, for he could not find a single thing in it that was "not subject to dispute." What he had been taught at school, he found, was unbelievable, incomprehensible, or doubtful.

He decided therefore to abandon books and learning from that "great book of the world," where, he thought, he might discover what he was seeking—a more exact type of reasoning and more certainty. But to his dismay, he found as much difference of opinion among practical men as among philosophers. Descartes chose to break completely with the past, start afresh, and build a system of knowledge upon the powers of human reason alone. Descartes's search for knowledge led him to the discovery not of the soul but of the mind, conceived as a separate substance or entity distinct from the body. This was to prove to be a discovery of momentous importance in philosophy.

What Descartes discovered was a new method of securing knowledge. He had been enormously impressed with the success and achievements of mathematics, and he suddenly saw that similar success might accompany his efforts were he to follow its procedure. What was therefore required was to abstract those rules that have been responsible for its success and use them in placing science and philosophy on a similarly sound foundation.

Analyzing the procedure used in mathematics, he learned that what was characteristic of it was that it began with very simple and clear ideas whose truth the mind was capable of apprehending directly and knowing with absolute certainty and distinctness. It then advanced step-by-step toward more complex truths, making sure that each step of the argument was indisputable. The mind achieved the first truths, Descartes saw, by way of *intuition* (a vision of such clarity that it left one in no doubt regarding the truth of what was apprehended) and the subsequent ones by way of *deduction* (a series of careful, clear, and certain inferences proceeding from what is obvious and simple to what is more complex and remote).

Knowledge required both procedures.

Being certain he had found the proper method and wishing to make sure he would not forget or neglect it, he recorded the four principles it embraced:

> The *first* was never to accept anything for true for which I did not clearly know to be such
> . . . to comprise nothing more in my judgment than was presented to my mind so clearly
> and distinctly as to exclude all ground of doubt. The *second*, to divide each of the difficul-
> ties under examination into as many parts as possible, and as might be necessary for its
> adequate solution. The *third*, to conduct my thoughts in such order that by commencing
> with objects the simplest and easiest to know, I might ascend by little and little, and, as it
> were, step by step, to the knowledge of the more complex. . . . And the *last*, in every case
> to make enumerations so complete, and reviews so general, that I might be assured that
> nothing was omitted. (*Discourse on Method*, Part II)

But is it possible to find in science and philosophy simple, clear, and obvious axioms on whose foundations we might construct this new system of knowledge, one that would be unquestionable? Descartes was not certain of this, but he was willing to try. He decided that from now on he would accept nothing as true unless he clearly and distinctly perceived it to be so, even if it turned out that he would have to discard the most honored and cherished beliefs. How should he go about this? It occurred to him that he might accomplish it by turning himself into a radical skeptic and doubting everything that could possibly be doubted. As he put it, "Because I wished to give myself entirely to the search after truth, I thought it was necessary for me to reject as absolutely false everything concerning which I could imagine the least ground of doubt." He determined to sweep away all his former opinions "so that they might later on be replaced, either by others which were better, or by the same, when I had made them conform to the uniformity of a rational scheme."

Once he began to apply this method of doubt, it quickly became apparent to him how uncertain indeed the knowledge he had been taught really was. He saw that he could without much difficulty doubt authorities, he could doubt common sense, he could doubt the testimony of the senses and memory, and he could doubt all the sciences based on these sources of knowledge. What could be clearer, as he reasoned to himself, than "that I am here, seated by the fire holding this paper in my hands?" But when I am asleep, I dream that I am sitting by the fire, and this makes me realize that "there are no conclusive indications by which waking life can be distinguished from sleep." But if the world and everything in it may thus simply be part of a dream, is it not similarly possible that this is true even of the sciences that deal with things? Although it is tempting to believe that mathematics and science are certain, for "whether I am awake or asleep, two and three together will always make the number five," yet it is possible to doubt that, too, for this world may be the creation of an evil demon who leads one to be deceived even in matters of this sort as well.

If I can doubt whether there really are such things as an earth and sky and external things, and whether two and three make five, he reasoned, can't I even doubt whether I am now presently doubting? Having uttered this, Descartes caught himself and came to realize that this was one thing he could *not* doubt, for obviously it was impossible for him to doubt that he was doubting! Doubting being a form of thinking, Descartes came to express the unquestionable truth he had finally discovered in the slogan, one of the most famous in all philosophy, "I think, therefore, I am."

This became Descartes's starting point—his Archimedean point of certainty on the basis of which he could now go on to construct a body of certain knowledge. "Remarking that this truth, *I think therefore, I am,* was so solid and so certain that all the most extravagant suppositions of the skeptics were incapable of upsetting it, I judged that I could receive it without scruple as the first principle of the philosophy that I sought."

Enquiring now what it was about this proposition that made it so certainly true, Descartes found it was the "clarity and distinctness" with which it forced itself upon him. He therefore decided to adopt this as his criterion of truth. If it would be absurd or nonsensical to deny the truth of a certain judgment, then that would constitute proof that the judgment in question was true. Any proposition will necessarily be true, in short, if it possesses this same extreme and peculiar kind of self-evidence.

But where is one to find other judgments as self-evident as the judgment "I exist"? In reflecting on this question, it struck Descartes that the judgment "A perfect Being exists" had the same peculiar kind of clarity and distinctness. He thought that like the judgment "I exist," it, too, once one understood what it conveyed, could not be logically doubted. For "by the name God," he reasoned, "I understand a substance which is infinite, independent, all-knowing, all-powerful and by which I myself and everything else, if anything else exists, has been created." This being so, how can I, a finite, imperfect substance, produce the idea of an infinite and perfect substance? I obviously cannot. Therefore, since ideas have causes, and since the cause must have at least as much reality as the effect, God alone must be the cause of the idea I have of Him.

It is doubtful that many will be as convinced of the obviousness of this proof of God's existence as Descartes was, nor was this the only proof he offered in behalf of the judgment. Nevertheless, he himself seems to have been convinced by it and proceeded to use it to establish his third and last major proposition—the existence of the external world. And his proof of this was simply that God, being good, would not deceive us. Although our ordinary judgments of perception are fallible and our senses at times deceive us, human knowledge, he came to conclude, is fundamentally reliable.

Although the existence of God is the second of the three major foundation stones of Descartes's system, having once set it in place, he tended to neglect it in favor of the other two. And these two—mind and matter, distinct substances, existing independently of each other, each capable of being known and studied apart from the other—came to constitute the main ingredients of his philosophy.

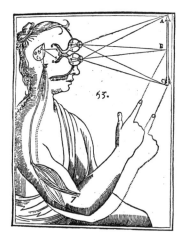

Diagram from Descartes's **Treatise of Man** *(1664)*

Historically, one of the important consequences of this **dualism** of mind and matter, which came to constitute the philosophy of Descartes, was that it separated philosophy from science, allowing each to pursue its separate domains uninhibited by conflict with the other (philosophy taking charge of the mind and investigating it and science being relegated to the study of matter and its laws of operation). Its major historical disadvantage, however, was that it bequeathed to philosophy a new and difficult problem, that of defining the relation between these two basic and utterly different realities. And this problem has continued to bedevil philosophy to this very day.

Nevertheless, this separation of the mind from the body or from matter came to be seen as Descartes's main contribution to philosophy. No philosopher before him had made the division as clearly and sharply as he had, and certainly no one before him had raised the mind to the level of matter, making it equal in importance. Mind and consciousness thus became, as they still are, the basic subject matter of philosophical investigation.

The immediate problem, however, was to define the relation between the two substances: If the two are as distinct as Descartes maintained, how do they come to interact with each other? Descartes himself believed the mind was "lodged" in the body ("as a pilot in a vessel") and was closely "united" with it. But how united? All subsequent philosophy, up to the present day, has been concerned with defining this relation: European rationalists have held on to the division, proposing ingenious methods of bridging it; the British empiricists have tried to dissolve the division by reducing the one to the other (by showing either how mind is derived from matter or how matter is derived from mind).

The first major European thinker to pick things up where Descartes left off was Spinoza.

Baruch Spinoza

Baruch Spinoza (1632–1677) was born in Holland, into a Portuguese Jewish family, refugees from the Spanish Inquisition. Sent to Hebrew school to study for the rabbinate, he was soon torn by doubts, unable to accept literally the teachings of the scriptures. He alarmed the Jewish community by expressing his doubts. Not at that time entitled to citizenship and fearful of reprisals for permitting heresy in their midst, they formally excommunicated him, placing a curse on his head and forbidding anyone from seeing or communicating with him. He was then 24 years old.

Spinoza took the news calmly and for the rest of his life lived a lonely, quiet existence in various places in Holland, earning his living by grinding and polishing lenses. He died at 44, the victim of tuberculosis, exacerbated by the glass dust he had inhaled practicing his vocation.

Only two of Spinoza's books appeared during his lifetime: one an exposition of Cartesianism titled *The Principles of Descartes's Philosophy* (1663) and the other, published anonymously, titled *Treatise on Theology and Politics* (1670). This second work became a milestone in biblical criticism, initiating the study of the Bible as a historical document. It was also one of the first works to advocate the separation of church and state, to stress the value of individual liberty and religious tolerance, and to argue for democracy as against the claims of monarchy and aristocracy.

> Thank God there are no free schools or printing . . . for learning has brought disobedience and heresy into the world, and printing has divulged them. . . . God keep us from both.
>
> —Sir William Berkeley,
> governor of Virginia, mid-1600s

But the dominant note of Spinoza's works was **pantheism**—the idea that since God alone truly is, everything must in some sense be God or be a part of God. This was not lost on his readers, and during his lifetime and for at least two centuries after his death, this aspect aroused intense and almost universal indignation and led him to be despised as an atheist. It was only in the late nineteenth century that he became venerated, as he still is, as a "God-intoxicated man" and the model of what a philosopher should be.

Spinoza's crowning achievement was the posthumously published book *The Ethics*, on which he began working in 1662 and into which he poured all his thought. It has come to be regarded as one of the most majestic of all philosophical works. It deals not only with ethics, as its title suggests, but also with such diverse subject matters as physics, metaphysics, and psychology. He named it *Ethics* because he believed that the purpose of philosophical investigation and thought is not just speculation but moral action as well.

In common with Descartes, Spinoza thought that we could achieve exact knowledge of reality if we followed the methods that had proven so successful in geometry. And so, starting with simple, clear, and distinct first principles, he went on to deduce the whole of what he thought was knowable concerning reality by using Euclid's geometry as his model. The result was a philosophical work consisting of a highly systematic arrangement of principles and axioms, all carefully and neatly demonstrated.

Spinoza chose as his starting point certain basic axioms that he believed were not arbitrarily hit upon but were vouchsafed by the mind as reflections of the true nature of

Baruch Spinoza (1632–1677)

things. And Spinoza's reasoning was the same here as Descartes's: Since these ideas had the requisite properties of being both clear and distinct and since every clear and distinct idea is true, a complete and systematic arrangement of them must give us a true picture of reality.

But, sad to say, although Descartes and Spinoza claimed to rely on the evidence of reason and both claimed their evidence to be infallible, the reasoning of the one turned out to be different from the reasoning of the other. For in the system of Spinoza, Descartes's dualism became transformed into a **monism**: The two Cartesian substances—mind and body—definitive of reality, became aspects of only one substance, which he called "Nature" or "God."

Spinoza arrived at this conclusion by working out the logical implications of Descartes's basic ideas more rigorously and more consistently than Descartes had done. Descartes had started with the clear and distinct idea of his own existence and went on to deduce the existence of God and then the world. But Spinoza recognized that since God is obviously prior to everything else—being the only truly independent substance there can be—we must begin with Him and by deduction try to discover whatever is true about us and the world. Furthermore, if "substance" is that which needs nothing other than itself in order to exist, then, strictly speaking, there can be only one substance, and everything else must be dependent on it. Consequently, thought and extension (Descartes's *two* other mutually independent substances) cannot really be separate substances but must be attributes of the one, single, independent substance, which is God.

God or Nature thus became for Spinoza the sole existent substance in the world. Whatever is "is in God, and nothing can exist or be conceived without God." Everything in the universe is dependent on Him, and God is the cause of all things and the principle within which all things find their being. Thought and extension, which had been conceived by Descartes as attributes of mind and body, are really, Spinoza went on to explain, themselves attributes of that one single substance—mind and body being really "modes" or modifications of those two attributes. Attributes, he went on to explain, are ways in which our intellect perceives this one basic and infinite substance. We as human beings perceive God in terms of only these two attributes, but there are in reality an infinite number of ways in which this one infinite and eternal substance can manifest itself.

Thought and extension being attributes of God and mind and body being modes of these attributes, it would not be correct to say that God is the creator of the world. God is the world. Similarly, since both thought and extension, or mind and body, are ultimately manifestations of this same basic substance, it would be incorrect to say that mind and body are separate and independent entities. They are really one, and what occurs in one finds its correlative occurrence in the other. Consciousness is thus not separate from body; it is simply "the idea of the body." The problem, therefore, of how mind can affect the body or how the body can affect the mind does not arise, for there is (e.g., as in the case of a concave and convex lens) a parallelism, not an inexplicable mysterious interaction between them.

These basic and, to Spinoza, simple and obvious metaphysical first principles entailed certain important consequences of a moral and practical sort. And in the remaining portions of his major work, *The Ethics*, Spinoza went on to explain what these were. First, since everything is in God or is God and everything therefore simply follows from the necessity of His nature, events must be seen as simply unfolding in the only possible way they can. It follows from this that, being part of God, we are not free to go our separate ways but are compelled to live lives whose destinies are fixed from eternity. And finally, this being so, nothing is in itself good or evil but only in relation to human interests. To God—and from "the aspect of eternity"—all is fair.

The consequence of all this, Spinoza argued, is that such human emotions as hope and fear, humility and repentence, envy and hatred, with which we are burdened, are useless and futile, for the future is unalterably fixed. We can free ourselves, however, from our bondage to these emotions (for being the bodily equivalents of mental ideas, they can be altered by knowledge) by striving through reason to achieve that identification with the order of the universe that will enable us to see how things must be the way they are. Spinoza calls this acceptance and love of our fate "the intellectual love of God." Its reward is "blessedness."

Gottfried Wilhelm von Leibniz

The last of the great rationalist philosophers on the European continent to try to solve the basic problem raised by Descartes was Gottfried Wilhelm von Leibniz, born in Leipzig, Germany, in 1646. With Leibniz, we have again that strange phenomenon: the boy genius. Not uncommon in the worlds of music and mathematics, it is rare elsewhere.

Mastering practically everything there was to master by the age of 20, Leibniz applied for a doctor of laws degree at the University of Leipzig. The professors turned him down, partly because of his age but partly also because they were jealous of his knowledge.

Incensed, he left his hometown for Altdorf, where the University of Nuremberg offered him the degree as well as a professorship. He accepted the degree, declined the professorship, and set himself to master whatever still remained—leading Frederick the Great, one of his patrons, later to describe him as a "whole academy in himself."

At 21, Leibniz entered diplomatic service, serving in the capacity of librarian, adviser, statesman, and international lawyer. Working every waking hour, he corresponded with scholars in 20 countries.

Leibniz (1646–1716; full name: Baron Gottfried Wilhelm von Leibniz)

It was at this time that he invented a computing machine that was in many ways a remarkable anticipation of our modern computers. He also planned and partially worked out an international language modeled on mathematics, a forerunner of the system of symbolic logic that was to come into its own some 200 years later.

In 1675, Leibniz discovered the differential calculus, and a year later, independently of Newton's slightly earlier work, he discovered the infinitesimal calculus. A long and bitter dispute arose as to who stole from whom, people taking sides along nationalistic lines: the French sided with Leibniz, the English with Newton. As a result, English mathematics fell behind for a century because the Newtonian notation was not as flexible as the Leibnizian, which the French adopted.

It was also at this time that Leibniz took up the librarianship at Hanover, a position he held until his death. When George of Hanover became King of England in 1714, Leibniz, because of the unfortunate repercussions of the controversy about the calculus, was not invited to follow the court to London. He stayed behind, embittered and neglected, and died two years later at the age of 70.

Although known as the best-of-all-possible-worlds philosopher, Leibniz's life, especially toward the end, was hardly idyllic. Acknowledged as the greatest thinker of his time, he died friendless and alone—only one man attended the funeral. As one acquaintance wrote, "He was buried more like a robber than what he really was, the ornament of his country."

Although Leibniz was a prolific writer, his best-known and still most widely read book is *Monadology* (1714), which he wrote in response to a request by a royal patron for a short account of his philosophy.

Like Spinoza's, Leibniz's work grew out of his reaction to the ideas of his predecessors. What Leibniz found wanting in the system of Descartes and Spinoza was their conception of substance. In his view, substance was not static but dynamic, and, furthermore, it did not consist of a single entity (as Spinoza had maintained) nor of two (as Descartes had held) but of many. Spinoza's monism and Descartes's dualism were replaced in Leibniz's system with a type of **pluralism**.

Although Leibniz's description of the nature of this basic stuff of the universe was somewhat reminiscent of Democritus's atoms, his conception of it was in reality quite different. Calling these basic units **monads,** he conceived them as unextended, endlessly diverse, throbbing centers of energy; each, furthermore, had the capacity of reflecting (some more clearly and more fully than others) the universe as a whole.

Our minds or souls, he suggested, are just such dynamic, immaterial monads, and what is true of our minds is true, in varying degrees, of all monads. They are all possessed of the same psychic, spiritual drives we find in ourselves and like us are endowed with powers of sensation and perception (or perhaps something analogous to what we know as "sensation" and "perception"), for the same principle, he argued, that expresses itself in the minds of humans is active in all of nature.

Every monad, having these powers of perception, however inchoate, perceives and represents the whole of the universe in itself. Each monad is, in a way, the universe in miniature or, as Leibniz expressed it, a "living mirror of the universe." Each monad, however, mirrors or represents the universe only with its own particular degree of clarity. It represents it, that is to say, only in its own way and from its own unique point of view.

He argued that there is thus no absolute division, as Descartes had mistakenly believed, between mind and body, or thought and extension, but a continuity between them, for what we find in nature are not minds and bodies but forces. These forces are possessed of varying degrees of perceptions, differing in clearness and distinctness, much in the same way that our own minds differ in this regard. In the very lowest monads, those of plants, perception is of a limited and primitive sort, and everything is obscure and confused; on the other hand, perception found among animals is of a much higher kind, one that we may call "consciousness." And in the case of humans, "consciousness" becomes even more refined and clear and turns into "self-consciousness."

But if monads are "mirrors of the universe," they are also "windowless." By this Leibniz meant that each monad, being in a process of evolution and busy realizing its nature by inner necessity, is neither determined nor influenced by anything outside it. Nor do monads need to be, for being miniatures of the universe they are not dependent on anything from without but possess implicitly or potentially within themselves everything they need to and will come to be. There cannot, therefore, be any interaction between monads.

But if neither Descartes's interactionism nor Spinoza's parallelism is what governs the unity within or between substances, what does? Leibniz's reply was that the unity, or "harmony," that we find was "preestablished" by God when He first created the universe. Monads, Leibniz explained, are like clocks that have been wound up together to keep the same time. Having been made by a perfect maker, they keep perfect time. Or, as he explained it, they are like "several different bands of musicians and choirs, playing their parts separately, and so placed that they do not see or even hear one another, nevertheless they keep perfect time together, by each following their own notes, in such a way that he who hears them all finds in them a harmony that is wonderful, and much more surprising than if there had been any connection between them."

Despite the prescient notion of substance, or matter, as essentially force or energy, a notion that was to come into its own only in the twentieth century, this theory of monads (and the solution to the problem of the mind and body it offered), although fascinating and intriguing, still continues to strike us as too fantastic to be believed.

THE EMPIRICISTS

What the three philosophers we have just looked at shared in common was a sublime confidence in the faculty of reason. The human mind, they believed, is so structured that by following the proper method, it is capable of arriving at certain knowledge of reality. Unfortunately, although each claimed to use that same faculty in the same way, each arrived at a remarkably different answer. Each assumed that what he could think "clearly and distinctly" with his mind was a reflection of what existed in the world outside, but what the three believed to so exist was impossibly contradictory. Depending on whom one chose to follow, the "stuff" of the universe turned out to be one, two, or many. These disparate accounts led their successors, the English empiricist philosophers, to question the basic, underlying premise shared by these three major continental thinkers. How reliable an instrument of knowledge is our faculty of reason? they asked. The first to do so was John Locke.

John Locke

John Locke (1632–1704) was born in Wrigton, Somerset, England. He was educated first at Westminster School, where he received a thorough grounding in the classics, and then at Oxford University, where he took his master's degree in 1658. He remained at Oxford to teach and pursue his studies in chemistry and medicine, to which he was becoming more and more drawn.

John Locke (1632–1704)

He was not destined to stay at Oxford, for in 1666 he met Lord Ashley (later the first Earl of Shaftesbury) and became his personal physician, friend, and confidant. This meeting and friendship was to determine Locke's own later fortunes, for Shaftesbury's attempt to exclude James II from the succession to the throne of England led to his dismissal and exile to Holland, and Locke followed him there.

In Holland, Locke met Prince William and Princess Mary of Orange, and when this couple ascended the throne of England after the bloodless revolution in 1688, Locke returned home with them.

Two years later saw the publication of the two works that were to make him famous both as a philosopher and as a political theorist. The first was *An Essay Concerning Human Understanding*, on which he had been working for some 20 years, and the second was *Two Treatises of Government*. Both these works were to prove enormously influential: the former on the whole history of philosophy, the latter on political history, providing the philosophical justification not only for the English Revolution of 1668 but also for the American Revolution of 1776, profoundly affecting the language and ideas of both the Declaration of Independence and the Constitution.

Locke's impassioned appeal for peace (the "state of nature is one of peace, good will, mutual assistance and preservation") and his arguments that (1) civil government derives its power from the consent of its members; (2) its purpose is the defense of individual liberty and property because men are "all equal and independent" and possess the natural rights to "life, health, liberty and possessions"; (3) in government the legislative branch is more important and authoritative than the executive; and (4) there should be a strict separation between these two branches and between church and state were all later to determine the course of the Western democracies.

What no doubt gave these ideas the attraction they had for him was the turbulent period through which he himself lived. The Thirty Years' War (1618–1648) overlapped the years of his own life, and during his lifetime he witnessed the execution of Charles I of England, the death of Cromwell, the Revolution of 1668, and the flight of James II. Elsewhere there occurred the rise of Louis XIV in France, Peter the Great in Russia, and Frederick I in Prussia. War and violence seemed everywhere, and in his political writings, he explored alternatives to the tyrannical solutions to which the world seemed to be reverting.

Locke's reason for undertaking his investigation "into the original, certainty, and extent of human knowledge, together with the grounds and degrees of belief, opinion, and assent" was not merely theoretical. Behind it lay the urgent desire to determine the sources and validity of the beliefs that brought people into such conflict with one another and caused so much bloodshed. He thought that if he could show how people's differing ideas resulted from their different experiences, they might become more tolerant of each other and thus avoid the agony of conflict and war.

An Essay Concerning Human Understanding opens with an investigation of the rationalist doctrine of innate ideas, the belief that the mind is endowed from birth with certain ideas and principles. However, there is no idea, Locke argues, that all men have and no principle that everyone accepts. Children and idiots, obviously, do not have such ideas or principles ready formed in their minds, so they cannot be born with them. To the objection that they are born with them but do not become aware of them until they reach the age of reason, he replies that there cannot be any ideas in the mind of which one is not aware. Besides, if reason is necessary to discover these ideas, these is no need for them to be innate (inborn). And with regard to morality, there is no single rule we can discover that is accepted by all societies; therefore, there cannot be any moral principle that is innate. This does not mean moral principles could not be proved by reason. The point is they are not innate.

Instead of imagining that we have true beliefs from birth, let us see, he says, whether we cannot trace our ideas back to their source in experience:

> Let us suppose the mind to be, as we say, white paper, void of all characters, without any
> ideas; how comes it to be furnished? Whence comes it by that vast store which the busy

and boundless fancy of man has painted on it, with an almost endless variety? Whence has it all the materials of reason and knowledge? To this I answer, in one word, from experience; in that all our knowledge is founded, and from that it ultimately derives itself.

That all knowledge comes from experience Locke now takes as his point of departure. The mind at birth, he says, is like a sheet of paper or blank tablet (tabula rasa) on which experience makes its marks. Experience furnishes us with sensations, and the mind reflects upon them. Sensations and reflections are the only two sources of knowledge that we have, and we are incapable of having an idea that does not come from one or the other of these two sources. **Ideas of sensation** (yellow, cold, bitter, hard, and so on) come to us through our various senses when some external object stimulates our sense organs; **ideas of reflection** (doubting, believing, knowing, reasoning, remembering, and so on) are the ideas we get from observing the operation of our own mind as it is employed about the ideas it already has. For the mind not only receives ideas from without but also thinks about ideas, has doubts, reasons, and so on, and these operations of the mind can be perceived by us just as we can perceive and observe colors, tastes, sounds, and so on.

The ideas the mind gets directly from sensation and reflection are simple. Once the mind has a store of **simple ideas**, it can repeat or compare or combine them in an infinite variety of ways to form new **complex ideas**. The number of simple ideas is very large, and we have names for only some of them. But the mind is not able to invent one new simple idea. A blind man, for example, has no idea of color. Most simple ideas come to us through one sense (e.g., color), while some come through two senses (figure and motion); some simple ideas we get from both sensation and reflection (pleasure and pain), and some simple ideas we get from reflection only.

The power of an object to produce an idea in the mind Locke calls a *quality* of the object. Sugar, for example, has the power to produce in us such ideas as white, granular, solid, and sweet. Some of these qualities resemble the objects that produce them, and some do not. Those that do Locke calls **primary qualities**; they include solidity, extension, figure, motion or rest, and number. Those that do not resemble the objects that produce them Locke calls **secondary qualities**. These consist of color, taste, sound, heat, and cold. These secondary qualities do not resemble any qualities of the object but are nothing more than powers to produce these ideas in us by means of the primary qualities in the object.

In the reception of simple ideas the mind is passive. The mind is concerned with the ideas it already has and is able to make new, complex ideas by combining, repeating, comparing, or abstracting from them. These complex ideas are made by the mind at will, and it is in this way that the mind furnishes itself with many more ideas than it originally receives from sensation and reflection. These new complex ideas formed by the mind may or may not correspond to something in the outside world.

There are three kinds of complex ideas: modes, relations, and substances. A **mode** is a complex idea of something that is thought of not as existing by itself but as dependent on, or as being a property of, a thing or substance (triangle, gratitude, number, and so on). **Relations** involve a comparison of one idea with another. Locke distinguishes between particular substances and pure substance in general. Particular **substances** are such things as gold, house, boy, and sugar. When we analyze our ideas of such particular substances, we find that they are combinations of several, separate ideas plus something else. Our idea of gold, for example, initially is a combination of simple ideas of sensation—color, extension, solidity, and so on. Although we think of this combination of simple ideas as capable of existing by itself, at the same time we cannot conceive of how they could do so except by supposing that there is some kind of support or bearer of ideas that we call substance. We think of this support as something besides the yellowness, the extension, the solidity. It is something that has all these or that supports all these and is thought of as the substratum of yellowness, hardness, and so on. This idea of support or substratum is the idea of pure substance.

When I examine the idea of pure substance in general, I find, Locke says, that I have no distinct idea of it at all. What then is it? In a famous phrase, Locke replies to this question that it is a "something, I know not what."

We can now state what **knowledge** is: "Knowledge is the perception of the agreement or disagreement of our ideas." It is plain that the mind cannot know things directly or immediately; it can know them only through the intervention or mediation of ideas. Knowledge, therefore, cannot extend further than one's ideas do. We have certain knowledge when we actually do perceive the agreement or disagreement of our ideas, and we have real knowledge when our ideas conform with or correspond to the reality of things.

The question that now inevitably arises in relation to Locke's theory of knowledge is, of course, this: If all we know are ideas and not the things themselves, how can we know that there is a conformity or correspondence between our ideas and reality? What justifies us in maintaining that there is a likeness between our perceptions and the things that produce them in us, if what we know are perceptions only? To prove such a correspondence, we would need to step outside our perceptions in order to compare them with the substances that cause them, and how can we do that? How can we step outside ourselves?

Locke's fatal error in his account of our situation was to posit a world we could know only through our ideas, one consisting of things held together by mysterious, unknowable substances. By doing so, had left himself open not only to the inevitable question of how he could know what was unknowable but also to the further question of how he could know such a thing exists at all.

George Berkeley

George Berkeley (1685–1753) was born in Kilkenney, Ireland, in 1685. At the age of 15, he entered Trinity College, Dublin, where he studied mathematics, logic, languages, and philosophy. In 1707 he received his master's degree, and two years later he was ordained

George Berkeley (1685–1753)

as a minister in the Church of England. Elected a fellow of the college, he remained there until 1713.

It was during this period, while still in his twenties, that he composed the literary and philosophical works on which his fame rests. The first was his *Essay towards a New Theory of Vision*, concerned with the manner in which we perceive the distance, magnitude, and position of objects. It appeared in 1709 when he was only 24 years old. It was followed a year later by his *Treatise concerning the Principles of Human Knowledge* (1710), containing his main philosophical ideas. (A second volume of this work, which he lost in manuscript, was never rewritten.) Three years after the appearance of the *Treatise*, Berkeley published a more popular version of its main themes in a work titled *Three Dialogues between Hylas and Philonus*.

In 1713, Berkeley left the college for London. After spending several years there and several in touring Europe, he returned to Ireland, where he conceived a plan for building a college in Bermuda devoted to "the reformation of manners among the English in our western plantations, and the propagation of the Gospel among the American savages." In preparation, he wrote a poem, *America, or the Muse's Refuge*, that gave expression to his almost messianic vision of this new land. The poem concluded with the following stanza:

Westward the Course of Empire takes its Way,
The four first Acts already past.
A fifth shall close the Drama with the Day,
The world's great Effort is the last.

Because of a navigation error, Berkeley's ship landed in Newport, Rhode Island, instead of Bermuda. Financial support for the planned college failed to materialize, so Berkeley decided to remain in Newport, where during the next three years he succeeded in starting divinity schools both there and in Connecticut as well as aiding the young universities of Yale and Harvard with donations of property and books.

Upon his return to England, he was named Bishop of Cloyne. Moving to his diocese in southern Ireland, he remained there for the next 18 years. In 1752 he settled with his wife and family in Oxford, where he died peacefully a year later at the age of 68.

Berkeley agreed with Locke that the materials of our knowledge are ideas—ideas of sensations and reflection and ideas formed by the help of memory and imagination. In addition, there is something that has the ideas, and this is mind, soul, spirit, or simply oneself. The mind is not the same as an idea but is rather what has or perceives and knows ideas. Ideas exist in it.

In all this Berkeley agreed with Locke: ideas of reflection (thoughts, feelings, volitions) can obviously exist only in the mind, for their very existence consists in being perceived by a mind. The same is true of our ideas of sensation: they, too, like thoughts and mental images, can exist only in the mind perceiving them. And it had been admitted by Locke that certain ideas of sensation—the secondary qualities—exist only in the mind and are not like anything existing apart from mind, while certain other ideas of sensation—the primary qualities—are copies of things or qualities existing outside the mind, and these things (extension, figure) actually do exist in external objects. External objects actually have extension, motion, and so on, and our ideas of these are more or less faithful copies of them.

But Berkeley now asked, How do we know that some of our ideas resemble qualities actually existing in external objects? On what ground can we say that the color of an object exists only in the mind, while shape really exists apart from mind? To be able to say that some qualities resemble the things in question and some do not, we would have to be able to compare an idea with the actual quality in the external object. But this is impossible since what we can perceive immediately is only the sensation and not the real object. In short, if the secondary qualities are subjective, the same must be the case with the primary qualities. Furthermore, if what we know consists of ideas and ideas only and if an idea cannot be compared with a "thing" but only with another idea, what evidence is there that physical objects exist at all?

The arguments with which Berkeley went on to reinforce these questions seem irrefutable. Is the shape or other sensible quality that is supposed to exist in an external object, he asked, perceivable or not? If it is perceivable, then it is an idea or sensation and exists in the mind; if it is not perceivable, how can we say that the sensation or idea we perceive resembles it? Besides, how can a sensation or an idea be like something that is not a sensation or an idea? The qualities of external objects, furthermore, are supposed to be relatively stable, but our sensations are constantly changing with changes in our sense organs, and how can sensations that constantly change resemble qualities that are supposed to be fixed? If one of these resemblances of the quality in the object is the faithful one, which one is it? Which is the real shape of the coin that appears round from one angle and oval from another?

According to Locke, extension, shape, and so on actually exist in objects apart from our perception, whereas color exists only in the mind of the perceiver. But is it possible to see a shape without a color? It would seem not. On the contrary, we infer the very existence of the primary qualities from the secondary ones. We would not know that an object took up space except by *seeing* a colored patch, *touching* something hard, and so on. All arguments that can be produced to show that secondary qualities exist in the mind can be used to show that primary qualities do so, too.

If there is nothing in an object except the qualities and if the qualities are dependent on experience, it follows, Berkeley concluded, that the object itself is dependent on experience. In short, if the "being of a color" means its being perceived and if the "being of a sound" means its being heard and thus for the other qualities, then the complex of qualities we call an object must owe its being to the combined perception of its qualities. And if this is so, then "to be is to be perceived"—*Esse est percipi*. This became Berkeley's famous thesis and summary of his philosophical position.

But, you will ask, doesn't matter exist? To this he replied that if by matter you mean some imperceptible and nonsensible entity, then as far as our senses are concerned, it simply does not exist; but if by matter you mean some inert, unthinking substance that has extension, figure, solidity, mobility, and so forth, then the very notion is contradictory since extension, figure, and so on cannot exist outside the mind. Therefore, matter in the usual sense of the word does not exist, and the belief that it is a "something, I know not what" is meaningless.

But if Locke was mistaken in believing in the existence of matter, he was not mistaken concerning the existence of mind or spirit. Mind, soul, or spirit (Berkeley used these terms interchangeably) does exist. The mind or soul, he said, is simple, undivided, and active. It is what perceives ideas and operates about them. We do not and cannot have an idea of mind or spirit; we can, however, form a "notion" of it. We know that it exists because we know that in addition to ideas there must be something that perceives these ideas, and this something is what we call mind or spirit.

To return, however, to matter. If matter, you will say, does not exist, then nothing in the physical world is real, and surely this is absurd. Surely, you will say, the tree I perceive is a real tree and similarly with the other things I encounter all around me. Berkeley's reply to this was that he did not deny the reality of the physical world. Together with everyone else, he believed his senses and believed that the objects he perceived by their means were the real things. His views were simply a combination of two views that used to be held separately—one by the common person, the other by the philosopher. The common person had always believed that the things he immediately perceived were real; the philosopher had always held that the things he immediately perceived were in the mind. What Berkeley was now saying was simply that what we perceive is real but obviously only mental.

One of the important advantages in seeing our situation in this light, said Berkeley, is that it removes all doubts concerning the possibility of knowledge. For as long as we suppose that there is a physical reality that can exist independently and unperceived, we shall remain in doubt as to whether our perception faithfully represents this reality to us. It is the belief in an independently existing reality that leads to doubt. But once we realize that the things we perceive are real and that these things exist in the mind, then we can once again trust our senses.

But one question still remains: if the real is what we perceive, then how can we know when we are perceiving a real object and when we are perceiving only an illusion? We can distinguish between the real and the imaginary, Berkeley replied, by noting such things as recurring patterns (when a perception is connected in a regular manner with previous and subsequent perceptions) and whether the perception depends on our will (as in fantasies).

But, you may still wonder, if the reality of things depends on our perception, does that mean that when I leave this room, everything ceases to exist? Berkeley's reply to this was that a tree that is struck by lightning in a dense forest and that crashes to the ground still makes a noise and that the distant stars still continue to exist in the daytime when we no longer see because God is there to perceive them!

This strange turn of his argument, one of the strangest in all of philosophy, has led many to poke fun at it. Among the earliest examples is the following pair of limericks attributed to Ronald Knox:

There was a young man who said, "God
Must think it exceedingly odd
That this little tree
Should continue to be
When there is no one about in the quad"

Reply:

"Dear Sir, your astonishment's odd;
I am always about in the quad,
And that's why this tree
Will continue to be
Since observed by
Yours faithfully,
God."

But however strange Berkeley's conclusion may appear, given the basic premise—that the only things we can know are ideas—the rest seems indeed to follow of necessity. For matter, as he has tried to show, is not the cause of ideas. Aside from the idea being meaningless, it is simply not conceivable how an unthinking substance could be the cause of ideas. And the ideas that we have must have some cause, for we ourselves are not their cause. And if matter is not their cause nor we, then it must follow that some other spirit or mind is. And this is conceivable because we ourselves are the cause of our ideas (as when we daydream), and so we have experience of a mind causing ideas in a mind. Therefore, it is conceivable that one mind may cause ideas in another, and this other mind or spirit must be God.

We can infer from the order of things, Berkeley added, what sort of spirit this is. It is, he says, one that is all-wise, all-powerful, and all-good.

Starting from Locke's epistemological premises, Berkeley built on them a view that was its diametrical opposite—Locke's realism or **materialism** (the doctrine that the world consists of material things and nothing else) transforming itself, almost magically, into a strict **idealism** (the doctrine that the only things that can be known to exist are ideas).

And this is very much what Berkeley had hoped to achieve, for both skepticism and atheism, he believed, result from a belief in materialism, and by denying the existence of matter, he had eliminated these twin evils.

David Hume

The last of the three great British philosophers to rely upon sense experience alone for knowledge of reality was David Hume. Hume carried the tradition of Locke and Berkeley—that nothing should be accepted as knowledge unless it has been acquired through sense experience—to its logical conclusion. His predecessors, he argued, had not followed this principle rigorously; they had in fact, he believed, violated it.

Like Locke and Berkeley before him, Hume took the primary data of human knowledge to be perceptions and reflections about perceptions. But he made a distinction they did not make, between "impressions" and "ideas." **Impressions** are the sensations, passions, emotions, desires, and so on we experience; **ideas** or thoughts are copies of impressions. Ideas differ from impressions only in that ideas are faint, whereas impressions are vivid. We remember the impressions, which are the primary data of our knowledge, by way of these "faint images" of them, and we can have no idea that is not a copy of an antecedent impression.

Some of these faint images or ideas are simple and exactly resemble their antecedent impressions; other ideas are complex, which the mind forms by means of various operations, and may not resemble anything of which we have ever had an impression—such as the idea of a unicorn.

Once we realize, said Hume, that each complex idea must be made up of simple ideas, every one of which must be a copy of an antecedent impression, we are able to see that a good deal that has been said by philosophers is simply nonsense. For if a word is to mean anything, it must stand for an idea, which must be a copy of an antecedent impression, and one must be able to show from what impression this idea has been derived. If one cannot do this, then there is no idea, and the word is meaningless. This means that a word such as *unicorn* has meaning because we can show the antecedent impressions of which this word is a complex representation. But there are some words that cannot be shown to have any such antecedent impressions. And this is the case, said Hume, with the word *substance*.

Berkeley was quite correct, therefore, when he rejected the notion of a material substance. We have no sense impression, as Locke himself admitted, of such a thing, and therefore we should not say—as Locke, unfortunately, did—that our impressions are caused by such an external material substance (by that "something, I know not what"). But neither can we say with Berkeley that our impressions are caused by some spiritual substance (a "soul," a "self," or a "mind"), for we have no sense impressions of such a thing, either. That notion, too, is therefore meaningless. What, then, is the soul or self?

> The soul, as far as we can conceive it, is nothing but a system or train of different perceptions, those of heat and cold, love and anger, thoughts and sensations; all united together,

but without any perfect simplicity or identity. Everything that exists is particular: and therefore it must be our several particular perceptions, that compose the mind. I say, *compose* the mind, not *belong* to it. The mind is not a substance, in which the perceptions inhere. We have no idea of substance of any kind, since we have no idea but what is derived from some impression, and we have no impression of any substance either material or spiritual. We know nothing but particular qualities and perceptions. *(A Treatise of Human Nature)*

Since we know nothing of an external world or of an internal self, we cannot, Hume concluded, know the origin of our impressions. The only things we can know are merely impressions and ideas. We believe, of course, in the existence of an external world and in the existence of a self, but no logical justification can be given for such beliefs. Metaphysics, therefore, which purports to investigate the nature of a reality independent of us, is impossible, for such an investigation is beyond us, requiring us to go, as it does, beyond our experience, and this we cannot do.

This being so, what kind of knowledge, according to Hume, are we capable of having? Two kinds, Hume replied: knowledge concerning "relations of ideas" and knowledge concerning "matters of fact." The first kind is arrived at by logical reasoning and issues in the kind of knowledge we have in a discipline such as mathematics; the other is arrived at by observation, not by logical reasoning. This does not mean that reasoning is not involved in the latter; it is, but the reasoning, being grounded in empirical fact, cannot have the certainty of the former.

> What peculiar privilege has this little agitation of the brain which we call *thought*, that we must make it the model of the whole universe?
>
> —**David Hume**, *Dialogues concerning Natural Religion*

For example, I hear a sound at the door (a matter of fact), and I reason from this to the fact that a person is there; or I see a brick being thrown at a window, and then I see the window shatter and reason that the one event is the cause of the other—meaning by this not merely that the one event preceded the other in time or was adjacent to it in space but that there is some necessary connection between the two. Distinguishing between a sheer coincidence and real causation in terms of this notion, we say that the cause necessitates, or compels, the effect. And once having found such a causal connection between *A* and *B*, we feel that we can predict with complete confidence that the next time *A* happens, other things being equal, *B* will follow—that it must follow.

But, Hume asked, what is this causal relationship? What is this necessary connection? Has anyone ever observed it? All one ever observes is the constant, temporal conjunction of two events, one of which is prior to another. And since that is all, strictly speaking, we ever observe, that is all we ought to admit.

But, you may ask, said Hume, if sequence in time and contiguity in space are all we observe, how do we ever get the idea of a causal bond or connection? To this he replied that we get the idea from custom or habit: after observing the sequence *A–B* many times, we come by sheer habit, or psychological conditioning, to expect *B* after *A*. And this feeling of expectation is the only impression upon which the idea of cause rests. What is certain is that we do not find this necessary connection in experience, for all that experience ever provides us with are particular instances of associated facts and not general or universal necessary relations or connections between facts. Since therefore a large part of our investigation of matters of fact depends on such causal relations, our knowledge must be considered both limited and uncertain.

The upshot of Hume's investigation is thus an extreme form of intellectual **skepticism**. By pushing Locke's and Berkeley's analysis of knowledge to its logical conclusion, he showed that we cannot be sure of the existence either of a self or of an external world or even of the law of cause and effect, the foundation of science.

Locke's realism, which in Berkeley's hands became transformed into idealism, has now in turn become transformed in Hume's hands into a full-blown skepticism.

THE KANTIAN SYNTHESIS

The two philosophical traditions we have just outlined—continental rationalism and British empiricism—each reached, as we have seen, a kind of dead end. The rationalists professed absolute confidence in reason, but the reasoning of one differed profoundly from the reasoning of the other. Their neglect of experience led to the construction of ambitious systems of thought, which, for all their brilliance of speculation, struck those of a more scientific turn of mind as merely castles in the air, lacking solid foundation.

The outcome of empiricism was similarly surprising and disappointing. Empiricism prided itself on its attachment to experimental science, yet when it faced the task of giving an intelligible account of some of the basic concepts underlying science itself—such as substance, mind, and cause—it proved unable to do so. Hume, by refusing to make any concessions to rationalism, came to assert, as we saw, that none of these concepts had any empirical meaning whatsoever: a "thing" was just a collection of sensations, the mind or self a "bundle of perceptions," and there was no such thing as a causal connection, only a series of "loose" or "separate" events.

Each system pursued in isolation thus came to an impasse: rationalism ending in dogmatism and empiricism in skepticism (**dogmatism** meaning a supreme confidence in the truth of one's own beliefs). Each side, however, seemed on strong ground when it attacked the other and pointed out its weaknesses although inadequate when it came to propose its own solutions. Each seemed strong, that is to say, precisely where the other was weak; human reason may not be sufficient to provide us with a knowledge of reality, as the empiricists emphasized, but it was certainly necessary in order to do so; and experience may not be the only source of our knowledge, as the rationalists argued, but it was certainly a major one. The one school seemed to have neglected the role of experience in knowledge and the other the role of reason.

What seemed to be required at this point in the investigation of the foundation and sources of knowledge was an attempt to synthesize the contributions of each of these two major movements, using the insights of one of these approaches to correct the errors of the other. The philosopher who undertook this task was Immanuel Kant.

Immanuel Kant (1724–1804) is without question the greatest figure in modern philosophy. He revolutionized practically every field of investigation he touched. Kant was born in Königsberg, a seaport in East Prussia. He lived in or near this small city all his life, never traveling more than a few miles from it. His parents belonged to the lower middle class and were members of a devout Protestant evangelical sect called Pietists. They were all deeply religious, and Kant himself remained so all his life.

Kant entered the University of Königsberg at the age of 16, intending to embark on a career in theology. By 22, however, both his parents had died, and, along with his three sisters and one brother, Kant now had to make his own way as best he could. He supported himself for the next nine years by being a private tutor in several families of the East Prussian nobility.

At age 31 he returned to the university for further study. On completing his doctorate, he was appointed instructor, and he remained in that position for 15 years. In 1770, at the age of 46, he was finally elevated to professor, a position he held to his retirement in 1797.

Although originally intending to embark on a career in theology, Kant gradually found himself attracted to science and then finally to philosophy. His first published work was not in theology or philosophy but in physics: *General History of Nature and Theory of the Heavens*, published in 1755. For 25 years after this work appeared, he published only occasional papers, using his time to formulate his own original and revolutionary philosophy.

Then in one decade he published five great works: *Critique of Pure Reason* (1781), *Prolegomena to Any Future System of Metaphysics* (1783), *Foundations of the Metaphysics of Morals* (1785), *Critique of Practical Reason* (1788), and *Critique of Judgment* (1790).

Kant attached great importance to the difference between the works he wrote before the *Critique of Pure Reason* and those that followed it. The former he regarded as devoid of interest. "Through this treatise," he wrote, "the value of my earlier metaphysical works was totally destroyed." When a new edition of his complete works was projected, he wished it to begin with *On the Form and Principles of the Sensible and the Intelligible Worlds* (1770), which, though not yet an embodiment of the critical philosophy, represented an important step toward it.

Kant did not come to the new views contained in the *Critique of Pure Reason* suddenly.

In the beginning of his career and for a long time afterward, the philosophy he taught and believed in was rationalism. This was the dominant school in German universities at that time. But Kant's interest in and knowledge of empirical science led him to see certain difficulties in this philosophy so that he gradually became more and more dissatisfied with it. And then, somewhere between 1756 and 1762, he came upon a translation of

Hume's *Enquiry concerning Human Understanding* (1748), which had an enormous impact on him. Kant was the first major thinker to appreciate the full force of Hume's argument. It led him to break with rationalism.

In a famous paragraph in the *Prolegomena*, Kant tells us of the effect this reading of Hume had on him:

> I openly confess that my remembering David Hume was the very thing which many years ago first interrupted my dogmatic slumber, and gave my investigations in the field of speculative philosophy a quite new direction. I was far from following him in the conclusions to which he arrived by considering, not the whole of his problem, but a part, which by itself can give us no information. If we start from a well-founded, but undeveloped thought which another has bequeathed to us, we may well hope by continued reflection to advance farther than the acute man to whom we owe the first spark of light.

Hume, Kant tells us here, not only started him thinking but gave him a clue to follow. What this clue was we will soon see. What is interesting here is that he apparently planned to out-Hume Hume. Hume, he believed, did not go far enough, stopping at skepticism; by continuing Hume's line of thought, he suggested, we should be able to arrive at a more satisfactory solution.

The Problem as Kant Saw It

The word *critique* in the title of Kant's work is borrowed from English literature and means "a critical examination"—in this case of the nature and operation of "reason." The work opens with these words of the preface:

> Human reason has this peculiar fate that in one species of its knowledge it is burdened by questions which, as prescribed by the very nature of reason itself, it is not able to ignore, but which, as transcending all its powers, it is not able to answer.

Human reason, or understanding, Kant is saying here, is doomed to ask questions it is apparently fated not to be able to answer. This is the human predicament as he sees it, and his attempt at a critical examination of human reason is designed to throw light on this predicament.

The attempt, however, is also very much within the spirit of his age, as he goes on to point out. This was the eighteenth century, the period of the Enlightenment, a period that prided itself on its critical spirit and whose watchword was Reason:

> Our age is, in especial degree, the age of criticism, and to criticism everything must submit. Religion through its sanctity, and law—giving through its majesty, may seek to exempt themselves from it. But they then awaken just suspicion, and cannot claim the sin-

cere respect which reason accords only to that which has been able to sustain the test of free and open examination.

This was an attitude inspired by admiration for the achievements of reason in natural science, especially in Newtonian physics.

But, Kant goes on to say, when we look more carefully into this praise of reason, when we inquire into its foundations, we find a sorry state of affairs. Metaphysics, the supreme work of reason, lies in ruins and in disrepute. At one time she was regarded as the Queen of the Sciences, but now she is met with scorn: a matron outcast and forsaken, she mourns like Hecuba. Her government under the administration of the dogmatists (rationalists) was at first despotic. Gradually, through internecine wars (rationalists competing among themselves) her empire gave way to complete anarchy, and so the skeptics (the empiricists), "a species of nomads, despising all settled modes of life, broke up from time to time all civil society." Happily, he says, they were few in number and could not completely destroy the empire, although they did a great deal of damage. In more recent times the "celebrated Locke" tried to put an end to all these controversies by proposing a "physiology of the human understanding." This attempt to cast doubt upon the pretensions of the Queen of all the Sciences, by tracing her lineage to vulgar origins in common experience, failed to accomplish its task. This has been recognized as a fictitiously invented genealogy, and metaphysics has continued to uphold her claims. And so now we have a return to dogmatism but one that is greeted with complete indifference.

But indifference to such matters, Kant says in a striking passage, is not compatible with being human. We should not therefore abandon our attempts to achieve this knowledge we so deeply desire. Although it is thought that all methods have been tried and found wanting, there is still one remaining at our disposal that has yet to be tested. This is the method of criticism of pure reason.

> I do not mean by this a critique of books and systems, but of the faculty of reason in general, in respect of all knowledge after which it may strive *independently of all experience*. It will therefore decide as to the possibility or impossibility of metaphysics in general, and determine its sources, its extent, and its limits—all in accordance with principles. The subject of the present enquiry is the question, how much we can hope to achieve by reason, when all the materials and assistance of experience are taken away. [Kant's italics]

And so Kant will now once again undertake to reconsider and reconstruct the foundations of knowledge to see what it is we can or cannot be certain about.

In this preface to the first edition of his work, he expresses some doubts, as he will continue to do, here and in other works, about his powers of expression. He might have made, he says, the work clearer and easier to comprehend had he used more examples and illustrations, but this would have made the work too bulky, and it is that already. In any case, such examples and illustrations are necessary only from a popular point of view, and "this work can never be made suitable for popular consumption." He ends the preface by making the bold claim that he had solved forever the main questions of philosophy.

In his preface to the second edition of the *Critique*, Kant returns to this note of what it is or is not possible for us to know. How can we put any faith in human reason, he asks, if in one of the very things that we most desire to know, reason not merely forsakes us but lures us on by false hopes only to cheat us in the end? But are there, perhaps, any indications that the true path has still to be found and that by starting afresh we may yet succeed where others failed?

Obviously, if we are going to succeed, a thorough reconstruction will be necessary. He goes on to refer to the examples of scientific discovery, in geometry and in physics, noting that scientific discovery comes not from passive observation but from an activity on our part. Galileo, he says, did not just watch balls rolling down an inclined plane: he conceived a theory of what was happening and then devised an experiment to confirm or reject his theory. He approached nature with certain definite ideas of his own, with certain hypotheses, and forced nature to answer his questions. This teaches us that "reason has insight only into that which it produces after a plan of its own."

Kant goes on to show how this moral can be of benefit in reconstructing philosophy. All previous philosophies—including both rationalism and empiricism—had started from a common view about the nature of mind and its relation to the world of objects. They assumed that the human mind was set over against a world of objects, which it tried to know but to the nature of which it contributed nothing. The object had been thought of as merely given to the mind; the mind had nothing to do with the making of the object. Beginning with this point of view, it is no wonder that both rationalism and empiricism ran into difficulties. Rationalism was unable to explain how its innate principles were capable of giving us knowledge of this independent reality (for how could we be certain there was a conformity between the ways of the mind and the ways of things?), while empiricism (with the belief that the mind was a passive observer) was unable to explain how we could ever attain anything more than collections of past observations lacking all predictive power.

It was this basic assumption, underlying both modes of philosophy, that Kant questioned. For if the human mind is to succeed in achieving a knowledge of objects, then these objects cannot be independent of the mind. The mind cannot be simply a spectator; it must itself contribute actively to the nature of the objects that confront it in experience. For again, the mind can know only that which it itself makes.

Now this is certainly clear in the case of the mathematical sciences. The objects of mathematics (yards, feet, inches, and so on) are objects we have made, and hence they are entirely knowable and also, consequently, certain. But what Kant will try to show in his *Critique* is that the mind, instead of being a passive spectator, also contributes something to the nature of *all* objects, including physical objects, and this fact is the key to their intelligibility.

314

This reversal of point of view—of making objects depend on the mind instead of vice versa—is compared by Kant to the revolution in astronomy brought about by Copernicus:

> Hitherto it has been assumed that all our knowledge must conform to objects. But all attempts to extend our knowledge of objects by establishing something in regard to them *a priori*, by means of concepts, have, on this assumption, ended in failure. We must therefore make trial whether we may not have more success in the tasks of metaphysics, if we suppose that objects must conform to our knowledge. This would agree better with what is desired, namely, that it should be possible to have knowledge of objects *a priori* determining something in regard to them prior to their being given. We should then be proceeding precisely on the lines of Copernicus's primary hypothesis. Failing of satisfactory progress in explaining the movements of the heavenly bodies on the supposition that they all revolved round the spectator, he tried whether he might not have better success if he made the spectator to revolve and the stars to remain at rest.

And if we try this same sort of thing in metaphysics, or philosophy, we shall find, says Kant, that just as some of the motions the stars were thought to possess were not really due to them but to us, so similarly certain of the characteristics objects have will be seen as not due to some external reality but to us, to the work of the mind.

In the concluding portions of his preface to the second edition of the *Critique*, Kant goes on to share with his readers some of the results he expects to achieve. If we accept the standpoint of the Copernican revolution, he points out, then we shall be able to prove rigorously that certain knowledge of reality is possible and thus be in a position to reply to Hume's skepticism. But we will discover that the only reality we can truly know is that which is given to us in sense experience. We will see that we cannot have knowledge, in the proper sense of that word, of anything lying beyond experience. In

---

With the appearance of Kant former systems of philosophy, which had merely sniffed about the external aspect of things, assembling and classifying their characteristics, ceased to exist. Kant led investigation back to the human intellect, and inquired what the latter had to reveal. Not without reason, therefore did he compare his philosophy to the method of Copernicus. Formerly, when men conceived the world as standing still, and the sun as revolving round it, astronomical calculations failed to agree accurately. But when Copernicus made the sun stand still and the earth revolve round it, behold! Everything accorded admirably. So formerly reason, like the sun, moved round the universe of phenomena, and sought to throw light upon it. But Kant bade reason, the sun, stand still, and the universe of phenomena now turns round, and is illuminated the moment it comes within the region of the intellectual orb.

—**Heinrich Heine, *Religion and Philosophy in Germany***

particular, we will come to see that we cannot and never will be able to establish three points that have been important to traditional philosophy: the existence of God, freedom, and immortality.

But although this is fatal to the usual claims of rationalism, which professes to be able to prove such ideas, Kant insists that we can find any meaning and any value in these ideas only if knowledge of them is *not* possible. And this would seem to follow from our basic premise, for if knowledge is restricted to things we can experience, then if God were knowable, he would have to be a thing of a physical sort, bound by the limitations characteristic of human beings. Such a God would lose all meaning for us. Similarly with the notion of freedom and immortality—if these ideas are to have any meaning for us, they must refer to a sort of reality lying beyond our empirical, phenomenal world.

And so Kant, toward the end of the preface, makes a remarkable assertion: "I have therefore found it necessary to deny knowledge of God, freedom, and immortality in order to find a place for faith."

If it thus appears that Kant does come after all to agree with Hume that we really cannot have knowledge of the things we so desperately wish we did, we shall also see that he will show that we are in possession of a good deal more knowledge than Hume believed.

The Solution to the Problem

Kant begins his introduction to the *Critique* by summarizing what he takes to be the correct insights of both empiricism and rationalism. He says that "there can be no doubt whatever that all our knowledge begins with experience," for in no other way could our faculty of knowledge get any material to work upon. It is experience, he says, that gives us "the raw material of our sense impressions." In the order of time, therefore, we have no knowledge prior to experience, and with experience all our knowledge begins.

To think that we can have knowledge without experience (as the rationalists contended) would be the same—making use of a remarkable and memorable analogy—as if a dove were to imagine that since it can easily fly through air, it could with equal, if not more, ease fly through empty space.

The fact, however, that all our knowledge begins *with* experience (which is the essential truth in empiricism) does not mean that it all originates *from* experience. The contribution the mind itself makes to its knowledge of things must be taken into account as well, for the mind is not a passive observer but takes an active role (and this is the essential truth in rationalism) in organizing and imposing form on the material that comes to it in experience.

If we could somehow combine these two basic insights, we might be able to achieve a solution to the problem of what it is we can or cannot know and what it is we can or cannot be certain about. What Kant does here is to translate these basic insights into strictly logical terms and by their means to go on to pose as clearly as possible the really significant question, doing so in a way that will make it amenable to a logical solution.

This question first suggested itself to him as a result of his reflections on Hume. We will soon look at the passages in Hume that occasioned it. Hume, he thought, almost stumbled on it himself; he probably would have if he had not stopped short at skepticism.

To fix the question more clearly both for himself and the reader, Kant resorts to some technical terminology. Any knowledge that we might possess or wish to convey to others would, first of all, need to be expressed or conveyed in the form of statements, statements that could then be judged to be either true or false. Although it is customary now to call such statements **propositions**, the term Kant uses is "judgments." A proposition has two basic components: a *subject*, about which something is stated, and a *predicate*, what is stated about the subject.

Some judgments we make, Kant points out, are **a priori**; that is, we can know them to be true apart from experience. An example is the judgment or proposition that 7 plus 5 equals 12. Such judgments have two distinguishing marks: universality and necessity—they are true everywhere and with certainty. In contrast are judgments that are **a posteriori**; they are derivable with the help, at some point, of sense experience. "The grass is green" would be an example of such a judgment.

There are, in addition, two other significant features about judgments. Some are **analytic propositions**: they are propositions in which the predicate is contained in the subject, as in "A bachelor is an unmarried male." In making such a judgment, we are simply drawing out, or analyzing, the nature of the subject term of the proposition. This being so, the predicate term in such propositions adds nothing to the subject, and the propositions therefore do not provide us with any new knowledge.

In contrast, there are judgments, such as "The house is burning," that are **synthetic propositions**. In synthetic judgments the predicate is not identical with the subject. We may analyze the subject term of such a judgment ad infinitum and never elicit from it the knowledge contained in the predicate term. And we cannot do so in the case of such judgments because the predicate is not part of the subject and therefore cannot be found there. Synthetic judgments, unlike analytic ones, do therefore tell us something new and are informative.

These distinctions overlap, giving rise to two types of propositions; those that are *analytic a priori* and those that are *synthetic a posteriori*. An analytic a priori proposition would be any truism: "A is A," "A bald-headed man is one who has no hair on his head," and so on. These propositions are necessarily and universally true, but they are also empty and uninformative, the predicate term merely explicating the subject term. A synthetic a posteriori proposition, on the other hand, is a proposition in which we record an empirical observation ("The grass is green").

Such propositions are informative but lack universality and necessity.

According to Hume (although he did not use these terms to describe them), these two are the only kinds of propositions we can have. The following is the famous passage in the *Enquiry* (which proved so suggestive to Kant) where Hume enunciated his view:

> All the objects of human reason or inquiry may naturally be divided into two kinds, to wit, "Relations of Ideas" and "Matters of Fact." Of the first kind are the sciences of Geometry, Algebra, and Arithmetic, and, in short, every affirmation which is either intuitively or demonstratively certain. That the square of the hypotenuse is equal to the square of the two sides is a proposition which expresses a relation between these figures. That three times five is equal to the half of thirty expresses a relation between these numbers. Propositions of this kind are discoverable by the mere operation of thought, without dependence on what is anywhere existent in the universe. Though there never were a circle or triangle in nature, the truths demonstrated by Euclid would forever retain their certainty and evidence. Matters of fact, which are the second objects of human reason, are not ascertained in the same manner, nor is our evidence of their truth, however great, of a like nature with the foregoing. The contrary of every matter of fact is still possible, because it can never imply a contradiction and is conceived by the mind with the same facility and distinctness as if ever so conformable to reality. That the sun will not rise tomorrow is no less intelligible a proposition and implies no more contradiction than the affirmation that it will rise. We should in vain, therefore, attempt to demonstrate its falsehood. Were it demonstratively false, it would imply a contradiction and could never be distinctly conceived by the mind.

Hume was fully aware of the vast implications of his position here. He pointed them out in the devastating passage with which he brought his book to a close:

> When we run over libraries, persuaded of these principles, what havoc must we make? If we take in our hand any volume; of divinity or school metaphysics, for instance; let us ask, Does it contain any abstract reasoning concerning quantity or number? No. Does it contain any experimental reasoning concerning matters of fact and existence? No. Commit it then to the flames: for it can contain nothing but sophistry and illusion.

We thus possess, according to Hume, only two kinds of propositions: a priori truths (his "relations of ideas"), which are really only analytic, meaning that they do not extend our knowledge about the world but tell us only about the interconnections of our ideas, and a posteriori truths (his "matters of fact"), which are really only synthetic, meaning that they merely summarize what we have observed and cannot serve therefore as predictions of future experience. A priori propositions, according to Hume, are indeed universally true, but they say nothing, for they are empty of content; and a posteriori propositions may be true, but because they cannot be universalized, they are useless. Hence Hume's skepticism.

But once having seen the dichotomy presented by Hume in his terms, Kant wondered whether we might not have within our reach still a third type of proposition, one that possesses the best features of the two admitted by Hume—namely, a proposition that is synthetic and a priori. So he asked himself the momentous question: How are synthetic a priori propositions possible? This would be a most valuable kind of proposition to have—to say the least—for as a priori it would be universally true, and as synthetic it would have an important content to it and could serve as a premise for valuable inferences and predictions about areas of natural events not yet observed or observable.

It might be thought that Hume must have considered the possibility of the existence of such a third type of proposition but simply dismissed it as either meaningless or impossible. Once we realize, however, how strange the very idea of the possibility of such a proposition is, the occurrence of the idea does not seem so inevitable. For the possession of such a proposition, or this type of knowledge, would be a most remarkable thing indeed, and our first inclination, assuming the idea of it did occur to us, would be to reject it as a piece of pure fiction. For, we might ask, how could it be possible for us, or our minds, to attain to a kind of knowledge that is significant or important (not trivial as in the case of analytic propositions) and yet certain and universal in scope by way of pure thought alone?

The difficulty is that if these are synthetic propositions, the subject and the predicate are two distinct notions. By what right can we say that nevertheless they are necessarily connected in some way, so that the proposition "S is P" is always true? This problem does not arise for analytic propositions, for here P is just part of S. It does not arise for synthetic propositions, for they do not assert any necessary connection. But it does arise for synthetic a priori propositions.

Hume saw this as a problem limited to causation and solved it by denying its existence. The causal axiom is synthetic: every synthetic proposition rests on experience (or is a posteriori), and therefore we cannot be sure of its universality or necessity (as we would if it were a priori).

Kant was certain, however, that the causal axiom is not an a posteriori but an a priori truth and that therefore all events are subject to it. But Kant also realized that the problem Hume was raising was not limited to causation; he realized that the question was much wider, although the causal axiom was an important example of it. The question was really whether it is possible for us to have this type of knowledge at all. And this was the form in which Kant decided to tackle the question.

The general question (how are synthetic a priori propositions possible?), if solved, would answer, he realized, three special problems, each again much wider than the question about causation originally posed by Hume: how such a discipline as mathematics is possible, how such a discipline as physics is possible, and, in the light of these, whether such a discipline as metaphysics is possible.

The three main sections of Kant's work—the Transcendental Aesthetic, the Transcendental Analytic, and the Transcendental Dialectic—are devoted to an exploration of these three main questions. His attack consists in carrying through the Copernican revolution—that is, showing that just as the motions of the stars are not really due to themselves but to our own motion, so certain of the characteristics objects have are not inherent in them but rather due to us—to the work of the mind. It was the failure to see this that had been responsible for the previous impasses. If the mind were merely a passive spectator of objects, a priori knowledge of a synthetic kind would be impossible. But on the assumption that the mind is active, that it does and must contribute something to the nature of objects of experience, we can see how such synthetic a priori knowledge is indeed possible.

Our cognitive situation, Kant argues, is similar to what it would be if we were compelled (to make use of a well-worn analogy) to wear blue spectacles we could not remove. We would be able to predict something about every object we saw, namely, that it would be colored some shade of blue. Nothing could be perceived by us without having this blue color imposed on it. We would consequently have some a priori information about any possible future object of experience. There would, of course, be differences between objects that we could not predict (e.g., red things would appear darker than pink things). But on one point we would be certain: whatever we experienced would be experienced as colored some shade of blue.

Now suppose that the mind imposes, by laws of its own, certain conditions on what comes to it in experience. The resulting objects of experience—called **phenomena** by Kant—would bear the stamp of the mind's activity. This would make possible synthetic a priori assertions. If the mind legislates in part for the nature of phenomena—that is, that phenomena bear upon them the imprint of the mind's projections—then we can know in advance something about their nature: that part of their nature that would be due to mind.

These a priori elements contributed by the mind to the nature of phenomena fall into two main groups: the a priori elements relating to the way we *sense* objects and the a priori elements relating to the way we *think about* objects. The mind, that is to say, senses the material that comes to it in certain ways (imposes certain forms of sensuous intuition on it), and it comes to understand it in certain characteristic ways (organizes it by way of certain conceptual patterns or "categories"). These are the two separate modes of organization, or structuring, imposed by the mind on the raw material supplied it in experience. The finished products are the objects or phenomena of experience, but since certain elements in the finished product are due to the mind, they are therefore predictable ("the mind has insight into that which it produces after a plan of its own"). It is thus possible for us to have a priori knowledge of a synthetic kind.

According to Kant, it is our faculty of "sensibility" that imposes the forms of sensuous intuition on the material that comes to it in experience, and it is our faculty of "understanding" that imposes its conceptual categories on the objects it thinks about. The task of investigating the a priori forms imposed by the mind by the former faculty is undertaken in the first of the three main divisions of the *Critique* (the Transcendental Aesthetic), while the a priori elements imposed by the mind through its faculty of understanding are undertaken in the second of these three main divisions (the Transcendental

Analytic). In the last of these three divisions (the Transcendental Dialectic), Kant investigates the intellectual elements offered by "reason" (in the narrow sense of the word) and shows that unlike the contributions made by sensibility and understanding, what reason offers is not valid of experience.

Space and Time

"Transcendental Aesthetic" is a technical way of identifying a discussion concerned with sense perception. By "transcendental," Kant means to isolate the factors that make possible the kind of sense perception we as human beings are subject to. It is concerned, to put it a little more technically, with the analysis of the condition (or preconditions) presupposed by knowledge. It is a method of investigation that starts with some facts about our experience and then asks, What are the conditions that make this fact possible, that explain this fact?

Kant himself gives the following definition of **transcendental knowledge**: it is, he says, "all knowledge that is concerned, not with objects, but with the way in which a knowledge of objects may be gained, so far as that is possible *a priori*." In a sense, of course, this is what all of Kant's philosophy is about: an investigation of the conditions under which knowledge is possible.

But here we are concerned with the investigation of the conditions (or the a priori elements) involved in perception. Is perception merely a matter of opening our eyes and our other sense organs to what may be inscribed or imprinted on them by things external to them, or is the situation somewhat more complicated?

Are there, perhaps, certain universal and necessary conditions imposed by the mind in order for objects to be perceived by us the way they are? Kant, of course, argues that we do impose such features on phenomena. He argues that when we abstract from our perception of objects all conceptual and perceptual differences (e.g., the fact that the thing in question is a kitchen table and not a dining room table and that it is brown rather than yellow) and anything else we might be capable of so abstracting or removing, we shall find remaining two factors we will not be able to remove: *spatiality*, the notion of this bare something as having extension and figure, and *temporality*, the notion of it as existing now. Space and time remain, it is Kant's argument, because they are due to our mind, and this is why we cannot think them away.

This will undoubtedly strike the reader as very curious. Does this mean that, according to Kant, space and time are not real but subjective—a kind of phantasm of the mind? The answer is yes and no. Kant himself had gone from an absolute theory of space, as embraced by Newton (the notion of it as being a kind of box or receptacle, more fundamental than matter, in which things are located), to a relational theory, as embraced by Leibniz (that it is nothing apart from the relations among objects and arises from their manner of organization), to, finally, his own theory that space is a form of perception, belonging to the subjective constitution of our own mind, "apart from which it cannot be predicated of anything whatever."

Kant goes on to produce a number of highly condensed arguments in support of this new view of the nature of space and time. Of these probably the most convincing and illuminating is the suggestion that our experience of externality is, on the level of bare sensation, nonspatial. We have sensations of this object or that object, and the sensations in question, although they differ in quality, do not, as bare sensations, differ in terms of their different spatial locations. The spatiality they come to possess, therefore, is something that we give to them. The representation of space, far from being derived from external experience, as we might be inclined to believe, is what first makes such experience possible. As a subjective form that lies ready in the mind, it precedes experience and cooperates in producing it. Were the representation of space not within us, the sensation of external objects would not be capable of being experienced by us as spatial.

This may still seem like a remarkable and unbelievable view to maintain. Are not things simply "out there"? Why should we believe that anything more is needed than simply to open our eyes and observe things located where in fact we find them? The fact is we have long forgotten how things really were when we first opened our eyes to the world and what a struggle it was to generate the space in which we came to locate these so-called external objects.

Now that Kant has shown what the nature of space is, he can go on to show how this view of it (and *only* this view of it) renders comprehensible the possibility of a certain body of synthetic a priori knowledge based on space.

But what body of knowledge is based on the phenomenon of space? The answer, of course, is geometry, which is the study of space. What is interesting and relevant here about geometry is that it gives us new truths that do not seem to rest on an analysis of mere concepts alone. It is not, in other words, a body of purely analytic propositions. Let us consider Kant's own example: the proposition that a straight line is the shortest distance between two points. This is very much *like* the proposition that a bachelor is an unmarried male, for here, too, we do not find it necessary to verify the proposition. We *know* it is true. Yet, unlike the example of the bachelor, we do not know it to be true because of the meaning of the term *straight*. For nothing in that term tells us about "shortest." The concept of *straight* only defines direction or quality of line; it says nothing about quantity. So it is not analytic, albeit a priori. It must therefore be an example of that strange hybrid proposition—the synthetic a priori.

We have here then an example of a piece of knowledge that has the characteristics of universality and necessity that, were space not as defined by Kant, would be completely inexplicable.

Let us consider other "facts" about space (and time), otherwise similarly inexplicable, such as the knowledge that there is and can be only one space or that time is irreversible. We are certain about all these things. They are not simply brute facts we happen to have discovered about our universe. We *know* this is the way our universe is, and we cannot conceive that it could be otherwise. We know this to be so without our having any evidence in support of it—or even thinking that such evidence is necessary. (As in the similar case of our bachelor: we haven't interviewed every bachelor in the world to see whether it is indeed the case that all bachelors are unmarried males, nor do we feel we need to; we know it for a certainty.)

But in the case of space, this seems strange. This is not our ordinary reaction to ordinary facts of the world, and the certainty in question seems more appropriate to analytic than to synthetic propositions. But it ceases to be strange, Kant argues, once we come to realize that we are dealing with a very peculiar phenomenon—a space we carry around with us, which conditions everything experienced in its terms. And this is why we do not have to worry about running into a triangle (say, one on Mars) to which Euclid's theorems may not apply. As long as we continue to experience, we will continue to do so in terms of the kind of space illuminated by Euclid's geometry.

This is indeed what gives this particular discipline its peculiar certainty. The knowledge it provides is certain because it is based on a space whose properties are descriptive not of some independent, external reality but of an inner, subjective, mind-dependent one.

Does this mean, then, that space and everything in it is unreal? Kant's answer to this is that if by things you mean things as they are in themselves, then space does not define them and is not real. But if you mean things as we experience them, then it is both true of them and real enough. For space is only the way in which we, as human beings, possessed of the kind of nature and cognitions descriptive of us, happen to experience the world presented to us. This is not the only way it can be experienced; certainly this is not the way a tiny insect experiences it, nor is it the way angels, if they exist, experience it. Doubtlessly, there are aspects and ways of viewing reality that are completely closed to us. But for human beings space and time are the only ways in which that reality can be perceived by us.

This does not mean we live in a world of illusion; it does mean that our world is a human world and that the knowledge we have of it is a human knowledge. If it is an illusion, it is a universal one. This is both unfortunate and fortunate—unfortunate since what we obviously know about this reality is infected by that human viewpoint and fortunate in that, although that knowledge is therefore necessarily limited, we need not doubt its certainty. And that is our ultimate dilemma or predicament: the very thing that enables us to know certain things is the very thing that makes it impossible to know other things. If I am compelled to wear blue spectacles all my life, to return to that useful analogy, I can know in advance and with certainty the color of any object of my experience, but I also know that I cannot ever know what its real color is, assuming it is colored.

But the deeper truth of all this is that we are part of the fabric of this universe. We have been fashioned for it, and it has been fashioned to fit us. We are very much like that little dove or that little fish in the ocean—if I may stretch Kant's analogy somewhat—who, noticing the way the air or the water fits so nicely around its wings or fins so that they seem to belong together, is led to believe that those wings or fins are not really part

I admit that all that is said here is really only an image and a figure, and in part also hypothetical; but we stand at a point to which thought can scarcely reach, not to speak of proof.

—Arthur Schopenhauer,
The World as Will and Idea

of its body but of the air or water that surrounds and envelops it. And it is the same with us. Space and time are our wings and fins, and despite the perfect fit between them and the things they embrace, we must recognize that they belong to us and are part of us and are not of the things or events they so perfectly match.

Space and time, Kant would therefore say, are real enough. But because they have been fashioned for us and define our particular being, they do not define the life of other possible beings and therefore cannot be said to be real in themselves.

And this is what Kant means when he speaks of a world of phenomena or appearances and a world of **noumena**, or things-in-themselves. The world of appearances is not a world of illusion; it is the world as it must appear to creatures constituted as we are. How the world is in itself we cannot know. But to know that much—that it must appear the way it does because of the way we are—and really know it is to know a great deal.

As the great German pessimist philosopher Arthur Schopenhauer, who regarded himself as the only true successor to Kant, expressed it,

Kant's teaching produces in the mind of everyone who has comprehended it a fundamental change which is so great that it may be regarded as an intellectual new-birth. It alone is able really to remove the inborn realism which proceeds from the original character of the intellect, which neither Berkeley nor Malebranche succeed in doing, for they remain too much in the universal, while Kant goes into the particular, and indeed in a way that is quite unexplained both before and after him, and which has quite a peculiar, and, we might say, immediate effect upon the mind in consequence of which it undergoes a complete undeception, and forthwith looks at all things in another light. Only in this way can anyone become susceptible to the more positive expositions which I have to give. On the other hand, he who has not mastered the Kantian philosophy, whatever else he may have studied, is, as it were, in a state of innocence; that is to say, he remains in the grasp of that natural and childish realism in which we are all born, and which fits us for everything possible, with the single exception of philosophy. Such a man then stands to the man who knows the Kantian philosophy as a minor to a man of full age. (*The World as Will and Idea*, pp. xxv–xxvi)

Understanding: Organizing Experience

The rest of Kant's argument, as it is set out in the Transcendental Analytic and Transcendental Dialectic, we may discuss more briefly since it takes almost a lifetime to master Kant's thought, and all we wish to do here is simply understand the idea behind it.

Just as Kant has shown that the a priori forms of sensibility (space and time) are the necessary conditions of objects being objects of perception to us, so he now goes on to show how certain forms of the understanding (he calls them "categories") are necessary conditions of perceived objects being objects of thought for us. Knowing what the necessary conditions are (and they turn out to be simply the laws of thought), we can know a priori those truths about the world that are functions of these conditions.

For example, one of the ways we as human beings form judgments about the things in this world is by way of the "if-then," or hypothetical, relationship. Thus, we say such things as, "If it rains then the party is called off," "If you drop this glass, it will break," and so on. These all have the same form: "If P then Q." P is the ground, and Q is the consequent.

It is typical for our understanding to function in this way: it always must find "reasons" or grounds for things. If we could be sure that this tendency to organize our thoughts in this manner is matched by the way things are themselves organized, then we could be certain that in the phenomenal world there must be things corresponding to P and Q such that P is the explanation of Q. Such things, or events, are what we call causes and effects. What Kant does in the Transcendental Analytic is to prove not only that there is such a correspondence but that there must be one.

The proof extends over quite a number of chapters, costing Kant, as he put it, "the most pains"; in the words of one of the great Kantian scholars, H. J. Paton, "The crossing of the Great Arabian Desert can scarcely be a more exhausting task." But if its elaboration is complicated, its key idea, like the idea of space and time being our air and water, is basically simple. Just as nothing is capable of being perceived by us except through the forms or by means of space and time, so similarly his argument here is that nothing is capable of being experienced by us unless organized in certain ways. If something is to be an object of experience for me, it must be put in a form absorbable by me, one capable of being understood by me. What are the ways in which we understand, apprehend, or absorb things? One of them is by way of the ground–consequent relation, and its corresponding, analogous relation in the world of things in the principle of causation. If, therefore, we are going to continue to think, we will do so by way of such logical relations, and if our experience will continue to be meaningful, we need never fear that the principles that make them meaningful will cease to apply. Should they do so, such a world would be inconceivable and inexperienceable by us and would simply cease to exist—just as a world not perceived in terms of space and time is impossible for us.

So as we can see, Kant bases his case on the necessity we have to experience the world and things in it in ways familiar to us. That need tells us something ultimate about ourselves, and since we are part of the fabric of this world, it tells us something objectively valid about it.

The clue to this basic truth Kant owed to Hume. And it had to do with Hume's questioning of the principle of causality—although, as we have pointed out, Kant came to see it as not limited to the problem of causality. Hume had noticed that the causal relationship was a synthetic one. He then had, as a strict empiricist, contended that all synthetic judgments have to be established through experience. But experience tells us only what is, not what must be, and so the principle cannot be justified and cannot be proven.

But why do we nevertheless believe in it? We do so, Hume replied, as a result of custom and habit. The curious thing about this explanation is that it presupposes causes. There is no reason, Hume is saying (without realizing the irony), for believing in the existence of causal connections; but the reason he assigns for our having a belief in the existence of causal connections presupposes the existence of causal connections. It is caused by habit. So Hume, as Kant observed, had to presuppose the existence of causation to account for its nonexistence!

Kant's attempt to understand this curious fact led him to the development of the *Critique* with its doctrine of subjective forms and categories, which, because they define our experience, are therefore objectively valid of our world.

Reason

But we have other determinations as well—those that issue from reason—and in the last division of the *Critique*, Kant takes these up. Unlike the forms of sensibility and the categories of the understanding, the ideals of reason have no objective validity. They may define us, but they do not define the world they try to penetrate. It is natural, for example, for our understanding to seek causes, to seek causes of those causes, and so on, as far back as one can seek them out. Reason, wearying of a seemingly endless regression but deeply committed to the search for causes and assured of their nearness, reaches for them and asserts them. An end to the series of causes, it thinks, must necessarily exist, absolutely necessary as it is, to think it. And so reason goes on to posit it—meaning by this, of course, that it posits God, the originator of the series of causes and its first cause.

Thus, as Kant says toward the end of the *Critique*, "In all peoples, there shine amidst the most benighted polytheism some gleams of monotheism, to which they have been led, not by reflection and profound speculation, but simply by the natural bent of the common understanding; as step by step it has come to apprehend its own requirements." Kant means that we are led to this search for God (and freedom and immortality) by deep tendencies in our nature. But this determination to define a reality lying beyond our world, through forms (causal series as in this example) applicable only to this world, must always remain suspect.

And so we are brought back here to two images struck at the very beginning of this intricate journey Kant has taken us on. The first are the opening words to the *Critique* regarding our human predicament of being doomed to ask questions that we cannot answer (Is there a God? Are we free? Is our soul immortal?), and the second is that of the dove, who, cleaving the air in its flight and feeling its resistance, might imagine it would do so much better in empty space. But, like it, we have to remind ourselves that our wings (forms, categories, ideals) are made for this world; they are not made for worlds that are alien to them and for which they are not fitted.

> My husband, T. S. Eliot, loved to recount how late one evening he stopped a taxi. As he got in, the driver said: "You're T. S. Eliot." When asked how he knew, he replied: "Ah, I've got an eye for a celebrity. Only the other evening I picked up Bertrand Russell, and I said to him, 'Well, Lord Russell, what's it all about?' And, do you know, he couldn't tell me."
>
> —Valerie Eliot, letter to the *London Times*

We must therefore settle for this world; we have after all, no other choice.

Where do things stand now? Let us observe first that philosophic problems, even when they appear to be resolved, have a tendency to become manifest again in another age as a result of its own peculiar concern and dilemmas.

We certainly see this in the case of the dispute between rationalism and empiricism in our own time. The question of whether everything comes from reason or from experience has surfaced once again in our own questions concerning genetics and education. Is human behavior a learned response based on social *nurture*, as contemporary "empiricists" contend, or is behavior based, as contemporary "rationalists" contend, on innate human *nature*?

A great deal of the drive toward equal education in the past several decades has come from the belief that differences in intelligence and school performance are due more to environmental than to hereditary factors. More recently, however, some geneticists have argued that heredity is more decisive. Undoubtedly, both play a role, but the question is their relative importance. No one needs to be reminded of the profound social and political implications of this current issue. No Kantian has yet emerged to synthesize the findings of these two schools of thought, and the solution continues to elude us.

The second thing we might observe is that even a philosophical position that may have proven successful in resolving the issues of its age in language meaningful to that

---

In 1907 William James wrote of the philosophy to which he had devoted the last 10 or 12 years: "I fully expect to see the pragmatist view," so he called this philosophy, "run through the classic stages of a theory's career. First, you know, a new theory is attacked as absurd; then, it is admitted to be true, but obvious and insignificant; finally, it is seen to be so important that its adversaries claim they themselves discovered it."

age but not to ours does not become completely obsolete. A residue tends to remain and continues to exert its influence on its successors. And this has been the case with the thought of Immanuel Kant. Very few today may still agree with his overall solutions, yet his philosophizing, especially his terminology, continues to exert its influence even on those who completely disagree with him. Very few now draw the line between the analytic and synthetic where he did, yet the analytic–synthetic distinction, bequeathed by him, continues to be one of the most intensely investigated issues in philosophy.

But it is not only individual problems or the language in which a philosopher has dealt with them that continue to survive in the work of successive generations. There is also a certain general thrust to a philosophy that leaves its imprint on successive generations of philosophers who try to reinterpret its insights in terms meaningful to them and their new understanding of the way things are. And this, too, has been the case with the philosophy of Kant.

His work has tended to divide the world of contemporary philosophy into two camps: those who have refused to abide by the limits of reason as set by him and have gone on to describe what lies beyond them and those who have confined their activities to further inquiries concerning those limits and what lies within them. The former, beginning in the nineteenth century with the so-called post-Kantian idealists (including such popular twentieth-century philosophers as Camus and Sartre), have been absorbed mainly with describing our psychological, moral, and social condition, the latter with our metaphysical and logical condition. Both owe much to this enormously gifted eighteenth-century philosopher.

SUMMARY

1. Epistemology studies the nature, sources, limitations, and validity of knowledge. The questions it asks itself are, How do we know, and how certain can we be of it?

2. There are two main sources of knowledge: reason and experience. Although both sources would seem to be intimately involved in knowledge, historically the question has tended to divide philosophers into two camps: those who placed their stress on reason and those who placed it on experience.

3. Philosophers who chose reason as our only trustworthy source of knowledge came to be called rationalists. These thinkers—Descartes, Spinoza, and Leibniz—shared a number of characteristics: they all lived in Europe, all believed that reason by itself is capable of arriving at a true knowledge of reality, all believed in the doctrine of innate ideas, their model of the perfect science was mathematics, and their test of whether our ideas are true was intuition: "the absence of doubt in the unclouded and attentive mind."

4. Philosophers who chose experience as our prime source of knowledge came to be called empiricists. These thinkers—Locke, Berkeley, and Hume—also shared a number

of characteristics in common: they all lived in Britain; all put their faith in experience as our main source of knowledge, doubting whether human reason is capable by itself of arriving at anything more than a few basic propositions about reality; all believed that the mind at birth is a tabula rasa, utterly blank of ideas; and their test of truth was external, not internal: ideas are true if they correspond with what we can find in the outside world.

5. Each school, by proceeding on its assumptions, arrived at a dead end. Rationalism professed absolute confidence in reason's ability to arrive at a perfect knowledge of reality, yet the results each rationalist achieved differed markedly from those achieved by the others. Descartes's reasoning led him to dualism, Spinoza's to monism, and Leibniz's to pluralism. Empiricism prided itself on its attachment to experimental science, yet in the end none of the major empiricists was able to give an intelligible account of some of the basic concepts underlying science itself. Locke had to admit that substance was "a something, I know not what"; Berkeley said that if we do not have an "idea" of the self, we nevertheless have a "notion" of it; and Hume said that what we call causes are only a series of "loose" or "separate" events.

6. Immanuel Kant tried to rescue what was valuable in these two schools of thought by means of a new attack on the problem of knowledge. He came to realize that each school had arrived at an impasse because of a wrong assumption about the mind's relation to the world. If we are to understand how knowledge is possible, we must come to see, Kant argued, that the mind is not, as both rationalism and empiricism assumed, totally independent of the world of objects it tries to know but rather contributes something to that world. Kant tried to identify this contribution in the *Critique*.

7. The *Critique* is divided into three main parts: the Transcendental Aesthetic, the Transcendental Analytic, and the Transcendental Dialectic. The first deals with the faculty of sensibility and shows how synthetic a priori propositions are possible in mathematics. The second deals with the faculty of understanding and shows how synthetic a priori propositions are possible in natural science. The third deals with the faculty of reason and shows how and why the a priori elements offered by it and the claims made on their behalf by traditional metaphysics are not possible.

8. Although Kant's contribution to our understanding of these matters was profound, much still remains unsettled and in doubt. As a result of these philosophic labors, however, we now see more clearly that the source of an idea cannot guarantee its validity (as rationalism had mistakenly believed); that the importance of empirical evidence lies not so much in being the source of ideas (as empiricism also mistakenly thought) as in being a means of testing and confirming them; that the process of information gathering, in order to be fruitful, must be guided (and Kant was right about this) by leading questions or hypotheses; but (and here is where he was probably mistaken) that the dream of an absolutely certain science built of synthetic a priori propositions is impossible.

KEY TERMS

a posteriori	monads
a priori	monism
analytic propositions	noumena
complex ideas	pantheism
dogmatism	phenomena
dualism	pluralism
empiricism	primary qualities
epistemology	propositions
idealism	rationalism
ideas	relations
ideas of reflection	secondary qualities
ideas of sensation	simple ideas
impressions	skepticism
knowledge	substances
materialism	synthetic propositions
mode	transcendental knowledge

REVIEW QUESTIONS

1. What are the major questions traditionally posed by epistemology?

2. How do rationalism and empiricism differ?

3. According to Descartes, what are the two means by which the mind achieves truth? What four principles did his method embrace? What was the conclusion, which became the starting point of his philosophy, that Descartes's method led him to?

4. How did Spinoza reconcile Cartesian dualism?

5. What was Leibniz's response to Spinoza's monistic and Descartes's dualistic notion of substance?

6. What was Locke's distinction between ideas of sensation and ideas of reflection?

7. What did Locke mean by "qualities" of objects? What two types of qualities did he distinguish?

8. What objection did Berkeley raise to Locke's notion of primary and secondary qualities?

9. Having argued that matter is not the cause of ideas, how did Berkeley affirm the idea of mind or spirit?

10. What distinction did Hume make between "impressions" and "ideas"? What conclusions did this distinction lead him to with regard to material substance? spiritual substance? metaphysics itself?

11. What did Hume conclude about causality?

12. How did Kant attempt to synthesize continental rationalism and British empiricism?

■ Reading

Meditations on First Philosophy

RENÉ DESCARTES

First Meditation: What Can Be Called into Doubt

Some years ago I was struck by the large number of falsehoods that I had accepted as true in my childhood, and by the highly doubtful nature of the whole edifice that I had subsequently based on them. I realized that it was necessary, once in the course of my life, to demolish everything completely and start again right from the foundations if I wanted to establish anything at all in the sciences that was stable and likely to last. But the task looked an enormous one, and I began to wait until I should reach a mature enough age to ensure that no subsequent time of life would be more suitable for tackling such inquiries. This led me to put the project off for so long that I would now be to blame if by pondering over it any further I wasted the time still left for carrying it out. So today I have expressly rid my mind of all worries and arranged for myself a clear stretch of free time. I am here quite alone, and at last I will devote myself sincerely and without reservation to the general demolition of my opinions.

But to accomplish this, it will not be necessary for me to show that all my opinions are false, which is something I could perhaps never manage. Reason now leads me to think that I should hold back my assent from opinions which are not completely certain and indubitable just as carefully as I do from those which are patently false. So, for the purpose of rejecting all my opinions, it will be enough if I find in each of them at least some reason for doubt. And to do this I will not need to run through them all individually, which would be an endless task. Once the foundations of a building are undermined, anything built on them collapses of its own accord; so I will go straight for the basic principles on which all my former beliefs rested.

Whatever I have up till now accepted as most true I have acquired either from the senses or through the senses. But from time to time I have found that the senses deceive, and it is prudent never to trust completely those who have deceived us even once.

Yet although the senses occasionally deceive us with respect to objects which are very small or in the distance, there are many other beliefs about which doubt is quite impossible, even though they are derived from the senses—for example, that I am here, sitting by the fire, wearing a winter dressing-gown, holding this piece of paper in my hands, and so on. Again, how could it be denied that these hands or this whole body are mine? Unless perhaps I were to liken myself to madmen, whose brains are so damaged by the persistent vapours of melancholia that they firmly maintain they are king when they are paupers, or say they are dressed in purple when they are naked, or that their heads are made of earthenware, or that they are pumpkins, or made of glass. But such people are insane, and I would be thought equally mad if I took anything from them as a model for myself.

A brilliant piece of reasoning! As if I were not a man who sleeps at night, and regularly has all the same experiences while asleep as madmen do when awake—indeed sometimes even more improbable ones. How often, asleep at night, am I convinced of just such familiar events—that I am here in my dressing-gown, sitting by the fire—when in fact I am lying undressed in bed! Yet at the moment my eyes are certainly wide awake when I look at this piece of paper; I shake my head and it is not asleep; as I stretch out and feel my hand I do so deliberately, and I know what I am doing. All this would not happen with such distinctness to someone asleep. Indeed! As if I did not remember other occasions when I have been tricked by exactly similar thoughts while asleep! As I think about this more carefully, I see plainly that there are never any sure signs by means of which being awake can be distinguished from being asleep. The result is that I begin to feel dazed, and this very feeling only reinforces the notion that I may be asleep.

Suppose then that I am dreaming, and that these particulars—that my eyes are open, that I am moving my head and stretching out my hands—are not true. Perhaps, indeed, I do not even have such hands or such a body at all. Nonetheless, it must surely be admitted that the visions which come in sleep are like paintings, which must have been fashioned in the likeness of things that are real, and hence that at least these general kinds of things—eyes, head, hands, and the body as a whole—are things which are not imaginary but are real and exist. For even when painters try to create sirens and satyrs with the most extraordinary bodies, they cannot give them natures which are new in all respects; they simply jumble up the limbs of different animals. Or if perhaps they manage to think up something so new that nothing remotely similar has ever been seen before—something which is therefore completely fictitious and unreal—at least the colours used in the composition must be real. By similar reasoning, although these general kinds of things—eyes, head, hands, and so on—could be imaginary, it must at least be admitted that certain other even simpler and more universal things are real. These are as it were the real colours from which we form all the images of things, whether true or false, that occur in our thought.

This class appears to include corporeal nature in general, and its extension; the shape of extended things; the quantity, or size and number of these things; the place in which they may exist, the time through which they may endure, and so on.

So a reasonable conclusion from this might be that physics, astronomy, medicine, and all other disciplines which depend on the study of composite things, are doubtful; while arithmetic, geometry and other subjects of this kind, which deal only with the simplest and most general things, regardless of whether they really exist in nature or not, contain something certain and indubitable. For whether I am awake or asleep, two and three added together are five, and a square has no more than four sides. It seems impossible that such transparent truths should incur any suspicion of being false.

And yet firmly rooted in my mind is the long-standing opinion that there is an omnipotent God who made me the kind of creature that I am. How do I know that he has not brought it about that there is no earth, no sky, no extended thing, no shape, no size, no place, while at the same time ensuring that all these things appear to me to exist just as they do now? What is more, since I sometimes believe that others go astray in cases where they think they have the most perfect knowledge, may I not similarly go wrong every time I add two and three or count the sides of a square, or in some even simpler matter, if that is imaginable? But perhaps God would not have allowed me to be deceived in this way, since he is said to be supremely good. But if it were inconsistent with his goodness to have created me such that I am deceived all the time, it would seem equally foreign to his goodness to allow me to be deceived even occasionally; yet this last assertion cannot be made.

Perhaps there may be some who would prefer to deny the existence of so powerful a God rather than believe that everything else is uncertain. Let us not argue with them, but grant them that everything said about God is a fiction. According to their supposition, then, I have arrived at my present state by fate or chance or a continuous chain of events, or by some other means; yet since deception and error seem to be imperfections, the less powerful they make my original cause, the more likely it is that I am so imperfect as to be deceived all the time. I have no answer to these arguments, but am finally compelled to admit that there is not one of my former beliefs about which a doubt may not properly be raised; and this is not a flippant or ill-considered conclusion, but is based on powerful and well thought-out reasons. So in future I must withhold my assent from these former beliefs just as carefully as I would from obvious falsehoods, if I want to discover any certainty.

But it is not enough merely to have noticed this; I must make an effort to remember it. My habitual opinions keep coming back, and, despite my wishes, they capture my belief, which is as it were bound over to them as a result of long occupation and the law of custom. I shall never get out of the habit of confidently assenting to these opinions, so long as I suppose them to be what in fact they are, namely highly probable opinions—opinions which, despite the fact that they are in a sense doubtful, as has just been shown, it is still much more reasonable to believe than to deny. In view of this, I think it will be a good plan to turn my will in completely the opposite direction and deceive myself, by pretending for a time that these former opinions are utterly false and imaginary. I shall do this until the weight of preconceived opinion is counter-balanced and the distorting influence of habit no longer prevents my judgement from perceiving things correctly. In the meantime, I know that no danger or error will result from my plan, and that I cannot possibly go too far in my distrustful attitude. This is because the task now in hand does not involve action but merely the acquisition of knowledge.

I will suppose therefore that not God, who is supremely good and the source of truth, but rather some malicious demon of the utmost power and cunning has employed all his energies in order to deceive me. I shall think that the sky, the air, the earth, colours, shapes, sounds and all external things are merely the delusions of dreams which he has devised to ensnare my judgement. I shall consider myself as not having hands or eyes, or flesh, or blood or senses, but as falsely believing that I have all these things. I shall stubbornly and firmly persist in this meditation; and, even if it is not in my power to know any truth, I shall at least do what is in my power, that is, resolutely guard against assenting to any falsehoods, so that the deceiver, however powerful and cunning he may be, will be unable to impose on me in the slightest degree. But this is an arduous undertaking, and a kind of laziness brings me back to normal life. I am like a prisoner who is enjoying an imaginary freedom while asleep; as he begins to suspect that he is asleep, he dreads being woken up, and goes along with the pleasant illusion as long as he can. In the same way, I happily slide back into my old opinions and dread being shaken out of them, for fear that my peaceful sleep may be followed by hard labour when I wake, and that I shall have to toil not in the light, but amid the inextricable darkness of the problems I have now raised.

Second Meditation: The Nature of the Human Mind, and How It Is Better Known than the Body

So serious are the doubts into which I have been thrown as a result of yesterday's meditation that I can neither put them out of my mind nor see any way of resolving them. It feels as if I have fallen unexpectedly into a deep whirlpool which tumbles me around so that I can neither stand on the bottom nor swim up to the top. Nevertheless I will make an effort and once more attempt the same path which I started on yesterday. Anything which admits of the slightest doubt I will set aside just as if I had found it to be wholly false; and I will proceed in this way until I recognize something certain, or, if nothing else, until I at least recognize for certain that there is no certainty. Archimedes used to demand just one firm and immovable point in order to shift the entire earth; so I too can hope for great things if I manage to find just one thing, however slight, that is certain and unshakeable.

I will suppose then, that everything I see is spurious. I will believe that my memory tells me lies, and that none of the things that it reports ever happened. I have no senses. Body, shape, extension, movement and place are chimeras. So what remains true? Perhaps just the one fact that nothing is certain.

Yet apart from everything I have just listed, how do I know that there is not something else which does not allow even the slightest occasion for doubt? Is there not a God, or whatever I may call him, who puts into me the thoughts I am now having? But why do I think this, since I myself may perhaps be the author of these thoughts? In that case am not I, at least, something? But I have just said that I have no senses and no body. This is the sticking point: what follows from this? Am I not so bound up with a body and with senses that I cannot exist without them? But I have convinced myself that there is absolutely nothing in the world, no sky, no earth, no minds, no bodies. Does it now follow that I too do not exist? No: if I convinced myself of something then I certainly existed. But there is a deceiver of supreme power and cunning who is deliberately and constantly deceiving me. In that case I too undoubtedly exist, if he is deceiving me; and let him deceive me as much as he can, he will never bring it about that I am nothing so long as I think that I am something. So after considering everything very thoroughly, I must finally conclude that this proposition, I *am*, I *exist*, is necessarily true whenever it is put forward by me or conceived in my mind.

But I do not yet have a sufficient understanding of what this "I" is, that now necessarily exists. So I must be on my guard against carelessly taking something else to be this "I," and so making a mistake in the very item of knowledge that I maintain is the most certain and evident of all. I will therefore go back and meditate on what I originally believed myself to be, before I embarked on this present train of thought. I will then subtract anything capable of being weakened, even minimally, by the arguments now introduced, so that what is left at the end may be exactly and only what is certain and unshakeable.

What then did I formerly think I was? A man. But what is a man? Shall I say 'a rational animal'? No; for then I should have to inquire what an animal is, what rationality is, and in this way one question would lead me down the slope to other harder ones, and I do not now have the time to waste on subtleties of this kind. Instead I propose to concentrate on what came into my thoughts spontaneously and quite naturally whenever I used to consider what I was. Well, the first thought to come to mind was that I had a face, hands, arms and the whole mechanical structure of limbs which can be seen in a corpse, and which I called the body. The next thought was that I was nourished, that I moved about, and that I engaged in sense-perception and thinking; and these actions I attributed to the soul. But as to the nature of this soul, either I did not think about this or else I imagined it to be something tenuous, like a wind or fire or ether, which permeated my more solid parts. As to the body, however, I had no doubts about it, but thought I knew its nature distinctly. If I had tried to describe the mental conception I had of it, I would have expressed it as follows: by a body I understand whatever has a determinable shape and a definable location and can occupy a space in such a way as to exclude any other body; it can be perceived by touch, sight, hearing, taste or smell, and can be moved in various ways, not by itself but by whatever else comes into contact with it. For, according to my judgement, the power of self-movement, like the power of sensation or of thought, was quite foreign to the nature of a body; indeed, it was a source of wonder to me that certain bodies were found to contain faculties of this kind.

But what shall I now say that I am, when I am supposing that there is some supremely powerful and, if it is permissible to say so, malicious deceiver, who is deliberately trying to trick me in every way he can? Can I now assert that I possess even the most insignificant of all the attributes which I have just said belong to the nature of a body? I scrutinize them, think about them, go over them again, but nothing suggests itself; it is tiresome and pointless to go through the list once more. But what about the attributes I assigned to the soul? Nutrition or movement? Since now I do not have a body these are mere fabrications. Sense-perception? This surely does not occur without a body, and besides, when asleep I have appeared to perceive through the senses many things which I afterwards realized I did not perceive through the senses at all. Thinking? At last I have discovered it—thought; this alone is inseparable from me. I am, I exist—that is certain. But for how long? For as long as I am thinking. For it could be that were I totally to cease from thinking, I should totally cease to exist. At present I am not admitting anything except what is necessarily true. I am, then, in the strict sense only a thing that thinks; that is, I am a mind, or intelligence, or intellect, or reason—words whose meaning I have been ignorant of until now. But for all that I am a thing which is real and which truly exists. But what kind of a thing? As I have just said—a thinking thing.

What else am I? I will use my imagination. I am not that structure of limbs which is called a human body. I am not even some thin vapour which permeates the limbs—a wind, fire, air, breath, or whatever I depict in my imagination; for these are things which I have supposed to be nothing. Let this supposition stand; for all that I am still something. And yet may it not perhaps be the case that these very things which I am supposing to be nothing, because they are unknown to me, are in reality identical with the "I" of which I am aware? I do not know, and for the moment I shall not argue the point, since I can make judgements only about things which are known to me. I know that I exist; the question is, what is this "I" that I know? If the "I" is understood strictly as we have been taking it, then it is quite certain that knowledge of it does not depend on things of whose existence I am as yet unaware; so it cannot depend on any of the things which I invent in my imagination. And this very word 'invent' shows me my mistake. It would indeed be a case of fictitious invention if I used my imagination to establish that I was something or other; for imagining is simply contemplating the shape or image of a corporeal thing. Yet now I know for certain both that I exist and at the same time that all such images and, in general, everything relating to the nature of body could be mere dreams and chimeras. Once this point has been grasped, to say "I will use my imagination to get to know more distinctly what I am" would seem to be as silly as saying "I am now awake, and see some truth; but since my vision is not yet clear enough, I will deliberately fall asleep so that my dreams may provide a truer and clearer representation." I thus realize that none of the things that the imagination enables me to grasp is at all relevant to this knowledge of myself which I possess, and that the mind must therefore be most carefully diverted from such things if it is to perceive its own nature as distinctly as possible.

But what then am I? A thing that thinks. What is that? A thing that doubts, understands, affirms, denies, is willing, is unwilling, and also imagines and has sensory perceptions.

This is a considerable list, if everything on it belongs to me. But does it? Is it not one and the same "I" who is now doubting almost everything, who nonetheless understands some things, who affirms that this one thing is true, denies everything else, desires to know more, is unwilling to be deceived, imagines many things even involuntarily, and is aware of many things which apparently come from the senses? Are not all these things just as true as the fact that I exist, even if I am asleep all the time, and even if he who created me is doing all he can to deceive me? Which of all these activities is distinct from my thinking? Which of them can be said to be separate from myself? The fact that it is I who am doubting and understanding and willing is so evident that I see no way of making it any clearer. But it is also the case that the "I" who imagines is the same "I." For even if, as I have supposed, none of the objects of imagination are real, the power of imagination is something which really exists and is part of my thinking. Lastly, it is also the same "I" who has sensory perceptions, or is aware of bodily things as it were through the senses. For example, I am now seeing light, hearing a noise, feeling heat. But I am asleep, so all this is false. Yet I certainly *seem to* see, to hear, and to be warmed. This cannot be false: what is called "having a sensory perception" is strictly just this, and in this restricted sense of the term it is simply thinking.

From all this I am beginning to have a rather better understanding of what I am. But it still appears—and I cannot stop thinking this—that the corporeal things of which images are formed in my thought, and which the senses investigate, are known with much more distinctness than this puzzling "I" which cannot be pictured in the imagination. And yet it is surely surprising that I should have a more distinct grasp of things which I realize are doubtful, unknown and foreign to me, than I have of that which is true and known—my own self. But I see what it is: my mind enjoys wandering off and will not yet submit to being restrained within the bounds of truth. Very well then; just this once let us give it a completely free rein, so that after a while, when it is time to tighten the reins, it may more readily submit to being curbed.

Let us consider the things which people commonly think they understand most distinctly of all; that is, the bodies which we touch and see. I do not mean bodies in general—for general perceptions are apt to be somewhat more confused—but one particular body. Let us take, for example, this piece of wax. It has just been taken from the honeycomb; it has not yet quite lost the taste of the honey; it retains some of the scent of the flowers from which it was gathered; its colour, shape and size are plain to see; it is hard, cold and can be handled without difficulty; if you rap it with your knuckle it makes a sound. In short, it has everything which appears necessary to enable a body to be known as distinctly as possible. But even as I speak, I put the wax by the fire, and look: the residual taste is eliminated, the smell goes away, the colour changes, the shape is lost, the size increases; it becomes liquid and hot; you can hardly touch it, and if you strike it, it no longer makes a sound. But does the same wax remain? It must be admitted that it does; no one denies it, no one thinks otherwise. So what was it in the way that I understood with such distinctness? Evidently none of the features which I arrived at by means of the senses; for whatever came under taste, smell, sight, touch or hearing has now altered—yet the wax remains.

Perhaps the answer lies in the thought which now comes to my mind; namely, the wax was not after all the sweetness of the honey, or the fragrance of the flowers, or the whiteness, or the shape, or the sound, but was rather a body which presented itself to me in these various forms a little while ago, but which now exhibits different ones. But what exactly is it that I am now imagining? Let us concentrate, take away everything which does not belong to the wax, and see what is left: merely something extended, flexible and changeable. But what is meant here by "flexible" and "changeable"? Is it what I picture in my imagination: that this piece of wax is capable of changing from a round shape to a square shape, or from a square shape to a triangular shape? Not at all; for I can grasp that the wax is capable of countless changes of this kind, yet I am unable to run through this immeasurable number of changes in my imagination, from which it follows that it is not the faculty of imagination that gives me my grasp of the wax as flexible and changeable. And what is meant by "extended"? Is the extension of the wax also unknown? For it increases if the wax melts, increases again if it boils, and is greater still if the heat is increased. I would not be making a correct judgement about the nature of wax unless I believed it capable of being extended in many more different ways than I will ever encompass in my imagination. I must therefore admit that the nature of this piece of wax is in no way revealed by my imagination, but is perceived by the mind alone. (I am speaking of this particular piece of wax; the point is even clearer with regard to wax in general.) But what is this wax which is perceived by the mind alone? It is of course the same wax which I see, which I touch, which I picture in my imagination, in short the same wax which I thought it to be from the start. And yet, and here is the point, the perception I have of it is a case not of vision or touch or imagination—nor has it ever been, despite previous appearances—but of purely mental scrutiny; and this can be imperfect and confused, as it was before, or clear and distinct as it is now, depending on how carefully I concentrate on what the wax consists in.

But as I reach this conclusion I am amazed at how weak and prone to error my mind is. For although I am thinking about these matters within myself, silently and without speaking, nonetheless the actual words bring me up short, and I am almost tricked by ordinary ways of talking. We say that we see the wax itself, if it is there before us, not that we judge it to be there from its colour or shape; and this might lead me to conclude without more ado that knowledge of the wax comes from what the eye sees, and not from the scrutiny of the mind alone. But then if I look out of the window and see men crossing the square, as I just happen to have done, I normally say that I see the men themselves, just as I say that I see the wax. Yet do I see any more than hats and coats which could conceal automatons? I *judge* that they are men. And so something which I thought I was seeing with my eyes is in fact grasped solely by the faculty of judgement which is in my mind.

However, one who wants to achieve knowledge above the ordinary level should feel ashamed at having taken ordinary ways of talking as a basis for doubt. So let us proceed, and consider on which occasion my perception of the nature of the wax was more perfect and evident. Was it when I first looked at it, and believed I knew it by my external senses, or at least by what they cast the "common" sense—that is, the power of imagination? Or is my knowledge more perfect now, after a more careful investigation of the nature of the wax and of the means by which it is known? Any doubt on this issue would clearly be foolish; for what distinctness was there in my earlier perception? Was there anything in it which an animal could not possess? But when I distinguish the wax from its outward forms—take the clothes off, as it were, and consider it naked—then although my judgement may still contain errors, at least my perception now requires a human mind.

But what am I to say about this mind, or about myself? (So far, remember, I am not admitting that there is anything else in me except a mind.) What, I ask, is this "I" which seems to perceive the wax so distinctly? Surely my awareness of my own self is not merely much truer and more certain than my awareness of the wax, but also much more distinct and evident. For if I judge that the wax exists from the fact that I see it, clearly this same fact entails much more evidently that I myself also exist. It is possible that what I see is not really the wax; it is possible that I do not even have eyes with which to see anything. But when I see, or think I see (I am not here distinguishing the two), it is simply not possible that I who am now thinking am not something. By the same token, if I judge that the wax exists from the fact that I touch it, the same result follows, namely that I exist. If I judge that it exists from the fact that I imagine it, or for any other reason, exactly the same thing follows. And the result that I have grasped in the case of the wax may be applied to everything else located outside me. Moreover, if my perception of the wax seemed more distinct after it was established not just by sight or touch but by many other considerations, it must be admitted that I now know myself even more distinctly. This is because every consideration whatsoever which contributes to my perception of the wax, or of any other body, cannot but establish even more effectively the nature of my own mind. But besides this, there is so much else in the mind itself which can serve to make my knowledge of it more distinct, that it scarcely seems worth going through the contributions made by considering bodily things.

I see that without any effort I have now finally got back to where I wanted. I now know that even bodies are not strictly perceived by the senses or the faculty of imagination but by the intellect alone, and that this perception derives not from their being touched or seen but from their being understood; and in view of this I know plainly that I can achieve an easier and more evident perception of my own mind than of anything else. But since the habit of holding on to old opinions cannot be set aside so quickly, I should like to stop here and meditate for some time on this new knowledge I have gained, so as to fix it more deeply in my memory.

■ Questions for Discussion

1. Explain Descartes's *method of doubt*. By applying this method, what does Descartes show about most of our mathematical, scientific, religious, and everyday beliefs?

2. There is something, according to Descartes, we cannot possibly doubt. What is that, and how does Descartes go about proving that this is so?

■ Reading

Plato's Theory of Forms

A. E. TAYLOR

Excerpted from A. E. Taylor, *Platonism and Its Influence* (New York: Longmans, Green & Co., 1927).

The leading ideas of Plato's theory of the nature and objects of scientific knowledge can be stated very simply. Thinking is not the same thing as the having of sensations; it is not literally true that "seeing is believing." All thinking is *judgment* and needs to be expressed in *propositions*, and no proposition is the mere record of the occurrence of a sensation. With Plato, as with Kant, the distinction between thought and sensation is fundamental. He neither, like the Associationists, regards thinking as a kind of attenuated "sensation," nor, with Leibniz, treats sensation as a kind of confused thinking. This is one reason why Plato, like Kant, is accused by his opponents of dividing the universe into "two worlds."

Again, not all thinking is knowledge or science. We have to distinguish what we really know from what we merely think or believe. For (1) we are perfectly sure of what we know and we can say exactly what it is; when we only think or believe, we are not sure, and we often are unable to formulate our belief with any precision. (2) If a man really knows a proposition, he can "give and receive argument" about it; he can produce rational grounds for his conviction of its truth. This cannot be done when you merely think or believe. (3) Knowledge can be communicated only by the production of good and sufficient grounds, but you can get men to share a mere belief, as skilled advocates in the Law Courts or on the political platform habitually do, by appeals to their emotions or prejudices.

The distinction just drawn is to be understood in an ontological and not in a merely psychological sense. It answers to a real difference of character between *objects* of which it is possible to have knowledge and those about which we can at best have opinions or beliefs. If the truths of science are certain, definite, and apprehended with intellectual necessity, the objects known must have a character which is unvarying, completely determinate and wholly luminous to the intellect. Science must thus be concerned with what is eternal, definite, and through and through intelligible, and with nothing else. Typical examples of a realm of such objects are yielded by mathematics and again by ethics. Triangles or circles and their properties are the same independently of all variations of place and date; their characters are wholly determinate, and determined by conditions of which the geometer is completely aware. Plato holds that the same is true of the objects of the moralist's study—good, right, the virtues. But if there are objects which are always "in the making" and never fully made, whose very "being" is change

341

or development, their characters will be fluid, changing with place and date, and our statements about them will always be liable to revision; in such statements there will always be an extra-rational element of mere given "brute" fact. This distinction between what is eternal, fully determinate, and wholly intelligible, and what is temporal, fluid, and weighted with an element of inexplicable "fact" is precisely the distinction between a realm where we are dependent wholly on thinking and a realm in which we have to take the reports of our senses about the occurrence of something at a given place and time as data for our thinking. It is only when the data of our thinking contain no such elements, that thinking leads to the results with the character Plato demands of everything that can be called science. Knowledge is attained only by the activity of "the mind by herself, apart from the instruments of sense-perception," and this is the historical reason why we still continue to speak of "pure" mathematics or "pure" ethics. Where the mind is dependent on the "instruments of sense" we have only beliefs or judgments which Plato will not dignify with the name of knowledge. The distinction thus corresponds fairly with that drawn by some modern thinkers between the "timeless" realm of ideals or values and the "temporal" realm of "actual" facts. But Plato is convinced that only what can stand the most rigid scrutiny of the intellect really *is*. Hence he calls the "ideals" of pure thinking "what is," and speaks of the "actual" and "sensible" as something "which never is but is always becoming." The whole of what we call "nature" or "the sequence of events" the system of interconnected facts revealed by our senses, is thus, in Plato's view, outside the range of knowledge proper; it is only by a loose use of language that we give the name "science" to our convictions about it. Strictly speaking, what the "natural" sciences have to tell us is no more than "likely stories."

This does not mean that we are not to pursue the "natural" sciences, or that any one "story" about such matters is as likely as another. If nature is always "in the making" our stories about it can only be provisional, and can never have the finality of mathematics or ethics, but that is no reason why we should not aim at coming as near to finality as we can. The more we look for definite order and law in the sensible world, the more we shall find of it, though we shall never wholly get rid of the element of brute fact for which no reason can be assigned except that "you see it happens so." Our "stories" will always be provisional, subject to revision as our stock of "facts" grows, but, for that very reason, they will always be "progressive." If the element of unaccountable brute "fact" in nature cannot be completely eliminated, we can at least set ourselves to diminish it without limit, and it is just in this that the true work of "physical science" lies.

These are the thoughts which lie at the bottom of what has commonly been called the "Platonic theory of Ideas." The name is better avoided because in English the word "idea" conveys associations which are quite misleading. The *ideai*—"figures," "patterns," "forms"—of which we read in Plato are in no sense "states" or "processes" of our minds, nor is their existence supposed to depend on the existence of any mind whatever. The Forms are just those absolutely determinate objects of thinking which, in Plato's language, "are" and do not "become" and which it is the business of science to know completely. We may, if we like, call them "concepts," provided that we remember two things: (1) they are that which is known, not the act or process of knowing it; (2) their existence does not depend on that of a mind which "conceives" them; minds know them but do not make them. More exactly, we might say that a Form is that which is *denoted* by a significant universal term. Such examples as "the number 2" in arithmetic, "the regular pentagon" in geometry, "the exactly right act" in morals, will illustrate for us what is meant. No Form is apprehended by sense-perception. We never see a "perfect circle" or two absolutely equal lengths; we do not meet with absolute and perfect moral goodness in the life of any man of flesh and blood. Yet the world of pure thought and that of the senses are not simply disconnected. We do see figures which approximate in different degrees to circularity, and we meet some men who are nearer moral perfection than others. In such cases, we know what it is that is being approximated to, we know that it is only approximated to, not reached, and, often at least, we can say which of two figures or of two men, approximates more nearly to circularity or to goodness. Plato expresses this by saying that sensible things "partake of" or "participate in" Forms, and again by saying that the Form is a "model" of which the sensible thing is a "copy" or "imitation." Aristotle tells us that the second of the formulae, that of "imitation," was originally Pythagorean. Plato himself indicates that the metaphor of "participation" comes from Socrates. It is important to remember that, as there is nothing sensible which does not "participate" in a Form or Forms, so there is no Form which is not "participated" in by something sensible.

The proper object of knowledge is always a Form. Yet it is certain that when we begin our life on earth as babies we do not bring ready-made knowledge of the Forms with us. Plato knows nothing of such a crude doctrine of "innate ideas" as is often erroneously imputed to Descartes. Our earthly life begins with sensations which the baby does not know how to interpret. How do we advance to the apprehension of the Forms? How, in fact, do we learn to know? In the *Phaedo* Socrates says that though sense-experience does not directly exhibit the Forms, it *suggests* them to us. If I see the portrait of an absent friend or some article belonging to him, I am not seeing my friend, but what I do see "reminds me" of him, suggests the thought of him. So I never see a perfectly straight line, but the sight of sticks which are more or less crooked suggests the thought of the perfect straightness which I do not see. Sense-experience exhibits a series of more remote or closer approximations to an "ideal limit," and so suggests the ideal limit itself. This is what is really meant by the doctrine that all learning is "being reminded" of something. The standing Platonic illustration of this is that by drawing a suitable figure and asking the right questions you can get a lad to see for himself the truth of a geometrical proposition which he has never been "taught." The point is that though sensation does not directly reveal scientific truths, as the empiricists suppose, it is always pregnant with them. The truths have to be discovered by an effort of thinking, but sense-experience starts the effort by suggesting to a mind which can think, as well as feel, truths which it does not disclose.

■ Questions for Discussion

1. How does Plato's theory of forms relate to rationalism?
2. How does it relate to empiricism?
3. How does it relate to Kant's theory?

CONTEMPORARY DIRECTIONS

■ The Analytic Tradition

EARLY IN THIS ACCOUNT of philosophy we discussed the life and thought of Socrates, one of the greatest philosophers of all time, and it is perhaps appropriate to end our account (or begin to end it) with Bertrand Russell, who resembles him in so many respects.

BERTRAND RUSSELL

When one thinks of a philosopher in our modern age, the name likely to come to mind is Bertrand Russell.

Russell was born in 1872 and died in 1970. His life was rich and fruitful, eventful and turbulent, filled with both much despair and many triumphs.

Russell's parents, who were close friends of John Stuart Mill, died when Russell was a child, and he, together with an older brother, was raised in the house of his paternal grandfather, the first Earl Russell. The family had been eminent in British politics and society for centuries, especially noted for their strong liberal leanings, despite being

---

Philosophy is to be studied, not for the sake of any definite answers to its questions, since no definite answers can, as a rule, be known to be true, but rather for the sake of the questions themselves; because these questions enlarge our conception of what is possible, enrich our intellectual imagination and diminish the dogmatic assurance which closes the mind against speculation; but above all because, through the greatness of the universe which philosophy contemplates, the mind also is rendered great, and becomes capable of that union with the universe which constitutes its highest good.

—Bertrand Russell, *The Problems of Philosophy* (1912)

347

Bertrand Russell (1872–1970)

members of the peerage. These strong liberal tendencies seemed to have been passed on to Russell, but in his case they did not lead to the position of prime minister (as it had in the case of his grandfather and great-grandfather) but to jail—once during World War I for "pacifism" and again, more briefly, in the early 1960s for taking part in nuclear disarmament demonstrations.

They also led, however, to the Order of Merit, Britain's highest honor, and the Nobel Prize, awarded him in 1950.

Always along with the acclaim there was public hostility—including an outcry against his appointment to teach philosophy at the City College of New York in 1940. The judge who upheld the suit brought against the Board of Education, which made the appointment, declared at the time that in offering the position to Russell the college was "in effect establishing a chair in indecency." Russell recorded the "honor" on the title page of his book *An Inquiry into Meaning and Truth*, reproduced here. It was his fiftieth publication.

Long before the appearance of this book, Russell succeeded in securing a place for himself in the history of philosophy with the publication, in collaboration with his teacher and mentor, philosopher-mathematician Alfred North Whitehead (1861–1947), of *Principia Mathematica* (1910–1913)—a work described by the American philosopher W. V. O. Quine as "one of the great intellectual monuments of all time."

This groundbreaking work has had an immense impact on twentieth-century thought and technology. The technological revolution we have experienced and continue to experience especially as a result of various advances in computer science owes much of its impetus to this pioneering work. In addition, the social revolution we have experienced in the West, especially in America, with its more enlightened and liberated (or perhaps overly "permissive," as its critics would say) views and attitudes toward child rearing, marriage, women, work, and so on, owes much to Russell. No doubt in time it will be seen that the new social world we now inhabit was in good part also fashioned by him in the series of nontechnical social and political works that came from his pen, such as *Marriage and Morals, In Praise of Idleness*, and *Has Man a Future?*

In light of their actual impact, it may seem ironic to us now that he should have wondered, as he sometimes did, whether these works and the enormous energies he expended on them could or would ever bear fruit. The following passage, written in a reflective moment, captures not only this mood but much of the sort of person he was:

When I come to what I myself can do or ought to do about the world situation I find my-self in two minds. A perpetual argument goes on within me between two different points of view which I will call that of the Devil's Advocate and that of the Earnest Publicist. . . . The voice of the Devil's Advocate is, at least in part, the voice of reason. "Can't you see," says this cynical character, "that what happens in the world does not depend upon you? Whether the populations of the world are to live or die rests with the decisions of Khrushchev, Mao Tse-Tung and Mr. John Foster Dulles, not with ordinary mortals like ourselves. If they say 'die,' we shall die. If they say 'live,' we shall live. They do not read your books, and would think them very silly if they did. You forget that you are not living in 1688, when your family and a few others gave the king notice and hired another. It is only a failure to move with the times that makes you bother your head with public af-fairs." Perhaps the Devil's Advocate is right—but perhaps he is wrong. Perhaps dictators are not so all-powerful as they seem; perhaps public opinion can still sway them, at any rate in some degree; and perhaps books can help to create public opinion. And so I per-sist, regardless of his taunts. There are limits to his severities. "Well, at any rate," he says, "writing books is an innocent occupation and it keeps you out of mischief." And so I go on writing books, though whether any good will come of doing so, I do not know.

This passage is taken from a book published in 1956 (hence the reference to the po-litical figures of the day, all dead now) titled *Portraits from Memory*. But it is Russell's technical works in philosophy—his *Principles of Mathematics* (1903), *Principia Mathe-matica*, and *Philosophy of Logical Atomism* (1918)—and not his social and political writ-ings that are of concern to us here. They prepared the ground, as we will see, for the philosophy of Wittgenstein, whose theme that we are prisoners of language was to dom-inate the world of philosophy in the twentieth century.

It had been recognized since the beginning of philosophy that in some way logic and mathematics are connected—for example, the two disciplines, and only they, pro-ceed by way of necessary inference—but the nature of this connection had never been made clear. Russell and Whitehead, building on Whitehead's earlier work, undertook to make this connection. Although *Principia Mathematica* is attributed primarily to Whitehead, Russell's contributions are not insignificant, and Whitehead always consid-ered him a coauthor of the work. Together, they came to the conclusion, demonstrated in *Principia Mathematica*, that the fundamental principles of mathematics are really a development of some quite simple, elementary, logical notions. The various fields of mathematics itself had already been shown to be reducible essentially to arithmetic ("the arithmetization of mathematics"), and what Whitehead and Russell now did was to show that the fundamental ideas of arithmetic itself (numbers, addition, and so on) could be developed from some purely logical concepts. This program of the unification of mathematics and logic was carried out by Russell and Whitehead with the aid of a new type of symbolism, and the resulting work came to be designated **symbolic** (or mathematical) **logic**.

The immediate impetus for undertaking this task was the emergence of certain perplexing contradictions (called logical paradoxes) in the branch of mathematics known as set theory. Unless these paradoxes could be resolved, mathematics was in danger of losing its claims to certainty. By showing that classical mathematics is to a large degree a subdivision or an extension of logic and possessing therefore its rigor and exactness, Russell and Whitehead succeeded in confirming the essential correctness of classical mathematics and thus dispelling the dismay that mathematicians were beginning to experience.

Although this was a notable achievement in itself, no less notable was the effect its findings had on the emergence of a new conception of the nature of philosophy. For *Principia Mathematica* gave rise to the belief that what it had uncovered or discovered was a kind of *ideal* language, one that correctly *pictured* or *mirrored* reality, a reality unfortunately distorted by ordinary, natural languages, arisen, as these have, in a haphazard manner over centuries. This being so, the job of the philosopher, in describing as accurately as possible what there is, is to trace philosophical problems and confusions to their true sources in language and thus solve or resolve them, aided in this task by the use of the precise symbolism of *Principia Mathematica*.

These seemingly revolutionary theses, first enunciated in *Principia Mathematica* and further explored in some of Russell's subsequent works—the theses that what we are immediately and directly acquainted with is language, that language mirrors reality, and that the job of philosophy is to correct the distortions created by the languages in use—came to acquire the force and thrust they did in the hands of Russell's pupil and colleague Ludwig Wittgenstein, who combined them in such a way as to form a powerful and explosive mixture. The approach they developed is referred to as **linguistic philosophy**.

LUDWIG WITTGENSTEIN

Ludwig Wittgenstein (1889–1951) was born into a wealthy, gifted, and cultured Viennese family. He was educated at home until he was 14 and then was sent to technical schools. He first went to England in 1908 at the age of 19 as a research student in the Department of Aeronautical Engineering in the University of Manchester, where he was occupied in the design of a jet engine. He left Manchester for Cambridge in 1912 to study with Russell. (Whitehead had departed Cambridge for University College in London in 1910.)

Wittgenstein's own reading of *Principia Mathematica* had made him realize that his true interests lay in pure mathematics and logic rather than in engineering. Russell recognized his extraordinary gifts at once and tried to encourage him in his work in logic and mathematics. But Wittgenstein, never really at ease in the company of others, spent less than two years at Cambridge before retiring to complete seclusion in Norway.

At the outbreak of World War I in 1914, he returned to Austria and joined the army, using his leisure time to compose the *Tractatus*. He was captured by the Italians in 1918 and spent some months as a prisoner of war. From his prison camp he sent the manuscript of this remarkable little book (containing only some 80 pages) to Russell, who recognized its importance but did not manage to secure its publication until 1921, and then only in a learned journal that, as it happened, ceased publication after that issue.

Russell's influence is evident throughout the work, which opens with the following statement to the reader:

The book deals with the problems of philosophy, and shows, I believe, that the reason why these problems are posed is that the logic of our language is misunderstood. The whole sense of the book might be summed up in the following words: what can be said at all can be said clearly, and what we cannot talk about we must pass over in silence.

Thus the aim of the book is to set a limit to thought, or rather—not to thought, but to the expression of thoughts: for in order to be able to set a limit to thought, we should have to find both sides of the limit thinkable (i.e., we should have to be able to think what cannot be thought).

It will therefore only be in language that the limit can be set, and what lies on the other side of the limit will simply be nonsense.

The book then goes on to state—in a cryptic, elegant, and aphoristic style—that "the world is everything that is the case": that it consists of "facts, not things"; that we "picture" these facts to ourselves in propositions or sentences; and that, therefore, how such sentences come to be significant is the big mystery of both language and philosophy. All this is explored in seven main propositions, numbered 1 to 7, and everything else is a comment on one of these propositions (and given a number with one decimal place—e.g., 1.1, 2.1), a comment on one of these comments (given a number with two decimal places—e.g., 1.11, 2.11), or a comment on one of the comments on a comment. This neatness stands in stark contrast with the inner turmoil of Wittgenstein's life, one troubled by several suicides in his immediate family, constant fear of impending insanity, and tragedy.

Wittgenstein ended this first book of his, the only one to be published in his lifetime, with the following propositions—very much in the style of the entire book:

6.53 The right method of philosophy would be this. To say nothing except what can be said, i.e., the propositions of natural science, i.e., something that has nothing to do with philosophy: and then always, when someone else wished to say something metaphysical, to demonstrate to him that he had given no meaning to certain signs in his propositions. This method would be unsatisfying to the other—he would not have the feeling that we were teaching him philosophy—but it would be the only strictly correct method.

6.54 My propositions are elucidators in this way: he who understands me finally recognizes them as senseless, when he has climbed out through them, on them, over them. (He must so to speak throw away the ladder, after he has climbed up on it.) He must surmount these propositions; then he sees the world rightly.

7. Whereof one cannot speak, thereof one must remain silent.

Thinking that he had thus solved all philosophical problems, Wittgenstein followed his own advice and gave up philosophy. For the next 10 years, he occupied himself with working as a gardener, teaching school, and designing a house for his sister in Vienna.

Then in 1928, after hearing a lecture given in Vienna by the famous Dutch mathematician L. J. Brouwer, he found himself interested once again in philosophy and decided to return to Cambridge. His *Tractatus*, published some eight years earlier and already famous, was accepted as his doctoral dissertation, and with Russell acting as one of the members of his "thesis" committee, he was awarded a Ph.D. in June 1929. He had given away the considerable fortune he had inherited from his father and now lived in great simplicity on the stipend from his position as philosophy tutor at Cambridge.

Ludwig Wittgenstein (1889–1951)

Although working feverishly at philosophy once again, he published nothing during these years. However, he dictated notes to his pupils, and these notes achieved a wide underground circulation. Although they proved mystifying to most of their readers—because of the novelty of both their themes and their manner of exposition—their impact and influence in Britain and the United States was enormous. These notes (composed between 1933 and 1935) came to be known as the *Blue Book* and the *Brown Book*, titles deriving from the color of the covers on the original copies.

In 1949, Wittgenstein completed a lengthy manuscript, originally begun in 1936, that was published posthumously as *Philosophical Investigations*. It has come to be regarded as the chief work of his later period. It is also thought to represent a sharp break with the philosophy of the *Tractatus*, although, as we will see, there is much in common between it and the earlier work.

What also did not change was the manner of presentation. Although the discussion in the later book is not nearly as cryptic and aphoristic as that in the *Tractatus*, much else remains the same. In his preface to *Philosophical Investigations*, Wittgenstein describes its style and contents in these words:

> The thoughts which I publish in what follows are the precipitate of philosophical investigations which have occupied me for the last sixteen years. They concern many subjects: the concepts of meaning, of understanding, of a proposition, of logic, the foundations of mathematics, states of consciousness, and other things. I have written down all these thoughts as remarks, short paragraphs, of which there is sometimes a fairly long chain about the same subject, while I sometimes make a sudden change, jumping from one

topic to another. It was my intention at first to bring all this together in a book whose form I pictured differently at different times. But the essential thing was that the thoughts should proceed from one subject to another in a natural order and without breaks.

After several unsuccessful attempts to weld my results together into such a whole, I realized that I should never succeed. The best that I could write would never be more than philosophical remarks; my thoughts were soon crippled if I tried to force them on in any single direction against their natural inclination. And this was, of course, connected with the very nature of the investigation. For this compels us to travel over a wide field of thought criss-cross in every direction. The philosophical remarks in this book are, as it were, a number of sketches of landscapes which were made in the course of these long and involved journeyings.

Wittgenstein lectured off and on at Cambridge from 1930 to 1947, when ill health forced him to resign his post. For three years during World War II, he served as hospital orderly and laboratory assistant. And both before and after the war, his restlessness forced him to seek solace, as it had done in earlier years, in living in seclusion for extended periods of time in Norway and sometimes in Ireland. He finally returned to Cambridge from Ireland when he discovered he was suffering from cancer. He died on April 29, 1951.

The Philosophic Task

While Wittgenstein's work perceptively and, in some ways, radically alters the approach to exploring the "troubles in our thoughts" caused by our attempts to make sense of the world, his is obviously not the first of the modern philosophical works to address the matters. Indeed, it is not even exclusively a modern matter. Although this struggle began properly with Locke, its seeds have been present in philosophy from its very beginnings. Thus, in trying to shake our faith in things as they appear to us, to plant a seed of doubt in our minds to make us aware of other possibilities, philosophy has from the very beginning set itself a task that has no competitors—certainly not among scientists. For scientists are not, qua scientists, interested in investigating what the world is really. They are happy to accept it as it is. Whether perhaps it is simply illusion is not a question that bothers them or that they feel a need to entertain. Their job is to describe the phenomenal world—that is, the world as they find it, the world as it appears, which is a big enough task in itself. To wonder whether a phenomenon is somehow at least one remove from something more deeply real is not of interest to them. But it is of central concern to the philosopher.

There is another way of putting all this which may be even more illuminating. We are all—philosophers, scientists, theologians—concerned with trying to explain things. Each of us, however, has a different ideal of explanation: the kind of explanation that will satisfy the scientist will not satisfy the philosopher, and the kind that will satisfy the philosopher may not satisfy the theologian.

Suffice it to say that to explain a thing is to try to reduce it into terms that the mind can absorb and accept, which involves, among other things, presenting it in such a way that the mind can accommodate it and come to rest with it. If the mind cannot accommodate or absorb it, the thing remains a mystery. For, again, to make a thing intelligible means to process it in such a way that the mind can take it up and absorb it. And this means reducing or translating it into terms endemic to the mind so that in taking it up, it will find it acceptable and satisfying—in short, *reasonable.*

Now if this is what, partially at least, is involved in making a thing intelligible to us, then we can begin to see why science can carry us only so far and why perhaps even philosophy can carry us only so far as well—that is to say, why science is not enough and why perhaps even philosophy, ultimately, is not enough. Let us consider, for example, the experience of pain or the phenomenon of sight. Without trying to be either technical or exact, a scientific explanation of pain or sight might take this kind of direction: the reason why, broadly speaking, you feel pain when a pin is stuck into your skin is because the pin strikes nerve endings, thereby producing pain; or in the case of sight, what makes you see things or have images of things that lie outside the mind is light rays that strike the object, travel to the retina of the eye, and produce there an image of the object. But, we might ask, are these truly explanations of the phenomena in question? Why should touching nerve endings in the skin produce pain? What connection is there between these two? Is there not a mystery here? And similarly with the phenomenon of sight: however intimately these rays of light may enter into the image that is their end product, they are, after all, only rays of light and not the image, and this will be true regardless of what we may in future learn to substitute for the more precise cause here. It will still be impossible for us to see why the two should be connected in this way and how the one, although different from the other, is yet the same as (or not different from!) it. Yet, of course, from a logical and philosophical point of view, until we are somehow told how this is so, we cannot say we *understand*, although the scientists' work may indeed be finished once he or she has brought together cause and effect.

This point can be put even more sharply when a more strictly philosophical problem is at stake—say, for example, the problem of evil. To try to answer the question of why there is evil in the world by finding evidence for it in such things as earthquakes, famine, war, and disease would, of course, be absurd. For, as we saw in chapter 1, in asking such a question what we want to know are not the efficient causes of evil (which is all the scientist is interested in and which we know only too well) but rather why there is evil in the world *at all*. We want an explanation that will somehow make evil *reasonable* (i.e., acceptable) to us. Trying to tell ourselves what evil is and how it comes to be is not sufficient. And since this is all science can tell us, we are not satisfied with the scientific explanation.

The Direction of Modern Philosophy

The realization that the philosopher's task is somehow radically different from the scientist's arose only slowly and gradually. The struggle has generally been carried on in the area of epistemology, and Locke was probably the first philosopher to try to address the issues, although he was not always successful in his efforts. Thus it is that we find him remarking in such studies as *Examination of Malebranche* and *Remarks upon Mr. Norris's Books* that no one can tell how ideas are caused and produced in the mind. For motion can produce only motion, and how motion can produce perception is entirely inexplicable. Or, as he puts it again in a memorable passage in the former work, "Impressions made on the retina by rays of light I think I understand; and motions from there continued to the brain is perhaps something I can perceive; and that these produce ideas in our minds, I am willing to believe—but how all this is accomplished is incomprehensible." It is something, he adds, that we simply must ascribe to God, whose ways are past finding out.

But although Locke seemed mildly aware that there is a kind of mystery here that science can never hope to unravel, he also seemed curiously unable to resist the thought and hope that the discovery and development of finer instruments would allow us to penetrate this mystery and give us an ultimate account of the origin of ideas and what lies behind them—a hope that, as he explained, was the reason for his own "extravagant conjectures" concerning such future "experimental" discoveries. This shows how far he still was from seeing the real nature of the problem. The philosophical developments and insights since Locke, including those of Wittgenstein, have enabled us to see that such hopes are entirely in vain, for what stands in our way are not barriers of a physical sort (which science could learn in time to overcome) but barriers of a logical sort that can never be overcome.

It was David Hume who, in the case of causation, was the first to generalize the ideas Locke was trying to get at and to bring them clearly before our minds. And it was Kant who was to see this merely as the first step in a whole program whose design was to show how very personal our knowledge is and that ultimately what we can know and what we come to know are only ourselves. Now Hume, by undermining our confidence in causal explanation, made it possible for others who followed not only to adopt a more sophisticated attitude toward science and scientific explanation but also a more sophisticated attitude toward philosophy and its own peculiar tasks. Whether this was Hume's intention is irrelevant. The point is that other philosophers could not fail to see that if causal explanation fares so badly with such empirical phenomena as sensations and images, it could hardly fare better with such problems as, for example, the existence of God, immortality, evil, and so on. Here, much more so than with such empirical phenomena as images and sight, the language of causes is hopelessly inadequate.

For some philosophers the language of reasons (i.e., attempting a *logical* rather than a *causal* account or explanation) seemed a possible solution here. But whether these philosophers succeeded in making out their case or not, it was the disenchantment with causal explanation that led them to see their own tasks and goals in a new light and gave them renewed confidence to prosecute them in their own ways. It now became clear that there are some questions that science is all too obviously unable to answer—most notably because these questions are of an entirely different nature than those it can and has dealt with successfully. This is the point, I think, of Wittgenstein's own comment in his *Notebooks* regarding the "urge towards the mystical." It comes, he says, "of the non-satisfaction of our wishes by science. We *feel* that even if all *possible* scientific questions are answered our *problem* is *still not touched at all.*"

Philosophical attempts to answer these questions (What is knowledge? What can we be certain of? What can we know?) in the way now seen to be demanded by them opened up new and startling insights. Doing so consisted in turning our attention away from the idea of knowledge as being representative and reproductive and toward seeing it as itself productive and creative. It consisted in turning away from the conception of the mind as a photographic plate registering whatever impinges on it and toward regarding it as a kind of self-regulating computer that will respond only to materials prepared and processed for it and that it is specifically designed to absorb. It consisted in seeing that the mind can respond only to that which it can absorb and accommodate; unless the materials presented to the mind have been translated into its terms, properly programmed for it, it will not answer us. The key to our problems, therefore, lies in discovering what these terms of reference of the mind are: what it can accommodate and absorb and what it cannot, what it does understand and what it does not.

Picture Theory

One of the difficulties in trying to describe Wittgenstein's philosophy is that he does not really have a "philosophy," as we usually understand that term, to describe. As we have noted, his books are essentially collections of remarks on diverse and seemingly unrelated topics.

This, however, does not mean that there are no philosophical theories to be found in Wittgenstein's writings or to be abstracted from them. Among these theories the fundamental one has to do with the way language holds us captive by generating certain "pictures" in our minds of the way things are or must be. Although this doctrine tends to undergo various changes as we move from the work of his early period (which deals with the philosophy of logic) to that of the middle period (which deals with the philosophy of imagery) to that of the late period (which deals with the philosophy of language), it is without doubt the closest thing to a unifying thread in his writings. It would be best, therefore, to concentrate our attention on it.

Wittgenstein's interest in "pictures" begins very early. In a brief passage in his *Notebooks* (dated November 15, 1914), he says, "That shadow which the picture as it were casts upon the world: How am I to get an exact grasp of it? Here is a deep mystery." The mystery Wittgenstein is here referring to—how is it that language can refer to reality?—has occupied philosophers from the beginning. It has not always been posed in these terms, and it is perhaps part of Wittgenstein's greatness and ingenuity that he was able to do so. However, neither the problem nor even some of Wittgenstein's proposed solutions to it are without precedent.

Nor is the problem merely an academic one. For how indeed is it that two things that are as different from each other as words and things are yet able to stand for each other? From one point of view, nothing perhaps could be simpler, for, after all, as we might be tempted to argue, by convention certain sounds have come to stand for and be associated with certain objects in our experience, and on the occasion of their use, these sounds simply bring these objects to our minds. But to say this does not, of course, solve our problem, for it leaves unclear the very point at issue: How it is that such things as sounds—which are, again, so different from such things as tables and chairs—are yet able to recall them to our minds and stand for them? And if it should be said that it is not the sounds themselves, of course, that do so but rather the images these sounds generate in our minds that manage it, then not only does this, again, leave unclear how it is possible for such unlike things as images (which are mental) and chairs and tables (which are not) to stand for each other, but it also raises the related and equally difficult problem of how it is possible for such things as words to arouse in our minds such things as images, seeing that words are words and images are images.

Kant struggled with this problem. Having arrived in his chapter in the *Critique of Pure Reason* on the "Schematism of the Categories," at the point where, in order to bring his argument to completion, he was compelled to show how it was that the categories applied to reality, he was faced with the problem of trying to relate things that were completely conceptual in nature (the categories) to things that were completely perceptual or sensuous in nature (objects). Related they obviously were, but how? What Kant believed he needed (naively, as we now see it) was some "third thing"—something that, being both "intellectual" and "sensuous," would mediate between the two and show how one was or could be an exemplification of the other. Kant thought he had found what he wanted in the "transcendental schema." But the exact nature of this "transcendental schema" and what there was about it that made him believe it could perform this miracle no one has ever properly been able to say. For, after all, even if such a third thing were indeed involved here, being a separate entity, two further "third things" would be required to connect it to each of the two things it was to connect and so on ad infinitum. And if we were to suggest that it was not some separate entity that brought these two together but something inherent in the two things themselves, what reason would there be to suppose that the two were indeed separate? Either, therefore, as we are now tempted to say, categories and objects are separate and nothing can conceivably bring them together, or they are not separate and require nothing to do so.

It would be a mistake to think that these logical objections, however disturbing they may be to Kant's formulation and solution of the problem, are irrelevant to Wittgenstein's statement of it. As we will soon see, this is not at all so. As everywhere else in the *Critique of Pure Reason*, Kant's purpose in this chapter, like Wittgenstein's in the *Tractatus*, was to define the conditions of significance and intelligibility. Kant's argument was that in itself and as such, the world is alien to the mind and therefore unknowable to it. For it to become knowable, it must in some way be mindlike. It must contain within it elements of rationality—something, that is, that our concepts can take up and absorb. This something Kant found in its structure and order: this is what is rational about the world, and that is what the mind can absorb. It is also, he tried to show in this chapter on schematism, what the mind knows when it comes to know the world.

If that is indeed Kant's argument, then we are obviously only a short step away from the position of the *Tractatus*. For if the mind, according to Kant, can absorb only that which is like itself, then, in a sense even more fundamental than Wittgenstein intended it, "the limits of my language" are indeed "the limits of my world," and language becomes the only reality with which we need concern ourselves.

The **picture theory** of Wittgenstein's *Tractatus*, like Kant's parallel theory of the transcendental schema, has caused endless trouble to those who have tried to grapple with it. "We picture facts to ourselves," he says enigmatically at 2.1. "A picture," he adds at 2.12, "is a model of reality." How is this possible? It is possible because, as he puts it, "In a picture objects have the elements of the picture corresponding to them" (2.13); or, put otherwise, "In a picture the elements of the picture are the representatives of objects" (2.131). A picture, he says, "is attached to reality; it reaches right out to it" (2.1511); "it is laid against reality like a ruler" (2.1512).

But the important question is, How do "pictures" manage to "reach out" in this way and become such "models" of reality? Not unlike Kant, Wittgenstein replies that pictures are able to do this in virtue of possessing "something in common" with what they depict (2.16 and 2.161), and what they have in common with reality is "logical form" (2.18). Thus, a picture can depict any reality whose form it has. It is this that enables a "proposition," for example, to picture reality, for a proposition is in fact a picture or a model of reality (4.01).

Wittgenstein is quite aware that a proposition (one "set out on the printed page, for example") does not at first sight "seem to be a picture of the reality with which it is concerned." "But no more," he adds, "does musical notation at first sight seem to be a picture of music, nor our phonetic notation (the alphabet) to be a picture of our speech. And yet these sign-languages prove to be pictures, even in the ordinary sense, of what they represent" (4.01).

One might object that neither music nor the phonetic system even remotely resembles musical sound or speech, but again what he obviously has in mind here is their common formal or logical patterns and not anything strictly pictorial. This seems at least to be indicated by such further remarks as "It is obvious that a proposition of the form a R b [a is related to b] strikes us as a picture. In this case the sign is obviously a likeness of what is signified" (4.012). "They are all constructed," he remarks again at 4.014, "according to a common logical plan." "That is what constitutes the inner similarity between these things which seem to be constructed in such entirely different ways" (4.0141).

He notes further, in a manner remarkably reminiscent of what Kant had said, that this is what, as a matter of fact, lies behind the possibility "of all imagery, of all our pictorial modes of expression," for logical form is more fundamental and prior to the imagery and the strictly pictorial characteristics. These are, he suggests, a later product and, in a sense, even unnecessary. For, as he says at 4.016, "in order to understand the essential nature of a proposition we should consider hieroglyphic script, which depicts the facts that it describes. And alphabetic script developed out of it without losing what was essential to depiction." In other words, alphabetic script stands for Wittgenstein to hieroglyphic script in the same relation in which schemata stand to images for Kant. In both cases what enables the hieroglyphics or images to function in the way they do is not anything pictorial or iconic about them but rather the logical patterns they inscribe for us.

Interpreting Wittgenstein's account in this way tends to remove some of the objections that have frequently been raised against it. Thus, for example, it has sometimes been objected that while it may be true that propositions may "refer" to reality, "state" things about it, "describe" it, and so on, they cannot, strictly speaking, *represent* or *picture* it. To criticize Wittgenstein in this way, however, is to misunderstand his point here. What obviously, according to him, permits the proposition to "picture" the facts it describes is simply, as in Kant, the logical structure it shares with them and not anything sensual, which it obviously does not possess in common with them. Propositions, that is to say, can picture facts not because they are identical, or *homomorphic*, with them but rather because they are structurally similar, or *isomorphic*, with them.

What perhaps has tended to mislead readers is that they have thought Wittgenstein is speaking here about the way ordinary sentences picture ordinary, everyday objects, whereas what Wittgenstein seems to be concerned with are not ordinary sentences and ordinary, everyday objects but rather unordinary, primitive or elementary propositions and the way they depict what he calls *states of affairs*.

If it is indeed true that what is involved are not ordinary sentences but something bordering on the conceptual (i.e., "states of affairs"), then to say the one "pictures" the other is not any longer to say anything very startling. For "picturing," far from representing or applying anything like a mirror image, obviously implies something far different from it. That this must be so seems to be clear from Wittgenstein's reference to hieroglyphic script. For, after all, even hieroglyphic script does not in any ordinary sense "depict the facts that it describes." If it did, even a child would be able to decipher it. Yet he describes this as a "depiction."

In other words, like Kant, Wittgenstein is obviously still dealing with matters that are far removed from ordinary or familiar events and with the mirror images in which we tend on that plane occasionally to conceive them. Not that these pictures, as we might say with Kant again, are always "completely congruent with the concept" they are designed to depict. On the contrary, that is precisely how confusions arise. For they arise from the fact, according to Wittgenstein, "that the apparent logical form of a proposition," as already pointed out by Russell, "need not be its real one" (4.0031). Although this diagnosis has also given rise to a good many objections and has often struck readers as superficial, in view of the simple and primitive nature of the linguistic or conceptual structures dealt with here, it is not perhaps, after all, entirely unconvincing. For if successful communication is, theoretically, a matter of using sentences that logically match or are congruent with the states of affairs they describe, then obviously any incongruence in the match will tend to lead to confusion. And on that level of discourse, where we are dealing with such bare and abstract possibilities, a simple failure in our ideography is all that is needed to bring this about.

Although viewing Wittgenstein's *Tractatus* picture theory in the light of Kant's parallel theory enables us to meet some of the objections that have been raised against it, there remains one objection this comparison cannot succeed in removing: If what enables the proposition to function in the way it does is the common logical structure it shares with that which it depicts, how can we ever be certain that it does indeed so depict it? Can we step out of language in order to compare the two? It would seem that we cannot.

Unfortunately, Wittgenstein's answer to this question is not only less satisfactory than Kant's but a good deal more mysterious. "In order to be able to represent logical form," he points out, "we should have to be able to station ourselves with propositions somewhere outside logic, that is to say outside the world" (4.12), and, of course, we cannot do that. And we cannot do that, for, again, "what finds its reflection in language, language cannot represent. What expresses *itself* in language, we cannot express by means of language" (4.121). But this, he says, does not mean that we are entirely trapped in language. What cannot be *said* can yet be shown. Thus it is that while it is true that a picture cannot depict its pictorial form, it can yet display it (2.172). And similarly with propositions: While it is true that they cannot represent logical form, this does not prevent them from mirroring it (4.121). "There are, indeed," as he reassures the reader toward the end of the *Tractatus*, "things that cannot be put into words" (6.522). "They *make themselves manifest*"; they are, he ends by saying, "what is mystical."

Misleading Pictures

It is interesting that when Wittgenstein returned to philosophy some 10 years later, it was precisely this question of how language comes to signify ("solved" so mysteriously in the *Tractatus*) to which he once again directed his attention. In this new period of his thought, he came to see that his old conception of language as being a mirror of reality was somehow mistaken. He decided therefore to make a fresh start—or what at first sight appeared to him to be a fresh start.

Briefly, he came to see that far from being a mirror whose sole object is to reflect reality, language is a tool capable of many uses. Since the failure to take note of this peculiar feature of language was something he shared with other philosophers, he came to regard this as not only responsible for his own former impasses but also at the root of the impasses of his fellow philosophers. And thus was born what he regarded as his new mission: to show others how they, too, had been misled by language.

In carrying out this mission, Wittgenstein seems to have been caught between two opposite drives. He realized that he had discovered what he called a "new method" of doing philosophy. Anxious to test it, he proceeded to apply it to all kinds of situations and problems, sometimes with startling results. In fact, so startling did these results appear to him that their elaboration tended to absorb him in their own right and to overshadow his prime object—the articulation of his new theory of language.

The picture theory that gradually emerges in his later works is, like the one found in the *Tractatus*, designed to show us how it is that we become trapped in language. Unlike the *Tractatus* theory, however, the trap here is not a deep-rooted, irreversible one but a manageable one: that is, it is one we can free ourselves from, given the proper insights. These insights involve becoming aware of certain peculiarities of language. The first of these has to do with the nature of words; the second, with the nature of sentences; and the third, with certain aspects of our psychology.

What particularly struck Wittgenstein about words was that despite the numerous and diverse roles they play, the mental images they generate do not always keep up with the new usages but tend to lag behind them. And it is the same with the sentences we form with these words: While the facts of our experience are unlimited and enormously varied, the forms of language, or sentence structures with which we are compelled to describe and record them, are few. The dangers of misdescribing and misrecording these facts are thus unlimited. What, finally, feeds and is in turn fed by these tendencies toward economy in language is our own mental attitudes, which strive always toward unity, simplicity, and economy. And this tendency, too, does violence to the multifarious nature of our experience.

Mainly, however, what he came to see at this point in his thinking was that a different, more literal sort of "picturing" seems to take place in language, one that,

---

At one of the at-homes, Wittgenstein related a riddle for the purpose of throwing some light on the nature of philosophy. It went as follows: Suppose that a cord was stretched tightly around the earth at the equator. Now suppose that a piece one yard long was added to the cord. If the cord was kept taut and circular in form, how much above the surface of the earth would it be? Without stopping to work it out, everyone present was inclined to say that the distance of the cord from the surface of the earth would be so minute that it would be imperceptible. But this is wrong. The actual distance would be nearly six inches. Wittgenstein declared that this is the kind of mistake that occurs in philosophy. It consists in being misled by a picture. In the riddle the picture that misleads us is the comparison of the length of the additional piece with the length of the whole cord. The picture itself is correct enough: for a piece one yard long would be an insignificant fraction of the length of the whole cord. But we are misled by it to draw a wrong conclusion. A similar thing happens in philosophy: we are constantly deceived by mental pictures which are in themselves correct.

—**Norman Malcolm**, *Memoir of Wittgenstein*

more than anything else, seems to be responsible for our philosophic puzzlement and confusion.

In order to understand a word, says Wittgenstein, we must know its use. With a great many words, a certain picture represents for us both its meaning and its use. This is the case, for example, with the word *chair*. One of the great benefits of this tendency of words to arouse pictures of what they represent is that it guarantees that we will all use these words in the same way. In other cases, however, these pictures are very misleading. An example, he says, is the word *particle*, which, unfortunately, is no longer used in such a way that the picture has any use. For rather than guaranteeing that we will use the word in similar ways, new uses to which old words are put tend rather to have the reverse effect. And this will be so whenever the words in question no longer continue to be used in their ordinary and familiar ways. Then the words are misleading—and understandably so, for the pictures they create lead us to expect the wrong things—and with obvious results.

On the contrary, we may go even further than that. If something about a certain subject or problem "charms or astounds" us, Wittgenstein says we may conclude that it is because we have been captivated by "the wrong imagery." Imagery of this sort is a function of metaphors, and such metaphors remain "fishy" as long as they are "exciting." When we begin to see these things in their true light, the amazement and excitement simply vanishes. Thus, for example, certain parts of mathematics are regarded as "deep." "But the apparent depth comes from a wrong imagery. It is pedestrian as any calculus." Yet that is precisely the way people were misled about the infinitesimal calculus when they mistakenly believed that it treated of infinitely small quantities. It is because we think of such things in terms of such misleading images (e.g., in terms of sizes, as here) that we go wrong. The amazement and excitement such things inspire in us should be taken as a sign that we have simply been misled.

Wittgenstein speaks in these mathematical writings of "charm," "excitement," "amazement," and so on, but it is easy to see how these expressions give way in the other works to such more familiar ones as "puzzlement," "wonder," and "confusion." That transition is to be found, in fact, in these writings themselves. He remarks, for example,

> There is one kind of misunderstanding which has a kind of charm . . . we say that the line intersects at an imaginary point. This sets the mind in a whirl, and gives a pleasant feeling of paradox, e.g. saying that there are numbers bigger than infinity. . . . He has employed a sensational way of expressing what he has discovered, so that it looks like a different kind of discovery . . . he describes a new state of affairs in old words, and so we don't understand him. The picture he makes does not lead us on. By the words of ordinary language we conjure up a familiar picture—but we need more than the right picture, we need to know the correct use. (Math Notes[1])

And this is precisely where such new notations, Wittgenstein emphasizes here, fail us so badly. The fact is that "in an overwhelming number of cases people do have the same sort of images suggested by words. This is a mere matter of fact about what happens in our minds, but a fact of enormous importance." In this light, it is not difficult to see why and how confusions arise. For all that is really necessary is for us to use familiar words in unfamiliar ways. The pictures aroused will be correct enough, but, of course, they will be misleading. And it is in such misleading pictures, he concludes here as well, "that most of the problems of philosophy arise."

These remarks echo ideas expressed in the *Tractatus*. "A sign," he says there, "is what can be perceived of a symbol" (3.32). But one and the same sign can be common to two different symbols, as is so often the case in our language. No harm is done as long as we realize they are signifying two quite different things and really therefore belong to two different symbols. But this is not always the case. "In the proposition, 'Green is green,'" for example, "where the first word is the proper name of a person and the last an adjective—these words do not merely have different meanings: they are *different* symbols" (3.323). This is, of course, an obvious example and not likely to mislead anyone. It is, however, in this way that "the most fundamental confusions are easily produced (the whole of philosophy is full of them)" (3.324). "In order to avoid such errors we must make use of a sign-language that excludes them by not using the same sign for symbols and by not using in a superficially similar way signs that have different modes of signification: that is to say, a sign-language that is governed by *logical* grammar—by logical syntax" (3.325). We need here only replace *sign* by *image* and *symbol* by *word* to see the close correspondence between the two picture theories and how little indeed Wittgenstein needed to change in his original theory as he moved from the *Tractatus* to the *Philosophical Investigations*.

Language Pitfalls

This second attempt to describe the way language pictures reality was not Wittgenstein's last. He went on to explore still a third view of language, built on this second one, one more detailed and more fully developed yet just as intriguing. This third view was not so much concerned with the genesis of confusion arising from the pictures generated by words as with the confusions stemming from our misunderstanding of what he now called the "grammar" of words.

A good example is the ancient problem regarding the nature of time. Trying to solve this problem in the way we might try to solve the problem regarding, say, the ultimate constituents of matter and not succeeding very well has tended to make us think that these philosophical entities are very queer things, that they are, as Wittgenstein puts it, "things hidden, something we can see from the outside but which we can't look into. . . . And yet nothing of the sort is the case. It is not new facts about time which we want to know. All the facts that concern us lie open before us" (*Blue Book*, p. 6). But it is the use of the noun time and the form in which we pose this question that misleads us into dealing with it in an impossible way. If we would look into the "grammar" of that word, we would no longer be puzzled and would know quite well how to use it. And that is all we mean by it.

But unfortunately, the question "What is time?" that so puzzled St. Augustine, like ordinary scientific questions, appears to ask for something else—for some factual information—and this, says Wittgenstein, leads us to deal with it as if it were indeed an ordinary scientific or empirical question. But this is obviously wrong and not what is wanted here. We do not see this because the puzzlement expresses itself here in a misleading way by means of the form of the question "What is . . . ?" But this question is simply, in this case, an utterance of "unclarity, of mental discomfort . . . comparable with the question 'Why?' as children so often ask it"—a question that like "What is . . . ?" "doesn't necessarily ask for either a cause or a reason" but is simply an expression of puzzlement (*Blue Book*, p. 26).

It is little wonder, therefore, that such questions cannot be answered by providing information but only by coming to recognize their cause, which lies in certain "contradictions" in the grammar of the words used. "St. Augustine, we might say, thinks of the process of measuring a length: say, the distance between two marks on a travelling band which passes us, and of which we can only see a tiny bit (the present) in front of us" (*Blue Book*, p. 26). Thinking of time in terms of such an analogy—of such a picture embedded in the notion of "measuring" common to the two cases—he naturally became puzzled as to how it could be done; how, that is, it should be possible for one to be able to measure time. For the past, as he himself put it, can't be measured, as it has gone by, and the future can't be measured because it has not yet come; finally, the present can't be measured, for it has no extension. What, then, is time?

If time were indeed like such a passing band (the part that is to be measured not having arrived yet and the other part already gone by), we would certainly not be able to measure it by laying, say, a ruler alongside it. To solve this puzzle, says Wittgenstein, what we must do is to come to see that we mean quite a different thing by *measurement* when applied to a band continuously passing by us and when applied to such a thing as time. It is because we try to apply such words rigidly and consistently and find that we cannot that we run into difficulties and become bewildered. We fail to see that we are really victims here of a kind of equivocation, that the same word may have quite different meanings when used in different contexts. "The problem may seem simple, but its extreme difficulty is due to the fascination which the analogy between two similar structures in our language can exert on us" (*Blue Book*, p. 26). Like children, we find it hard to believe that one word can have two meanings.

Wittgenstein goes on to generalize this point. "Philosophy, as we use the word, is a fight," he says, "against the fascination which forms of expression exert upon us" (*Blue Book*, p. 27). It is an attempt "to counteract the misleading effect of certain analogies" (*Blue Book*, p. 28). "The man who is philosophically puzzled sees a law in the way a word is used, and, trying to apply this law consistently, comes up against cases where it leads to paradoxical results" (*Blue Book*, p. 27). What we must try to do is to undermine and loosen this rigidity of mind and counteract the effect these misleading analogies have upon us.

Two aspects of Wittgenstein's analysis here are important. The first is his view, apparently, that what makes us particularly prone to these pitfalls in language is a certain mental laziness or lack of alertness. If we have come to understand a term in a certain way, we have a tendency to continue to understand it that way, come what may. Mentally, it is easier and requires less energy to do this than to be constantly alert to changing circumstances. Unfortunately for us (and here we come to Wittgenstein's second point), certain features of language tend to collaborate to sustain this mental laziness. One feature is the highly analogical character of language, which tends to lull us into thinking that there is more unity and uniformity in the facts recorded than there really is. Wittgenstein never tires of emphasizing the hypnotic effect this feature of language has on us. "We aren't able to rid ourselves of the implications of our symbolism" (*Brown Book*, p. 108), he says at one place. "We are led into puzzlement by an analogy which irresistibly drags us on." Or again, "A picture held us captive. We could not get outside it, for it lay in our language and language seemed to repeat it to us inexorably" (*Philosophical Investigations* I, p. 115).

Wittgenstein doesn't want to claim that all analogies necessarily lead to the kind of confusion he describes here or that all analogical thinking is bad. There are no doubt many analogies that are, from this point of view, entirely harmless, and many of them are extremely useful. "When we say that by our method we try to counteract the misleading effect of certain analogies," he qualifies his remarks here, "it is important that you should understand that the idea of an analogy being misleading is nothing sharply defined. No sharp boundary can be drawn round the cases in which we should say that a man was misled by an analogy. The use of expressions constructed on analogical patterns stresses analogies between cases often far apart. And by doing this these expressions may be extremely useful. It is, in most cases, impossible to show an exact point where an analogy begins to mislead us. Every particular notation stresses some particular point of view" (*Blue Book*, p. 28).

"The cases," however, "in which particularly we wish to say that someone is misled by a form of expression are those in which we would say: 'He wouldn't talk as he does if he were aware of this difference in the grammar of such-and-such words, or if he were aware of this other possibility of expression' and so on."

To make this point clearer Wittgenstein draws our attention to a host of different examples. "It might be found practical," he points out, "to call a certain state of decay in a tooth, not accompanied by what we commonly call toothache, 'unconscious toothache' and to use in such a case the expression that we have toothache, but don't know it. It is just in this sense that psychoanalysis talks of unconscious thoughts, acts of volition, etc. Now is it wrong in this sense to say that I have toothache but don't know it? There is nothing wrong about it, as it is just a new terminology and can at any time be translated into ordinary language. On the other hand it obviously makes use of the word 'to know' in a new way" (*Blue Book*, pp. 22–23).

But unfortunately, the new expression not only leads us to think that we have done more than we actually have but also calls up for us "pictures and analogies which make it extremely difficult for us to go through with our conventions" (p. 25). And this in turn creates puzzlement and gives rise to bad philosophy.

Thus, by the expression "unconscious toothache," for example, we are "misled into thinking that a stupendous discovery has been made, a discovery which in a sense altogether bewilders our understanding; or else you may be extremely puzzled by the expression (the puzzlement of philosophy) and perhaps ask such a question as 'How is unconscious toothache possible?' You may then be tempted to deny the possibility of unconscious toothache; but the scientist will tell you that it is a proved fact that there is such a thing, and will say it like a man who is destroying a common prejudice. He will say: 'Surely it's quite simple; there are other things which you don't know of and there can also be toothache which you don't know of. It is just a new discovery.' You won't be satisfied, but you won't know what to answer." But obviously what has been overlooked by these disputants is, inter alia, the fact that these other things we "don't know of" are things that, unlike having a toothache, we "don't have." And what puzzles us is the fact that since a toothache is something "we have," we ought, normally speaking, "know of it." The new notation, although not unintelligible, does not seem to provide room for this and thus runs into conflict with the old. This generates confusion and puzzlement.

It is the same with the so-called discoveries of psychoanalysis and all the disputes and confusion they have caused. "Can we have unconscious thoughts, unconscious feelings, etc? The idea that we can has revolted many people. Others again have said that these were wrong in supposing that there could only be conscious thoughts, and that psychoanalysis had discovered unconscious ones." Both, however, were confused about what had really happened. "The objectors to unconscious thought," for example, "did not see that they were not objecting to the newly discovered psychological reactions, but to the way in which they were described. The psychoanalysts on the other hand were misled by their own way of expression into thinking that they had done more than discover new psychological reactions; that they had, in a sense, discovered conscious thoughts which were unconscious. The first could have stated their objection by saying 'We don't wish to use the phrase "unconscious thoughts"; we wish to reserve the word "thought" for what you call "conscious thought."' They state their case wrongly when they say: 'There can only be conscious thoughts and no unconscious ones.' For if they don't wish to talk of 'unconscious thought' they should not use the phrase 'conscious thought,' either" (*Blue Book*, pp. 57–58).

These disputes and difficulties can be cleared up by recognizing that they are essentially verbal, that what is being disputed are not the facts of the case—whatever they may be—but simply their description. It is this confusion of the grammatical with the experiential that has led philosophers to say typically metaphysical (i.e., paradoxical) things. This is also what has led them to believe that they have somehow stumbled upon some very striking scientific or empirical discoveries when as a matter of fact they have merely used words in consistently and therefore systematically misleading ways. If there is anything actually new that they have accomplished, here it is to forge some new conventions regarding the uses of words and speaking about them. To do this, however, is not to discover anything new or startling about any of the things described by these expressions. In the end it is simply a matter of making new notations. Philosophers, however, have not as a rule been aware that that is all it is.

That this third, more generalized view of the way we are misled by language is intimately connected with the second view concerning the image-generating capacity of language is clear from numerous other passages scattered throughout Wittgenstein's writings, where both views seem to exist side by side. Let me illustrate this with one or two examples.

"The new expression misleads us," he says in the *Blue Book*, "by calling up pictures and analogies which make it difficult for us to go through with our conventions. And it is extremely difficult to discard these pictures unless we are constantly watchful" (p. 23). Now we can be so watchful, he goes on, by asking ourselves at such times "*How far does the analogy between these uses go?*" We can also try to construct "new notations, in order to break the spell of those which we are accustomed to." In view of what we have seen Wittgenstein say about "pictures," we can perhaps now understand, much better than was possible before, the deeper implications of these remarks: why, for example, he should say that it is extremely difficult to discard these pictures; how being watchful in the way he suggests will enable us to do so; and why he should speak of the whole process in the terms he does ("go through with our conventions," "spell," "notation," and so forth). The same may be said of a good many other passages in the *Blue Book*.

Although such discussions tend to be more puzzling without these further aids, occasionally they are, as we now see, surprisingly explicit and clear. His remark on page 43 of the *Blue Book* is a case in point. "The scrutiny of the grammar of a word," he says there, summarizing his results, "weakens the position of certain fixed standards of our expression which had prevented us from seeing facts with unbiased eyes. Our investigation tried to remove this bias, which forces us to think that the facts must conform to certain pictures embedded in our language."

The Tyranny of Words and Pictures

To see how Wittgenstein came to connect his thoughts about this picture-generating capacity of language with his later thoughts on the nature and sources of philosophical confusion, we need to turn to the *Philosophical Investigations*.

The trouble with our failure "to get away from the idea that using a sentence involves imagining something for every word" is, he argues in volume 1, that we do not realize that we do all sorts of things with words—turning "them sometimes into one picture, sometimes into another" (p. 449). Furthermore, such pictures are often "only like an illustration to a story" and from it alone it is mostly impossible "to conclude anything at all"—for only "when one knows the story does one know the significance of the picture" (p. 663). But mainly, of course, the trouble with such pictures is that they seem "to fix the sense unambiguously when this is not at all the case." On the contrary, "the actual use, compared with that suggested by the picture," is "muddied" (p. 426).

Certainly language has this effect on us—"the picture is there"; nor need we necessarily dispute its "validity in any particular case." But we do "want to understand the application of the picture" (p. 423). And not only is this often lacking, but other pernicious effects result as well. Or, as he puts it in volume 2, "what this language primarily describes is a picture. What is to be done with the picture, how it is to be used, is still obscure. Quite clearly, however, it must be explored if we want to understand the sense of what we are saying. But the picture seems to spare us this work: it already points to a particular use. This is how it takes us in" (p. vii).

To save ourselves from being taken in, we ought always to ask, Does reality accord with such pictures? (I, p. 352). These pictures seem "to determine what we have to do, what to look for, and how," but they do not really do so. They seem "to make the sense of the expressions unmistakable" but in fact prove to be utterly misleading (p. 352). For example, "what am I believing in when I believe that men have souls? What am I believing in, when I believe that this substance contains two carbon rings? In both cases there is a picture in the foreground, but the sense lies far in the background; that is, the application of the picture is not easy to survey" (p. 422). In ordinary circumstances such words and the pictures they generate "have an application with which we are familiar. But if we suppose a case in which this application is absent we become as it were conscious for the first time of the nakedness of the words and the picture" (p. 349), of how "idle" such pictures are (p. 291). In the end we must simply regard them as "illustrated turns of speech" (p. 295), which stand "in the way of our seeing the use of the word as it is" (p. 305).

In restating, as I have tried to do here, Wittgenstein's position in terms of this new idea and emphasis, I have, of course, taken some liberties with the order of his own exposition. This has been necessary in order to make it possible for us to look at such remarks in the *Philosophical Investigations* as, for example, "philosophy is a battle against the bewitchment of our intelligence by means of language" (p. 109), "a simile that has been absorbed into the forms of our language produces a false appearance" (p. 112), "a *picture* held us captive" (p. 115), and so on, in the way in which we ought now, perhaps, to look at all Wittgenstein's remarks regarding the genesis of philosophical confusion.

One of the values to be derived, it seems to me, from doing so is that it enables us to meet an objection that must strike every reader who tries to come to terms with Wittgenstein's attack on philosophy. One is often tempted to object that it seems preposterous to attribute the rise of various metaphysical theories, complex as they often are and supported by subtle and intricate arguments, to such seemingly absurd and unbelievable causes. Surely, one is inclined to say at such times that it is pure fancy to suggest that St. Augustine's puzzlement about time arose in this way. On the contrary, to try to dismiss it in such a high-handed manner is itself simply absurd. For, after all, what proof is there that such an analogy even occurred to him during his deliberations on this problem?

But from what has been said here, it could perhaps be argued that it is really not Wittgenstein's intention to try to base his case, here or elsewhere, on any such claims. His point seems rather to be that our questions (about time or anything else) are often products of our tendency to look at these things through misleading pictures (whatever these may be at any one occasion or for any one particular philosopher). On the other hand, should it be argued that he did indeed intend to be a good deal more specific, then the whole question simply becomes an empirical one. To settle it, we would need to ask people whether, for example, in thinking about the flow of time they had in their minds, however dimly (as he seems to suggest in the *Brown Book* that they apparently do—see pp. 107–8), some notion of the flow of logs down a river. We might, by investigating it in this way, discover that either they had something else in the back of their minds (Must it be *logs*? Could it not be, perhaps, clouds floating across the sky?) or, more probably, nothing at all. But this is probably not what Wittgenstein has in mind here. His point seems rather to be that the general tendency of language is to generate pictures in our minds (this is a fact of language and is essential to his case) and that this being so, it simply cannot fail to have an adverse effect on thinking. Such pictures, being often incongruent with the facts that they are designed to explain, must prove misleading.

It is perhaps this general fact about language (and not any one particular picture he need necessarily defend) on which he seems mainly to base his case. This is what, for example, his remarks about symbolism in his later works seem to entail. "Thus it can come about," he says, "that we aren't able to rid ourselves of the implications of our *symbolism*." We become "obsessed" with it—an analogy that "irresistibly drags us on" and leads us into confusion (*Brown Book*, p. 108).

The symbolism or ideography of which he speaks is obviously of a much more complicated kind than the one discussed in the *Tractatus*. But like it, it is designed to show how language, by failing to be congruent with the states of affairs it is designed to depict, gives rise to difficulties. Both doctrines, that is to say, are designed to be descriptive of certain very general and universal aspects of the operation of language.

Wittgenstein and Our Philosophic Tradition

In being concerned with these questions and in exploring them the way he did, it might appear as if Wittgenstein and the contemporary analytic and linguistic philosophy he influenced so profoundly are very remote from the central concerns of philosophy. Although many have believed this to be so, in an important sense what Wittgenstein tried to achieve can be seen as lying very much in the direct line of development of philosophy and that he was occupied with what has always been central to it.

Let us begin with a remark found in Wittgenstein's *Notebooks*: "The great problem round which everything that I write turns is: Is there an order in the world a priori, and if so what does it consist in?" (p. 53). This attempt to find the true structure or order of the world and make sense of it is what philosophy, as we have seen, has traditionally been conceived to be mainly concerned with.

Like all great philosophers before him, Wittgenstein tried to show that the world as it appears to us appears so as a result of the conceptual system we use in organizing it, and since this system is essentially a human one, we are in a fundamental sense our own prisoners. How to break free of this prison, how to come to see the way things really are—this is the theme around which all philosophy turns.

Some of philosophy's most memorable passages have been devoted to describing this condition in which we find ourselves. Among the greatest of these is Plato's **allegory of the cave** in his most famous work, the *Republic*.

As an illustration of the degree to which our nature may be enlightened or unenlightened, Plato says, imagine the condition of men imprisoned in a dark and deep underground cave. They are chained to their seats and are able to move neither to the right nor to the left. They have been there from birth and sit facing the wall of the cave. It is a deep cave, and the long, winding entrance behind them permits no light to enter. Somewhat farther behind them there is a wall or partition and behind this wall a path or track. Farther back still a fire is burning. Along this track people walk to and fro, carrying all sorts of objects (figures of men, animals, and so on) that project above the partition. As they walk by, some talking, some silent, the fire casts shadows of these figures onto the wall of the cave facing the prisoners. But the prisoners, like their modern counterparts in movie theaters, see neither the fire nor the people whose shadows are reflected on the wall of the cave. They see only the shadows; they are aware of nothing else. But from these shadows that they see and that they take to be real things and from the echoes they hear, they form, after perhaps much trial and error, various theories, some, as we might suppose, highly ingenious—perhaps that these activities of which they are spectators generally last for periods of some eight hours a day and only five days of the week. To this knowledge they add, in the course of time, further bits of insight, and thus they pass their existence: the only one they know.

But now suppose, says Plato, we released one of these prisoners and brought him to the rear. He sees the wall and the track, the fire burning in the distance, the people and the objects which they carry, and the prisoners sitting below watching the shadows. Not accustomed to such intense light, he shuts his eyes in pain and disbelief. He is seized with fear and is overcome by an urge to return to the more familiar and comfortable condition of the darkness of the cave. In time, however, his eyes become accustomed to the light, and he comes to see that what he once took to be real things were indeed only shadows, and an intense desire possesses him to return to the cave to tell the others what he has seen.

Suppose we now follow him there. The other prisoners have not seen the wall, the men, or the fire. They see him descending into the cave, falling, and stumbling, for the cave is dark, and it is difficult for him to find his way about. They laugh and jeer at him, for his movements are absurd. "He has gone up," they say, "only to come back with his sight ruined." He begins, however, to tell them about the great fire burning and about the partition and the statues and the other things he has seen, but it sounds absurd to them. Obviously it is not worth one's while, they say, even to attempt the ascent. But he is undaunted and persists in enlightening them. They become annoyed, and their laughter now turns to anger. They instruct him to keep his peace and not disturb them, or else they themselves will silence him. And that, concludes Plato, with obvious allusions to Socrates, is what they will do should an opportunity present itself.

This parable is Plato's way of expressing his belief that the world may, for all we know, be quite other than what it appears to be—that with regard to it, we are or may be in a state of human and universal deception.

Ever since Plato, philosophers have tried to come to understand more clearly the source and nature of this universal deception. Spinoza, another philosopher whom we have already encountered, believed that a good deal of it originated from our belief in the purposiveness of nature. Why, he asked himself in his *Ethics*, are people so prone to believe this about nature? What is it that stands in their way of seeing that the facts are quite the contrary, namely, that "nature has no particular goal in view" and that everything in it "proceeds from a sort of necessity, and with the utmost perfection" (p. 75)?

Partly, he answers, it is due to ignorance of natural causes and partly to the human propensity to seek and believe only that which is useful to us. "Herefrom it follows, first, that men think themselves free inasmuch as they are conscious of their volitions and desires, and never even dream, in their ignorance, of the causes which have disposed them so to wish and desire. Secondly, men do all things for an end, namely for that which is useful to them, and which they seek" and nature, too, behaves similarly:

> Thus it comes to pass that they only look for a knowledge of the final causes of events, and when these are learned, they are content, as having no cause for further doubt. If they cannot learn such causes from external sources, they are compelled to turn to considering themselves, and reflecting what end would have induced them personally to bring about the given event, and thus they necessarily judge other natures by their own. Further, as they find in themselves and outside themselves many means which assist them not a little in their search for what is useful, for instance, eyes for seeing, teeth for chewing, herbs and animals for yielding food, the sun for giving light, the sea for breeding fish, etc., they come to look on the whole of nature as a means for obtaining such conveniences. Now as they are aware, that they found these conveniences and did not make them, they think they have cause for believing, that some other being has made them for their use. As they look upon things as means, they cannot believe them to be

self-created; but, judging from the means they are accustomed to prepare for themselves, they are bound to believe in some ruler or rulers of the universe endowed with human freedom, who have arranged and adapted everything for human use. They are bound to estimate the nature of such rulers (having no information on the subject) in accordance with their own nature, and therefore they assert that the gods ordained everything for the use of man, in order to bind man to themselves and obtain from him the highest honor. Hence also it follows, that everyone thought out for himself, according to his abilities, a different way of worshipping God, so that God might love him more than his fellows, and direct the whole course of nature for the satisfaction of his blind cupidity and insatiable avarice. (*The Chief Works of Benedict De Spinoza*, pp. 75–76)

"Thus the prejudice," Spinoza concludes this brief history of natural religion, "developed into superstition, and took deep root in the human mind; and for this reason everyone strove zealously to understand and explain the final causes of things; but in their endeavor to show that nature does nothing in vain, i.e., nothing which is useless to man, they only seem to have demonstrated that nature, the gods, and men are all mad together." Consider, he urges, the result:

Among the many helps of nature they were bound to find hindrances, such as storms, earthquakes, diseases, etc.: so they declared that such things happen, because the gods are angry at some wrong done them by men, or at some fault committed in their worship. Experience day by day protested and showed by infinite examples, that good and evil fortunes fall to the lot of pious and impious alike; still they would not abandon their inveterate prejudice, for it was more easy for them to class such contradictions among other unknown things of whose use they were ignorant, and thus retain their actual and innate condition of ignorance, than to destroy the whole fabric of their reasoning and start afresh. They therefore laid down as an axiom [deserting in the process the very principle with which they began] that God's judgment far transcends human understanding.

Spinoza goes on to try to correct these misconceptions, asserting the doctrines for which he is noted, that "final causes are mere human figments," that "everyone judges of things according to the state of his brain," that names may be names of nothing at all, and so on.

Spinoza's account is interesting not only because of the nature of its doctrines (important as they are) but also because of the effect their exposition is designed to have on the mind of the reader. And this is of deflation and disillusionment. Like Plato before him and Wittgenstein after him, the task Spinoza has here set himself is to free the mind from the pictures and illusions that have captivated it and held it in bondage. It is an attempt to show that the world as we tend to experience it is very much a product of our own making, that as such and in itself, stripped of the illusions and deceptions prone to our ways of comprehending it, it is absurdly different from what we are inclined to take it to be.

When we turn to Wittgenstein, we find that he, too, has taken this, the unmasking of the illusions and deceptions to which we are so prone, as his main object. The passages I should like to quote here are directly concerned with our belief in "essences"—our tendency to think that there must be something in common among all the members of a class of things called by the same name. It is the kind of tendency to which, for example, Socrates apparently was especially liable. In the *Meno*, for example, he asks, "What is this thing which is called 'shape'? . . . Don't you see that I am looking for what is the same in all of them? . . . What is it that is common to roundness and straightness and the other things which you call shapes?" Clear and as natural as that kind of question must once have appeared, Wittgenstein would have us see that that is really a "complex question." For why should we assume, as he would ask, that there is such one common property or essence that runs through all such things? Surely, he would say, until we have settled that things share such common properties, it makes no sense to ask for them. Such questions are impossible to answer and produce puzzlement because they are often impossible questions. They keep the mind, as he puts it in his *Blue Book* and *Brown Book*, "pressing against a blank wall, thereby preventing it from ever finding the outlet. To show a man how to get out you have first of all to free him from the misleading influence of the question."

"Instead of producing something common," Wittgenstein explains in the *Philosophical Investigations*, "I am saying that these phenomena have no one thing in common which makes us use the same word for all—but that they are *related* to one another in many different ways. And it is because of this relationship, or these relationships, that we call them all [by the same name]. I will try to explain this" (emphasis added).

> Consider for example the proceeding that we call "games." I mean board-games, card-games, ball-games, Olympic games, and so on. What is common to them all?—Don't say: There must be something common, or they would not be called "games"—but look and see whether there is anything common to all. For if you look at them you will not see something that is common to all, but similarities, relationships, and a whole series of them at that. To repeat: Don't think, but look!—Look for example at board-games, with their multifarious relationships. Now pass to card-games; here you find many correspondences with the first group, but many common features drop out, and others appear. When we pass next to ball-games, much that is common is retained, but much is lost.— Are they all "amusing"? Compare chess with noughts and crosses [tic-tac-toe]. Or is there always winning and losing, or competition between players? Think of patience [solitaire] . . . we can go through the many, many other groups of games in the same way; we can see how similarities crop up and disappear.
>
> I can think of no better expression to characterize these similarities than "family resemblance"; for the various resemblances between members of a family: build, features, color of eyes, gait, temperament, etc. etc. overlap and criss-cross in the same way—. . . "games" form a family.

The kinds of number form a family in the same way. Why do we call something a "number"? Well, perhaps because it has a—direct—relationship with several things that have hitherto been called number; and this can be said to give it an indirect relationship to other things we call the same name. And we extend our concept of number as in spinning a thread we twist fiber on fiber. And the strength of the thread does not reside in the fact that some one fiber runs through its whole length, but in the overlapping of many fibers.

But if someone wished to say: "There is something common to all these constructions—namely the disjunction of all their common properties"—I should reply: Now you are only playing with words. One might as well say: "Something runs through the whole thread—namely the continuous overlapping of those fibers."

I can give the concept "number" rigid limits . . . but I can also use it so that the extension of the concept is not closed by a frontier. And this is how we do use the word "game." For how is the concept of a game bounded? What still counts as a game and what no longer does? Can you give the boundary? No. You can draw one; for none has so far been drawn.

"But then the use of the word is unregulated, the 'game' we play with it is unregulated."—It is not everywhere circumscribed by rules; but no more are there rules for how high one throws the ball in tennis, or how hard; yet tennis is a game for all that and has rules too. (*Philosophical Investigations* I, pp. 65–68)

It would be a mistake to think that Wittgenstein is interested here in merely unseating or unmasking **essentialism**—the belief in the existence of essences. Nor is he merely trying to point out that such questions as, for example, "What are games?" "What is beauty?" "What is justice?" and so on are really "loaded" questions that need themselves to be questioned before they are answered. What he is interested in showing is not that there are no such essences to be found but rather what this search for them, invited as it is by such questions, tends to do to us. For this desire for unity and this will to system, which such questions illustrate and invite, blunts and blinds our perceptions and sensitivities. It does violence to the multifarious nature of our experience, makes it easy for us to ignore what is exceptional in that experience, and leads us to take a contemptuous attitude to what is unique and individual in it.

In other words, this approach to the world tends to produce the illusion that the world really is as we have parceled it out by means of our concepts—that our conceptual net has really caught all there is to catch and nothing has gotten away. But how can we be sure of this? Perhaps some fish have not been caught and those that have are not at all representative of what there is to catch.

SUMMARY

1. The person who set the course of contemporary philosophy in the English-speaking world was Bertrand Russell. Through his contributions to mathematical logic and his

social and political activism, Russell was not only one of the major forces responsible for the revolution that has taken place in modern philosophy but also one of the major figures responsible for the social and technological revolutions that have taken place in the twentieth century.

2. Although Russell was the catalyst of the revolution in contemporary philosophy, it was his pupil, Ludwig Wittgenstein, who charted its course and gave it the tone and character that still marks it.

3. Taking his cue from Whitehead and Russell's *Principia Mathematica* (1910–1913), Wittgenstein went on to show in his first work, the *Tractatus*, that language, far from being a jungle as might at first be thought, has a definite structure and order to it, one that mirrors or pictures the structure of reality, and that the job of philosophy is to describe as accurately as possible what this structure is. In this way, philosophy may solve or dissolve, as the case may be, whatever philosophical problems might still remain.

4. Believing that he had solved all the problems of philosophy, Wittgenstein gave up its study for other occupations. By 1929, however, he returned to philosophy. Although he did not this time seek to publish the results of his new investigations, he did, around 1933, begin to circulate his new ideas in the form of two sets of lecture notes, one in a blue folder (the *Blue Book*), the other in brown (the *Brown Book*). The ideas presented there were at first regarded as representing a complete break with those contained in the *Tractatus* as well as being wholly unprecedented in the history of philosophy; however, neither of these views is now considered entirely accurate.

5. In retrospect, we can now see that Wittgenstein, like his predecessors in philosophy, was concerned in these later works with describing the conceptual systems we use, or are compelled to use, in our effort to arrive at a knowledge of reality—conceptual systems (language in his case) that, because of their very nature, must represent a veil between us and the reality they seek to glimpse. Philosophical theories, Wittgenstein therefore concluded, as he had in the *Tractatus*, being products of the distorting mirror of language, are necessarily confusions.

6. The philosophy inspired and set in motion by Russell and Wittgenstein, called linguistic analysis or analytic philosophy, has had its greatest vogue in English-speaking countries. On the European continent the philosophy that has been most dominant in the contemporary world has been existentialism, a school of thought that came into prominence following World War II.

KEY TERMS

allegory of the cave	picture theory
essentialism	symbolic logic
linguistic philosophy	

REVIEW QUESTIONS

1. In what respects did Bertrand Russell resemble Socrates? How did they differ?

2. According to Wittgenstein, how do words often mislead us? How do pictures do so?

3. What great task has philosophy, throughout its history, been absorbed with? To what extent was Wittgenstein occupied with this task as well?

■ Reading
"The Value of Philosophy"

BERTRAND RUSSELL

Excerpted from *The Problems of Philosophy* by Bertrand Russell, Oxford University Press (1912).

Having now come to the end of our brief and very incomplete review of the problems of philosophy, it will be well to consider, in conclusion, what is the value of philosophy and why it ought to be studied. It is the more necessary to consider this question, in view of the fact that many men, under the influence of science or of practical affairs, are inclined to doubt whether philosophy is anything better than innocent but useless trifling, hair-splitting distinctions, and controversies on matters concerning which knowledge is impossible.

This view of philosophy appears to result, partly from a wrong conception of the ends of life, partly from a wrong conception of the kind of goods which philosophy strives to achieve. Physical science, through the medium of inventions, is useful to innumerable people who are wholly ignorant of it; thus the study of physical science is to be recommended, not only, or primarily, because of the effect on the student, but rather because of the effect on mankind in general. Thus utility does not belong to philosophy. If the study of philosophy has any value at all for others than students of philosophy, it must be only indirectly, through its effects upon the lives of those who study it. It is in these effects, therefore, if anywhere, that the value of philosophy must be primarily sought.

But further, if we are not to fail in our endeavor to determine the value of philosophy, we must first free our minds from the prejudices of what are wrongly called "practical" men. The "practical" man, as this word is often used. is one who recognizes only material needs, who realizes that men must have food for the body, but is oblivious of the necessity of providing food for the mind. If all men were well off, if poverty and disease had been reduced to their lowest possible point, there would still remain much to be done to produce a valuable society; and even in the existing world the goods of the mind are at least as important as the goods of the body. It is exclusively among the goods of the mind that the value of philosophy is to be found; and only those who are not indifferent to these goods can be persuaded that the study of philosophy is not a waste of time.

Philosophy, like all other studies, aims primarily at knowledge. The knowledge it aims at is the kind of knowledge which gives unity and system to the body of the sciences, and the kind which results from a critical examination of the grounds of our convictions, prejudices, and beliefs. But it cannot be maintained that philosophy has had any very great measure of success in its attempts to provide definite answers to its questions.

If you ask a mathematician, a mineralogist, a historian, or any other man of learning, what definite body of truths has been ascertained by his science, his answer will last as long as you are willing to listen. But if you put the same question to a philosopher, he will, if he is candid, have to confess that his study has not achieved positive results such as have been achieved by other sciences. It is true that this is partly accounted for by the fact that, as soon as definite knowledge concerning any subject becomes possible, this subject ceases to be called philosophy and becomes a separate science. The whole study of the heavens, which now belongs to astronomy, was once included in philosophy; Newton's great work was called "the mathematical principles of natural philosophy." Similarly, the study of the human mind, which was a part of philosophy, has now been separated from philosophy and has become the science of psychology. Thus, to a great extent, the uncertainty of philosophy is more apparent than real: those questions which are already capable of definite answers are placed in the sciences, while those only to which, at present, no definite answer can be given, remain to form the residue which is called philosophy.

This is, however, only a part of the truth concerning the uncertainty of philosophy. There are many questions—and among them those that are of the profoundest interest to our spiritual life—which, so far as we can see, must remain insoluble to the human intellect unless its powers become of quite a different order from what they are now. . . . Has the universe any unity of plan or purpose, or is it a fortuitous concourse of atoms? Is consciousness a permanent part of the universe, giving hope of indefinite growth in wisdom, or is it a transitory accident on a small planet on which life must ultimately become impossible? Are good and evil of importance to the universe or only to man? Such questions are asked by philosophy, and variously answered by various philosophers. But it would seem that, whether answers be otherwise discoverable or not, the answers suggested by philosophy are none of them demonstrably true. Yet, however slight may be the hope of discovering an answer, it is part of the business of philosophy to continue the consideration of such questions, to make us aware of their importance, to examine all the approaches to them, and to keep alive that speculative interest in the universe which is apt to be killed by confining ourselves to definitely ascertainable knowledge.

Many philosophers, it is true, have held that philosophy could establish the truth of certain answers to such fundamental questions. They have supposed that what is of most importance in religious beliefs could be proved by strict demonstration to be true. In order to judge of such attempts, it is necessary to take a survey of human knowledge, and to form an opinion as to its methods and its limitations. On such a subject it would be unwise to pronounce dogmatically; but . . . we shall be compelled to renounce the hope of finding philosophical proofs of religious beliefs. We cannot, therefore, include as part of the value of philosophy any definite set of answers to such questions. Hence, once more, the value of philosophy must not depend upon any supposed body of definitely ascertainable knowledge to be acquired by those who study it.

The value of philosophy is, in fact, to be sought largely in its very uncertainty. The man who has no tincture of philosophy goes through life imprisoned in the prejudices derived from common sense, from the habitual beliefs of his age or his nation, and from convictions which have grown up in his mind without the cooperation or consent of his deliberate reason. To such a man the world tends to become definite, finite, obvious; common objects rouse no questions, and unfamiliar possibilities are contemptuously rejected. As soon as we begin to philosophize, on the contrary, we find . . . that even the most everyday things lead to problems to which only very incomplete answers can be given. Philosophy, though unable to tell us with certainty what is the true answer to the doubts which it raises, is able to suggest many possibilities which enlarge our thoughts and free them from the tyranny of custom. Thus, while diminishing our feeling of certainty as to what things are, it greatly increases our knowledge as to what they may be; it removes the somewhat arrogant dogmatism of those who have never travelled into the region of liberating doubt, and it keeps alive our sense of wonder by showing familiar things in an unfamiliar aspect.

Apart from its utility in showing unsuspected possibilities, philosophy has a value—perhaps its chief value—through the greatness of the objects which it contemplates, and the freedom from narrow and personal aims resulting from this contemplation. The life of the instinctive man is shut up within the circle of his private interests: family and friends may be included, but the outer world is not regarded except as it may help or hinder what comes within the circle of instinctive wishes. In such a life there is something feverish and confined, in comparison with which the philosophic life is calm and free. The private world of instinctive interests is a small one, set in the midst of a great and powerful world which must, sooner or later, lay our private world in ruins. Unless we can so enlarge our interests as to include the whole outer world, we remain like a garrison in a beleaguered fortress, knowing that the enemy prevents escape and that ultimate surrender is inevitable. In such a life there is no peace, but a constant strife between the insistence of desire and the powerlessness of will. In one way or another, if our life is to be great and free, we must escape this prison and this strife.

One way of escape is by philosophic contemplation. Philosophic contemplation does not, in its widest survey, divide the universe into new hostile camps—friends and foes, helpful and hostile, good and bad—it views the whole impartially. Philosophic contemplation, when it is unalloyed, does not aim at proving that the rest of the universe is akin to man. All acquisition of knowledge is an enlargement of the Self, but this enlargement is best attained when it is not directly sought. It is best obtained when the desire for knowledge is alone operative, by a study which does not wish in advance that its objects should have this or that character, but adapts the Self to the characters which it finds in its objects. This enlargement of Self is not obtained when, taking the Self as it is, we try to show that the world is so similar to this Self that knowledge of it is possible without any admission of what seems alien. The desire to prove this is a form of self-assertion and, like all self-assertion, it is an obstacle to the growth of Self which it desires, and of which the Self knows that it is capable. Self-assertion, in philosophic speculation as elsewhere, views the world as a means to its own ends; thus it makes the world of less account than Self, and the Self sets bounds to the greatness of its goods. In contemplation, on the contrary, we start from the non-Self, and through its Greatness the boundaries of Self are enlarged; through the infinity of the universe the mind which contemplates it achieves some share in infinity.

For this reason greatness of soul is not fostered by those philosophies which assimilate the universe to Man. Knowledge is a form of union of Self and not-Self; like all union, it is impaired by dominion, and therefore by any attempt to force the universe into conformity with what we find in ourselves. There is a widespread philosophical tendency towards the view which tells us that Man is the measure of all things, that truth is man-made, that space and time and the world of universals are properties of the mind, and that, if there be anything not created by the mind, it is unknowable and of no account for us. This view . . . is untrue; but in addition to being untrue, it has the effect of robbing philosophic contemplation of all that gives it value, since it fetters contemplation to Self. What it calls knowledge is not a union with the not-Self, but a set of prejudices, habits, and desires, making an impenetrable veil between us and the world beyond. The man who finds pleasure in such a theory of knowledge is like the man who never leaves the domestic circle for fear his word might not be law.

The true philosophic contemplation, on the contrary, finds its satisfaction in every enlargement of the not-Self, in everything that magnifies the objects contemplated, and thereby the subject contemplating. Everything, in contemplation, that is personal or private, everything that depends upon habit, self-interest, or desire, distorts the object, and hence impairs the union which the intellect seeks. By thus making a barrier between subject and object, such personal and private things become a prison to the intellect. The free intellect will see as God might see, without a *here* and *now*, without hopes and fears, without the trammels of customary beliefs and traditional prejudices, calmly, dispassionately, in the sole and exclusive desire of knowledge—knowledge as impersonal, as purely contemplative, as it is possible for man to attain. Hence also the free intellect will value more the abstract and universal knowledge into which the accidents of private history do not enter, than the knowledge brought by the senses, and dependent, as such knowledge must be, upon an exclusive and personal point of view and a body whose sense-organs distort as much as they reveal.

The mind which has become accustomed to the freedom and impartiality of philosophic contemplation will preserve something of the same freedom and impartiality in the world of action and emotion. It will view its purposes and desires as parts of the whole, with the absence of insistence that results from seeing them as infinitesimal fragments in a world of which all the rest is unaffected by any one man's deeds. The impartiality which, in contemplation, is the unalloyed desire for truth, is the very same quality of mind which, in action, is justice, and in emotion is that universal love which can be given to all, and not only to those who are judged useful or admirable. Thus contemplation enlarges not only the objects of our thoughts, but also the objects of our actions and our affections: it makes us citizens of the universe, not only of one walled city at war with all the rest. In this citizenship of the universe consists man's true freedom, and his liberation from the thraldom of narrow hopes and fears.

Thus, to sum up our discussion of the value of philosophy; Philosophy is to be studied, not for the sake of any definite answers to its questions, since no definite answers can, as a rule, be known to be true, but rather for the sake of the questions themselves; because these questions enlarge our conception of what is possible, enrich our intellectual imagination and diminish the dogmatic assurance which closes the mind against speculation; but above all because, through the greatness of the universe which philosophy contemplates, the mind also is rendered great, and becomes capable of that union with the universe which constitutes its highest good.

■ **Questions for Discussion**

1. The main value of the study of philosophy, according to Russell, is that it has an ennobling effect on our mind. What does Russell mean by that?

2. How would you put this to a friend wondering whether to take philosophy?

3. What would you say the main value of philosophy has been for you?

NOTE

1. An anonymous publication, based on Norman Malcom's notes of Wittgenstein's lectures.

CHAPTER ELEVEN

■ The Continental Tradition

I N THE PRECEDING CHAPTER, we began to examine the final chapters of the story that began with Socrates and his predecessors. The work of Bertrand Russell and Ludwig Wittgenstein marks a significant shift in the Anglo-American philosophical tradition that, in some ways, dates to those early British empiricists John Locke and David Hume. The other major branch of twentieth-century philosophical investigation, however, is perhaps best exemplified by the existentialists on the Continent. Interestingly, Wittgenstein plays a prime role in both streams. As we concluded the previous chapter with an examination of Wittgenstein's contributions to the linguistic philosophy tradition, so we use his contributions to linguistic philosophy's major rival as a launching point for the discussion of existentialism.

WITTGENSTEIN, EXISTENTIALISM, AND THE HISTORY OF PHILOSOPHY

Another important contemporary philosophical movement is **existentialism**. It arose in continental Europe and came into its own after World War II. The events of that terrible period of history made people feel that life was **absurd**, that there was no grand design to it, and that it was really meaningless. The old philosophic questions that were posed with such passion by Socrates—"What should we do?" "What can we believe?"—became burning issues once again. In their search for answers to these questions, some turned to religion, others to a new kind of humanism, and some, indeed, to nihilism.

This feeling of the absurd follows from the realization, they have suggested, that we inhabit a world devoid of human values, a world in which things simply are without having a sufficient reason for being as they are, a world we futilely try to make sense of. As remarkable as it may seem, Wittgenstein seems to have shared these feelings and views as well. "The sense of the world," he says in the *Tractatus*, "must lie outside the world." For in the world, he says, "everything is as it is, and everything happens as it does happen: in it no value exists—and if it did, it would have no value." For "if there is any value that does have value, it must lie outside the whole sphere of what happens and is the case. For all that happens, and is the case, is accidental. What makes it nonaccidental cannot lie within the world, since if it did, it would itself be accidental. It must lie outside the world." This being so—the world being accidental, arbitrary, and beyond good and evil—"it is impossible," he concludes, "for there to be propositions of ethics" (6.41–6.42).

Wittgenstein's handling of this concept of the absurd is of course different from that of his predecessors but not unrecognizably so. Although he does not speak of the world as being a "shadow" of itself (as Plato does), as a product of our "imagination" (as Spinoza does), or as a product of the "categories" (as Kant does), what he says about our conceptual system (or "net") that we use to make sense of it seems to amount to much the same thing. For like Plato, Spinoza, and Kant, he seems to have believed that the sort of world we are able to experience depends very much on the conceptual system we use in organizing it for ourselves and that here, too, we are under a kind of human and universal deception. In stressing this aspect of our human condition (an aspect that in its modern version is the all-embracing theme of existentialism), Wittgenstein shows himself to be part of this great philosophical or metaphysical tradition. It is a tradition to which he himself added a memorable chapter—his account in the *Philosophical Investigations* of the games people play. Like Plato's **parable of the cave** as described in the *Republic* and Spinoza's account in the *Ethics* regarding the common man's worship of God, this chapter is a study in the absurd.

In my view, the leading and dominant idea around which all philosophy turns is this insight regarding the existence of two worlds—the world of reality and the world of appearance, the world as it is in itself and the world as it appears to us. Although only the passages from Plato seem to deal directly with this question, we can see that in dealing with our conceptual frameworks in the way Wittgenstein and the other philosophers do, they, too, are very much involved in the same endeavor.

I do not wish to imply here that all the great philosophers are unanimous on this question. They are not. But what divides them are not goals, but means. In their goals, they are remarkably at one. They do not, however, always agree as to what constitutes the best methods for arriving at these goals. Another way of putting this would be to say that they agree in their conclusions but not in the proofs that have been provided for them. And on these proofs philosophers are still at work.

It is, I think, the same with both existentialism and linguistic philosophy. In their basic endeavor—which is to open people's eyes to their true condition—they are in agreement, as a quick comparison of the views expressed on these matters by representatives of these two movements reveals.

Douglas Steere, in introducing his translation of Søren Kierkegaard's *Purity of Heart*, sums up Kierkegaard's purpose and achievement in these words: "Kierkegaard conceived it his function as a writer to strip men of their disguises, to compel them to see evasions for what they are, to label blind alleys, to cut off men's retreats, . . . to isolate men from the crowd, to enforce self-communication, and to bring them solitary and alone before the Eternal Here he left them. For here that in man which makes him a responsible individual must itself act or it must take flight. No other can make this decision. Only when man is alone can he face the Eternal."

As for Wittgenstein, the proper task of philosophy, he says in Book I of the *Philosophical Investigations*, is to uncover "one or another piece of plain nonsense and of bumps that the understanding has got by running its head against the limits of language" (p. 119); its aim is "to teach you to pass from a piece of disguised non-sense to something that is patent nonsense" (p. 464); it is in this way that we can destroy the "houses of cards" and clear up "the grounds of language on which they stand" (p. 113). The result will be that our problems will "*completely* disappear" (p. 113)—for if the aim has been reached, "everything lies open to view and there is nothing to explain" (p. 126).

The differences between the two schools are no less illuminating. They differ in that one seems to be concerned with what might be called humanity's psychological and moral condition, while the other is concerned with humanity's intellectual and scientific condition. These emphases are revealed in the vocabularies of the two approaches. Thus, one speaks of absurdity, the other of nonsense; one speaks of despair, the other of confusion; one speaks of anguish, the other of puzzlement; one speaks of roles we play, the other of games we play; one speaks of shipwreck, the other of not knowing one's way about; and so on. Absurdity, despair, anguish, roles, and shipwreck are expressive of our psychological and moral states; their intellectual correlatives are nonsense, confusion, puzzlement, games, and so on. Even these different vocabularies, therefore, cannot hide the family resemblance of the two schools. But if their vocabularies disclose commonality, they also disclose a decisive separation. What this separation is—and what it implies—is what I now wish to consider.

The Philosophic Task, Again

Although existentialism and linguistic philosophy are alike in being involved in this great program—alike, that is, in exploring the "troubles in our thoughts" caused by our attempts to make sense of a senseless world—in interpreting these troubles in the psychological and human terms in which it does, existentialism certainly seems more involved in the exploration than linguistic philosophy, whose tendency is to become more and more scientific and concomitantly more and more trivial.

It is both strange and ironic that this should seem so, for in a sense it could be said that of the two, existentialism is a good deal closer to science and its methods and more sciencelike than linguistic philosophy. On the other hand, in dealing with these problems in the way it does, it may be said that it has failed to share in certain fruits, the labors of which have been carried on in philosophy for some 200 or 300 years now. To see this we have to consider some of the facets of the history of this struggle.

As we saw in the preceding chapter, a good portion of the modern history of philosophy can be read as a search to see just what the mind can, in this sense, come to terms with and accept. Wittgenstein's work belongs to this history. He came to see that since the life of the mind is simply language, its dissatisfactions are to be stilled not by confronting it with causes or reasons but rather, more simply, by clarifying and reordering its language. This is especially the case, he came to see, where philosophical issues are in question. The philosophic "What is . . . ?" does not ask for a cause or for a reason but is simply an expression of puzzlement and unclarity. It is to be relieved therefore not by trying to find a cause or a reason but by clarifying its terms, whose confusion initially gave rise to our perplexity.

It is in this sense that his own thinking on these matters may be regarded as lying in the same line of development as that of his predecessors in the history of philosophy. For in speaking as it often does of the openness of the future, of our existence in a world in which things simply are without a sufficient reason for being as they are, of our futile attempts to make sense of an essentially senseless world, and so on, existentialism is not thereby dealing with unrelated matters. However, if the price existentialism has had to pay for addressing the issues in the way it does is to appear less foundational than its competitor, it has had the satisfaction of knowing that its message has been both a comfort and a challenge to our times.

EXISTENTIALISM

If there is one concept that is a common property of existentialists, it is probably the concept of the absurd. This is not to say that all existentialists make use of this concept or that those who do so mean the same thing by it. Still, if the label existentialist has any meaning at all and if existentialists may be said to share anything in common, it is prob-

---

The relevance of philosophy for an understanding of current issues and events is, however, indirect rather than direct. Questions such as "Should marijuana be legalized?" or "Should abortion be freely available to any woman upon request?" are important and timely questions, but they are not philosophical questions. Philosophy cannot provide a direct answer to such questions, nor should it attempt to do so. What philosophy can and should do, however, is to clarify the kind of reasoning that is involved in our thinking about ethical issues with the hope of raising the discussion of these issues to a higher level of rationality than would otherwise be likely to occur. To represent philosophy as being directly concerned with such timely student concerns as abortion, drugs, homosexuality, the draft, and the like is, in my opinion, to trivialize philosophy and to defraud the students toward whom such pseudo philosophy is directed. Students have a right to expect that the insights gained from a serious study of philosophy will be relevant to the problems of tomorrow as well as to those of today.

—**William H. Halverson, *A Concise Introduction to Philosophy***

ably the desire to throw some light on our feeling of the absurd, whether they call it that or not.

Søren Kierkegaard

Søren Kierkegaard, Danish theologian and philosopher, is considered the father of existentialism. He was born in 1813 and died at a young 42. In his few short years he accomplished an enormous amount of work, writing many deep and profound literary, theological, philosophical, psychological, devotional, and polemical works, some of them published anonymously. These works—which bore such dramatic and striking titles as *Either/Or, Fear and Trembling, The Concluding Unscientific Postscript,* and *The Sickness unto Death*—made little impression on his fellow Danes and almost none at all on those outside his homeland. However, at the beginning of the twentieth century, his works were translated into German, French, English, and other languages and began to make an enormous impact on readers. This strange thinker, who had lived and worked much of his life as a near recluse and who generally was regarded by his contemporaries as a crank, had at last found his audience. Indeed, even though he has been dead for over a century, he feels and sounds like a contemporary of ours.

Søren Kierkegaard (1813–1855)

Kierkegaard distinguished three types of lives that are open to us: the aesthetic, the ethical, and the religious. The aesthetic is the life most of us lead most of the time. It is a hedonistic kind of life in which we seek sensual pleasure and an escape from boredom. When we fail to achieve fulfillment and life becomes more and more meaningless, we become frantic and desperate. In our despair we come to confront for the first time in our lives the question of what we should do. This question helps us approach a second stage of life—the ethical. Unlike the hedonistic stage, the ethical phase is marked by decision and commitment. Here, through choice, genuine individuality is attained. But it is still short of fulfillment. Rest, we come to discover, can finally be found only in the religious stage, where, defying all reason, we make a "leap of faith" and pledge our lives and selves to God—our only salvation.

Others who experienced the same impasse or impasses that Kierkegaard did and that he described with such profound insight and passion found themselves unable to accept Kierkegaard's solution. Psychologically unable to believe that God exists—accepting, rather, Nietzsche's pronouncement that, for all we know, He is dead—they tried to find a solution to the human predicament in humans themselves.

In several of his philosophical works, Kierkegaard argued for a type of skepticism, contending men are incapable of gaining any knowledge by their own means. If man is completely ignorant, then, Kierkegaard argued, he can overcome his sad state only by first recognizing it for what it is, and then by blindly and irrationally seeking for a solution by faith. He must believe that there can be direct contact between God and himself in his own life, though he cannot tell whether it is either possible or probable.

Johannes Climacus summed up these skeptical views in the Postscript by proclaiming that a logical system of knowledge is possible but an existential one is not. A logical system consists of a body of necessary truths derived logically from an initial set of concepts or definitions. An existential system, on the other hand, would be a body of necessary truths about the changing world of experience. Such a system cannot be discovered or constructed because we cannot know any necessary truths about factual or historical events.

—Avrum Stroll and Richard H. Popkin, *Introduction to Philosophy*

Life is meaningless only if one fails to make it meaningful, they argued. And only we can make it meaningful. There is no God in the universe and no absolute, genuine purpose to life. We are, indeed, alone—and absolutely free to do what we like. It is up to us to fill this void. It is up to us to find ourselves. Human beings have no special nature or essence, and there is no special plan or goal to life. We have only being or existence, and "being precedes essence" rather than the other way around, as philosophy had believed until now. We are not here to fulfill some preordained human essence but must, if anything, create one from scratch. We must make our selves, choose our own essences— with no guide whatsoever to help us. There are simply no rules for doing it and no one else to do it for us. We have been thrust into this world, and it is up to us to make of it what we can. Such freedom is indeed "dreadful," and the "anguish" we feel when we come to recognize our condition is real. But there is no "exit" from all this.

The person who popularized these terms—"dreadful freedom," "anguish," "no exit"—was Jean-Paul Sartre, whose name is almost synonymous with existentialism. But before we go on to consider Sartre's ideas, we must look briefly at a nineteenth-century thinker who is considered one of the founders and predecessors of existentialism, Friedrich Nietzsche.

Friedrich Nietzsche

Nietzsche was born in 1844 and died at the age of 55, his last 11 years spent in complete insanity. He started his career as a brilliant classical scholar at the University of Basel in Switzerland at the age of 24. He had not yet completed his doctor's degree at Leipzig, but the university, on the strength of his published writings and his teacher's enthusiastic recommendation, appointed him a university professor. The University of Leipzig then conferred his doctorate without examination.

His years at Basel and his life were not fated to be happy ones. His fascination with Wagner and Wagner's music and the highly controversial Wagnerian tone of his first major publication, *The Birth of Tragedy from the Spirit of Music*, alienated many. Ill health finally compelled him to resign his professorship. He was only 34. For the next decade he wandered about Europe in search for some place where his health might be restored. Writing furiously all the time, he published book after book during these years. The books were marked by great brilliance of style and biting sarcasm, bearing such titles as *The Dawn of Day, Joyful Wisdom, Thus Spake Zarathustra*, and *Beyond Good and Evil*. All expressed his revulsion toward contemporary—in his view decadent—European life and culture. In

Friedrich Wilhelm Nietzsche (1844–1900)

January 1889 he collapsed on a street in Turin, lapsing into insanity from which he never recovered.

Nietzsche's most famous remark is probably his announcement in *Thus Spake Zarathustra* (1883) that "God is dead." It is also his main message and, probably, the starting point of his entire philosophy of will and power. For if God is indeed dead, then we are accountable to no one but ourselves and there is no need to seek salvation somewhere beyond us. Nor is there any longer a need to subdue our nature, or dampen our spirits, or deny our will in hope of eternal rewards in another world. That idea is false and misguided, a product of the corrupting effect of centuries of Christianity with its life-denying ethic. Rather than subdue and deny our basic nature and impulses, we should revel in them, recognize that what in the past was called bad is really good and what was labeled good is really bad. Life is passion and the good life is passionate. "Man is something to be surpassed." To do so he must break the barriers and restraints of the past and affirm life's forces and energies, not wallow in pity and remorse, making life as small as possible. To continue to stifle our natural impulses and passions is to live the bankrupt and pitiful lives we see around us.

He felt that humankind's natural forces, held in check so long by Christian civilization, were bound to erupt and break loose. Nietzsche prophesied chillingly and accurately the devastation that would result (the world wars).

But if Nietzsche was correct about the deceptive calm of his age and the coming explosion, what are we to say about his account of humanity and its prospects? His remarks on this question are reminiscent of those of the ancient Greek philosopher Protagoras, whom we quoted in chapter 2: "Man is the measure of all things"—that is, human beings set the standards. But is it really the case that we set the standard, that we are lords over all creation and can, therefore, do what we wish? How can people be the

A remark of Haller's [the "hero" of *Steppenwolf*] gave me the key to this interpretation. He said to me once when we were talking of the so-called horrors of the Middle Ages: "These horrors were really nonexistent. A man of the Middle Ages would detest the whole mode of our present-day life as something far more horrible, far more barbarous. Every age, every culture, every custom and tradition has its own character, its own weakness and its own strength, its beauties and ugliness; accepts certain sufferings as matters of course, puts up patiently with certain evils. Human life is reduced to real suffering, to hell, only when two ages, two cultures and religions overlap. A man of the Classical Age who had to live in medieval times would suffocate miserably just as a savage does in the midst of our civilization. Now there are times when a whole generation is caught in this way between two ages, two modes of life, with the consequence that it loses all power to understand itself and has no standard, no security, no simple acquiescence. Naturally, every one does not feel this equally strongly. A nature such as Nietzsche's had to suffer our present ills more than a generation in advance. What he had to go through alone and misunderstood, thousands suffer today."

—Hermann Hesse, *Steppenwolf*

measure of all things when they are not the measure of themselves? Can we prevent ourselves from feeling pain and anguish? Can we say no to hunger and thirst? Are these not limitations? things that define us? things that set standards for us?

Despite these criticisms and limitations of Nietzsche's philosophy, what remains and what continues to have a powerful effect on so many thinkers is his profound advocacy that with God dead we now have only ourselves to rely on. In the early twentieth century this was a timely message. Many rose to its challenge, Jean-Paul Sartre among them.

Jean-Paul Sartre

Sartre was born in Paris in 1905. In the early 1930s he studied in Berlin, where he came under the influence of Edmund Husserl, an important and early German existentialist thinker. It was also in Berlin that Sartre wrote his novel *Nausea*, which to the very end of his career he considered his best work. It was in this book that he struck one of the major chords of his philosophy: that we are "trapped" in a world that is "contingent" and therefore without sense or purpose and that coming to recognize this fact fills us with nausea.

During World War II, Sartre was active in the French Resistance movement and was captured by the Germans. While in the prisoner-of-war camp, he read Martin Heidegger, another important early German existentialist and student of Husserl. This study led to Sartre's major philosophical opus, *Being and Nothingness* (1943). This was followed by numerous other works, both literary and philosophical, and eventually world acclaim. In 1964, Sartre was awarded the Nobel Prize in but, ever the rebel, refused to accept it.

Jean-Paul Sartre (1905–1980)

While in college he met a fellow student, Simone de Beauvoir, who was also to become a world-renowned playwright, novelist, and essayist. They carried on a lifelong and sometimes stormy relationship but never married. Sartre died in 1980 at the age of 74.

According to Sartre, it is our sad fate to find ourselves trapped in a world that makes no sense. Whether we like it or not, this fact is inescapable. Naturally, we try to make some sense of this senseless world, but without success. The world simply is as it is. There is no explanation that we can uncover for its existence or nature. Everything could just as well have been different—again, for no conceivable reason. And because there is no reason why the world should be one way rather than some other way, so similarly there seems to be no reason why we should live one sort of life rather than another, choose one course of action rather than another, or come to value one thing rather than another. Experiencing all this—coming to see the way we and the world really are—makes us dizzy and fills us with nausea.

What shall we do? We are aware that we are free to do what we like—and anything we like. The world being arbitrary and senseless, it doesn't matter what we do, for what difference could it make? Rather than finding this prospect pleasing, we find it "dreadful." We

---

Although we now know that deduction does not give us knowledge about the world, the philosophy of Descartes, with its quest for certainty, still influences philosophical thought, especially on the continent of Europe. The existentialists, whose theories can best be studied in the works of Sartre, are, like Descartes, dissatisfied with the uncertainty of empirical knowledge but, unlike Descartes, they realize that any search for certainty is a vain one. The world is as we find it, but there is no necessity in its being as it is; it might have been different. The laws of nature are not rules of logic, and we cannot deduce what the world is like from self-evident truths.

Such an inescapable conclusion causes the existentialist to look upon human life as absurd—absurd because it is devoid of logical sense. He longs to discover some necessity in things and events, and when he finds that he cannot, because the world is not a deductive system, he feels the situation to be intolerable. It is the realization that induction does not lead to necessary truths that produces the "nausea" which plays such an important part in the philosophy of Sartre and the existentialists.

—Frederick Vivian, *Thinking Philosophically*

are free to choose but can find no way to decide what to choose, there being no guides, signposts, or certainties in this absurd world into which we have been thrust. What to do then? Well, choose we must, for not to do so is to remain forever in the "nausea of existence." We must take the risk and choose and act, knowing that the choices may prove disastrous, but no other path exists to an "authentic" life and existence. In a world where there is no God, nothing more can be done than to make one's own decisions and heroically live by them. Any other life is no life at all.

As appealing as such exhortations are, particularly to humanists, they have not found favor with everyone. Linguistic philosophers, especially, have found much in this kind of philosophy to criticize. Existentialists, they have said, have in essence abandoned philosophy for literature. For philosophy has always been marked by careful, logical analysis and the piecemeal examination of problems and issues, but what we find in the pages of such writers as Sartre is emotion, exhortation, passion, pessimism, and even traces of nihilism.

In the excerpt that follows this chapter, taken from one of Sartre's famous pieces of writing, we shall see how Sartre himself defends existentialism against some of these typical reproaches. But, of course, it is not the case that existentialist writings are totally devoid of the sort of "research" or investigations more readily recognizable as philosophical. Certainly there is no lack of careful and serious analysis of issues in Sartre's works or in the writings of many of the other existentialist thinkers. So what is it that really bothers other philosophers—especially linguistic or analytic philosophers—about existentialists? Is it that, in fact, they are so very much alike—as startling as this may seem at first? Is it possible that Sartre and other thinkers and writers like him are really in a way linguistic analysts and that Wittgenstein, the linguistic analyst par excellence, is a kind of existentialist? I would like to suggest that there is a good deal of truth to this idea.

SUMMARY

1. Two of existentialism's main founders or predecessors—Søren Kierkegaard and Friedrich Nietzsche—were thinkers who lived in the nineteenth century. They were most concerned with the question of what people should do and what they should believe, seeing that the world is irrational and meaningless. Kierkegaard advocated that the solution to our problems lay in blind faith and trust in God; Nietzsche, believing that "God is dead," argued that the solution to our predicament must come from ourselves, in living life as fully and passionately as possible.

2. The twentieth-century philosopher whose name has become synonymous with existentialism is Jean-Paul Sartre. At the foundation of his thinking lies the belief that there is no grand design to the world and no meaning to it. It has no special plan or destiny, and the same is true of humanity. Prior philosophers were mistaken in thinking that essence precedes existence; the truth is that existence precedes essence. But rather

than allowing this fact to defeat us, we should make the most of what there is, trusting only in ourselves.

3. Although these two twentieth-century philosophical movements may seem worlds apart, on closer examination they are seen to have much in common: both share the belief in the arbitrariness of what exists—things simply are the way they are; they could easily have been otherwise—and both conclude that the world is devoid of value. In short, both believe the world is absurd and that life is meaningless (i.e., there is nothing necessary about what exists, nor does it have any value in itself). They differ, however, in what they conceive their primary jobs as philosophers to be: analytical/linguistic philosophers believe it is to describe, as far as it is possible to do so, the world's logical structure and properties; existentialists believe that the philosopher's task is to explore our resultant modern plight.

KEY TERMS

absurd   parable of the cave
existentialism

REVIEW QUESTIONS

1. What great task has philosophy, throughout its history, been absorbed with? To what extent were the existentialists occupied with this task as well?

2. How would you define existentialism and its main concerns?

3. How do the concerns of existentialism vary from the concerns of linguistic philosophy?

4. Which approach—existentialism or linguistic philosophy—do you find more satisfying? Why?

■ Reading

Existentialism and Humanism

JEAN-PAUL SARTRE

Excerpted from Jean-Paul Sartre, *Existentialism and Humanism*, translated by Philip Mairet (London: Methuen, 1948).

My purpose here is to offer a defense of existentialism against several reproaches that have been laid against it. First, it has been reproached as an invitation to people to dwell in quietism of despair. For if every way to a solution is barred, one would have to regard any action in this world as entirely ineffective, and one would arrive finally at a contemplative philosophy. Moreover, since contemplation is a luxury, this would be only another bourgeois philosophy. This is, especially, the reproach made by the Communists.

From another quarter we are reproached for having underlined all that is ignominious in the human situation, for depicting what is mean, sordid or base to the neglect of certain things that possess charm and beauty and belong to the brighter side of human nature: for example, according to the Catholic critic, Mlle. Mercier, we forget how an infant smiles. Both from this side and from the other we are also reproached for leaving out of account the solidarity of mankind and considering man in isolation. And this, say the Communists, is because we base our doctrine upon pure subjectivity—upon the Cartesian "I think": which is the moment in which solitary man attains to himself; a position from which it is impossible to regain solidarity with other men who exist outside of the self. The *ego* cannot reach them through the *cogito*.

From the Christian side, we are reproached as people who deny the reality and seriousness of human affairs. For since we ignore the commandments of God and all values prescribed as eternal nothing remains but what is strictly voluntary. Everyone can do what he likes, and will be incapable, from such a point of view, of condemning either the point of view or the action of anyone else.

It is to these various reproaches that I shall endeavor to reply today; that is why I have entitled this brief exposition "Existentialism and Humanism." Many may be surprised at the mention of humanism in this connection, but we shall try to see in what sense we understand it. In any case, we can begin by saying that existentialism, in our sense of the word, is a doctrine that does render human life possible; a doctrine, also, which affirms that every truth and every action imply both an environment and a human subjectivity. The essential charge laid against us is, of course, that of overemphasis upon the evil side of human life. I have lately been told of a lady who, whenever she lets slip a vulgar expression in a moment of nervousness, excuses herself by exclaiming, "I believe I am becoming an existentialist." So it appears that ugliness is being identified with existentialism. That is why some people say we are "naturalistic," and if we are, it is strange to see how much we scandalize and horrify them, for no one seems to be much frightened or humiliated nowadays by what is properly called naturalism. Those who can quite well keep down a novel by Zola such as *La Terre* are sickened as soon as they read an existentialist novel. Those who appeal to the wisdom of the people—which is a sad wisdom—find ours sadder still. And yet, what could be more disillusioned than such sayings as "Charity begins at home" or "Promote a rogue and he'll sue you for damage, knock him down and he'll do you homage"? We all know how many common sayings can be quoted to this effect, and they all mean much the same—that you must not oppose the powers-that-be; that you must not fight against superior force; must not meddle in matters that are above your station. Or that any action not in accordance with some tradition is mere romanticism; or that any undertaking which has not the support of proven experience is foredoomed to frustration; and that since experience has shown men to be invariably inclined to evil, there must be firm rules to restrain them, otherwise we shall have anarchy. It is, however, the people who are forever mouthing these dismal proverbs and, whenever they are told of some more or less repulsive action, say "How like human nature!"—it is these very people, always harping upon realism, who complain that existentialism is too gloomy a view of things. Indeed their excessive protests make me suspect that what is annoying them is not so much our pessimism, but, much more likely, our optimism. For at bottom, what is alarming in the doctrine that I am about to try to explain to you is—is it not?—that it confronts man with a possibility of choice. To verify this, let us review the whole question upon the strictly philosophic level. What, then, is this that we call existentialism?

Most of those who are making use of this word would be highly confused if required to explain its meaning. For since it has become fashionable, people cheerfully declare that this musician or that painter is "existentialist." A columnist in *Clartés* signs himself "The Existentialist," and, indeed, the word is now so loosely applied to so many things that it no longer means anything at all. It would appear that, for the lack of any novel doctrine such as that of surrealism, all those who are eager to join in the latest scandal or movement now seize upon this philosophy in which, however, they can find nothing to their purpose. For in truth this is of all teachings the least scandalous and the most austere: it is intended strictly for technicians and philosophers. All the same, it can easily be defined.

The question is only complicated because there are two kinds of existentialists. There are, on the one hand, the Christians, amongst whom I shall name Raspers and Gabriel Marcel, both professed Catholics; and on the other the existential atheists, amongst whom we must place Heidegger as well as the French existentialists and myself. What they have in common is simply the fact that they believe that *existence* comes before *essence*—or, if you will, that we must begin from the subjective. What exactly do we mean by that?

If one considers an article of manufacture—as, for example, a book or a paper-knife [letter opener]—one sees that it has been made by an artisan who had a conception of it; and he has paid attention, equally, to the conception of a paper-knife and to the preexistent technique of production which is a part of that conception and is, at bottom, a formula. Thus the paper-knife is at the same time an article producible in a certain manner and one which, on the other hand, serves a definite purpose, for one cannot suppose that a man would produce a paper-knife without knowing what it was for. Let us say, then, of the paper-knife that its essence—that is to say the sum of the formulae and the qualities which made its production and its definition possible—precedes its existence. The presence of such-and-such a paper-knife or book is thus determined before my eyes. Here, then, we are viewing the world from a technical standpoint, and we can say that production precedes existence.

When we think of God as the creator, we are thinking of him, most of the time, as a supernal artisan. Whatever doctrine we may be considering, whether it be a doctrine like that of Descartes, or of Leibnitz himself, we always imply that the will follows, more or less, from the understanding or at least accompanies it, so that when God creates he knows precisely what he is creating. Thus, the conception of man in the mind of God is comparable to that of the paper-knife in the mind of the artisan: God makes man according to a procedure and a conception, exactly as the artisan manufactures a paper-knife, following a definition and a formula. Thus each individual man is the realization of a certain conception which dwells in the divine understanding. In the philosophic atheism of the eighteenth century, the notion of God is suppressed, but not, for all that, the idea that essence is prior to existence; something of that idea we still find everywhere, in Diderot, in Voltaire and even in Kant. Man possesses a human nature; that "human nature," which is the conception of human being, is found in every man; which means that each man is a particular example of a universal conception, the conception of Man. In Kant, this universality goes so far that the wild man of the woods, man in the state of nature and the bourgeois are all contained in the same definition and have the same fundamental qualities. Here again, the essence of man precedes that historic existence which we confront in experience.

Atheistic existentialism, of which I am a representative, declares with greater consistency that if God does not exist there is at least one being whose existence comes before its essence, a being which exists before it can be defined by any conception of it. That being is man or, as Heidegger has it, the human reality. What do we mean by saying that existence precedes essence? We mean that man first of all exists, encounters himself, surges up in the world—and defines himself afterwards. If man as the existentialist sees him is not definable, it is because to begin with he is nothing. He will not be anything until later, and then he will be what he makes of himself. Thus, there is no human nature, because there is no God to have a conception of it. Man simply is. Not that he is simply what he conceives himself to be, but he is what he wills, and as he conceives himself after already existing—as he wills to be after that leap towards existence. Man is nothing else but that which he makes of himself. That is the first principle of existentialism. And this is what people call its "subjectivity," using the word as a reproach against us. But what do we mean to say by this, but that man is of a greater dignity than a stone or a table? For we mean to say that man primarily exists—that man is, before all else, something which propels itself towards a future and is aware that it is doing so. Man is, indeed, a project which possesses a subjective life, instead of being a kind of moss, or a fungus or a cauliflower. Before that projection of the self nothing exists; not even in the heaven of intelligence: man will only attain existence when he is what he purposes to be. Not, however what he may wish to be. For what we usually understand by wishing or willing is a conscious decision taken—much more often than not—after we have made ourselves what we are. I may wish to join a party, to write a book or to marry—but in such a case what is usually called my will is probably a manifestation of a prior and more spontaneous decision. If, however, it is true that existence is prior to essence, man is responsible for what he is. Thus, the first effect of existentialism is that it puts every man in possession of himself as he is, and places the entire responsibility for his existence squarely upon his own shoulders. And, when we say that man is responsible for himself, we do not mean that he is responsible only for his own individuality, but that he is responsible for all men. The word "subjectivism" is to be understood in two senses, and our adversaries play upon only one of them. Subjectivism means, on the one hand, the freedom of the individual subject and, on the other, that man cannot pass beyond human subjectivity. It is the latter which is the deeper meaning of existentialism. When we say that man chooses himself, we do mean that every one of us must choose himself; but by that we also mean that in choosing for himself he chooses for all men. For in effect, of all the actions a man may take in order to create himself as he wills to be, there is not one which is not creative, at the same time, of an image of man such as he believes he ought to be. To choose between this or that is at the same time to affirm the value of that which is chosen; for we are unable ever to choose the worse. What we choose is always the better; and nothing can be better for us unless it is better for all. If, moreover, existence precedes essence and we will to exist at the same time as we fashion our image, that image is valid for all and for the entire epoch in which we find ourselves. Our responsibility is thus much greater than we had supposed, for it concerns mankind as a whole. If I am a worker, for instance, I may choose to join a Christian rather than a Communist trade union. And if, by that membership, I choose to signify that resignation is, after all, the attitude that best becomes a man, that man's kingdom is not upon this earth, I do not commit myself alone to that view. Resignation is my will for everyone, and my action is, in consequence, a commitment on behalf of all mankind. Or if, to take a more personal case, I decide to marry and to have children, even though this decision proceeds simply from my situation, from my passion or my desire, I am thereby committing not only myself, but humanity as a whole, to the practice of monogamy. I am thus responsible for myself and for all men, and I am creating a certain image of man as I would have him to be. In fashioning myself I fashion man.

This may enable us to understand what is meant by such terms—perhaps a little grandiloquent—as anguish, abandonment and despair. As you will soon see, it is very simple. First, what do we mean by anguish? The existentialist frankly states that man is in anguish. His meaning is as follows—When a man commits himself to anything, fully realising that he is not only choosing what he will be, but is thereby at the same time a legislator deciding for the whole of mankind—in such a moment a man cannot escape from the sense of complete and profound responsibility. There are many, indeed, who show no such anxiety. But we affirm that they are merely disguising their anguish or are in flight from it. Certainly, many people think that in what they are doing they commit no one but themselves to anything: and if you ask them, "What would happen if everyone did so?" they shrug their shoulders and reply, "Everyone does not do so." But in truth, one ought always to ask oneself what would happen if everyone did as one is doing; nor can one escape from that disturbing thought except by a kind of self-deception. The man who lies in self-excuse, by saying "Everyone will not do it" must be ill at ease in his conscience, for the act of lying implies the universal value which it denies. By its very disguise his anguish reveals itself. This is the anguish that Kierkegaard called "the anguish of Abraham." You know the story: An angel commanded Abraham to sacrifice his son: and obedience was obligatory, if it really was an angel who had appeared and said, "Thou, Abraham, shalt sacrifice thy son." But anyone in such a case would wonder, first, whether it was indeed an angel and secondly, whether I am really Abraham. Where are the proofs? A certain mad woman who suffered from hallucinations said that people were telephoning to her, and giving her orders. The doctor asked, "But who is it that speaks to you?" She replied: "He says it is God." And what, indeed, could prove to her that it was God? If an angel appears to me, what is the proof that it is an angel; or, if I hear voices, who can prove that they proceed from heaven and not from hell, or from my own subconsciousness or some pathological condition? Who can prove that they are really addressed to me?

Who, then, can prove that I am the proper person to impose, by my own choice, my conception of man upon mankind? I shall never find any proof whatever; there will be no sign to convince me of it. If a voice speaks to me, it is still I myself who must decide whether the voice is or is not that of an angel. If I regard a certain course of action as good, it is only I who choose to say that it is good and not bad. There is nothing to show that I am Abraham: nevertheless I also am obliged at every instant to perform actions which are examples. Everything happens to every man as though the whole human race had its eyes fixed upon what he is doing and regulated its conduct accordingly. So every man ought to say, "Am I really a man who has the right to act in such a manner that humanity regulates itself by what I do?" If a man does not say that, he is dissembling his anguish. Clearly, the anguish with which we are concerned here is not one that could lead to quietism or inaction. It is anguish pure and simple, of the kind well known to all those who have borne responsibilities. When, for instance, a military leader takes upon himself the responsibility for an attack and sends a number of men to their death, he chooses to do it and at bottom he alone chooses. No doubt he acts under a higher command, but its orders, which are more general, require interpretation by him and upon that interpretation depends the life of ten, fourteen or twenty men. In making the decision, he cannot but feel a certain anguish. All leaders know that anguish. It does not prevent their acting, on the contrary it is the very condition of their action, for the action presupposes that there is a plurality of possibilities, and in choosing one of these, they realize that it has value only because it is chosen. Now it is anguish of that kind which existentialism describes, and moreover, as we shall see, makes explicit through direct responsibility towards other men who are concerned. Far from being a screen which could separate us from action, it is a condition of action itself.

And when we speak of "abandonment"—a favorite word of Heidegger—we only mean to say that God does not exist, and that it is necessary to draw the consequences of his absence right to the end. The existentialist is strongly opposed to a certain type of secular moralism which seeks to suppress God at the least possible expense Towards 1880, when the French professors endeavored to formulate a secular morality, they said something like this: God is a useless and costly hypothesis, so we will do without it. However, if we are to have morality, a society and a law-abiding world, it is essential that certain values should be taken seriously; they must have an *a priori* existence ascribed to them. It must be considered obligatory *a priori* to be honest, not to lie, not to beat one's wife, to bring up children and so forth; so we are going to do a little work on this subject, which will enable us to show that these values exist all the same, inscribed in an intelligible heaven although, of course, there is no God. In other words—and this is, I believe, the purport of all that we in France call radicalism—nothing will be changed if God does not exist; we shall rediscover the same norms of honesty, progress and humanity, and we shall have disposed of God as an out-of-date hypothesis which will die away quietly of itself. The existentialist, on the contrary, finds it extremely embarrassing that God does not exist, for there disappears with Him all possibility of finding values in an intelligible heaven. There can no longer be any good *a priori,* since there is no infinite and perfect consciousness to think it. It is nowhere written that "the good" exists, that one must be honest or must not lie, since we are now upon the plane where there are only men. Dostoevsky once wrote "If God did not exist, everything would be permitted"; and that, for existentialism, is the starting point. Everything is indeed permitted if God does not exist, and man is in consequence forlorn, for he cannot find anything to depend upon either within or outside himself. He discovers forthwith, that he is without excuse. For if indeed existence precedes essence, one will never be able to explain one's action by reference to a given and specific human nature; in other words, there is no determinism—man is free, man is freedom. Nor, on the other hand, if God does not exist, are we provided with any values or commands that could legitimize our behavior. Thus we have neither behind us, nor before us in a luminous realm of values, any means of justification or excuse. We are left alone, without excuse. That is what I mean when I say that man is condemned to be free. Condemned, because he did not create himself, yet is nevertheless at liberty, and from the moment that he is thrown into this world he is responsible for everything he does. The existentialist does not believe in the power of passion. He will never regard a grand passion as a destructive torrent upon which a man is swept into certain actions as by fate, and which, therefore, is an excuse for them. He thinks that man is responsible for his passion. Neither will an existentialist think that a man can find help through some sign being vouchsafed upon earth for his orientation: for he thinks that the man himself interprets the sign as he chooses. He thinks that every man, without any support or help whatever, is condemned at every instant to invent man. As Ponge has written in a very fine article, "Man is the future of man." That is exactly true. Only, if one took this to mean that the future is laid up in Heaven, that God knows what it is, it would be false, for then it would no longer even be a future. If, however, it means that, whatever man may now appear to be, there is a future to be fashioned, a virgin future that awaits him—then it is a true saying. But in the present one is forsaken.

As an example by which you may the better understand this state of abandonment, I will refer to the case of a pupil of mine, who sought me out in the following circumstances. His father was quarreling with his mother and was also inclined to be a "collaborator" [collaborators were French people who willingly cooperated with the Germans who occupied their country during World War II]; his elder brother had been killed in the German offensive of 1940 and this young man, with a sentiment somewhat primitive but generous, burned to avenge him. His mother was living alone with him, deeply afflicted by the semitreason of his father and by the death of her eldest son, and her one consolation was in this young man. But he, at this moment, had the choice between going to England to join the Free French Forces or staying near his mother and helping her to live. He fully realized that this woman lived only for him and that his disappearance—or perhaps his death—would plunge her into despair. He also realized that, concretely and in fact, every action he performed on his mother's behalf would be sure of effect in the sense of aiding her to live, whereas anything he did in order to go and fight would be an ambiguous action which might vanish like water into sand and serve no purpose. For instance, to set out for England he would have to wait indefinitely in a Spanish camp on the way through Spain; or, on arriving in England or in Algiers he might be put into an office to fill up forms. Consequently, he found himself confronted by two very different modes of action; the one concrete, immediate, but directed towards only one individual; and the other an action addressed to an end infinitely greater, a national collectivity, but for that very reason ambiguous—and it might be frustrated on the way. At the same time, he was hesitating between two kinds of morality; on the one side the morality of sympathy, of personal devotion and, on the other side, a morality of wider scope but of more debatable validity. He had to choose between those two. What could help him to choose? Could the Christian doctrine? No. Christian doctrine says: Act with charity, love your neighbor, deny yourself for others, choose the way which is hardest, and so forth. But which is the harder road? To whom does one owe the more brotherly love, the patriot or the mother? Which is the more useful aim, the general one of fighting in and for the whole community, or the precise aim of helping one particular person to live? Who can give an answer to that *a priori?* No one. Nor is it given in any ethical scripture. The Kantian ethic says, Never regard another as a means, but always as an end. Very well; if I remain with my mother, I shall be regarding her as the end and not as a means: but by the same token I am in danger of treating as means those who are fighting on my behalf; and the converse is also true, that if I go to the aid of the combatants I shall be treating them as the end at the risk of treating my mother as a means.

If values are uncertain, if they are still too abstract to determine the particular, concrete case under consideration, nothing remains but to trust in our instincts. That is what this young man tried to do; and when I saw him he said, "In the end, it is feeling that counts; the direction in which it is really pushing me is the one I ought to choose. If I feel that I love my mother enough to sacrifice everything else for her—my will to be avenged, all my longings for action and adventure—then I stay with her. If, on the contrary, I feel that my love for her is not enough, I go." But how does one estimate the strength of a feeling? The value of his feeling for his mother was determined precisely by the fact that he was standing by her. I may say that I love a certain friend enough to sacrifice such or such a sum of money for him, but I cannot prove that unless I have done it. I may say, "I love my mother enough to remain with her," if actually I have remained with her. I can only estimate the strength of this affection if I have performed an action by which it is defined and ratified. But if I then appeal to this affection to justify my action, I find myself drawn into a vicious circle.

Moreover, as Gide has very well said, a sentiment which is play-acting and one which is vital are two things that are hardly distinguishable one from another. To decide that I love my mother by staying beside her, and to play a comedy the upshot of which is that I do so—these are nearly the same thing. In other words, feeling is formed by the deeds that one does; therefore I cannot consult it as a guide to action. And that is to say that I can neither seek within myself for an authentic impulse to action, nor can I expect, from some ethic, formulae that will enable me to act. You may say that the youth did, at least, go to a professor to ask for advice. But if you seek counsel—from a priest, for example—you have selected that priest; and at bottom you already knew, more or less, what he would advise. In other words, to choose an adviser is nevertheless to commit oneself by that choice. If you are a Christian, you will say, consult a priest; but there are collaborationists, priests who are resisters and priests who wait for the tide to turn: which will you choose? Had this young man chosen a priest of the resistance, or one of the collaboration, he would have decided beforehand the kind of advice he was to receive. Similarly, in coming to me, he knew what advice I should give him, and I had but one reply to make. You are free, therefore choose—that is to say, invent. No rule of general morality can show you what you ought to do: no signs are vouchsafed in this world. The Catholics will reply, "Oh, but they are!" Very well; still, it is I myself, in every case, who have to interpret the signs. Whilst I was imprisoned, I made the acquaintance of a somewhat remarkable man, a Jesuit, who had become a member of that order in the following manner. In his life he had suffered a succession of rather severe setbacks. His father had died when he was a child, leaving him in poverty, and he had been awarded a free scholarship in a religious institution, where he had been made continually to feel that he was accepted for charity's sake, and, in consequence, he had been denied several of those distinctions and honors which gratify children. Later, about the age of eighteen, he came to grief in a sentimental affair; and finally, at twenty-two—this was a trifle in itself, but it was the last drop that overflowed his cup—he failed in his military examination. This young man, then, could regard himself as a total failure: it was a sign—but a sign of what? He might have taken refuge in bitterness or despair. But he took it—very cleverly for him—as a sign that he was not intended for secular successes, and that only the attainments of religion, those of sanctity and of faith, were accessible to him. He interpreted his record as a message from God, and became a member of the Order. Who can doubt but that this decision as to the meaning of the sign was his, and his alone? One could have drawn quite different conclusions from such a series of reverses—as, for example, that he had better become a carpenter or a revolutionary. For the decipherment of the sign, however, he bears the entire responsibility. That is what "abandonment" implies, that we ourselves decide our being. And with this abandonment goes anguish.

As for "despair," the meaning of this expression is extremely simple. It merely means that we limit ourselves to a reliance upon that which is within our wills, or within the sum of the probabilities which render our action feasible. Whenever one wills anything, there are always these elements of probability. If I am counting upon a visit from a friend, who may be coming by train or by tram, I presuppose that the train will arrive at the appointed time, or that the tram will not be derailed. I remain in the realm of possibilities; but one does not rely upon any possibilities beyond those that are strictly concerned in one's action. Beyond the point at which the possibilities under consideration cease to affect my action, I ought to disinterest myself. For there is no God and no prevenient design, which can adapt the world and all its possibilities to my will. When Descartes said, "Conquer yourself rather than the world," what he meant was, at bottom, the same—that we should act without hope.

Marxists, to whom I have said this, have answered: 'Your action is limited, obviously, by your death; but you can rely upon the help of others. That is, you can count both upon what the others are doing to help you elsewhere, as in China and in Russia, and upon what they will do later, after your death, to take up your action and carry it forward to its final accomplishment which will be the revolution. Moreover you must rely upon this; not to do so is immoral." To this I rejoin, first, that I shall always count upon my comrades-in-arms in the struggle, in so far as they are committed, as I am, to a definite, common cause; and in the unity of a party or a group which I can more or less control—that is, in which I am enrolled as a militant and whose movements at every moment are known to me. In that respect, to rely upon the unity and the will of the party is exactly like my reckoning that the train will run on time or that the tram will not be derailed. But I cannot count upon men whom I do not know, I cannot base my confidence upon human goodness or upon man's interest in the good of society, seeing that man is free and that there is no human nature which I can take as foundational. I do not know whither the Russian revolution will lead. I can admire it and take it as an example in so far as it is evident, today, that the proletariat plays a part in Russia which it has attained in no other nation. But I cannot affirm that this will necessarily lead to the triumph of the proletariat: I must confine myself to what I can see. Nor can I be sure that comrades-in-arms will take up my work after my death and carry it to the maximum perfection, seeing that those men are free agents and will freely decide, to-morrow, what man is then to be. Tomorrow, after my death, some men may decide to establish Fascism, and the others may be so cowardly or so slack as to let them do so. If so, Fascism will then be the truth of man, and so much the worse for us. In reality, things will be such as men have decided they shall be. Does that mean that I should abandon myself to quietism? No. First I ought to commit myself and then act my com-mitment, according to the time-honored formula that "one need not hope in order to undertake one's work." Nor does this mean that I should not belong to a party, but only that I should be without illusion and that I should do what I can. For instance, if I ask myself "Will the social ideal as such, ever become a reality?" I cannot tell, I only know that whatever may be in my power to make it so, I shall do; beyond that, I can count upon nothing.

Quietism is the attitude of people who say, "let others do what I cannot do." The doctrine I am presenting before you is precisely the opposite of this, since it declares that there is no reality except in action. It goes further, indeed, and adds, "Man is noth-ing else but what he purposes, he exists only in so far as he realizes himself, he is there-fore nothing else but the sum of his actions, nothing else but what his life is." Hence we can well understand why some people are horrified by our teaching. For many have but one resource to sustain them in their misery, and that is to think, "Circumstances have been against me, I was worthy to be something much better than I have been. I admit I have never had a great love or a great friendship; but that is because I never met a man or a woman who were worthy of it; if I have not written any very good books, it is be-cause I had not the leisure to do so; or, if I have had no children to whom I could devote myself it is because I did not find the man I could have lived with. So there remains within me a wide range of abilities, inclinations and potentialities, unused but perfectly viable, which endow me with a worthiness that could never be inferred from the mere history of my actions." But in reality and for the existentialist, there is no love apart from the deeds of love; no potentiality of love other than that which is manifested in loving; there is no genius other than that which is expressed in works of art. The genius of Proust is the totality of the works of Proust; the genius of Racine is the series of his tragedies, outside of which there is nothing. Why should we attribute to Racine the ca-pacity to write yet another tragedy when that is precisely what he did not write? In life, a man commits himself, draws his own portrait and there is nothing but that portrait. No doubt this thought may seem comfortless to one who has not made a success of his life. On the other hand, it puts everyone in a position to understand that reality alone is reli-able; that dreams, expectations and hopes serve to define a man only as deceptive dreams, abortive hopes, expectations unfulfilled; that is to say, they define him negatively, not positively. Nevertheless, when one says, "You are nothing else but what you live," it does not imply that an artist is to be judged solely by his works of art, for a thousand other things contribute no less to his definition as a man. What we mean to say is that a man is no other than a series of undertakings, that he is the sum, the organization, the set of relations that constitute these undertakings.

In the light of all this, what people reproach us with is not, after all, our pessimism, but the sternness of our optimism. If people condemn our works of fiction, in which we describe characters that are base, weak, cowardly and sometimes even frankly evil, it is not only because those characters are base, weak, cowardly or evil. For suppose that, like Zola, we showed that the behavior of these characters was caused by their heredity, or by the action of their environment upon them, or by determining factors, psychic or organic. People would be reassured, they would say, "You see, that is what we are like, no one can do anything about it." But the existentialist, when he portrays a coward, shows him as responsible for his cowardice. He is not like that on account of a cowardly heart or lungs or cerebrum, he has not become like that through his physiological organism; he is like that because he has made himself into a coward by his actions. There is no such thing as a cowardly temperament. There are nervous temperaments; there is what is called impoverished blood, and there are also rich temperaments. But the man whose blood is poor is not a coward for all that, for what produces cowardice is the act of giving up or giving way; and a temperament is not an action. A coward is defined by the deed that he has done. What people feel obscurely, and with horror, is that the coward as we present him is guilty of being a coward. What people would prefer would be to be born either a coward or a hero. . . . If you are born cowards, you can be quite content, you can do nothing about it and you will be cowards all your lives whatever you do; and if you are born heroes you can again be quite content; you will be heroes all your lives, eating and drinking heroically. Whereas the existentialist says that the coward makes himself cowardly, the hero makes himself heroic; and that there is always a possibility for the coward to give up cowardice and for the hero to stop being a hero. What counts is the total commitment, and it is not by a particular case or particular action that you are committed altogether.

We have now, I think, dealt with a certain number of the reproaches against existentialism. You have seen that it cannot be regarded as a philosophy of quietism since it defines man by his action; nor as a pessimistic description of man, for no doctrine is more optimistic, the destiny of man is placed within himself. Nor is it an attempt to discourage man from action since it tells him that there is no hope except in his action, and that the one thing which permits him to have life is the deed. Upon this level therefore, what we are considering is an ethic of action and self-commitment. However, we are still reproached, upon these few data, for confining man within his individual subjectivity. There again people badly misunderstand us.

Our point of departure is, indeed, the subjectivity of the individual, and that for strictly philosophic reasons. It is not because we are bourgeois, but because we seek to base our teaching upon the truth, and not upon a collection of fine theories, full of hope but lacking real foundations. And at the point of departure there cannot be any other truth than this, *I think, therefore I am*, which is the absolute truth of consciousness as it attains to itself. Every theory which begins with man, outside of this moment of self-attainment, is a theory which thereby suppresses the truth, for outside of the Cartesian *cogito*, all objects are no more than probable, and any doctrine of probabilities which is not attached to a truth will crumble into nothing. In order to define the probable one must possess the true. Before there can be any truth whatever, then, there must be an absolute truth, and there is such a truth which is simple, easily attained and within the reach of everybody; it consists in one's immediate sense of one's self.

In the second place, this theory alone is compatible with the dignity of man, it is the only one which does not make man into an object. All kinds of materialism lead one to treat every man including oneself as an object—that is, as a set of predetermined reactions, in no way different from the patterns of qualities and phenomena which constitute a table, or a chair or a stone. Our aim is precisely to establish the human kingdom as a pattern of values in distinction from the material world. But the subjectivity which we thus postulate as the standard of truth is no narrowly individual subjectivism, for as we have demonstrated, it is not only one's own self that one discovers in the *cogito*, but those of others too. Contrary to the philosophy of Descartes, contrary to that of Kant, when we say "I think" we are attaining to ourselves in the presence of the other, and we are just as certain of the other as we are of ourselves. Thus the man who discovers himself directly in the *cogito* also discovers all the others, and discovers them as the condition of his own existence. He recognizes that he cannot be anything (in the sense in which one says one is spiritual, or that one is wicked or jealous) unless others recognize him as such. I cannot obtain any truth whatsoever about myself, except through the mediation of another. The other is indispensable to my existence, and equally so to any knowledge I can have of myself. Under these conditions, the intimate discovery of myself is at the same time the revelation of the other as a freedom which confronts mine, and which cannot think or will without doing so either for or against me. Thus, at once, we find ourselves in a world which is, let us say, that of "inter-subjectivity." It is in this world that man has to decide what he is and what others are.

Furthermore, although it is impossible to find in each and every man a universal essence that can be called human nature, there is nevertheless a human universality of *condition*. It is not by chance that the thinkers of today are so much more ready to speak of the condition than of the nature of man. By his condition they understand, with more or less clarity, all the *limitations* which *a priori* define man's fundamental situation in the universe. His historical situations are variable: man may be born a slave in a pagan society, or may be a feudal baron, or a proletarian. But what never vary are the necessities of being in the world, of having to labor and to die there. These limitations are neither subjective nor objective, or rather there is both a subjective and an objective aspect of them. Objective, because we meet with them everywhere and they are everywhere recognizable:

and subjective because they are *lived* and are nothing if man does not live them—if, that is to say, he does not freely determine himself and his existence in relation to them. And, diverse though man's purposes may be, at least none of them is wholly foreign to me, since every human purpose presents itself as an attempt either to surpass these limitations, or to widen them, or else to deny or to accommodate oneself to them. Consequently every purpose, however individual it may be, is of universal value. Every purpose, even that of a Chinese, an Indian or a Negro, can be understood by a European. To say it can be understood, means that the European of 1945 may be striving out of a certain situation towards the same limitations in the same way, and that he may reconceive in himself the purpose of the Chinese, of the Indian or the African. In every purpose there is universality, in this sense that every purpose is comprehensible to every man. Not that this or that purpose defines man for ever, but that it may be entertained again and again. There is always some way of understanding an idiot, a child, a primitive man or a foreigner if one has sufficient information. In this sense we may say that there is a human universality, but it is not something given; it is being perpetually made. I make this universality in choosing myself; I also make it by understanding the purpose of any other man, of whatever epoch. This absoluteness of the act of choice does not alter the relativity of each epoch.

What is at the very heart and center of existentialism, is the absolute character of the free commitment, by which every man realizes himself in realizing a type of humanity—a commitment always understandable, to no matter whom in no matter what epoch—and its bearing upon the relativity of the cultural pattern which may result from such absolute commitment. One must observe equally the relativity of Cartesianism and the absolute character of the Cartesian commitment. In this sense you may say, if you like, that every one of us makes the absolute by breathing, by eating, by sleeping or by behaving in any fashion whatsoever. There is no difference between free being—being as self-committal, as existence choosing its essence—and absolute being. And there is no difference whatever between being as an absolute, temporally localized—that is, localized in history—and universally intelligible being.

This does not completely refute the charge of subjectivism. Indeed that objection appears in several other forms, of which the first is as follows. People say to us, "Then it does not matter what you do," and they say this in various ways. First they tax us with anarchy; then they say, "You cannot judge others, for there is no reason for preferring one purpose to another"; finally, they may say, "Everything being merely voluntary in this choice of yours, you give away with one hand what you pretend to gain with the other." These three are not very serious objections. As to the first, to say that it matters not what you choose is not correct. In one sense choice is possible, but what is not possible is not to choose. I can always choose, but I must know that if I do not choose, that is still a choice. This, although it may appear merely formal, is of great importance as a limit to fantasy and caprice. For, when I confront a real situation—for example, that I am a sexual being, able to have relations with a being of the other sex and able to have children—I am obliged to choose my attitude to it, and in every respect I bear the responsibility of the choice which, in committing myself, also commits the whole of humanity. Even if my choice is determined by no *a priori* value whatever, it can have nothing to do with caprice . . . on the contrary, man finds himself in an organized situation in which he is himself involved: his choice involves mankind in its entirety, and he cannot avoid choosing. Either he must remain single, or he must marry without having children, or he must marry and have children. In any case, and whichever he may choose, it is impossible for him, in respect of this situation, not to take complete responsibility. Doubtless he chooses without reference to any preestablished values, but it is unjust to tax him with caprice. Rather let us say that the moral choice is comparable to the construction of a work of art.

But here I must at once digress to make it quite clear that we are not propounding an aesthetic morality, for our adversaries are disingenuous enough to reproach us even with that. I mention the work of art only by way of comparison. That being understood, does anyone reproach an artist when he paints a picture for not following rules established *a priori*? Does one ever ask what is the picture that he ought to paint? As everyone knows, there is no predefined picture for him to make; the artist applies himself to the composition of a picture, and the picture that ought to be made is precisely that which he will have made. As everyone knows, there are no aesthetic values *a priori*, but there are values which will appear in due course in the coherence of the picture, in the relation between the will to create and the finished work. No one can tell what the painting of tomorrow will be like; one cannot judge a painting until it is done. What has that to do with morality? We are in the same creative situation. We never speak of a work of art as irresponsible; when we are discussing a canvas by Picasso, we understand very well that the composition became what it is at the time when he was painting it, and that his works are part and parcel of his entire life.

It is the same upon the plane of morality. There is this in common between art and morality, that in both we have to do with creation and invention. We cannot decide *a priori* what it is that should be done. I think it was made sufficiently clear to you in the case of that student who came to see me, that to whatever ethical system he might appeal, the Kantian or any other, he could find no sort of guidance whatever; he was obliged to invent the law for himself. Certainly we cannot say that this man, in choosing to remain with his mother—that is, in taking sentiment, personal devotion and concrete charity as his moral foundations—would be making an irresponsible choice, nor could we do so if he preferred the sacrifice of going away to England. Man makes himself; he is not found ready-made; he makes himself by the choice of his morality, and he cannot but choose a morality, such is the pressure of circumstances upon him. We define man only in relation to his commitments; it is therefore absurd to reproach us for irresponsibility in our choice.

In the second place, people say to us, "You are unable to judge others." This is true in one sense and false in another. It is true in this sense, that whenever a man chooses his purpose and his commitments in all clearness and in all sincerity, whatever that purpose may be it is impossible to prefer another for him. It is true in the sense that we do not believe in progress. Progress implies amelioration; but man is always the same, facing a situation which is always changing, and choice remains always a choice in the situation. The moral problem has not changed since the time when it was a choice between slavery and anti-slavery—from the time of the war of Secession, for example, until the present moment when one chooses between the M.R.P. [Mouvement Républicain Populaire] and the Communists.

We can judge, nevertheless, for, as I have said, one chooses in view of others, and in view of others one chooses himself. One can judge, first—and perhaps this is not a judgment of value, but it is a logical judgment—that in certain cases choice is founded upon an error, and in others upon the truth. One can judge a man by saying that he deceives himself. Since we have defined the situation of man as one of free choice, without excuse and without help, any man who takes refuge behind the excuse of his passions, or by inventing some deterministic doctrine, is a self-deceiver. One may object: "But why should he not choose to deceive himself?" I reply that it is not for me to judge him morally, but I define his self-deception as an error. Here one cannot avoid pronouncing a judgment of truth. The self-deception is evidently a falsehood, because it is a dissimulation of man's complete liberty of commitment. Upon this same level, I say that it is also a self-deception if I choose to declare that certain values are incumbent upon me; I am in contradiction with myself if I will these values and at the same time say that they impose themselves upon me. If anyone says to me, "And what if I wish to deceive myself?" I answer, "There is no reason why you should not, but I declare that you are doing so, and that the attitude of strict consistency alone is that of good faith." Furthermore, I can pronounce a moral judgment. For I declare that freedom, in respect of concrete circumstances, can have no other end and aim but itself; and when once a man has seen that values depend upon himself, in that state of forsakenness he can will only one thing, and that is freedom as the foundation of all values. That does not mean that he wills it in the abstract: it simply means that the actions of men of good faith have, as their ultimate significance, the quest of freedom itself as such. A man who belongs to some communist or revolutionary society wills certain concrete ends, which imply the will to freedom, but that freedom is willed in community. We will freedom for freedom's sake, and in and through particular circumstances. And in thus willing freedom, we discover that it depends entirely upon the freedom of others and that the freedom of others depends upon our own. Obviously, freedom as the definition of a man does not depend upon others, but as soon as there is a commitment, I am obliged to will the liberty of others at the same time as mine. I cannot make liberty my aim unless I make that of others equally my aim. Consequently, when I recognize, as entirely authentic, that man is a being whose existence precedes his essence, and that he is a free being who cannot, in any circumstances, but will his freedom, at the same time I realize that I cannot not will the freedom of others. Thus, in the name of that will to freedom which is implied in freedom itself, I can form judgments upon those who seek to hide from themselves the wholly voluntary nature of their existence and its complete freedom. Those who hide from this total freedom, in a guise of solemnity or with deterministic excuses, I shall call cowards. Others, who try to show that their existence is necessary, when it is merely an accident of the appearance of the human race on earth, I shall call scum. But neither cowards nor scum can be identified except upon the plane of strict authenticity. Thus, although the content of morality is variable, a certain form of this morality is universal. Kant declared that freedom is a will both to itself and to the freedom of others. Agreed: but he thinks that the formal and the universal suffice for the constitution of a morality. We think, on the contrary, that principles that are too abstract break down when we come to defining action. To take once again the case of that student; by what authority, in the name of what golden rule of morality, do you think he could have decided, in perfect peace of mind, either to abandon his mother or to remain with her? There are no means of judging. The content is always concrete, and therefore unpredictable; it has always to be invented. The one thing that counts, is to know whether the invention is made in the name of freedom.

Let us, for example, examine the two following cases, and you will see how far they are similar in spite of their difference. Let us take *The Mill on the Floss*. We find here a certain young woman, Maggie Tulliver, who is an incarnation of the value of passion and is aware of it. She is in love with a young man, Stephen, who is engaged to another, an insignificant young woman. This Maggie Tulliver, instead of heedlessly seeking her own happiness, chooses in the name of human solidarity to sacrifice herself and to give up the man she loves. On the other hand, La Sanseverina in Stendhal's *Chartreuse de Parme*, believing that it is passion which endows man with his real value, would have declared that a grand passion justifies its sacrifices, and must be preferred to the banality of such conjugal love as would unite Stephen to the little goose he was engaged to marry. It is the latter that she would have chosen to sacrifice in realizing her own happiness, and, as Stendhal shows, she would also sacrifice herself upon the plane of passion if life made that demand upon her. Here we are facing two clearly opposed moralities; but I claim that they are equivalent, seeing that in both cases the overruling aim is freedom. You can imagine two attitudes exactly similar in effect, in that one girl might prefer, in resignation, to give up her lover whilst the other preferred, in fulfilment of sexual desire, to ignore the prior engagement of the man she loved; and, externally, these two cases might appear the same as the two we have just cited, while being in fact entirely different. The attitude of La Sanseverina is much nearer to that of Maggie Tulliver than to one of careless greed. Thus, you see, the second objection is at once true and false. One can choose anything, but only if it is upon the plane of free commitment.

The third objection, stated by saying, "You take with one hand what you give with the other," means, at bottom, "your values are not serious, since you choose them yourselves." To that I can only say that I am very sorry that it should be so; but if I have excluded God the Father, there must be somebody to invent values. We have to take things as they are. And moreover, to say that we invent values means neither more nor less than this; that there is no sense in life *a priori*. Life is nothing until it is lived; but it is yours to make sense of, and the value of it is nothing else but the sense that you choose. Therefore, you can see that there is a possibility of creating a human community. I have been reproached for suggesting that existentialism is a form of humanism: people have said to me, "But you have written in your *Nauseé* that the humanists are wrong, you have even ridiculed a certain type of humanism, why do you now go back upon that?" In reality, the word humanism has two very different meanings. One may understand by humanism a theory which upholds man as the end-in-itself and as the supreme value. Humanism in this sense appears, for instance, in Cocteau's story *Round the World in 80 Hours*, in which one of the characters declares, because he is flying over mountains in an aeroplane, "Man is magnificent!" This signifies that although I, personally, have not built aeroplanes I have the benefit of those particular inventions and that I personally, being a man, can consider myself responsible for, and honored by, achievements that are peculiar to some men. It is to assume that we can ascribe value to man according to the most distinguished deeds of certain men. That kind of humanism is absurd, for only the dog or the horse would be in a position to pronounce a general judgment upon man and declare that he is magnificent, which they have never been such fools as to do—at least, not as far as I know. But neither is it admissible that a man should pronounce judgment upon Man. Existentialism dispenses with any judgment of this sort: an existentialist will never take man as the end, since man is still to be determined. And we have no right to believe that humanity is something to which we could set up a cult, after the manner of August Comte. The cult of humanity ends in Comtian humanism, shut-in upon itself, and—this must be said—in Fascism. We do not want a humanism like that.

But there is another sense of the word, of which the fundamental meaning is this: Man is all the time outside of himself: it is in projecting and losing himself beyond himself that he makes man to exist; and, on the other hand, it is by pursuing transcendent aims that he himself is able to exist. Since man is thus self-surpassing, and can grasp objects only in relation to his self-surpassing, he is himself the heart and center of his transcendence. There is no other universe except the human universe, the universe of human subjectivity. This relation of transcendence as constitutive of man (not in the sense that God is transcendent, but in the sense of self-surpassing) with subjectivity (in such a sense that man is not shut up in himself but forever present in a human universe)—it is this that we call existential humanism. This is humanism, because we remind man that there is no legislator but himself; that he himself, thus abandoned, must decide for himself; also because we show that it is not by turning back upon himself, but always by seeking, beyond himself, an aim which is one of liberation or of some particular realization, that man can realize himself as truly human.

You can see from these few reflections that nothing could be more unjust than the objections people raise against us. Existentialism is nothing else but an attempt to draw the full conclusions from a consistently atheistic position. Its intention is not in the least that of plunging men into despair. And if by despair one means—as the Christians do—any attitude of unbelief, the despair of the existentialists is something different. Existentialism is not atheist in the sense that it would exhaust itself in demonstrations of the nonexistence of God. It declares, rather, that even if God existed that would make no difference from its point of view. Not that we believe God does exist, but we think that the real problem is not that of His existence; what man needs is to find himself again and to understand that nothing can save him from himself, not even a valid proof of the existence of God. In this sense existentialism is optimistic, it is a doctrine of action, and it is only by self-deception, by confusing their own despair with ours that Christians can describe us as without hope.

■ Questions for Discussion

1. How does Sartre reply to the reservations and criticisms of existentialism?
2. How satisfying do you find these replies?

CHAPTER TWELVE

T HE ANALYTIC AND CONTINENTAL TRADITIONS garnered the majority of the attention paid to the academic practice of philosophy during the twentieth century. As a result, the dominant questions revolved around questions of language, logic, and knowledge. Some of the debates became so esoteric that it was not at all clear that philosophy had much to do with the practical, everyday lives of people.

Other deeply philosophical questions found their forum outside of the halls of academic philosophy and in the growing demands for equality and the recognition of the full humanity of all people. Largely unnoticed as a branch of philosophy, political activism born of nineteenth-century philosophical liberalism gave birth to cries for justice and equal rights. The women's suffrage movement of the late nineteenth century led to the feminist movement of the late twentieth, and John Rawls revolutionized political theory and practice with his groundbreaking "Theory of Justice." In this chapter, we will look first at the Theory of Justice that renders the notion of justice as a question of fairness before turning to one of the central questions of fairness, the rights and humanity of women.

JOHN RAWLS AND JUSTICE AS FAIRNESS

Theories of justice are centrally concerned with whether, how, and why persons should be treated differently. There is the deep and abiding prephilosophical intuition that people should be treated similarly unless there is a real and demonstrably relevant reason not to do so. In other words, if Bill and Ted have no relevant differences between them, then to treat them in different manners is unjustified and unjustifiable. Indeed, even if the two have considerable differences between them but none of the differences is relevant to the question at hand, then those differences cannot be used as justification for unequal treatment.

This notion of equal or fair treatment reflects a primal intuition. Children on a playground have at least a rudimentary notion of fairness—or perhaps a very intense notion of unfairness. While they may not be able to detect when they have treated another unfairly or when others have not been fair to each other, they have a very acute sense of when they themselves have been treated unfairly. The cry of "That's unfair" is one of the more common complaints of childhood.

John Rawls (1921–2002)

That primal intuition is more telling than is sometimes realized. Indeed, many of the debates surrounding questions of justice have their roots in that intuition. John Rawls revolutionized the discussion of human rights and political theory with his advocacy of a quite simple and yet deeply complex definition of justice. For Rawls, justice is fairness, and fairness is justice.

As compelling as such a conception is, however, it is quite difficult to establish fairness in any given situation. Every person brings to a situation a different set of beliefs, characteristics, abilities, desires, and commitments. Thus, in almost any situation, there will be competing desires, commitments, and principles that have to be weighed and adjudicated. Indeed, at times, those competitors are wholly incompatible. Further, the moral legislator is not in a position to render some objective decision, as she is also trapped within a perspective that is highly personal and colored with her own beliefs, desires, abilities, and so on. The lazy moral legislator might fall back to a simplified definition of fairness that amounts only to equality of treatment. However, the failings of such a view are apparent. Suppose two people, John and Jane, are admitted to a hospital for treatment. John is in need of dialysis, and Jane requires knee surgery. It clearly makes no sense to perform knee surgery on both of them, although this would be a simple case of equal treatment. So, the assumption that fairness means equality of treatment falls victim to a very straightforward counterexample.

The counterexample also gives rise to a view that makes more sense. John, in need of dialysis, should be treated as one in need of dialysis, while Jane should receive the knee surgery that she needs. Thus, fairness then amounts to treating each person in the manner that is appropriate to his or her situation, without regard for the differences between them that are irrelevant. For example, John should not receive dialysis because he is male, and Jane should not be refused surgery because she is female or vice versa. We would recognize that sex is not a relevant factor in either case.

At the same time, the reality of the social structure of modern society is that many decisions about everything from voting rights to medical care to taxation to educational opportunities are significantly influenced, if not straightforwardly determined, by factors and interests that are quite arbitrary. How, then, can one discern what is fair? Rawls proposes a thought experiment that is as insightful as it is radical.

The Original Position

Suppose everyone who was going to live with a particular set of social rules and structures was gathered in a room in which they would spell out all of the rules by which the society would be governed. These rules would not only include the laws and the political structures but would govern everything. Further, suppose that these rule makers would have no idea where in the society they would live. Thus, those gathered for the purpose of advancing the rules and principles that will govern their society are separated from the actual world in which they will live by a *veil of ignorance*. Behind this veil of ignorance, Rawls considers the social contractors to be in the **Original Position**. One of them could turn out to be a multimillionaire, while another would be a severely physically and mentally disabled person. Given that they have no prior knowledge of the role in society that each will play, Rawls supposes that they will construct the rules in such a way that those most disadvantaged in the society they will occupy are not further disadvantaged by the rules in place. Or, in another way, they will design the rules in such a way as to favor those whose positions are most tenuous and most in need of support. They will not disenfranchise those whose positions are most privileged in all likelihood, but they will most assuredly grant the most disadvantaged positions more benefits. This position of decision making, completely removed from any knowledge of their places in the society that they are constructing, is called the Original Position.

Clearly, the Original Position is a thought experiment that is impossible to produce. However, within political philosophy, there is a long tradition of using thought experiments to test our political intuitions and make the case for one kind of social contract or another. For Thomas Hobbes, the seventeenth-century political philosopher, the state of nature out of which grew the *social contract* that was the basis of any government was a state of war of each against all. Because of a need for protection of self and property, people would band together and enter into a contract in which they gave up many of their personal freedoms for a sense of security and protection. Thus, the authority of the government derives from the people surrendering total freedom and quite limited security for greater security and lesser freedom. John Locke, another of the early social contract theorists, argues that the only valid social contract is one in which the inalienable rights of people are recognized and protected. And even Plato, in his *Republic*, uses a thought experiment—the construction of the ideal city—in order to provide a justification for a political theory that upholds a rule of the "best," or an *aristocracy*. Thus, Rawls is in the tradition of the great political philosophers who appeal to a thought experiment to express a political ideal.

As a thought experiment, the Original Position is quite compelling because it draws out the deeply held intuitions toward fairness, or at least toward the avoidance of unfairness, by putting the self-interests of the participants in play. A person in the Original Position is hardly likely to advocate a completely unfair rule for the society when there is the very real possibility that once the participants take their places in that society, he will be on the receiving end of the disadvantage. Thus, while Rawls does not think that any society will be fair in the sense that all people achieve similar outcomes or even have the same opportunities, it will be fair because the method by which the governing principles or social contract was developed was procedurally fair.

The principles that emerge from behind the thick veil of ignorance will be the outgrowth of rational and self-interested perspectives and will exhibit a particular set of characteristics, on Rawls's view. They will be universal in form. In other words, they will apply to all people everywhere within the society. The principles would serve as the ultimate basis for deciding between competing claims and for settling disputes. They would also be coherent with the reasoned and reflective social judgments about the nature of justice. And, finally, they would serve to found a stable social structure that was both practical and plausible.

FEMINISM AND WOMEN'S RIGHTS

It might seem odd to reach back into the eighteenth century for a discussion of contemporary trends in philosophy, particularly with regard to feminism and the women's rights movement. However, within the twentieth century, greater attention began to be given to the philosophical founders of what blossomed into the suffrage movement and ultimately feminism. Chief among those early mothers of the movement was the early modern philosopher Mary Wollstonecraft.

Mary Wollstonecraft

Mary Wollstonecraft's voice is one of the first voices of women philosophers generally added to the canon of the modern period in Western philosophy. The absence of women's voices in the canon has come to be understood to be by no means on account of a lack of depth, sophistication, and/or creativity. Rather, contemporary scholars have come more and more to understand the significant loss to philosophical inquiry that resulted from the arbitrary exclusion of the voices of women philosophers. Wollstonecraft's until recent exclusion is a clear case of this arbitrariness and the attendant loss. Her most famous work, *A Vindication of the Rights of Women*, which followed her lesser-known work, *A Vindication of the Rights of Men*, by two years is a powerful criticism of the social, political, economic, and educational oppression of women and a compelling argument for the full inclusion of women in the public arena. It should be noted that *Vindication* precedes the better-known work of John Stuart Mill (*Subjection of Women*) by four decades and the granting of the franchise to women in the United States by 120 years.

Wollstonecraft was a direct victim of the suppression of women's voices. Despite the demonstration of a tremendous intellect from a very early age, she was excluded from "proper" English education and society. Without much formal education, she worked mainly as a writer and an editor, which is itself a testament to the breadth of her self-taught learning. Even with such impressive contributions to the arena of philosophical discourse, she has been, until recently, best known for the work of her daughter, Mary Wollstonecraft Shelley, author of *Frankenstein*.

Wollstonecraft's lack of educational opportunities during her formative years was never far from her mind or her writings. She argues, in *Vindication*, that the subjection of women and the relegation of women to second-class status or, worse, tied exclusively to hearth and home is the direct result of women's having been systematically denied the opportunity of education. As a protofeminist, Wollstonecraft is sometimes marginalized by the very feminist movement that owes much to her. This is probably due to the fact that she concedes that the women of her era are, in fact, inferior to men in the area of intellect. This marginalization is unfortunate because it reflects a very naïve reading of her work. She is not suggesting that the fact of intellectual inferiority is in any way a natural or essential feature

Mary Wollstonecraft (1759–1797)

of women. Instead, it is an accidental property of English society, a property caused by male oppression through the denial of education to women. Having been excluded from the opportunity of education, it is small wonder that a person so denied might, as a result, be uneducated. While this denial of educational opportunity will not entail a lack of education, it will tend, in a large population organized under such a system, to produce precisely that result as a common feature of the group thusly denied. Simply put, being a woman did not render one inferior; being systematically denied the opportunity to develop one's intellectual capacity tends to render one less intellectually capable. Since the education actually widely available to women was focused solely on passive aspects of beauty and servility, one should not express surprise that this is the general result. An alteration in the system would result not only in women having educational opportunity but also in the rightful assumption by women of equal political and social rights.

One of the canonical nineteenth-century philosophers deeply influenced by Wollstonecraft was John Stuart Mill, whom we have encountered previously in this volume. His *Subjection of Women* sets out as its thesis at the very outset of the work that the political and social structure that subordinates women to men is wrong in and of itself and is one of the chief causes of the slow progress of civilization. Within this work, Mill makes some use of Wollstonecraft's work as he levels devastating arguments against those opponents of women's rights. Let us look briefly at one of his most powerful refutations.

Mill's opposition, simply put, are all those who would argue that women ought be subject to men. One of the most common arguments put forward was that women were inferior to men because women's *nature* makes them subject to men, and thus the passage of legislation that accords with that fact is to be preferred because it is in keeping with *natural law*. Thus, women are to be excluded from the public sector, from owning property, from participation in politics, and from education because they are naturally incapable of owning, participating, and learning.

For these, Mill offers a series of analogies, each making this view more ridiculous than the last. Consider the occupation of blacksmithing. Is it necessary to pass legislation that people who are physically weak, infirm, or intolerant of high heat and pressure should be excluded from this profession? Indeed, isn't the profession itself sufficient to restrict those who cannot perform it, whether men or women, from pursuing it? And, if they pursue it and fail, this is sufficient to demonstrate their inability, quite independent of law. Simply put, if legislation is necessary to restrict action, then the actions are not an outgrowth of human nature; if the inferiority is a feature of nature, then no law is sufficient to enforce it. Thus, Mill puts the opposition in the unenviable and, indeed, untenable position of being caught between incompatible principles. To say that legislation is necessary to restrict women from the public sphere is just to say that nature does not so restrict them. To say that nature restricts them is just to say that legislation is unnecessary. They can have it one way or the other but not both. Since the only support for such legislation is appeal to nature, that path is cut off. Since the only support for the argument about nature is some appeal to social/legislative/doctrinal assertions, then that path is likewise eliminated. Thus, those who would argue that women are naturally and legislatively inferior to men are thwarted. Further, the arguments to restrict any rights accorded to men from women are refuted.

Simply put, Wollstonecraft (in the last part of the eighteenth century) and Mill (in the middle of the nineteenth) win. Their arguments, first hers and then his, utterly refute those who would marginalize and systematically oppress women. The philosophical battle is won. Yet it was nearly a century after Mill's *Subjection* and over 120 years after Wollstonecraft's death that women gained the right to vote in the United States. In the first part of the twenty-first century, civilization is still met with structural and systemic differences that are disadvantageous to women. Despite the success of Mill's arguments in support of his thesis that the subjection of women is wrong, despite the success of Wollstonecraft's arguments that women should enjoy the same education and rights men enjoy, this is still not universally recognized even within the United States and surely not within the rest of the world.

Carol Gilligan

The progression toward equal rights and equal regard socially, politically, and ethically has been slow and uneven. That there are clear biological differences between men and women is obvious. Whether those biological differences indicate any general differences with regard to **moral development** and perceptions of the world is an open question. The opposition to Wollstonecraft and Mill, an opposition that could trace its philosophical ancestry to Aristotle, would argue that there is indeed a significant difference and that, in virtue of that difference, women's experience of the world is inferior. Even after such a view was dispatched as intellectually dishonest and morally repugnant, the practice of excluding women's voices from important moral discussions was fairly common. A growing field within the study of psychology is a case in point. Theories of moral development became hot conversation topics in the latter half of the twentieth century. However, all of the

Carol Gilligan (1936–)

subjects in the field studies and experiments on moral intuitions and justifications/rationalizations used only males as test subjects. Carol Gilligan offered a different approach, conducting significantly similar studies with a substantially different population: females. Her view that women generally value different ethical principles and have different base perceptions of morality than men do was the conclusion of her studies and the subject of her most famous work, *In a Different Voice*.

It is important to recognize the importance of Gilligan's study. Given that men were the sole representatives in earlier studies and that, by far, the vast majority of philosophers weighing in on the subject of ethics were also male, it was generally thought that since women tended to "diverge from the standard," that was an indication of moral inferiority and, further, a developmental inferiority. Thus, from Aristotle forward into the mid-twentieth century, women were most often classified along with children in terms of moral capacity and development. From our examination of formal and informal logical fallacies in chapter 4, the flaws in such arguments should be obvious. Unfortunately, they were not. Fortunately, Gilligan's empirical work pointed these fundamental mistakes out.

Since research was done exclusively by and on males, it would not be strange to see that women would generally differ in some significant ways. However, it is straightforwardly **question begging** to assume that the conclusion that women are inferior follows. Instead, the better and more scientifically and logically valid approach is to take as the population for study the entirety of humanity. Gilligan notes that while men tend to value universal abstract principles in moral reasoning, women tend to focus on the self under question and the relational values it experiences. What emerges from her studies is a new perspective on moral theory, commonly called an *ethics of care*. As a competitor to the great ethical traditions that tend to focus on consequences or motives and intentions, the ethics of care puts forward the view that moral judgments are dependent on

419

shared norms and expectations, on the recognition of power and power differentials, on the development of consensus, and on the valuation of truth, reconciliation, and nonviolence. Care for the other becomes the universal obligation of morality.

While some criticism has arisen of Gilligan's work—for example, though she argues for a radical reevaluation of theories of moral development, her own theory is put forward as one that applies to all human beings but is an outgrowth of studies exclusively with women—it is also the case that her work is a much needed corrective to narrowly conceived views of moral development that arbitrarily privileged male experience of the world. As an intellectual descendant of Mary Wollstonecraft, Gilligan's work vindicates not only the rights of women but the development of a moral perspective that takes seriously the ways in which all people exist in a matrix of relationships that can be preserved only by attention to the value of each human being and the relationships that provide value to individual human lives.

Alison Jaggar

Following Wollstonecraft's contributions to arguments for women's education and rights and Gilligan's arguments elevating women's voices in the conversation concerning moral development, Alison Jaggar reevaluates the fundamental questions of modern philosophy itself, focusing her attention on questions of knowledge, or epistemology. In

Alison Jaggar

her work *Emotion in Feminist Epistemology*, she addresses the lingering devaluation of the emotional character of human life in developing knowledge and theories of knowledge.

From the time of the ancient Greeks, ruminations about the structure of knowledge and the nature of the mind have presupposed that reason and emotion are radically different and completely antithetical to one another. Aristotle famously goes so far as to use this distinction between reason and emotion to argue for a distinction in the human soul. From that distinction within the human soul—half rational, half emotional—he claims that women are inherently and of nature inferior to men. This is because he claims that the emotional part of the soul of a woman dominates her soul, while the rational part of the soul of a man has the capacity to rule his soul.

This view leads him to argue that women cannot truly attain full virtue but are relegated to the virtues proper to one whose emotions must be kept in check by the male to whom she is attached (first father, then husband). The view of ethics, for example, that arises from this dichotomy between rationality and emotion is a systematic rejection of any role for emotion in the formation of proper ethical maxims, character traits, or actions.

Much of the early feminist movement, from Wollstonecraft through the early twentieth century, obviously disagreed with Aristotle that women are inherently inferior to men and that the soul of a woman cannot be governed by rationality instead of the emotions. The odd assumption that tended to go unexamined and unassailed was that the center of virtue was with rationality. Emotions are important, but more because they were a force to be controlled and, further, a force to be carefully excluded from questions of knowledge, which was thought to be the product of cool and calculating rational deliberation. At best, the emotions, so the story goes, may well provide data about a given situation, but the data are inherently unstable, unpredictable, and undependable. Thus, such information cannot possibly be appropriate for the development of knowledge, which is supposed to be stable, have predictive force, and be dependable.

Jaggar challenges this notion of the inferiority of the emotions as a ground of knowledge. It should be noted here that Jaggar does not endorse, even tacitly, the Aristotelian notion of virtues of men (based on rationality) and virtues of women (based in emotion). In this, she also diverges from Gilligan. Instead, Jaggar argues that the nature of a human being involves both the emotions and the rational capacities. Since a full human being is both rational and emotional, it is improper to presuppose that one pole (the rational) is to be accentuated, while the other is to be attenuated. Rather, Jaggar argues that the emotions are "helpful and even necessary" to the development of knowledge. Because the emotions have been systematically and, frankly, arbitrarily excluded from the arena of knowledge and ethical discussions, it has resulted in skewed, lopsided, and fundamentally flawed epistemologies, metaphysics, and ethical commitments. The arbitrariness is somewhat obvious. She writes, "Just as observation directs, shapes and partially defines emotion, so too emotion directs, shapes, and even partially defines observation." Emotion is most often described as an active feature of the mind, engaged in the world while rationality is generally seen as a passive observer of the world. This separation between the two strikes Jaggar as a false dichotomy and one that does not actually represent the realities of the human experience of the world. Those philosophical positions that reject the reality of emotions in the formation of beliefs, in the development of reactive attitudes, and in the construction of compassion, sympathy, and empathy will remain fundamentally flawed because they appropriate only a subset of the data available to the human mind. The human being is, on Jaggar's view, capable of a wide range of emotion and a correspondingly wide range of rationality. Only by the recovery of the importance of emotion to epistemological speculations will the fullness of humanity be incorporated into philosophical, social, ethical, and educational theories, and only then will those theories have basis to claim relevance for life.

Susan Moller Okin

While Rawls radically alters the terrain of philosophical discussions about rights and the nature of **contractarian** political theory, Susan Moller Okin proposes important and meaningful correctives to Rawls's work. Considered by many to be the greatest feminist philosopher of the twentieth century, Okin left an indelible mark on the ways in which serious women and men think about the notions of sex, gender, and the roles of men and women in society. Her groundbreaking *Justice, Gender, and the Family* makes the radical (at the time) claim that notions of justice are not simply matters of jurisprudence or matters of public interactions. Instead, justice is simply misconceived at the outset if the concept does not apply to family and family roles.

One place where Okin and Aristotle agree is that the family or the household is the fundamental unit of society and the place that cannot be excluded from a discussion of justice. However, Okin's striking indictments of the Aristotelian assumptions of the inferiority of women and "women's roles" that have been adopted without much, if any, reflection are truly radical, suggesting the requirement of fundamental shifts in the notion of family, sex, gender, and justice.

Susan Moller Okin (1947–2004)

One of the most easily confused distinctions in modern scholarly discourse is the distinction between sex and gender. Confusing one for the other, even with the admirable attempt to avoid morally irrelevant distinctions based on misguided notions of sex and/or gender, is one of the more common mistakes made in contemporary debate. Okin not only preserves this distinction but also develops the implications that follow from that distinction that arise in the very language used to describe men and women. Sex is a matter or biology—there are males and females. Gender is a matter of roles. Gender roles are arbitrarily (or, at least, socially) constructed to preserve power differentials. These power differentials are then assumed to be reflective of the "way the world actually is" and as a result are then unreflectively recapitulated in language. For example, we speak of a man "fathering" a child and a woman "mothering" a child. However, in the former case, the "fathering" does not entail much more, necessarily, than a brief interlude long before the advent of the child in question. On the other hand, to "mother" is not seen so much as a representation of the biological propagation of the species as a nurturing and caretaker role. Historically, these roles bring with them stereotypes that put in place a division of labor within the household that is referred to as "man's work" and "woman's work." Those roles are then transferred to the wider society as certain arenas are seen as proper for men while others are seen as proper for women. For example, women continue to make considerably less money for equal work; to be underrepresented in legislative, executive, and judicial branches of government; and generally to be less welcome in the workforce outside of the roles of teacher, nurse, and so on—roles that reenact the gender roles within the household. Okin, here, gives an account of the ways in which socially structured worldviews compromise and marginalize women and their contributions to the social order. Here, she is clearly a descendant of Wollstonecraft and the early women's rights pioneers who put forward a *Declaration of Sentiments* at the Seneca Falls Conference in 1848. That *Declaration* is included in one of the readings that conclude this chapter and is deeply reflective of the contractarian theory of John Locke and the signatories to the Declaration of Independence.

On Okin's view, all of these social, political, and moral discrepancies are rooted in familial injustice, a familial injustice that she suggests is not eliminated by a veil of ignorance and the Original Position, which takes some social roles into account but ignores biological differences for the most part. As a result, the traditional work of women in the home is devalued in society and in the Original Position because it is unpaid labor, the labor of women outside the home is devalued because it is remunerated at a significantly smaller rate than her male counterpart, and the value of the labor of men outside the home is inflated because it is remunerated at a level above equal work performed by his female counterpart. At the root of this unfairness is the very common error of mistaking sex and gender.

In the first case, sex is irreducible. Women can become pregnant. Men cannot. However, to suppose that the gender differences that make appeal to this physical fact are anything more than arbitrary appeals to ancient patriarchal authorities is to engage in disingenuousness of a profound sort. Thus, only through the abolition of gender can justice be brought to the family, and only through the advent of justice in the family can justice be brought to civil society. Whether such an abolition is possible from a Rawlsian view is not clear. However, the intuition toward "justice for all" and "fairness" that runs through Rawls's work and the demand for fairness and equal rights in the feminist movement mark invaluable contributions to the development of civil society in the twenty-first century.

SUMMARY

1. John Rawls's Theory of Justice provides a framework for analyzing the deep moral intuitions that human beings have about fairness. His Original Position thought experiment is a compelling example that encourages an objective analysis of societal systems and the principles that undergird them while issuing universal, practical, and plausible methods of resolving conflicts between competing principles.

2. Mary Wollstonecraft and the early feminists prefigure the Rawlsian appeal to fairness by arguing that women have been unfairly excluded and, because of this unfairness, unjustly excluded from full participation in education, society, politics, and moral life. Despite devastatingly effective arguments against the societal subjection of women, differences in treatment persist.

3. Contemporary feminists have made significant contributions to theories of moral development (Gilligan), epistemology (Jaggar), and contractarian political and societal

theory (Okin) all of which have built on the foundational arguments offered by Wollstonecraft.

KEY TERMS

contractarian
fairness feminism
moral development

Original Position
question begging

REVIEW QUESTIONS

1. How does Rawls's Original Position address questions of fairness in the development of social and economic principles and systems?

2. How does Wollstonecraft's work influence Mill and his arguments against those who would relegate women to second-class status or worse?

3. How does Carol Gilligan's work serve as a corrective to the traditional approach to understanding moral development? How does her work express the intuition toward justice as fairness?

4. Alison Jaggar makes significant contributions to theories of knowledge. How does her reclamation of emotion alter the approach to epistemology?

5. What is the distinction between sex and gender? How does the confusion of that distinction cause problems for the ascription of full humanity to women? What are some of the implications, on Okin's view, of maintaining the careful distinction between the notions of sex and gender?

■ Reading

Declaration of Sentiments,
Seneca Falls Conference, 1848

When, in the course of human events, it becomes necessary for one portion of the family of man to assume among the people of the earth a position different from that which they have hitherto occupied, but one to which the laws of nature and of nature's God entitle them, a decent respect to the opinions of mankind requires that they should declare the causes that impel them to such a course.

We hold these truths to be self-evident; that all men and women are created equal; that they are endowed by their Creator with certain inalienable rights; that among these are life, liberty, and the pursuit of happiness; that to secure these rights governments are instituted, deriving their just powers from the consent of the governed. Whenever any form of government becomes destructive of these ends, it is the right of those who suffer from it to refuse allegiance to it, and to insist upon the institution of a new government, laying its foundation on such principles, and organizing its powers in such form, as to them shall seem most likely to effect their safety and happiness. Prudence, indeed, will dictate that governments long established should not be changed for light and transient causes; and, accordingly, all experience hath shown that mankind are more disposed to suffer, while evils are sufferable, than to right themselves by abolishing the forms to which they were accustomed. But when a long train of abuses and usurpations, pursuing invariably the same object, evinces a design to reduce them under absolute despotism, it is their duty to throw off such government, and to provide new guards for their future security. Such has been the patient sufferance of the women under this government, and such is now the necessity which constrains them to demand the equal station to which they are entitled.

The history of mankind is a history of repeated injuries and usurpations on the part of man toward woman, having in direct object the establishment of an absolute tyranny over her. To prove this, let facts be submitted to a candid world.

He has never permitted her to exercise her inalienable right to the elective franchise.

He has compelled her to submit to laws, in the formation of which she had no voice.

He has withheld from her rights which are given to the most ignorant and degraded men—both natives and foreigners.

Having deprived her of this first right as a citizen, the elective franchise, thereby leaving her without representation in the halls of legislation, he has oppressed her on all sides.

He has made her, if married, in the eye of the law, civilly dead.

He has taken from her all right in property, even to the wages she earns.

He has made her morally, an irresponsible being, as she can commit many crimes with impunity, provided they be done in the presence of her husband. In the covenant of marriage, she is compelled to promise obedience to her husband, he becoming, to all intents and purposes, her master—the law giving him power to deprive her of her liberty, and to administer chastisement.

He has so framed the laws of divorce, as to what shall be the proper causes of divorce, in case of separation, to whom the guardianship of the children shall be given; as to be wholly regardless of the happiness of the women—the law, in all cases, going upon a false supposition of the supremacy of man, and giving all power into his hands.

After depriving her of all rights as a married woman, if single and the owner of property, he has taxed her to support a government which recognizes her only when her property can be made profitable to it.

He has monopolized nearly all the profitable employments, and from those she is permitted to follow, she receives but a scanty remuneration.

He closes against her all the avenues to wealth and distinction, which he considers most honorable to himself. As a teacher of theology, medicine, or law, she is not known.

He has denied her the facilities for obtaining a thorough education—all colleges being closed against her.

He allows her in church, as well as State, but a subordinate position, claiming Apostolic authority for her exclusion from the ministry, and, with some exceptions, from any public participation in the affairs of the Church.

He has created a false public sentiment by giving to the world a different code of morals for men and women, by which moral delinquencies which exclude women from society, are not only tolerated but deemed of little account in man.

He has usurped the prerogative of Jehovah himself, claiming it as his right to assign for her a sphere of action, when that belongs to her conscience and her God.

He has endeavored, in every way that he could to destroy her confidence in her own powers, to lessen her self-respect, and to make her willing to lead a dependent and abject life.

Now, in view of this entire disfranchisement of one-half the people of this country, their social and religious degradation,—in view of the unjust laws above mentioned, and because women do feel themselves aggrieved, oppressed, and fraudulently deprived of their most sacred rights, we insist that they have immediate admission to all the rights and privileges which belong to them as citizens of these United States.

In entering upon the great work before us, we anticipate no small amount of misconception, misrepresentation, and ridicule; but we shall use every instrumentality within our power to effect our object. We shall employ agents, circulate tracts, petition the State and national Legislatures, and endeavor to enlist the pulpit and the press in our behalf. We hope this Convention will be followed by a series of Conventions, embracing every part of the country.

Firmly relying upon the final triumph of the Right and the True, we do this day affix our signatures to this declaration.

■ Questions for Discussion

1. In what ways, and why, in your opinion, does the Seneca Falls Declaration parallel the U.S. Declaration of Independence?

2. What reasons do the authors of the Seneca Falls Declaration give to support their claim of an "absolute tyranny" of man over woman?

3. In light of the legal, political, and economic changes in the United States, do you think that elements of the description of the situation of women still ring true? Explain.

■ Reading
"Two Types of Justice"

JOHN RAWLS

Excerpted from "Two Types of Justice" in *A Theory of Justice* (Cambridge, Mass.: Harvard-Belknap Press, 1971).

I shall now state in a provisional form the two, principles of justice that I believe would be chosen in the original position. In this section I wish to make only the most general comments, and therefore the first formulation of these principles is tentative. I believe that doing this allows the exposition to proceed in a natural way.

The first statement of the two principles reads as follows.

First: each person is to have an equal right to the most extensive basic liberty compatible with a similar liberty for others.

Second: social and economic inequalities are to be arranged so that they are both (a) reasonably expected to be to everyone's advantage, and (b) attached to positions and offices open to all.

There are two ambiguous phrases in the second principle, namely "everyone's advantage: and "open to all."

By way of general comment, these principles primarily apply, as I have said, to the basic structure of society. They are to govern the assignment of rights and duties and to regulate the distribution of social and economic advantages. As their formulation suggests, these principles presuppose that the social structure can be divided into two more or less distinct parts, the first principle applying to the one, the second to the other. They distinguish between those aspects of the social system that define and secure the equal liberties of citizenship and those that specify and establish social and economic inequalities. The basic liberties of citizens are, roughly speaking, political liberty (the right to vote and to be eligible for public office) together with freedom of speech and assembly; liberty of conscience and freedom of thought; freedom of the person along with the right to hold (personal) property; and freedom from arbitrary arrest and seizure as defined by the concept of the rule of law. These liberties are all required to be equal by the first principle, since citizens of a just society are to have the same basic rights.

The second principle applies, in the first approximation, to the distribution of income and wealth and to the design of organizations that make use of differences in authority and responsibility, or chains of command. While the distribution of wealth and income need not be equal, it must be to everyone's advantage, and at the same time, positions of authority and offices of command must be accessible to all. One applies the second principle by holding positions open, and then, subject to this constraint, arranges social and economic inequalities so that everyone benefits.

These principles are to be arranged in a serial order with the first principle prior to the second. This ordering means that a departure from the institutions of equal liberty required by the first principle cannot be justified by, or compensated for, by greater social and economic advantages. The distribution of wealth and income, and the hierarchies of authority, must be consistent with both the liberties of equal citizenship and equality of opportunity.

It is clear that these principles are rather specific in their content, and their acceptance rests on certain assumptions that I must eventually try to explain and justify. A theory of justice depends upon a theory of society in ways that will become evident as we proceed. For the present, it should be observed that the two principles (and this holds for all formulations) are a special case of a more general conception of justice that can be expressed as follows. All social values—liberty and opportunity, income and wealth, and the bases of self-respect—are to be distributed equally unless an unequal distribution of any, or is to everyone's advantage.

Injustice, then, is simply inequalities that are not to the benefit of all. Of course, this conception is extremely vague and requires interpretation.

As a first step, suppose that the basic structure of society distributes certain primary goods, that is, things that every rational man is presumed to want. These goods normally have a use whatever a person's rational plan of life. For simplicity, assume that the chief primary goods at the disposition of society are rights and liberties, powers and opportunities, income and wealth. These are the social primary goods. Other primary goods such as health and vigor, intelligence and imagination, are natural goods; although their possession is influenced by the basic structure, they are not so directly under its control. Imagine, then, a hypothetical initial arrangement in which all the social primary goods are equally distributed: everyone has similar rights and duties, and income and wealth are evenly shared. This state of affairs provides a benchmark for judging improvements. If certain inequalities of wealth and organizational powers would make everyone better off than in this hypothetical starting situation, then they accord with the general conception.

Now it is possible, at least theoretically, that by giving up some of their fundamental liberties men are sufficiently compensated by the resulting social and economic gains. The general conception of justice imposes no restrictions on what sort of inequalities are permissible; it only requires that everyone's position be improved. We need not suppose anything so drastic as consenting to a condition of slavery. Imagine instead that men forego certain political rights when the economic returns are significant and their capacity to influence the course of policy by the exercise of these rights would be marginal in any case. It is this kind of exchange which the two principles as stated rule out; being arranged in serial order they do not permit exchanges between basic liberties and economic and social gains. The serial ordering of principles expresses an underlying preference among primary social goods. When this preference is rational so likewise is the choice of these principles in this order.

In developing justice as fairness I shall, for the most part, leave aside the general conception of justice and examine instead the special case of the two principles in serial order. The advantage of this procedure is that from the first the matter of priorities is recognized and an effort made to find principles to deal with it. One is led to attend throughout to the conditions under which the acknowledgment of the absolute weight of liberty with respect to social and economic advantages, as defined by the lexical order of the two principles, would be reasonable. Offhand, this ranking appears extreme and too special a case to be of much interest; but there is more justification for it than would appear at first sight. Or at any rate, so I shall maintain. Furthermore, the distinction between fundamental rights and liberties and economic and social benefits marks a difference among primary social goods that one should try to exploit. It suggests an important division in the social system. Of course, the distinctions drawn and the ordering proposed are bound to be at best only approximations. There are surely circumstances in which they fail. But it is essential to depict clearly the main lines of a reasonable conception of justice; and under many conditions anyway, the two principles in serial order may serve well enough. When necessary we can fall back on the more general conception.

The fact that the two principles apply to institutions has certain consequences. Several points illustrate this. First of all, the rights and liberties referred to by these principles are those which are defined by the public rules of the basic structure. Whether men are free is determined by the rights and duties established by the major institutions of society. Liberty is a certain pattern of social forms. The first principle simply requires that certain sorts of rules, those defining basic liberties, apply to everyone equally and that they allow the most extensive liberty compatible with a like liberty for all. The only reason for circumscribing the rights defining liberty and making men's freedom less extensive than it might otherwise be is that these equal rights as institutionally defined would interfere with one another.

Another thing to bear in mind is that when principles mention persons or require that everyone gain from an inequality, the reference is to representative persons holding the various social positions, or offices, or whatever, established by the basic structure. Thus in applying the second principle I assume that it is possible to assign an expectation of well-being to representative individuals holding these positions. This expectation indicates their life prospects as viewed from their social station. In general, the expectations of representative persons depend upon the distribution of rights and duties throughout the basic structure. When this changes, expectations change. I assume, then, that expectations are connected: by raising the prospects of the representative man in one position we presumably increase or decrease the prospects of representative men in other positions. Since it applies to institutional forms, the second principle (or rather the first part of it) refers to the expectations of representative individuals. As I shall discuss below, neither principle applies to distributions of particular goods to particular individuals who may be identified by their proper names. The situation where someone is considering how to allocate certain commodities to needy persons who are known to him is not within the scope of the principles. They are meant to regulate basic institutional arrangements. We must not assume that there is much similarity from the standpoint of justice between an administrative allotment of goods to specific persons and the appropriate design of society. Our common sense intuitions for the former may be a poor guide to the latter.

Now the second principle insists that each person benefit from permissible inequalities in the basic structure. This means that it must be reasonable for each relevant representative man defined by this structure, when he views it as a going concern, to prefer his prospects with the inequality to his prospects without it. One is not allowed to justify differences in income or organizational powers on the ground that the disadvantages of those in one position are outweighed by the greater advantages of those in another. Much less can infringements of liberty be counterbalanced in this way. Applied to the basic structure, the principle of utility would have us maximize the sum of expectations of representative men (weighted by the number of persons they represent, on the classical view); and this would permit us to compensate for the losses of some by the gains of others. Instead, the two principles require that everyone benefit from economic and social inequalities. It is obvious, however, that there are indefinitely many ways in which all may be advantaged when the initial arrangement of equality is taken as a benchmark.

■ Questions for Discussion

1. Describe the two types of justice.

2. What is "justice as fairness"?

3. How does Rawls describe the Original Position and its use as a thought experiment that promotes justice as fairness?

A

accidental property According to Aristotle, these properties do not have any necessary connection to the essence of a thing.

a posteriori **propositions** Propositions that are derivable with the help, at some point, of sense experience.

a priori **propositions** Propositions we can know to be true apart from experience. *A priori* propositions are universal and necessary—true everywhere and with certainty.

absurd Glaringly irrational, illogical, or meaningless.

abusive *ad hominem* An unsound argument in which an attempt is made to prove a conclusion false by condemning the advocate of the conclusion.

accent Fallacy arising from ambiguity or confusion in emphasis.

altruism The practice of unselfish concern for the welfare of others.

amphiboly Fallacy resulting from faulty or careless sentence structure.

analogy A method of reasoning in which facts that are obscure or difficult to understand are explained by comparing them to facts that are already known or better understood and to which they bear some likeness.

analytic propositions Propositions such as "A bachelor is an unmarried male," in which the predicate is contained in the subject. Analytic propositions do not provide new knowledge.

anthropomorphism The assignment of human characteristics to nonhuman beings.

argument Reasoning in which one or more statements (the premises) are offered as support for some other statement (the conclusion).

atomism The theory, first propounded by Leucippus and further developed by Democritus, that the basic stuff out of which everything arises is atoms—tiny, indestructible particles, infinite in number.

B

begging the question The fallacy of simply repeating or restating a conclusion rather than providing proof for it.

bifurcation The fallacy of presuming that a certain distinction or classification is exhaustive and exclusive when in fact other alternatives are possible.

C

categorical imperative According to Kant, a strictly moral imperative that commands us to act purely from a sense of duty, following the dictates of reason rather than inclination or desire.

categorical proposition A simple, declarative sentence such as, "The sky is blue."

causation Concept that refers to the notions of cause and effect.

circumstantial *ad hominem* An unsound argument in which an attempt is made to prove a conclusion false by suggesting that the conclusion merely serves the advocate's own interests.

complex ideas According to Locke, ideas that are formed from the repetition, comparison, or combination of simple ideas derived from sensation and reflection. Locke identified three kinds of complex ideas: modes, relations, and substances.

compulsion The irresistible impulse to do something.

conclusion In an argument, the statement being supported by the premises.

contractarian An approach to ethics that allows to formulate key principles for personal and social duties based on the idea of contract or mutual agreement.

cosmology The branch of metaphysics concerned with the nature of the universe as a whole.

D

deductive argument Argument in which the conclusion is presented as necessarily following from the premises.

deontological theory Any theory that evaluates the rightness or wrongness of proposed actions in accordance with whether or not they conform to certain principles one feels bound to obey or follow regardless of their consequences.

desire Want of the individual on which it can act or not.

determinism The view that the whole realm of nature, including humans, is governed by the law of cause and effect.

dialogue Literary form used by Plato to present Socrates' method.

dogmatism A supreme confidence in the truth of one's own beliefs.

dualism In the philosophy of Descartes, the idea that mind and matter are distinct substances, existing independently of each other, each capable of being known and studied apart from the other.

E

efficient cause According to Aristotle, the triggering event that leads to the existence of an object.

emotivism The theory that moral concepts and the judgments in which they occur are not real concepts and real judgments but rather unverifiable expressions of emotion.

empiricism The view—held by Locke, Berkeley, and Hume—that experience is the primary source of knowledge and that the proper test of truth is external: Ideas are true if they correspond to what we find in the external world.

epistemology The area of philosophy concerned with the nature, sources, limitations, and validity of knowledge.

equivocation Using a word with two or more meanings during the course of an argument while acting as if the meaning of the word was being held constant.

essentialism The belief in the existence of essences.

essential property According to Aristotle, it is something that an entity *itself* has the power to do or become.

ethical hedonism The doctrine that pleasure is always intrinsically good and that it is the only thing that is intrinsically good.

ethics The area of philosophy concerned with how we should order our lives, what goals we should seek, and what should count with us most; the study of human conduct.

existentialism The belief that there is no grand design, that the universe is irrational and meaningless, and that we should therefore focus on the question of what to do and believe in the face of what is essentially an absurd situation.

F

fairness Primal intuition that people should be treated similarly unless there is a demonstrably relevant reason not to do so.

fallacies Arguments that appear to be sound but that for various reasons are not.

fallacies of ambiguity Unsound arguments that result from ambiguity in the meaning of words. Fallacies of ambiguity include amphiboly, accent, and equivocation.

fallacies of presumption Unsound arguments in which unfounded or unproven assumptions are presented in the guise of valid argument forms. Fallacies of presumption include arguments in which the facts are overlooked, arguments in which the facts are evaded, and arguments in which the facts are distorted.

fallacies of relevance Unsound arguments in which the emotional appeal of the language being used deceives us into believing that the premises are relevant to the conclusion being drawn when in fact they are not. Fallacies of relevance include genetic fallacy, abusive *ad hominem*, circumstantial *ad hominem*, *tu quoque*, and poisoning the well.

false analogy A fallacy of presumption in which certain cases are made to appear more similar than they really are.

false cause A fallacy of presumption in which two events are made to appear causally connected in a way they are not.

feminism Advocacy of women's political, economic, and social equality with men.

final cause According to Aristotle, the proper or natural end or purpose of a thing.

formal cause According to Aristotle, the organizing principle or form of an object.

freedom According to Hume the hypothetical ability to have chosen differently because of other beliefs or desires.

free will The idea that human conduct, rather than being determined by divine intervention or physical laws, is the result of personal choice.

G

genetic fallacy An unsound argument in which an attempt is made to prove a conclusion false by condemning its source.

golden mean Aristotle's conception of moral virtue as a mean between the vice of excess and the vice of deficiency.

good will According to Kant, the only thing that can be taken as good without qualification. Goodness of the will derives from the use of such faculties and gifts as intelligence, courage, and wealth in the service of duty.

H

hasty generalization In logic, the use of some isolated or exceptional case or event as a basis for a general conclusion.

hedonism The view that the proper end of human activity is pleasure or happiness.

hypotheses According to William James, anything that may be proposed for us to believe. Hypotheses may be *living* or *dead*.

I

idealism The doctrine that the only things that can be known to exist are ideas.

ideas According to Hume, copies of impressions differing only in that they are faint whereas impressions are vivid. We can have no idea that is not a copy of an antecedent impression.

ideas of reflection According to Locke, ideas (such as doubting, believing, reasoning, and remembering) that we get from observing the operation of our own mind as it is employed about the ideas it already has.

ideas of sensation According to Locke, ideas (such as yellow, cold, and hard) that come to us through our senses when some external object stimulates our sense organs.

impressions According to Hume, the sensations, passions, emotions, desires, and so on that we experience. Hume argued that impressions are the primary data of our knowledge.

indeterminism The belief that some events do not have causes but spring into being by pure chance without any relation to anything preceding.

inductive argument Argument in which the conclusion is presented as following from the premises with a high degree of probability.

intellectual virtues According to Aristotle, those qualities tied to our intelligence—including prudence, foresight, and wisdom—that deal with our ability to discover and recognize the rules of life we ought to follow.

intention The desire on which we have the will to act.

J

justice In Plato's view, a kind of disposition existing in each member of the just state to attend to his or her own proper business and not to meddle in affairs in which, by their nature, they lack competence.

just society According to Plato, a society where everything has its proper place and everyone does what is proper—that is, what their nature and talents prepared them best for.

K

knowledge In Locke's theory, the perception of the agreement or disagreement of our ideas.

L

liberty According to Hume, the power to act unforced by constraints and/or compulsion; freedom from coercion and/or compulsion.

linguistic philosophy The view, first explored by Russell and further developed by Wittgenstein, that what we are immediately and directly acquainted with is language, that language mirrors reality, and that the job of philosophy is to correct the distortions created by the languages in use.

logic The area of philosophy concerned with the formal principles of reasoning and the criteria for valid reasoning.

logical positivism *See* Vienna Circle

M

material cause Refers, according to Aristotle, to the material a thing is made of and in which change occurs.

materialism The doctrine that the world consists of material things and nothing else.

metaethics Inquiry into the nature of ethical theories; investigation not of what is right or wrong, good or evil but of the meanings of such terms as *right* and *wrong*, *good* and *evil*.

metaphysics The area of philosophy concerned with first principles and the fundamental nature of the universe.

Milesian school The earliest pre-Socratic philosophers: Thales, Anaximander, and Anaximenes. The Milesians sought a unitary source of being, attempting to identify the fundamental stuff out of which all else arose.

mode According to Locke, a complex idea of something that is not thought of as existing by itself but as dependent on, or as being a property of, a thing or substance.

monads Leibniz's term for the fundamental units of reality, which he conceived as unextended, endlessly diverse centers of energy, each of which has the capacity of reflecting, to one degree or another, the universe as a whole.

monism The theory that there is only one fundamental substance. Spinoza argued that mind and matter are attributes of this fundamental substance, which he identified as God.

moral development Concept that refers to personal development in the sense of becoming a socially responsible individual.

moral virtues According to Aristotle, those qualities tied to our character—including courage, modesty, and temperance—that deal with our ability to check our appetites and passions so that they will obey the rules recognized as good.

N

naturalism The belief that the order and events of the world can be understood through reason and scientific investigation.

noumena Things-in-themselves.

noumenal Refers to the essence of things, out of the causation of the physical world.

O

option According to William James, the decision between two hypotheses. Options may be living or dead, forced or avoidable, momentous or trivial.

original position According to Rawls a position in which those, constructing a society, do not have any prior knowledge of the roles they are going to play in that society.

P

pantheism The idea that everything must in some sense be God or be a part of God.

parable of the cave Plato's expression of the idea that the world may be quite other than what it appears to be. Plato likened our condition to that of men imprisoned in a cave. The prisoners face away from the cave's entrance and can only view shadows cast by people moving about outside the cave, with no real knowledge of who or what exists outside.

paradox A type of statement that leads to two contrary or contradictory conclusions.

phenomena According to Kant, objects of experience that bear the stamp of the mind's activity.

phenomenal This notion refers to the phenomenal world or the objects we experience through sense perception.

philosophy The attempt, using reason alone, to gain an understanding of ourselves and of the world we live in.

picture theory Wittgenstein's argument that, in the same way that pictures model reality because they have the same logical form as the reality they depict, a proposition—which is a picture or model of reality—can picture facts by virtue of the logical form it has in common with them.

pluralism The view that the universe is made up of more than one basic substance.

poisoning the well An unsound argument in which an attempt is made to place the opponent in a position from which he or she is unable to reply.

premises In an argument, the statements offered in support of the conclusion.

pre-Socratics The ancient Greek thinkers who lived and taught before the time of the great philosopher Socrates.

primary qualities According to Locke, qualities (ideas produced in the mind by an object) that resemble the object that produced them. Primary qualities include solidity, extension, figure, motion or rest, and number.

principle of universality Kant's fundamental moral principle that one should act only in a manner that he or she would will that all others act.

principle of utility Bentham's moral principle that only those actions, practices, and codes of law are worthy that promote the greatest happiness for the greatest number.

problem A type of statement that can be solved by rational, logical means.

propositions Statements, originally called "judgments" by Kant, that have two basic components: a subject, about which something is stated, and a predicate, what is stated about the subject.

prudential imperative According to Kant, an imperative that tells us that we ought to do certain things if we wish to achieve certain ends.

psyche The human soul; that part of a person that is most truly the self.

R

rationalism The view—propounded by Descartes, Spinoza, and Leibniz—that reason alone is capable of arriving at a true knowledge of reality and that the test of truth is intuition: "the absence of doubt in the unclouded and attentive mind."

rational psychology The subdivision of metaphysics concerned with the nature of the soul.

rational theology The subdivision of metaphysics concerned with the existence and nature of God.

reactive attitudes According to Strawson expressions within human life which involve participation with others in interpersonal human relations, e.g. resentment, gratitude; the heart of human interaction.

reason The ability to think and draw conclusions.

relations According to Locke, complex ideas that involve a comparison of one idea with another.

S

secondary qualities According to Locke, qualities (ideas produced in the mind by an object) that do not resemble the object that produced them. Secondary qualities include color, taste, sound, heat, and cold.

simple ideas According to Locke, ideas the mind gets directly from sensation and reflection.

skepticism The position that real knowledge of things is impossible, that there is no such thing as truth.

Sophists A group of ancient Greek teachers who, in exchange for high fees, offered instruction in rhetoric, discourse, and politics. The Sophists fell into disrepute when they began to attack the established system of law, ethics, and religion.

soundness In logic, the result when the premises of an argument are true and its conclusion validly derives from them.

substance According to Locke, a kind of complex idea about the pure substance that supports our ideas about particular substances. Locke says that pure substance is "something, I know not what."

supernaturalism The belief that the order and events of the world result from a divine or supernatural power.

sweeping generalization The assumption that what is true under certain conditions must be true under all conditions.

syllogism An argument composed of categorical propositions.

symbolic logic The unification of mathematics and logic carried out by Russell and Whitehead, who demonstrated that the fundamental ideas of arithmetic could be developed from purely logical concepts.

synthetic propositions Propositions such as "The house is burning," in which the predicate is not identical with the subject. Synthetic propositions provide new information.

T

technical imperative According to Kant, an imperative that commands us to do certain things if we want to achieve certain ends.

teleological theory Any theory that evaluates the rightness or wrongness of proposed actions by the results that will issue from them.

theodicy A justification of the goodness of God given that there is evil in the world.

Thomism The theological and philosophical teachings of Thomas Aquinas.

transcendental knowledge According to Kant, "all knowledge that is concerned, not with objects, but with the way in which a knowledge of objects may be gained, so far as that is possible *a priori*."

truth In logic, whether the premises and conclusion of an argument accord with the facts.

tu quoque An unsound argument in which the person advocating a position is charged with acting in a manner that contradicts the position taken.

U

unconscious According to Freud, the repressed complex of desires, impulses, and fears that are unknown to the conscious mind but that profoundly influence mental activity and behavior.

utilitarianism The position, propounded by Bentham and Mill, that the only proper standard of morality is the principle of the greatest happiness of the greatest number.

V

validity The correctness with which the conclusion of an argument has been inferred from its premises; whether the conclusion follows from its premises.

verification principle The principle, used by the Vienna Circle to examine the traditional problems of philosophy, that a statement is meaningful only if it can be empirically verified; otherwise it is a pseudo-statement lacking cognitive significance.

Vienna Circle A group of thinkers, centered around Moritz Schlick in the 1920s, whose goal was to make philosophy scientific and rigorous. Using the test of empirical verifiability, the group concluded that many of the traditional problems of philosophy were actually pseudo-problems and needed to be superseded by the positive activity of exposing the nonsense of the past and replacing it with the logical clarification of the concepts and achievements of science. The movement eventually came to be known as logical positivism.

virtue Right conduct; acting in accord with what is good.

Z

Zeno's paradoxes A set of paradoxes devised by Zeno to support the idea that change or motion is impossible. The most famous of these—each dealing with movement in space, change of position—are the paradox of Achilles and the tortoise, the race track paradox, and the flying arrow paradox.

TEXT CREDITS

Aristotle. *Physics*, from *The Physics of Aristotle*, trans. R. P. Hardie and R. K. Gaye, http://classics.mit.edu/Aristotle/physics.html. First published in 1864. Provided by the Internet Classics Archive.

Aristotle. *Prior Analytics*, book I, chap. 1–4, trans. A. J. Jenkinson, http://classics.mit .edu/Aristotle/prior.html. Provided by the Internet Classics Archive.

Aristotle. *Nicomachean Ethics*, trans. Terence Irwin (Cambridge, Mass.: Hackett, 1999), pp. 1–5, 13–17, 29–35, 44–47, 150, 284–287.

Cornford, F. M. "Ionian Science before Socrates," from *Before and After Socrates* (Cambridge: Cambridge University Press, 1950), pp. 1–28. Reprinted with the permission of Cambridge University Press.

Descartes, René. "Meditations on First Philosophy," from *The Philosophical Writings of Descartes,* vol. 2, ed. John Cottingham, Robert Stoothoff, and Dugald Murdoch (New York: Cambridge University Press, 1984), pp. 12–23. Footnotes are omitted. Reprinted with permission of Cambridge University Press.

Hume, David. "Dialogues Concerning Natural Religion," from *The Philosophical Works of David Hume,* vol. 2 (Edinburgh: Adam Black and William Tait; and Charles Tait 1876).

Hume, David. *Treatise on Human Nature,* book 1, sect. 4, 1st ed. 1739. Ed. Selby-Bigge (Oxford: Clarendon Press, 1896).

James, William. "The Will to Believe," from *The Will to Believe, an Address to the Philosophical Clubs of Yale and Brown Universities.* First published in the New World, 1896.

Plato. *Apology,* from *The Dialogues of Plato,* trans. Benjamin Jowett (New York: Random House, 1937).

Rawls, John. "Two Types of Justice" from *A Theory of Justice* (Cambridge, Mass.: Harvard-Belknap Press, 1971), pp. 60–65.

Russell, Bertrand. "The Value of Philosophy," from *The Problems of Philosophy* (Oxford: Oxford University Press, 1912).

Sartre, Jean-Paul. "Existentialism and Humanism," from *Existentialism and Humanism*, trans. Philip Mairet (London: Methuen), pp. 23–56.

Stanton, Elizabeth Cady, et al. *Seneca Falls Conference, Declaration of Sentiments,* 1848.

Taylor, A. E. "Plato's Theory of Forms," from *Platonism and His Influence* (New York: Longmans, 1927), pp. 29–37.

PHOTO CREDITS

p.7: THALES (640?–546 B.C.). Greek philosopher and scientist. Antique Greek sculpture. © The Granger Collection, New York; p.19: DEMOCRITUS (c460–c370 B.C.). Greek philosopher. Hellenistic bronze bust. © The Granger Collection, New York; p. 48: SOCRATES (470?–399 B.C.). Greek philosopher. © The Granger Collection, New York; p.53: PLATO (427?–347 B.C.). Greek philosopher. Line engraving, French, 1584. © The Granger Collection, New York; p. 71: SOCRATES (c380–c450). Greek philosopher. The Death of Socrates: wood engraving, German, 19th century. © The Granger Collection, New York; p.91: ARISTOTLE (384–322 B.C.). Greek philosopher. Roman marble bust. © The Granger Collection, New York; p.161: SCHOOL OF ANCIENT ATHENS (center detail of Plato, left, and Aristotle). Fresco, 1509–10, by Raphael. © The Granger Collection, New York; p.168: IMMANUEL KANT (1724–1804). German philosopher. Steel engraving, German, 19th century. © The Granger Collection, New York; p.176: JEREMY BENTHAM (1748–1832). English jurist and philosopher. Line and stipple engraving, English, 1837. © The Granger Collection, New York; p.179: JOHN STUART MILL (1806–1873). English philosopher and economist. © The Granger Collection, New York; p. 207: SAINT THOMAS AQUINAS (1225?–1274). Italian philosopher: Italian engraving, 1812. © The Granger Collection, New York; p. 221: DAVID HUME (1711–1776). Scottish historian and philosopher. Line engraving after the painting, 1766, by Allan Ramsay. © The Granger Collection, New York; p. 234: BLAISE PASCAL (1623–1662). French scientist and philosopher. Line and stipple copper engraving, French, 18th century. © The Granger Collection, New York; p. 237: WILLIAM JAMES (1842–1910). American philosopher and psychologist. © The Granger Collection, New York; p. 290: RENE DESCARTES (1596–1650). French mathematician and philosopher. Oil on canvas by Frans Hals. © The Granger Collection, New York; p. 294: DESCARTES: TREATISE OF MAN. Woodcut from Rene Descartes "Treatise of Man," 1664, illustrating his theory that perceptions travel from the eyes to the pineal gland, which then allows "humors" to pass to the muscles to produce response. © The Granger Collection, New York; p. 296: BARUCH SPINOZA (1632–1677). Dutch philosopher. © The Granger Collection, New York; p. 298: LEIBNIZ (1646–1716). Full name: Baron Gottfried Wilhelm von Leibniz. German

S. MORRIS ENGEL is professor emeritus of philosophy at York University in Toronto, Ontario. Previously, he taught at the University of Southern California for twenty-five years.

ANGELIKA SOLDAN is associate professor of philosophy and government at the University of Texas at Brownsville and Texas Southmost College.

KEVIN DURAND is associate professor of philosophy at Henderson State University in Arkadelphia, Arkansas.